An Economic History of London, 1800–1914

In 1800 London was already the largest city in the world. Over the course of the next century its population grew rapidly to reach over 7 million by 1914. It was also the wealthiest city, a major manufacturing, services and financial centre and the first city to have extensive networks of suburbs connected to the centre by public transport systems.

Historians have often depicted London after the Industrial Revolution as an industrial backwater, that declined into the mass exploitation of labour through 'sweating', dominated by City and merchant interests. This book instead argues that London was a centre of nineteenth-century British economic growth. Modern economic theories of cities are used to explain the causes of metropolitan economic development and emphasis is placed on the changing role of the metropolis within Britain and the wider world economy.

The evolution of London did not occur on purely free market terms. Transport, infrastructure and public services were all regulated and considerable debate took place over the proper boundaries of private enterprise, municipal endeavour and state regulation. So, the supply of urban services is an important component of metropolitan history, particularly in the changing relationship between government and private endeavour.

Individual chapters comprehensively survey a wide variety of topics including: population and migration; employment and industry; the standard of living; changes in retailing and leisure; housing and suburbanisation; transportation; the utilities of gas, water and electricity; post and telecommunications; individual industry studies; the City and finance; social welfare and local government.

This fascinating history will appeal to a wide audience from amateur to specialist interests in economics, history, urban studies and geography. Those whose interest is in understanding the development of London are given new insights into a key period in the formation of the modern city.

Michael Ball is Professor of Urban Economics at South Bank University, London. **David Sunderland** is a former Research Fellow of South Bank University, London.

Routledge Explorations in Economic History

1 **Economic Ideas and Government Policy**
Contributions to contemporary economic history
Sir Alec Cairncross

2 **The Organization of Labour Markets**
Modernity, culture and governance in Germany, Sweden, Britain and Japan
Bo Stråth

3 **Currency Convertibility**
The gold standard and beyond
Edited by Jorge Braga de Macedo, Barry Eichengreen and Jaime Reis

4 **Britain's Place in the World**
A historical enquiry into import controls 1945–1960
Alan S. Milward and George Brennan

5 **France and the International Economy**
From Vichy to the Treaty of Rome
Frances M. B. Lynch

6 **Monetary Standards and Exchange Rates**
M. C. Marcuzzo, L. Officer and A. Rosselli

7 **Production Efficiency in Domesday England, 1086**
John McDonald

8 **Free Trade and its Reception 1815–1960**
Freedom and trade: Volume I
Edited by Andrew Marrison

9 **Conceiving Companies**
Joint-stock politics in Victorian England
Timothy L. Alborn

10 **The British Industrial Decline Reconsidered**
Edited by Jean-Pierre Dormois and Michael Dintenfass

11 **The Conservatives and Industrial Efficiency, 1951–1964**
Thirteen wasted years?
Nick Tiratsoo and Jim Tomlinson

12 **Pacific Centuries**
Pacific and Pacific Rim economic history since the 16th century
Edited by Dennis O. Flynn, Lionel Frost and A. J. H. Latham

13 **The Premodern Chinese Economy**
Structural equilibrium and capitalist sterility
Gang Deng

14 **The Role of Banks in Monitoring Firms**
The case of the Crédit Mobilier
Elisabeth Paulet

15 **Management of the National Debt in the United Kingdom, 1900–1932**
Jeremy Wormell

16 **An Economic History of Sweden**
Lars Magnusson

17 **Freedom and Growth**
The rise of states and markets in Europe, 1300–1750
S. R. Epstein

18 **The Mediterranean Response to Globalization Before 1950**
Sevket Pamuk and Jeffrey G. Williamson

19 **Production and Consumption in English Households 1600–1750**
Edited by Mark Overton, Jane Whittle, Darron Dean and Andrew Haan

20 **Governance, The State, Regulation and Industrial Relations**
Ian Clark

21 **Early Modern Capitalism**
Economic and social change in Europe 1400–1800
Edited by Maarten Prak

22 **An Economic History of London, 1800–1914**
Michael Ball and David Sunderland

An Economic History of London, 1800–1914

Michael Ball and
David Sunderland

London and New York

To Aslı Ball
whose understanding, support and forbearance made this book possible

First published 2001
by Routledge
2 Park Square, Milton Park, Abingdon, Oxon, OX14 4RN

Simultaneously published in the USA and Canada
by Routledge
270 Madison Ave, New York NY 10016

Routledge is an imprint of the Taylor & Francis Group

Transferred to Digital Printing 2006

Typeset in Baskerville by Florence Production Ltd, Stoodleigh, Devon

British Library Cataloguing in Publication Data
A catalogue record for this book is available from the British Library

Library of Congress Cataloguing in Publication Data
Ball, Michael.
An economic history of London, 1800–1914 / Michael Ball and David Sunderland.
p. cm. – (Routledge explorations in economic history ; 22)
Includes bibliographical references and index.
1. London (England)—Economic conditions. 2. London (England)—History—1800–1950. I. Sunderland, David, 1958– . II. Title. III. Series.
HC258.L6 B35 2001
330.9421–dc21 00–050994

ISBN10: 0–415–24691–1 (hbk)
ISBN10: 0–415–40640–4 (pbk)

ISBN13: 978–0–415–24691–0 (hbk)
ISBN13: 978–0–415–40640–6 (pbk)

Contents

Tables

Figures

Acknowledgements

The authors and publishers would like to thank the following for granting permission to reproduce material in this work:

The Belknap Press for permission to reprint Figure 1.1 from *The Government of London. 1855–1889: The Metropolitan Board of Works, the Vestries, and the City Corporation* by D. Owen, Cambridge, Mass.: The Belknap Press of Harvard University Press, © 1982 by the President and Fellows of Harvard College.

Academic Press for permission to reproduce Figure 5.1 from 'Trends in real wages in Britain 1750–1913' by N. F. R. Crafts and T. C. Mills in *Explorations in Economic History*, Volume 31, 176–194, © 1994 by Academic Press, reproduced by permission of the publisher.

Blackwell Publishers for permission to reprint Figure 8.1, originally published in *Urban Economics: An Introduction* by Alan W. Evans, Blackwell Publishers, 1985, page 105.

Routledge Publishers for permission to reprint Figure 8.2, originally published in *Slums and Slum Clearance in Victoria* by J. A. Yelling, Allen & Unwin, 1986, page 56.

Blackwell Publishers for permission to reprint Figure 8.3, originally published in 'Urban housing problems' by J. C. Spensley, *Journal of the Royal Statistical Society*, lxxxi, © 1918 Royal Statistical Society.

Macmillan Press Ltd for permission to reproduce Figure 8.4, originally published in *Building Cycles and Growth* by J. P. Lewis, Macmillan Press Ltd, 1965, page 171.

Ashgate Publishers Limited for permission to reproduce Table 15.1, originally published in *From Artisans to Paupers: Economic Change and Poverty in London 1790–1870* by D. Green, 1985, page 219.

Every effort has been made to contact copyright holders for their permission to reprint material in this book. The publishers would be grateful to hear from any copyright holder who is not here acknowledged and will undertake to rectify any errors or omissions in future editions of this book.

Part 1

Economics and urban history

1 This city

Nineteenth-century London was a place of firsts and superlatives: the capital of the first industrial nation; the largest and richest urban agglomeration in the world; the first city with extensive mass suburbanisation, to name but a few. It was also a city of contrasts which could be seen in the extremes of wealth and poverty; in dynamic, successful industries alongside declining ones; in people at leisure and those locked in the most menial drudgery; and in new architectural and civil engineering wonders next to acres of dilapidation.

Identifying such distinctive features and how they changed over time is at the heart of any narrative urban history. Yet, the characteristics of any city cannot simply be described. There needs to be an explanation of how things came about and there is no shortage of explanations within the wide literature on London's history. What is noticeable, however, is how little use has been made of modern economic theories, particularly those falling within the ambit of urban economics. To claim this is not to beat the drum of professional jealousy nor to suggest that economics can explain all, but rather to suggest that developments in nineteenth-century London were mainly stimulated by what are now reasonably well-understood economic processes.

This viewpoint is at variance with many histories of London because they tend to identify a uniqueness in the character of the metropolis at the centre of their explanations. Uniqueness can certainly be found and as a theme it has a long pedigree. The capital city of the United Kingdom, the leading world power by the 1820s, was a special place that caused wonderment at its vastness. At the same time, its scale filled many contemporary observers with horror, mixed with pride at the scale of the human endeavour needed to create it. Yet, the causes of the growth of London were generally regarded as something of a mystery. Other cities in Britain, like Manchester, had burst forth out of virtually nothing at the end of the eighteenth century, but they could be seen to be a product of the new industrial capitalist society. The same forces transformed London but this was not so obvious because there were few of the features that spawned the industrial towns of the Midlands and North. Near it were no coalfields; there was no intense specialisation in heavy industry or textiles; nor was London even a focal point for a network of surrounding industrial towns.

Only one thread of argument seemed to explain London's existence. Despite all its apparent modernity, the metropolis was a unique throwback to a bygone mercantilist age: with its scale generated by the conspicuous consumption of the wealthy, the world-wide tentacles of the City and Empire, and a terrible exploitation of a mass of poor people. Uniqueness was clearly important within this interpretation, because, if it was extrapolated to the nation as a whole, this view was revolutionary in content but, when localised to the capital, it was believed by many who were hardly radical in their general politics. This explanation had a powerful effect on what was seen as London – an image that has persisted in much of the literature until today. The capital was like Wilde's Dorian Gray. The proud architectural and cultural face of Georgian, Victorian and Edwardian London existed because of the hidden picture that was the inner-suburban industrial districts and the poverty associated with them. The problem of London was contained in the misleading geographical metaphors of the West End versus the East End and the City versus Industry.

Heaven and hell were found just a few streets away from each other, as commentators noted with a regularity that never seemed to flag or bore, and this theme filled a flood of novels, amateur reports and official inquiries. This viewpoint of London as the unique jewel-encrusted terror helped to promulgate a horror of large cities and suburban sprawl that is still such a common English characteristic today. It also has become the standard way of explaining nineteenth-century metropolitan development. The problem is that it does not make much economic sense.

The economic dimension

Urban life started over four thousand years ago, when human beings combined specific building technologies with ways of organising society to create densely populated living spaces. Since then, many different types of society have found urban living useful, and technological change has made the potentials of city existence manifoldly apparent. Yet, it was not until the nineteenth century that countries larger than city states became structured as predominantly urban ones. Britain was the first country to experience that shift, and London towered above all its other cities in size, wealth and productive capacity – housing over a fifth of England's population by 1900. The cause, of course, was associated with the development of modern capitalist societies – a process in which Britain took the initial lead.

Urbanisation went along with industrialisation and sustained economic growth. These inter-linked processes subsequently spread through other countries and continue to encompass more areas of the globe. In today's Third World can be seen the fastest urban growth rates ever, and it is estimated that over half the world's population will live in urban areas within a decade, so the process looks set to continue for the foreseeable future and undoubtedly beyond. In many senses, therefore, the growth of London in the nineteenth century represents the first example of this modern phenomenon and its economic history is interesting for that reason alone.

The technical and organisational characteristics of capitalist cities, moreover, make them highly amenable to economic analysis. Clustering does not arise in such societies through some pre-conceived plan but through the responses to market forces of a multitude of individuals and firms. The foundation of urban organisation is consequently that of markets – the stuff of economic analysis. The strong positive impact that cities make on the productive potential of society overall, and the social ills which go along with it, in addition, make an economic analysis of cities important for an understanding of general economic development. (It is one of the professional paradoxes of economics that modern growth theory has tended to ignore the urban dimension when looking at the causes of economic growth.)

This is not to say that the antecedents of metropolitan growth in the nineteenth century were unimportant, nor that some sudden break can be seen in the way in which Britain's capital city functioned. Even so, from the later decades of the eighteenth century, five important new characteristics are discernible.

The first was that London's population began to expand continuously at the fast rate of around a fifth every decade. This growth continued for over 150 years until the suburbs spilled far beyond the juridical area of the metropolis. City growth, in other words, was a self-sustaining process – no longer linked to government and aristocratic behaviour but to market relations.

The second new characteristic was that traditional work practices had noticeably given way after centuries of slow dissolution, so that nineteenth-century London industry was, in the main, openly competitive and exhibited overtly capitalist behaviour.

The third feature was an increasingly commonplace separation between workplace and residence amongst all urban social classes. It was also widely believed, and desired, that all families should have their own separate accommodation with no shared facilities. The transformed way of living was so pervasive that by the end of the nineteenth century home-working and overcrowding were generally being condemned as social evils rather than the facts of life they had been for centuries before. These separations transformed the physical structure of cities into their modern, functionally distinct areas and helped to define many urban problems in terms of work and home and getting between them. The processes by which they came about in London are central themes of this book.

The fourth characteristic was particularly significant in nineteenth-century Britain. There was a marked specialisation of the country's regions in particular economic activities and the rapid appearance of major cities in the areas where manufacturing became important. London, therefore, was not alone. An array of other urban areas simultaneously existed, in what came to be called 'conurbations', but with notably different features from each other and the metropolis – reflecting the differing industrial specialisations of the regions in which they emerged. London, consequently, was the first amongst many. This influenced its development and provided a means by which to compare its development.

Finally, from around the 1820s, another facet of nineteenth-century urban development became significant, in that the technologies of urban life were subject to widespread change with many radically transformed. Public transport, for instance, from being virtually non-existent for most social groups became more widespread, and its motive power slowly shifted from the horse to steam and electricity, below ground as well as on it, and finally to the petrol engine. This prodigious and unexpected series of innovations, and their subsequent application to metropolitan life, lasted throughout the period up to 1914. Further additions could be made to the list of relevant and important discoveries and new organisational capabilities, and they would include many of today's urban technologies that are now taken for granted. Then they were new but highly expensive to install. Some of the most notable were street lighting; extensive paved, drained and cleansed roads; sanitation and fresh, piped water for the masses; gas and electricity; the telegraph and telephone; new types of long-distance transport, and ways in which travel was related to cities via stations and ports. The scale of these new inventions, their speed of adoption and the enormous costs of providing them were a unique event of the period from around the 1820s to the 1920s.

The rapidity of change, moreover, made investing in the new technologies of urban living a highly risky business. Most of all, the content of urban life was changed beyond recognition. New words had to be invented to deal with the spatial forms and lifestyles that were made feasible. The new technologies enormously increased the spatial spread of cities, expanded hugely the amount of fixed capital required to make urban areas function and made sustained economic growth viable at last in major cities.

Technologies are only socially useful when some agency turns them into viable products. With regard to the new urban technologies that transformed nineteenth-century London, most were provided by private interests, with local government supreme in only a few. Rules and regulations were put in place to affect the ways in which those private firms operated and invested. Some were fixed by Parliament or by public urban agencies, others arose from the detailed histories of the organisations involved and the nature of the competitive contexts in which they found themselves. Organisations and institutional practices, therefore, are important in understanding the history of the metropolitan economy during this period. Contemporary observers were well aware of this fact and there were widespread debates about the functioning of particular industries and the efficacy of new urban technologies. Controversy particularly raged over urban infrastructure and over the ways in which it should be provided with champions of the private and public sectors and, even on occasion, private–public partnerships. Debates, none the less, went beyond simple public–private polarisations to question what forms of regulation were needed, how to avoid monopoly abuse and the means to encourage change.

Institutions were also significant with regard to social policy, labour markets and other key areas of the economy, such as the City, the docks and the structure of consumer industries. London government during the period, similarly, is often regarded as woefully inadequate because of the earlier institutional framework from which it developed and the lack of change in it. This negative description may be debatable but the impact of urban governance on infrastructure provision, private as well as public, was none the less substantial.

To talk of markets, consequently, is not to deny the significance of the broader contexts in which they exist. Whether unregulated market outcomes or constraints on them dominated is a matter of historical and empirical enquiry. The theme of markets and institutions pervades the analyses contained in this book, but when interpreting the available evidence most weight is put on market outcomes. This is partly because, empirically, market processes were more likely to be causally important than some hypothesised monopoly, hidden influence or act of political manipulation. In addition, a market approach provides a means by which to link together the distinct aspects of urban economic development, and underlies standards through which to evaluate change.

The inter-dependence of urban activities is central to an economic analysis of cities. The close spatial proximity of both similar and distinct activities gives cities their economic rationale – their big technological benefit over other potential forms of human existence. Alongside the mutual gains of proximity, there is a competitive element, because each urban activity competes for scarce urban resources. Such competition is predominantly over labour and land, as capital is more mobile. Because the overall productivity of an urban economy grows over time, however, the outcome is generally not a zero-sum game of winners and losers. Growth leads to extra facilities in a city, and a wider spatial spread of the urban area. These alter and improve urban resource availability (at least up to the point of excessive congestion). Within the overall process of city growth, some activities expand, and others will be in absolute or relative decline. Some activities may leave the city altogether, because it is no longer profitable for them to be there at the prevailing urban input prices. Competition for scarce urban resources has forced them out, leading to a restructuring of the city's industrial profile.

Inter-connectedness, in both its mutually reinforcing agglomeration and restructuring competitive aspects, is consequently another general theme of this book, and represents one of its distinguishing features, as many general city histories tend to treat urban activities in isolation. Again, with inter-connectedness, institutional frameworks, specific contexts and first-mover advantages are important. The dock companies, for example, when they were given powers to build new docks were simultaneously handed control of the spatial structure of a large part of East London. Even when they clearly could no longer compete with other activities for an urban location, they still used the land – more because of the sheer cost of converting redundant dockland to any other urban use than because of any land ownership titles they held.

The docks illustrate a parallel point. Urban districts change very slowly because of built environment costs: the need to create new built structures and to demolish or refashion existing ones when they become economically redundant. Added to these physical construction issues when contemplating the transformation of whole neighbourhoods are problems associated with multiple property ownership, legal rights and the difficulties faced by the affected local community. Commitment to a particular activity, consequently, has long-term ramifications for an urban district.

Only when the gains from change were so great did large-scale urban renewal take place in nineteenth-century London. The most spectacular, short-run, neighbourhood changes were caused by the building of transport facilities, which destroyed and divided neighbourhoods on a grand scale. Despite this, over the longer term, there was a radical transformation of most of the pre-existing eighteenth-century urban area, from which only the best West End locations remained untouched. By the 1900s, the city of a century before had been divided into a commercial core of the West End and City of London and an inner-industrial area of factories, workshops and low-income housing. Yet, this process was gradual and unplanned and was only possible because it was so. In other European cities, states were transforming their capital cities but in England private capital was the main instigator. One consequence of piecemeal, private urban renewal was that the street and broader urban pattern of previous centuries still predominated in the nineteenth century on to which new growth was added. This helps to explain the continuing and incessant complaints of congestion, and oddities such as the fourteen mainline railway termini built in central London.

The call of economic analysis

The scale of scholarship related to retrieving information about London's development has been substantial and its quality high. These histories come from a number of disciplinary backgrounds. Some are generalist, others are political, social or geographic, but few are economic. In most of them, therefore, economic processes are mentioned only descriptively or in passing. Even so, strong conclusions are frequently made about the nature of the metropolitan economy. Keynes once famously wrote of practical men that they were 'slaves of some defunct economist'[1] and, whether their economists are defunct or not, many histories of London contain poorly articulated, implicit economic theories.

Recognition of a lack of explicit economic analysis has led some historians to call for an economic history of nineteenth-century London. Cannadine, for instance, in a perceptive essay originally written in 1983, suggests that such a history is essential if any progress is going to be made in understanding urban change during this period.[2] In some senses, his hopes for an economic history are too high, as there is simply insufficient data on so many facets of metropolitan economic life for definitive views to be possible. An economic history, furthermore, is only as good as its explanations, which requires use of appropriate theories as part of the analysis. Theories also offer guidance when data are poor by enhancing the ability to interpret the information that exists.

Cannadine's essay, in addition, contains a succinct statement of a common view of the capital.

> The difficulty is that nineteenth-century London was such a success story in some ways that historians cannot cope with it, and such a fable of failure in others that they do not want to. From one standpoint, London was the Cinderella of nineteenth-century cities, the inert, lifeless embodiment of economic backwardness, class fragmentation, political marginality, municipal stagnation and administrative chaos; while the provinces blazed the trail in economic growth, class formation, political radicalism, municipal reform and administrative progress.[3]

In this view, the three themes of economic backwardness, a failure to deliver adequate urban public services and unequal wealth form a triangular causality explaining metropolitan change – with backwardness at its apex. This sentiment can be found in many other texts as the reviews in later chapters show. Yet, each of the three categorisations can be questioned. The detailed historical evidence outlined in later chapters, for example, contradicts the notion that London was industrially backward. As a manufacturing centre, it grew enormously over the century, with the changing composition of its industries broadly corresponding to the predictions of competitive market theory. Rather than backward, London's nineteenth-century industrial structure was instead distinct from those of the northern industrial towns. Moreover, as London manufacturing moved further and further away from its pre-industrial capitalist origins as the nineteenth century progressed, the metropolitan industrial landscape expanded to encompass many of the new manufacturing sectors that growth and technical development were creating. This helped to encourage a convergence between key elements of the metropolitan economy and those in the rest of the country as a whole.

London became less industrially specialised between 1800 and the early 1900s but, even so, over a third of its huge workforce remained employed in manufacturing, making it one of the largest manufacturing centres in the country. The First World War, therefore, was not the source of a sharp break in manufacturing practices from 'traditional' craft-based activities to new factory-based 'modern' industries that led to a boom in metropolitan industry during the inter-war years. This structural-break view of inter-war industry is a common one but it is predicated on a misunderstanding of the pre-1914 situation. As new industries prospered in the nineteenth-century metropolis, predictable continuity in the nature of change is a more reasonable interpretation of the early twentieth-century dynamic.

Another recent perspective has many underlying similarities with the idea of London as a manufacturing backwater, but it has a more optimistic view of long-term metropolitan economic growth. It again links three perceived features of the nineteenth-century London economy. This time the points of the causal triangle are made up of, at its base, London as a centre of wealth/empire, on one side, and a service-orientation, on the other, and, at its service apex, the City as a world financial centre. Yet, this perspective itself leads to a distorted understanding of the metropolitan economy, as Chapter 4 will suggest, by exaggerating and misinterpreting the role of some of its components. It is interesting to note that, as with the previous causal triangle, all its three points are economic in character. Causal economic theories are consequently again recognised as central to the subject matter of city development.

The structure of the book

The chapters that follow aim to cover a wide range of issues associated with the economic history of nineteenth-century London. They are divided into seven major parts. This is done not simply for completeness but also because of the importance of understanding the influence of varied parts of its massive economy, and the inter-connections between them, on the ways in which London changed. However, the reader who wishes to dip into particular themes will find that each chapter, apart from the conclusions, can be read as a stand-alone individual piece – although some of the interconnections would be lost by such an approach. The following paragraphs indicate the themes of each chapter of the book.

The first part includes this introductory chapter and another one that outlines some basic urban economic theory, relating it to the nature of the nineteenth-century metropolis. Part 2 uses this theory in its overview of the capital's economic history. Chapter 3 analyses population and migration. This is followed by an examination in Chapter 4 of the city's changing industrial structure, the relative importance of manufacturing and services, and the nature of labour markets and employment practices. Chapter 5 considers information on wealth, poverty and the standard of living – where the notion of exceptionally widespread metropolitan poverty is argued to be an exaggeration. Part 3 then begins to look at the components of London's economy. The three chapters in it deal consecutively with factors that transformed the face of the city: marked changes in the characteristics of shopping, leisure and housing provision from mid-century onwards. They highlight the fact that mass markets were becoming more important for British industry – a process in which London played an important part as the largest population centre by far. Apart from examining the new mass suburbanisation, Chapter 8 also investigates the ways in which private housing was provided and the associated land development process, particularly the use of the long building lease.

Suburbanisation leads on to the fourth part of the book dealing with infrastructure. Chapter 9 considers improvements in travel between London and elsewhere with the advent of stagecoach services, railways and ships. Included in it is a history of the docks. Chapter 10 looks at the development of public transport, which changed the metropolis from a predominantly pedestrian city into one criss-crossed by a wide variety of different transport systems. In these transport histories, emphasis is placed on institutional structures and the economic behaviour of agencies within them. Chapter 11 deals with the other utilities apart from transport: gas, water, electricity, the telegraph, telephones and wholesale markets.

Part 5 turns to a detailed analysis of sectors of the London economy and relates their histories to industrial change in Britain as a whole. It provides detailed sector-specific evidence that complements the arguments previously presented in the overview of London's industrial structure in Chapter 4. Chapter 12 examines manufacturing industry, paying particular attention to developments in the industries most associated with nineteenth-century London, those providing clothing and other consumer goods. Chapter 13 looks at service labour, from the humble servant and clerk to the prestigious professions. Then Chapter 14 focuses on the financial and other activities taking place in the square mile of the City of London.

Part 6 examines welfare and local government issues. Local government is looked at in two distinct ways. One of the growing pressures on it was the provision of a wider range of welfare services. Though reformed in the 1830s, the Poor Law remained a locally operated and funded activity. Local administration, in addition, towards the end of the century came to be regarded as a key vehicle for changing national urban and social policies. From being a moribund backwater, it became a key battle area for national political parties and their local coalitions. In view of the significance of local welfare programmes, they are examined separately from the administrative functioning of metropolitan governance, in Chapter 15, and integrated with simultaneous developments in private and charitable welfare provision. The changing administrative structure of London's government is then discussed in Chapter 16 in the context of theories of local public goods.

The final part consists of only one chapter, the concluding one, where the themes are drawn together and an assessment is made of the economic problems of nineteenth-century London and the lessons that can be drawn from them.

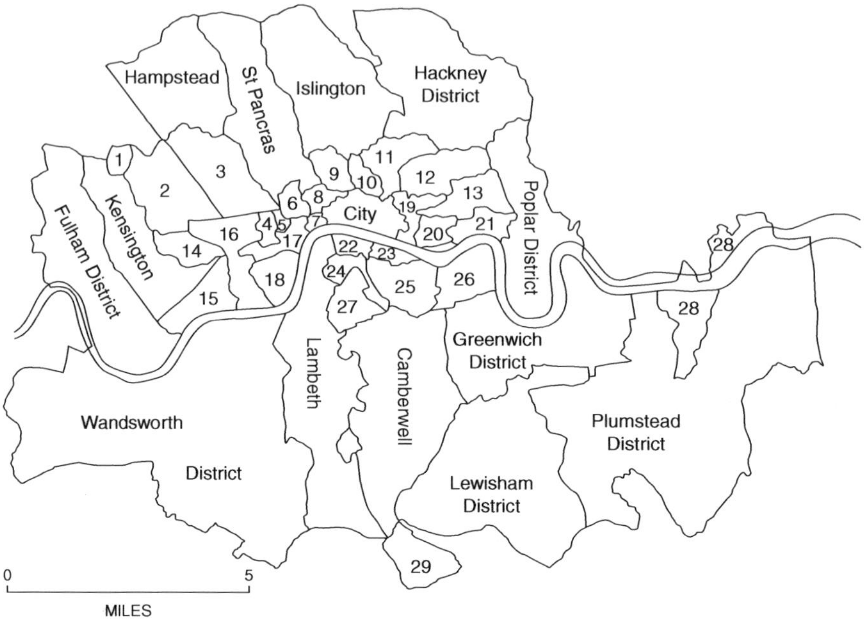

Key to the numbered districts on the map of London showing the area of the Metropolitan Board of Works, based on Edward Stanford's map of 1872.

1 Kensal Green, detached part of Chelsea
2 Paddington
3 St Marylebone
4 St James, Westminster
5 St Anne, Soho, detached part of Strand District
6 St Giles' District
7 Strand District
8 Holborn District
9 St James and St John, Clerkenwell
10 St Luke, Middlesex
11 St Leonard, Shoreditch
12 St Matthew, Bethnal Green
13 Hamlet of Mile End Old Town
14 Part of Westminster District
15 Chelsea
16 St George, Hanover Square
17 St Martin-in-the-Fields
18 Remainder of Westminster District
19 Whitechapel District
20 St George-in-the-East
21 Limehouse District
22 St Saviour's, Southwark, District
23 St Olave District
24 St George The Martyr, Southwark
25 Bermondsey
26 Rotherhithe
27 St Mary, Newington, Surrey
28 Woolwich
29 Penge, part of Lewisham District

Figure 1.1 The extent of administrative London: vestries and Metropolitan Board of Works areas, 1850s to 1880s

Source: Owen, 1982, 200.

Note: The London County Council Area from 1889 was the same as the Metropolitan Board's.

Defining London

The definitions of London used are based on two juridical areas. The first is the County of London, the area defined for the London County Council in 1889, and the second is Greater London. The extent of the County of London is shown in Figure 1.1. The County took over the area run by the Metropolitan Board of Works, which is what the map, drawn in 1872, actually refers to. Greater London as an administrative area only came into existence in the 1960s, and represents the area covered by the current Greater London Authority, but it is a useful definition of the capital in the late nineteenth century as well. In the literature, however, the definition of Greater London during the period varies depending on the author and statistical sources in question. The City, in contrast, is clearly defined, as it refers only to the area administered by the Corporation of London whose boundaries remained the same. This is the location of the modern financial district and is often known as the Square Mile. To avoid confusion, City, when referred to in capitals, means the Square Mile, and city, in lower case, is used when reference is being made to London as a whole.

By the second half of the nineteenth century, the suburbs of London had expanded across the County line and, by 1914, into some areas beyond the Greater London boundary. Nevertheless, many parts of outer Greater London remained rural – to be filled up with development in the interwar years. The formal ways of delineating London, therefore, do not correspond with the true economic and social geography of the city, which, as can be seen, increasingly crossed such lines. From a data point of view, this creates considerable difficulties. Most published data refer to the County of London, which means that a part of suburban London's economic activity falls outside of it. The latter is combined with the rest of the surrounding 'Home' Counties. Some data, however, exist that do encompass Greater London. As a result, the text tries to be careful in its description of London, citing either the County or Greater London wherever relevant. Yet, it should be remembered that these two definitions do not describe the true geographic range of the metropolis at any point in time. (Publishing economics have made the provision of detailed maps impossible here, so the reader may wish to avail her or himself of a modern map of the City when specific locations are being discussed.)

Laxity with the definition of the nineteenth century, in contrast, is applied here. For simplicity, and in recognition of the break in normal economic development represented by the First World War, the phrase 'the nineteenth century' is generally meant to imply the whole of the period from 1800 to 1914.[4]

2 Economics and London's history

Introduction

This chapter considers general economic explanations for the existence and growth of cities.[1] In the context of nineteenth-century London, economic theory is important for three reasons. First, it enables deductions to be made about real world economic processes. These can then bring life to the historical information available. Second, economic theory enables clear expression of the interconnectedness of urban economic activity; and, third, it helps to identify the way in which London's economy related to the wider national and international ones.

A core concept is that of agglomeration economies. They are generated by the crowding together of economic activities into an urban area, and increase with city size. Such clustering provides mutual benefits to producers and consumers, lowering their costs and extending their range of options. Another key component is the notion of competition for the resources of a city: its labour, land and other inputs. There are simultaneous processes of mutual benefit and adversarial competition – or attraction and repulsion – that determine which activities are undertaken in a city and how they change over time. Together they help to explain why London was of the size it was, the activities in which it specialised and the spatial structure of the urban area.

Economic theory for many is an arid subject. The models of economists may seem too abstract and based on too many simplifying assumptions to be of use in investigating a particular city's economic development. It could be argued that cities are too full of rigid, long-lasting built structures to correspond to the flexibility assumed in many economic models.[2] City dwellers, moreover, do not have the simplified rational behaviour attributed to them.[3] Such criticisms of assumptions, however, tend to miss the point. All deductive analysis is abstract and, hence, makes 'unrealistic' assumptions. Just as modern geologists in their quest to understand mountain building are gaining insights through assuming that solid mountains act like fluids, so does economic analysis benefit from its assumptions.

Analysis, nevertheless, if it is to aid the understanding of London's economic development has to bring in a wider range of factors than those provided by urban economic theory alone. Urban development, for example, is path-dependent in the sense that what already exists influences the future trajectory of growth. This is most obvious in the evolution of city transportation systems, but it is also apparent in the institutional frameworks within which economic activity takes place. Analysis also has to be sensitive to such factors as the prevailing state of technology.

These determinants of urban economic life and general comments on their effects on London in the nineteenth century, therefore, are the themes of much of the rest of this chapter.[4] Transport costs are examined first, followed by the impact of economies of scale in production and consumption. An analysis of agglomeration economies and diseconomies is then undertaken and their role in influencing the growth and size of the metropolis outlined. The importance of considering institutions in the capital's evolution is then argued for. After this, some issues related to infrastructure and urban politics are considered and, finally, the role of London in the wider national economy is examined.

Transport

The production of goods and services requires the movement of inputs to points of production and outputs from them to consumers. The location of economic activity can consequently be viewed as a problem of transport cost minimisation. Transport costs affect location when they are a significant component of total costs. This is likely to occur when the scale of production is such that large amounts of inputs are needed and the volume of output is too great for a local market alone. Not all industries are like that: some are ubiquitous – traditional bakers and repair shops, for example; others are relatively footloose and could set up profitably at many locations. But most face situations where some inputs are bulky and expensive to ship and their markets are found at different places from some of their inputs. Transport costs will then pull firms towards input sources or their main markets. It is unlikely that producers will locate at intermediate points between a source of a bulky raw material and a main market, because such locations are not minimum total transport cost points. Intermediate places require extra handling charges and, hence, higher total transport costs. They also face the disadvantage that transport charges tend to fall per kilometre travelled with greater distance. Industries where the cost of transporting the raw material is high relative to that of the final product, therefore, generally locate near the site of that raw material; whereas when finished products are more bulky, difficult or expensive to move producers locate at the site of a major market.

This simple distinction provides a good rule-of-thumb for many London-based manufacturing activities. Bulky input-using industries are relatively absent and consumer goods and government purchase industries are strongly represented. Such nineteenth-century industries as iron and steel, most heavy engineering and all textiles – prodigious consumers of coal and other bulky inputs – gained no benefit from locating in the capital; whereas consumer-oriented industries had strong attachments towards it, including clothing, furniture, drinks, foodstuffs, printing and light engineering. London, as a result, was and would always be distinctive as a manufacturing centre from the industrial regions of the Midlands and North.

An exception to the rule about intermediate locational points occurs when there is a transshipment point, such as a seaport. There, raw materials inevitably have to be handled as they are moved from one transport mode to another. This encourages firms dealing in bulky imported raw materials to set up at transshipment points. In consequence, another reason is offered for London-based manufacturing industries – its port. In particular, stimulation was given to import-processing industries, such as foodstuffs and timber-related activities, which included shipbuilding before the advent of ironclad ships.

Services have other locational pulls. For some of them, those that are consumed as they are produced, locating near to consumers is imperative. Domestic service, retail facilities and the like consequently follow consumer demand; as do non-manufacturing production activities, like building, water provision and, in the nineteenth century, gas and electricity production and supply. Transport similarly is primarily population driven. Some other service activities need to locate in places that maximise their market area (like department stores) or to be near to the functions that they serve (for example, lawyers and public administration). Other ones, like finance, gain from good information and pools of skilled labour and, so, benefit considerably from locating at places where extensive intermediation takes place. Given its role in Britain, therefore, London was a place with thriving service activities.

Scale economies

The importance of scale

Cities would not exist without economies of scale in production.[5] If there were no economies of scale, the existence of transport costs would cause production activity to be small and evenly spread across the places where people live – and they would themselves have no economic reason to group together. There would no incentive for densely clustered urban activity. This even spread does not occur, because scale economies are pervasive in production, consumption and in the provision of public goods and facilities. They have limits, however, and after certain sizes unit costs tend to rise. The exact points at which economies of scale are exhausted depend on the specific production process and prevailing technology, but, one hundred or more years ago, efficient production levels tended to be at far smaller outputs than today. The result was the more general existence of efficient, small enterprises across a wide range of industries. This affected the structure of production activities throughout the country, including the metropolis. The effect can even be seen in the industry that for some exemplifies the industrial revolution, cotton textiles. Studies of the Lancashire cotton industry have suggested that small and medium-size firms were more cost-efficient than the largest mills in the 1830s and 1840s.[6]

Some of the major scale economies derive from the principle of specialisation. Craft workers, for instance, are considerably more productive when they undertake a limited number of skilled tasks. But to specialise they need to be able to sell large volumes of output, and a large city provides that opportunity. Such craft workers may also be linked to others in complex divisions of labour. Nineteenth-century London exhibited this type of scale economy extensively and was the home to a wide array of, often inter-connected, craft specialisms.

With industrialisation from the eighteenth century, scale increasingly became associated with factory production. Factories were steam powered, so it is often believed that they must have mainly been located on the coalfields. By deduction, London is then regarded as a place with few factories.[7] Scale economies combined with transportation costs, however, suggested otherwise. The locational balance was tipped towards London when the relative cost of transporting the finished commodity was greater than that of inputs found elsewhere; when its port and railhead facilities gave a metropolitan location a transport cost advantage; when the necessary inputs were generally available everywhere; or when the most expensive input was labour.

As by far the most concentrated, richest consumer market in Britain, the pull of a metropolitan location was strong. Once there, scale economies could be achieved within a single plant or through networks of producers specialising in particular parts of the division of labour, depending on the industry in question. The range of goods produced in the nineteenth century was obviously far smaller than now – partly because average incomes were much lower and many of today's consumer goods still had to be invented. Even so, the capital bristled with manufacturing activity. Much took place in small workshops or in people's homes. At the other end of the scale, the heavier, larger plant-oriented activities included many of the materials needed to build and equip houses, commercial buildings and other built structures – such as paint, linoleum and iron castings; others were in industries creating intermediate inputs for the client London industries – such as many of those in chemicals and imported raw materials processing; further large enterprises could be found in a range of activities – such as drinks, food processing, consumer durables and transport equipment. There were, for example, several relatively large plants producing pianos (the nineteenth-century equivalent of the television). Government armaments, energy production, brewing and transportation also generated large employment sites in the capital.

Increasing economies of scale

Over the course of the nineteenth century, the optimal scale of production grew and the costs of transport fell. After mid-century it became increasingly possible for firms in consumer-oriented industries to supply the national market from plants sited at one or two locations. Firms began to use marketing, branding and other means to achieve country-wide presences. London, as the country's largest consumer market by far, was an excellent place to locate a nationally oriented plant, and such businesses started to appear in the capital, adding more factories to the capital's tally. A good example is margarine. In the main, none the less, nineteenth-century branded goods production occurred at provincial locations, rather than in the capital, for reasons that are explored in Chapter 6.

Yet, even though scale economies did increase, Britain was still generally characterised by relatively small plant and firm sizes in comparison to those emerging in Germany and the USA. Some have put this down to entrepreneurial failure;[8] while others attribute it to the characteristics of activities in which contemporary Britain specialised and the relatively small size of the domestic market.[9] Whatever the reason, as the largest manufacturing centre in the country, London was unlikely to buck the 'small is beautiful' trend. It also had a strong handicraft, small workshop tradition – bringing path dependency to its nineteenth-century industrial structure.

Scale economies in consumption and transport

Scale economies exist in consumption and transport as well as in production. Large urban areas enable advantage to be taken of scale economies in the consumption of goods consumed collectively or via networks. Such scale affects existed in the provision of utilities – gas, water, electricity and communications (mail, telegraph and telephone); public facilities like parks, art galleries and museums; and cultural and entertainment complexes, such as theatres. The new rail and tram transport systems also contained inherent scale advantages because of their high fixed costs and large capacities. Public transport was particularly important in the nineteenth century, as few, affordable, private means of transportation existed beyond walking. Dense networks of regular public transport thus greatly increased the mobility of urban residents.

Again, scale economies in both consumption and transportation increased during the nineteenth century. For the utilities, in the early part of the century, diseconomies often set in at outputs far below those feasible with London's population size. This created fragmented provision but, as technologies improved, scale benefits in many of these activities began to be reaped for very large populations, especially in sewerage, water and gas. This increased potential efficiencies in their provision; yet, the extent to which the prevailing institutional arrangements were up to reaping those scale benefits is another matter (see Chapter 11).

Urban hierarchies and scale economies

Urban hierarchies arise because of the existence of scale economies. Some activities can only be supported in towns above a certain population threshold – larger cities then provide those facilities for a range of smaller towns in their hinterlands. Examples are specialist shops, cultural facilities, market exchanges and law courts. A hierarchy arises because progressively 'higher-level' activities require ever larger local population bases and bigger hinterlands. Towns and cities in a country can then be ranked on the basis of the functions existing within them. In the case of nineteenth-century Britain, London towered above all other urban areas in the range and scale of the functions operating there.

Agglomeration economies and diseconomies

So far the location of economic activity in nineteenth-century London has been explained mainly in terms of costs and benefits internal to a particular firm or activity – focusing on transport costs and economies of scale. There are a further range of benefits that arise from the joint existence of many activities and from the size of a city itself. They are part of a general type of economic effect known as an externality. Such 'external' benefits or costs are associated with the existence of a particular activity but they do not influence its scale, which is determined by the marginal costs and revenues directly borne by the decision-making unit (be it a firm, a car driver, etc.). The pollution caused by a firm discharging contaminated water into a river is a classic external cost. The benefits to a beekeeper of a nearby orchard, or the reverse benefit of the keeper's bees for the orchard holder, are textbook external benefits. Cities generate many external benefits and costs. They arise from the concentration and interaction of separate activities and are, thus, the consequences of agglomeration.

Agglomeration economies can be divided into those that improve the productive potential of a particular industry, known as *localisation economies*, and those that spread across a variety of urban activities, termed *urbanisation economies* – although, in practice, the two may be hard to distinguish. Such benefits, furthermore, are not limited to businesses but extend to consumers and workers and differentially affect specific social strata. Consideration of agglomeration economies has to be primarily deductive because it is extremely difficult to measure most agglomeration benefits and, hence, direct empirical evidence is weak even for modern cities. Indirect evidence of their overall existence, none the less, is compelling because firms and people are willing to pay much more to locate in large cities, which they would only do if they are more than compensated for those costs by the benefits they gain.

Business gains from agglomeration

Localisation economies

Particular industries gain much from clustering together – an effect that may have consequences for the way in which production is organised. Clustering enables specialised out-sourcing and leads to a greater amount and variety of available shared inputs. Firms, small craft workshops or even home-workers can set up to provide some specialist manufactured input or some service because they supply a pool of firms. Economies of scale may result in each part of the production process which could not have been achieved if every firm had undertaken all the activities themselves. The paradox may arise that individual firms and plants may be smaller than if all aspects of production were unified into one plant but, at the industry level, greater scale economies are achieved.

Firms producing products subject to considerable variations in demand can use such networks to avoid high fixed costs and bankruptcy. Rather than having to set up a costly and inflexible production system, networked firms need only purchase particular inputs when required – spreading the costs of such flexibility across a wider range of agencies. This pooling effect tends to reduce variability for individual enterprises and enables the remaining fluctuations more easily to be priced into overall costs. Capital may also be cheaper, especially working capital, as proximate firms may be more willing to extend trade credit or lend a sub-contractor longer-term funds, if they are local, well-known and can easily be monitored. The evolution of the clothing and furniture industries in nineteenth-century London exhibits such networking gains.

One way of thinking about particular agglomeration benefits is that they reduce the transaction costs of market exchange. The effort to search out information and to strike deals is considerably lowered by clustering. Formal and informal institutional arrangements evolve, so that firms, workers and suppliers know, and are accustomed to, the ways in which business is conducted. With lower transaction costs in the market place, the benefits of integrated production under the auspices of one firm are diminished.

Particular types of industry especially benefit from these clustering effects. Many are characterised by a lack of standardisation in the products they produce – fashionable clothing is one London instance, precision instrument engineering is another. When long standardised product runs can be made, and demand is stable, unified, factory-based mechanised processes may be cheaper. In which case, agglomeration benefits are far less and a plant may well be set up in a non-metropolitan area because little extra is derived from a city location.

A related clustering benefit is that of complementary industries congregating in order to use by-products. Gas production, for example, led to such spin-offs. The extensive metropolitan tanning industry grew out of the huge number of livestock brought to the capital to feed its population, augmented by imported skins and furs. Glue factories and other animal rendering processes were other outcomes. Even polluting industries may encourage other polluters to set up near them, because their existence depresses local land values and, hence, creates cheaper places to locate. Outer East London's noxious industries exhibited such clustering dynamics and so did laundries in the west.

For some industries, continuous information is essential in order to lower the risks of doing business. The news might be about changing demand and supply conditions in volatile markets, new products and fashions, process innovations, political intrigue, ships arriving at port or plain gossip. Whatever the need, the imperative to cluster to obtain and share information can be great. Prior to the advent of telephones, let alone modern electronic equipment, acquiring news at distant locations was very costly and slow. The draw of the capital city as a source of information on many activities was immense as a result.

Labour market effects also arise. If firms in an industry locate near to each other, a pool of labour used to its customs, practices and skills grows up in the residential districts around. Firms, therefore, are less likely to experience difficulty in obtaining labour and can rely on its quality and dependability. Training costs can be spread and employment varied in relation to demand.

The overall result of these localisation economies are that 'industrial districts' arise, as Alfred Marshall termed them.[10] Nineteenth-century London had a large number of these industrial districts, so that the geography of activities across the city revealed particular local specialisms.[11] Their existence also affected the residential structure of the city, with many working-class residences attracted towards them and middle-class ones avoiding them and their smoke and pollution.

Urbanisation economies

The benefits of urban agglomeration that are not specific to a particular industrial sector come in a variety of guises: innovation, scope and insurance effects are three of the most significant.

INNOVATION

It has been argued that cities are places where ideas can spill over into new areas, encouraging innovation. There is a milieu of intellectual hardware – universities and other places of advanced learning. (Given the limited existence in nineteenth-century Britain of seats of learning, their metropolitan concentration was an important endowment of the capital.) Capital cities, moreover, are locations where professionals are likely to meet, including at the headquarters of their accredited bodies. In a major city, designers can easily pick up on new trends in fashion and apply them to their own products. Scientists, engineers and others meet frequently outside of the narrow confines of workplaces and come up with new, cross-fertilised, ideas. The modern epitome of such spillovers is California's Silicon Valley – yet, in the pre-motor car era, large cities were far more likely to play that role. Intellectual feedback was complement by the available range of skills and equipment in a large city. The wide range of easily obtainable skills and parts to facilitate experimentation, for example, helps to explain the significance of the Clerkenwell instrument engineering district in a number of nineteenth-century British inventions (including the early machine gun). Similar arguments can be made regarding services: financial innovations, for instance, were a virtual City prerogative.

SCOPE

A greater range, or scope, of activities is made possible in big cities. Specialist services can be set up, for example, in the knowledge that they can draw business from across a wide range of sectors. Accountants, business lawyers and advertising agencies are three such examples – and London was the British centre for all three in the nineteenth century. Diversity has also been suggested to have the effect of smoothing the impact of the business cycle, as different industries enter recessions at distinct points in time and some are worse affected than others.

INSURANCE EFFECTS

Industrial diversity may help sustain an urban economy through structural economic change. If a city is a single-industry town and technical change or shifts in demand lead to that industry's demise, the locality faces severe economic difficulties. Whereas, if a wide variety of industries exists, the urban area as a whole experiences only limited impacts from any such structural change, so the knock-on effects are limited and laid-off workers find it far easier to be re-employed. This is an example of the risk-pooling, insurance-type, effects of the economic life of large cities.

Another such effect arises in property markets because property developers and housebuilders have a wide range of potential purchasers of their new buildings and so are less vulnerable to the behaviour of a few potential clients. The City of London, for instance, was almost entirely rebuilt for commercial use in the nineteenth century but needed no planner or principal client.

Consumption and labour market effects

The agglomeration principles that apply to firms have parallels in consumption and labour supply and will only briefly indicated here as they are similar to those for business. In contrast to a small town or rural locality, consumers in big cities benefit from the array of outlets there – which intensifies competition between sellers, reduces search costs and widens consumption opportunities. At a social level, the potential number of personal contacts is large, even though the city is still big enough generally to ensure the personal anonymity so loved by the majority of city dwellers.

In labour markets, workers are in good bargaining positions with a large array of potential employers bidding for labour. Skills are also more likely to be matched with available job opportunities. Periods of unemployment are reduced, as workers have a range of alternative opportunities when one job comes to an end. The higher productivity of labour in the city also leads to higher earnings for many skills. Workers may additionally acquire a range of skills and dexterities from urban living, and be socialised into a way of life some carry with them to other localities, where the practices are then emulated. Many young people go to large cities to learn skills, so that large cities often have a disproportionate share of a nation's youth. Nineteenth-century London was such a youthful city.

All of the consumption and labour market benefits described so far either refer to scale or urbanisation economies. But localisation ones exist as well, with consumption districts replacing the industrial districts of business. Cultural activities, for example, often share common inputs (actors, artists, musicians, etc.). Fashion vultures need to see and be seen. Groups of socialites, professionals, scientists, clergy and politicians congregate to talk about whatever they want to talk about. The sexes congregate and mix according to contemporary practice. Games may start in the street, on common ground or in the parks of the more regulated Edwardian era. The list is endless.

Social group differences

Agglomeration benefits affect various social groups differentially. The upper class derived considerable gains from the social networks and possibilities for luxury consumption available in nineteenth-century London and flocked to it as a result. Businessmen and financiers profited from the scale of the market and the concentration of British finance in the City. Middle-class professionals' earning opportunities were enhanced in London by its place at the top of the British urban hierarchy, with many of the best jobs available there and the range of openings the greatest. All three of these social groups could also enjoy the rich cultural and entertainment life of the capital.

The situation of the poor was somewhat different. They did not frequent the delights of the West End and their job and living possibilities were much more restricted. None the less, their situation was relatively improved by living in a large city like London. Unskilled earnings were often greater than elsewhere, even if part of the benefit was lost in higher rents. There were also more opportunities to find work within the capital's casual labour markets. Low-income households, in particular, were far more likely to find some sort of work for more members of the family than in many other places with their narrower employment structures. Other income opportunities were also greater in the form of street selling, begging and busking. Personal support networks could be found in the dense slums of the inner city.

Spatial differentiation between social groups inevitably is great in a large city, because of the pressure of land values. This can be seen in nineteenth-century London as much as anywhere else. Only the rich could afford to live in the better-off neighbourhoods – though there were hidden pockets of poverty even in these areas. The poorest, furthermore, could not afford to commute on the new transport systems to the suburbs like other social strata. Social policies designed to alleviate the lot of the poor, moreover, intensified spatial separation because they were overwhelmingly paid for out of property taxes and so involved a substantial redistribution from the better-off. The latter tried to avoid this through sustaining a localised 'vestry' structure of poor rate support, so that the vestries in which the better-off lived for much of the century paid a far low poor rate. The other option was to leave the city centre and move to suburbs beyond the remit of the tax net, which the middle classes did in droves as soon as transport systems made it feasible.

Some authors have suggested that the extent of class segregation in nineteenth-century London was mainly driven by a paranoid fear in the minds of the middle classes about the mob.[12] The fear was that East would one day meet West in an apocalyptical political crisis. Rational economic calculation, however, probably did the job of spatial segregation far more thoroughly – especially as the century progressed and metropolitan land-use patterns were transformed.

The costs of urban growth

If cities provide agglomeration benefits why do they not grow forever? The answer, of course, is that along with the good comes the bad – in this case, several costs tend to grow with city size. Large urban areas, therefore, expand in size until the costs of being there start to exceed the benefits for a sufficient number of people and firms, so that the flow of emigrants from the city begins to outweigh that of new immigrants. The increasing costs of agglomeration are those associated with doing business and living – and are transmitted through the land market, transport costs and local taxes – plus further problems of pollution and congestion.

Land market effects

The clustering of economic activities in a large urban area forces land prices to rise. The rents on business premises are consequently higher, as are housing costs. Once extensive commuting became commonplace, moreover, thousands faced the expense and time of the trek to and from work. These housing and travel costs then feed through into wages, so that labour costs for employers rise. If they rise continuously, they will eventually halt employment growth. Data on housing rents show that London rents, in fact, were far higher than elsewhere in Britain, although general housing conditions were better than in most other British cities. Property costs for businesses were also high. The transformation of the City of London, for example, went along with huge increases in office rents and land values.

These increases in land rents and housing costs, however, were being counteracted by improvements on the supply side, so that the city continued to grow. The amount of available land grew exponentially as ever more distant suburbs were opened up. Technical improvements in transportation and other infrastructure provision, and extensive investments in them, made this possible; whilst rising incomes brought the suburban lifestyle within reach of millions of Londoners.

Not all of the effects of rising land costs were negative for urban growth. For one thing, the structure of the city was re-ordered through the demolition and rebuilding stimulated by land value gains. Some attractive and historic buildings may have been unfortunately destroyed but the economic efficiency of the city was enhanced, which helped to sustain its growth. Higher-level service activities became concentrated in the core and much manufacturing industry was set up in an inner urban ring, circling the centre in all but the west, and the suburbs stretched to the horizons and beyond. In this way, London became the world's first, giant, spread-out city. In contrast to the modern megalopolis, however, employment activity was strongly centrally focused.

Higher land costs, furthermore, are not simply a cost in a large city, as the housing and other buildings, and the land on which they sit, belong to someone. Property costs, in other words, are transfer payments from tenants to building and ground landlords and to the lenders of mortgages. There is good reason to believe that much rental income remained, at least initially, within the confines of the metropolitan economy, as its recipients were fellow Londoners. Landowners and ground landlords are perhaps the most well-known receivers of rent, yet their share of housing rent was relatively small and probably declined over time. Far more significant in terms of the flow of funds were housing landlords and mortgage holders. They were mainly not the rich but middle-income individuals and many of them would have lived in the capital. Rents raised their incomes and wealth, thereby indirectly affected the pattern and scale of demand in the city.

Pollution and urban health

Another limiting factor on a city's economic well-being is pollution. Urban pollution today predominantly means bad air, excessive noise and visual signs of dereliction and decay. Two hundred years ago, it was much more directly associated with death. Polluted water, inadequate sewage disposal, rotting rubbish, combined with poor diets and ignorance, enabled the transmission of a wide variety of killer diseases. Frequent, soot-laden smog added further deaths by encouraging the ravages of tuberculosis and bronchitis. Life expectancy was low. London's population growth in the eighteenth and early nineteenth centuries was consequently held back by a very high death rate.

Added to the costs of living in London for much of the time period, therefore, was the probability of a much shorter life span when compared to rural living. The behaviour of the rich helped them to minimise the risks. They came to the capital for relatively short periods of time, for events like the Season, and otherwise lived in rural mansions. Yet, all classes were affected by the threat of disease when residing in the capital, with the poor the most vulnerable because of their diets and bad living conditions. This cost of being in London fell dramatically over the course of the nineteenth century, so that life expectancy was the same as the, by then, much higher national figure at the century's end.[13]

This very considerable improvement in longevity and the quality of life is not measured in monetary data on incomes, but it clearly represented a major gain in the standard of living. The contribution that urban improvements made to the reduction in the death rate is unclear, but vast sums were spent on them. The only aspect that saw no sign of progress was the smogs that continued to debilitate or kill people in the capital until the Clean Air Acts of the 1950s.

Congestion

Congestion increases the monetary expense and time of travel. Such delays to people and goods raise urban costs, reduce mobility and lower the potential size and spread of an urban area.

Any additional vehicle driven on to an already crowded street further slows down the traffic, so that other users of the thoroughfare are subject to extra delay. The external cost of an additional vehicle on a road is thus the sum of the costs of any extra delays imposed on other users. Above moderate levels of congestion, these will usually far outweigh the benefit derived from the additional journey itself. Even so, a little congestion is generally a good thing because it means an expensive public asset is being used to its full capacity. Yet, in the absence of other means of traffic restraint, congestion tends to rise above such socially optimal levels because individual road users do not bear the costs they impose on others when deciding whether to undertake a journey. Similar effects can occur with pedestrians, because walking speeds are hampered on crowded streets. Given the high population densities of pre-motorised cities, with walking the prime means of getting about, streets could be extremely crowded, and hence congested, all day long.

Even public transport and dock systems were subject to delays. The rail network built in the 1860s linking Charing Cross, Cannon Street, Farringdon and London Bridge, for example, was infamous for the delays at its over-used junctions almost as soon as the lines were built. Most road vehicles by the second half of the century, in London, as in other cities, were for public transport, and narrow streets and junctions would form huge bottlenecks for horse (and later motor) buses, trams and other vehicles all day long. Traffic rules were rudimentary and buses could career from one side of the road to the other to pick up passengers as there were no controls on where they could stop until late in the century. Congestion in the Port of London reached crisis point during the Napoleonic Wars.

Congestion is as old as urbanisation. There has never been a golden age, when city streets were uncrowded all day long. The ancient Romans complained about gridlock and nineteenth-century London was a city where the situation just seemed to become worse and worse as more and more vehicles were driven on to its streets and its pedestrian population multiplied. Surface travel by any means in the city centre did not improve noticeably over the course of the nineteenth century. Developments in public transport, and far greater efficiencies in inland and seaborne transportation, may have lowered travel costs in important ways but, city-wide, road transport remained poor.[14] Many new roads were built, others were improved and legislation was toughened to remove impediments, like street markets, but the extra building and other measures failed to keep road capacity in line with the growth in traffic.

An early form of road-pricing existed in the first half of the century as many roads into and out of London were subject to tolls, as were most of the bridges across the Thames. These tolls were immensely unpopular – the poor were excluded from using bridges as a result of the tolls, and the press was full of real or imagined complaints of monopolistic abuse. In contrast to modern road-pricing ideas, fixed rates were charged that did not directly reflect the degree of congestion. By the 1860s, the chorus of complaint had led to the abolition of the final tolls. The democratic right to delay others had won out.

Traffic delays certainly raised costs for London businesses and residents. As with modern congestion, any delay was an affront to most of those who experienced it, though the true economic effects of congestion should not be exaggerated.

Local taxes

The final cost of agglomeration is the local taxation necessitated by the provision of public goods[15] (such as roads, street lighting and parks) and services (such as health regulation) by local government. Growth in local government expenditure in nineteenth century has been likened to the tide: concern would grow over a lack of public provision, to be met by a howl of ratepayer reaction as the cost of the schemes rose, and subsequent curtailment of improvement plans, in an ever-repeated cycle.[16] London was no exception but, in its case, the cost of local government almost continuously rose, especially after the 1850s.

Higher rate bills encouraged some firms to quit the capital and others to follow the better-off by moving to the outer suburbs. The impact on businesses, and their levels of activity and employment, nevertheless, depended on the usefulness to them of public expenditure. Expenditure that indirectly lowered wage costs (say, by improving the possibilities of commuting) or that made people healthier would not necessarily have been an aggregate business deterrent, as the resultant lower labour costs would have offset the extra taxes. Similarly, expenditure on roads and other urban infrastructure improvements could directly aid business profitability. Much of this type of expenditure, furthermore, was concentrated in the West End and City where many businesses were located.

Businesses, moreover, were taxed on the rateable value of the property they used, rather than the value of their turnover or profits. This would have encouraged them to economise on property in their activities but not necessarily to contemplate quitting the metropolis. The overall impact of growing local property taxes on firms and aggregate levels of employment is consequently uncertain. Yet, even so, the burden of the rates grew substantially, which must have had some effects. Working conditions, in addition, were made worse by the incentive to economise on building space that property taxes induced.

Agglomeration economies – the whole picture

Table 2.1 summarises the benefits and costs of agglomeration.

Table 2.1 Economic factors benefiting and restricting urban growth

Beneficial factors

- The 'friction' of distance and scale economies
- Size of local consumer and intermediate good markets
- Specialisation and the division of labour
- Scale economies in transportation, utilities and public goods
- Shared inputs in production and consumption
- Pools of specialised labour
- Information availability – production, consumption and labour
- Risk minimisation and insurance
- Competitive markets
- Transaction cost lowering
- Innovation enhancing
- Substitute goods and resale markets
- Diversity

Costs restricting growth

- Real wages
- Land costs
- Housing costs
- Pollution
- Congestion
- Local taxes

London's employment and population growth were both very rapid right up until 1914. In order for this to have happened, the agglomeration benefits derived from being in the capital must have be increasing faster than the extra costs of locating there. On the demand side, this suggests that the productivity of labour and other inputs was rising at a healthy rate. To achieve this, agglomeration economies were continually being refashioned and improved upon in ways that are part of the narrative that follows in subsequent chapters.

The significance of path dependency and institutions

The interaction of the benefits of locating in London and the costs of being there at any point in time determined the size of the capital and the activities taking place there. Yet, change was not an easy or fluid process. Simple inertia played an important part, so change could be a long drawn-out process. Inertia, moreover, need not be irrational, once account is taken of the uncertainty and transaction costs of moving.

Change, in addition, depended on what there was to be altered. This made London's economic development 'path-dependent'.[17] Path dependency can be seen at the regional level in London's ascendancy in the British economy, which had evolved in the centuries before 1800. Many of its nineteenth-century roles were thereby predetermined – for example, being the major urban consumer market in Britain, one of the country's largest ports, the international finance centre and the seat of government and law. The benefits of these prior attributes were then magnified as the British economy continued to grow during the century. Path dependency can also be seen in the types of industrial district that evolved because, once there, their benefits encouraged others to join in.

One of the clearest examples of path dependency can be seen in the institutional framework of economic life in the capita, and institutional theory can help to explain the implications. There are two aspects to institutional analysis: organisations and institutions. Organisations are the functional bodies that exist in particular areas – firms, governments, unions and the like. Institutions are the prevailing rules and practices by which the organisations operate and interrelate with each other, which may be formal procedures or informal ways of doing things and implicit boundaries to behaviour. A frequent analogy is that of a professional sport with its teams (organisations) and rules of play and success (institutions). The two-fold distinction, moreover, is somewhat of a heuristic device because the two aspects, organisations and institutions, obviously interact closely. Rules can be embedded so deeply within organisational structures that it is difficult to conceive of one without the other, as could be said, for example, of many practices in the nineteenth-century City. Keeping the two aspects in mind, none the less, is still useful. Institutions in the combined sense are important because they are the conduits through which economic processes work themselves out. Informal institutional practices on who could be hired, what work they could do, and the pay they received were, for example, important in the functioning of the capital's labour markets. In fact, they were far more pervasive than any formal trade union activity.

Areas in which institutions and path dependency were perhaps the most significant were in relation to the supply of urban services in transport, property and the utilities. Interesting questions are whether London had a particular set of institutions distinct from those in other parts of urban Britain and whether they were suited to the tasks at hand? The answer to the first question is undoubtedly yes. Despite common national and legal frameworks and increasing national conformities in local politics, London institutions remained supremely distinct. Their efficiency, to reply to the second question, was distinctly mixed, as later chapters will show.

Many of the 'urban supply' institutional frameworks were set up, or ordained, by Parliament. This not only occurred with the structure of local government and changes within it but also with transportation, innovations in communications and with the utilities. Private institutions, for instance, were given monopoly powers over transportation routes and in the spatial provision of water and gas. They were also given rights of compulsory land purchase but usually could not recoup any of the 'betterment' to adjacent land values that their activities created. Within the land market, and in housing provision, central and local government set down regulatory rules in the form of building regulations and controls, and favoured new 'social housing' landlords over private ones from the 1860s onwards. With regard to land law, Parliament tended to favour landowners over land users.

Once set up these institutional frameworks affected outcomes. The institutional context under which the enclosed docks were built in the East End, for instance, and the way in which dock activity moved down river, had fundamental impacts on the economic geography of the east and south-east of the city, as Chapter 1 has already noted. Path dependency, in this case, meant that individual docks affected the local urban spatial structure long after they had become economically unviable (which had already happened to several of them by the middle of the nineteenth century). The costs of filling them in and reorganising the local infrastructural fabric were too expensive for any private organisation to contemplate, so large areas lay in sub-optimal use for over a century.

Urban infrastructure

Growth and increasing capital intensity

Infrastructure here is used in the broad physical sense of the means by which the built form of a city is linked to form a whole and connected to other places. It includes the road network, inter- and intra-urban public transportation systems, communications, power networks for heating, lighting and industry, water supply and, finally, sewerage. These facilities form the physical core of any city and their provision affects how fast a city can grow, its shape and size, the success of business enterprises there and the quality of life enjoyed by its citizens.

As has already been noted, these were generally provided by specific private institutions set up or, in modern terminology, 'regulated' by Parliament. In London, two features of infrastructure provision stand out: how much existed and who provided it.

In 1800, the infrastructure was poor in relation to the vast amount of investment that then occurred over the next 114 years. In part, of course, this was because much of what were to become key elements of any city's urban infrastructure had yet to be invented. Each successive wave of innovation then had enormous impacts on the functioning of London as a city. The nineteenth-century city experienced equally as much effect from transport innovations as the twentieth-century city did from the motor car. The innovations stretched from the steam railway through the electric underground and tram to the motor bus. These helped to make London the largest city in the world and the first one with widespread suburbs linked by intra-urban transportation systems to the city centre. All these innovations, moreover, required large initial investments in groundwork and equipment.[18] The switch from labour-intensive to capital-intensive technology was equally great in the port, with ships moored at quaysides or in the river – and served by lighters – giving way to an extensive network of enclosed docks.

In the field of power, coal remained the main source of domestic heat and candles the main source of domestic light, but, first gas (mainly for public lighting until towards the end of the period), then, falteringly, electricity, appeared. They each used capital-intensive production and distribution systems that grew in optimal scale over time. In a broadly similar way, the traditionally inadequate supply of fresh water was revolutionised by a series of technical innovations in storage, piping and pumping and, once again, they were associated with a considerable increase in the use of expensive fixed capital. Sewage disposal was also transformed by the advent of disposal via underground systems of sewers. In communications, the postal service was highly labour-intensive but, from mid-century, it was supplemented, initially by the capital-intensive telegraph and later by the telephone.

Monopoly and collusion

The tendency towards monopoly and collusive agreements can be seen in all private sector infrastructure activities in nineteenth-century London, as Part 4 shows. Water and gas firms carved up localities and fixed prices. Railway and tram companies specialised in particular areas and trod gingerly around each other's territories. One bus company remained dominant for much of the period. The underground railway system was unified under one owner, even before lines were completed, and, eventually, one large firm had effective control over most of the bus, tram and underground networks. When collusion failed, excess capacity and poor profits could last for many years, as occurred for several periods in the docks and for railways south of the river.

These events did not occur by chance and similar tendencies are common in all cities. Infrastructure projects have 'natural monopoly' characteristics which influence the behaviour of firms within them. Because of their high initial fixed investments, average costs fall in these activities as greater volumes are produced. If there is competition, all firms incur losses as each competitor can price down to short-run marginal costs. Where one supplier has a larger market share than others, it will have lower unit costs and, therefore, be able to drive the others out of business. Given the scale of the sunk costs of each producer, moreover, the associated price war is likely to be lengthy and fierce. There are then two possible outcomes. In one, only a monopolist remains and it can restrict output below optimal levels, raise prices and threaten price wars to deter new entrants. In the other scenario, collusive agreements are reached between the existing firms, so that markets are shared out and prices maintained. Collusion is easier across space, as each firm can be allocated an exclusive territory.

Was London's infrastructure, consequently, in the hands of rapacious monopolies that restricted supply and made unreasonable profits? The answer is mixed, because it depended on how contestable these markets were. As the individual histories considered later show, many of them were contestable to a degree and technical innovations played a major part in stimulating competition.

Contestability depends on the existence of the threat of a new entrant if an incumbent firm tries to take advantage of its monopoly position. Although entry does not actually have to occur (firms simply have to be worried about it), evidence about the situations in which new entry does actually take place allows some judgement of the real competitive situation of transport and utility undertakings. New entry was most noticeable in nineteenth-century London in public transport. For instance, the monopoly bus operator from mid-century, the London General Omnibus Co., faced a major new entrant in the 1880s and then, later, a flood of new firms with the development of the motor bus. Buses were the easiest sector to enter, with relatively low fixed capital requirements and limited cost benefits of greater scale. This meant that, even when collusive agreements or a single firm existed, small firms could still enter and nibble at the pricing strategies of the incumbents. Moreover, each transport mode was subject to a degree of competition from others and the options open to passengers increased substantially as the century progressed.

Spatial monopoly was less contestable, especially if the territories were protected by Acts of Parliament. Technical change would still play its part, however, as occurred in the gas industry from the 1860s onwards when there was a major merger movement. Later, furthermore, gas was to face the threat of electricity. Water was the least contestable, which is perhaps why it was the most unsuccessful of the infrastructural industries over the period. Governments tried to regulate it and painstakingly slowly managed to improve the controls and incentives, but ultimately failed to put in an adequate regulatory environment that combined targets on quality, investment and profitability, and it was eventually brought into public ownership in 1905.

The regulation of natural monopoly

Governments need to enter into regulation of private infrastructure schemes for three reasons: competition, eminent domain and externalities.

- *Competition*: Monopolistic tendencies are inherent, as noted above. There is no direct evidence of monopoly-busting or competition-encouraging activity by governments over London's infrastructure. Quite the contrary. On occasions collusive agreements would be given legal status – as in gas and water – on the basis of the 'public interest'. Sometimes, though, price ceilings were imposed – as with workmen's tickets. Yet, it could still be argued that, through the ability of new entrants to get Parliamentary permission for their schemes, governments none the less did encourage contestability. The Parliamentary process was much complained about but was vastly quicker, easier and cheaper than today's mammoth inquiries. So new dock companies and railways, for example, appear at regular intervals.
- *Eminent domain*: All infrastructure schemes interfere with the prevailing urban fabric and so companies involved require powers to dig up roads, tunnel or compulsorily buy up land and property on which to build facilities. Through its power of eminent domain, the state can confer these powers and simultaneously set the terms of compensation for existing property owners. These powers overwhelmingly favoured existing property owners, which considerably raised the cost of both public and private sector infrastructure projects. Infrastructure providers, moreover, through their facilities often improved adjacent land values but were legally unable to recoup a share of this betterment through financial measures or via property development. Doubtless, nineteenth-century London would have seen far more infrastructural schemes – from grand avenues to subways – if these formulae had favoured infrastructure providers more.
- *Externalities and distributional effects*: Infrastructure schemes imposed costs on some activities (for example, inner city housing, pollution and congestion) and provided benefits to others. The scale of proposed schemes, moreover, could swamp the city. In the 1840s and, again, in the 1860s, large parts of central London were threatened with demolition by rail projects.[19] Investors, moreover, could make bad decisions and overbuild facilities with detrimental effects on the functioning of the city.

> Governments, by having to transfer their power of eminent domain to specific projects, therefore, were drawn into land-use and infrastructure planning long before planning became a formal government activity.

Nineteenth-century Parliament needed no encouragement to indulge its capacity to affect the physical structure of the capital. Political whim and influence seem uppermost in affecting the decisions made, rather than operating under rules drawn up on an analytical basis or through the building up of a cadre of disinterested experts similar to today's land-use and traffic planners. It has been argued that rational criteria were brought to bear in the debates and evidence of the armies of expert witnesses presented to Parliamentary committees.[20] Amongst a wide variety of topics, the congestion impacts of termini locations were calculated in the 1840s; in the next decade, sheep and other animals were counted by surprisingly alert enumerators in relation to the potential relocation of Smithfield, and people and vehicles were noted on entering and leaving the City to identify causes of congestion. The methods used, none the less, were no match for modern sophisticated cost-benefit analyses. But, perhaps, what was worse was that each deliberation tended to be piecemeal, so that there was rarely a realistic conception of the future of London and any particular scheme's place within it. Broader perspectives did appear as the century progressed, with infrastructure policies increasingly being based on perceived solutions to urban ills. Whether this was progress, however, is less certain. Supposed solutions soon became political totems, especially after the formation of the LCC, and were rarely subject to much rational evaluation and, with the exception of a few cases like the main sewer system, failed to achieve their exaggerated claims. Isolated initiatives and buckets of wishful thinking unfortunately still dominate urban planning and politics, so modesty about the present is needed when being critical of such ancient and revered practices.

London in the British economy

Cities in competition

One common approach to understanding the relationship of cities to wider national and international economies is to treat an urban area as though it was identical to a firm in a highly competitive industry.[21] Cities then 'compete' with each other for such things as jobs and favourable government policies. The consequences, it is often claimed, are that successful ones grow and the less favoured decline, in parallel to similar claims about nations solely competing over international trade.[22]

Although there is no denying the importance of competition at the local level in winning public policy dispensations, to view cities solely as competitors is misguided. Few large cities are single-firm or even single-industry entities, especially a global giant like London, so that the fortunes of particular firms are not the main causes of their prosperity. Cities, moreover, tend to specialise in the activities that they are best at: leading to long-run mutual gains. Such outcomes are the results of the benefits of trade and specialisation. The associated mechanisms by which the activities of any urban area come into being and change determine the trajectory of its comparative advantages. Trying to understand them leads to far more fruitful lines of enquiry than the crude city competition metaphor.

Segmented or integrated regional growth?

In an entirely different stream of literature from city competition debates, historical geographers and other historians have adopted two contrasting positions on British regional development in the nineteenth century. One highlights differences between regions, arguing that regional economic development was spatially segmented so that each region was, in effect, a distinct economic island within the British Isles. The other viewpoint focuses on the inter-linkages between British regions and identifies similar sets of processes and convergence in several key regional attributes, so that Britain was more regionally integrated than the segmentalists assume.[23] The debate is founded on the regional industrial geography of newly urbanising Britain, which was generally one of intense specialisation and a heavy reliance on world markets – textiles and coal in Lancashire (cotton) and the West Riding (wool); metals, chemicals, heavy engineering and coal in the North-East, West-Central Scotland and South Wales; and small-scale engineering, metals and coal in the West Midlands. Places with coal, iron ore and fast-running streams became identified with Victorian Britain's industrial lead and role as 'workshop of the world'. London's industries, in contrast, are often regarded as small-scale and focused, apart from the City, on domestic, even local, markets. Consequently, they exhibited few of the characteristics of those industries that formed the standard image of the industrial revolution.[24]

The segmented regional growth model is based on observations about the new regional pattern of industrial, capital and labour markets from the mid-eighteenth century onwards. It is argued that during the industrial revolution wage growth diverged and favoured the North;[25] that most industrial capital and commercial credit was raised locally – at least until the 1840s;[26] and that regional social structures were distinct and remained so. The separation is qualified, none the less, because centralising, London-based, influences slowly reasserted themselves after the advent of rail travel, but this predominantly led to a dualism in Britain's regional economic development between the capital and the manufacturing regions.[27] These spatial divisions have been encapsulated most strongly in claimed social divisions between industrialists from the 'North' and a financial/commercial and landed oligarchy centred on London. North and South in this view had opposed economic interests, with southern finance and commerce having a bias towards the international economy and imperialism at the expense of real northern industry.[28] When stated in a strongly causal way, these regional divisions become assertions about the relative degrees of political power exercised by northern industrialists and a metropolitan oligarchy. The North never managed, according to this view, to out-manoeuvre the South. The United Kingdom resembled a union that was economically crippled by a backward-looking South, contrary to experience in the USA, and economic decline beckoned while resurgent post-civil war America boomed. So, according to this view, spatial and social differentiations had far more influence on British economic development than economic analyses of market processes would forecast.

A market approach to British economic development would be very different from this segmented position and closer to the integrated regions perspective. To consider such regional economic fusion, the theories of market integration and urban economic analysis outlined earlier in the chapter would be used to explain events in nineteenth-century regional development, and evidence for regional convergence would be sought. If input endowments are different between regions (say, some are more natural resource-rich than others), a standard economic analysis based on regional comparative advantages would predict major differences in the industrial composition of regions as a result of trade between them. A simple two-region trade model of a coal-rich 'North' and a labour-rich 'London', for example, would lead to the North exporting goods that used a lot of coal in their production to London in exchange for more labour-intensive goods. Merely to identify regional industrial differences, therefore, is not sufficient justification for the segmented view.

Price formation offers a useful test of the two views. The segmented approach would predict limited price convergence across regions in specific markets – which ones would depend on the claimed nature of the segmentation. A market approach conversely would predict price convergence across regions for both outputs and inputs (in line with the predictions of the Heckscher-Ohlin-Samuelson model). For output and possibly capital markets, if free trade and factor mobility existed, the price convergence should be rapid but, with labour, the process might be long drawn-out because it involves extensive migration of labour to higher real wage regions.[29] Thus, evidence of higher wages in the North at the end of the eighteenth century would be argued to be caused by the technological shock of the new industries setting up there and the slow migration of workers to those districts in response to the resulting higher wages, which would then decline again relative to other regions as local labour supplies improved.

In reality, markets were often imperfect so that these adjustment processes were weakened or delayed. One of the causes of imperfection is the effect of distance, especially in a society with only limited and generally expensive means of transport and communication. Improvements in transportation consequently should lead to greater price convergence. The enormous technological improvements in transport during the nineteenth century should, therefore, have encouraged processes of price convergence.

To accept the possible existence of imperfect markets, therefore, is to still believe in a causal structure related to market processes; whereas the segmented approach concentrates on the causes and consequences of the segmentation, which are by definition non-market in nature.

Price differences alone, moreover, do not necessarily imply a lack of convergence tendencies. Labour in London, for example, had to be paid more than elsewhere to compensate for the high cost of housing. Regional price differences could similarly arise in capital markets, particularly in the early years of the nineteenth century. If a 'northern' capital market appeared entirely local in character with all industrialists funded by local lenders, this may be because of the advantages of local knowledge in reducing risk and of proximity in reducing transaction costs. A London financier would then have to charge a higher interest rate to compensate for these disadvantages and, thus, be priced out of the market unless local savings are in short supply. The absence of London finance in a region or locality consequently cannot be taken as proof that the City was 'ignoring' that region. Careful account has to be taken to explain interest rate differences, when they arose, in standard financial market terms before the segmentation view can be justified.

The actual extent to which regional industrial structures and prices were converging requires extensive empirical investigation. Aspects are considered in Chapter 4 (industrial structure), Chapter 5 (prices and wages) and Chapter 14 (financial markets). Broadly, they suggest that convergence processes were occurring – supporting the pervasive market rather than the segmented economy view.

Conclusion

An economic analysis of London aims to identify the characteristics of the city that made it a productive place. The economic attributes of London were part of the overall contemporary productive potential of the British economy and many aspects of the metropolitan economy were, therefore, nationally determined. The ways in which capital and labour were used in the metropolis were generally of higher than average national productivity because of the agglomeration benefits of the world's largest city. Growth in London was important for overall national economic growth as it probably contained more than a fifth of the productive potential of all British industries and services. (No data existed but its share of the national population was around 14 per cent alone.) As a region of Britain, the metropolis had comparative advantages across a wide variety of activities, but only in the case of a few sectors, such as international finance, was national activity overwhelmingly centred there. London was not so much in competition with the rest of Britain but an integral part of an increasingly unified national economy. In this way, to adapt the cliché, what was good for London was good for the British economy as a whole.

Part 2

London's economy and people

3 Population and migration

Introduction

The people of a city are its most basic economic resource. This chapter surveys the population growth of London in the nineteenth century and its causes. Because the ten-year population census started in 1801, the information some of the richest available. As in all major cities up to the nineteenth century, life in London was often a short experience before disease carried off the urban dweller.[1] Cities then stopped being such unremitting killers, which helps to explain the rapid expansion in urban populations. Even so, uncertainty still arises over the causes of major changes in life expectancy and birth rates. As urban areas continued to expand, Britain was transformed from a predominantly rural society to an urban one, the first major economy to experience such a change. London led the pack in terms of consistent growth, with its population rising by around a fifth each decade.

Population growth was the result both of natural increase – that is, births exceeding deaths – and net migration inflows from other areas. To determine the reasons behind the expansion, it is, therefore, necessary to examine death and birth rates and migration flows. These tasks are undertaken below, after the broad pattern of London's population growth is described and compared to those in other contemporary British cities and elsewhere in the world.

Size and growth

The growth of London

Deciding on what was the actual population of London at any point in time depends on whether the County or the Greater London spatial area is defined as London. As Chapter 1 has already noted, neither administrative area is an ideal guide to the size of the metropolitan area. The population of the continuous built-up area of the capital is somewhat exaggerated on both definitions, because in the County and the outer areas making up the rest of Greater London there were many free-standing

Table 3.1 The growth of London's population, 1801–1911

	County of London	*Greater London*	*London as % of Greater London*	*% change in County of London*	*% change in Greater London*
1801	959,310	1,096,784	87		
1811	1,139,355	1,303,564	87	19	19
1821	1,379,543	1,573,210	88	21	21
1831	1,655,582	1,878,229	88	20	19
1841	1,949,277	2,207,653	88	18	18
1851	2,363,341	2,651,939	89	21	20
1861	2,808,494	3,188,485	88	19	20
1871	3,261,396	3,840,595	85	16	20
1881	3,830,297	4,713,441	81	17	23
1891	4,227,954	5,571,968	76	10	18
1901	4,536,267	6,506,889	70	7	17
1911	4,521,685	7,160,441	63	0	10

Source: Census.

towns and villages at the beginning of the nineteenth century. But, as the century progressed, the built-up area spread over much of the County and into the surrounding districts and, by the end of the period, the Greater London area became the most meaningful of the two as the spatial definition of the extent of the capital. By the 1900s, none the less, even the Greater London area was too small, with suburbs growing up in the adjacent parts of surrounding counties.

Table 3.1 presents the basic statistics of this growth. In 1801, the County had just under a million people living in it. By 1911, its population stood at 4.5 million. This was the peak level for the County because for almost every decade subsequently it has lost population. By 1981, the number was down to 2.5 million. The 2 million extra people packed into the County area just prior to the First World War indicates how high the population densities of nineteenth-century cities were in comparison to modern ones.

Growth of the County faltered from the 1860s as transport improvements led to extensive suburbanisation on the fringes of the capital. Ex-County suburban growth meant that, overall, London continued to expand throughout the nineteenth century, with ten-year population percentage growth rates in the high teens and low twenties. By the 1900s, however, even the expansion of the Greater London area began to slow down – in part because extra suburbs were now being added beyond the Greater London border.

A greater importance of the outer suburbs is indicated in Table 3.1 by the proportion of the population of the metropolis living in the County area. Up to 1861, 87–89 per cent of those living in Greater London actually resided in the inner area delineated by the County. Then the County's share gradually fell, so that by 1911 less than two-thirds of Londoners lived within its boundaries. This had important implications for local governance because the jurisdiction of the London County Council (LCC), set up in 1889, was the County of London area. At its inception, therefore, a quarter of Londoners lived outside of its remit, and over a third twenty years later. Centralised city government was consequently stymied from its inception (see Chapter 16).

The population of London on its broad definition still grew in the inter-war years, but at a slower rate than before 1914. The maximum population was reached in 1941, when the number of people living in the metropolis peaked at 8.6 million. By 1991, the number of Londoners was down to 6.4 million – with virtually all of the decline occurring within the County area. (By the 1940s more people lived in London's suburbs beyond the County area than within it.) From the inter-war years, London ceased to be a stand-alone urban entity but, instead, became a less population-dense hub of a wider metropolitan agglomeration spread across south-east England. For the purpose of this study, which looks at the years before 1914, however, it can be treated as a separate urban agglomeration in the economic and social senses as well as in pure administrative terms.

London's growth compared

The growth of London was part of a general process of urbanisation taking place during the transformation of Britain into the first industrial nation. In 1801, for example, 36 per cent of the British labour force worked directly in agriculture; yet, by 1901, the proportion had dropped to only 9 per cent,[2] and the proportion of the national population living in urban areas rose from a third in 1801 to almost four-fifths in 1911.[3] London gained considerably from the rural to urban shift, and the County increased its share of the population of England and Wales from 11 per cent in 1750 to 14 per cent in 1911. Other cities in the industrial regions also grew dramatically during the period – with Manchester, for example, almost starting from nothing in the mid-eighteenth century. (The growth rate of the northern conurbations was exceptionally fast in the first half of the century, but faltered from then onwards.) By 1901, more than half of the population of England and Wales lived in provincial towns and cities, but no other British city managed to reach a solitary million, let alone Greater London's 7 million plus (21 per cent of the population of England), before 1914 – even when their non-city jurisdiction suburbs are included. The capital consequently dwarfed other urban areas and consolidated its position at the peak of Britain's urban hierarchy.

In England and Wales, the shift from a predominantly rural–small town society into an urban one was proceeding at a faster rate than anywhere else in the world. Between 1800 and 1850, the proportion of the population of Britian living in towns of 10,000 or more was growing at a rate that was at least twice as fast as other rapidly urbanising countries. But, by the second half of the century, several other countries had almost caught up with England's urbanisation rate. In Western Europe, the fastest urbanisers were parts of what became Germany, France and Belgium; elsewhere they were countries experiencing large inflows of European migrants – Australasia, the USA, Argentina and Chile. So, as urbanisation spread, other parts of the world were catching up with Britain's urban way of living by the early decades of the twentieth century. Later, from the 1950s, the urban revolution spread to the Third World where vast cities have been created. Yet, in the nineteenth century, London towered above the other large cities in the world. Its population in 1890, even on the narrower County of London definition at 4.2 million, was far greater than that of its nearest rival, New York–New Jersey at 2.7 million, and bigger than that of Chicago, Philadelphia, St Petersburg and Istanbul combined (the world's seventh to tenth largest cities, respectively). No other major city in the world, furthermore, had such a large share of its country's population.[4]

Household patterns in London were somewhat different from those found elsewhere in England and Wales because of its structural position within British society. At least from the 1840s, the capital contained a relatively smaller proportion of males and females under the age of 14, but a far larger percentage of 15- to 34-year-olds: a reflection of the scale of immigration into the metropolis. There were also more men and women aged between 35 and 54. This younger average age of the London adult population meant that they were more likely to be single or childless, if married. There were fewer aged over 55 – partly because many previous migrants as they aged returned to their home villages or towns, where living was cheaper and family support more available.

Explaining the growth of London's population

Deaths

Two hundred years ago, cities and town were unhealthy places. In 1811, the life expectancy of someone born in London was only 30; eleven years less than someone born in the countryside. In some other large towns, such as Manchester and Liverpool, life was even shorter. (Life expectancy is an average figure. As many young infants died, a person who lived to adulthood could expect to live longer than this.) Gradually, over the course of the century, urban life became healthier and, by 1911, life expectancy in London had risen to 52. Longevity also became more homogeneous throughout the country.[5]

Within London, mortality varied according to sex and area of residence. In his study, Woods found that in 1861 more males died in childhood and infancy than females, with the highest number in the central areas.[6] The geographic distribution of deaths, however, was affected by whether people died at home. As nearly 15 per cent of London deaths occurred in public institutions, districts containing large numbers of workhouses and general hospitals exhibited higher than normal death rates. A similar effect arose for areas with large numbers of lodging houses, because such places were often the last refuge of those unable to work through illnesses contracted elsewhere.[7]

The death rate in the eighteenth century was particularly bad, but after 1802 baptisms in London finally began to exceed burials, because of a lower incidence of killer diseases.[8] Mortality fell rapidly from the late eighteenth century and almost half the gain occurred among the very young, aged under 2.[9] London Bills of Mortality suggest that a major part was played by a reduced incidence of convulsions, the main killer of children and infants. Convulsions had been responsible for a quarter of all London deaths in 1750. By 1800, the proportion had dropped below a fifth and steady improvement occurred up to the late 1840s, by which time convulsions were the cause of only 2 or 3 per cent of deaths. Fever mortality, caused by typhus amongst other things, also improved during this period. In the second half of the eighteenth century, 10 to 15 per cent of deaths were due to it, but by 1830 its impact was small. The final cause of early nineteenth-century mortality improvements was a marked fall in the incidence of tuberculosis. It had risen sharply at the end of the eighteenth century, carrying off thousands of Londoners and leading to over a quarter of all deaths in peak years. After 1830, the illness abated and it represented only around a tenth of all deaths from the mid-century onwards. The incidence of smallpox and pneumonia-related deaths also declined.[10]

Why the virulence of these diseases decreased at this time is something of a mystery, especially as living conditions in the capital during the early years of the nineteenth century were probably exceptionally bad, partly because of the effects of the French Wars.[11] There was overcrowding; poor water quality; worsening air pollution; and the price of bread, the staple foodstuff, was high. Matossian has tried to relate the mortality improvements to changes in lifestyles.[12] Although part of the fall in smallpox deaths may have been due to a weakening in the toxicity of the disease, she suggests that lower general fever mortality may be attributable to an increase in the number of hospitals. Their greatest benefit was to isolate infectious patients from the populace as a whole. Diet may also have contributed. The incidence of tuberculosis may have been reduced by greater consumption of potatoes, because they lacked the fungi strains found in badly stored grains that increase susceptibility to the disease. More breast feeding and a growing use of potato, or potato-starch bread, to supplement breast milk rather than the traditional rye bread, the grain most prone to fungi invasion, may have reduced the number of infant deaths from convulsions. Closely correlating health improvements with changing material conditions, however, is hard. There was little decline in bread consumption during the early nineteenth century when tuberculosis deaths began to decline. The scientific case for links between rye ergot and convulsions and grain mytoxins and tuberculosis is also far from conclusive. Convulsion mortality, furthermore, appears to have been no higher in areas where rye flours were used than elsewhere.[13] An alternative explanation for the decline in the recorded incidence of tuberculosis and fever emphasises the inexact nature of contemporary medical science, so there could simply have been a change in terminology and diagnosis rather than any real improvement in health.

The years from the mid-1840s, when comprehensive recording of deaths started, to the 1860s were punctuated by several bouts of unusually high death rates, and the capital seems to have fared far worse than the country as a whole. Some of them related to cholera epidemics and, thus, may have resulted from problems of water supply and sewerage considered in later chapters. From the late 1860s, however, London mortality rates gradually declined and they began to coincide with those of the country by the end of the century. They were noticeably better in 1905 than those for other large English cities, other European capitals and New York. Improvements in survival rates started first among younger people, aged between 2 and 35. By the 1890s, older adults were experiencing the effects and, a decade later, the most vulnerable began to benefit – the elderly and those less than a year old.[14]

In the country as a whole, and probably also in London, the drop in adult and child mortality between the 1850s and 1890s was related to a lower incidence of five diseases: typhus and typhoid; scarlet fever; tuberculosis; cholera, dysentery and diarrhoea; and smallpox.[15] The reasons behind the weaker virulence of these diseases are again uncertain. As the rate of mortality decline varied across social classes, with the poor the most susceptible to disease, an important factor may have been improvements in working-class diets. This is the essence of the view of McKeown and his colleagues who studied the mortality data in detail in the 1960s and 1970s; whereas medicine they regarded as virtually useless.[16] A general reduction in family sizes from the 1870s, in turn, allowed more and better-quality food to be distributed to each family member – although no evidence of actual working-class family consumption habits exists. Rising living standards and dietary improvements were responsible for approximately half of the mortality fall, helping most in lowering the incidence of tuberculosis and, to a lesser extent, typhus.[17]

This emphasis on food as an explanation for reductions in the death rate has sparked substantial controversy. Against it, for example, are studies of contemporary working-class eating habits. These suggest that up to the First World War, at least, diets continued to be heavily dependent on starchy sources of energy, and that improvements in the consumption of animal products were limited to very small amounts of dairy goods, largely fats and milk.[18] Improved nutrition, at best, probably had only a limited effect on the declines in diphtheria, typhus, influenza and syphilis and played no part in the reduction of typhoid fever or smallpox. Other evidence, nevertheless, highlights the likely significance of diet. For one thing, food expenditure was a high proportion of average household budgets, so any increase in income probably significantly raised consumption and quality levels, and falls did the opposite. Variations in food intake would have been especially marked for households whose income was irregular, and for many more during times of unemployment and recession. The effect of food intake could also be seen in the shorter stature of working-class people in relation to their middle- and upper-class compatriots. Over 40 per cent of all military conscripts from 1917 to 1918 were deemed unfit for frontline service[19] – an indicator at that late date of earlier hungry or malnourished childhoods. If diet is related to resistance to infection as well, the McKeown view is persuasive.

Alternative explanations for the reduction in death rates centre on public health measures – improvements in water supplies, sanitation and housing – and on better medical science. McKeown and Record are optimists, believing, for example, that sanitary and water reforms were responsible for a quarter of the total national fall in deaths.[20] Luckin disagrees for London specifically, arguing that by the end of the 1890s, 31 per cent of all Londoners still had no access to a constant water supply.[21] In the case of medical improvements, a partial defence of the medical profession has been mustered. Some lives were saved by greater hospitalisation and the introduction of anaesthetic surgery in the 1850s, antiseptics in the 1870s, and diphtheria and smallpox immunisation. By 1900, 30 per cent of all metropolitan typhoid sufferers received treatment as in-patients, although general hospitals tended to refuse admission to those with infectious diseases.[22] Overall, though, the influence of medicine was probably small. London was relatively well served by doctors, with a doctor/patient ratio in the 1860s over twice as high as that for England and Wales.[23] Doctors' medical capabilities, however, were limited, the clientele overwhelmingly middle-class and, at least in 1861, there appears to have been no statistically significant link between the number of medical practitioners in an area and the rate of mortality.[24]

Other suggested reasons for the decline in London death rates and their convergence with national levels include greater migrant disease immunity, changes in disease characteristics, climate and immigration, and improvements in municipal health provision for children. By the late nineteenth century, migrants to the capital may have been more immune to diseases than their earlier counterparts. This arose because of the general increase in personal mobility throughout the country, associated with transport improvements and a more urban social structure, which meant that few areas of Britain avoided exposure to diseases previously concentrated in large urban areas. With regard to the diseases themselves, some changed in behaviour. The reduced incidence of scarlet fever, for example, was responsible for approximately a fifth of the national fall in mortality.[25] At least part of the fall in deaths from smallpox and, perhaps, diphtheria and whooping cough was due to alterations in the characteristics of these diseases independent of human intervention. Climate changes also helped, as in the case of the fall in bronchitis deaths from the early 1890s, which may have been related to the late-century return of warmer winters, reducing coal consumption and, thus, air pollution. Lower mortality from typhus may have been associated with the gradual fall in immigration from Ireland where the disease had a greater hold; rates remained high in Dublin and Belfast and in north-east and north-west England, the only areas with continuing Irish immigration. It also appears likely that child mortality was influenced by the factory legislation of the 1860s and 1870s designed to protect working children. Extra municipal welfare, provided for children under the aegis of the London School Board and its LCC successor, may have improved immunity as well.

Infant mortality

London infant mortality was somewhat higher than that of England and Wales, from the 1860s to the 1890s. It only began to decline in the late 1890s, and then quickly tracked national changes.[26] The causes are again shrouded in controversy. Apart from the general influences affecting adults, noted above, there were several specific factors. A major one was the effects of improvements in mothers' and babies' nutrition levels and standards. By the 1870s, rising real incomes were pushing progressively more households above the meagre subsistence threshold. As more women began to benefit, the proportion of healthier babies became noticeable in the aggregate statistics by the 1890s. These healthier children were better fed in the first year of their lives than many babies had been in previous generations. Breast feeding came back into vogue, and cow's milk was more readily available and of a better quality. For the very poor, free milk distribution depots appeared; the first in the capital opened in Battersea and Finsbury in 1902 and 1904 respectively.[27]

Food was not the only factor. Greater attention was paid to infant rearing practices. More widely available general education played a part, as did the provision of more specific child-related information. Particular schemes to provide education in child health were opened for the poor and others. In London, shortly after its establishment, the Finsbury Milk Depot began to distribute advice to parents and, in 1907, a formal school for new mothers was established in St Pancras. The reduction in family size allowed more care to be taken of infants, and the associated wider use of contraception enabled women to spread pregnancies over a longer time period. The 1902 Midwives Act established a central midwives board, giving it powers to examine midwives, lay down rules governing their conduct and act as a disciplinary body. Finally, the 1897 extension of the Infant Life Protection Act reduced the abuse of infants in the care of people other than parents.[28]

Birth rates

After a gradual rise in the first three quarters of the nineteenth century, London birth rates began a rapid descent, which continued well into the twentieth century. In these changes, the capital closely followed national developments. Prime causes of the increase in fertility were the growth of job opportunities and the associated rise in real incomes, both of which encouraged more and earlier marriages. By 1861, in the country as a whole, women on average were aged 24.6 when they married (24.9 in London) as compared to 25.5 in the early eighteenth century.[29] The subsequent falls in the birth rate from the mid-1870s were the result of a drop in the average number of children born within marriage, particularly from 1870 to 1930. Average completed family sizes fell from nearly six in the late eighteenth century to five by 1860 and just over two by 1920.[30] Factors accounting for the decline in the birth rate are again clouded in uncertainty. The influences affecting death rates were probably important – incomes, food intake, drinking water, sanitation, lifestyles and health education. Contraceptive methods also became widespread, but no particular hypotheses on the timing of the changes correspond well with the available data.[31]

Migration

Migration to London took two forms: temporary and permanent. Temporary migrants came to the capital for only part of the year and were particularly prevalent in the first part of the century. They were mainly rootless travelling workers, who moved to the city during the 'Season' to obtain casual work, and agricultural workers who spent their winters in the capital.[32] Permanent immigrants were continually attracted to London on a scale and with a constancy not experienced anywhere else in Britain between 1800 and 1914.

Over the seventy-year period from 1841 to 1911, the net population gain due to migration was one and a quarter million people. As a proportion of the total population of Greater London, however, net migration was slowing, down from 12 per cent in the decade 1841–51 to 4 per cent in the decade 1891 to 1901. In the first decade of the twentieth century, the net movement was even reversed, with 230,000 people lost to the metropolis; yet this may partly indicate the scale of suburbanisation that was starting to occur beyond the metropolitan boundary. With its myriad of employment opportunities, high wages and relative immunity from the trade cycle, London attracted immigrants like no other British city after the 1840s, as by then the expansion of the northern cities was slowing. The inflow between 1841 and 1911 was 28 per cent higher than that of eight large Midland and northern towns and cities combined (namely Birmingham, Hull, Leeds, Leicester, Liverpool, Nottingham, Manchester and Sheffield).[33]

Migrants to London came from all over Britain and the world. During the years from 1851 to 1891, a tenth of migrants came from abroad and a similar proportion from Scotland and Ireland. Of those from England and Wales, distance played an important part, with a decline in migrant numbers at greater distances from London – although the shares from each region varied from decade to decade. The impact on the population of London can be seen in information for 1911, when 46 per cent of non-London-born men came from somewhere else in the South-East; 29 per cent from Scotland, Ireland and overseas; 16 per cent from the Midlands and North; and 10 per cent from the South-West. The continuing low-wage, rural nature of southern England, its proximity and the cheaper costs of transport to London are the likely reasons for its dominance as a source of London migrants; whereas, for more distant regions, costs rose and information about opportunities in the metropolis declined, making another British city or emigration from the UK the more likely preferred options. Migrants might also have been encouraged to move to the capital by the existence of relatives and friends already there, so that the weight of the South as an origin would have been perpetuated.

In general, the skilled tended to move longer distances than the unskilled, and those from adjacent counties were more likely to move straight to London than those from further afield, who made their way to the capital in two or more stages (for example, country to small town, then to London). Most were young, single, and largely semi- and unskilled. Between 1851 and 1901, for England and Wales, 81 per cent of inter-county migrants were aged 15 to 34 and the remainder were children.[34] Although no proportions are available, it seems likely that more women than men migrated because of the limited opportunities for women in rural areas and the attractions of urban domestic service.

There was also a significant number of out-migrants – that is, people born in London who either moved to a different British region or emigrated from the country. London-born movement to the rest of England and Wales was high. The number represented around 40 per cent of all those coming to London from Britain and overseas in 1851–61 and a substantial 89 per cent in 1881–91, reflecting both the scale of nineteenth-century mobility and the central place of the metropolis within it. The rise in those leaving the metropolis was substantial over time – up from 116,000 between 1851 and 1861 to 359,000 between 1881 and 1891. Some migration was simply a shift to an expanding suburb in an adjacent county, but this cannot explain the majority – 53 per cent of out-movers between 1881 and 1891, for instance, went to eastern and South Midland counties, with only 27 per cent to the rest of the South-East.[35] A pattern of national migration with London at the hub as the most common source and origin was found by Pooley and Turnbull in their analysis of data on individual family histories.[36]

English- and Welsh-born immigrants

Few of the English and Welsh immigrants entered the capital's traditional industries. Most lacked the necessary skills, entry to some trades was hereditary, and general unskilled occupations were unattractive. Instead, many undertook work in which they already possessed some skill. For those coming from rural areas, activities related to the countryside were popular. In the 1890s, for example, according to Booth, 55 per cent of millers, 58 per cent of saddlers and 63 per cent of milk sellers were not born in London.[37] Migrants also predominated in building: rural apprenticeships were thought to be superior to the less formalised training that often occurred in London, while the nature of the work put strength and endurance at a premium. Others went into drapery, a trade dominated by Welshmen and Cornishmen who preferred to employ their fellow countrymen; or into the gas, brewing and transport industries, where employers were attracted by the strength, adaptability and lack of trade union membership of newcomers to the capital. Most of those moving to the metropolis settled in the outer suburbs – either in an area close to their place of origin or in one where friends or relatives lived. This affected neighbourhood composition: in 1881, for example, 73 per cent of the residents of the inner industrial area were London-born, compared to only 60 per cent in the rest of the capital.[38]

Ethnic minority groups

The search for a better standard of living is the main impetus for people to move between countries and immigrants from overseas did come to London during the nineteenth century, but on nothing like the scale of the movements of population to the Americas and Australasia. A recent study argues that nineteenth-century emigration levels from European countries were determined by wage gaps between the source and destination country – wages in the USA, for example, were far higher than in Europe where most of its immigrants came from; by the age structure of the source population – because people tended to move in their twenties before they had children; and, finally, by the number of previous migrants from the same location, as they were a source of information about the new country for would-be immigrants and provided support during the early phases of emigration.[39] Movement into Britain from abroad was unimpeded, so the explanation for the low share of foreign-born in the metropolis, therefore, probably lies in the lower average earnings there relative to other emigrant destinations and in the absence of large numbers of previous immigrants from all but a few places.

The two biggest non-British-born groups were the Irish and the Jews. By the nineteenth century, both already had well-established London communities that clustered together because of social ties, a common experience of extreme poverty, or as protection against the prejudice and hostility of others. Substantial Irish communities were first established in the fourteenth century. They expanded rapidly in the eighteenth century, when many of the Irish harvesters attracted to Britain by the agricultural revolution began to spend their winters in London.[40] Jews began to settle again from 1625, after Cromwell lifted the medieval ban on them. Their numbers increased from the 1750s with the arrival of Poles and Germans fleeing persecution and, by 1800, the capital had a Jewish population of between 15,000 and 20,000.[41]

An upsurge in Irish migration occurred in the first part of the nineteenth century.[42] Population pressures, economic crises and a series of poor harvests forced many to take advantage of new, cheap steamer fares and sail to England. By 1841, more than 3 per cent of London's population was Irish. The mass emigration from Ireland caused by the 1846–8 potato famine led to a further influx, so that, by 1851, the number of Irish-born in London had reached 109,000. The general growth of London's population at the time, none the less, meant that they were still a small proportion of the total population – only 5 per cent.[43] Unlike most of the English who moved to the metropolis, many of the Irish were already married with children – indicating the importance of the push of extreme poverty in Ireland rather than the lure of the better living standards that had attracted others. Almost half were married, with at least one child, and most were unskilled.[44] They found work in the docks, building industry, railway construction, other casual trades and, in the case of women, heavy domestic work. Many settled in Holborn, St-Giles-in-the-Field, Whitechapel and the St Olave part of Southwark – ancient Irish centres close to the main labour markets for casual work.[45] Engels's descriptions of the Irish living in Manchester indicate the low esteem in which many held them.[46] Similar contemporary tales were related about those living in London. The Irish rookery – the old-fashioned word for a slum neighbourhood – is something of a myth, however – with poverty, rather than ethnic exclusivity, determining the social and ethnic mixes of such neighbourhoods. Like many other migrants to London, the Irish-born were present throughout the city and, even when clustered together, they hardly ever formed more than 50 per cent of the population of a census district.[47]

The great influx of Jewish immigrants occurred from the 1880s. In the first half of the 1880s, between 20,000 and 30,000 Jews from overseas settled in London and, by 1900, the city's Jewish population numbered approximately 120,000.[48] They came overwhelmingly from Russia, Poland and Romania, escaping poverty and persecution. Eastern Europe was experiencing rapid population growth. The resultant drastic fall in living standards fuelled traditional enmities. In Russia, the Temporary Laws of May 1882, which were not repealed until the 1917 revolution, restricted Jews' mobility and rights of residence.[49] Most who could travelled to the New World, but London and Western Europe offered cheaper alternatives. Unscrupulous agents also tricked travellers into thinking they were going to New York rather than to shorter destinations, like London.

On arriving in London, their behaviour was similar to that of some more recent immigrant groups. Settlement was initially concentrated, with the majority living in the East End of London. There, they found cheap housing within walking distance of the docks, their point of disembarkation. The East End also contained most of the Jewish-owned businesses, offering them employment, and it was the main centre of Jewish social, cultural and religious life. Support could be obtained from friends and relations, or organisations like the Jewish Board of Guardians. Places like the Jews' Shelter provided help during the first few months of residence.[50]

The degree of spatial concentration of Jewish immigrants was consequently high. In 1891, 82 per cent of the Russian- and Polish-born inhabitants of London were found in Whitechapel, St George-in-the-East and Mile End Old Town, an area of just two square miles.[51] Many came with skills from previous urban existences, and found skilled and semi-skilled jobs in the clothing trades – which contained over a quarter of working-class Jews – boot and shoe manufacture, and the furniture and tobacco industries. Anti-semitism grew, with Jews being accused of virtually everything from the usual lexicon of racial abuse. In particular, it was claimed that they stole jobs, encouraged de-skilling, cut wages in the already badly paid casual trades, and pushed up housing rents. As with more recent immigrants, myth took over from reality. Yet anti-Semitism undoubtedly clouds historical descriptions of life and living standards in the East End and its trades in the last decades of the nineteenth century.

People from other parts of the globe also came to London to try their luck – pushed by poverty at home and the prospect of a better life in London.[52] Other significant overseas immigrant groups included Italians, South Asians, Chinese, Africans and those from the Caribbean. However, although significant in particular districts, their overall numbers were relatively low.

Italian migrants first came at the end of the Napoleonic Wars, when poor economic conditions in northern Italy forced young males to leave. They settled in Hatton Garden and Saffron Hill and took up occupations influenced by kinship and village ties, such as street performers and statuette makers and peddlers, with the more skilled producing mirrors and precision instruments. A second wave of immigration occurred in the 1880s and 1890s, again initiated by agrarian crisis and rapid Italian population growth. These newcomers entered a wider variety of employments than their forerunners. The activities were still specific, none the less: such as jobs in the building trades, knife grinders, barbers, itinerant ice-cream vendors and café proprietors. The construction of Clerkenwell Road and Rosebery Avenue broke up the traditional Italian quarter, forcing the community to become more widely dispersed. St Pancras, Islington and Westminster and, particularly, Soho became the new homes for the Italian community.

London's immigrants from the Indian subcontinent were ex-sailors, servants or professionals. The ex-sailors, known as lascars, came from Bengal, the Punjab and the West Coast of India. They remained in England either after jumping ship or on becoming too ill to complete their return voyage. Most lived near the docks in Stepney and, later, Poplar and Canning Town as the docks moved down river. They earned their livelihoods as peripatetic street entertainers, sweepers and servants or as hawkers and market traders selling scarves, spices and herbs. Numbers grew from mid-century, due to the expansion of the lascar workforce with the introduction of steamships, with many more shipping lines from London to the Far East then employing Indians as stokers and crew. From mid-century, Asian professionals began to live in London – lawyers, doctors, retired civil servants and merchants.

Employment at sea was similarly the route through which a lot of the Chinese, African and Caribbean residents of London arrived. The number of Chinese settlers grew rapidly from the 1860s, following the Opium Wars and the opening up of Chinese ports to the West. By the 1880s, a Chinese community was established in Limehouse. Most, at first, worked in dock-related occupations but, later, opportunities opened up in the laundry business. The first Chinese laundry opened in Poplar in 1901 and, ten years later, East London possessed over thirty such establishments. African sailors largely came from West Africa and British Somaliland. The community they joined was comprised of former slaves brought into the country during the eighteenth century as domestic servants. In 1857, the Strangers' Home for Asians, Africans and South Sea Islanders was opened in Limehouse.

Emigration

As well as the centre of immigration, London was also an important source of emigrants from the UK. Between 1861 and 1900, around 420,000 London-born left Britain, 16 per cent of all males and 20 per cent of females emigrating.[53] Some emigrants, though, might simply have used the capital as a stepping stone to raise enough money through metropolitan work for expensive fares, as they had done in the previous centuries.[54] The relatively young age structure of the capital would also have encouraged emigration, as would the good links to previous Londoners who had emigrated.

An unusually large proportion of British emigrants were women, who in the 1860s and 1870s made up almost half of the total. Net female emigration then fell, not because fewer women left but because for some reason a far greater proportion of women returned than men. Whatever their sex, a remarkably high number of British emigrants returned home at some point – 40 per cent of those leaving the country between 1864 and 1914, for example, came back to Britain.[55]

Generally those who emigrated were poor and unskilled, but had raised sufficient funds to pay their passage. Many travelled to Australia as it was the only destination that could directly be reached by emigrant ship from London. Others went to America, particularly New York, whose labour markets contained similar activities to those in London. Information on economic conditions in such areas was widely available to the potential migrant from the letters of earlier emigrants and the experiences of returning ones.

4 Work and industry

Introduction

Along with the rapid growth in population, the economy of London expanded substantially during the nineteenth century. This chapter looks at employment and the changing industrial structure of the capital. It relies on the main statistical source available, the census, which, from 1841, included questions on employment. This enables a picture of industry to be built up, but it has limitations, both in terms of definition and geographical spread, particularly when the capital expanded beyond the boundaries of the County of London. As well as looking at the general picture, and changes within it, the information examined here enables consideration of some important questions about the role of London in the wider British economy. There are a number of commonly held views about London's uniqueness that do not seem to conform to the available information.

Backward and service-oriented?

The size and diversity of London's industries were unparalleled in any other city or urban region in the country but were frequently small-scale and did not conform to the development of modern industry taking place elsewhere in Britain.[1] The difference has led to a common interpretation of the development of manufacturing and service industries in nineteenth-century London. Specific arguments are examined later, but the overall perspective is one that suggests that manufacturing seemed increasing backward, as it predominantly relied on workshop production using traditional handicraft techniques rather than factories and modern machinery. Producers then gradually succumbed to the pincer effects of competition. A squeeze in output markets arose from cheaper and better-equipped firms in the provinces and abroad. Pressures in input markets sprang from rising land, labour and other costs, with other activities in the capital increasingly bidding more for their use. So, by the 1860s, manufacturing was in crisis and much of what was left was 'sweated' industry organised in a system of sub-contracting and casual labour to 'exploit' the mass of London poor. This claimed transformation explains the scale of poverty in the capital believed to exist in the latter part of the nineteenth century, with the switch to exploitation creating thousands of low-paid workers trapped in the East End and other inner industrial districts. A significant part of the labour force was, thereby, forced into greater poverty.

In this approach, the trajectory of economic development is said to have taken on a dual form. For alongside the immiserisation of the inner city, some modern production industries grew up. But, above all, services took over as the dynamic part of the London economy and blossomed under the lead of the merchanting activities of the City, with its supremacy in world financial and commodity markets. This view of London's economic development during this period, consequently, looks backwards to a specific picture of the 'take-off' industries in Britain's industrialisation and forward to the late twentieth century with London's concentration on financial services. Variants would put less emphasis on the stylised 'factory' view of the industrial revolution by recognising the continuation nationally of much workshop and domestic production, but the trajectory in metropolitan industry is still essentially the same.

This broad interpretation will be called here the 'immiserisation thesis'. The description of it above is obviously a simplified one, but in variants it has constituted the conventional wisdom on the London economy for many years. It is most sophisticatedly advocated in influential books by Hall (1962a) and Stedman Jones (1971), yet the hypothesis has an even longer pedigree stretching back into the nineteenth century: the authors of the *Report on the Sweated Trades* (1886) were early proponents. It is also a dominant theme in the seminal works of Shepard.[2] Three other significant writers, Barker (1989), Green (1991 and 1995) and Schwarz (1992), are supporters. Johnson (1996) and Godley (1996), in contrast, have been two recent critics.

The view is open to dispute both in its interpretation of British economic development and in its description of the London economy. Many modern analyses of the 'industrial revolution' emphasise a much more gradual rate of change in the British economy and place a greater role on the domestic economy, on small-scale activity and the slow spreading out across the regions of a complex, urban, integrated economy.[3] The London economy, moreover, did not possess the characteristics suggested by the immiserisation thesis. Nineteenth-century finance, for example, was unlike present-day financial services, as Chapter 14 shows, and the same could be said for other services. Finance, in fact, was far less important as an economic activity in London than figures on the scale of the contemporary export of capital would suggest.

Although finance undoubtedly did expand during the nineteenth century, so did many other of the capital's economic activities; ones that employed vastly more of its huge workforce – in manufacturing as well as services. London's advantages as the wealthiest and largest consumer market in the country, the greatest and most diverse source of skilled labour, and its central position in the nation's transport networks sustained a large manufacturing presence throughout the period – especially in direct consumer goods or in processes feeding into them. The overall nature and content of Britain's manufacturing activities changed as the century progressed, and heavy industry continued to cling to the coalfields and ports of the industrial regions. Of particular importance to manufacturing in London was that rising incomes, technical innovations, and the adoption of marketing all slowly created a national mass market in a broadening range of consumer goods. This shifted 'modern' national industry away from producing for a narrow range of export markets towards a widening range of home markets. Firms in London were well placed to take advantage of these new and expanding domestic markets – in metal bashing (vehicles etc.), chemicals, electricals, food processing, clothing, furniture and elsewhere. Some very large firms, by contemporary standards, set up amongst the swarms of small firms in the capital from the mid-century onwards.

The expansion of consumer-related industries using modern technology is often seen as part of a metropolitan industrial renaissance of 'new industries' in the 1920s and 1930s.[4] However, it would seem more appropriate to see the inter-war years as the continuation of a dynamic that had been going on for a least half a century before. There was no crisis of London manufacturing industry in the 1860s nor in later decades; neither did it simply slide into technologically outmoded sweating. Hence, there could be no subsequent inter-war renaissance sixty odd years later. What happened, instead, was that the structure of London manufacturing industry continuously changed and expanded from 1800 to 1914; and, according to the information available from mid-century, the broad split between manufacturing and services stayed roughly the same.

At the same time, other parts of the country caught up with the capital's pre-eminence in certain activities' as the national economy broadened and deepened, although regional specialisation remained strong throughout the period. Despite such regional specialisation, there was a fall in the nationally-weighted share of London's employment in many industries. This again has been seen as a loss of competitive edge for the capital. Yet, in only a few sectors did London actually lose employment. The reduction in shares, more reasonably, indicates a three-way process in which nationally the decline of agricultural employment and the rural-urban shift continued, London diversified its industrial structure, and the rest of the country began to focus more on expanding local and domestic markets. The breadth of economic activity generated in nineteenth- and early twentieth-century London, and the dynamics it created, were then to protect the capital from a succession of economic upheavals and to keep it at the forefront of British economic developments during the rest of the twentieth century.

These themes require substantial elaboration and justification. Differences in interpretation of a limited range of statistics are perhaps inevitable, but the available employment data are only part of the argument, as several of the underlying themes of much of the rest of the book relate to these issues. The development of mass market systems in retailing and leisure activities, and the spread of suburban communities, were necessary components of the continued strength of London's consumer-orientated manufacturing. Technical change led to new products and to a changing array of agglomeration benefits and costs. Evolving transportation systems played their part, as did the greater role of government in providing urban public goods. Before subsequent chapters take up these themes, the statistical case needs to be put first and hypotheses about the characteristics of the metropolitan economy related to that data.

The next section deals with the available information in the population censuses on work and industry, and the problems faced when interpreting the data. After that, there is an examination of employment by industrial sector from 1851 to 1911 for the County of London area, and the respective roles of manufacturing and services. The difficulties arising from the spread of London's suburbs beyond the County boundary are subsequently examined. After this the gender breakdown of work and then trade union activity are described. This is followed by analysis of the degree of concentration of particular national industries in the London area, showing the broad base of industry there. The scale of firm sizes in the metropolis is then investigated. The final section considers the impact of Britain's changing role in the international economy and its consequences for London.

Using the employment data from the census

The nineteenth-century ten-year censuses are an invaluable source of information, but for employment purposes there are several problems. The data contained in the 1801 census are of little worth, as people are classified into only three sectors – agriculture; trade, manufacturing and handicrafts; and other – and there is no uniformity of treatment in the enumeration of women, children and domestic servants. The 1811, 1821 and 1831 censuses are little better. Returns were collected for entire families rather than individuals and the information is again classified into just three categories. Wishing to improve the usefulness of the information obtained, the 1841 census takers returned to the surveying of individuals rather than families, and split employment into 877 occupations. Unfortunately, these categories are not consistent with those adopted from 1851.[5] This chapter consequently only uses data from the 1851 and subsequent censuses. Lee (1979) reworked the census data to provide a more accurate detailed breakdown of employment by industrial sector for the regions of Britain, and his tables for London and the surrounding counties form the basis of the analysis here.

The classification of industries in the census in Lee's tables is based on the official 'Standard Industrial Classification' (SIC) of 1968. This groups all activities into twenty-seven sectors ranging from agriculture to public administration and a further 'not classified' category. The unclassified group unfortunately is large and variable. This makes it difficult to trace industrial change because some of the apparent variation may be accounted for by movements over time between the unclassified and other categories. The industrial groupings themselves are broad-brushed, hiding much useful detail, particularly over a sixty-year period when some industries declined and others grew from nothing, confounding attempts neatly to pigeonhole activities into clearly identifiable 'industries'.

The original recording of the census information creates some other difficulties. Householders often provided inaccurate employment details; many had a number of occupations, but listed only one; and most failed to list female relatives' temporary or part-time work. Similar, enumerators recorded those retired, in hospital and in prison as employed in their previous occupation and had difficulty classifying jobs with obscure titles. When transforming the raw data into SIC categories, problems arise with census takers' failure to make a distinction between industrial and occupational classifications. Lee, therefore, had to place such occupations as labourers and clerks etc. into the 'not classified' category.

Nineteenth-century statisticians, furthermore, had the unfortunate tendency, in modern eyes, of grouping the whole chain from inputs through manufacturing processes to distribution and retailing as part of one industry. A clothing wholesaler, for example, would appear as a clothing manufacturer rather than part of the service sector associated with this particular activity. The dividing line between manufacturing and service industries, thereby, becomes clouded, which might be said to give a bias towards manufacturing away from services.

The biggest problem occurs between distribution, a service activity, and the manufacturing of foodstuffs, because many retailers of foodstuffs made some or all of the items they sold and so were classified under manufacturing. A similar, but small, problem occurs with other manufacturing industries.[6] Some of the effects can be seen for 1911, when a more accurate categorisation came into existence, as Lee provides data by which the old and new classifications can be compared – and the results are shown in the appropriate section below.

Yet the confusion is not entirely a statistical quirk, because the separating line between manufacturing and services was often blurred, with organisations straddling the divide, as is still the case today. This occurred not only in food and drink – for instance, the manufacturing processes in London's clothing and furniture industries were often organised by wholesalers (see Chapter 12). A sharp division between several manufacturing and service activities, therefore, cannot be held up as credible. Some 'services' only existed as part of an extended 'manufacturing' process, rather than representing some distinct, competing, higher-order, urban activity – supporting the view of the nineteenth-century statistician. Inevitably, the significance of classifications depends on the questions being asked and investigated using the data. In so far as the question is one of the extent to which manufacturing is replaced by services, the problem may not be so great after all because of the organic link between some services and their associated manufacturing industries.

Difficulties also arise with the geography of a large city like London. The population census is based on where people live, not on where they work. When people commute, as they increasingly did, a misleading picture of the industrial geography of a large city may result. The bias, moreover, varies across income groups as the better-off are more likely to commute further. When dealing with employment in a city as a whole, these differences may not matter, if most people live within its administrative boundaries. This was not the case in nineteenth-century London, especially in later decades as the population spilled over into the surrounding districts. Manufacturing industry was decentralising as well, while the services that were not immediately associated with local population tended to concentrate in the centre. County of London data, consequently, miss the commuting bankers, brokers and other service workers who poured into London's central stations from the outer suburbs during the rush-hours at the turn of the new century. But they also miss much manufacturing spreading up the Lea Valley, to the east and elsewhere around London's fringes. Fortunately, it is possible to undertake some analysis to see how sensitive results are to the spatial extent of the metropolis. This is done after presentation of the basic County of London information, and the results suggest that these problems again may not be so large as to make the County-level analysis unrepresentative of the broader Greater London economy.

Employment

Between 1851 and 1911, employment in the County of London doubled from 1.1 million to 2.2 million;[7] a somewhat faster growth rate over that time than for the residential population, which increased by 88 per cent from 2.4 to 4.5 million. The share of those in employment as a proportion of the total population rose slightly from 46 to 48 per cent.

What is interesting about this rapid industrial expansion over a sixty-year period is that it was broadly spread across most industrial sectors, with only agriculture and shipbuilding recording absolute falls in employment. In fact, the prime division between production activities and services seems to have remained stable throughout the decades. Geographically, the capital remained by far the largest single concentration of manufacturing activity in Britain.

As Table 4.1 shows, production industries (that is, manufacturing plus construction, electricity, gas and water) constituted 47 per cent of County employment in 1851 and 45 per cent in 1911; whereas services accounted for 43 and 45 per cent at those two dates respectively. Table 4.1 shows some minor variations over the years in the broad industrial groupings. Not much should probably be made of these slight changes, however,

Table 4.1 Industrial sector shares, 1851–1911

Sector	*1851*	*1861*	*1871*	*1881*	*1891*	*1901*	*1911*
Agriculture, mining, etc.	2	1	1	1	1	1	1
Manufacturing	40	40	36	35	36	37	38
Construction, electricity, gas & water	7	7	7	8	7	8	7
Miscel. services (domestic, etc.)	25	24	24	24	23	22	22
Other services	10	10	10	10	10	11	12
Transport	8	9	9	10	11	11	11
Not classified	7	7	12	11	12	11	9
All production industries	47	48	44	43	43	45	45
All services	44	43	43	44	44	44	45
Totals	100	100	100	100	100	100	100

Source: Own estimates based on Lee, 1979.

which may simply arise from statistical noise in the data because of deviations in the number of jobs that could not be put into specific industries, as the 'not classified' category in the table indicates. Another reason for slight variations is that the business cycle has temporally varying effects on employment across the sectors, with some leading and others lagging changes in the overall level of economic activity. So, a particular point in time when a census is taken may see some sectors with temporally higher or lower employment than longer-term trends would suggest.

To an extent, the scale of manufacturing is exaggerated in the Series A data in Table 4.2, because of the above-mentioned problem of classifying many distributive jobs as manufacturing ones. Lee's more accurate Series B data are shown in Table 4.2 for 1911 and compared to the Series A information. Under the improved classification, production industries drop by a full 10 per cent in employment importance and services rise by 10 per cent. Table 4.2 also shows a similar consequence of adopting the Series B categorisations for Britain as a whole – with manufacturing declining by 8 per cent and service employment rising by the same amount. On either count, London had pretty much the same share of manufacturing as the nation all together – 29 per cent of employment compared to 31 per cent nationally according to the Series B estimates. London's big and obvious deficits were in agriculture and mining and in their place were extra services.

Obviously, it would be ideal to have the better classification for the whole nineteenth century but it is unavailable, so Lee's Series A employment data have to be used to enable changes over time to be examined. One useful assumption is that the classification error in Series A was constant throughout the period – it is then possible to consider the dynamics of industrial change from 1851 to 1911. If this assumption is incorrect, however, the errors significantly affect only two manufacturing industries,

Table 4.2 The impact of the reclassification of occupations on industry shares, London and Great Britain, 1911

	London		*Great Britain*	
	A	*B*	*A*	*B*
Agriculture, mining, etc.	1	0	15	14
Manufacturing	38	29	39	31
Construction, electricity, gas & water	7	7	7	7
Miscel. services (domestic, etc.)	22	22	16	16
Other services	12	21	9	17
Transport	11	12	8	9
Not classified	9	9	7	6
All production industries	*45*	*35*	*46*	*38*
All services	*45*	*55*	*33*	*41*
Totals	100	100	100	100

Note: A and B refer to the two classifications in Lee, 1979. Rounding errors make slight differences in totals.

as they accounted for much of the reclassification into distribution. The most important change occurs with food, drink and tobacco, which fall by 4.5 per cent of total employment in Series B compared to Series A, and, secondly, textiles fall by 1.5 per cent to near obscurity. Taken together, these two industries account for almost two-thirds of the 9.3 per cent increase in distributive trades between the two series. The full differences between the Series A and Series B occupation data are shown in Table 4.3. The following sections, therefore, derive conclusions on the assumption that the Series A data are generally indicating the true dynamics of industrial change in the capital from the 1850s onwards.

A decline of manufacturing?

Both the rapid growth in jobs and the stability of the shares of employment in the broad sector groupings question the common view that manufacturing within the capital declined during the second half of the nineteenth century. There is no evidence in these data of a decline when measured in terms of the number of jobs – quite the opposite, in that the number of people employed in manufacturing actually virtually doubled between 1851 and 1911 from 432,000 to 826,000.

It would, of course, be useful to see whether a similar picture is derived from data on output, rather than employment, but they do not exist. With no output and capital stock information, productivity differences cannot be examined either. Because of differences in productivity between sectors, the value-added contribution of each sector of the London economy to national income unfortunately cannot be ascertained either. Employment

Table 4.3 The impact of the reclassification of occupations on London's industrial structure, 1911

SIC		*Series A*	*Series B*	*B–A*
1	Agriculture, etc.	0.4	0.4	0.0
2	Mining and quarrying	0.4	0.0	–0.4
3	Food, drink and tobacco	6.9	2.4	–4.5
5	Chemicals and allied industries	1.1	0.7	–0.4
6	Metal manufacture	1.2	0.3	–0.9
7	Mechanical engineering	1.5	1.5	0.0
8	Instrument engineering	0.4	0.4	0.0
9	Electrical engineering	1.0	0.9	–0.1
10	Shipbuilding and marine engineering	0.1	0.1	0.0
11	Vehicles	0.9	0.9	0.0
12	Metal goods not elsewhere specified	1.4	1.9	0.5
13	Textiles	2.1	0.7	–1.4
14	Leather, leather goods and fur	1.5	1.0	–0.5
15	Clothing and footwear	10.6	9.8	–0.8
16	Bricks, pottery, glass, cement, etc.	0.4	0.3	–0.1
17	Timber, furniture, etc.	3.1	2.7	–0.4
18	Paper, printing and publishing	4.8	4.2	–0.6
19	Other manufacturing	0.8	1.1	0.3
20	Construction	6.1	6.0	–0.1
21	Gas, electricity and water	0.6	0.5	–0.1
22	Transport and communication	11.0	12.2	1.2
23	Distributive trades	1.8	11.1	9.3
24	Finance, etc. and business services	1.3	1.9	0.6
25	Professional and scientific services	5.0	5.0	0.0
26	Miscellaneous services	22.1	22.1	0.0
27	Public administration	4.1	3.1	–1.0
Not classified		9.2	8.7	–0.5
Total		100	100	0

Source: Own calculations based on Lee, 1979.

Note: SIC 4 is not applicable for this date.

data alone, therefore, bias the real output contributions of London industries. Lower productivity activities, in particular, would have employed far more people than their contribution to total output. The significance of higher valued-added ones are consequently under-represented.

Not only is the evidence of manufacturing decline absent from the employment data, but the dynamics of industrial development shown in the data also do not conform to the predictions of the 'immiserisation thesis'. A necessary condition for its hypotheses to be valid is that employment grew fastest in what are seen as labour-intensive, low-productivity, manufacturing industries. This is not the case in the information presented in Table 4.4, which gives the full 28-group classification of employment percentage share from 1851 to 1911. The industries normally associated with arguments about sweating and casualisation – clothing, footwear and furniture – actually become relatively less important over time, even though

Table 4.4 Employment by industrial sector, 1851–1911 (per cent)

SIC		*1851*	*1861*	*1871*	*1881*	*1891*	*1901*	*1911*
1	Agriculture, etc.	1.5	1.2	1.0	0.7	0.8	0.5	0.4
2	Mining and quarrying	0.6	0.5	0.4	0.4	0.4	0.4	0.4
3	Food, drink and tobacco	6.4	6.0	5.9	5.6	6.1	6.2	6.9
5	Chemicals and allied industries	1.1	1.0	1.0	0.8	0.9	1.0	1.1
6	Metal manufacture	2.0	1.9	1.8	1.7	1.7	1.4	1.2
7	Mechanical engineering	0.9	1.3	1.1	1.1	1.2	1.7	1.5
8	Instrument engineering	0.6	0.6	0.5	0.4	0.4	0.4	0.4
9	Electrical engineering	0.0	0.0	0.0	0.1	0.3	0.6	1.0
10	Shipbuilding and marine engineering	0.5	0.6	0.4	0.3	0.2	0.2	0.1
11	Vehicles	0.6	0.6	0.6	0.6	0.5	0.6	0.9
12	Metal goods not elsewhere specified	1.1	1.0	1.1	1.0	1.0	1.3	1.4
13	Textiles	4.0	3.3	2.7	2.3	2.2	2.2	2.1
14	Leather, leather goods and fur	1.4	1.5	1.4	1.5	1.4	1.4	1.5
15	Clothing and footwear	14.8	14.7	12.0	11.6	11.3	10.8	10.6
16	Bricks, pottery, glass, cement, etc.	0.7	0.5	0.4	0.4	0.4	0.4	0.4
17	Timber, furniture, etc.	3.2	3.8	3.7	3.3	3.1	3.2	3.1
18	Paper, printing and publishing	2.4	3.0	3.3	3.9	4.5	4.6	4.8
19	Other manufacturing industries	0.5	0.6	0.7	0.7	0.8	0.7	0.8
20	Construction	6.4	6.8	7.0	7.7	6.6	7.3	6.1
21	Gas, electricity and water	0.2	0.3	0.3	0.3	0.5	0.6	0.6
22	Transport and communication	8.5	9.2	9.4	9.9	11.4	11.3	11.0
23	Distributive trades	1.6	1.4	1.5	1.5	1.5	1.4	1.8
24	Finance, etc. and business services	0.1	0.3	0.5	0.6	0.7	0.9	1.3
25	Professional and scientific services	5.5	4.9	4.8	5.2	4.9	4.9	5.0
26	Miscellaneous services	25.0	24.4	23.8	24.5	22.6	22.0	22.1
27	Public administration	3.0	3.3	3.1	2.6	2.9	3.4	4.1
Not classified		7.4	7.3	11.6	11.2	11.7	10.7	9.2

Source: Own estimates based on Lee, 1979.

Note: SIC 4 is not applicable for this time period.

the absolute growth in jobs in these industries was substantial. Clothing and footwear, in particular, dropped from 15 to 11 per cent of total employment between 1851 and 1911, because employment in these industries only grew by 43 per cent; whereas manufacturing as a whole expanded by 100 per cent. (Chapter 12 argues anyway that they were not entirely the low-productivity activities that is often implied.)

Again, uncertainty arises over the statistical validity of some of the fall in clothing and footwear's share because greater use of sub-contracting and home-working in these sectors may have led to more under-recording of jobs over time in the census. Offsetting that qualification, however, is the nature of the industries that were increasing their employment share, which were not low value-added ones. These included engineering and vehicles (excluding shipbuilding), and printing and publishing, which were overly represented in the outer suburbs and in which technological change and capital investment were raising labour productivity substantially. Together these dynamic sectors increased their share of employment by the same percentage as the decline experienced by the so-called sweated trades.

The significance of London as a manufacturing region remained strong throughout the period. It contained 12 per cent of national manufacturing employment in both 1851 and 1911 (see Table 4.5). The County area is also a poor indicator of the true national influence of the Greater London region's manufacturing capabilities, which are better approximated by adding the Home Counties' manufacturing presence to the County data. This is done in the second row of Table 4.5, and it shows that this broader metropolitan area was home to almost a fifth of British manufacturing jobs in 1911, and only one other region had a greater share of manufacturing: the north-west of England, the centre of the cotton industry. Many of the so-called 'manufacturing regions', therefore, had far fewer manufacturing jobs than the broad metropolis. Any claim that the general industrial peculiarities of the capital created an anti-manufacturing bias in the policy makers who lived in its milieu seem wide of the mark, as suggested, for example, by Cain and Hopkins.[8] From the terrace of the new House of Commons, the vista was of factories belching smoke from the industrial districts of Lambeth and Southwark. London-bound politicians, consequently, did not have to travel like Cobbett had done decades before to realise that Britain was now a manufacturing nation. Obviously, the composition of manufacturing industry was different in London from many of those other regions – but to contrast London and what are usually termed 'the industrial regions' in the Midlands and North is to undertake special pleading for the latter's heavy and textile industries rather than to confront a 'finance-service-consumption' metropolis against 'productive manufacturing' provincial regions.

The shift in London's manufacturing structure indicating in the data corresponds to the economic theory outlined in Chapter 2. London manufacturing, according to that viewpoint, rather than declining over time, was adjusting so that the industries that benefited the most expanded there. This process continuously pushed out the older activates that could no longer compete for a metropolitan location. The agglomeration advantages of the capital that were suggested in Chapter 2, included, among other things, its large consumer market; pools of skilled labour and the other network effects of industrial districts; an ability to adjust to market

Table 4.5 Selected regional shares of national manufacturing employment, 1851–1911 (per cent)

Region	*1851*	*1911*	
		Series A	*Series B*
London	12	12	12
London + 5 Home Counties	16	20	18
North-West	19	21	22
Yorkshire & Humberside	12	12	12
North	4	5	5
Scotland	14	12	12
Wales	3	3	3
Great Britain	100	100	100

Source: Own estimates based on Lee, 1979.

Note: The five Home Counties are Essex, Hertfordshire, Middlesex, Surrey and Kent.

information more quickly than at non-metropolitan locations; and an ability to deal with risk better. The growth of a mass consumer market and new technologies across a wide range of industries in the second half of the nineteenth century increased the attractiveness of locating in large urban agglomerations, so that London manufacturing moved along with the leading edge of contemporary economic change rather than sank into exploitation.

Why was a location in a large urban area so important for so many manufacturing enterprises, when the ties are much weaker today? There is a danger when looking back of forgetting the much higher relative costs of transportation for goods and people a hundred or more years ago, and the poor quality of the means of communicating complex short-term information, apart from through direct face-to-face contact. Much manufacturing activity was consequently wedded to large urban size.

The process of industrial change was stimulated by relative changes in factor prices in the capital. Competition between London-based firms for the scarce inputs of labour and land raised the price of both of them over time. Some manufacturing firms consequently would increasingly find it unprofitable to remain in London. As they folded or moved to the provinces, they would complain about high land and labour costs, but London manufacturing employment still grew fast because the quitting firms were replaced by other firms taking advantage of London's agglomeration benefits. Merely to report the plight of the declining firms and industries in such a dynamic context, as a number of the immiseration interpretations have tended to do, is to give a misleadingly partial picture of decay; when expansion was, in fact, the order of the day.

Dynamic services?

Arguments suggesting that services were the leading light of the London economy are of more recent origin, stemming from work written predominantly since the 1980s. Lee (1981 and 1984) claims that London and the South-East accounted for a relatively large share of the growth of service employment, and that services, and London in particular, were responsible for a relatively large part of UK productivity improvements and output growth. Michie (1997) has supported this view. Rubinstein in a series of publications[9] adopts a variation of this argument by suggesting that, as London had such a concentration of the nation's wealthy, it was inevitable that such demand pressures would push services to the forefront of its economy. Cain and Hopkins (1993) adopt a similar, but somewhat more complicated, position on the service role of London in their own notion of 'Gentlemanly Capitalism'.

Although service employment did double from employing almost half a million in 1851 to almost a million in 1911 – supporting these views of a dynamic service sector – service's overall share of employment was static because both services and manufacturing were expanding in tandem. The service-centred view, however, is shown to be on even weaker ground when the composition of such activities is examined, as Table 4.4 highlights. Half or more of service employment was in miscellaneous services, the bulk of which was domestic service, and the share still remains high, at 40 per cent, in the re-adjusted data for 1911. In this sense, Rubinstein is right about the impact of London's wealth on the scale of service employment, but one of the consequences was to draw labour (especially women) away from the production of marketable goods and services. This servant effect would probably have also raised the cost of labour in London and, thus, discouraged to an unknown extent both manufacturing and non-domestic service activity from locating in the capital. Transport was the second largest service sector, with a slowly rising share of total employment over the period. Outside of servants and transport workers, service employment in the capital shrinks to only a tenth (or a fifth on the new 1911 classification because of the greatly enhanced role of distribution) of the workforce, with only a slight increase in its share in the 1900s.

Nineteenth-century service jobs, moreover, should not be equated with the high valued-added intellectual skills of many of today's occupations. Even many manual activities in modern services are associated with high utilisation of capital equipment and leading-edge technology, as exemplified in modern supermarkets. In contrast, many service jobs in the nineteenth century involved heavy manual labour, little or no capital equipment, and substantial over-manning because of an abundance of cheap hands. Many service jobs consequently were low productivity, and they were also poorly paid ones. The distributive trades, miscellaneous services and transportation, in particular, were the places in the SIC taxonomy where many of the poor and desperate would end up: selling on the streets, running errands and delivering messages, trying their luck at the dock gates, and hauling or carrying loads through the streets. The ready availability of cheap labour of this type, or even of more respectable sorts, encouraged London service firms to be proliferate with labour – cabs permanently on hand, hourly postal deliveries and thousands of waiting messengers are but a few examples. This characteristic can still be experienced today in the service activities of large Third World cities – the masses of porters in stations and hotels, waiters in restaurants, assistants in shops and people set on petty tasks. Relatively high-productivity services, on the other hand, such as finance and the higher echelons of clerical work, employed only a small proportion of London's total workforce (Table 4.3 and Chapters 13 and 14 below). It can be concluded that London did have more service jobs than elsewhere in Britain, but there was a dualism within them. On the one hand, there were a greater number of servants and a wide availability of menial, low-paid jobs, and, on the other hand, there existed an expanding set of higher-value service businesses. But they did not negate the significance of manufacturing.

In terms of their productivity and their contribution to the value-added produced, given the arguments above, it is not clear that London's services were, in general, more productive than its manufacturing activities. Total factor productivity estimates for the UK as a whole, in any case, suggest that, in the period from 1856 to 1913, transport, communications and commerce's productivity growth rates lagged behind those of manufacturing.[10] Other estimates suggest that service productivity increases were only half those in manufacturing across the same period and less than the average for the UK economy as a whole.[11] This, of course, is not to say that services in London were in the doldrums – far from it – but to emphasise them is to give a partial picture of employment and industry.

The impact of commuting

The industry and residences that spilled over into the surrounding Home Counties of Middlesex, Hertfordshire, Essex, Kent and Surrey are obviously missed out when only the County area is considered. Moreover, as the census is residence-based, people's employment is registered at the place where they live rather than where they work. This means that employment in the County is likely to be understated, and that of surrounding counties overstated, because of commuting. Unfortunately, there is no easy way of resolving the problem of accounting for the commuters. The difficulty becomes more acute as the century and suburbanisation progressed. In order to assess the likely effects, rough estimates can be made of potential commuters into London.

Because of subsidised workmen's tickets, not all commuters would have been in middle-class occupations. But, to consider the sensitivity of the County results to non-County commuting, a strong assumption can be

Table 4.6 'Commuting' service industry shares in total employment by region, 1911 (per cent)

SIC	*London*	*Middx*	*Kent*	*Surrey*	*Essex*	*Herts*	*NW*	*Y&H*	*Britain*
24	1.9	3.0	1.4	2.8	2.0	1.8	1.4	1.0	1.3
25	5.0	6.3	5.2	7.1	4.6	6.0	3.0	3.0	4.0
27	3.1	2.8	7.9	3.8	3.4	1.6	1.2	1.2	2.4

Source: Own estimates based on Lee, 1979.

Note: Lee's Series B employment data are used. NW = North-West. Y&H = Yorkshire and Humberside. SIC 24: Finance, etc. and business services; 25: Professional and scientific services; and 27: Public administration.

made that only those working in finance, professional services and administration (SICs 24, 25 and 27) in the Home Counties commuted into the County, to see whether it significantly alters the balance between service and manufacturing employment in London. The comparison is made for 1911 when long-distance commuting was greatest.

Table 4.6 shows the shares of these SICs in total employment in counties around London, in the North-West and Yorkshire for comparison, and for Great Britain as a whole for 1911. It can be seen that the Home Counties all have higher employment shares in these sectors than the national average, with the exception of Hertfordshire in public administration, and that the industrial North-West and Yorkshire had lower than average shares. Much of the higher share occurs in SIC 25, which includes teachers. It could be the case that education was better provided for in the Home Counties, but a maximum estimate of commuters could be that all the excess over the national shares of employment in the Home Counties is actually identifying commuters to London from those counties. When these calculations are made, a total of 90,000 'commuters' are identified.

Such numbers of commuters have a significant effect on employment in these SICs in the capital, suggesting that as many as 30 per cent of those working in them in London commuted from outside of the County area. However, these activities still remain relatively small elements of the London economy as a whole, and the share of these SICs in total London employment only rises from 10 per cent to 14 per cent. It should be remembered that this estimate is based on the extreme assumption that all the excess over the national average were commuters and that no one working in other sectors – including manufacturing – commuted across the County boundary, which is highly unlikely given the scale of working-class suburbs in the ex-County north-east and the extensive network of workmen's fares to them. Such estimates do not suggest the need for a radical review of earlier statements about employment patterns in London because of cross-County boundary commuting.

Sexual divisions of labour

London contained a larger proportion of women in its working population than Great Britain as a whole. In the country at large, around 30 per cent of the workforce were women in 1851, and the proportion stayed constant throughout the rest of the period, with a slight drop after 1891.[12] In London, women were more strongly represented at around 35 per cent of the workforce, with a slight rise after 1901. The huge metropolitan demand for servants accounts for most of the extra significance of women, with many entering domestic service as single, young female migrants into the city.

In 1851, 43 per cent of men worked in manufacturing, 7 per cent more than in the rest of the country where agricultural employment was still large. Another 10 per cent were found in construction, gas and electricity; 3 per cent in agriculture and quarrying; and 32 per cent in services. The manufacturing proportion, however, then fell by about 5 per cent as male employment grew faster in other parts of the London economy. The share of national male employment in manufacturing rose as the capital's declined and, by 1881, the shares were identical and remained so in later decades.

Tens of thousands of other men worked in services and the construction, electricity, gas and water industries. The proportion employed in construction and the utilities, in 1851, was two percentage points higher than nationally, though the rest of the country caught up with this share by the 1900s. With little agriculture to speak of, men were more likely to be occupied in services in the capital than elsewhere and this distinction remained throughout the period. In 1851, almost a third of men worked in services, compared to only 15 per cent in the country overall. Services became more important over time as a source of male employment throughout the nation, but London retained its distinctiveness with 40 per cent of men working in London services compared with 27 per cent nationally in 1911. In the rest of Britain, industrial agglomerations still remained islands in a sea of agriculture; whereas service activity – spread throughout the urban area – took on that encompassing role in the capital. In 1851, the largest male employer was a service sector, transport and communications, with 13 per cent of the total male workforce. Second was construction and then two manufacturing industries, clothing and footwear. Sixty years later, transport and communications continued to employ more men than any other sector, increasing its share to 17 per cent of the total, but construction had been relegated to the third largest employer by miscellaneous services.

Men were spread across all industries, but women were mainly employed in the services – with two-thirds there in 1851. The percentage in manufacturing did increase after 1881, as women were substituted for men in a growing number of manufacturing activities. Data on women's work, unfortunately, are less accurate than for men. It seems likely that the census greatly underestimated female participation in the labour market throughout the period. Many of the jobs undertaken by women were poorly recorded or missed out altogether by census takers, especially if women worked casually or intermittently; in activities such as street trading and scavenging; and also when they worked together with husbands or fathers. The 1851 census's suggestion that just under half the women in the capital worked is consequently likely to be a substantial underestimate. So female workforce participation rates in the metropolis were probably as high as they are today, or even higher.

The census information may constitute a better indicator of the distribution of women in the labour market than of their absolute number, because the missed-out trades were spread across a similar range of activities to those actually enumerated. The majority of women, for instance, were to be found in tasks classified under miscellaneous services, in particular in domestic service, laundering and street trading. Female employment in manufacturing was concentrated in trades not associated with the most physically demanding work, such as clothing and footwear; food, drink and tobacco; and paper, printing and publishing.

Segmented labour markets and trade unions

One area where evidence of segmented markets in the nineteenth century is strong relates to labour. One factor that kept women out of particular jobs was the attitude of employers, male workers and their unions to women. Male trades in both manufacturing and services fought to exclude independent women and young people in an attempt to sustain labour scarcity and, hence, higher rates of pay. Clothing, printing and shoemaking are three good examples. Women and minors, however, did work in some trades as part of a family unit tied into the tasks assigned to their husbands or fathers.

The battles over male exclusivity intensified as the century progressed because technological developments encouraged the use of machinery operated by women in place of male handicraft labour.[13] In some service activities, furthermore, male dominance of the better positions came under threat, particularly in clerical work. Yet employers as much as unions maintained the sexual division of labour in some sectors. Many jobs in transport, for instance, which was the largest male employer, could have been done by women but only a few were employed.

The use of women was often associated with the 'de-skilling' of a production process. This involved a move away from a skilled male handicraft organisation of production to one in which more machinery was used with possibly more 'putting out' of tasks to sub-contractors and home-workers. Women and juveniles were cheaper than the male craft workers and they also possessed different skills – such as greater dexterity – and so greater mechanisation led to men being replaced by them.

De-skilling, of course, is an emotive term, implying that the traditional male handicraft work is inherently better than any other sort of manual work, as well as being better paid. The higher pay of skilled men depended on them being able to restrict entry to their trades. A series of such trade restrictions were broken down over the course of the century. A first phase arose predominantly as a result of the political swing against combinations of workers and later actions were related to battles over technical change. Such technical change, moreover, could be in the organisation of the whole chain of production and distribution, as emphasised by Chandler in his examination of the development of mass production in the USA.[14] Changes in the relations between manufacturers and retailers, as he showed, stimulated developments in manufacturing methods.

Bespoke tailoring offers examples of both the impact of changes in labour legislation and new relationships between retailing and production. Change, particularly a greater use of out-working, was encouraged by the 1814 repeal of the Elizabethan apprenticeship statutes, which already had been flouted for a long time; but the greater pressures came from ready-made clothes and the rise of the 'show shop', in which garments were displayed and orders made up elsewhere, because both of these developments threatened the role of traditional workshops. Trade unions attempted to oppose these changes, but were generally unsuccessful. In 1827 a strike to prevent the spread of the use of female out-workers collapsed, and further industrial action in 1834 failed to restrict out-working or to maintain artisan wages.[15] The later introduction of the sewing machine revolutionised the clothing trades and led to even more female employment. In clerical work, the typewriter tipped the balance away from men. In printing, however, men were more successful at keeping new technology under craft operations.

These examples illustrate that segmented labour markets generally are unlikely to be permanent. It is hard, consequently, to judge their overall impact on the employment structure of London's economy but it was probably small. Some firms, such as printers, undoubtedly left the capital in order to avoid craft restrictions but, in general, there is limited evidence of successful trade union activity to protect skilled male jobs for long against pressures for change.

Trade union activity was relatively weak in the capital throughout the period, partly because of the fragmented structure of workplaces but also because it was easy for employers to find alternative labour and for workers to find new jobs in such as large labour market, so that the conditions for long drawn-out successful strikes were undermined. Altogether, only 294 labour disputes were recorded in London between 1790 and 1870.[16] It has recently been suggested that this indicates a high degree of militancy and was the tip of an iceberg of confrontational labour relations, contrary to the standard view of great quiescence.[17] As an indicator of militancy, however, it is rather weak because it suggests that there were only 3.3 disputes a year on average. Many disputes, furthermore, were concentrated in a small number of industries. Building and shoe-making had the most, representing a third of all disputes. Strikes until the 1880s, furthermore, were limited almost entirely to skilled workers and they were a minority of the labour-force.

The number of disputes was greatest in building and construction, where craft loyalties and the need of firms to complete contracts gave unions greater power – although union effectiveness depended considerably on the building cycle and the type of work.[18] Their industrial strength gave building workers considerable influence in London labour politics.[19] The London Trades Council, for example, was founded in the aftermath of an 1861 builders' dispute. It aimed to co-ordinate the activities of all London trades. In this, it was not particularly successful, and it stayed aloof from the new national Trades Union Congress. Yet it began to have some political influence with the rise of Radical Liberalism and, later, the Labour Party. It was probably at the peak of its influence prior to 1914 during the period of Progressive control of the London County Council.

The unskilled had little chance of combining because of the nature of their employment, so that unions were craft preserves. Most of the so-called new model unions, founded nationally in several skilled trades from the 1850s, had their headquarters in London. They brought new levels of administrative efficiency and offered their members friendly society-type benefits. By the turn of the century, engineering unions, particularly the Amalgamated Society of Engineers, had significant and important footholds in London's engineering trades and, as the hub of the nation's transport system, unionisation in transport became important in London, as national unions developed. Only from the 1880s did unionism of the unskilled achieve any significant proportions, but even then many unions were short-lived or ineffectual.

Formal bans on women or other unwanted social groups in particular areas of work were often unnecessary because informal institutional arrangement kept jobs available only for narrow groups of men. Entry to better-paid occupations was restricted by the need for training, which excluded most adults who were too old to enter apprenticeships, and meant that opportunities for younger workers were limited because of the cost and exclusiveness of the apprenticeship system. In some places, jobs were handed down from father to son; elsewhere information on available work was passed verbally around tight, exclusionary groups. It is probably because of such factors and the specialisation of sub-districts of the city, like the docks, that Hobsbawm was led to argue that the London labour market was highly fragmented and localised.[20] As many people walked to work, in what by the end of the period was a widely spread-out city containing many specialised industrial districts, this image of fragmentation is reinforced. However, Hobsbawm may well have exaggerated the degree of localisation by emphasising the quantitative spatial characteristics of labour markets, rather than their contestability and, hence, the ability of potential interlopers to affect wages and conditions. Even quantitatively, there is much contrary evidence of intense competition for work and there was also notable movement between industrial sectors, especially lower down the status hierarchy.

Divisions between skills and between artisans and less respectable, unskilled workers remained strong, and even perhaps intensified in the years prior to 1914. This occurred despite contemporary heady socialist rhetoric which suggested that the working classes had a unified class interest. In the London labour market that communality was often hard to see, given the scale of competition for work in some sectors and the limits on entry imposed by workers powerful enough to enforce such controls.

The concentration of industries in London

So far, the importance of particular industries for the London economy has been considered. This section considers the significance of London for specific industries nationally. A simple way to consider this issue is to calculate location quotients to indicate the national role of each metropolitan activity. They are estimated as the national share of employment in a specific London industry divided by the overall share of London in total national employment. So, if the location quotient of an industry is greater than 1, employment in it in London is more than the average distribution of jobs in the country would suggest.

Two relevant features can be drawn out from location quotients. First, metropolitan industries can be identified that were nationally concentrated there or were only weakly represented. Second, the changing degree of specialisation of the London economy can be examined. These issues are now considered in turn.

Industrial specialisms

The types of industries that London specialised in can be examined by ranking the location quotients at the time of the 1851 and 1911 censuses for the twenty-seven Standard Industrial Classifications. A location quotient of 1 indicates that London at the time had just the same amount of employment in an industry as a country as a whole. Construction was such an average industry – the same amount of building work, in other words, was going on in the capital as in the rest of the country. A location quotient of 2 would indicate that twice as much employment in a sector existed in London as would be expected in terms of London's general share of national employment.

Tables 4.7 and 4.8 group the industries of 1851 and 1911 into four levels of concentration based on arbitrary, but plausible, divisions in the value of the location quotients (lq): industries that were strongly concentrated in London (lq > 1.5); concentrated ones (lqs from 1.5 to 1.3); national average presence (lq from 0.8 to 1.2); and, finally, below-average presence (lq < 0.8).

Table 4.7 The concentration of industries in London, 1851: a ranking of location quotients

	Strongly concentrated			*Strongly concentrated*	
18	Paper, printing and publishing	3.1	27	Public administration	2.0
8	Instrument engineering	2.5	22	Transport and communication	1.9
21	Gas, electricity and water	2.5	23	Distributive trades	1.8
19	Other manufacturing industries	2.3	24	Finance, etc. and business services	1.7
5	Chemicals and allied industries	2.1	26	Miscellaneous services	1.7
14	Leather goods and fur	2.1	15	Clothing and footwear	1.6
25	Professional and scientific services	2.0	17	Timber, furniture, etc.	1.6
	Concentrated			*Below-average presence*	
3	Food, drink and tobacco	1.5	16	Bricks, pottery, glass, cement, etc.	0.7
10	Shipbuilding and marine engineering	1.4	6	Metal manufacture	0.6
11	Vehicles	1.3	13	Textiles	0.3
	Average presence		2	Mining and quarrying	0.2
			1	Agriculture, etc.	0.1
7	Mechanical engineering	1.2			
20	Construction	1.2			
12	Metal goods not elsewhere specified	1.1			

Source: Own estimates based on data from Lee, 1979.

In 1851, the most concentrated industries are classic capital city ones for the period. London is the focus of printing, specialist handicraft engineering, developments in gas and water and leather because of the large amount of meat consumption and the port. These production industries are followed by service ones again associated with capital city status: the professions, government, transport, distribution and finance. Apart from agriculture, under-represented are building materials, metals, textiles and mining, plus some of the growth industries of the industrial revolution whose locations are influenced by the distribution of natural resources and the coalfields.

By 1911, some industries had declined notably. Chemicals had moved beyond the County boundary or were expanding elsewhere nearer the coal needed for the newer discoveries. Shipbuilding had collapsed. By 1911, a range of consumer goods and contemporary advanced technology industries were the most strongly over-represented in London. Moreover, they are all manufacturing rather than service industries, so that the six most concentrated industries remained production rather than service ones over the sixty-year period. The concentrated group includes many service sectors, some of which are still over-represented because of the

Table 4.8 The concentration of industries in London, 1911: a ranking of location quotients

Strongly concentrated			*Concentrated*		
14	Leather, leather goods and fur	2.2	23	Distributive trades	1.5
18	Paper, printing and publishing	2.2	22	Transport and communication	1.4
8	Instrument engineering	2.0	26	Miscellaneous services	1.4
17	Timber, furniture, etc.	1.8	21	Gas, electricity and water	1.3
9	Electrical engineering	1.6	24	Finance, etc. and business services	1.3
15	Clothing and footwear	1.6	27	Public administration	1.3
19	Other manufacturing industries	1.6			
Average presence			*Below-average presence*		
5	Chemicals and allied industries	1.2	7	Mechanical engineering	0.5
25	Professional and scientific services	1.2	6	Metal manufacture	0.4
3	Food, drink and tobacco	1.1	16	Bricks, pottery, glass, cement, etc.	0.4
20	Construction	1.0	13	Textiles	0.3
11	Vehicles	0.8	10	Shipbuilding	0.2
12	Metal goods not elsewhere specified	0.8	1	Agriculture, etc.	0.1
			2	Mining and quarrying	0.1

Source: Own estimates based on data from Lee, 1979.

uniqueness of London as the capital city – finance, public administration, transport and distribution. In contrast, professional and scientific services – health, education and the professions – had greatly expanded in the rest of Britain since 1851 and, hence, had lost their general metropolitan concentration.

The capital city argument should not be overdone. Most service activity existed simply because of the enormous size of the city's population with all the attendant demands that were thereby generated for utility, transport and personal services (including domestic service, which is a large proportion of the miscellaneous services category). By 1911, in its service activities, London had a diverse range commensurate with its size, rather than a clear concentration on particular areas. The industries in which London was still weak were, unsurprisingly, agriculture, mining and the heavy and textile industries. If the outer suburbs beyond the County boundary had been included in the analysis, some of the concentrations would have been higher, particularly in the engineering and chemicals trades.

The decline of specialisation

Inspection of the location quotations reveals that most declined significantly between 1851 and 1911. These declines were almost universal, as can be seen in Table 4.9, which shows the location quotients at ten-yearly intervals from 1841 to 1911. Yet the prime cause of this change had little to do with the metropolis itself but rather with the shift away from agriculture in the rest of the country. The result was a general expansion of urban employment, including in London, and a broadening of manufacturing and service employment in the provinces, as Britain became a wealthier, more technically advanced, urbanised society. To an extent, the rest of Britain could be said to be catching-up with what was already happening in the metropolis and, by doing so, was weakening the concentration of some activities there.

It is tempting to argue that declining location quotients indicate a weakening in the competitiveness of London industry in relation to provincial counterparts, but that interpretation is misleading. The relative decline in London specialisms was inevitable because nationally labour was being transferred from agriculture into manufacturing and services, and the geographical endpoints of rural-urban migrations were widespread rather than simply focused on movement to the metropolis.

Surveying the concentrations of industry in Table 4.9 highlights the advantageous position of London in the broader British economy just prior to the First World War. It had a very diverse industrial structure, with a wide range of growth industries, and poor representation in the volatile staple export industries. This was to prove of enormous benefit when the staples began to decline in the 1920s.

The size of firms

In Chapter 2, it was argued that large cities have strong tendencies to have a large array of small firms. This is because such firms benefit most from agglomeration economies and clustering into industrial districts. This was undoubtedly the case for London. In 1851, for example, the census suggests that 86 per cent of employers employed fewer than ten workers and three-quarters fewer than five.[21] The generally accepted fact, therefore, is that metropolitan enterprises were small. It is recognised that several giant plants existed – for instance, the Royal Arsenal employed about 12,000 during the Boer War and the Stratford Works of the Great Eastern Railway employed about 7,000 in 1910[22] – but these are generally regarded as the exceptions that prove the proverbial rule. Firm size in Britain was generally quite small.[23] The question is whether London firms were smaller than the contemporary British average. The evidence that is available suggests that conventional wisdom about the distinctiveness of London firm sizes might be exaggerated.

The view that London was a city of petty producers appears to be supported in the writings of contemporaries like Henry Mayhew. The

Table 4.9 Location quotients for London industries, 1841–1911

	Industry	*1841*	*1851*	*1861*	*1871*	*1881*	*1891*	*1901*	*1911*
1	Agriculture, etc.	0.1	0.1	0.1	0.1	0.1	0.1	0.1	0.1
2	Mining and quarrying	0.1	0.2	0.2	0.1	0.1	0.1	0.1	0.1
3	Food, drink and tobacco	1.5	1.5	1.4	1.3	1.2	1.1	1.1	1.1
5	Chemicals and allied industries	2.1	2.1	1.8	1.6	1.4	1.3	1.3	1.2
6	Metal manufacture	0.7	0.6	0.5	0.5	0.5	0.5	0.4	0.4
7	Mechanical engineering	0.8	1.2	1.2	0.8	0.7	0.6	0.6	0.5
8	Instrument engineering	3.1	2.5	2.4	2.1	1.8	1.7	1.7	2.0
9	Electrical engineering	–	–	–	–	3.8	2.8	1.8	1.6
10	Shipbuilding and marine engineering	0.9	1.4	1.3	0.8	0.6	0.4	0.2	0.2
11	Vehicles	1.6	1.3	1.3	1.1	1.1	0.9	0.7	0.8
12	Metal goods not elsewhere specified	1.1	1.1	0.8	0.9	0.8	0.8	0.8	0.8
13	Textiles	0.4	0.3	0.3	0.2	0.2	0.2	0.3	0.3
14	Leather, leather goods and fur	1.6	2.1	2.2	2.0	2.1	2.0	1.9	2.2
15	Clothing and footwear	1.6	1.6	1.5	1.5	1.4	1.4	1.5	1.6
16	Bricks, pottery, glass, cement, etc.	0.6	0.7	0.4	0.4	0.4	0.4	0.4	0.4
17	Timber, furniture, etc.	2.0	1.6	2.1	2.2	2.1	2.0	1.8	1.8
18	Paper, printing and publishing	3.3	3.1	3.0	2.8	2.6	2.6	2.3	2.2
19	Other manufacturing industries	2.6	2.3	2.7	2.5	2.3	2.2	1.7	1.6
20	Construction	1.1	1.2	1.2	1.1	1.1	1.1	0.9	1.0
21	Gas, electricity and water	3.4	2.5	2.2	1.7	1.5	1.4	1.2	1.3
22	Transport and communication	1.9	1.9	1.8	1.8	1.6	1.5	1.4	1.4
23	Distributive trades	1.6	1.8	1.9	1.6	1.5	1.5	1.5	1.5
24	Finance, etc. and business services	1.7	1.7	1.6	2.1	1.6	1.4	1.3	1.3
25	Professional and scientific services	2.0	2.0	1.8	1.6	1.5	1.4	1.3	1.2
26	Miscellaneous services	1.5	1.7	1.5	1.4	1.4	1.4	1.4	1.4
27	Public administration	1.7	2.0	1.6	1.5	1.4	1.4	1.4	1.3

Source: Own estimates based on data from Lee, 1979.

Note: SIC 4 is not applicable for this time period.

investigations undertaken by Mayhew, however, may give a biased view of overall firm sizes, because his focus on the poor meant that he ignored many of the manufacturing trades with large plants where they were thinly represented. The census, similarly, may give an inaccurate impression of firm size. It is believed to have underestimated the actual number of firms in existence, perhaps by half, partly because it centred attention on manufacturing and construction. It can be misleading about the size of firms, as well, especially as it lists those companies employing women separately; thereby understating the size of firms employing both men and women.

The census also had problems distinguishing between firms and the self-employed. Rather than containing more very small firms than the rest of the country, London in fact had fewer firms employing between one and four workers, but more masters who worked alone or failed to state the number of journeymen employed. Over 43 per cent of the capital's masters employed, or claimed to employ, no workers, as compared to 28 per cent in the North-West and 38 per cent in Yorkshire, for example.[24]

The size structure of nineteenth-century London firms, consequently, is in some doubt. It is highly likely, given the capital's industrial structure, that many small enterprises prevailed, but in a considerable number of activities large plants existed as well. The utilities of gas and water are cases in point, as are the many transportation companies, bank headquarters and, towards the end of the period, the myriad of government and other public entities. Larger firms also prevailed in some heavier industries, in food processing, some consumer durables and drinks. Towards the end of the century, moreover, the multinationals entering Britain frequently set up a large plant in the environs of the capital. London, rather than simply having a mass of small enterprises by the end of the century, more likely had a bimodal distribution – with many small firms but also a disproportionately high number of very large firms.

Perhaps the strongest evidence of the existence of many large plants is provided by the survey of the location of larger metropolitan employers undertaken by the 1905 Royal Commission on Traffic in London. It provided maps showing all establishments in transport, the utilities and manufacturing employing more than 100 people in 1904. There were literally hundreds of factories and works of such sizes, as can be seen in Figure 4.1, which shows most of the inner industrial areas from Vauxhall in the west to the Isle of Dogs in the east. Large-scale plants were scattered throughout the capital's industrial districts – although they are under-represented in the East End, which may have misled historians as that district has been the focus of most historical enquiry on London's industries.

In terms of the geography of London's larger industry, the Royal Commission's maps show that there is a concentration in Holborn and Clerkenwell between the City and West End; and in the south in inner Southwark and Bermondsey and along the environs of the Surrey Canal. More larger establishments are spread along the rivers, canals and docks

Figure 4.1 Principal factories and works in inner London, 1904

T = Tobacco; C = Clothing; W^D = Wood; TY = Timber Yard; D = Distillery; L = Leather; PW = Printing Works; RW = Rope Works; IF = Iron Foundry; IW = Iron Works; BF = Brass Foundry; MW = Mineral Water; W = Wharf; WH = Warehouse; GD = Goods Depot; FS = Fire Station; CW = Chemical Works; BR = Breweries; LD = Laundries; B = Bookbinding.

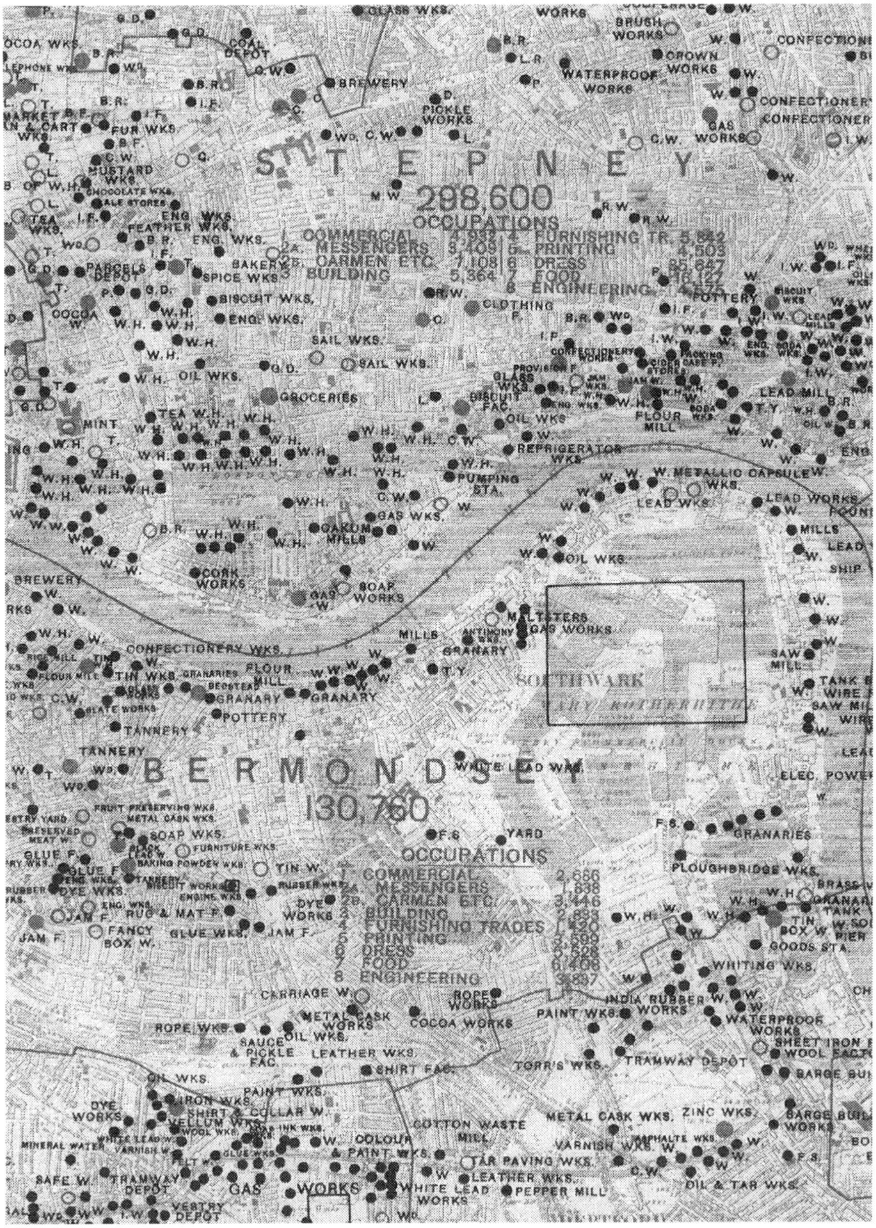

Figure 4.1 continued

Employees in factories: Circle > 100; Black dot > 200; Grey dot > 500; Square/polygon > 1000.

Source: Royal Commission on London Traffic, 1905.

to the east. To the west, the density is less but there are notable concentrations in Westminster and Chelsea, along the river in Lambeth, Battersea and Wandsworth. To the north, Camden, Kentish Town and Holloway contain less concentrated industrial districts. Further out in the west, only Brentford close to the Thames constitutes an industrial district. Northwards, Tottenham, Enfield and Edmonton contained notable industries close to the Lea Navigation. Eastwards, Stratford and the lower Lea Valley contain many plants employing more than a hundred hands; while Millwall and the two Royal Docks each employed more than 1,000; as did the Gas, Light and Coke Company's Beckton works and the Royal Arsenal and Siemens's facilities in Woolwich. Yet, elsewhere, great swathes of suburbia, from Hackney anti-clockwise round to Lewisham and Blackheath, contain few works, apart from transport depots. The outward spread of industry, therefore, was limited and piecemeal – a situation that changed radically after 1914.

Several examples give the flavour of the size of some plants and the range of industries they cover. The Borough of Poplar had 12 plants employing between 200 and 500 involved in starch, match, cocoa and biscuit making, shipbuilding and repair, indiarubber, clothing, metals and iron bridges. In addition, five factories employed more than 500, making vehicles, matches, stained paper and gas. St Pancras had eight establishments employing 200 to 500: two piano works plus fabricators of locomotives, false teeth, mineral water, plaster, ammunition and a bookbinders. Camberwell had six large plants, mainly associated with clothing. Battersea had a soap factory employing more than 500. Westminster had both a clothing factory and a printing works of such size. Furthermore, in it were thirteen establishments in the 200 to 500 category, among which were five printing works and plants for making jam, gas, engineering products, clothing and beer. These plant sizes by no means matched the giant plants already being established in the USA and Germany but were quite large in the context of contemporary British industry. Thus, the idea that pre-1914 London had no large places of employment, in contrast to the so-called industrial regions of Britain, is somewhat of a myth.

Large companies existed for several reasons. They might be in industries that required large amounts of fixed capital, as in printing, engineering and margarine and sugar processing. The London printing industry contained six of the largest printers in the country. Other large plants existed because firms wanted to be near to their main market and some possessed local monopolies in industries with considerable economies of scale, such as gas.

London also attracted a disproportionate number of the large multinational firms that came to Britain from the 1850s onwards.[25] In 1885, nine, out of a total of seventeen, of such firms' plants in Britain were in the South-East. Later, the proportion stayed much the same with, in 1907, 55 out of a total of 110. The first foreign producer to settle in the capital was the American gun manufacturer Colt, which set up a factory in 1853.

It was followed by the German Ohlendorff and Co., which manufactured guano fertiliser; the French fan manufacturer Ettlinger; and Siemens, which established a telegraphic factory in Finsbury in 1858, and a sea cable plant at Woolwich in 1863.

The changing structure of London's industry

Industrial change over the course of the nineteenth century was obviously enormous and London unsurprisingly shared in those changes. The predominantly artisanal economy of the early nineteenth century[26] was slowly transformed into a way of life more familiar to modern eyes. The long-term forces in this process were technical change, rising living standards and the resulting shifts in the composition of demand, new patterns of international trade and the shifting attractiveness of the rapidly expanding metropolis for particular types of activity.

The transport revolution from the 1830s transformed the barrier of distance, with the new rail network enabling the agriculture of more distant counties to be adjusted to feed the giant London population. Manufacturers could also far more easily serve the London market from provincial locations, and, similarly, London firms could take advantage of a much deeper and more extensive national market. The near monopoly over London consumers that metropolitan manufacturers had previously enjoyed was severely weakened. Even the wealthy London brewers saw their market successfully invaded by companies from the Midlands by the 1870s.

Not only did innovations in transportation alter the relationship between the capital and the rest of the country but they also made the continued expansion of London possible. Without them, rising congestion, housing shortages and escalating land prices would have slowed urban growth considerably. Changes in manufacturing and distribution, furthermore, were associated with new ways of selling goods to consumers. Shops became more important in the distribution of goods and served an expanding mass market. This transformed the West End into the locus of what was then the most affluent mass market in the world containing many large retailers operating from department stores and new multiple chains. Suburban shopping centres grew up to complement these developments in the city centre. Alongside the larger shops and chains were a myriad of smaller ones taking advantage of the huge metropolitan consumer base to specialise in particular lines. The new mass markets and the ways in which goods were sold, in turn, altered the structure of many of London's consumer goods industries, particularly in sectors like clothing and furniture.

London, like the rest of Britain, was affected by the growth of what has been termed the 'Atlantic economy' and its increasing integration from mid-century onwards. The term is used to describe the geographic area of the Americas and Western Europe, linked via the Atlantic, and added to it are other areas of recent European expansion, notably Australasia, that exported foodstuffs and raw materials. In the first half of the century,

O'Rourke and Williamson argue, the Atlantic economy had been characterised by limited commodity trade and migration, high tariffs and undeveloped capital markets. As a result, its economies tended to diverge from each other.[27] Starting with the repeal of the British Corn Laws in 1846, trade liberalised. This was followed by subsequent enormous improvements in transport and communications. The overall result was that these economies became more integrated as trade expanded, countries industrialised, and capital and labour migrated. Technological advances across a wide range of industries became more easily disseminated between countries. New sources of agriculture produce and raw materials were opened up, so that primary commodity prices tumbled. One consequence of greater integration into a global economy was that a long, slow process of convergence in living standards and prices was observable. Convergence was dampened somewhat by the surge of innovations in the USA from the 1890s, which gave it a substantial productivity lead over other countries and this was reflected in local factor incomes. Further integration was hampered by restrictive trade policies that emerged again in the USA after the Civil War, and through reactions in continental Europe countries to the impact of cheap food imports on their large agricultural sectors, but Britain retained its free trade stance throughout.[28] Yet the world economy had been irrevocably changed.

What are the implications of these developments in the Atlantic economy for London? The effects were profound, especially as they were occurring alongside parallel changes in the domestic economy, driven by the same transportation and communication factors. Some only will be mentioned briefly here as the consequences form part of the histories outlined in the later chapters. One of the most significant was the fall in the price of agricultural foodstuffs after 1870 and the decline of arable agriculture in Britain. At a national scale, the switch to overseas imports sustained the drift of population from rural to urban areas and, by this time, the great expansions of the northern cities were over and subsequent urbanisation was more diffuse – with the exception of London which continued its spectacular growth. Falls in the price of agricultural land also encouraged the outward spread of cities, a process in which London's suburbanisation towered over that of other cities. Cheaper agricultural produce, in addition, gave a substantial boost to British urban workers' living standards and they could now afford to spend more on housing and to buy a wider range of products, such as clothing and furniture. London enterprises – from transport companies, through retailing and leisure, to manufacturing – could rely on a greater mass of relatively affluent consumers. Developments in industries as diverse as furniture and trams, thus, received an impetus from the new world economy. In contrast, the resurgence of British imperialism and the expanded tropical Empire seem to have had comparatively little impact on the metropolitan economy.

Not all the changes benefited every metropolitan industry. Free trade led to the demise of several traditional London industries, such as watch and luxury shoe-making. Others were affected by strong competition from imports as other European countries industrialised. The large London piano-making industry, for example, found it increasingly difficult to keep up with French and German producers. The re-imposition of tariffs in Europe induced further change. Offsetting them were the new overseas markets that were opening up as a consequence of large-scale European emigration, to which several London industries began exporting – including clothing and furniture.

Finally, the Atlantic economy gave an enormous boost to the activities of the City. As the world centre for commodity trading, the greater volume of international trade stimulated its commodity markets. On the finance side, City firms discounted much of the finance associated with international trade as world money and capital markets became more integrated, and many foreign institutions were attracted to London. The new issues market, merchant and clearing banks all gained from the enormous export of capital from Britain to fund expansion elsewhere in the Atlantic economy.

Developments in the nineteenth-century metropolitan economy, consequently, cannot be viewed parochially. The role of London in the national economy changed over time as did Britain's position internationally. The rivalry between nation states that led to rejuvenated imperialism and, ultimately, the horrific world wars of the twentieth century was not the only factor in international relations. The co-operative elements associated with expanding economic and financial relations were fortunately of greatest significance for London's economic growth. The technological advances, which did so much to transform London as they did other cities, were public knowledge at a world scale. In fact, many transport innovations were imported to the capital from overseas, often via foreign entrepreneurs; and similar processes occurred across a wide variety of other activities from clothing and shoe-making to electricity and foodstuffs. When looking at the detailed events in the capital's economic history, as later chapters do, it is important to bear in mind these broader global changes. But, before moving on to them, the standard of living in nineteenth-century London is first considered in the next chapter.

5 Wealth, living standards and poverty

Introduction

Capital cities of all countries contain extremes of wealth and poverty. Many contemporary and modern views of nineteenth-century London echo the refrain of opulence for the rich and extreme misery and deprivation for the poor. It is easy, however, for emotion at the apparent lack of social justice of this state of affairs to cloud interpretation of the available data. Descriptions of wealth and poverty alone do not tell much about the overall distribution of income in a city and how it was changing. Nor do they identify whether the situation was typical of the time or specific to a city, like London. Was it actually true that the distribution of income was more unequal in the capital city than elsewhere in Britain?

Causality is also in question because conclusions are strongly affected by whether it is thought specific economic processes in a city generate poverty. Some writers, such as Stedman Jones (1971) and Green (1995), suggest that such London-specific characteristics contributed to poverty, particularly through the functioning of its casual labour and housing markets and through the 'de-skilling' of artisanal labour. Associated with such distributional issues is the general standard of living of the city's population. Was it higher in London than elsewhere, how did it change over time and why? These topics form the themes of this chapter but, unfortunately, the theory and data that can be worked with are insufficient to give clear answers; therefore, pointers to likely outcomes only can be given.

Difficulties arise in any discussion of the distribution of income and the standard of living over definitions, data availability and interpretations of them. With regard to the nineteenth century, these issues are amplified – and they become even worse when a particular city is considered, rather than the nation as a whole. London fares better than most cities in the information available. Henry Mayhew walked its streets in the 1850s examining the lives and poverty of the ordinary populace. Then, roughly fifty years later, a unique, path-breaking survey of poverty was undertaken by Charles Booth and his colleagues. Both provide detailed and copious evidence on working-class earnings and poverty; and of great assistance as well are data from income tax returns and Poor Law records.

Yet, two surveys only provide snapshots and say nothing of the periods before or in between. Those surveys themselves need critical evaluation. The official returns, moreover, are only partial in coverage. Similar problems arise with regard to wealth and income measures, because everyone had strong incentives to hide their income and wealth from the taxman's and others' prying gazes.

What is perhaps worst when trying to evaluate the distribution of income and changes in living conditions is that little can be accurately said about the living standards of the great mass of the population in between the very rich and the very poor. The relative importance of wealth and poverty in the capital and how it changed consequently is unclear. The actual standard of living of the average Londoner can only be guessed at from contentious standard of living estimates, limited wage data, old photographs and the physical remains of the houses contemporary Londoners lived in.

The attractions of a large city to the rich and poor were outlined in Chapter 2. Unfortunately, theory does not say what the resultant share of each group is likely to be in the overall distribution of income. Even if the poor were attracted to the metropolis or were born and remained there, so were millions of others who prospered. The share of poverty in London's population as a whole, consequently, could have been diminishing over time, even if it is believed that the absolute numbers in poverty were rising.

This chapter cannot possibly undertake a full survey of the potential pitfalls of historical standard of living and distributional studies, but some signposts are necessary as the information is presented. The first section examines wealth, which is followed by an investigation of middle-class incomes. After this, changes in the general working-class standard of living over the period are considered – an exercise that requires surveys of available data on variations in the cost of living, housing rents and money wages; consideration of the relation between wages and average annual earnings; and a comparison of London earnings with elsewhere. This, finally, leads on to the incidence of poverty and its causes.

Wealth

Capital cities traditionally attract the very wealthy, especially if they are the seat of national government and centres of business and luxury consumption. This was the case throughout Europe in the nineteenth century, including London. The politics, economy and sheer size of the USA, Canada and many other British dominions and colonies, in contrast, divided these functions between a number of cities. Given its role in the British urban hierarchy, it is no surprise that London contained many of the nation's wealthy. The linkages of the rich to the capital and its economy, however, were multi-faceted.

Many affluent Britons had London residences rather than directly derived their riches from the metropolis. A large number of the nation's wealthy had some sort of London address but many were used for only part of the year. The assets of such itinerants, moreover, were based on land held elsewhere, mining and other non-London industry, or derived from overseas activities, especially financial investments.

A preference of the rich to live in London, or make extended visits to it, had much to do with the particular set of agglomeration benefits that they derived from being there. The gains in political influence and social standing and the opportunities for particular forms of luxurious enjoyment were manifold. These benefits for the wealthy influenced the structure of demand in the capital and supply responded accordingly. The resultant scale and external economies in the supply of luxury consumption goods and services made a wider range of them available than elsewhere in the country. Demand and supply, therefore, fed on each other to enhance agglomeration benefits. The inward and outward flow of the wealthy in relation to the London Season, however, created considerable seasonal fluctuations in luxury demand, which affected businesses and workers active in those areas.

The rich also took over much central urban land for their residences and leisure activities and also monopolised the most esteemed suburbs. In doing so, they competed with other activities for scarce space, raising land values in the process. Over time, none the less, the relative influence of the wealthy on the overall operation of the London economy declined because mass consumption grew to represent a much greater source of demand.

One source of information on the rich in this period is probate returns made at death. Until the late nineteenth century, probate returns excluded real property (buildings and land) and some settled property, so the wealth of the landed magnates is absent. The most prolific analyst of probate returns has been Rubinstein.[1] He has used his results as justification for interpreting British economic history as a conflict between a 'gentlemanly capitalism' – based in London and deriving its wealth predominantly from the commercial and financial activities of the City – and 'industrial capitalism' operating in the provinces. The wealth and close social connections with the highest in the land of the metropolitan commercial and banking elite, he argues, enabled them to influence economic policy and the development of the British economy to the detriment of industrial interests.

No one disagrees with the integration of wealthy society in London, with capitalists mixing with aristocrats – how could it have been otherwise? But Rubinstein's division between commercial and industrial capitalists, and its use by other historians, has led to considerable criticism. The causal chain of his argument that economic development is determined by government economic policy, which is, in turn, controlled by a commercial elite is weak in all its links.[2] Yet, even if it cannot be easily demonstrated that a City elite was a collective equivalent of an *éminence grise* to successive nineteenth-century British governments, the question still remains of whether London was the place to become seriously rich because of the uniqueness of its industrial structure, including finance, or, once account is taken of its size, was the probability of becoming rich much the same as in other parts of the country?

Probate data

Rubinstein estimates that, of the forty British fortunes worth £2 million or more left between 1809 and 1914, twenty belonged to Londoners.[3] This conclusion identifies the metropolis as a uniquely special place to become rich in nineteenth-century Britain, and the reason, according to Rubinstein, is the capital's economic structure, containing as it did the commercial and financial activities of the City.

The capital features extremely highly as a location for the rich in the early years of the century, with almost two-thirds of half-millionaires and above residing there. Yet Rubinstein's data show that as the wealthy increased in number in the country as a whole during the next hundred years, the importance of London diminished, so that by the First World War only 44 per cent of the richest gave a London address. A marked decline can also be seen in the national significance of London for the second rung of wealth – those leaving between £100,000 and £500,000 – in the probate data between 1809 and 1869, which Rubinstein analysed as well.[4]

Rubinstein's belief in the overwhelming significance of the City as a source of wealth has been widely criticised. Berghoff suggests, using a different probate sampling procedure, that the industrial revolution created a new group of provincial rich that displaced London from the top in the wealth hierarchy.[5] He concludes that there were roughly equal shares of industrialists and City bankers within the very wealthy in Britain. Perkin also disagrees with the belief that millionaires came mainly from commerce and finance, suggesting that there were as many rich industrialists as merchants, bankers and insurance underwriters.[6] Most recently, Nicholas has challenged Rubinstein's whole approach.[7] He points out that those leaving half a million or more left only a small proportion of bequest wealth – 3 per cent in 1858 and 10 per cent in 1900–1 – so that, whatever is concluded about who the very wealthy were, little can be said about the general regional distribution of wealth from it. He instead draws a broader sample of businessmen and finds that the distribution of wealth in London was not significantly different from other regions and that there was no significant difference in wealth creation between industry, on the one hand, and commerce and finance, on the other.

Nicholas's conclusions make sense if a reasonable degree of competition is assumed within the economy as a whole. In such situations, capital would flow into and out of sectors until the rates of return were roughly equalised, and this implies that different industrial sectors should broadly produce rich people in proportion to their significance in the economy. This could not always happen as monopoly restrictions might be long-lasting – land ownership, in particular, was highly concentrated within the aristocracy and tied up in family settlements.[8] But nineteenth-century manufacturing is generally regarded as competitive and so is the financial sector. That capital flowed towards the areas where it achieved the greatest return can also be seen in the enormous export of capital from Britain and the way it which it varied in line with changes in rates of return in Britain.[9] If one sector of the economy was churning out millionaires, consequently, it is to be expected that capital and talent would have flowed towards it.[10] (This process can be seen with the internet in modern times.) Those flows then bring down rates of return in the over-achieving sector to more usual levels and thus reduce the possibilities of becoming rich there.

One further factor that needs to be brought into consideration is the riskiness of any line of business. The more risky, the greater will be the dispersion of winners and losers, but the average wealth creation will be the same as in a less risky business, assuming the same average risk-adjusted return. Using information on the wealthy at death, therefore, is to concentrate on the winners only. The low-risk industry in such circumstances will create less rich people at the end of any time period than a risky one; yet it is producing wealth at the same average rate. It just happens simultaneously to be producing fewer losers and bankrupts. So, even if some industries are found to produce proportionately more rich, this may simply indicate that they are more risky than average, rather than highlight some hidden special favours. Eighteenth- and early nineteenth-century finance was very risky. So reported declines in the proportion of the super-rich in banking over time may simply indicate that the riskiness of finance was declining relative to other economic activities. New industries and ones subject to substantial innovation would also tend to be more risky, and successful businesses would be more likely to be protected by patents and, thus, more rich are likely to be created in them than in existing mature industries. Both finance and retailing were subject to much innovation, as later chapters show, and, therefore, are likely to figure significantly in wealth data. But alongside the winners would have been many who lost all, taking their backers' investments with them.

Probate returns, finally, give information for men who generally died in their seventies and eighties. As Rubinstein himself points out, they therefore highlight the conditions for wealth creation decades before when these men made their money. The conditions for wealth creation at a specific point in time cannot be gleaned from them as a result.[11]

General wealth

Probate returns only record wealth at death. The savings and assets owned by the less prosperous, but still comfortable, members of society as a result are likely to be strongly under-represented in them. Most people, when they could, saved for older age, changing family circumstances and periods of ill-health or unemployment, and after such wealth has been drawn down in face of such needs, it obviously leaves no trace at death when probate returns are made. Unfortunately, however, it is not possible to find out accurately the wealth of living Londoners or the role that economic activity in the capital played in creating and distributing that wealth. In particular, the wealth embodied in the housing stock, which today represents about a half of all personal sector wealth, was in the nineteenth century quite widely owned. Because of the much higher value of buildings in London than elsewhere in Britain, moreover, housing would have been a more significant conduit for metropolitan wealth creation. Ground leases helped to make their noble, commoner and corporate owners rich, but such leases represented only a fraction of the full capital value of commercial or residential buildings. As Chapter 8 shows, most of the housing stock was held on lease or owned outright by people of relatively modest means acting as housing landlords and funded by the equally modest holders of private mortgages. A major part of the metropolis's capital stock – its housing – consequently had a diffused ownership structure. It could be argued, therefore, that the metropolis, rather than intensifying the national mechanisms through which wealth was concentrated, as Rubinstein and others strongly feel, may have provided openings for its greater diffusion via real property.

It is clear, none the less, that the City was not the only source of wealth: manufacturing, urban commerce and housing provision all played their parts as well. Nor was London the only place to become wealthy, because the provinces offered many manufacturing and commercial opportunities as well. The towering pinnacle of wealth in nineteenth-century Britain, at least until the 1880s, moreover, was still land.[12] Urban land-holdings were making a few magnates very rich but most landed wealth related to agricultural rents and mineral royalties – and of the latter two London had virtually none.

Middle-class income

London was the focus of middle-class income as well as a haunt of the rich. Some well-paid, middle-class professions were heavily concentrated there. But, again, the actual incidence of the middle classes and the incomes they enjoyed is unclear.

Using income tax returns, Rubinstein (1993) has suggested that the capital's middle classes throughout the century accounted for at least a quarter of the income of that social group in Britain as a whole. This share, he argued, far outweighed those of their counterparts in industrial regions, like Yorkshire and Lancashire. London's percentage of total British middle-class income fell during the first half of the century from 40 per cent to a low of 27 per cent; it then rose rapidly to reach 45 per cent in 1911/12.[13] The changing shares may reflect the growth of the industrial regions during the first half of the century and the resurgence of London activities in the second, as Rubinstein suggests, but doubts about the data make such an interpretation questionable. In the first place, no income tax was assessed from the end of the Napoleonic Wars until 1842, so much weight has to be put on the comparability of the returns from the early war-time part of the century with those of the mid-century, if the changes in regional shares between those dates are to be believed. Similarly, later alterations in tax rules and variations in the efficiency of the inspectors' nets may have played a part in determining subsequent, apparent regional shares.

Another possibility is that the income tax data have a higher-order service and, hence, London bias. Britain's industrial structure was dominated by a mass of small, unincorporated businesses and family ownership. Along with the rural middle class of prosperous farmers, the owners of those businesses were probably adept at minimising their true incomes. This may have been less possible for the professionals and others over-represented in the capital. If this hypothesis is true, an exaggerated middle-class income share for London results. Countervailing this bias is the fact that income from real property is excluded from the tax returns examined – the Londoners who invested in it presumably benefited more than most because of the high property rents there. (Women taxpayers are also not recorded.)

The major problem with using tax returns to measure the spatial distribution of the middle class is the unclear boundary that defines the middle class. The tax band below which no tax was paid varied in the nineteenth century from £60 in the early period to £100 to £160 later. Rubinstein (1993) assumes that anyone above the prevailing threshold is in the 'middle class'. This leads to an enormous estimate of the size of this metropolitan social grouping. He calculated that 41 per cent of London males paid tax in 1861, compared with only 13 per cent in Lancashire and 11 per cent in Yorkshire.[14] Yet it is hard to believe that so many Londoners were actually middle-class – many clerical and skilled workers would have been paying tax as well. Perkin estimates from national data on male earnings in 1909, for example, that 46 per cent of insurance clerks paid income tax, 44 per cent in banking, 37 per cent in central government, 28 per cent in local government, 23 per cent in industry and trade and 10 per cent in the railway companies.[15] The occupational structure of London employment and the relatively high earnings there were consequently catching far more in the tax net than simply the prosperous.

Other estimates of the size of the middle class put it far lower as well. The middle-class occupations associated with the industrial structure analysis, presented earlier in Chapter 4, do not suggest that London's employed middle class were proportionately that much different in scale from urban Britain as a whole. The evidence from location quotients, reported in Table 4.9 (see p. 78), for instance, gave no preponderance to London with regard to the 'professional and scientific services' category. For the early decades of the century, Schwarz, using data on income and housing taxes, categorises the metropolitan income hierarchy into a 2–3 per cent upper income group with over £200 a year; a 'middling classes' group constituted another 16–21 per cent on incomes averaging £80 to £130; another 7–8 per cent were shopkeepers; around 4 per cent were self-employed non-building industry artisans; employed artisans made up another quarter; and the remaining half were semi- and unskilled.[16] These estimates of the middle class are broadly in line with those at the end of the century, when Booth in the 1890s put the figure for the middle classes all together – that is, the lower, middle and upper parts of it combined – at 18 per cent. This corresponds closely to national information on occupations and class for 1911, where 20 per cent count as middle-class, with the rest part of the working class (2 per cent foremen, 33 per cent skilled, 34 per cent semi-skilled and 12 per cent unskilled).[17]

Contemporary fiction and other qualitative material attest to the scale of the metropolitan middle class, but whether the available information provides accurate pictures of metropolitan and provincial incomes is in some doubt. In the absence of further information, the null hypothesis cannot be rejected that the middle class in London was no different in relative size from that of the country as a whole. This conclusion, if true, still gives London a much larger middle class than any other British city, but simply because of its size rather than because of its economic structure.

The distribution of income and wealth: the national context

Conclusions about the distribution of income and wealth in London have been shown to be fraught with difficulties by examining evidence for the very rich and the middle class. Does the literature on the country as a whole help? One conclusion from it is that wealth and income distributions were similar up until the 1870s to what they had been in earlier agrarian times from at least the late seventeenth century. From the late 1860s, however, there was then a marked shift towards greater equality because of the decline of landed incomes and a gradual rise in incomes from employment.[18] Lindert in his survey,[19] however, argues that in terms of socio-economic groupings a clear increase in inequality occurred from 1760 to 1815, with landlords and wholesale merchants gaining at the expense of the middle and lower classes. This shift is less apparent in terms of the available information on the richest 10 per cent of the population though, because the likes of landlords and merchants became significantly smaller proportions of the growing British population. Furthermore, he argues that there was no real decline in inequality until the beginning of the twentieth century. Inequality in mid-Victorian society was particularly marked, with the richest 5 per cent of UK households receiving 41 per cent of all incomes – a share that was significantly less equal than in other contemporary European and North American countries.

Whether this is representative of the London situation is unclear. The penchant of the landed wealthy and others to live in rural mansions weakened the pull of the metropolis at least for most of the year, in contrast to, say, French or American society. In addition, it was noted earlier that international commerce as a source of wealth was in relative decline and was being supplemented by a broader range of sources of wealth. Finally, the massive expansion of house-ownership in London from the 1860s, albeit frequently as landlords, may have created a nineteenth-century-style 'property owning democracy' not experienced elsewhere in the country, because of the capital's relatively high housing costs. So, London undoubtedly reflected the national situation, but its absence of agriculture, dispersed real property ownership and higher-productivity activities probably narrowed rather than extended inequality. The 'significant improvement after 1870' view of national changes may be more relevant to the metropolitan situation, consequently, than the one that postpones change to a later date.

Working-class living standards and the cost of living

Nineteenth-century living standards are one of the most contentious areas of debate in nineteenth-century British economic history. Controversy is permanent because of the limited wage series available, although the statistical techniques used have improved over time and a gradual consensus is emerging. Unfortunately, no continuous reliable series exist at all for London itself, so that inferences generally have to be drawn from national views. This does not matter much if prices and earnings between regions move in tandem. Evidence of regional convergence in prices and of regional disparities in earnings, therefore, has to be considered. As a result of doing all this, some reasonable broad-brushed inferences can be made about London living standards and influences on them.

The cost of living and regional price convergence

The cost of living in London depended on both national and local factors. National markets increasingly determined the prices of most products and movements in the overall price level; whereas local influences related to the efficiency of London's markets and distribution mechanisms in keeping prices low and the high cost of housing relative to the rest of the country.

Non-housing costs

Crafts and Mills's national cost of living index from 1750 to 1913 is presented in Figure 5.1. Looking at long-run trends, prices rose through the second half of the eighteenth century and then inflation accelerated during the French Wars, particularly during the poor harvest years of

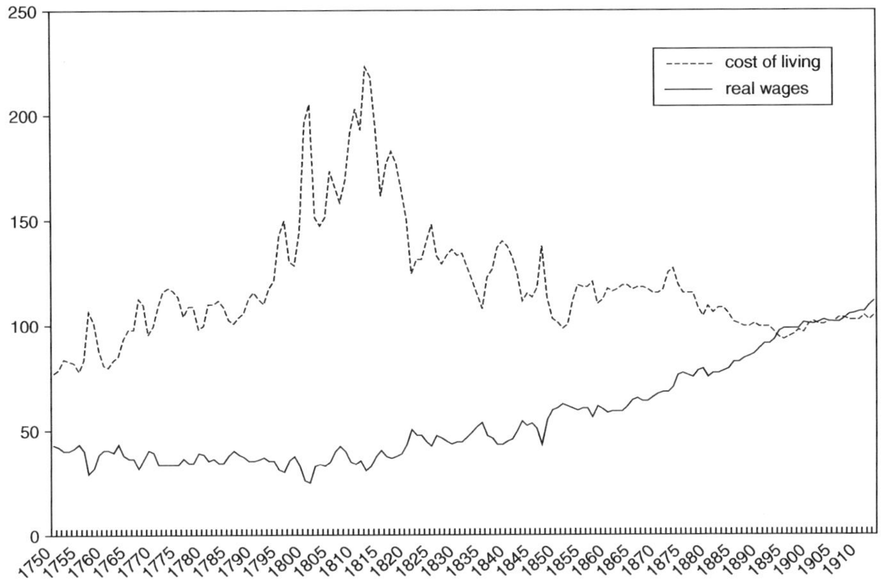

Figure 5.1 The cost of living and real wages in Britain, 1750–1913
Source: Crafts and Mills, 1994.

1811 and 1812, but fell with wars' end, with the exception of 1816 and 1817 when harvests again failed. The trend was then flat from the mid-1830s until the 1870s, albeit with some notable cyclical swings. In general, the cost of living is volatile until mid-century due to the impact of harvests in a country still with strong regional differences and few grain imports. After that, there was a marked shift to a regime of reduced short-term price volatility. This indicates the extent to which Britain had moved towards an integrated network of national and international food sources, which helped to smooth out the price effects previously caused by temporary local shortages. From the mid-1870s, a period of deflation ensues until the mid-1890s, after which inflation is apparent.

Changes in national cost of living data, apart from housing, probably reflect the general experience of the metropolis. There are only limited reasons for thinking that London prices were much different from the rest of the country for most tradable goods and services. With its central role in national transportation and distribution systems, prices in London were more likely to correspond to national ones than was the case for more remote regions. Other countries in Europe, with less developed national markets, had far greater variations in regional prices than Britain. Any marked divergence in London prices with those elsewhere would have created substantial arbitrage opportunities for merchants to exploit. The retail price of bread in the capital from 1824–1900, for example, was governed by the price of wheat and was only slightly higher than that in Scotland's capital, Edinburgh. In the 1790s, it was reported that beef prices in meat-producing Rutland were only 1d per pound below those in London.[20] Later, in 1815, Manchester, Liverpool and the larger Lancashire towns all quoted provision prices comparable to those in the capital.[21]

One later study does put London prices higher than those in some provincial cities. In 1905, the Board of Trade published an index based on the cost of a representative weekly basket of commodities consumed by an average family in various towns and cities. This survey suggested that the larger industrial towns of the Midlands and North were somewhat cheaper than the capital, mainly because of lower-priced coal – by 9 per cent in the case of Birmingham. Within London, the same study indicated that prices tended to rise from the centre to the outer suburbs. What weight should be given to this single study is unclear. Yet it does indicate that not all costs can be equalised across space, because of differences in transport costs. Coal was the prime source of heat and bulky, and London was further away from coalfields than most other large towns. Further, spatial factors may have generated cost of living differences as well. Higher London property and labour costs may have outweighed any scale economies the capital had in distribution over other urban areas. Any resultant higher input costs would then have been passed on to metropolitan consumers. If such cost differences did actually exist, regional arbitrage possibilities could not have brought prices in London entirely into line with those elsewhere, although the effects for most working-class goods are likely to have been small.

Housing costs

Land is immobile, so competition cannot harmonise land prices and property rents. Land scarcity in London and the weight of economic activity located there pushed up housing costs well above those in other parts of the country throughout the nineteenth century. The Crafts and Mills cost of living index does include a component for housing costs but such national averages can be highly misleading for the capital. A 1905 Board of Trade rent survey found, for example, that London rents were 32 per cent higher than those in Newcastle, 61 per cent more than in Manchester, and 69 per cent above those in Birmingham and Bradford.[22] To have the same standard of living as their provincial counterparts, therefore, London workers would have to have received noticeably higher money earnings to be compensated for their higher housing costs.

Detailed information on housing rents is hard to come by. As housing was such an important component of working-class living costs, and because it has been cited in a number of studies[23] as the prime cause of rising living costs in London,[24] it is worth considering the weakness of the rent data in some detail. The fundamental problem is that housing is heterogeneous, due to differences in location and quality, which makes it difficult to compare like with like. Furthermore, the composition of the stock in a district and its quality and desirability alter significantly over time, particularly in the fluid context of nineteenth-century residential mobility. Most cited data on housing rents during this period are anecdotal statements by people wishing to make a particular case, rather than detailed, statistically accurate studies, so their validity must be treated with considerable suspicion. Witnesses to the Royal Commission of Housing for the Working Classes, 1884–5 are commonly cited, but its Report provides no tabular information. The only witness cited in the Report actually did an unspecified 'survey' of 1,000 dwellings and claimed that 'rents in the congested districts of London are gradually getting higher', which helps very little.[25] The 1905 Board of Trade study cited above also looked at changes in rents over a twenty-year period from 1880 to 1900 by examining changes in rate assessments. This gives greater accuracy but still faces the problem of heterogeneity.

The Board of Trade information on rents across time is presented in Table 5.1, where working-class housing is broadly defined in terms of the relevant annual gross rental values for London, the rest of Britain and twenty large British provincial towns respectively. (Actual household rents were far lower than those shown because many houses were subdivided.) The heterogeneity problem comes to the fore immediately: because it explains why the rise is fastest in Britain as a whole rather than in the largest towns. This occurred not because rents actually rose faster in rural areas and small towns, but because of the continued movement of people from the countryside, where rents were low. This meant that over the course of the period more of the total working-class housing stock was made up of higher urban rent ones. A similar problem arises in comparing London and the provincial towns. Many higher than existing quality working dwellings were built between 1880 and 1900. In the provincial towns, these would mainly have been built within municipal boundaries, whereas in London a lot were erected beyond the County boundary. Even if cities' housing stocks were changing in exactly the same way, therefore, London on the County definition alone would seem worse.

It is also interesting to note in Table 5.1 that the large urban areas exhibit a common cycle of faster and slower rent rises – indicating the significance of building cycles. As real rents rose, landlords and builders would be encouraged to supply more homes, bringing rents down again. Long-term trends in rents, consequently, are difficult to discern in the price fluctuations associated with the building cycle.[26]

The Board of Trade also asked town clerks in the capital to undertake surveys of the same houses over the same twenty-year period from 1880 to 1900. This is still not a perfect comparison as many supposedly identical dwellings may not be in the same state of repair, especially over such a long time period. Their significance in the overall stock, which they are supposed to represent, also changes over time because subsequent new building would have added distinct types of dwelling altering the overall

Table 5.1 Changes in working-class rents (including rates), London and elsewhere, 1880–1900 (per cent)

	London (gross rental value under £50 p.a.)	*Rest of Great Britain (gross rental value under £20 p.a.)*	*20 large British provincial towns (gross rental value under £20 p.a.)*	*Identical London houses*
1880–5	5	4	4	3
1885–90	–1	4	1	1
1890–5	8	6	7	4
1895–1900	2	10	5	5
1880–1900	14	25	18	13

Source: Parl. Paper, 1905, lxxxiv, 35.

composition of the stock. At a more micro level, finally, neighbourhood desirability may change and this was especially important during the last decades of the nineteenth century when suburbanisation was in full swing. The information derived, none the less, is useful as a comparison with the previous data, and is given in the last column of Table 5.1. The differences between it and the first column show the extreme sensitivity of the rent results to the samples from which they were taken.

Data problems apart, several conclusions can be gleaned from surveys of rent. The most obvious is that, within the metropolis, housing rents were greatest in the desirable and the crowded districts at or near the centre, and that they fell towards the suburban fringe with suburban differences depending on distance, class composition and dwelling sizes.[27] To gain the benefits of lower suburban rents, many had to commute, adding transportation costs to household budgets to a much greater degree than in other cities.

The actual impact of transportation on the average cost of living in London is unknown. The impact of rents is also hard to determine. Rents varied enormously from street to street and district to district and, as noted above, no reliable measures of their average incidence exist. For what they are worth, several sources suggest that housing costs were rising as a proportion of incomes. In the 1790s, the London working man supposedly spent approximately an eighth of his income on housing.[28] The increase in population and street clearances are generally blamed for causing the proportion to rise to a fifth in the 1840s, despite increases in average real wages over the period. In the East End, clearances for railways, industrial buildings, warehouses and street improvements led to further rises. By the 1880s, average London wages had risen further; yet, in 1887, in St George-in-the-East residents were paying between 20 and 30 per cent of their wages in rents, compared with 14 to 28 per cent forty years previously. By modern private market standards, these shares of housing costs in disposable incomes are not exceptional. Yet, for the very poor, the burden

Table 5.2 Indices of London annual rental values

	All houses under £30 gross rental value		*All houses under £50 gross rental value*		*All houses*	
	With rates	*Excluding rates*	*With rates*	*Excluding rates*	*With rates*	*Excluding rates*
1880	89	93	88	92	92	97
1885	93	97	92	96	96	99
1890	92	96	91	95	94	97
1895	98	99	98	99	99	100
1900	100	100	100	100	100	100
Percentage increase 1880–1900	13	7	14	9	8	3

Source: Adapted from Parl. Paper, 1905, lxxxiv, 47.

Note: Rents are in nominal prices.

of rents could be particularly high. In Clerkenwell, St Luke's, St Giles and Marylebone, in the 1880s for example, 80 per cent of the poor paid more than a fifth of their income on housing and 45 per cent between a quarter and a half of their income.[29]

It is often argued from these data that housing costs in London were rising substantially in the second half of the century. Comparison, however, is difficult across a forty-year period. One problem is that the composition of the population in a specific locality may well have altered over such a long time, so that average incomes there were different. In the inner areas, higher-earning skilled workers in general and the most successful in specific occupations would have joined the exodus to the suburbs to be replaced by poorer households, so that income levels in those localities were probably falling over time. Even if rents had not changed, consequently, a rising local income rent share would have occurred anyway. Moreover, the experience of specific inner districts may not be representative of the capital as a whole.

The Board of Trade surveys cited earlier provide some help. Indices from its survey of London rents for the years 1880 to 1900 are presented in Table 5.2.[30] Three cumulative categories are shown: houses with a gross rental value of under £30; then those under £50; and, finally, all houses. Rents with and without rates are also included. The £50 and under rental houses were primarily occupied by the working classes. Several conclusions can be drawn from this information. First, cyclical effects can be seen, with rents, excluding rates, rising and falling in line with demand and the building cycle – declining in the late 1880s and rising in the turn of the century boom. It is therefore difficult to strip out trends from these cyclical variations. Overall, none the less, the rents of the cheaper properties rose faster than the average for all houses. The all housing rent index, in fact, is virtually flat in trend. As the final column of Table 5.2 includes the cheaper as well as the better housing, it is probable that nominal rents on better houses were actually falling, because the weighting of the overall stock towards low-value homes was high. The cheapening of housing was occurring because suburbanisation was having its beneficial supply side effects. It was improving the total quantity and average quality of housing (the latter, for example, through greater suburban amenities and larger floor areas and plot sizes), and helped to hold down rents throughout the city by dispersing demand over a wider spatial area.

As the general price level was slowly moving upwards from the early 1890s, real middle-class rents were falling faster than the nominal data would suggest. Once account is taken of inflation, even the real rental growth of cheaper dwellings is unlikely to have been high and, in many neighbourhoods, they would also have been falling in real terms. Once cyclical effects and inflation are taken into account, consequently, these data do not suggest an overall increase in London rents from the 1880s to 1914 and may indicate significant real falls – with the better-off probably enjoying the greatest benefit. This conclusion has to be tentative, however, given the quality of the data. Moreover, there were significant spatial variations within the metropolis, as are examined below.

The picture of housing costs is also different when rate payments are included in the rent indices that are given in Table 5.2. The percentage increases are then noticeably higher than for rents alone, indicating that rate demands were growing. Rates were also a disproportionate burden in the poorer inner city areas, raising the housing costs of those on low incomes. Rising public expenditure, and the local tax burden to pay for it, were thus having increasing impacts on the living costs of Londoners in the closing decades of the century. Rates, rather than rising rents, were the issue. A paradox was the part of the rate income that was being raised to deal with poverty under the auspices of the Poor Law, yet its relative burden was greatest on the poor themselves through their housing costs. In St George-in-the-East in 1848, for example, 21 per cent of a baker's low wages went on housing (3s 10d out of 18s 6d), as opposed to only 14 per cent of better-paid coopers' earnings (3s 8d out of 25s 5d).[31]

The general downward direction of housing costs was not experienced in all districts but the causes of these changes are complex. Inner city transportation was improving, opening up areas where rents may once have been lower because of poor communications. The expansion of trams and buses, and the prospect of the tube, for example, may account for the rises in rents in northern districts during the twenty years up to 1900, as reported in the same Board of Trade study cited above. Increases were approximately 17 per cent in Hampstead, St Marylebone and St Pancras; 10 per cent in Islington; yet only 1 per cent in Stoke Newington.[32]

In the last twenty years of the century, eastern working-class rents rose rapidly – in Stepney by a third. The faster increases can be seen in Table 5.3, where further use is made of the above-mentioned Board of Trade

Table 5.3 Changes in rents in working-class streets in North, South, East and West London, 1880–1990 (per cent)

District	*1880–5*	*1885–90*	*1890–5*	*1895–1900*	*1880–1900*
Northern Boroughs (5)	2	0	5	3	12
Eastern Boroughs (3)	8	3	3	9	25
Southern Boroughs (7)	3	0	1	5	10
Western Boroughs (5)	–1	0	8	4	11

Source: Parl. Paper, 1905, lxxxiv, 39.

Notes: Rents include rates and are in nominal prices. Parentheses contain number of boroughs studied.

study and its survey of identical houses. There seem to have been two surges in East End rent increases in the years 1880–5 and 1895–1900. The causes, however, could be many. Demand could have increased, for example, for several reasons: firms and jobs may have moved out eastwards; communications improved so that eastern rents caught up with those elsewhere; or periodic influxes of immigrants may have created local shortages. The differences in rent increases between parts of the city, nevertheless, show the difficulty of adjusting the cost of living for changes in rents, because the individual experience of housing costs was so varied.

Wages

Crafts and Mills's index of cost-of-living-adjusted real wages in Britain from 1750 to 1913 is shown in Figure 5.1. Their statistical analysis leads them to conclude that the trend of real wages was static from 1750 to 1813, grew steadily from 1813 to 1903 at a trend of 1.2 per cent a year, and stagnated again after that.[33] Overall between 1813 and 1913 real wages rose three and a quarter times.

These results seem to contrast with Schwarz's conclusions – based on a long wage series for London bricklayers for the period 1700 to 1860.[34] He suggests that real wages in London fell substantially – by 40 per cent – between 1750 and the late 1790s/early 1800s, and real wages did not again reach their mid-eighteenth-century level until the 1830s/1840s. Arguments for a crisis in the London economy during the era of initial British industrialisation can be built up on such foundations. Yet the difference between Crafts and Mills's real wage stagnation and Schwarz's collapse lies solely in the cost of living indices each uses. Schwarz deflated his money wage series, using cost of living indices estimated earlier by Phelps-Brown and Hopkins in the 1950s and by Lindert and Williamson in the early 1980s.[35] If his money wage series is deflated by Crafts and

Mills's own cost of living index instead, the two estimates of real wages are virtually identical. This correspondence is unsurprising as early nineteenth-century British wage estimates rely heavily on London and southern England sources. In fact, Crafts and Mills used Schwarz's money wage data for the years 1797–1819, either weighted with other series or alone, and for 1819 to 1855 they used Bowley's information on building labourers.[36]

As the 'London' real wage series is virtually identical to the 'national' one until 1860, it is tempting to extrapolate further on in time. Unfortunately for the London observer, the national wage series become more sophisticated in the later years as a greater number of data sources are available. Crafts and Mills use Feinstein's new estimates of average earnings from 1880 onwards, which are truly national in coverage and deal with a far greater range of occupations.[37] Even so, London is likely to have broadly followed national trends (though with a qualification about regional convergence discussed below). A reasonable conclusion, in summary, seems to be that wages in London were stagnant in the first decade and a half of the century, grew steadily for decades afterwards and then stagnated again in the decade before the First World War.

Annual earnings

The actual, annual take-home real income of Londoners, and hence their standards of living, are not simply determined by the real wages paid to a household's principal earner. Other factors included non-monetary payments, the presence of other forms of household remuneration, the form and regularity of earnings and the types of job done. Furthermore, earnings and wages of workers within a single occupation vary enormously, as an inspection of Booth's copious survey data reveals, so that average data are only that, rather than describing the real experience of individual workers.

Non-wage payments and other sources of household remuneration

Wage rates exclude allowances in kind, such as beer and fuel provided by the employer, tipping, the rewards from commonly accepted pilfering, and the existence of customary allowances in addition to the wage.[38] Although the latter slowly disappeared, some still existed into the twentieth century. They took a variety of forms: dock coopers, for example, had the right to the contents of broken barrels on ships, tailors to cloth scraps, known as 'cabbage', and Admiralty yard shipwrights to unwanted 'chips' of wood. Bus conductors, especially before ticketing was introduced late in the century, would also supplement the driver's and their incomes with undeclared passenger fares.

Overall, such non-wage benefits could form substantial increments to monetary payments. In so far as they declined in importance during the nineteenth century, the improvement in real living standards is exaggerated for the occupations that benefited from them. Tipping, however, probably rose significantly rather than declined.

The principal wage earner's main job was generally not the sole source of working-class income. To have only one male breadwinner, in fact, became an important indicator of higher social status. According to Booth in the 1890s, the employment of wives and older children could increase the wages of barge builders by 9s 6d a week and those of bookbinders by 8s 11d.[39]

The regularity of pay and employment

Many did not receive a regular weekly money wage. Among them was the vast army of underemployed – including the many hawkers and peddlers – and those employed erratically on piece rates. Others worked in gangs and sold their labour for a lump sum in the docks and building. Finally, many of the better-paid jobs within the middle-class professions were based on a fee paid for a service rendered, settlement of which was often delayed and erratic.

Each of these factors needs to be borne in mind for the occupations they affected, because they alter the reality of actual earnings away from the apparent returns as measured by other occupations' wage rates. Frequently, the expected earnings to be gained from a particular occupation were far less than the headline incomes of those who made it to the top of their occupation. This was especially true for the professions. For every successful lawyer, doctor, journalist, writer and architect, for example, there would be a number of fellow entrants to each calling who did not quite make it. The expected earnings in these better-paid occupations, therefore, were far less than the recorded data on the successful would suggest.

Seasons, casuals and cycles

As few trades followed the same seasonal pattern, workers could adjust and dovetail one seasonal occupation with another or co-ordinate their own seasonal work with that of other family members. So, depending on the time of year, clock-makers would turn to the manufacture of gas meters; harness producers became boot-makers; gas stokers entered the building trade; and dockers switched to street selling. In Southwark and Bermondsey, husbands worked in the docks and the leather trades in the summer and their wives in the fur pulling and hat sectors in the winter.

Such job-switching strategies would also only work in the aggregate if the demand and supply of seasonal labourers continuously balanced each other out, which was rare, particularly in periods of economic downturn. The mid-1860s saw much distress because of a sharp recession. In January 1891, 285,000 men were unemployed because of the freezing conditions, one-third of the male labour force.[40] Slack times, though, were not necessarily accompanied by poverty. The high wages of the more skilled seasonal workers were often sufficient to tide them over. Others relied on relatively sophisticated systems of personal credit. Most shops and landlords were willing to provide credit as they expected to be repaid when trade picked up. Recourse could additionally be made to pawnshops, which, in 1830, numbered 342 licensed houses and 600 unlicensed or 'dolly' shops.[41]

Casual labour was employed for short periods of time and was largely unskilled or semi-skilled. The difference from common day labour is hard to discern, but seems to relate to the daily frequency with which employment was won. A day labourer could be fully employed for long periods of time, whereas a casual was not. Although it is difficult to determine exact numbers, Stedman Jones believes that casuals and their families comprised around 10 per cent of the London population – about 400,000 people.[42] But he based that estimate solely on classifying all the lower categories of workers found by Booth as casual.[43] As Booth's analysis itself had weaknesses (see below), this is undoubtedly an extrapolation too far. The real number of casuals was probably far less[44] and would vary across the trade cycle.

Green has argued that the irregularity of earnings became worse over the first half of the century, so that by the 1860s those involved in manufacturing faced 'growing uncertainty and irregularity of employment for all but the most skilled workers, and this, rather than any fall in wages, constituted the main threat to working-class living standards in the capital'.[45] This argument is a variant of the immiserisation thesis discussed in Chapter 4, one which recognises that general living standards did rise but that London workers tended to miss out on them.

Green reaches his conclusions by suggesting that earnings were far more uncertain than wage data alone would suggest, and they had become more precarious because of the replacement of artisan-regularised skilled labour with less skilled jobs. He does this by mustering evidence on business cycles, bankruptcies, failed strikes and de-skilling. Yet, when viewed in aggregate, the argument is unconvincing. To identify fluctuations in individual activities is not to prove that they continuously moved together. The argument of Chapter 2, instead, was that such fluctuations tended to balance each other out in a large city. Much weight is also put on a structural crisis in the mid-1860s. This was a time when a severe depression hit London, but it was one caused by the exceptional financial crisis following the collapse of Overend Gurney rather than by long-term trends.[46]

Schwarz, a few years earlier, adopted a similar argument to Green's in his analysis of the impact of industrialisation on London. He emphasises the problem of judging average living standards from limited data on real wages. Many payments were non-monetary, he argues, and seasonality and the trade cycle were significant factors lowering earnings.[47] He suggests that the pool of semi- and unskilled labour was far larger than the available job opportunities throughout the first half of the century, so that many remained at near subsistence levels. Employers, where they could, would substitute less skilled for skilled labour in the same manner as argued by Green. More industries slid into sweating to the extent that there was a 'crisis' of the old artisanal manufacturing system.[48] Growth from 1800 to 1840 in London, he believes, also trailed behind that of other regions and was slower than in the late eighteenth century.[49] Although this relative stagnation complements the argument about the crisis in artisanal manufacturing, the conclusion is questionable given the limited data series offered to support it and the absence of modern de-trending techniques. In addition, both his arguments about cycles and seasonality suffer from the same aggregation difficulties as those of Green. Moreover, it can be wondered why other alternative activities did not spring up to employ the endless, cheap, under-used resource of labour, if it actually existed.

In relation to de-skilling, the employment of male skilled labour was actually growing rapidly during the period Green considers, 1800 to 1870, according to his own data. In 1800, there were around 100,000 London-based artisans and, by 1848, the number had probably doubled.[50] Such growth implies a rising, rather than a falling, demand for skilled work; although, within the global sum, there would have been several trades in decline – such as silk weaving and watch-making. With such growth rates in skilled labour use, it is hard to believe that the price of skilled labour in general was not rising in order to attract the migrants necessary to fill the jobs. The switch in some trades towards less skilled workers, therefore, could have partly been a reaction to an input whose cost was increasing significantly rather than a concerted attempt to drive down the wages of all London workers. Furthermore, with greater opportunities opening in manufacturing, less skilled men, women and youths now had wider choices of work, which should have improved their earnings. Finally, in the late 1840s, skilled workers were probably 28 per cent of the total male workforce.[51] This is undoubtedly a significant proportion of the labour-force, but it still represents a minority, and the proportion of the skilled subject to erosion of the job privileges would have been even smaller still. The experience of skilled workers who lost their trades or who were subject to wage cutting, therefore, cannot be said to be representative of the working population as a whole.

Conclusions on the standard of living

As the introduction to this chapter noted, it is hard to come to any firm conclusions about Londoners' living standards over the course of the period from 1800 to 1914 because of the absence of good data and the varied experiences of individuals. Even so, the issues covered here can provide several pointers.

Londoners' wages probably rose more than threefold over the period. Although many workers did not receive a regular wage, there is no reason to expect that their activities, on average, fared any better or worse than jobs where a regular wage was paid, with a modicum of competition in labour markets. Furthermore, a simple hierarchy of occupational earnings is misleading as successive wage surveys – from Booth onwards – find wide dispersions of earnings within occupations as well as between them.[52]

A qualification is that the wage data discussed earlier are mainly based on skilled wages. Labour market segmentation and the changing supply and demand balances in unskilled labour markets may have meant that some unskilled workers fared worse. There is, however, no clear way of knowing about long-term, unskilled living standards. Yet, even if there is uncertainty over unskilled real income changes, occupational shifts would have enhanced average take home pay as the century progressed.

Housing costs were noticeably higher in London than elsewhere but there is no evidence, from the 1890s onwards at least, that metropolitan households suffered from ever-rising housing costs. In fact, it seems that real rents may have been falling across the city as a whole during or after the 1880s. As suburbanisation had been going on at a rapid rate by then for many decades, moreover, it should not be assumed that the 1880s were a watershed between years of rising and falling real rents. Particular localities in the capital, however, were subject to sudden surges in rent levels. The extent to which these were micro-adjustment processes within broader metropolitan settings or the effects of some local exigency are generally unclear. Overall, however, it was probably not the case that London housing costs depressed London living standards to any great extent. Instead, earnings were higher than those in other regions to compensate for the extra costs of living in the capital – an issue that is taken up further in the following section.

London wages and regional convergence

Over the long term, economic theory would suggest that wages between regions tend to converge once differences in cost-of-living are taken into account. This occurs because some firms quit high-cost areas in search of lower wage costs, while workers move to the better-paid regions, with the result in the static case that wages rise in the initial low-wage areas and fall in the high-wage areas. With growth, wages in all areas are rising; therefore, low-wage regions 'catch-up' to higher-wage ones over time. Spatial variations in wages, therefore, depend on the state of labour market conditions in particular cities and regions and the ability of labour and firms to migrate between them.

As migration is the main stimulus to convergence, the process can be expected to take a long time and will be influenced by the contemporary demographic structure of the labour-exporting region. Modern research suggests that regional income-per-capita changes take seventy years to smooth out three-quarters of an initial difference, based on historic data from the USA and Western Europe.[53] Labour markets alone might move more quickly, but the process is likely to be slow and uneven. Greater convergence might be expected in skilled labour markets (assuming no technological obsolescence) than in unskilled ones because skilled workers are likely to be more mobile over longer distances.

Any intervening shocks are likely to intensify disequilibria between regional labour markets. A process of convergence, therefore, might never end up producing equal real wages between regions because intervening shocks overlay any convergence that might slowly be happening. Two huge shocks disturbed British regional labour markets from the late eighteenth to the early twentieth centuries: the first was the growth of the industrial towns and cities during the industrial revolution; and the second was the crisis in agriculture following the opening up of world markets from the 1870s. Both of these were associated with significant inter-regional and rural–urban migrations and overlay the long-term shift of employment away from agriculture to urban industries.

Most of the available British regional wage data concern money wages rather than real wages. Many regional price differences were slowly eaten away during the period, as noted above, but housing cost differences were not. Relative differences in regional housing costs, moreover, are likely to vary over time as rents are determined by local demand and supply balances, which themselves take a long time to adjust. Differences in housing costs, therefore, mean that measuring convergence in money wages alone is unreliable.

There are several other reasons why money wages might permanently differ. The consumption possibilities in large towns – the big city/bright lights effect – may induce movement towards cities, even in the absence of higher real wages. Furthermore, the risk of unemployment may be less in the capital than elsewhere, meaning that earnings in localities with higher risks have to be adjusted downwards to compensate for the greater threat of redundancy. The Lancashire cotton towns, for example, were subject to periodic lay-offs to a greater extent than many London industries, and real wages in those towns would need to be adjusted downwards to take account of this. Further factors inhibiting real wage equality come from non-competitive market situations. Institutional barriers to recruitment in specific localities tend to keep wages in specific occupations from converging. Several such barriers in London were discussed in the previous chapter. Finally, 'efficiency wage' theory suggests that some firms like to pay above the going wage to retain better-quality staff. This view correlates with empirical findings that suggest that the firms in growing, successful industries pay their staff more. Nineteenth-century London had many of these growth industries, and so its real wages might have been higher than average as a result.

Carpenters' and agricultural labourers' wages are the main data sources used in the literature to consider regional wage convergence and they are believed to represent well general skilled and unskilled wages respectively.[54] They show that, throughout the nineteenth century, London retained its position as the highest money wage region. Industrialisation in the North during the second half of the eighteenth century and in the early nineteenth century seems to have lowered the wage differential between London and the North – with the North moving towards London levels. According to Hunt, carpenters' wages in Manchester rose from 64 to 88 per cent of London ones in the thirty years between 1760 and 1790 and then stabilised around that ratio for the next 100 years or so. In Scottish cities, convergence was from a low base and took longer but by 1906 Edinburgh carpenters were earning around 85 per cent of London rates, whereas they had only been paid 40 per cent in 1765.[55] In his early work, Hunt had also concluded that labour markets became more integrated from 1850 to 1914.[56]

The picture was different for agricultural labourers. In the late 1760s, the South-East and East Anglia were the high-wage regions and the West Midlands, North of England and Scotland were the low-wage areas, earning a third or so less. Thirty years later, at the height of the industrial revolution, the picture was transformed – with the North of England now a high-wage zone, while the South Midlands had become a low-wage zone. A hundred years later, some counties around London – Kent, Surrey and Middlesex – remained high-wage ones, as did the North of England. Yet the low-wage counties were now firmly in the south and west of England, including Essex.[57] Demographic differences between counties partly explain these changes. Yet the most obvious influences were the proximity of the new industrial towns in the North, so that agriculture had to compete for labour, raising relative wages, and the relative lack of urban job opportunities in the South, apart from the counties adjacent to London. The decline of tillage from the 1870s particularly affected southern grain-producing counties like Essex. The greater decline in southern wages must have encouraged migration to London, although many from the West Country went to South Wales in the 1870s and 1880s, but insufficient numbers moved to reduce supply enough to raise agricultural wages.

Boyer and Hatton partly take account of cost of living differences in their study of carpenters' and agricultural labourers' wages, and they find that agricultural wage differentials were growing in the second half of the century.[58] This may have been because agricultural labour markets were segmented or, perhaps more likely, because of slow adjustments to the different regional impacts of the switch to imported food. For urban wages, of most interest in the context of London, they found that the metropolis was poorly correlated with other regions when it came to short-run changes in wages – which may reflect the greater intensity of the building cycle in the capital and its impact on carpenters' wages – but integrated with every other English region over the long run.

Sharp differences in wage rates throughout Britain still remained, nevertheless, by the 1900s. Table 5.4 compares indices of wage rates in building, engineering and printing for London and a selection of other towns in 1905. In the table, towns are ranked according to the wages paid to skilled building workers, part of the late nineteenth-century 'labour aristocracy', whose relative remuneration is presented in the second column. The

Table 5.4 Board of Trade wage comparison for London and various other towns, 1905 (London = 100)

Town	*Building*		*Engineering*		*Printing*
	Skilled	*Labourers*	*Skilled*	*Labourers*	
London	100	100	100	100	100
Birmingham	98	100	91	83	88
Manchester and Salford	95	92	91	83	90
Hull	91	101	92	94	82
Newcastle	90	89	89	89	90
Dover	87	83	–	–	64
Leeds	87	94	85	–	91
Ipswich	86	86	75	79	72
Bradford	83	85	87	96	85

Source: Parl. Paper, 1908, cvii, xxxiv.

ranking roughly makes sense in terms of the size of towns and the ranking for skilled engineers approximates to that of builders. This tends to support the theoretical hypotheses about convergence in skilled wages, outlined above. For unskilled workers and printers, however, the rankings are not the same. The difference for printers may be accounted for by their greater unionisation and worker-based control of entry and local earnings. The unskilled workers' lack of correlation suggests that unskilled labour markets are more dependent on contemporary local labour market conditions. Even so, London labour overall generally received relatively higher wages than elsewhere.

The final regional comparison is presented in Table 5.5. The 1905 Board of Trade survey, cited above, also calculated a real wage index for the major regions of England and Wales. Differences in rents and prices were applied to money wages to derive a 'real wage' index. The problems of doing this have already been raised, but the real wage index shown in Table 5.5 presents some interesting conclusions. The real skilled wages of London and the industrial regions of England and Wales, given likely errors in the data, are shown to be pretty much the same; whereas the more rural areas of the southern and eastern counties had significantly lower real wages. If these data are right, they suggest that, at least for skilled workers, regional wage convergence was occurring. The literature suggests that significant regional labour market differences remained by 1914 but that London was the best integrated with the rest of the country. This is perhaps unsurprising given the shape of the national transport system and the significance of London in inter-regional moves, as highlighted by Pooley and Turnbull.[59]

If convergence processes occurred in skilled earnings between London and other regions during the nineteenth century, the trajectory of real

Table 5.5 Board of Trade real wage comparison for skilled men in London and elsewhere, 1905

	Rents and prices	*Wages*	*'Real wages'*
Lancashire and Cheshire	84	87	104
London	100	100	100
Midlands	85	85	100
Yorkshire	87	84	97
Wales and Monmouthshire	89	86	97
Northern counties and Cleveland	90	86	96
Eastern counties	88	76	86
Southern counties	93	80	86

Source: Parl. Paper, 1908, cvii, xl.

wage earnings must obviously have been different in order for them to be converging. As London was the initially high real wage centre, wage growth must have been faster elsewhere during periods of catch-up. This raises concerns over using nationally derived wage growth series for London. In fact, the national real wage data of Crafts and Mills cited earlier used London wages as its national measure until the 1880s, so their index may understate national wage increases if other regions were catching up with London before then. The problem for London specifically arises after 1860 when metropolitan wage increases are likely to have been less than national ones, if other regions' wages were actually catching up with London. This effect, however, should not be interpreted as the capital falling behind, because London was still at the highest level of real wages in Britain; while the process of catch-up was associated with migration from other regions into London, increasing labour supply there and so moderating metropolitan wage increases relative to other regions. More skilled workers, in other words, were living in the high-wage centre over time, and average living standards, therefore, rose as a result.

The conclusion about the integration of the London labour market into the national economy is also important as it gives more credence to the belief that standards of living in London were no worse than elsewhere and generally better – although other major industrial cities were catching up in later years' as was to be expected. It also further reinforces the belief that hypotheses about the immiserisation of the metropolitan workforce during the nineteenth century are wide of the mark. Furthermore, the evidence suggests that the Victorian London economy was actually behaving in ways posited by the economic theories being used in this book.

Poverty

The extent of poverty

The amount of poverty in London is again difficult to determine. There was certainly a perception among middle-class observers that the capital contained relatively large numbers of poor. This view, however, may have been influenced by the increasing visibility of the poor, as those with means moved to the suburbs, and by the London-based intellectual elite's lack of direct and detailed knowledge of conditions in the capital and elsewhere.

Henry Mayhew chronicled the lives of street folk in the 1850s,[60] and a succession of writers, including Dickens, Greenwood,[61] and Mearns,[62] provided dramatic and sensational descriptions of individual lives amongst the metropolitan poor. No attempt to measure poverty in aggregate was made until the 1890s when the Liverpool ship-owner and amateur statistician, Charles Booth, made his study of the *Life and Labour of the People of London*.[63] At first sight, his findings appear to confirm social reformers' perceptions of the city. Booth estimated that four of his eight classes lived in poverty, and that the poor constituted 31 per cent of the population, 35 per cent of those in the East End, and 40 per cent of the working class. By comparison, Joseph Rowntree, who defined his poverty line as 'the minimum expenditure for the maintenance of physical health', discovered in 1899 in York that 28 per cent of that city's population and 43 per cent of its working class lived in poverty.[64] These numbers shocked educated observers then and since.

Booth's meaning of poverty, however, included the state of 'having no surplus' and exhibiting certain personal characteristics as well as those living 'in want'. If the latter definition is adopted, only two of Booth's classes were seriously deprived: class A, 'occasional labourers, semi-criminals and loafers', and class B, the very poor. Together these two lowest classes constituted only 8 per cent of the population in London and 12 per cent in the East End. The rest of the poor were in classes C, 'intermittent earnings', and D, 'small but regular incomes'. They were, to quote Booth, 'neither ill-nourished or ill-clad according to any standard that can reasonably be used'. Instead, they had no 'surplus', which essentially meant that they had to work regularly and did not have a particularly comfortable existence. The rest of the working class – slightly over half of the County's population – existed in 'some relative comfort and security', according to Beatrice Webb, one of Booth's helpers. Classes A and B alone, therefore, fell within a more usual definition of relative poverty. Booth classified them as 'those whose means are insufficient [for a decent independent life] according to the usual standard of life in this country'. The definitions of poverty used by Rowntree, Booth and others were, thus, based on comparisons with what were felt to be acceptable contemporary living standards, coloured by a particular classification of the population that placed them within a hierarchy of the labour market. Those who had no relationship whatsoever with the labour market, such as some of the elderly, did not feature within the survey – although poverty might be proportionately high amongst them.

The results are affected by the methods used to create them, which were subject to contemporary as well as later critical comment. Booth's survey technique left much to be desired by modern standards. It was not a survey of households and their incomes but the opinions of household circumstances held by his enumerators – school board officers going about their daily business of trying to ensure that children attended school. No house-to-house survey was undertaken; rather these opinions were scaled up to represent geographic areas by like-minded observations of the quality of particular houses and streets. Housing quality was poor and disrepair high in the older, inner city where most of the poor lived. Yet the correlation between house condition and outright poverty must have been highly imperfect, especially as housing was rented and landlords could be reluctant to repair. Income, apart from that of main earners, was also neglected. Booth was also unaware of the benefits of random sample surveys, which enable accurate predictions of the circumstances of a population to be made with far fewer resources than a full survey of the population would necessitate. Rowntree in York deliberately based his survey in York on Booth's 'street impression' approach, even though he had already collected copious information on incomes, which he did not use in his poverty estimate. The correspondence of his and Booth's findings thus has much to do with the similarity of their dubious methodologies rather than the actual incidence of poverty in the two places.

Moreover, there is the usual problem of defining the geographic extent of London. Booth, for example, found that 31 per cent of the population was in 'broad poverty' on his standard and 8 per cent suffered real poverty. Yet that was for the LCC area only and by the 1880s the poor were spatially concentrated in the East End and inner south. The picture is less clear for Greater London as a whole, including the vast suburbs that lay beyond the LCC boundary where a notable proportion of the better-off lived. If the outer suburbs had been included, the measured incidence of poverty would undoubtedly have been lowered significantly.

In summary, the poverty line drawn by Booth was arbitrary,[65] hard to define, poorly measured and inconsistently applied to ill-defined income groups, while the proportion of the metropolitan population to which it referred was exaggerated by excluding the suburbs and including a tendentiously large group at risk of poverty though not actually poor in terms of the criteria laid down. The accuracy of Booth's survey, consequently, must be brought into question. It was based on an approach that is likely to have exaggerated the extent of serious poverty amongst particular occupational and social groupings.[66] As a result, it has been argued by some modern historians that it is better to regard Booth's survey as one on employment and occupation, and that it was fired by particular social theories and policy recommendations to improve low wages.[67] That his social classes are primarily based on types of employment, and the survey is tilted towards the work of the main wage earner, are the prime stimuli to this view. Booth held to the theory of a hopeless residuum at the bottom of the labour market and was keen to remove it to rural labour colonies in order to improve the competitive position of the classes above.[68]

Booth's emphasis on the peculiarities of the London labour market in creating poverty was at the end of a long line of Victorian thinking that believed that both the causes and solutions to poverty were essentially local in nature. Local labour and housing markets helped to create the problem, along with the moral laxity of many of the poor. The London's East End was believed by Booth to exhibit the worst outcome, and he was surprised to find that inner South London actually had a worse incidence of poverty.[69] The social policy perspectives resulting from such a localised causality had, unsurprisingly, city-level policy recommendations. Exhortation, voluntary local visiting and the national/local structure of the Poor Law were mainstream policy instruments along with some housing market reform, suburbanisation and limited local labour market regulation added towards the end of the period. Influential radical views were again localised in perspective – notably in the municipalisation movement and in arguments that the poor should be press-ganged into rural labour-camps. By the 1900s, however, the focus had changed to the national level. Army recruitment for the Boer War, debates over national efficiency in the face of foreign competition, fashionable eugenics, and the broadening number of towns subject to poverty investigations changed perceptions away from local labour and housing markets to national-level issues. Family circumstances also become clearer causes of distress – especially old age, ill-health or death of the main wage earner, large family sizes and poor or non-existent education and training.[70] Yet the local has persisted in writings about London's poverty, with Booth's surveys as the principal source of proof.

The geography of poverty

Poverty was predominantly an inner city phenomenon around the central City and West End core, and the spatial distribution of the poor changed in accordance with the outward spread of those districts over the course of the century. Using Booth's definition of poverty and a factor analysis of various social indicators, Green (1995) found that in 1840 the poorest districts circled the City – stretching from St Luke in the north to Bethnal Green in the east and Rotherhithe and Southwark in the south. The very poorest area was Bermondsey, followed by Bethnal Green, St George, Southwark and Shoreditch. By 1870, poverty had extended east to the riverside districts of Stepney, Poplar and Greenwich, which had expanded over the period but were all badly affected by the recent collapse of shipbuilding. Of the five poorest areas, just one, Bethnal Green, retained its position, being joined by St George-in-the-East, Stepney and Camberwell.[71] Once the impact of the demise of shipbuilding had worked its way through, the distribution of poverty would again have changed, with greater growth in the inner south by the time of Booth.

The wealthiest areas exhibited a similar process of decentralisation, but the West End remained strong because of the spatial concentration of contemporary wealthy society. All the richest parishes were in the West End in 1840 – led by St George, Hanover Square, then St James, Westminster and St Martin-in-the-Fields. By 1870, there had been some out-migration to the northern and southern suburbs, with Islington and Kensington now featuring in the five most wealthy districts.[72] Suburbanisation continued to change the picture somewhat. In the 1890s, Booth found the largest concentration of the wealthier G to H classes in the west, north and outer south.[73]

Poverty and the workhouse

Another source of information that has been used to identify changes in poverty is returns from the Poor Law Guardians on the number of paupers living in workhouses ('indoor relief'). Some relevant results from a study by MacKinnon (1994) are given in Table 5.6. It can be seen that London for all categories of poor had consistently far higher rates of indoor relief than the North (classified as England from the Midlands northwards). In the early 1870s, the London ratio for able-bodied men, for example, was over four times that of the North. The proportion of indoor paupers also rose over time in both areas. MacKinnon highlights some of the problems of using these data. These include changing rules on the availability of outdoor relief and improvements in the quality of workhouses and their infirmaries, which were pushing and persuading progressively more of the destitute into the workhouse (see Chapter 15). The conclusion reached, even so, is that conditions in casual urban labour markets were deteriorating. This attributes an urban causality to the rise of poverty.[74]

Other London-specific factors not associated with the labour market may, however, have also been at work. The persistently greater rate of entry to the workhouse in London was, in part, due to the high proportion of metropolitan households that were recent migrants and, thus, had few informal support systems. High housing costs, overcrowding and the ease of eviction in the capital were also likely to push more of the elderly and infirm, as well as the able-bodied destitute, into the workhouse. The proportion of fit men entering the workhouse in the North, moreover, was growing rapidly, suggesting that something was changing in the northern economy or in the application of the Poor Law there. Use of these data as evidence of deteriorating casual urban labour markets consequently is questionable.

One influence on poverty was the operation of the Poor Law. With the advent of the New Poor Law in 1834, the share of national income spent

Table 5.6 Indoor pauperism, London and the 'North', 1870–90

	Fit males (as percentage of those aged 25–64)		*Fit females (as percentage of those aged 25–64)*		*Non-able-bodied males (as percentage of all males aged 65+)*	
	North	*London*	*North*	*London*	*North*	*London*
1870–4	0.06	0.24	0.13	0.29	3.90	11.2
1875–9	0.08	0.17	0.13	0.19	4.73	12.7
1880–4	0.09	0.20	0.15	0.20	5.13	14.4
1885–9	0.10	0.25	0.13	0.20	5.40	15.3
1890–4	0.14	0.34	0.13	0.22	5.25	14.9
1895–9	0.18	0.35	0.14	0.22	5.71	15.8
1900	0.20	0.33	0.15	0.21	6.00	16.2
1905–9	0.25	0.43	0.16	0.23	6.62	17.7

Source: Adapted from MacKinnon, 1994, 285.

Note: The 'North' consists of W. & N. Midlands, N.W., Yorkshire and Northern census divisions.

on poor relief gradually fell from 2 to 1 per cent of national income and remain there for the rest of the century (though, with growth, 1 per cent of 1900's national income was a greater sum than 2 per cent of 1830's). Levels of support remained roughly the same, but it became less easy to obtain relief.[75] Towns, in addition, tended to be less generous than the country – presumably because rate-paying urban dwellers gained less direct economic benefit than seasonal labour-hiring farmers and landlords. Within the countryside, furthermore, the arable areas were more generous than pastoral ones, with the low-wage, rural South East tending to be the most generous.[76] This operation of the Poor Law in rural regions, therefore, may have stopped a flood of distressed agricultural labourers from entering the capital's labour market and pushing down wages there.

Conclusions about poverty

In many accounts of the period, the scale of poverty in nineteenth-century London is regarded as dire. This was certainly true of many contemporary accounts and Parliamentary inquiries, which modern writers have used as their reference sources. Yet, without disparaging the severe hardships that many millions must have endured, nineteenth-century poverty in urban Britain has to be put into context. Poverty as a social issue was 'discovered' in the nineteenth century and all the literature essentially refers to relative deprivation by using measures of 'want' based on value-laden measures of need and idealised consumption patterns for low-income families. By doing so, contemporary middle-class incomes, values and accepted wisdom were being contrasted and applied to those of the lowest economic stratum. It is easy to agree with the minimal nature of the poverty standards laid down and be saddened by the often heart-rending descriptions of the miserable lot of the poor. None the less, any statements and information derived from these studies should still be critically examined and their relative nature borne in mind.

Whatever is concluded about poverty in the capital during the nineteenth century, moreover, it is almost certain that other places and times have been worse for those at the bottom of the social scale. It should be remembered that few Londoners actually experienced starvation during the period, though many suffered from meagre diets, ill-health and shortened lives. The sight of the poor dying in the streets was rare, thanks in part to the hated Poor Law. And it should be remembered that few other countries at the time offered any official assistance to the destitute whatsoever.

The capital had benefits for the poor in greater job and other income-generation opportunities. The downsides for them were that earnings would still be meagre, the cost of housing was high and big city life lacked informal support systems for some city dwellers. When incomes dried up, the plight of many of London's poor was dire – leaving little option but the workhouse. The scale of serious poverty at the end of the century should not be exaggerated, though. It was nowhere near the 'more than 30 per cent' often attributed to Booth.

Several factors suggest that a lower share of poverty than Booth's headline figure is the more realistic view. The theory in Chapter 2 suggested that a large growing city generates good earnings for many and would attract the poor. The London economy certainly was expanding fast and so offered many employment opportunities. This may have kept poverty at bay, for all but the unfortunate and those who middle-class reformers were convinced would never work – the residuum. Yet this does not explain why the poor – or particularly those from the adjacent poorest agricultural districts – did not flood into the capital to improve their low prospects.

This would suggest that the social policies towards the poor in London and the structure of its economy had some effect in limiting the influx of the poor. Many poor people would have been put off from trying their luck in the capital by several factors. The cost of housing, as noted above, was relatively high and the legal possibilities for informal housing, squatting or sleeping in the street – so common in the modern Third World – were limited. The policing of such activities, moreover, became much stricter over time as part of public health measures. Migration patterns, in addition, caused many earlier migrants to the city to return eventually to their place of birth, where job prospects for someone trained in London but of advancing years could be far greater than they would have been by remaining in the capital, especially for women on leaving the domestic service or clothing industries. Moreover, the value of any accumulated savings would have been greater in the provinces and housing costs cheaper. The Poor Law also returned some immigrants back to their place of origin and, as argued previously, may have helped to keep the southern rural poor in their place. An added deterrent for those who thought they would remain destitute in the capital was the far greater probability of ending up in the workhouse than elsewhere, as shown in Table 5.6.

These mechanisms taken together formed a network of spatial exclusionary measures that was a key aspect of contemporary economic and social policy towards the poor. Though to the modern mind they might seem heartless, to the Victorian social reformer they limited the flood of the poor, so that London never experienced the mass migration of the destitute to it as has occurred in many modern Third World cities.

Booth's survey took place at the end of what was likely to have been four decades of quite rapid real wage growth. In the mid-century and earlier, far more of the population would probably have been in extreme poverty. Rising living standards dragged many social cohorts out of the threat of poverty, even if not into a life of affluence. One rough estimate reckons that, because of low earnings, the contemporary occupational structure in the East End in 1813 would have put 40 per cent of the population in serious poverty, *if they had families* – which a significant number did not.[77] That statement would have been less applicable a hundred years later.

One of the benefits of economic growth is that more and more people are pulled out of bare subsistence. The evidence overall does not suggest that London had an adverse role in generating poverty. Rather, getting by in the richest city in the world offered more opportunities than most other places.

Part 3

The transformation of London

6 Retailing and the new mass market

Introduction

One of the most visible signs of economic change in the nineteenth century was the expansion of shopping. Less obvious to the naked eye were simultaneous changes elsewhere in the distributive chain and the growing distance between producer and consumer as the intimacy of the small artisanal workshop gave way to the anonymity of the shopping street. Shops were already common in London by the 1800s and sold a wide variety of goods. Half of them probably sold food and drink;[1] others were pure retailers in areas such as haberdashery (dress accessories and sewing items), drapery (textile fabrics) and a variety of luxury goods; yet more were the front selling areas attached to small or large workshops. What changed over the century was the length of the distributional chain and the roles and organisation of shops. London was not especially innovative, with much change imitated from new practices elsewhere. Yet the shift was a profound one for the urban economy and it altered the city's street life and micro-geography.

Developments in retailing were stimulated by improving living standards and by technical changes in production, distribution and enterprise organisation. The 'mass market' was emerging, especially in foodstuffs, basic household goods and clothing. As one of the richest consumer markets in the world, moreover, the impact of these changes was substantial in terms of the number of retail outlets that emerged, the effects on the household economy, the consumer markets producers faced, and the evolving pattern of the new suburbs. At the centre of the metropolis, the West End was made the focus of urban consumption by the new retailing technology; while one of the traditional aspects of commerce in the City was greatly reduced in importance.[2]

The new forms of retailing, furthermore, helped to break down traditional, regionally based production and consumption patterns. In relation to production, new 'branded' consumer goods could be sold throughout the country, so national, rather than local, markets were the focus of suppliers. London had few specific locational advantages for producers that could operate from one large plant, and they predominantly set up in cheaper locations elsewhere – for example, Lever in Port Sunlight in Cheshire, Cadbury in Bourneville, near Birmingham, and Rowntree in York. In trades where mass production did not take place via the technology of the single plant but via interlinked networks of producers, as in clothing and furniture, the agglomeration benefits of the metropolis meant that they expanded there, as Chapter 12 will show.

In Chapter 2, it was noted that retailing has specific geographical patterns – from the highly localised convenience store to the specialist that drew clients from a wide area. Only large cities could support the latter and the metropolis was an obvious place for such suppliers to locate. As specialist consumption was the virtual monopoly of the wealthy in the early nineteenth century, it was inevitable that activities like the best tailors, dressmakers, jewellers, clock-makers, carriage and piano producers were usually found in the capital, and visiting them was an excuse to go 'up to town'. London retailing in this sense had served a national market for centuries, but by the late nineteenth century and the Edwardian years a much wide range of the population gained benefits from such 'higher-order' retail clustering. The new forms of retailing, in particular, gave the West End and its environs a large array of department stores, intermingled with multiples and specialists and there was intense competition between all of them. This made it the best location in the country to shop, so that the capital's role at the top of the national retailing hierarchy became even more preponderant.[3]

An examination of the development of metropolitan shopping habits thus has to consider a range of aspects, from the convenience and keen prices demanded in food shopping, through to the activities that can survive only by attracting clients from a broad geographical area. Examined first is traditional street selling. This went through a long period of peaceful co-existence with shops, before slowly dying away by the end of the century. The characteristics of nineteenth-century shops are then considered; followed by the growth of branded goods and their impact on London industry; and next is considered the expansion of multiple chains, co-operative societies and department stores. The final section comments on the consequences of the new ways of shopping for London's households and industry.

Costermongers and hawkers

Goods had been bought on London streets since it was founded. As late as the 1850s, the cries of some 41,000 itinerant street sellers still resounded – one for every sixty-three residents.[4] Yet, fifty years later, they hardly existed except in the poorest areas. Congregating in market areas, or tramping up to fifteen miles a day through residential streets in all weathers, the life of a street seller could be hard and offered only meagre returns. Hawkers were often reluctant traders therefore, victims of unemployment or illness, attracted to the profession by its ease of access. Many were women. Little start-up money was needed. Barrows, baskets and trays could be hired by the day or week from dealers. Goods sufficient for one or two days' trading could be acquired on credit, or by using a day loan procured from wealthier traders, shopkeepers or publicans. Legal constraints on street trading were limited, encouraging many to try their luck. The 1832 Police Act gave the police discretionary powers to confiscate the goods of tradesmen obstructing the highway, but there were few arrests. Only 361 and 334 cases of obstruction were brought before London magistrates in 1832 and 1837 respectively, and less than half led to the forfeiture of goods, according to a contemporary commentator.[5] Despite the ease of entry and exit for this line of activity, some established street traders, none the less, could have a reasonably good business – one that was passed down through the generations.

A significant amount of street trading was undertaken by 'costermongers'. They sold fruit and vegetables and also fish – particularly once railways had brought the price of fish down to levels that the general populace could afford. According to Mayhew in the late 1850s, around half of the costermongers inherited the trade from their fathers. Most bought their supplies from a wide range of wholesale markets. At mid-century, they purchased half of the fruit and vegetables sold at Covent Garden and three-quarters of Billingsgate's fish.[6]

Less numerous, though of equal importance, were street sellers dealing in cooked food, drink and manufactured goods. Many working-class families lacked, or could not afford to heat, an oven and generally cooked food in pots, which restricted choice. Ready-made meals and drinks were much in demand – a need met by countless food and drink hawkers. Their wares were sometimes self-prepared but, more generally, were obtained from wholesalers and drinks suppliers. Mayhew in the early 1860s reckoned that 124 million oysters were sold on the streets annually and counted 500 soup and eel traders, 300 whelk-sellers, 300 tea and coffee stall keepers, 300 sellers of sheep's trotters, 500 of muffins, and 1,500 of ginger-beer. New treats included ice-cream from 1850 and fried fish at around the same time.[7]

Street dealers in manufactures, such as crockery, glassware and metalwork, either sold their goods for cash or bartered them for old clothes, subsequently sold to second-hand clothes exchanges. Again, the goods were either made by the hawkers themselves or, more usually, bought from specialist wholesale markets known as 'swag' shops. Numbering around 150 at mid-century, swag shops were often large-scale establishments, employing up to 200 people, and were locationally concentrated. Glass and crockery shops, for example, were to be found in Spitalfields, and haberdashery wholesalers in Bishopsgate. More expensive working-class goods, such as furniture and clothing, were sold in the street by tallymen, who encouraged custom by offering credit. Although their lending terms were generally high, few of their customers earned enough to be able to save for such purchases nor could they obtain credit in shops.

Street markets

Street markets one or two hundred years ago largely sold foodstuffs, particularly fruit, vegetables and meat, although some specialised in second-hand goods. The relationship between itinerant street trading and street retail markets was close, because such markets were obvious places for street sellers to congregate, and they often graduated to market stall holding. Market traders themselves would use costermongers to sell their unsold stock.

London contained a large number of markets, many of which dated from medieval times and survive today.[8] The most well known were Leadenhall, Middlesex Street (Petticoat Lane) and Brick Lane in or close to the City; the New Cut in Lambeth; Clare Market off the Strand (now the site of the London School of Economics); Berwick Street in Soho; Shepherd Market in Mayfair; and the Brill in Somers Town. As the suburbs expanded in the nineteenth century, new street markets were set up to service them. The centre of Brixton, for example, was designed to incorporate a mixture of partly covered and open street markets (the shopping arcades are an inter-war addition). The proud use of innovatory electricity there is remembered in the street names – Electric Avenue and Electric Lane.[9]

The longevity of street markets was encouraged by the ever-rising cost of shop rents and the proximity of wholesale markets, which enabled street markets to continue to compete on price and quality. Owners of land rights in market areas, either the local landowner or vestry, had a strong incentive to keep the markets going, because they derived a good income from charging traders a fee for the right to pitch a stall. Gradually, the number of markets in the centre fell – due to the growth of shops, suburbanisation and attempts to alleviate traffic congestion that forced them off main roads. The 1875 Public Health Act contained provisions threatening street market practices, which local authorities should have enforced, but implementation was lax in London. Many markets survived through the century; in 1900, for example, a London County Council survey noted over 100.[10]

A nineteenth-century innovation was the development of sheltered premises for street traders in enclosed markets. Such markets became popular in London, though to a lesser extent than in the rest of the country. There was a bad start with the financially unsuccessful Hungerford Permanent Market in 1833 – part of which burnt down in 1854, and all of which was demolished in 1862 for the erection of Charing Cross Station.[11]

Milk

Milk production was an agricultural activity with a close link to retailing. In many instances, this would be literal, with the cows stalled behind the shop where the milk was sold. London's milk supply came from suburban dairy farms, urban cow keepers, and increasingly from rural areas surrounding the city and beyond, after the advent of the railway and the introduction of stricter sanitary regulations. At the start of the century, the milk was mainly sold by Irish and Welsh women, who contracted with a suburban supplier for the daily produce of a specific number of cows. After milking 'their' cattle early each morning, these women then undertook the arduous task of carrying the milk into central London in heavy pails hung from a wooden beam slung over their shoulders, where they sold it to passers-by. Such itinerant trading continued to the end of the century.

From the 1840s, milk also began to be sold by the dairies themselves, in general convenience stores, and by specialist retailers. As the city grew, there was a rise in the demand for milk and this was met by an increase in the number of cow keepers. The city's physical expansion brought it into neighbourhoods where many cow keepers and their dairies had traditionally been located. By 1840, most Londoners lived within walking distance of a dairy, and this encouraged many dairies to turn to retailing.

Railways began to transport milk from 1845, when the Eastern Counties Railway conveyed supplies overnight from Brentford and Romford in Essex. Although the milk was much shaken and often sour, particularly in hot weather, by 1850, 800,000 gallons a year arrived by rail. However, most milk at this time still travelled by road (2.5 million gallons) with the bulk of supplies produced by town cows (12 million gallons).[12] In 1865/6, an outbreak of rinderpest destroyed 80 per cent of the London herd, and the lack of a local supply caused the demand for rail-transported milk to soar. By 1866, 7 million gallons, almost half the capital's supply, was brought by rail from over 200 stations around the South-East.[13] Having discovered the superior quality of country milk, few returned to the town product. Helped by refrigeration and the introduction of more stringent city cow-shed hygiene regulations, the railways by 1890 delivered 84 per cent of the milk consumed in the capital and, by 1910, they had almost totally captured the market with a 96 per cent share.[14]

The greater demand for milk led to its sale developing in general stores, 4,421 of which stocked supplies in 1883. There was also a growth of specialist 'dairy' shops, unassociated with the previous dairies that had housed town-based cows and, by 1883, they numbered a substantial 1,941. They sold, in addition, butter, eggs, margarine and some groceries, and first appeared in the West End and the City. In 1910, 76 per cent of these dairy shops were single-shop enterprises, but large operators ran the remainder and they sold much greater volumes. Examples of the large firms were Express County Milk (founded in 1864) and the Aylesbury Dairy Co. (1866). Amongst these volume sellers concentration was high, with ten chains owning 40 per cent of the branches. Many were subsequently taken over by margarine producers to guarantee outlets for their products (see p. 137).[15] Doorstep delivery began at mid-century and was controlled by independent traders. They would make up to three deliveries a day to prevent souring.

By the turn of the century, therefore, the majority of the capital's milk was being transported by rail from Essex, Suffolk, Wiltshire, East Dorset, Somerset and the Midlands. Large wholesalers gained scale economies and so dominated the trade. They built depots near rural railway stations, allowing the milk to be cooled before despatch, and in the adjacent creameries summer milk surpluses were converted into butter and cream. Wishing to sustain demand, the majors sold the milk at the same price throughout the year, despite the fact that farm prices varied considerably between winter and summer. Many small, ephemeral firms were attracted by the high summer profit margins, but the sector continued to be dominated by a small number of large distributors. By 1914, there were four majors – the Wiltshire United Dairies; the Great Western and Metropolitan Dairies; the Dairy Supply Co., the wholesaling subsidiary of Express Dairies; and F. W. Gilbert.[16] It was difficult for others to gain a permanent footing because of high costs of entry, and the benefit to existing firms of their strong links with retailers and farmers who supplied scarce winter milk. Milk thus is an example of an industry whose production left the capital because of the growth of new forms of transportation and distribution, but it was one in which there remained a close link between metropolitan outlets and non-metropolitan producers.

Shops

Shops were generally small at the start of the century and directly owned by the shopkeeper, who employed assistants, often their relatives, and live-in, sometimes unpaid, apprentices. Despite low investment in wares and displays, the cost of setting up a store in the capital was still high – £50 to £200 for apothecaries, and £1,000 to £5,000 for woollen drapers, for example. The rewards though were great. In 1798, over a third of London households liable for tax were retailers, and three-quarters of those shopkeepers who paid tax were in the three highest tax categories.[17]

The most profitable retail establishments were in the City and, increasingly, in the West End. The location of particular types of shops, furthermore, seems to have corresponded to the well-known principles of retail location, which continued until the advent of the mall and superstore: locate where the greatest number of people pass by and, when specialised, stay central to maximise the population catchment area. On the main thoroughfares, therefore, would be found a broad mix of establishments to attract the general and casual shopper and the ones in a hurry. Specialist shops would cluster in cheaper side streets, because shoppers were more likely to have the time to make specific trips to them and to appreciate being able to compare products and prices. Geographical specialisation was strong. St James's Street, for example, contained hatters, tailors, shoe-makers and gunsmiths; along with shirtmakers, wigmakers and tobacconists in nearby Jermyn Street. The district catered primarily for a male clientele. Covent Garden and the Strand, in contrast, largely served female clothing needs. Both Piccadilly and Oxford Street as main streets contained a wide range of shops, though from the 1820s the northern side of Oxford Street began to be dominated by linen drapers and haberdashers. Elsewhere in London, the types of shops depended on the consumption patterns of the local populations, with residential-oriented shops selling foodstuffs in local high streets – such as butchers, bakers and general food traders – and specialist and generalist dry goods shops concentrated in suburban centres.[18]

The craft route into shopkeeping was a common one, because many craftsmen sold their own goods directly. This sector began to decline with the spread of mass-produced goods, though significant numbers survived in tailoring, footwear and watch-making. Market traders occasionally moved up the retailing career ladder to become shopkeepers, via the intermediate stage of a stall in a market hall.

Shops and street traders were not necessarily antagonistic towards each other. Most shopkeepers were willing to tolerate traders because they served a different market by selling poorer-quality produce. Their presence also helped to attract shoppers to a locality. The dividing line between the two types of retailing activity was in any case fluid because, when times were hard, many shopkeepers were forced to hawk goods themselves. Shops, however, gradually grew at the expense of street traders, for both demand and supply reasons. The biggest demand factor undoubtedly was economic growth. With higher incomes, people bought more and demanded a wider range of goods and services. As the benefits of growth trickled down the social hierarchy, shopping became a mass activity. Customers, especially the middle-class ones, in addition had more time to visit shops. They were increasingly likely to live in the suburbs and travel into town for their less frequent, expensive purchases; whereas day-to-day items were bought by them or their servants in local suburban centres. This central–local retailing pattern was to survive for much of the twentieth century. A retail hierarchy emerged consequently in nineteenth-century London, of local, suburban and city centre shopping functions, especially in the forty years prior to 1914. Improvements in transportation, particularly after the dense network of buses, trams and underground lines came into existence, gradually reinforced the hierarchical specialisation of retail areas.

On the supply side, technical improvements, most notably improved interior lighting, made shops more viable. The quality of dry goods, and of foodstuffs like cheeses, benefited considerably from protection from the elements afforded by the addition of chilling facilities in the latter decades of the period. Book-keeping and ordering provided better information and financial control, and watchful proprietors could more easily monitor staff than in the hurly-burly of the street. Using shops enabled both economies of scale and scope to be achieved over the street seller. As they offered a wider variety of higher-quality and cheaper goods, shops had a competitive edge and gradually displaced street selling.

Shops provided fewer advantages for fruit and vegetables, the selling of which remained concentrated in street markets. Their freshness depended on the speed of the distribution from farm to consumer, so that the street seller could still be more competitive. Working-class households for convenience would often use a local shop or seller of processed food during the week, and use street markets at the weekend for their major shopping.

Changes slowly occurred in the practices and organisational structures of shops. Over the period, more retailers began to display goods, set fixed, clearly-marked prices, and sell only for cash. Shop owners started to live away from their shop premises, and paid managers and supervisors became more common. Retailing, like manufacturing, was transforming from a personal relationship into a more de-personalised mass market, although the small, family-owned and -run shop remained the mainstay of the capital's retailing structure.

Another nineteenth-century retailing innovation was the arcade. First built in Paris, the shopping arcade reached London in 1817/18 with the construction of the Royal Opera and Burlington Arcades. They maximised shop frontages in relation to internal space, made use of cheaper inter-building strips of land, and potential thieves could easily be excluded. Arcades provided a sheltered, more pleasant, fashionable shopping experience and were precursors of the modern shopping mall. Many of the arcades that sprang up have long since disappeared,[19] as the expansion of specific retailing establishments in them was severely restricted by the limited space available, and the arcades could not compete with the facilities in department stores once they became commonplace.

Bread-making

As one of the most basic foodstuffs, bread-making illustrates the shift in the nature of retailing and the new relationships it brought between retailer and consumer. Production had to be local in nature to ensure freshness – but the feasible catchment area expanded from the near-confines of the bakery to city-wide and beyond by the end of the century. Health measures in this case encouraged innovation and larger-scale production.

The Bakers' Company lost its guild controls in 1805. Bread prices were freed in 1815, after which time the industry was open to all comers, and fierce competition was associated with serious adulteration. From the 1880s, firms became larger and wholesalers became more common. Mechanisation and new methods of distribution encouraged the growth of these larger firms. From 1887 to 1911, the number of bakehouses in London fell from 4,000 to 2,722 and, by the mid-1890s, a dozen produced bread solely for wholesale and began to dominate the market.[20]

Until the 1901 Factory and Workshop Act, approximately half of the bakehouses were below street level. Up to the 1880s, much dough was hand-kneaded by sweating, semi-naked journeymen in often vermin-infested premises that lacked proper sanitation and ventilation. After this time, in response to competition from the major firms and greater public concern over quality, conditions improved and even the smaller bakeries began to adopt dough-kneading machines. Other techniques changed as well. Most small bakers originally used wood-fired ovens, but then adopted scotch ovens, heated by a small external coke furnace, and even Vienna steam ovens. Traditional bakeries remained but with new techniques, quality levels and noticeable competition from large firms producing for the wholesale market. Now bread could be sold in a variety of retail outlets and via the expanding number of restaurants and other eating places.

Branded goods

Branded and packaged goods, especially in foodstuffs and household goods, grew to have a significant influence on the British retail market from the 1880s onwards. The production technologies used were often new, but relatively simple, and brands were marketed nationally on the basis of quality, price and reliability. For goods like cigarettes, jams, sweets, biscuits, mustard, chocolate, soaps, starch, paints and pills, a handful of brands became household names. The fortunes of London producers varied considerably in relation to branding and it is worth considering a few of them. Sugar, cigarettes, soap, candles and pharmaceuticals illustrate the nature of the changes that branding brought and the varying consequences for London producers.

Sugar and confectionery

Sugar refining was brought to the capital by Germans in the first half of the sixteenth century. Sugar at this time was a luxury, but supply gradually increased and its price fell with the colonisation of the West Indies and the setting up of the colonial sugar plantation economy. London's sugar refineries were close to the Sufferance Wharves where the raw sugar from the West Indies was landed. By the nineteenth century, sugar had become an essential part of even working-class diets, with annual per capita national consumption of around 25 pounds in the late 1840s.[21] Until the 1850s, the London industry prospered, producing loaf sugar, broken into lumps by retailers, white and yellow crushed sugar, and a small amount of brown sugar and treacle. The business was generally small-scale. In 1823–4, the East End contained eighty-two refineries employing over a thousand refiners and many others.[22]

The industry then declined in the metropolis. Continental refiners could supply sugar more cheaply after the 1860 Free Trade Act, especially from France and Belgium where loaf sugar producers were subsidised by the state. The source of the raw material was also switching from exclusively cane sugar imported into London and Liverpool from the West Indies, to beet sugar, some of which was grown in Britain, but most was imported from Central Europe. At the outbreak of the First World War, two-thirds of Britain's sugar consumption was imported from Austria-Hungary alone.[23] The remaining sugar refining in the UK inevitably moved away from the ports previously associated with the West Indian trade and individual plants operated at a far larger scale of output. The resultant decline in plant numbers was substantial. In 1800, there had been a hundred metropolitan refineries, two-thirds of the British total; yet, by 1900, there were only four – although this was still a quarter of those remaining in Britain.[24]

By the 1850s, London's sugar refineries were concentrating on specialist products for the mass market, generally sold under proprietary brand names. They were relocating to the Silvertown area of East London, because of its deep-water facilities – ideal for the larger vessels carrying raw materials that were unable to enter the Pool – a good rail link in the form of the North Woolwich Railway, and later weaker pollution controls outside the County boundary. One London firm, Manbre, however, successfully continued to compete in the national market from its riverside site in Hammersmith.[25]

The Liverpool refiner, Henry Tate (benefactor to the Tate Gallery, opened in 1897) built his seven-and-a-half-acre Silvertown refinery in 1878 to exploit his patent to produce sugar cubes using the Langen process. The cubes proved highly popular and, in 1908, the refinery was doubled in size. It additionally produced 'pieces' of yellow sugar and, from around 1900, granulated sugar – such diversification guarding against the swings in tastes. Abram Lyle built his eleven-acre Silvertown works in 1880. It largely produced his branded 'Golden Syrup', a type of treacle, and the firm prospered. Just over forty years later, in 1921, the two firms amalgamated to form Tate and Lyle.[26]

Alongside the branding of sugar products, a large number of major national brands emerged in chocolate, other sweets and jams. None, however, originated from London producers. Instead, firms such as Cadbury, based outside Birmingham, used high-volume, modern methods to produce nationally advertised goods. Country-wide distribution was by rail and orders were won and monitored by the companies' own sales forces rather than through traditional intermediaries. Most of these firms' production facilities were located away from the main urban centres. Non-conformist ownership was common. On occasion, model villages were built for some of the workforce. Relative land and labour costs and the loss of locational advantage with the decline of cane sugar may account for the lack of success of London firms.

Cigarettes

Like sugar, tobacco industries had thrived in the capital with its twin advantages of the port and a major market. Yet, with the introduction of cigarettes, branding and the widespread popularity of this new way of smoking, metropolitan producers declined markedly in relative national importance. Most London firms were small. By far the largest was Lambert and Butler, established in Clerkenwell in 1834, which in 1870 had a capitalisation of £87,200, only slightly below that of the Bristol producer, Wills and Co., the country's largest tobacco company. Wills was the first company to adopt national branding and the advertising of cigarettes, in the 1880s, after it obtained exclusive rights to the use of some major cost-reducing machinery – most importantly, the Rose tobacco packing machine.[27] The London trade was turned into a relative backwater by the national success of Wills. By 1901, in stark contrast to thirty-one years before, Lambert and Butler had a capitalisation of only £754,300 against Wills's £6.9 million. In that year, the two, along with thirteen other companies, amalgamated to form Imperial Tobacco in an attempt to beat off the challenge of the American Tobacco Co., which, through Ogdens, its British subsidiary, was threatening to corner the UK market.[28]

Soap

In the eighteenth century, London was the country's main producer of soap. Towards the end of the century, however, dominance was lost to Merseyside. That area had better access to coal, which was used in large quantities, as well as good facilities for the import of tallow, palm oil, and crude alkali in the form of kelp. By the 1820s, Merseyside was making twice as much soft soap as the capital and, fifteen years later, 50 per cent more hard soap.[29] The extent of the increase in national demand, however, meant that the change was a relative one, and the London industry continued to prosper. Removal of excise duties in 1853 further stimulated demand.

Soap was produced from bones and fats supplied from London slaughter-houses, restaurants and private houses, imported barilla and later synthetic alkalis. Toilet soap manufacturers often used hard yellow soap as their raw material, reboiling, refining and perfuming it. The major processes were undertaken by men, while women wrapped and boxed the finished product.[30]

London's industry fared worse towards the end of the century in the face of competition from Lever. That firm, based at Port Sunlight on Merseyside, revolutionised soap marketing and selling by introducing vertically integrated production, strong brands and national distribution systems. London firms seem to have made little attempt to match this competition.[31]

Candles

Many soap-makers also made candles and tallow. Tallow is a white fatty solid made by melting down animal fat. Tallow manufacture was a noxious industry and so was located in the city's industrial districts by the river.

Many candles were used for domestic light throughout the nineteenth century, with gas and electric lighting only becoming commonplace in working-class housing in the next century. Whether made of beeswax or tallow, they were initially made by dipping, rolling or pouring. By the 1890s, however, most were manufactured in metal moulds, using stearin, a mixture of fatty acids.

Candle-making was highly seasonal. It took place mostly in winter, when demand was high and candles were more likely to set rapidly. The main producer was Prices Patent Candles. It adopted the strategies of other successful consumer goods firms in that it innovated and developed national brands and distribution. Established in 1830, the firm produced candles from coconut fat in factories in Battersea and Vauxhall. After developing the composite candle in 1840, it underwent rapid expansion, with employment rising to 700 in 1849. A further plant was set up in Birkenhead, close to Liverpool – the main location for imported palm oil. The company also moved upstream in the production process by purchasing a thousand acres of coconut plantation and several coconut crushing mills in Ceylon. Concerned at the growth of gas and electric lighting, the company diversified in the 1890s and began to produce gas and, later, petrol engine oil and white spirit. London's sea links, its market size and a large labour market able to absorb seasonal fluctuations in labour requirements had helped to produce a national market leader.

Pharmaceuticals

In 1800, the pharmaceutical industry was based in Finsbury, close to the spice and drug auctions. Production was small-scale and generally unmechanised. The industry grew rapidly in the first quarter of the century because of technological developments, improvements in medical care and trade liberalisation.[32] In the second half of the century, major London producers included Howards and Sons – with a six-acre Stratford plant employing 250; May and Baker (1834) of Battersea – between 1860 and 1900 their employees rose from 30 to 100;[33] and Burroughs Wellcome, which in 1885 began to produce drugs at a former paper mill in Deptford.[34]

Burroughs Wellcome was founded by two Americans and soon became known colloquially as the 'Yankee Chemist'. Other British producers of the time were making branded products for the retail trade using licensed American processes and undertaking little research. In contrast, Burroughs Wellcome modelled itself on US contemporary practice and developed marketing and research capabilities similar to theirs.[35] It invested heavily in the research and development of new drugs, which were marketed aggressively at home and abroad to hospitals and doctors, as well as to the over-the-counter trade. In Chapter 2, innovations were argued to be a hallmark of large cities, and the location of pharmaceuticals production illustrates that effect. A London firm, Burroughs Wellcome became a market leader; yet most UK firms' production facilities were elsewhere in the country.

Failure in branded goods?

This brief survey of several London industries by no means encompasses all the brand goods that emerged from the 1850s onwards. It does, however, illustrate some general principles of the location of factories making them. Most branded goods were relatively light in weight, used simple technologies in their production and were focused on providing for basic consumption needs for the broad mass of the population. With the comparatively short distances between locations in Britain, the manufacture of such products often did not have to be located near to the main markets, so that the input costs associated with labour, land and raw materials had a greater influence on location than market demand. Although the precise locations of facilities were often influenced by the idiosyncratic histories of individual entrepreneurs, they tended not to be in the capital because input costs were higher there. London's large market tended to induce a metropolitan location only when another locational characteristic came into play as well. With the above goods, it was possibly the port – as in the case of sugar – along the lines of the impact of transhipment points on transport costs highlighted in Chapter 2. In candle-making, the large labour market helped as well; whereas with pharmaceuticals, the city's role as an innovation seedbed seems to have been influential. Innovation alone, however, was insufficient. In dye-stuffs, for example, Sir William Perkin, in 1856, had invented the first process for making dyes by chemical synthesis,[36] but his Greenford plant in suburban London did not prosper and the technology was taken up in Germany, rather than anywhere in Britain, and helped to form the basis of that country's industrialisation. The market for pharmaceuticals was more susceptible to new products, however, and it is interesting that the most successful London producer, Burroughs Wellcome, employed many research staff in contrast to other British firms; so another metropolitan attribute – a large skilled labour market – was important to it but not them.

Similar factors can be seen to operate elsewhere. Mineral waters are a relatively 'low-value to bottled-weight' product, but Schweppes succeeded in developing international brands in tonic water and ginger ale from its original eighteenth-century Drury Lane origins. It had decentralised to Hendon by the 1890s, but its brand was built up on setting up other production and bottling facilities around Britain and overseas, thereby overcoming the problem of weight and limiting exports from London. This case, thus, is different from the others mentioned above in that transport costs were a bigger problem – and one resolved by having more geographically spread plants as turnover increased.

Even if London producers did not do particularly well in relation to the late nineteenth-century rise of branded goods, this should not be interpreted as a 'failure'. Rather, the attributes of the capital were better suited to other economic activities. This can be seen even within the food, drink and tobacco sectors where most of the branding took place. London employment grew in these fields, which by no means suggests failure, but rather indicates that many activities in these spheres were still bound to local populations and that the switch from domestic to imported foodstuffs benefited London-based firms.

As branding and mass-marketing expanded in the twentieth century, it might be supposed that metropolitan industry was further disadvantaged. Yet this was not to be the case. Later, branded electrical and other consumer durables were to be more sophisticated and require far greater amounts of skilled labour – so that London in the inter-war years was to prove an ideal location for them.

The rise of the multiple

Multiple shops are chains of retailers owned by the same company, often using a standard format of design, products, value and service quality. An invention of the nineteenth century, they are another example of branding in retailing. Consumers could feel confident of value, product range and quality in standardised outlets. Multiple retailing developed where consumer convenience was significant. As a result, multiples were especially important in foodstuffs and in other frequently purchased items, and were mainly found in suburban shopping centres and at transport termini. The initial setting up of chains of new outlets by enterprising retailers was spurred on by recognition that there was a finite number of customers who would come to one location, no matter how good the shop. Rather than expanding existing premises, successful shopkeepers therefore found it more profitable to open new branches.

In 1800 multiple retailing was unknown in London, apart from some fashionable shops with branches in the Spa towns where customers spent part of the year. True multiples first appeared in the 1850s. They started in specialist retailing activities: selling goods traditional retailers lacked the facilities to handle or were reluctant to sell because of uncertain demand. W. H. Smith profited by spotting the opportunity of railway passengers' reading needs. His newspaper and magazine business combined retail outlets with speedy wholesale distribution. He opened branches in all the major London stations as well as throughout the country; eventually becoming one of the few Victorian entrepreneurs to succeed in politics. Another early example was the Singer Manufacturing Co., one of the first US multinationals to come to Britain. It faced the distinct problem of setting up a national network of outlets and repair shops for the sewing machines mass-produced in its new Scottish plant. The multiple shop gave it a High Street presence throughout the country and quality control over a network of repair and spares outlets. London was a focus of its activities because of the importance of the clothing industry there – an industry that Singer machines revolutionised (see Chapter 12). Multiples then gradually spread to the footwear, meat and grocery trades. In footwear, the multiple arose when some retailers became willing to carry large stocks of factory-produced shoes, such as London-based E. Rabbits and Pocock Brothers. As regards groceries, the London pioneers were Walton Hassell and Port, and John Sainsbury, who, having run a dairy in Drury Lane since 1869, opened a second in Kentish Town in 1876, near where he lived, and a third in Croydon before expanding to many other suburban centres.

In butchery, multiples grew with the import of chilled meat from Argentina and elsewhere. Foreign meat suppliers found that traditional butchers were reluctant to sell their produce. Two British firms – Eastman and Nelson – seized the opportunity to set up an extensive network of shops specialising in cheap foreign meat. They acquired their own refrigerated ships and facilities in Argentina and set up a nation-wide retailing network. Despite their success, they could not compete with the scale economies of US firms. Thus two-thirds of British meat imports from South America at the outbreak of the First World War were shipped by US meat packers.[37] Other British meat importers fared well. W. R. Fletcher, for example, specialised in imported Australian lamb.

One London firm grew from a small Smithfield business to become the world's third largest meat packing company by the 1920s, with its headquarters still in Smithfield. The Vestey family set up Union Cold Storage (UCS) in the 1880s to store and transport perishable foods. With rapid expansion, it developed scale economies that induced the above-mentioned multiples of Eastman and Nelson to close down their own overseas facilities and use those of Union Cold Storage. The Blue Star Line was founded in 1911 as a shipping subsidiary, and the previously mentioned Fletcher business was acquired in 1910. A few years after this, the Vestey family bought up most of their competitors. The scale of the firm's activities in the first decades of the twentieth century made Union Cold Storage one of Britain's largest enterprises by share value. By 1923, it was the world's largest meat retailer, with one-third of British refrigerated storage capacity and two-thirds of multiple butcher outlets.[38]

Multiples spread in other lines of retailing in the 1890s. Tailors selling factory-produced goods, such as G. A. Dunn and Hope Brothers, began to open multiple branches. Limited company chemists, like Nottingham-based Boots, free from 1880 to call themselves chemists and druggists, began to establish chains and sell patent medicines. At the turn of the century, London became home to stores developed elsewhere in the UK or overseas, such as the American company Woolworth. The initial expansion of multiples was financed mainly through ploughed-back profits, and most enterprises expanded into near by localities. Unsurprisingly, therefore, most of the chains originating in London remained purely metropolitan at first. National expansion by London firms only occurred in the 1890s after some of them adopted public limited status and then had the capital to establish country-wide presences. The new joint stock company status also facilitated organisational restructuring by encouraging the use of professional managers in distant stores. Julius Drew and J. Musker, for example, began with a shop in Edgware Road. They then started to trade as the Home and Colonial Stores with branches throughout the South. Only in the 1890s did they expand to Leeds and Birmingham; yet by 1903 they had 400 branches nation-wide.[39]

The growth of the multiple was induced by a number of factors. These reflected changing trends in supply with the move away from domestic agriculture to imported foodstuffs, the switch from craft to factory production and the greater range of consumer goods available in late Victorian and Edwardian Britain. Multiples also offered competitive prices by limiting the number of goods sold in order to purchase in bulk goods with a high turnover. In this way, profit margins could be kept low – 0.5 per cent on sales in the case of meat retailing – and the return on capital high. They minimised costs by refusing credit, eliminating home deliveries, adopting fairly simple shop fittings, and introducing strict and standardised branch stock control systems.[40] Such shops, moreover, set new standards in quality and service. Their retailing areas were attractively laid out and kept immaculately clean, with long opening hours that extended from 7 a.m. to 11 p.m. on weekdays and to midnight on Saturdays. New sales techniques were successfully tried – such as adopting a uniform shop layout and advertising through handbills and sandwich-board men. (London already had a thriving advertising industry.)[41]

These characteristics were all aimed at the growing urban working class. In contrast, multiples failed to attract the custom of the poor, who required credit, and of many in the middle class, who demanded a greater choice of goods and ordering, delivery and monthly account services. This left much of retailing to the small shop, the specialist 'quality' retailer, the department store and the co-op. Consequently, by 1900, for the UK as a whole, multiple retailers accounted for under 5 per cent of total sales. Growth, however, continued so that, by 1915, multiples, department stores and co-operatives taken together had around a fifth of British retail sales and were selling 31 per cent of groceries, 44 per cent of footwear, 23 per cent of women's apparel and 20 per cent of furnishings.[42]

Vertical integration

The narrow lines of basic necessities meant that the multiples could reap the benefits of economies of scale in their production and distribution. The Lipton and Home and Colonial chains, for example, sold a narrow range of products – tea, sugar, bacon, ham, margarine, butter, cheese and eggs – and they moved into owning their producers and processors, overseas as well as in the UK. This was encouraged by the fact that the optimal scale of production was not high for these types of goods and so a small number of outlets could consume the entire output of a production facility. It also meant that British retailers, unlike some of their US counterparts, did not require large management structures and bureaucracies to run their businesses. (Large headquarters offices for British firms, in general, were not to appear until the inter-war years.) London, as a result, had no particular pull over the location of such enterprises in the way that cities like Chicago did in the USA. The impact of multiples on London industry, however, was large because they now controlled important elements of the distribution chain of working-class necessities and simple luxuries. This function had been under the control of indigenous London industry for the metropolitan population for centuries before. Clothing and furniture were two metropolitan industries that were thereby affected, and the consequences for them are examined in Chapter 12.

In some cases, greater economies of scale in either production or distribution led to firms in those fields acquiring or setting up chains of retailers. The Singer Sewing Machine company, as was noted above, set up its own British network of shops. The Vestey family, also described above, used their advantages in meat production and distribution to dominate meat retailing. A similar development occurred between grocery chains and margarine firms. Margarine was invented in 1869, using animal fat, and by 1876 Britain was importing over a million tons a year. Production only came to Britain in 1889, almost two decades after the first imports. By this time margarine sales were high, scale economies in production were important and vegetable oils were increasingly being used in its manufacture. The capital soon contained a number of margarine producers – Maypole in Southall, Van de Berg and the English Margarine Co. in Fulham, and Jurgens down river at Purfleet. They could take advantage of the port for imports of raw materials, and London's large consumer base and transport links to the rest of the country. Maypole Dairy was a large retail multiple that became a major margarine producer with properties in West Africa; and Van de Berg and Jurgens were subsidiaries of the two Dutch firms that dominated the European business. The latter two targeted Britain because it was the world's largest market for margarine.

These three firms competed aggressively. They bought up retailers to ensure outlets for their goods; so that Britain's grocery multiples were one by one taken over by them. By 1926, the two Dutch companies controlled six of the eight largest grocery chains in Britain – and the erstwhile competitor, Maypole. Later they were to form parts of the Unilever conglomerate.[43]

London's retail co-operatives

Co-operatives first appeared in London in 1760 when Woolwich and Chatham shipwrights set up their own co-operative corn mill. Societies for the retail sale of goods began to be formed in the 1820s and particularly grew in numbers from the 1840s.[44] Originally selling groceries and provisions, they slowly extended their range of goods to bread, meat and tobacco and eventually to drapery, boots, furniture and household utensils. All goods were unadulterated – a major issue of concern in the nineteenth century – sold for cash and from 1863 mainly obtained from the Co-operative Wholesale Society. Members received a dividend based on purchases.

Compared with the north of England, co-operative societies were under-represented in London, probably because of its large number of competing retail outlets, in contrast to the scattered urban structure that had spawned the northern co-operative movement. Competition amongst retailers in Britain's nineteenth-century large cities kept the price of foodstuffs lower and quality higher than elsewhere. Industrialisation in the north of England, in contrast, had led to a dispersed pattern of relatively small towns. Rochdale in Lancashire, where the Co-operative movement was founded, is a classic example. There was consequently less pressure to form societies in London, outside of certain peripheral parts of the metropolis, such as Woolwich. In 1900, Lancashire had nine societies with a membership of over 11,000; the capital had just one of the same size.[45]

London, even so, had a disproportionate number of middle-class societies that imitated the Co-operative principle and were formed in the 1860s and 1870s. Unlike their working-class counterparts, membership of these societies was limited to certain professional groups and profits were distributed in relation to shares held. By 1879, for example, the Civil Service Association had a turnover of over £1 million and 31,800 members, while the Army and Navy Society had sales of over £1.5 million.[46]

Department stores

Department stores took advantage of economies of scope by selling a wide range of products, as well as economies of scale by operating in large buildings at locations to which many middle-class families would be attracted. They served the demands of the middle classes in the ways that the multiples did with necessities for the working classes.

The department store had long forebears in London. Harding Howell and Co. had sold goods – arranged by item and room – at Schomberg House, Pall Mall in 1796, and bazaars began to appear in the West End in the 1830s and 1840s.[47] These bazaars generally comprised large central halls, with or without galleries or upper floors, which housed stalls and counters to rent. Some of the most well known included the Soho on the north-west corner of Soho Square, which sold millinery, lace, gloves and jewellery; the Pantechnicon in Belgrave Square, a centre for the sale of carriages, furniture, wine and toys; Oxford Street's Pantheon, famous for its retail picture gallery and the wide range of goods sold; and the Baker Street horse bazaar, whose small-holders dealt in harnesses, carriages, stoves and ironmongery.

The true department store emerged in the 1850s, generally through expansions of drapery shops. The demand for textile materials and for sewing accessories was then undergoing a rapid growth. Most middle-class women of the time still had their clothes made at home. With fashion putting emphasis on the importance of unique designs, their interest in ready-to-wear apparel was limited. The arrival of the sewing machine and the paper pattern helped to make this domestic task easier, with a better end result. In response to the new strong demand, many long-established drapery stores began to extend their premises and increase the number and range of articles sold. Well-established drapers in the heart of the West End took the lead, including Dickins and Jones (originally founded under the Dickins name in 1790), Peter Robinson (founded in 1833) and John Marshall (founded in 1837).[48]

At the same time, entrepreneurs like William Whiteley entered the sector in response to its profitability. Stores opened by new entrants were generally away from the centre in fashionable inner suburbs, such as Bayswater, Kensington and Knightsbridge, where property could be obtained relatively easily and cheaply. Whatever their origin, the initial enterprises then quickly grew through amalgamation. They adopted the strategy of purchasing adjacent properties until they owned an 'island' site, or street block, and were thus less affected by competition from nearby retailers.[49]

In the 1890s, both central and suburban department stores began to be purpose-built – a trend that began in 1877 with Bon Marché in Brixton. The trend reached its peak at the turn of the century with the creation of the main Harrods building during 1905 and, in 1909, the construction of Selfridges' Oxford Street store. High rents and rates encouraged intensive use of sites by stores, and recent technical developments in building enabled them to be housed in spacious, multi-storey premises. In order to attract customers, the interiors frequently had highly ornate fittings. Stores established in the middle-class suburbs helped to stimulate further retail development in the locality. A list of them identifies many nineteenth-century middle-class shopping centres – Jones Brothers opened a store on Holloway Road, Arding and Hobbs at Clapham Junction, Pratts in Streatham, Sayers and Sons in Ealing and B. B. Evans on Kilburn High Road.

Two developments stimulated the growth of the department store – transport improvements and an expanding middle class. Better and cheaper transport after the 1850s increased the number of people visiting the West End and encouraged the growth of suburban shopping centres. A prime reason for the department stores' success was their capture of the price-conscious, middle-class market. This social group wished to acquire the symbols of prosperity but were generally ignorant of high fashion and so were reluctant to use the specialist shops patronised by the upper classes. By buying in bulk, the big stores offered varied lines and competitive prices. Unlike specialist retailers, they displayed and priced all wares and employed many staff to advise customers. They also made every effort to stock the latest products and provide a range of free services, including toilets, art galleries and a Christmas grotto.

Three of the largest department stores were Whiteleys, Harrods and Selfridges. William Whiteley opened his first store in Westbourne Grove in 1863 and, at first, sold ribbons, lace, trimmings and fancy goods. The demand for these items prompted him to move into other products, like silks, linen, mantles and drapery. By 1867, his shop contained seventeen separate departments. It had a turnover of £43,000 and a profit of approximately £4,500 a year. Over the following decade, he took over other premises in Westbourne Grove and started selling dresses in 1868, gentlemen's outfits in 1869, boots and hats in 1871, and furnishing drapery in 1872. He also began to deal in non-drapery items, opening a house agency and refreshment room in 1872, a dyeing and cleaning service in 1874, a furniture department in 1875, and a customer bank – the deposits of which were used to finance the expansion of the store. Despite fires which severely damaged the shop premises in 1882 and 1887, the firm continued to grow in the 1880s at the same location. In the 1890s, it moved into the production and cultivation of some of the goods sold. Factories were established for the manufacture of furniture and, in the 1890s, land was acquired in Hillingdon, Middlesex and Hamworth, near Hampton Court, for the cultivation of flowers, strawberries and fruit trees and the raising of cattle and pigs. By 1906, the firm grew a large proportion of the fruit and vegetables sold, the store employed a staff of 6,000 – with 400 more on the various farms – and it had a turnover of over £1 million.[50] The store moved to Queens Road (now Queensway) in 1911, four years after the unfortunate Whiteley had been shot in his office by a man claiming to be his illegitimate son.

Whiteley's closest pre-1914 competitors were probably Harrods and Selfridges. The former was established by Charles Henry Harrod, the owner of a grocery store in Stepney (1833) and a wholesale business in East Cheap, who in 1849 took a financial interest in a grocery shop in Brompton Road. Under the management of his son, Charles Digby Harrod, the latter store began to sell patent medicines, perfumery and stationery, and by 1871 had a turnover of £1,000 a week, employing in 1880 approximately 100 staff. Like Whiteley, Harrod continually added sales departments and diversified upstream into production and other areas. In 1893, a furniture depository was opened in Barnes and several bakeries and workshops were established in West London. By 1913, the store had nine floors, a turnover of £4 million, profits of £309,227, and four years later employed around 6,000.[51]

Selfridges was the largest purpose-built department store to be built in the capital. It was opened in 1909 by the American, Gordon Selfridge, using capital from another London store owner, Sam Waring of Waring and Gillow located further east in Oxford Street, on condition that Selfridges did not sell furniture – an agreement that Selfridge kept for many years. The shop employed over 1,000 staff and attempted to entice customers away from Whiteleys and Harrods with the sheer luxury of its decor and the provision of a range of new services, including a silence room, a library, an information bureau, and an American barber's shop and soda fountain. Three years after opening, a roof garden was added, followed in 1913 by a 'seaside' children's play area. After a slow start, the store proved highly successful, generating in 1914 profits of £131,546.[52]

Other significant stores included John Lewis, Barkers, Debenhams, Schoolbred, and Maples. Barkers of Kensington was established in 1870 by John Barker, one of William Whiteley's managers and, by 1893, had forty-two separate departments.[53] Debenham and Pooley opened their Wigmore Street store in 1791 and had it enlarged and entirely rebuilt in 1883 and 1907/8 respectively. The company had a larger wholesale trade than its counterparts, and by the end of the century had offices in Paris, Brussels and Copenhagen.[54] Schoolbred founded in 1820 at first sold linen, woollen and silk goods and carpets and only moved into furnishing in the 1880s. Failing to develop a customer account business and owned by a family more interested in careers in the army and navy than in retailing, it grew relatively slowly. By comparison, its main Tottenham Court Road competitor, Maples, went from strength to strength. Opened in 1841, the store sold everything required to furnish a house, including linens, ironmongery, crockery and ornaments; in 1901 it introduced one of the first store hire-purchase schemes; and in the twentieth century it established warehouses and workshops in Buenos Aires and Paris.[55]

The employees of the new multiple and department stores and other shops were largely female, attracted to the work by its relatively high social status and its physically undemanding nature compared to domestic service and manufacturing industry. Drawbacks were the poor wages paid, often further reduced by fines for trivial offences like bad time-keeping, and the long working hours. The 1886 Shop Hours Regulation Act restricted working hours for those below the age of 18 to a still substantial seventy-four hours a week, but did nothing for adult staff.[56] Young people were predominantly employed – between a third and a half of workers were less than 21 years old – and few remained in the trade beyond the age of 40. Women were expected to leave on marriage, and the constant standing, lack of fresh air and poor food caused bad health. Unsurprisingly, shop assistants between the ages of 25 and 45 in 1886 experienced a high death rate of 9 per cent.[57]

The impact of shops

The change in shopping patterns up to 1914 both reflected and encouraged profound transformations in London life and labour. Shops themselves were major employers by the end of the period. A new, if not well-paid, avenue was opened for respectable women's work. At the same time, the shop squeezed out street selling, with a considerable loss of employment, and closed off one means of earning a meagre income for the poor. The number of retail establishments in London was subsequently closely linked to the contemporary size of the city's population but, in addition, the expansion of speciality shops and large department stores encouraged ever more people to visit London primarily for the purpose of shopping.

In 1873, department stores, multiples and co-ops had a tiny share of national retail sales, but, by 1915, they accounted for around a fifth.[58] In London's suburban and central shopping districts, the percentage was likely to have been even higher.

Shops were part of the change in the London economy caused, as elsewhere, by the growth of mass urban markets. Stores were the places from which households bought their much greater volume of purchases than that bought by previous generations. Those purchases also were no longer overwhelmingly of traditional, domestically grown, foodstuffs and a few simple manufactured goods. Now, far greater emphasis was put on buying imported and processed foods and on a wider range of mass-produced, manufactured items. The range of goods, nevertheless, was still nothing like that of today and much would have comprised clothing, furniture and a few cooking items.

This shift in consumption patterns created many opportunities for London producers. Not only was demand far larger than at the beginning of the century, but also the range of goods that could be made was much greater. The higher share of retail purchases satisfied by imports stimulated port turnover and wholesale activities. Others, however, lost out in the change to large-scale retailing of mass-produced goods. The metropolis's traditional industrial base was centred on craft activities. With the exception of certain luxury sectors, shops now demanded standardised products available for bulk purchase, and they wanted to be able to change specifications quickly in response to changing fashions and levels of demand. Many craft producers were unable to cope, but others in London responded by developing a new organisation of craft production suited to the mass market (see Chapter 12).

Inevitably, London demand became more decoupled from London supply with the growth of mass retailing. Consumption expenditure was less centred on unprocessed foodstuffs brought in from the countryside and locally produced craft manufactures, as it had been in the early 1800s. The capital, instead, became the market for producers from all over Britain and the world, and branded goods became much more important. In Adam Smith's terminology, the greatly extended market increased the division of labour, with some activities undertaken in London and others elsewhere. Yet, as most of the extra demand was new – a product of economic growth – this reformed division of labour did not lead to a displacement of jobs away from London. Instead, employment continued to expand there, much of it in consumer goods industries. The expansion, even so, was on a new basis. London firms were less protected by the friction of distance and so industries only prospered if a metropolitan location offered them a competitive advantage. The types of benefit offered were discussed earlier in Chapter 2; and so, unsurprisingly, metropolitan industry increasingly began to reflect the changing array of agglomeration economies.

The final point to note about shops is their importance in suburban development. The fashionability of new residential areas and the success of housing developments in the new suburbs could be strongly influenced by the quality of local shopping facilities. The location of a good department store, in particular, would encourage people to move to a neighbourhood. The contrast that emerged between rich and poor suburbs intensified with the growing importance of these local shopping centres. In working-class districts, there would be far more local, corner shops – extending credit, or tick, to their low-income clientele. The shops in the latter type of local centre were also likely to be smaller in scale with no department store nearby. The visual distinctions between neighbourhoods were becoming stronger on social class lines.

7 Leisure and pleasure

Introduction

Over the course of the nineteenth century, Londoners' consumption of leisure increased. Although still long, working hours gradually shortened; legally enforceable 'bank' holidays were introduced; living standards rose; and the very conception of leisure changed from a rest from work to an activity that could be pursued for its own sake.

At the same time, there were profound shifts in the leisure activities undertaken. Changes in work organisation and suburban migration reduced work-centred entertainments. Trade feasts, carnivals and other outings all slowly disappeared. Amusements became more commercialised and sophisticated. Education increased literacy levels and expectations. The destruction of many activities was achieved as a result of the campaigns of moral reform bodies, such as the Christian Socialists, and Evangelicals, like Wilberforce and More. Their actions led to the suppression of such atavistic sports as bull and rat baiting; the end of public executions; restrictions on drinking hours; and the closure of annual fairs and pleasure gardens. The Methodist and temperance movements, however, were relatively weak in the capital, and few wholeheartedly embraced the more morally acceptable diversions of the church, physical exercise and good literature.

Changes in leisure activities brought substantial changes in London industry and employment. Thousands of new jobs were created, for example, in new industries, such as hotels, music halls and cinema, and, yet more, in vastly expanded newspaper and magazine publishing. At the same time, traditional London producers began to experience competition from the provinces as the costs of distance diminished and national brands grew up. The brewers were a case in point. Elsewhere, mechanisation and standardisation encouraged some activities to leave for cheaper locations – as occurred in printing. It is useful, therefore, to link the history of changes in leisure to changes in some of the industries associated with it.

Not all leisure activities are covered in this chapter and some of the things examined as leisure, such as religion, would not be classified as such by all. The most time-consuming non-work activity, however, was not religious observance but drinking, and this is considered first, both in terms of where and what was drunk and the changes experienced by London producers. After this, the hotel trade and eating out are examined. The demise of several gruesome or exuberant traditional pastimes, such as public hangings and fairs, follows and, then, the growth of the theatre, music hall and cinema. Culture and church are next, followed by the associated industries of piano- and organ-making. Finally, reading, publishing and printing are examined.

Drinking and brewing

The bane of eighteenth-century London had been gin – 'the mother's ruin'.[1] Gin had been introduced into London from Holland at the time of William III. Easy to make, free of tax and sold without licence, it soon became the capital's favourite drink and led to many early deaths. Concern over health slowly led to reform. As a result of these restrictions, consumption in the country as a whole fell from 13.5 million gallons in 1734 to 9 million gallons in 1743. Over time, tax on the spirit rose inexorably. Such was the success of the legislation that by 1794 Westminster contained only 957 gin retailers, as compared to an estimated 2,200 in 1750.[2]

Regulation had converted gin-making from a small, backroom operation spread throughout the metropolis into a highly concentrated business by the end of the eighteenth century, and London firms distilled most of the country's gin. Nineteenth-century production was dominated by four distillers: Seager Evans (1805) based at Millbank; Gilbeys, which opened its Clerkenwell gin distillery in 1872; Booth (1770); and James Burroughs (1863). That three of these firms were founded in the nineteenth century attests to the still profitable nature of the business. The drink slowly lost its adverse connotations and London had become synonymous with its production in a way the Scottish Highlands are for malt whisky. (A historical curiosity was the Lee Valley Distillery, which at Stratford annually produced 155,000 gallons of malt and 305,000 of grain whisky during the late nineteenth century, using water from the New River – but 'London' malt has not survived.)[3]

Though the gin panic was long past, people in the nineteenth century still drank prodigious amounts of alcohol. At the beginning of the century, thirty-four gallons of beer per head were drunk annually in England and Wales and, after a decline, consumption was at the same level again in 1876. According to Burnett's high estimates almost £3 per head of population was spent on beer in 1850.[4] Actual drinking patterns would have varied enormously between towns and social groups. But, whatever the precise figures for individual households, drink undoubtedly had a large impact on working-class budgets, with many spending a third to a half of their income on it.[5] This was one of the causes of poverty that so concerned reformers like Booth. Yet there were some rational reasons for the national love of pubs and beer. Pubs were usually warmer and more comfortable than many homes. Hard manual trades, like building and foundry work, required the consumption of large amounts of liquid at a time when good-quality water was hard to come by. Leisure alternatives were also limited.

Although in many central and working-class areas pubs were crowded together, compared to elsewhere in the country the drinking habits of Londoners may have been relatively moderate, if evidence from the end of the century is representative. In 1896, the capital had a pub density of 393 residents per pub, lower than any other major English city. In comparison, Leeds had a density of 345 per pub, Liverpool 279, Sheffield 176, and Manchester 168.[6] Some home brewing no doubt occurred, which should be added to the total consumption of drink; yet the amount produced in this way was probably relatively small because of the restrictions of urban living.

Londoners' seeming moderation was probably related to the comparative absence of occupations requiring great physical exertion, the larger middle class than in many industrial towns, and the relatively tight restrictions on drinking. It has been estimated that there were 1,810 pubs in the City and Westminster in the early part of the century,[7] giving a high ratio of 150 persons per pub, which seems to suggest that there was a significant decline in drinking establishments over the years. This decline may have arisen from the structural and regulatory factors already mentioned, but counter to this indicator of greater temperance was the growing diversity of places to drink – beer houses from 1830, more numerous clubs and places of entertainment and, finally, greater consumption at home by using the services of off-licences and wine and spirit merchants. There were also more alternative leisure pursuits in the capital, and expensive land might have discouraged the setting up of new drinking places.

National consumption of beer fluctuated considerably in the nineteenth century. It fell from the mid-1830s to the 1850s, and then rose again to record heights in the 1870s. From mid-century it was also overwhelmingly a man's drink, with women preferring tea or spirits.[8] From the 1870s peak, growth in England and Wales slowed, and in the 1900s demand actually fell, with consumption dropping in the ten years between 1899 and 1909 by 14 per cent.[9] Explanations for this decline include the appearance of alternative leisure activities, the rise of the temperance movement, and the migration of urban populations to relatively pub-free suburbs; the latter especially damaging for London demand. From 1900, sales were also affected by pressures on working-class living standards, increases in national taxation, and higher licence duties that fell disproportionately on the large, highly assessed, pubs common in the capital.[10]

Brewers and the tied system

In the early years of the century, brewing companies were some of the most successful, richest and most highly capitalised enterprises in the capital. Twelve large breweries accounted for approximately half of production in 1780, and for 85 per cent in 1830.[11] Scale economies were consequently important and growing. London brewers had been some of the first to use Watt's steam engines, and the leading firms were producing 2 million barrels a year at the end of the Napoleonic Wars, possibly a fifth of national output. Small firms also existed – there were ten times as many breweries below the top dozen for most of the period, spread throughout the metropolis.

Most breweries had a 'tied' retail trade, whereby pubs only sold one brewer's beers. This trend had developed in the mid-eighteenth century and, by 1830, almost half of London's pubs were tied houses. Publicans as a result could not play one brewery off against another and the brewers had assured outlets for their large-scale production facilities. Tying was achieved through the purchase of public house leases or, more commonly, by giving publicans loans for the purchase or improvement of their businesses in return for an agreement to sell only their beer. To become a publican was relatively easy. Taking into account the loans obtained from breweries in return for the exclusive sale of their products, in the 1880s a beer house could be acquired for £300 to £400 and a pub for £1,200. The returns, however, were often meagre and beer sales had to be high to cover the cost of borrowings, which encouraged premises to stay open so that landlords worked long hours. They also had strong incentives to adulterate beers in order to increase profits. The practice only ended after the passage of the 1872 Adulteration of Food, Drink and Drugs Act, which empowered local authorities to recruit public analysts, and the introduction by breweries of strength tests on all returned beers.[12]

Tying fundamentally affected the economics of brewing, because brewers' holdings of property and loans to publicans, rather than the value of their brewing production and distribution equipment, were the principal reasons why they were such highly capitalised enterprises. The tied system encouraged a proliferation of pubs, moreover, because any firm wishing to expand output had to open new ones. This, as well as drinking habits, may explain the extraordinary number of pubs by early twenty-first-century standards.

Data on tied houses are available for Whitbread from 1830 to 1875 and show that the vast majority (65–75 per cent) of its beer was sold through tied houses. Owned-house beer sales peaked at a fifth of the total in 1850 but declined rapidly after 1860. This fall-off in ownership occurred as a result of Whitbread putting greater emphasis on offering loans to publicans rather than owning outlets outright. By 1875, outlets tied by loans accounted for almost three-quarters of sales.[13] Whitbread's strategy of shifting from owned pubs to tying via loans probably reflects the greater incentives to sell beer that indebted pub owners had over salaried managers, plus a desire to reduce the capital the brewery had to invest in property in order to assure outlets for its drinks.

As well as in pubs, beer was also sold in beer houses, gentlemen's and working men's clubs, and off-licences. Beer houses were created by the

1830 Beer Houses Act, when the duty on beer was cut to encourage the poor to drink beer rather than gin, and this resulted nationally in 40,000 new drinking establishments within five years.[14] There was a distinct social geography of the different types of establishment. Beer houses, for example, sold only beer and were concentrated on the side streets of the poorer working-class districts. Public houses sold a wider range of alcohol and were found in better-off working-class areas, transport nodes and commercial districts. They were usually located in prominent positions, often on street corners and concentrated on main thoroughfares.

From the 1830s, the number of beer houses in London rose from around 1,200 to peak at 4,000 in 1870, while pubs grew from around 4,500 to over 6,000 over the same period. Expansion then stopped, and beer-house numbers fell from the 1870s, and pubs were on the decline from the 1900s. The faster growth of beer houses up to the 1870s presumably reflects the outward spread of working-class suburbs, as beer houses were far cheaper to set up than a pub.[15] An important cause of the decline in outlets was tightening regulation of drinking licences – encouraged by pressure from the growing temperance movement in the 1870s. As the number of licences fell, the value of each rose and pub prices rocketed as brewers competed with each other for outlets.[16]

Brewing in a changing market

The number of breweries per capita was greatest in the early part of the century; then over forty London breweries were closed from the 1830s to the 1850s, as profits declined with falling beer prices due to reduced demand and the extra competition induced by the Beer Houses Act. From 1850, as demand increased again, new firms entered and the range of beers brewed widened, so that the number of breweries in London by the 1880s had again risen to its 1830s level.[17] With around 110 breweries in the 1880s, the capital was supplied by local producers, and the number suggests that the costs of transporting beer within the metropolis were high, so that breweries had relatively small catchment areas.

Many breweries were located within easy reach of the river. Movement by water cheapened the transport of raw materials (including coal) and the distribution of the finished product. Hops were brought in from Kent and malt came from Hertfordshire – and from East Anglia after railways reduced the cost of transport. Southwark was the centre of the buying, selling and storage of hops, and a Hop Exchange was opened in Southwark Street in 1866. Brewery workforces were small, predominantly male and relatively highly paid. In 1889, one of the biggest brewers, Trumans, employed only 400 workers and the Red Lion brewery 200.[18]

The types of beer produced changed over time as the result of changes in drinking habits and technology. At the start of the century the large brewers – Barclay Perkins, Trumans, Whitbread, Reids, and Calvert and Hoare – mainly brewed strong porter beer. Tastes then changed towards less strong beer, so that from the 1820s there was increased consumption of mild ale and, from the 1850s, pale ale. The London porter brewers responded only slowly to these market-driven changes. Well-established, monopolistic and complacent, they were controlled by relatively large numbers of partners. This ownership pattern made innovative management difficult. Active partners tended to manage particular aspects of the business – brewing, public house management, accounting, distribution, etc. – so that change which altered internal organisational structures was hard to achieve.[19] Varying partners' shares of the issued capital was also difficult, as was any development that would disturb market agreements with other producers. They also faced technical problems that discouraged a switch from porter to ale brewing. The capital's water supply, in particular, with its high carbonate and low sulphur content, was far from perfect for ale brewing, producing a beer with relatively poor taste and colour. The brewers' problems, however, were ameliorated by growth in the overall level of beer demand after 1850, so that an absolute decline in porter output only occurred in the 1870s.

London's traditional brewers were not averse to resorting to cartels to limit competition, nor to allowing publicans to adulterate their products to maintain profitability and the value of pub leases. Two Parliamentary inquiries, in 1850 and 1853–4, noted that the London brewers had an agreement to sell barrels of beer at a uniform price. The brewers also made no attempt to ensure that publicans did not adulterate their products, but rather created incentives for them to do so. Agitation for better-quality beer was high in the 1850s, both in the media and in politics. Investors recognised an opportunity: in 1851, for example, the Metropolitan Brewing Company was set up with a substantial capital of £50,000 'to supply the public with genuine beer'.[20] Tighter regulation from the 1870s, however, greatly curtailed adulteration.

Eventually, the porter brewers re-equipped and began to brew ale in significant quantities. The delay, however, led to the growth of the London ale brewers: Courage, Charrington, Boss and Allsop, and Mann, Crossman and Paulin. Between 1830 and 1880, Courage, for example, increased its annual output from 10,000 to 250,000 barrels. These new brewers produced their own ale in London but, along with some porter houses, they began to buy provincial ale, take over country breweries and open their own pale ale breweries outside the capital to serve their London outlets. By doing so, they took advantage of fast rail transport and sidestepped the problems of water quality in London. In the early 1870s, three London firms – Trumans, Charrington, and Mann, Crossman and Paulin – all opened breweries in Burton-upon-Trent.

Despite these strategic moves, ale brewers in Edinburgh, Dublin, Burton-upon-Trent and elsewhere gained a foothold in the London market; Lacons of Great Yarmouth, for example, increased its sales in the capital from 43,000 barrels in 1858 to 100,000 barrels in 1871. The optimal size of breweries was becoming greater, following scientific discoveries in the

1870s, and this encouraged firms to seek out more distant markets. The new technologies made it possible to transport good-quality beer over considerable distances and improvements in rail freight made such distances feasible. As a sign of the times, when St Pancras Station was built in the 1870s its basement was purposely-designed to handle thousands of beer barrels from Burton. The London beer market was being opened up to national competition, with consequent effects for local producers, parallel to developments occurring in the retailing of general foodstuffs and consumer durables. The slow response of some of the traditional metropolitan producers to their changing market place disadvantaged them. Consequently, by 1880 metropolitan producers brewed only two-thirds of the beer consumed in the capital, as opposed to four-fifths in 1830.[21]

The new brewing environment persuaded more firms to go public and induced a wave of brewery amalgamations. In 1860, only six breweries had their shares quoted on the London Stock Exchange; by 1885 they had risen to eighteen – but after that many converted, so that by 1906 over 300 brewers were listed.[22] Many London breweries joined in this switch from partnerships to joint stock, limited liability status. The original partners generally kept control of the new companies through extensive equity ownership. When the Reid brewery was floated, for example, its ordinary shares were completely taken up by the original partners, but the public took up half of the company's £2 million of capital through allocations of 5 per cent preference and mortgage debenture stock. Between 1890 and 1899, £86 million of brewery debentures and preference shares were issued.[23] Brewery owners, thus, could extend their capital base significantly and limit their financial exposure, whilst retaining control. Flotation also made mergers more easy as the partners of the old independent businesses could be compensated with newly issued shares. Some of the major London breweries took advantage of their new financial status to merge with each other and provincial concerns: Watney, Combe, Reid was one of the biggest mergers with £15 million worth of securities issued in the business in 1898 – the combination had been a stepwise process with Watney and Combe linking together earlier in the late 1880s.[24]

Flush with funds and keen to guarantee outlets for their beers, brewers intensified their national control over pubs through the tied system, so that tied premises increased from 70 per cent of all licences in 1886 to 95 per cent by 1913.[25] London was no exception. Taking advantage of contemporarily low interest rates, brewers began to purchase the leaseholds of free public houses, particularly those of high-class businesses unlikely to be included in any future legislation to close down poor-quality establishments. From 1895 to 1902, leaseholds were purchased at a rate of 500 per year; so that by 1907 Whitbread, for example, owned £2 million worth of properties, as compared to only £26,000 in 1886.[26] Although these acquisitions helped to protect individual brewers' markets, they did little to improve the sector's general prosperity. Many of the pub businesses bought were overvalued and the breweries faced high charges on the debenture and preference stock issued to finance their purchases.

Traditional draught producers were also threatened by bottling. Technical innovations improved the quality of beer in bottles, and its cost fell in the 1890s and 1900s after the introduction from the United States of chilling, filtering, carbonisation and pasteurisation techniques and the development of bottle making, washing, corking and labelling machines. Some, mainly non-London, brewers – Burton-based Bass and Worthington and, most successfully, Irish-based Guinness – used these new bottling technologies to develop nationally known, branded bottled beers, shunning the traditional route of expanding pub ownership. They succeeded in making significant inroads into the beer market and stimulated the propensity to drink at home.

The earliest and most enthusiastic London bottler was Whitbread and much of its late-century success was due to this strategy. It began bottling in 1869 and, by 1912, sold as much as 440,000 bottles a year, 45 per cent of its output. Other London brewers were more wary; the market was highly competitive, off-licences were not 'tied' to particular breweries, and production was less profitable than the cask trade. Nevertheless, by 1903, a further seven London brewers were producing bottled beer, with four more entering the market the year after. The actual bottling was generally undertaken by independent firms with exclusive agreements with brewers. By far the largest was M. B. Foster and Sons of Woolwich and Marylebone, which had links with Bass, among others, and claimed to be the largest bottler in the world.[27]

Overall, the fortunes of the London breweries varied depending on the strategies they adopted. The new ale-producing interloper, Mann, Crossman and Paulin, soon matched the output of the traditional breweries, and, along with Whitbread, enjoyed meteoric growth in the 1890s and 1900s. In contrast, Trumans' period of steady growth was from 1830 to 1870, as the adjacent East End expanded – with beer production falling sharply after the mid-1870s.[28] Overall, the history of the nineteenth-century London brewers is one in which institutional structures are important, because ownership structures and cartels left the traditional firms flat-footed when changing technology and tastes altered market conditions.

The changing role of pubs

At the start of the century pubs had an important economic function. The London coaching inns, clustered in Borough High Street, Bishopsgate and Piccadilly, were the equivalent of railway termini – selling coach tickets, serving passenger needs and stabling coaching horses. Other pubs provided public meeting places. Government *laissez-faire* and religious control of education meant that few public buildings or schools were available for meetings. Consequently, a whole host of organisations met in pubs, including friendly societies, building clubs and trade unions. From the 1820s, many pubs, known as singing saloons, also offered musical and theatrical entertainment, provided at first by customers and later by professionals.

By the end of the century, however, pubs were largely places of recreation. Coaching inns disappeared with the coming of railways and, in new central commercial areas, many pubs had switched to serving the commuter market. Central London hostelries tending to straddle the traditional east–west main routes and to a lesser extent the expanding north–south ones. Their meeting-place and entertainment functions declined in importance for several reasons. Voluntary bodies increasingly provided places where organisations could meet; whilst singing saloons were damaged by the rise of the music hall and tighter regulations.

Over the period, both the layout and the social roles of pubs changed. In the 1830s, bars began to appear in place of the previous table service, and areas were created in front of bars where customers could freely move around. In the 1860s, pubs were enlarged and made more sumptuous, and new bars were introduced to separate different types of customer. A higher standard of finish encouraged greater middle-class use by both sexes during the 1880s and 1890s.

Gentlemen's and working men's clubs

Exclusivity and choice of drinking acquaintances led to specialist drinking and entertainment establishments for different social strata. Gentlemen's clubs catered for the upper-class male, and during the century changed from subscription establishments to clubs owned and run by the members themselves. Many were long-established, such as Whites and Boodles, but most – around forty – opened during the course of the century. Examples include the Union (1805), which in 1824 built an £18,000 clubhouse in Trafalgar Square and had a membership of 800; and the United (1815), the second military club after the Guards, which had a membership of 1,400 by 1819 and a Smirke-designed clubhouse in Charles Street. Also in Charles Street, off of Berkeley Square, was the Portland – devoted to cards with a small exclusive membership of 100.[29]

The gentlemen's clubs' working-class equivalent, the working men's club, appeared at mid-century. Their role was greatest in industrial Lancashire and Yorkshire, but London had the third largest number.[30] By the 1880s and 1890s, most had acquired a beer licence and were owned and operated by their members. Offering unadulterated cheap beer, music hall-type entertainment, dancing and billiards, they greatly increased their membership, and in some places contributed to the fall in pub numbers.

Wine merchants

Wine merchanting was a long-established London trade serving the consumption habits of the middle class and wealthy, and Britain had been the world's major wine market outside of the wine-making regions for a long time. During the Napoleonic Wars, London merchants prospered as French ones were excluded by an embargo on French imports. Further stimulus came in the 1830s, because many alehouses reacted to competition from new beer houses by diversifying into wines and spirits and becoming taverns. According to the *London Post Office Directory*, the capital in 1851 contained 800 wine merchants.[31]

Growth was fastest in the 1860s and 1870s as the move to free trade led to sharp cuts in the import duty on wine. The government also passed the Single Bottle Act which enabled any shopkeeper to obtain a licence for the sale of wine, and permitted owners of eating houses to take out an annually renewable licence that allowed wine to be consumed on their premises.

The main wine merchants reacted faster and more successfully to market change than did most of the London brewers. Each had its own strategy, influenced by its initial market position, and they ended up with different outcomes. Two of the largest were Bishop and Gilbey – each had a strategy of expanding the spatial area over which their businesses operated and moving upstream into drinks production.

As well as acting as merchants, the old-established Bishop family also produced Stone's Original Ginger Wine. The company's sales of bought and manufactured wine more than doubled from 190,000 gallons in 1816/17 to 400,000 gallons in 1848, but then fell sharply to less than 160,000 gallons in 1869, due to the competition from cheaper wines. To diversify, the firm in the 1880s began to blend its own whisky and to distil its own gin. It adopted the brewers' strategy of buying public houses to minimise competition.[32]

Gilbey, in contrast, only began to sell wine in 1857 from premises in the West End – an operation set up by two young brothers back from the Crimea. It found a market gap by initially concentrating on cheap, new-quality South African vintages which benefited from lower colonial import duties. Demand proved so great that by the end of its first year the company had 20,000 customers and had to move premises. Tax reductions in the early 1860s made traditional wine-producing areas more competitive and the firm began to deal in French wines. It passed all of the reduction of duty on to customers, unlike its competitors, and with growing sales it took over the Pantheon (a large ex-theatre turned art gallery) in Oxford Street. Innovative direct links were made with wine and cork growers. It moved its bottling, storage and distribution facilities to Camden Town to take advantage of lower rents and the good transport links by rail and canal to the port and the rest of the country. By 1889, it had 2,510 agents spread throughout the UK. Its huge facilities dominated Camden Town. Like the Bishop family, Gilbey diversified into blending whiskies and distilling gin, and the Roundhouse in Camden became a bonded warehouse where spirits were matured in fifteen giant vats and bottled, in an early example of re-using redundant railway buildings. In 1875 Gilbey bought its own 470-acre Bordeaux chateau and, in 1887, began the take-over of three Scottish distilleries, which together produced over 300,000 gallons of whisky.[33]

Off-licences

Off-licences were largely found in middle-class areas and again prospered at the end of the century. Suburban land sale and lease contracts often precluded the building of pubs, and the middle class, aware of the relationship between temperance and respectability and with warm comfortable homes, preferred to drink in private.

Several wine merchants set up chains of off-licences or sold to middle men, as illustrated by the examples of Bishop and Gilbey above. Others were stimulated to enter the sector as suburban London spread out. The Victoria Wine Co., for example, sold its wines through its own string of retail off-licences, which additionally dealt in spirits, coffee, beer and mineral waters. By 1879, the company owned sixty-three shops in London and others in Bristol, Brighton and elsewhere, and had a large cellar and bottling plant in London, which in 1880 processed almost 440,000 bottles of wine and spirits.[34] It is an example of a multiple spreading out from a London base.

Hotels

Hotels represent a nearly new nineteenth-century industry at which London excelled. Most innovations were copied from abroad – especially from France in terms of style and cuisine and from the USA in terms of organisation, facilities and scale. The industry was also an important employer with the larger hotels having hundreds of staff.

In the late eighteenth century, visitors to London stayed in rooms in private lodging houses rented by the day, week or month, or in the stagecoach inns concentrated in the City, Holborn and Southwark. Hotels only began to appear in the 1800s, largely opened by French chefs, who had fled to England after the French Revolution, or by retired butlers, who understood the tastes and ways of the wealthy. In 1803, for example, the French chef Grillion opened a hotel he named after himself in Albermarle Street, which was later patronised by Louis XVIII on a visit in 1814. These hotels catered for a largely male clientele and, unlike the coaching inns, had no public dining rooms. They prospered with the rise in the number of travellers after the expansion of rapid and cheap stagecoach travel. Their success was encouraged by the culinary skills of some of the owners and a policy of charging high prices. In 1814, for instance, the Pulteney charged the Grand Duchess of Russia £210 for just one week's stay.[35]

The coaching inns were clustered on the main approach roads into the city. In 1799, at least a dozen coaching inns with courtyards existed, for example, on the east side of Borough High Street, south of London Bridge. After the advent of rail travel, they lost a large proportion of their clientele. Having reinvested little of their profits in improvements in the quality of their accommodation, they found it difficult to attract new custom. Many went down-market, and others folded.

The first two railway hotels were built at Euston by the London and Birmingham Railway at a cost of £55,000. The Victoria (not to be confused with the later railway station of the same name), west of the station, was completed in 1839 and offered sleeping accommodation plus an unlicensed coffee house. The Adelaide, opened a year later, served as a hotel-cum-club. Both were successful, earning a return on capital of 6 per cent, but, at first, they were not imitated by other railway companies.[36] The needs of railway passengers were being met by others and neither shareholders nor Parliament supported the diversification of railway company interests. It was thus fifteen years before the next railway hotels were constructed – by the Great Northern and Great Western Railways at their main London terminals, King's Cross and Paddington respectively. These cost £35,000 and £60,000 and were again a great success, encouraging yet others to enter the field. These early establishments were quite stark but, by the 1860s, newly built stations came complete with splendid hotels – in 1861 the Grosvenor at Victoria; in 1865 the Charing Cross Hotel, with a mock medieval cross in its forecourt; in 1867 the Cannon Street Hotel, larger than that at Charing Cross; and, in 1872, the 250-roomed Midland Grand at St Pancras. The latter was regarded as one of the most sumptuous hotels of its day, and cost £438,000.[37] It boasted hydraulic lifts, a grand gothic staircase and innovative fireproofing, though water was still taken by hand to the rooms and suites. The best architects were used for these later hotels. The tradition was followed when the Holborn Viaduct Hotel opened in 1877; the Great Eastern at Liverpool Street in 1884; and the Great Central, incongruously large, in front of Marylebone in 1899. Yet, by the turn of the century, the railway hotel boom was well and truly over. The neighbourhoods of the railway termini were becoming increasingly seedy, and clients searched for more sumptuous accommodation in the West End.

The Langham (1865) in Portland Place started a new style in grand hotels. It cost £300,000 with 600 rooms and private suites and expensive furnishings.[38] The Prince of Wales opened it in a great extravaganza and the hotel remained the height of fashion until after the First World War (it was reopened as a hotel in the 1990s). The Savoy was opened in 1889, and introduced even greater luxury. Its founder, D'Oyly Carte (of Gilbert and Sullivan fame), hired as its manager Europe's best hotelier, Cesar Ritz, a reflection of the importance to grand hotels of contacts and reputation in the attraction of a clientele. D'Oyly Carte later set up a network of similar hotels, acquiring and upgrading Claridge's in 1895 and opening the Coburg (now Connaught) in 1896. Ritz in 1905 opened his own hotel, the Carlton in Haymarket, and a further hotel named after him was built to his own specifications by the Blackpool Building and Vendor Company in Piccadilly in 1906;[39] this, incidentally, was London's first major steel-framed building. At the turn of the century, the splendid Russell and Imperial Hotels of identical design were opened in Russell Square; with the latter scandalously demolished in the 1960s.

In the second half of the century, therefore, the number of hotels multiplied rapidly, largely because of the 1862 Companies Act and the adoption by companies of limited liability status, which encouraged investment. Many small hotels emerged, as well as the larger ones discussed above. Hotel owners also began to follow their counterparts in America by providing better and extended services. The Savoy was the first 'modern' hotel. It contained seventy bathrooms compared with its nearest rival's four; provided 24-hour service; and had electric lighting and lifts. Its success led to the construction of others, including – as well as the already mentioned Ritz, Russell and Imperial – the Piccadilly (1908), the Hyde Park (1908), and the Goring (1910) in Victoria. Unfortunately, just as many of these were opening their doors to their first guests, the inflation generated by the Boer War caused the demand for accommodation to fall. In addition, London had by this time far too many hotels. In the years before the First World War, therefore, the sector experienced severe economic difficulties and even the larger establishments were forced to cut prices and offer new services to attract custom. The Ritz, for example, in 1906–8 made a loss of £50,000.[40]

Eating out

At the start of the century, meals could be obtained in coaching inns, hotels, chop houses and coffee houses. The West End coffee houses were the forerunners of the gentlemen's clubs and, in 1760, they numbered over 500, of which the aforementioned Whites in St James Street, plus the Grecian and the Cocoa Tree, were famous.[41] Pubs played their part by providing cooked vegetables and their customers added meat bought from local butchers and given to the pub's staff to cook.

All these ways of eating, however, were deemed unsuitable for middle-class women, who generally ate at home. This situation changed in the 1860s with the arrival of the better railway hotels, the dining rooms of which welcomed women, and later with the appearance of restaurants such as the Holborn, the Criterion and the Gaiety. Women were also welcome in tea and coffee shops. These began to appear in the 1870s, when several temperance societies opened them. By 1879, the capital contained 100 such establishments, many of which offered food and entertainment. Often mismanaged and of poor quality, most had relatively short life spans.

The temperance societies' role in the serving of tea was soon followed by commercial companies. One of the first was the Aerated Bread Co., which opened a tea and snack café in 1884. (The company's once large bakery in Camden is now the site of a Sainsbury superstore.) They were spread throughout suburban London. The success of the ABC cafés, which in 1893 numbered over sixty, led to the establishment of Pearce's Refreshment Rooms, catering for low-income Londoners; Lockharts, which in 1893 operated fifty coffee rooms; and a small number of tea shops run by Express Dairies.[42]

The style, scale and operation of such cafés were then revolutionised by the business methods of J. Lyons. With capital of £120,000, he opened his first establishment in 1894 on the south side of Piccadilly and it was soon followed by others. They served light refreshments and meals from early morning until late at night, and were largely patronised by lower middle-class office workers during the day and cinema and theatre-goers in the evening. In 1904, the firm also opened a 'popular café', which offered cheap table d'hôte dinners and became the forerunner of the Lyons' Corner House, the first of which opened in 1909 on the corner of Coventry Street and Rupert Street and seated 2,000.[43] The prestige of the famous central London location was then used to spread Lyons' establishments throughout the country.

Spectacles: hangings, fairs and pleasure gardens

Londoners' main sources of entertainment in the first half of the century were the performing arts, public hangings – which in the 1840s could draw crowds of 40,000 to Newgate[44] – fairs and pleasure gardens. The performing arts were transformed by the growth of concert halls, theatres, music halls and art galleries, which turned them into major businesses and organisations. The other three disappeared. Public hangings were abolished in 1868 – following animal fights and torturing into obscurity. Fairs were similarly regulated out of existence and pleasure gardens could not compete with the dynamics of urban change.

Fairs

There were three types of fair: annual carnivals, seasonal fairs and spontaneous events, which celebrated special occasions, such as the freezing of the Thames, royal jubilees, etc. Annual carnivals, and May and autumn fairs took place at their old historic locations. Their original function was not entertainment but the selling of labour and produce – labourers were still being hired at fairs in metropolitan Essex even in the 1830s. Increasingly they began to concentrate on entertainment alone and incurred the wrath of the authorities as a result. In 1830–4, almost half of Bartholomew fair was given over to exhibitions, animal and human freak shows, plays and pantomimes, agility displays and waxworks.

Attendances were high – in 1843, 200,000 visited Stepney fair – but the unruliness of many of the activities and occasional bouts of drunken rioting attracted the attention of social reformers. Pressure was placed on magistrates and few remained after the suppression of the prestigious Bartholomew and Greenwich fairs by the City Corporation in 1857.[45]

Pleasure gardens

Many of the attractions offered by fairs could also be found in the pleasure gardens that had ringed the city for many generations.[46] Their location shifted as the city expanded and the land on which they sat became too valuable, but as an entertainment form they survived well into the nineteenth century. In return for an entry fee, visitors to privately owned pleasure gardens were able to admire the plants and flowers, watch fireworks, juggling displays and mock tournaments, or take part in boat races, pigeon shooting matches and other diversions. In 1786, 61,000 people were said to have attended a celebration in fancy dress at Vauxhall Pleasure Gardens, including the Prince of Wales; and even in the 1850s attendances of 27,000 people a day were not uncommon.[47] (Vauxhall Gardens lay to the south of Black Prince Road, SE1; most of the site was redeveloped by the LCC in the 1950s as the Vauxhall Gardens Estate.) Though extremely popular at their height, pleasure gardens gradually disappeared as better entertainments grew and their land was sold for residential development.

Their closest successors were the re-sited Crystal Palace, moved to Sydenham after the 1851 Great Exhibition as the centre-piece of a great amusement park, and the Alexander Palace opened at Muswell Hill in 1873 as a rival. Housed in a 220-acre park and based on an earlier exhibition's buildings, the latter failed to match the success of its southern rival.[48] Both, like the earlier pleasure gardens, were set up on the then suburban fringe, where land was cheap. Yet their scale and the permanence of their buildings were far greater than their forebears, and the entertainments offered in them were more regularised, cultural and 'family-oriented' – befitting the changed moral climate. To enable large crowds to attend events, such as Crystal Palace's famous firework displays, dedicated rail lines and terminals were built.

London suburban pursuits were to an extent superseded by the seaside excursion. Cheap railway fares, the 1871 Bank Holiday Act, and Saturday half-days allowed many of the working class to go on day excursions; and the middle class and artisans started to have week-long holidays at the seaside. In response, a range of resorts developed on the south coast and package holiday organisations were established, such as those of Frames and Sir Henry Lunn.[49]

Theatres, music halls and cinemas

Theatres

At the start of the nineteenth century, dramatic theatre was theoretically restricted to Covent Garden and the Theatre Royal, Drury Lane: the only two theatres that possessed royal letters of patent permitting the presentation of plays. In reality, the numerous theatres distributed around the West End and on the Surrey side of the Thames circumvented the regulation by presenting 'illegitimate dramas' – light comedies, burlesques and melodramas – and, in 1843, the Theatre Regulation Act abolished the monopoly.

The ownership of theatres and the presentation of plays were separate activities, as is still commonly the case today. Theatre owners rented their auditoriums to managers, who put on a play or a series of plays with the financial backing of 'angels', that is, private investors. The first great period of theatre building occurred from the 1820s to the 1840s and was particularly concentrated in the City and East End. The East End contained six theatres offering 17,600 seats per night, around a third of the then total London capacity. Theatre construction then halted for almost thirty years, largely due to economic depression and oversupply, only reviving in the late 1860s. Later building was concentrated in the West End, such as along the new Shaftesbury Avenue where six new theatres were built between 1888 and 1907, and the 'Theatre District' came into being. By 1911, the capital possessed fifty-four theatres, twelve more than in 1843, with a total seating capacity of almost 67,000.[50]

In 1800, theatre managers were generally businessmen, but as the century progressed they were increasingly former actors. These actor-managers would often appear in the plays they produced and, to build up a faithful audience, specialised in a particular type of play. A good example, in the early 1900s, was the Lyceum under the management of Henry Irving.

The number of actors retained by theatre companies was large, particularly before the 1860s when most theatres operated a repertory system, presenting a different play each night or each week. The rise of the middle class and the provincial theatre-goer allowed managers to introduce long runs of a single play and to reduce company sizes, though the fashion for crowd scenes and the practice until the 1880s of writing tickets out by hand caused staff numbers to remain high. Costs were recouped from ticket sales, the renting of bars and other refreshment areas to outside contractors, cloakroom fees, the sale of playbills and, from the 1870s, programmes. After falling in the first half of the century, ticket prices rose. Traditional practices, such as the half-price ticket (which permitted admittance at half price at the end of the first act and from 1825 after 9 p.m.) were generally phased out.[51]

Prices varied considerably depending on the location of the theatre. In 1873, ten, and, in 1879, thirteen, West End theatres charged at least 10s for a stall seat; while the Britannia, the East London and the Pavilion in the East End sold 1s stall seats. The financial viability of West End theatres in the last quarter of the century was so good that it encouraged more building and the gradual demise of theatres elsewhere.[52] The pull of a West End location highlighted agglomeration benefits – steady audiences for long runs could be achieved there, the pool of acting talent and behind-scenes staff was greatest, people could be sped home easily on the new metropolitan transport systems, and it was fashionable to go out in the West End – and the option, at least as a treat, was opening to an ever-wider proportion of the city's population and its visitors.

Music halls

More popular than the high-brow theatre was the music hall, which developed after the 1850s from the singing saloon and song and supper rooms. The first hall, the 1,700-seat Canterbury in Lambeth, was built in 1852 by Charles Morton. Shortly afterwards he opened a second hall, and in 1861 the Oxford in Oxford Street. The success of these ventures brought others into the sector. In 1860, the 3,500-seat Alhambra, Leicester Square, the largest hall in the country, opened its doors. By 1866, the capital contained 33 halls, with an average capacity of 1,500. Growth was then more subdued until the mid-1880s, when the opening of the restyled London Pavilion inaugurated a period of de luxe halls or variety theatres. Production facilities became more elaborate and the open-plan nature of the earlier auditoriums gave way to fixed stall seating and more pronounced audience segregation.[53]

Entry costs to the sector were relatively high. The average capitalisation of halls in 1866 was £10,000, most of which was raised privately.[54] Running costs were similarly heavy and increased throughout the century, due to a rise in artiste salaries, greater sophistication and scale in the staging of acts, and an increase in the number of performers on each programme. Expenses were recouped partly from takings at the door, but largely from 'wet money' – sales of drinks and refreshments. Audiences were at first largely lower middle/working-class males attracted as much by the availability of drink as by the entertainment.

Music halls, in general, were viewed with suspicion and distaste by the middle classes and reformers tried to have them closed down. From 1889 the LCC regulated the content of shows, purging much of the material regarded as indecent; restricted the sale of alcohol; and banned prostitutes from the halls. This resulted in more middle-class and female patronage. At the same time, halls began to be acquired by large groups, in particular Moss Empires, which owned the Hippodrome, and Oswald Stoll, the operators of the Coliseum (now home to the English National Opera).

Despite the large size of many of their auditoriums, music halls were less numerous in London than elsewhere. In 1868, for example, the capital possessed just 10 per cent of all UK halls.[55] Unlike theatres, music halls were more widely spread through working-class districts, though they were still concentrated in the West End.[56]

Cinemas

First shown in 1896 at Regent Street Polytechnic, moving pictures were initially added to the end of music hall shows. The first cinemas appeared in the early 1900s in large converted buildings – including a former workhouse in Upton Park, an empty chapel in Tolmers Street (which survived as a cinema until the 1970s), and a closed-down skating rink in Camden Town. Later safety and licensing requirements forced many of the converted cinemas to close and to be replaced by purpose-built auditoriums. One of the earliest purpose-built cinemas was the Electric in Islington, opened in 1908. This was followed by the 1909 Finsbury Park Cinematograph Theatre, and, among others, the Electric, Portobello Road, and Brixton's Electric Pavilion and Cinematograph Theatre (now part of the Ritzy).[57]

Cinemas were introduced into the capital far more rapidly than elsewhere in the country and it was almost immediately the centre of the British film industry. By 1911, London possessed a total of 94 cinemas with an average seating capacity of 590.[58] By 1913, the metropolis contained 497 buildings showing films, at suburban as well as central locations, as compared to only 90 in Manchester and 40 in Birmingham. Most of the cinemas were owned by individuals, though a significant number were part of chains. The most important chain owner was Montagu Alexander Kyle, who before going bankrupt in 1914 built three cinemas in 1909, a further eight in 1910 and another five in 1911, all of which were in London.[59]

Film-making

Film-making developed from 1895 when the Hatton Garden electrical engineer Robert W. Paul built the country's first moving picture camera, taking advantage of Edison's failure to patent his discovery in Britain, and began to produce short movies and newsreels.[60] The industry was at first located in and around Charing Cross Road, especially in Cecil Court, known as 'Flicker Alley'. The area was close to the centre of London, the source of news; the theatre district and its set designers, directors and actors; the leading theatrical agents; and the larger music halls, which showed films as part of their variety bills. Needing space, the studios migrated to the suburbs – often to converted buildings (including an ex-roller-skating rink, a power station and a dance hall) to cheapen costs. Some were purpose-built, as with the French Gaumont Company's new studios at Lime Grove, Shepherd's Bush; but central offices and distribution centres remained firmly wedded to the West End in a classic suburban/city centre separation of operating functions. The industry, however, failed to have the domestic impact of producers in France, Germany and the USA. In 1910, 36 per cent of films shown in London were French and another 25 per cent American; and the situation deteriorated for the home film-makers to the extent that, by 1926, only 5 per cent of cinema programmes were British (that is London) made, with most of the rest by now American in origin.[61]

Museum and church attendance

The nineteenth century was the time when personal improvement through cultivated leisure was promoted as a worthwhile pastime. This trend led to the construction, in central, north and west London, of many new museums, art galleries and concert halls. Spatial concentration can again be seen as museums and galleries were centred on the West End and the new Kensington site opened up after the 1851 Great Exhibition. Private galleries and agencies tended to cluster around particular streets in the West End, especially in Mayfair, near to their affluent clientele. In addition, a huge Royal Aquarium opposite Westminster Abbey was opened in 1876, at a cost of £200,000, as an unsuccessful private venture (it was sold to the Methodists for the building of their Central Hall in 1903); and, more successfully, London Zoo in Regent's Park was set up, opening in 1828.[62]

The scale of public cultural building was far greater than it was in the twentieth century, and it helped to encourage the drift of fashion and social activity westwards. Funding for these enterprises was a mixture of public and private donations and profit-seeking investment. For example, royal initiative after the 1851 Exhibition, aided by Parliamentary funding, led to eighty acres of land being purchased south of Hyde Park for museums, concert halls, colleges and premises for learned societies – from which came the Albert Hall and the South Kensington museum quarter. Houses were developed on part of the site to help fund the public buildings.

A further activity encouraged by moral reform bodies was church attendance. At mid-century, 37 per cent of Londoners attended the Sunday services of one of the city's 1,097 places of worship – 57 per cent being Church of England services and a further quarter Presbyterian, Baptist or Independent ones.[63] Many people were involved in the numerous dramatic societies, sewing circles, sports clubs and mutual improvement societies run by churches during the week. Church attendance, however, was far lower than elsewhere in the UK. In the South-East and North Midlands, for example, 60 per cent and 63 per cent respectively of the population went to a Sunday service. There were also far higher attendances at all denominations' churches in the outer middle-class suburbs than in the inner working-class areas of the capital.[64]

Church building and 'restoration' to contemporary taste were big business in a city with so many central churches, expanding middle-class suburbs rich in donations, and poorer districts with many souls that benefactors felt needed to be saved. Church building helped to create the reputations of many aspiring architects, and kept builders, organ makers and others in business. The first surge of funding in the nineteenth century came from Parliament as thanksgiving for the outcome of the Napoleonic Wars – £1.5 million was spent on 38 new London churches between 1818 and 1828. A further impetus occurred with the setting up of the Metropolitan New Churches Fund in 1834 – leading to 78 new churches. Overall, between the 1830s and 1850s, the Bishop of London consecrated almost 200 new churches. A new Bishop of London's fund started in 1863, with royal patronage, raised another £1 million to contribute to the costs of a further 41 churches.

The other denominations added their share – though generally on a less grand scale. Parsimony was not always the case: the Methodists' imposing Central Hall in Westminster could seat 2,700 and was completed in 1911. Somewhat earlier, after a lengthy period of fund gathering and planning, the Catholic Church finally had a huge new London base, Westminster Cathedral, built over 300 years after the Reformation and completed in 1903 on the site of a women's prison, whose foundations helped to save on costs. Its interior was left unfinished on grounds of economy.[65] The end was nigh for this remarkable period of church building and restoration.

Churches were also demolished, with population movements and, particularly, the rebuilding of the City. Between 1841 and 1908, the greatest period of change, twenty churches disappeared under City rebuilding.[66]

Piano and organ manufacture

If no nineteenth-century suburb was complete without a church or two, resplendent with the massed pipes of a booming organ, then no middle-class residence was a home without a piano. Many places of entertainment also needed musical instruments. London was the major production centre for pianos and organs in the nineteenth century, and for many other instruments. By the 1850s, there were over 200 piano-makers.[67]

Pianos and organs are bulky, so it made sense to locate in the largest market to minimise transport costs. As the cultural centre of the country, home to a large middle class and experiencing substantial suburban church building, London assured a high metropolitan local demand for both instruments. Since they were made of wood, moreover, the skills used in the capital's large furniture industry were of advantage as well, and during slack periods workers could turn to cabinet making when they were laid off, especially during spring and summer when sales were slow.

Firms set up purpose-built plants and moved pianos around them on assembly-line principles. The moving parts of instruments were not as bulky as the frames, nor were the pipes with organs, so over time they were increasingly out-sourced. Most manufacturers produced only the back, case and sounding board of the piano, buying the actions – keys, pedals, rollers, etc. – from local and foreign manufacturers, and pipes from London and German producers. London firms also faced competition from larger rivals in France, Germany and, later, the USA.

Pianos were made by a few, well-known, companies producing high-quality instruments, with cheaper ones made by a large number of small, often one-person, firms. Materials were also given to artisans who completed the job for a fixed price on the manufacturer's own premises, with the help of assistants whom they employed themselves. This system and the specialist skills needed encouraged clustering of firms and small workshops. Camden Town, with its excellent canal and rail links, was an important centre for piano works, with over ten large establishments there at the turn of the century; and other producers were spread eastwards along the Regent's Canal and north into Kentish Town. By 1911, there were still 133 piano firms in London – and only three elsewhere in the country – but the industry was being decimated by German competition.[68] The backward-looking, craft-based production methods of metropolitan producers could not keep up with the better-quality, more mechanised producers overseas, selling up-to-date instruments in volumes that enabled them to reap substantial economies of scale.

The history of the largest London piano producer, Broadwoods, illustrates that locational advantage could not keep at bay either poor judgement or bad luck. In the mid-1830s, it was producing over 3,000 instruments a year at two factories – one of which was large, consisting of four three-storey buildings with a workshop over half a mile in length. Its sales, however, collapsed in the late 1840s, largely due to the emergence of French piano makers, led by Evards of London and Paris, who produced more fashionable instruments. (Note that the Paris firm set up a subsidiary in London, presumably to take advantage of the same locational benefits as the domestic producers.) In 1856 the main Westminster factory burnt down and, although it was rebuilt, the firm never recovered as it failed to switch to the high-quality upright piano that became the market leader.[69]

Growth in organ building was particularly strong in the 1860s, encouraged by the construction of new churches. In 1807, there were thirty organ builders, mostly small craft enterprises; by 1857, the number had grown to forty-six; and it then more than doubled to ninety-six in 1862. One of the most important London organ manufacturers was the Bishop family. Their company was established in 1807 and innovated by developing the composition pedal, the flute-like clarabella stop and the concussion bellows. The firm had a small staff – twenty-two in 1847 – and a complex network of local sub-contractors – obtaining parts from thirty-three local suppliers in 1851.[70] This illustrates, once again, the emphasis within much of nineteenth-century London manufacturing on craft-based, 'flexible' production. Requiring room for expansion, in 1899 the company moved part of its production to a site in Baker Street and the remainder to Ipswich.

Reading, printing and publishing

Literacy levels were relatively high in London and reading skills were encouraged because they were far more useful than in, say, a contemporary rural area. This greater literacy is indicated in data based on whether men and women signed their own names on marriage registers. Between 1861 and 1870, 10 per cent of men and 16 per cent of women were signing with a mark in London and Middlesex. This compares favourably with all other English counties: in Kent, for example, the shares were 20 and 19 per cent respectively, and, in Lancashire, 24 and 45 per cent. Being able to write one's name may indicate only limited reading skill, but it is still a useful guide, though the data are for rural-dominated counties, so whether metropolitan literacy levels were any better than in any other large urban area is less clear.[71]

The advent of compulsory schooling improved reading abilities nationwide, so that, by the turn of the century, literacy had spread throughout the country. In this respect, the provinces may have caught up with the capital in the late nineteenth century – or, alternatively, the rest of the country caught up with the major cities. In terms of general education, none the less, ignorance generally ruled, as schooling for the vast majority of the population remained rudimentary throughout the period. The Education Acts of 1870 and 1902 provided for primary and secondary schooling respectively, and education of some sort was compulsory from 1876. Much was funded from local property taxes and education became the second biggest item of national public expenditure after the armed forces in the 1900s.[72]

The general level of literacy and the partial spreading out of good education meant that there was a ready audience in London for printed material. This fact, plus the demands of central government, the legal system and finance – all of which were centred on London – and the many other local needs for printed material, made the capital the undisputed centre of the printing and publishing industry throughout the period. Greater integration of the national market helped to enhance its position at a far higher scale of activity, so that employment in the industry doubled between 1851 and 1911, with actual employment rising from 26,000 to 103,000. Its locational bias in favour of London was consistently one of the highest of all industries – in 1851, it employed 36 per cent of the national workforce and, by 1911, it still had 26 per cent.[73]

There was also a long-established newspaper and book industry in London. During the French Revolution there were fourteen London dailies. By 1855, however, there were only ten, as *The Times* rose to dominance and because of the expense of setting up new rivals. Circulation was at first relatively low – *The Times* sold only 38,000 a year nationally between 1836 and 1851. Readerships though were far higher. Papers could be hired from hawkers, were available in coffee shops and pubs, and were bought by working-class 'reading clubs'. Sales then rose from the 1850s, largely due to the fall in prices. Advances in printing technology allowed production to increase from 6,000 copies per hour to 100,000 per hour; railways reduced distribution costs; and in 1855 advertisement taxes and newspaper stamp duty were abolished, followed in 1861 by paper duty. Newspaper circulations then again increased in the 1880s when the advent of 'new journalism', based on interviews and gossip columns and greater literacy, allowed papers such as the *Daily Mail* to reach a new mass readership.[74]

Book publishing was strongly focused on the capital, as the centre of literary circles and creative, if often unsuccessful, talent. Books could be bought in the growing number of specialist bookshops, or hired. The large-circulation book trade produced lurid or macabre novels but also the works of more serious writers, usually in weekly parts. Prices were low, particularly after the mechanisation of binding in the 1840s and later advances in printing, and such books were widely available from itinerant traders. Libraries were far scarcer. Before mid-century, general reading libraries were operated by the London Mechanics Institute and private companies, who charged a fee for their use, though some offered free facilities to the poor. The first municipal library was opened in Gloucester Place in 1854 by the St Marylebone vestry. The majority of metropolitan local authorities, however, were unenthusiastic supporters of libraries, and by 1898 the County of London contained just 48 public libraries, used by only 137,000 borrowers out of a population of millions.[75]

Many printing activities were traditionally located in Holborn, and particularly around Fleet Street.[76] In 1855, 37 per cent of firms could still be found in a rectangular area north of Blackfriars Bridge (see Figure 4.1, pp. 80–1). This area was near to St Paul's, for ecclesiastical business and book selling, and next to the legal quarter, a great source of business; it was also conveniently located between the City and the West End. Over time, printing works became bigger and many moved away, but publishers remained and the new mass newspaper industry set up there, with their presses keeping the printing tradition alive. By the First World War, Fleet Street was dominated by newspaper and magazine publishers, and ancillary activities such as news-gathering agencies. Their clustering highlights the classic agglomeration benefits of information gathering and dissemination and the availability of a skilled workforce.

Already by the nineteenth century, printing was relatively capital-intensive and large-scale. At mid-century, six of the largest printing firms in the country were located in London.[77] William Clowes, the capital's biggest printer, for example, employed over 600 people at mid-century.[78] The workforce comprised unskilled machine operators and skilled compositors, who set, proof-read and dismantled the type. Because of the heavy and dirty nature of the work and the influence of unions, no women were employed as operators. Technical change was substantial over the course of the period. In composition, the introduction of machines in the 1850s led employers to replace some men with women. The London Society of Compositors, however, strongly resisted female recruitment[79] and, by 1891, only 5 per cent of those employed were women.[80] With regard to juveniles, the various unions were less successful and the proportion of those aged below 20 years rose from 22 per cent in 1851 to 29 per cent in 1871.[81]

Unlike newspaper printing, which had to be located close to copy writing because of the transient nature of the information newspapers provide, book printers and binders had more leeway over where to locate, especially after the advent of rail travel and better communications. Rising land prices and regulatory controls in their traditional central locations consequently encouraged several to migrate to small towns in the provinces from the 1870s – to places like Aylesbury, Tonbridge and Beccles. Moreover, as firms by then were highly mechanised, they no longer required a pool of skilled labour. London wages were also far higher than elsewhere, due to the strength of the unions. In 1890, the capital's book printers earned from 36s to 38s per week, compared to 27s in Perth and around 26s in Aylesbury and Ipswich.

Among the first to leave were Unwins in 1871, and Clowes, which set up a works in Beccles, Suffolk in 1873. By 1900, most of their counterparts had followed their lead and only two significant firms remained: Eyre and Spottiswoode, cushioned by their Bible business, and Cassells, who reaped large profits from the advertisements that appeared on the covers of their penny books, so both were interested in the prestige of a London address. Similar cases can be identified in other parts of the printing industry with some firms encouraged to quit the capital to find lower input costs. Hall in his study of London industry uses printing and publishing as an example of where London industry could not remain competitive in the face of mechanised provincial industry.[82] His point is correct for businesses that came no longer to benefit from metropolitan agglomeration economies, as became the case with several large printing firms able to mechanise long production runs of popular books and other items. Yet, for much of the rest of the industry, London still had a substantial draw. As the employment data show, the decentralisers were more than replaced by firms that found it imperative to remain at the centre of sources of news, publishing business and skilled printing labour.

Conclusion

The failure of nineteenth-century British firms to adopt techniques discovered elsewhere is a perennial complaint, but it is certainly not justified for many leisure and cultural activities in London. Style and fun were already internationalised. Foreign fads such as roller-skating or bicycling were picked up with alacrity, as was the cinema, which proved to be a far more durable means of mass entertainment. On occasion, organisation methods and marketing were also copied from abroad, as in the hotel trade.

Few economic histories make much of leisure time, but in understanding the economic development of nineteenth-century London its importance is high, and one of the prime reasons why people enjoyed urban living. Leisure activities could make the deprivations suffered by many in other aspects of their life more bearable. Visitors were encouraged to come to London by their existence, stimulating demand for other activities as well. Leisure facilities developed their own urban geography and helped to forge the identity of localities within the capital. Entertainment in its varied forms was a major employer in the metropolis, on a scale that grew considerably throughout the century.

Modern location theory puts considerable emphasis on the cultural characteristics of cities as locational inducements for business. Nineteenth-century London had culture and entertainment without parallel. Such pleasures of life, as well as grinding economic necessity, must have helped to encourage firms and people to locate there. London's role as the nation's culture centre also helped to reinforce its position within the British urban hierarchy. This also happened with sport. Although not covered here, the growth of spectator sports towards the end of the century inevitably meant that London would be the most common venue for national finals and major sporting events.[83]

Locational and social factors were important within the city. Few leisure pursuits crossed the class boundaries in content and location – though cinema was to be a great leveller. Drinking establishments, for example, were socially separated and this had implications for where they were located – a gentlemen's club had to be in the smartest district and working men's clubs where the working classes congregated. The pull of the centre was strong, and the popular entertainment areas were just a street or two away from exclusivity, just as they are today. Along with retailing, the leisure industries helped to convert the West End into a place with classic capital city centre functions linked to suburbs by a growing transport network.

8 Suburbanisation and housing

Introduction

During the nineteenth century, London was transformed from a city that covered a relatively small area to a large, sprawling metropolis with suburbs linked to the centre by an extensive public transport system. Rapid population growth, rising living standards and new social values combined to created an enormous demand for single family homes. The physical separation of workplace and home, which had started in earlier centuries, accelerated to encompass most social strata over the period.[1] Domestic life, furthermore, became increasingly privatised with a new, greater differentiation of a household's living space from that of its neighbours. The suburbs, encouraged by prevailing building regulations,[2] mainly grew up as uniform acres of terraced housing facing each other across paved and drained streets behind railways, old turnpikes and the repaved, but often still narrow and winding, lanes that had existed before urban expansion.

An additional sharp boundary arose between the home and street with the eradication of old popular forms of living which had predominantly been based on street life and extensive use of open spaces. In contrast, in the expanded city, the new suburban open spaces were well-policed street pavements or fenced-off parks. Entertainment, for better or worse, ceased to be informal and was instead commercialised, specialised and regulated, as Chapter 7 has already noted.

Central and local government had no planning controls for most of the era, although they acquired some weak ones in 1909; yet they still extensively intervened in suburban development through building regulations, which influenced the design of houses and street layouts, and through the consequences of property taxes imposed on housing. Most local public services and the Poor Law were funded out of the rates charged on real property. Local government finance, consequently, was intertwined with housing provision, so that each had significant impacts upon the other. Nationally, the tax system was adjusted in favour of housing supply with the abolition of the window tax (1851) and other duties on bricks (1850), glass (1860) and timber (1866).

The public sector, none the less, was principally a passive player in suburbanisation, providing limited services after an urban neighbourhood had grown up. Instead, prodigious expansion required the channelling into housing development of large amounts of private capital and labour. Over the course of the period from 1800 to 1914, millions of dwellings were built in London. The rate of new building, however, was not steady but rather was punctuated by a series of building cycles that lasted far longer than the normal nineteenth-century business cycle. Reasons for this cyclical behaviour are investigated below.

Specific institutional structures existed in nineteenth-century housing provision that are no longer present today and, in London, these had their own peculiar characteristics. The vast majority of the population rented rather than owned. To facilitate new building, landowners and developers laid out estates, frequently using the device of the ground lease, and a multitude of small builders erected the actual dwellings, mainly selling the improved leases on to landlords who then let or sublet the properties until the leases finally became due. This structure of housing provision disappeared during the First World War. Since then, housebuilding in London, as elsewhere in Britain, has been predominantly based on owner occupation and subsidised building for rent by local authorities and housing associations, using freehold land in the main. Some have argued that the demise of the nineteenth-century private-rental structure of housing provision was the product of a terminal crisis in its economic functioning;[3] whereas others have suggested that a severe cyclical crisis in the Edwardian years and strong anti-landlord political intervention during and after the Great War were the real causes.[4] This debate is important for the understanding of housing policy in London, because it influences the interpretation made of the attempts by the Victorians to resolve the housing problems of their capital city. The housing and property tax nexus is considered here, while the housing policy debate itself is left until Chapter 15.

Bad housing and severe shortages were manifold, particularly in the first half of the century. With housing needs outstripping the available supply, the poorest bore the brunt of the deficiency of housing. Living in dilapidated inner city and East End slums, their lives were made even more miserable by the overcrowding caused by a loss of much inner city housing land to commercial uses, railway building and road improvements. Philanthropic housing bodies tried to improve the situation and were at the forefront of housing policy debate, but their actual impact was limited, as Chapter 15 will show. The spread of working-class suburbs from the 1860s with the advent of cheap, mass forms of public transport did much more to relieve the situation, but considerable pockets of inner city slums remained. In fact, it was during this period, in reference to London, that the word 'slum' came into general use.[5]

The LCC, when it was established, treated housing as a priority but, although it built slightly under 10,000 dwellings at a cost of £2.9 million prior to 1914, this had only limited influence on the available housing supply in such a large city.[6] Attempts to do more were always quickly lost in political wrangles and the sheer size of the costs involved. In addition, it was not clear to many that state-subsidised housing was the answer – even amongst socialist supporters of the LCC. The attempts that arose to find a 'third' way between state and profit-maximising provision have a particular resonance with the housing debates of the present day.

This chapter considers the theory of how a private market system creates suburban expansion and the consequences for the urban economy of such growth. It was into this process that governments and philanthropists wished to intervene with their housing schemes for the poor. The dilemmas they faced were not simply a product of Victorian reluctance to interfere with the rights of private property, but were probably more the product of a stark conflict. Everything that raised the cost of private sector housing provision lowered the profitability of private renting and with it reduced the available private supply. Government initiatives in the housing sphere did substantially raise private costs and so ended up crowding out private supply. Private costs were forced up, either through minimum standards legislation, which landlords had to meet (or in slum areas avoid), or through higher property taxes raised to pay for urban improvements, new public transport links or council housing. The crowding-out effects of higher taxes and competing public sector housing supply could result in well-meant attempts by government to improve the housing conditions of the poor actually ending up making them worse, because of the overwhelming reliance during this period on local property taxes to fund urban welfare expenditure. This argument is developed further in Chapters 15 and 16.

Here, the market processes operating in nineteenth-century London housing provision, and their outcomes, are examined: first, by looking at the spread of the suburbs and the economic consequences of their growth; second, by examining the impact of building cycles; third, by considering the ways in which suburban houses were rented and built, including an investigation of the roles of the landlord, landowner, developer and builder and the significance of the devices they used, like the ground and building lease. As part of this, the problem of the rates is discussed. Because of the importance of explaining the mechanisms and effects of suburbanisation and housing provision this chapter contains more theory than some of the others.

The spread of the suburbs

The shape of London

By the end of the eighteenth century, London had already spread out from the tight core of the City, the immediate south bank of the river, and the environs of Westminster.[7] The wealthy residential West End had grown up, filling part of the annual social calendar for the nation's elite; while the new bridges thrown over the Thames had stimulated middle-class developments to the south. Further east, the docks and ancillary industries were encouraging the spread of adjacent housing for those working in them; to the south-east, the military complexes in Greenwich and Woolwich had induced the growth of a virtually distinct township reached primarily by the river. Some wealthy Londoners, moreover, had already discovered the delights of 'urbanised village' living, residing in the commodious small developments erected for them in the then more desirable villages, like Clapton and Clapham, spread along the roads out of London.

The spatial pattern of this pre-1800 expansion had been different from what was to follow over the subsequent century. The cause was the virtual absence of public transport. Only the wealthy, who could afford coaches and the time to travel, could bear the cost of commuting any significant distance. And, even for many of them, the attractions of the proximity afforded by living centrally were greater than the benefits of cheaper suburban housing. For the rest of the population, the constraints of walking kept them within narrow residential confines. Not surprisingly, therefore, residential population densities were high throughout the urban core; even relatively so in the prosperous districts. Modern developers of middle-class housing, for example, would rarely contemplate the building densities and shared internal walls of an eighteenth-century London middle-class terrace. Below the wealthy, for most people housing was overcrowded and had only rudimentary facilities shared with adjacent dwellings. Not surprisingly, much more of life was therefore spent outside the home on the unpaved streets and poorly regulated open spaces, or in the pubs, beer houses, gin palaces and other public meeting places, than was to be the case a hundred or so years later.

The spatial shape of expanding London in the early 1800s is interesting. Unlike many other European cities, its growth was not constrained by defensive city walls, nor, once more bridges were erected, did the Thames represent much of a barrier. Lying in the middle of a flat basin, bound to the north and south by low hills, there were few physical barriers to suburban development, apart from the difficulty of draining much of the low-lying marshland. Even so, the metropolis had an odd shape that was roughly rectangular, which was caused by the competing pulls of the City and the West End. This urban shape was soon to be transformed by the advent of horse-drawn public transport and the building of more turnpike roads. Developments then spread out along and behind the main thoroughfares leading out of the older eighteenth-century city structure, which themselves were being improved – meaning that greater distances could be more easily and safely travelled. So, by the 1830s, most of the earlier urbanised villages had been joined up to the capital by housebuilding along the main roads, with further villages drawn into the urban net. Additional new buildings spread out into the countryside in the new neighbourhoods erected adjacent to the older town structure – much of Islington and Bayswater being classic City and West End instances of this phenomenon. Growth was slow and constrained by the need to introduce horse-drawn public transport and the limitations of this mode of travel (see Chapter 10). The overall effect, in terms of urban form, of this pattern of suburban expansion was to give expanding London geographically a rough star-shape, at least up to the late 1840s.

During this period, in the suburban fringes, the better-drained land would be first sought out, because prevailing technology and speculative builders' habits led to persistent dampness in housing built on marshy land.[8] Thus, large tracts of land in the new suburbs were at first left empty because of land-quality problems or due to an absence of adequate transport beyond the main thoroughfares. In the working-class suburbs to the east and south-east, this effect was less pronounced. The quality of the land used for their often meagre dwellings was of less concern, as using it provided cheaper, if damp, accommodation. Sources of employment were also moving outwards in conjunction with these neighbourhoods, with the spread down river of the enclosed docks and some of the heavier, manual industries.

By the 1870s, the previous star urban shape is no longer discernible. By then, railways criss-crossed the urban area, complemented by local horse-drawn feeder transport and walking. Sewerage and drainage had also improved. Railway building tended to lead suburban development in the south and the west, as inspection of contemporary Ordnance Survey maps shows. The lines, however, were not usually built in anticipation of such suburban traffic, but instead reflected competition over routes to and from London by the mainline railway companies. The possibilities they created for suburban development were thus mainly a spin-off from other objectives.

Technical changes in overall infrastructure provision, and the substantial investments associated with them, took a long time to put into place, but they finally enabled the full extent of the urban area to be filled in by development. This gave London a new, circular geographic shape. This was the almost universal type of urban morphology appearing at the time in the new major capitalist cities of the world, most notably in the United States, as described by Weber in the 1890s and later in the sociological models of Park and Burgess in the 1920s.[9] Some natural barriers had to be respected as the suburbs expanded: such as the Lea Valley to the north-east and the constraints of the hills to the north and south. Yet even these were partly overcome as drainage and public transport continued to improve; so that by 1914 the city stretched an even greater distance, while keeping its broadly circular form.

In the years prior to the First World War, the capital had spread out well beyond the boundaries of the old County of London. To the east and north-east, this spilling over the administrative boundary was partly due to the fact that the geographic limit of the County of London had been drawn much closer to the city centre than elsewhere (see Figure 1.1, p. 12). Residential suburbs and industrial areas as a result rapidly grew up there in such ex-County districts as West Ham:[10] well-connected by transportation links to the rest of the capital and further afield, but outside of the regulatory controls and property taxes imposed within the County. This spread the East End out beyond the confines of the formal definition of London. Located close to the river and the newest docks, these eastern suburbs became the site of noxious industries, most notably Beckton's giant gas works (complemented by Greenwich's to the south). Other chemical industries set up there, as well as noxious trades and firms attempting to avoid the scrutiny of County factory inspectors. In addition, the valley of the River Lea provided similar benefits, so that industry spread up its banks through Hackney, Tottenham and Edmonton to Enfield. The policy of the Great Eastern Railway in running many working men's suburban trains encouraged further working class suburbanisation to the east and north-east; although they were not offered on some lines, such as that to Ongar, so the neighbourhoods around them remained solidly middle-class.[11] The easterly movement of industry also led to the suburbanisation of some lower-income households;[12] whereas those moving into other suburban districts were mainly the middle classes, clerks and other better-paid service sector workers, and craft manual workers.

Those living in the suburbs had either moved from elsewhere in London – either to improve their housing or to set up home for the first time – or they were in-migrants to London, who frequently formed the majority of new suburbanites. Dyos, for example, calculated that 40 per cent of immigrants to South London between 1841 and 1881 were from the metropolitan area or Surrey and Kent; 28 per cent from the rest of the South-East; and most of the rest from the West, East Anglia and the Midlands, with a growing proportion moving down from the northern industrial towns in the last decades of the nineteenth century.[13]

Technical developments in transport and other infrastructure had key parts to play in creating and moulding the suburbs. They overcame the physical barriers of distance and terrain and enabled a dramatic fall between 1800 and 1914 in the cost of urban travel. With reduced travel costs and frequent services on several alternative public transport modes, more and more social strata over the period could enjoy the benefits of lower-density suburban living. The suburbs, even so, became highly socially stratified. Victorian and Edwardian concerns with social status helped to encourage this segregation, which was far greater than in the late eighteenth century when the Duke of Bedford had to physically restrain the *hoi polloi* from entering his Bloomsbury estate by erecting gates and employing gatemen. Now distance and variations in transport costs and housing rents did the job far more effectively in the suburbs. On occasion, middle-class groups would protest at the threatened introduction of cheap transport to their districts in the form of trams or working men's rail tickets, bringing with them lower-income groups as neighbours. Yet, in the main, if they or their offspring were prepared to move out further with each improvement in transport, they could find the neighbourhoods they desired. A similar suburban segregation occurred throughout the social scale and became a common feature of most cities.[14]

In terms of the broad social structure of nineteenth-century London, contemporary views on health and air pollution encouraged the better-off to avoid low-lying areas and to take advantage of the prevailing westerly winds and the Northern and Southern Heights. They had to move ever further out as the more popular, dense suburbs began to encroach on their previously low-density neighbourhoods. Their poorer suburban brethren tended to be concentrated to the north-east and south-east, with the least well-off in the inner east and south-east where new dock and industrial development had not pre-empted the available space. Such a broad description is inevitably a crude generalisation, however, with many parts of the city containing pockets of distinct social mixes.

Suburban industry and employment

The spatial extent of suburban industrial districts was far less than that of housing. Residences are generally the most prodigious consumers of urban space. In modern British cities, for example, about half of urban land is covered by them.[15] Industries moved outwards to take advantage of lower land prices and the new, cheaper transportation systems. Many of the places where the industries described in Part 5 below were located were themselves rural areas in 1800. Such industrial districts, as has been noted, tended to be concentrated in clusters and, even after the advent of rail transport, locational pressures meant they still often clung near to the river, waterways and canal sides.

New suburban shopping centres and the expanding transport systems provided alternative, non-manufacturing, sources of suburban employment, servicing the needs of their local communities. Jobs in construction would also have had a city fringe bias as the tide of new building passed through particular districts. Finally, at a growing rate over the period, schools, hospitals, asylums and other public facilities were set up in the suburbs, offering further sources of employment. Some of these new jobs would be low-paid or casualised, in the nineteenth-century metropolitan tradition, which helps to explain the prevalence of pockets of poverty throughout the city.

The suburbanisation of employment, consequently, did not mean that everyone had to travel to and from the city centre to work. This puts the importance of transportation in context, because, once formed, suburbs have their own dynamics. The majority of suburbanites, even at the end of the period, in fact did not use public transport to reach the urban core but, instead, had local jobs or ones near enough that they could walk or cycle to work.[16] None the less, it was still the possibility of such intra-urban journeys that triggered off the expansion of most suburbs. This was not simply because of the key importance of central city commuters to suburban expansion, but also because incorporation into the urban transport network meant that many of the economic advantages of the wider urban agglomeration could be enjoyed by local suburban households, workers and firms.

Population density gradients

The significance of the shifts in transport technology for the nature of the physical expansion of London can be grasped by examining changes in population densities at greater distances from the city centre over the course of the nineteenth and early twentieth centuries. The relevant data are available for London in a study by Clark (1951). He calculated average population densities on a radius from the city centre (taken as Charing Cross) for a sample of census years from 1801 to 1941, and his data are shown in Figure 8.1.

It can be seen in the diagram that in 1801 population density drops dramatically at greater distances from the urban core, with very low densities even three miles away from the centre. Between 1801 and 1841, there was then an outward shift in the density function. This was caused by the interaction of two effects: one suburban and the other working in the urban core. Developments in public transport up to 1841 helped to increase densities in the inner suburbs but its limitations meant that the urban

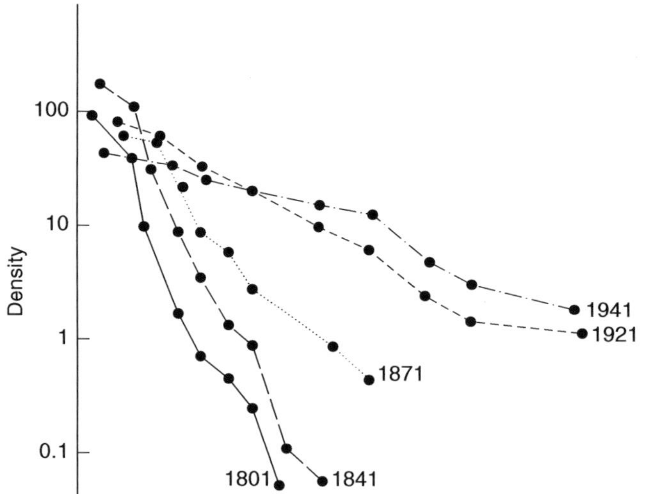

Figure 8.1 London density gradients, 1801–1941

Source: Evans, 1985, 105. Based on Clark, 1951.

Note: The vertical axis is in logarithms highlighting the exponential nature of the density gradient.

fringe expanded only slowly. Meanwhile, in the city centre, population pressures and the loss of central city housing land had caused overcrowding to become worse. Public transport then as the century progressed had a far greater impact on urban densities. By 1871, the urban fringe had moved a far greater distance from the city centre as the urban rail network encouraged millions to set up home in the suburbs. Even so, central densities, although somewhat improved, remained extraordinarily high – a characteristic that remained until after the Second World War. The slope of the density gradient had also flattened by the 1870s. This was caused more by an increase in suburban densities than through an easing of inner city overcrowding.

Much higher densities existed in suburban areas because of the greater efficiency and scope of the available transportation networks and the simultaneous movement to the suburbs of employment. As new suburbs developed, they were less likely to contain the pockets of vacant land common in earlier ones, poorly served by public transport, to be infilled later. In the already existing suburbs, apart from infilling, the older, low-density developments were being refashioned or rebuilt, raising their population densities, as Dyos (1961) describes in detail for Camberwell; meanwhile the agricultural land remaining between the earlier suburbs was being drawn into urban use. The scale of the suburbanisation of London was such that these increases in suburban population densities occurred as the city spread further outwards, even though the total built-up area of the city was expanding faster than the increase in its radius. (This is because the area of a circle is πr^2, where r is the radius.) These processes were further enhanced with the advent of the underground, tram and motor bus, so that even higher suburban population densities resulted, as represented by the much flatter population density gradient for 1921. By then, overcrowding in the city centre had been reduced somewhat, but the greatest effect over the course of the period had been the spreading out of the suburbs and the increased density of the populations living in them.

London densities were by no means the worst in Britain: in 1868, London's population per acre was 40, the same as Edinburgh's and much less than Glasgow's 87 and Liverpool's 96. To a great extent, this reflects the higher standard of living in London and the greater responsiveness of the housing supply. If not the worst, the problem nevertheless was a persistent one. Its inner city population densities were not to fall significantly until the 1950s and 1960s with the advent of major slum clearance programmes and a general movement out of London, leading to substantial falls in its overall population.

The residential choice process

Although changes in population density can be ascribed to transportation developments and population pressures, all the same they still arose from the private decisions of millions of nineteenth-century Londoners to move out to the suburbs. A simple model of residential location helps to explain their choice. If it is assumed, for ease of argument, that all jobs are in the city centre and people only travel to and from work, households when making the choice of where to live can trade-off the cost in time and money of travelling a greater distance against the benefit of lower suburban land values and, hence, cheaper housing. At some distance, the extra cost of travel will just match the savings in housing costs for each household, depending on their preferences and incomes and the gradients of travel costs and house rents. Each household chooses to locate at this optimal point. Households with higher incomes have a greater demand for housing and, hence, are likely to gain the most from living in distant, low-density suburbs. The land price gradient reflects these choices, with the cost of land falling with greater distance from the city centre and, therefore, the rents of the (quality-adjusted) housing built on it. The better-off in this model end up, seemingly paradoxically, living on the cheapest land – at the urban fringe.

The lowest-income households, in contrast, end up living on more expensive inner city land – by crowding together in low-quality homes to outbid other potential land uses. This concern for centrality arises because the poor have a limited demand for housing because of their meagre incomes, while all work opportunities, by assumption, are at the city centre, so they gain little from spending money travelling to the suburbs to take advantage of cheaper housing costs. Such spatial choices and constraints are then reinforced by environmental improvements in the better neighbourhoods and degradation in the poorer ones. Any fall in transport costs encourages more people to move to the suburbs to gain the benefit of cheaper land values, so the city expands, with the better-off moving further out and the original low-density suburbs converted to higher density for those further down the income hierarchy.

Spatial differences in rents for a modest three-roomed dwelling were surveyed in 1905. The pattern of rents declines with distance from the centre, ranging from 10s 3d a week in Holborn to 5s 3d in Enfield and Edmonton in the suburban north. Rents were also affected by social status, with, for example, rent levels higher in the west than in the east at equivalent distances from the centre.[17] Thus, although the residential location model is extremely simple, it does seem to capture the essence of the suburbanisation processes operating in nineteenth-century London. Moreover, relaxing some of the assumptions makes the model able to explain some of the greater complexity of actual location choices, without undermining its basic principles. For example, the very poor may have suffered in economists' speak from a 'lumpiness' in the profile of housing and transport costs – that is, minimum amounts of either had to be bought before they could be used. This means that they could not optimise in the way hypothesised above. They may have already been spending more of their incomes than they would wish on housing, caused by the need for a minimum necessary space for shelter and warmth, and may have been unable to afford the cost of a daily public transport journey to work, making slum housing in the inner city their only option. Modern evidence from the US,[18] for example, indicates that low-income households do not increase their housing consumption much with rises in incomes; whereas middle- and upper-income groups do.

Contemporary housing reformers suggested that such lumpiness effects may well have existed, with their common complaint that the poor would not spend any more on housing to improve their living conditions.[19] Yelling, in contrast, cites evidence that households moving into the LCC's Boundary Street estate spent more on their new housing – though the tenants moving into Boundary Street were not the poorest of households.[20] The poor may also have had a strong preference for living in a central location as part of their survival strategy, because this was where the benefits of agglomeration for them were at their greatest.

Intra-urban industrial location

In the residential location model, it was assumed that all employment is located in the city centre. With firms, this assumption is not particularly useful. Instead, it is better to consider where particular employment activities are likely to locate throughout a city.

The importance of centrality for many firms was highlighted earlier, in Chapter 2. A central location maximises the benefits of agglomeration and the activities that gain the most are able to outbid others – these tend to be higher-order service sector activities. They do not include many manufacturing firms because they use processes that are more land-intensive, so they set up or move to the suburbs to take advantage of cheaper land prices. The relative importance of centrality or cheaper land, however, varies between activities depending on the types of agglomeration benefit each gains. Moreover, by clustering together, suburban firms involved in interlinked processes can still gain many external economies. Networks of labour and suppliers for particular activities emerge in particular parts of the city, encouraging firms in them to locate in specific districts to take advantage of the resultant external economies. Other industries that use similar inputs may also cluster in the same vicinity to take advantage of the external economies, thereby creating areas with similar characteristics, such as the handicraft industries of East London's inner industrial belt. Yet more firms evolve in the suburbs to serve local populations in retailing and other ventures.

All will generally locate near to good transport links for easy shipment of their products, assembly of inputs, or to enable the maximum number of customers to come to their premises. The noxious ones tend to crowd together as their negative environmental impact depresses land values from which they can take advantage. This decentralisation of industry, by creating employment opportunities in the suburbs, is at variance with the initial assumption in the intra-urban locational model of all employment being located in the city centre.

The suburban employment nodes that emerge induce similar behavioural responses in residential location decisions to the original 'everyone works in the centre' formulation. The eventual locational pattern, thus, is one derived from central city workers and suburban node workers both trading off distance against lower housing costs. Land values peak in the city centre and there are ancillary peaks around suburban nodes.

Other factors can be added to the model to make it more sophisticated (and horrendously complex). It can be extended to encompass more activities than just work – such as shopping and leisure pursuits. It can also be complicated by imposing a pre-existing social and physical geography that itself engenders its own relatively attractive locations – rivers, hills and prevailing winds (very important when smog exists), parks, high-status neighbourhoods and so on. The high cost of demolishing existing buildings adds future complications. Rapid transit around a city, moreover, is structured by the contemporary pattern of main roads, railways and other means of travel. Agglomeration economies, in addition, to not simply exist at one point, such as the city centre, but decay as firms or individuals move away from their loci.

All of these factors make formal modelling a difficult exercise but that does not obviate the basic principles of location within a city. The question now is what do they imply for the understanding of London's nineteenth-century urban structure?

The pattern of nineteenth-century location

Intra-urban location theory taken all together would predict that, for nineteenth-century London, the central areas are given over to high value-added business uses. Around this centre are low-income inner suburbs and small workshops taking advantage of centrality but saving on accommodation costs in a similar way to the poor. Beyond them lies an expanding outer ring of suburbs, housing the rest of the population and industry. Income levels and land-intensive industry rise towards the suburban fringe. Suburban industry would be clustered, with its locations influenced by the geography of the available transportation links and physical geography. Several parts of the suburbs would be taken over by the most environmentally damaging activities; furthermore, as these tend to have bulky inputs, such locations are likely to be adjacent or near to water transportation. These predictions broadly conform to the situation in London in the nineteenth century.

By 1906, up to a quarter of a million people were commuting by train into the City and West End from the inner and outer suburbs and, with tram and bus journeys added, perhaps one man in four commuted by public transport.[21] Of the other three-quarters of suburban working men, some would have walked to the centre while many others would have been employed locally. Where the commuters came from depended on their income and social status, as delineated in the characteristics of the suburbs that fanned out around the city centre.[22] Suburbanisation, in fact, spread into the working classes decades earlier. In the 1880s, for example, four predominantly working-class London suburbs were the fastest-growing places in England and Wales – Willesden, Leyton, Tottenham and West Ham.

In reality, urban location decisions are complicated matters influenced by available supply, household circumstances and social connections. The suburbs of Victorian London may have been socially segregated to an extent not seen before but they still invariably contained some social mixing rather than being purely homogeneous. Greater complexity is shown in a map of Booth's results for streets containing a majority of households in his two lowest categories of income, as shown in Figure 8.2. Poverty was concentrated in the inner city, as predicted, but pockets of deprivation were spread throughout the urban area. Poor streets were scattered throughout an inner circle around the City, declining in frequency with greater distance from the city centre. These neighbourhoods had been developed mainly in the seventeenth and eighteenth centuries, so much

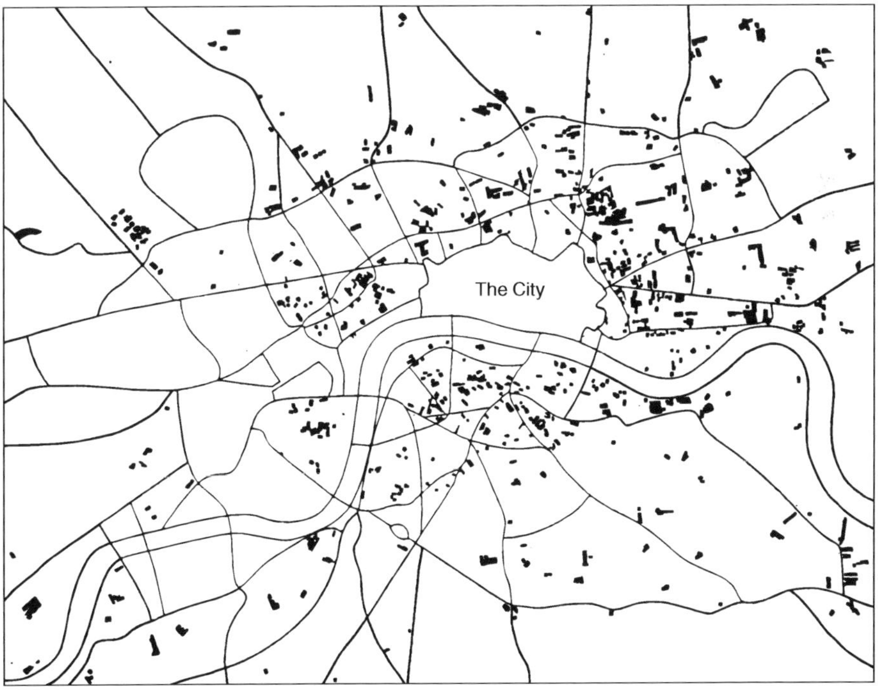

Figure 8.2 Poverty streets, 1889

Source: Yelling, 1986, 56.

of the housing there was already old. Some of it had filtered down from middle-class dwellings to slums and most had been subject to years of neglect. Many of the industries of London were also concentrated in these districts. Booth's results on overcrowding again highlight a concentration in the inner districts, particularly in the northern and eastern inner areas, plus a notable pocket south of the river around Waterloo.

Some evidence of declining house rents with rising travel costs to the city centre can be found in a 1900 LCC survey, which examined working-class housing costs at various destinations from Waterloo Station and the costs of third-class fares to them. The weekly rent of 8s 1d for two or three rooms around the station fell to 6s 9d by Vauxhall, rising somewhat in the more desirable suburbs of Wandsworth and Wimbledon, and falling to 5s 6d for a much larger cottage in distant Sunbury – but, there, 5s a week had to be paid in train fares back to Waterloo.[23] Extra strains on suburban living were incurred by working-class commuters to the centre in the form of their long working hours and early or late starts and the fact that the suburbs afforded fewer female employment opportunities and, hence, could lower family income. Transport costs were consequently not the only part of the actual residential location decision.

Many of the highest-income households, even at the end of the century, were still located in the West End because of the importance of centrality for the consumption of political and leisure activities. Even so, the broad geographic picture corresponds to the predictions of the simple, modern location model, with the poor concentrated in the inner urban areas; most of the middle class in the more distant suburbs; and the respectable working class in an intermediate ring or on the suburban fringes where industry had also set up.

This conclusion places in context the housing problems of nineteenth-century London. Rather than being unique, they are common outcomes of the development of a large, predominantly market-driven, urban area; added to which there were London-specific supply-side institutional and geographic processes by which housing and neighbourhoods were created and transformed over time. This conclusion in no sense is meant to underrate the severity of the housing conditions of the poor in the capital during this period, but rather to suggest that the solutions to the problem lay as much in finding ways to raise pitifully low incomes as in dealing with any inefficient working of the housing market itself.

One final aspect of the suburbanisation of London was the relatively slow spreading out of inner city industry. Many substantial plants remained in the inner industrial districts right up to 1914. There might be two reasons why industry remained tightly bound. The first is the inertia caused by the external benefits of industrial districts, so that once formed in a particular district they continued to exert a strong hold over industrial location. The other factor was the constraints imposed by the contemporary transport network, which may have encouraged firms to stay centrally located. One particular problem may have been the reluctance of rail companies to provide siding facilities at many suburban locations – an issue taken up in Chapter 10.

Effects of suburbanisation on housing costs and supply

By drawing in ever more land from agricultural to urban use, suburbanisation enabled the supply of housing to be considerably increased without generating continuing large increases in land values at the urban fringe. It enabled the classic English two- to three-storey suburban terrace and garden to be reproduced by the million in the metropolis, in contrast to the far denser cities emerging in most of the rest of urbanising Western Europe. Mansion blocks did develop in inner areas in response to the higher land values there, for those in the middle class with small families and a liking for central city life. The philanthropic housing associations also built blocks of central flats, but the suburban terrace was the overwhelmingly popular form of mass housing. Increasingly over the century, however, the middle classes took advantage of lower suburban land values to live in semi- and fully-detached homes: of which Bedford Park in Chiswick is a classic and innovative instance.[24]

The impact on housing costs can be seen most clearly when it is assumed that there is no population growth. In that situation, falling transport costs and greater resultant suburbanisation lead to a fall in the demand for housing at the centre and, with that demand reduction, lower central housing rents would ensue. In this way, the housing costs of the inner city poor decline as well. London clearly did not have zero population growth in the nineteenth century. Moreover, suburbanisation was not at a sufficient rate actually to reduce housing demand in the centre, as was shown in the population density evidence cited above. This was because population increases and inner city housing losses combined to outweigh the rate of growth of the suburbs. Yet the reduction in density in the central areas by the 1870s does suggest there was some such absolute effect in the later part of the period. Relatively, the point is far stronger: without suburbanisation, housing costs and the housing conditions of many nineteenth-century Londoners would inevitably have been far worse. As the main thrust of suburbanisation occurred from the middle of the century onwards, housing shortages were most acute up until then.

The impact on London business costs

The falls in intra-urban transport costs throughout the century and the spreading out of the suburbs had the indirect effect of stimulating economic growth in the capital by reducing the costs of doing business there. The reasoning is easiest to understand in the context of the simple model above, where all employment is located in the central city and there is no net immigration to the city, and then to assume that there is a transport innovation encouraging further suburbanisation. A fall in transport costs was argued above to lower overall housing costs. This raises living standards so that workers could be paid a lower wage for the same standard of living. With lower wage bills, the profitability of firms grows and more set up. Extra jobs and higher factor incomes result.

This situation is unlikely to be stable, however, as the extra employment has to be taken up by someone. Initially, the higher labour demand will raise wages again and, weakening the 'no migration' assumption, migrants will be attracted to the city as a result, taking up some of the employment and dampening the upward pressure on wages. The city's population grows in consequence and its geographic area increases. Additional agglomeration economies arise because of the greater scale of economic activity and larger overall urban population. These positive growth effects are then weakened, but not negated, by the further pressures on housing costs induced by the housing demands of the extra population, and by greater congestion costs in the city centre.[25]

Did such effects happen in nineteenth-century London? The answer is yes, qualified by the fact that there were many other pressures on wage costs – most notably the increase in living standards throughout the century and variations in the cost of living. If there had been little suburbanisation, wages would have had to have been far greater because housing costs would have been higher, and the capital would have been a much smaller place in consequence as employment would have grown at a slower rate. More tangible evidence can be gleaned from the limited available data on rents. The earlier data on housing costs, given in Chapter 5, suggest that, at least from 1880 to 1900, housing rents may actually have been falling in real terms, despite continued population growth. It is perhaps no surprise that this period was the one when some of the most notable innovations in suburban transportation in London were occurring and the average amount of suburban housebuilding was at its greatest. It is also interesting to note that the fall in housing rents was greatest for middle-class dwellings, precisely the social stratum which was likely to benefit most from the suburbanisation generated by transport improvements. As such people were more likely to work in services than manufacturing, moreover, this housing cost effect would have shifted London wage costs in favour of service activities.

Suburbanisation, in summary, was not simply about finding better and cheaper places for nineteenth-century Londoners to live. It simultaneously breathed life into the broader London economy via its effects on wage costs and agglomeration economies, enabling it to grow in the way it did. The positive economic benefits of this spreading out of the suburbs during this period cannot be too highly stressed, as the process of decentralisation is often given a bad press: both in Victorian times and today. Policy since the 1940s has dramatically swung away from facilitating the spreading out of London, to one of dramatically arresting the tendency.[26] The consequences for the London economy have probably been as unfortunate since then as they were propitious in the years to 1914.

Housing development

The ways in which most housing was provided had evolved over the previous century and a half. The forms of finance, a multitude of small-scale landlords, building and development practices, property taxes and the prevalence of leasehold land ownership did not alter much from the late eighteenth century. The significant change in nineteenth-century London was the emergence of a mass market for new housing, the like of which had never been seen before. The demand stimuli to the booming housing market were continued population growth, rising incomes, falling transport costs and new social mores. The supply response by the thousands involved was vigorous, with landowners, developers, housebuilders, mortgage lenders and investors in rental housing all eager to profit from the radical physical transformation of London. The outcome was not simply a much greater housing stock, but also one that was much healthier, more spacious and of better building quality. It has been estimated that housing quality doubled nationally from 1811 to 1910, with much of the increase occurring between 1850 and 1870.[27]

The design styles were also carried over from earlier periods, to be reshaped somewhat by taste and new building regulations. London developers had already recognised the cost advantages of the terraced house. It maximised the number of separate family dwellings facing any given length of street because its rectangular form extended back from a narrow front; while, with little load to bear, the foundations and brick structure could be flimsy. This type of building and the street layout in which it was placed also meant that little infrastructure expenditure was required. Where ground conditions permitted, roads were thrown up on embankments above the original ground level, saving on expensive digging. Building foundations were minimal and the houses' basements were erected to the height of the raised road, to cope, it was hoped, with any rising damp.[28] (It was the dampness of nineteenth-century basement accommodation that made them such a well-known resort of the poorest households and cheapest workplaces.)

For the grandest homes, squares could be inserted and relatively cheap columns, pilasters and stucco-work attached to the houses' front walls in often beautiful parodies of a palace or country house. There were costs to households in terms of privacy, ventilation and light, and in the endless uniform dreariness of the meaner suburbs, but there were compensations in the built form's cheapness. As well as saving on capital costs, in contrast to the mansion blocks more common elsewhere in Europe at the time, terraced housing could be built on a piecemeal basis. This lowered development risks, as capital was not locked up in unsold houses when the market turned sour, which it frequently and unexpectedly did. It could take years as a result for a street of terraced houses to be completed.[29]

Plots in a new street, furthermore, could be leased out to separate builders, introducing flexibility into the supply of inputs. The relatively low levels of capital investment required further encouraged small builders to enter development. The multitude of potential purchasers of building plots, therefore, made it difficult for large land development companies to emerge, able to cream off the gains from building at the expense of the landowner or builder – a common situation in other European countries. The initial suburban extensions after these mechanisms were worked out were built from the time of Charles II in what now seem to be areas in the heart of the city – Covent Garden, Red Lion Square, other areas to the north of Holborn, St James's, Soho and, most spectacularly, the West End districts of Mayfair and Marylebone. The transference of the approach to lower-income housing was also well-established, especially in the east and south-east.[30]

Histories of individual nineteenth-century London residential developments, particularly for the wealthy, are extensively documented and their stories will not be retold here.[31] Rather of interest are the organisational and market mechanisms through which housing development took place, the agencies involved, and the consequences in terms of housing supply. The organisation of housebuilding elsewhere in Britain, especially England, was similar, of course, though the ways of the capital were to some extent unique. Much of the reason for institutional continuity was that the earlier structures of housing provision were well suited to the situations prevailing in the nineteenth century.

At the core of the contemporary structure of housing provision was the fact that housing was being built for rent. Agencies entered housing to profit from that fact in the most effective ways, so that a complex structure evolved in which lease holding was an integral, if often misunderstood, part.

Rental housing and the mortgage market

Few Londoners owned their own homes, renting them instead. Homeownership grew towards the end of the period amongst the middle classes, and some of the better-off suburbs of the 1900s were being constructed predominantly for owner occupation.[32] Yet it was comparatively rare, partly because the tax system was not biased towards owner occupation as it was later. Furthermore, most contemporary mortgages could be called in at a moment's notice – imposing a risk in housing finance that was generally more effectively borne by landlords.

Housing landlords were usually not wealthy individuals – rather, rental housing was seen as a good investment for those with savings they wished to invest profitably to fund consumption later in life. Shopkeepers, widowers, skilled workers, clerks and others were all part of the landlord class, as well as the occasional full-time property owner and wealthy individual. It has been estimated that half of UK houses just prior to the First World War were owned by those leaving less than £5,000 at death, with many house owners having much more limited assets.[33] Property had its ancient mystique as a safe, long-term investment, but the available evidence suggests that investment flows into rental housing, and hence the amount of housebuilding, were influenced by prevailing housing returns relative to other outlets for funds.

House rental could be a risky business – risks that pushed up required returns and viable rents, and which periodically threatened capital values. Rent levels once houses were let, for example, tended to be slow to adjust to changes in demand-and-supply conditions. Lease terms meant that rents could only be periodically adjusted, with landlords reluctant to cut rents and tenants resistant to increases. Changes in interest rates or property taxes in such circumstances could bring grief to the financial calculations of a landlord. Non-payment of rents was common, especially in poorer neighbourhoods, with hard-pressed households doing a 'midnight flit' to avoid the landlord (this helps to explain the very high mobility common in those areas). Added to non-payment risks was the threat of vacancy, when no tenant could be found. Vacancies tended to grow when the supply of housing outstripped demand, and shrunk when a surge of demand coincided with moribund housebuilding.

The return landlords required from rental housing before investing in it depended on the alternatives available to them. It has frequently been suggested that nineteenth-century housing landlords were trapped into owning homes by the limited investment alternatives open to them. This argument, initially put forward by the 1914 Liberal Land Enquiry Committee, suggests that mid-nineteenth-century local capital markets were not very deep, in the sense of a narrow range of opportunities open to small investors, which trapped them into becoming small landlords.[34] As soon as other investment alternatives developed, via friendly societies, municipal bonds, overseas investment and the like, as they increasingly did from the last quarter of the nineteenth century, investors withdrew from housing, precipitating a structural crisis in its provision. This view of the nineteenth-century landlord seems misplaced and with it the claimed early twentieth-century structural crisis of private renting.

One difficulty with this argument is that it ignores the well-developed private mortgage market, which enabled many landlords to borrow and, thereby, gear up the returns on their own capital in ways remarkably similar to modern property developers. Those who did not wish to rent houses and incur the administrative costs and housing market risks could indirectly participate in housing provision via the private mortgage market. This means of finance was organised by solicitors and other professionals as a conduit for local savings. The loans could be instantly recalled, earning a rate of interest slightly above that of gilts, to compensate for the greater risk of default, with the principal repaid in full at the end of the term. As low-risk investments, they, rather than being a landlord, deserve the claim 'as safe as houses'.

By the 1870s, building societies were extolling the use of their payment-by-instalment mortgages, but generally landlords still preferred the cheaper, more flexible, private mortgage market. Even as late as the 1950s, over half of all house mortgages were still funded in this way. Before 1914, around 80 per cent of UK houses were mortgaged up to two-thirds of their value, indicating the extent to which landlords relied on loans to fund their operations, which hardly suggests they were trapped in housing.[35] If the range of small investment opportunities did increase towards the end of the nineteenth century, modern portfolio theory would suggest that this might raise the target rate of return for housing through the greater choice of savings instruments. This might lead to somewhat higher rents, but that hardly warrants the claim of a structural crisis. There was no shortage of funds for housing, as long as investment in it could earn the risk-adjusted, prevailing general rate of return.

Via the mortgage market, housing was closely linked to the contemporary capital market, including overseas investment. This connection to financial markets has been found in recent work that shows a clear influence of changes in long-term interest rates on the number of property transactions in the London area (Middlesex) after 1770.[36] Because of these key links to other investment markets, rises in interest rates would cause house prices to fall, as such increases raised the yield required from housing rents in order for them to match alternative investment opportunities. Inflation would also erode the real value of sticky rental incomes – another influence depressing house prices. Such factors affected the return from renting throughout the period, so years of falling as well as rising house prices were common. These short-run rent and cost relationships would then slowly percolate through to determine the overall demand-and-supply balance via the rate of housebuilding and extent of repair and maintenance.

On the supply side, periods when landlord costs were increasing faster than rents would depress housebuilding. A growing house shortage would then result. This would push up rents, making the yields from house ownership rise again, which, in turn, would stimulate housebuilding. The demand for housing would be stimulated by the rate of inward migration to London, which itself was influenced by the prevailing state of employment growth and wages. Surges of demand for suburban homes, moreover, would be created by developments in transportation technology and consequent investment. As new transport systems were installed in particular districts, more households would move into them or, alternatively, industry would decentralise, generating local employment opportunities. Eventually, the gains from transport improvements would be exhausted as housing filled the available land served by them and housebuilding would decline. One of the most well-known instances of this process was the spectacular growth of Golders Green in North London after the underground station was built in green fields in the 1900s.[37]

Building cycles

The short- and long-run stimuli to demand in the capital would lead to more houses being built until an overhang of vacant dwellings brought on a building depression once again. As the vacancy rate rose, housebuilding declined and it then grew again as the stock was taken up.[38] Long reaction lags in these inter-relationships between demand and supply would make the cycles cover extended time periods. In London, these seem to have averaged around eighteen years in length from the 1780s to the 1900s.[39] Such long building cycles were a common nineteenth-century phenomenon – identified as the Kuznets cycle, after its discoverer.[40]

Accurate data on housebuilding in London (or Britain) for the whole of the nineteenth century do not exist. No housing data are available at all before the 1850s, so surrogates for housebuilding are used in compiling estimates – such as surveyors' fees from new building, which include non-housing construction as well, or transactions deeds which also include existing buildings.[41] As London spilled out of its administrative boundaries, furthermore, it becomes more difficult to identify suburban building in the available data. The approximate situation in the second half of the century is shown in Figures 8.3 and 8.4, derived from two different sources. The vacancy link to cycles is highlighted in Figure 8.3, with building cycle there inversely correlated with the number of empty houses. Empty properties represented about 5 per cent of the London stock on average but fluctuate considerably around that level.

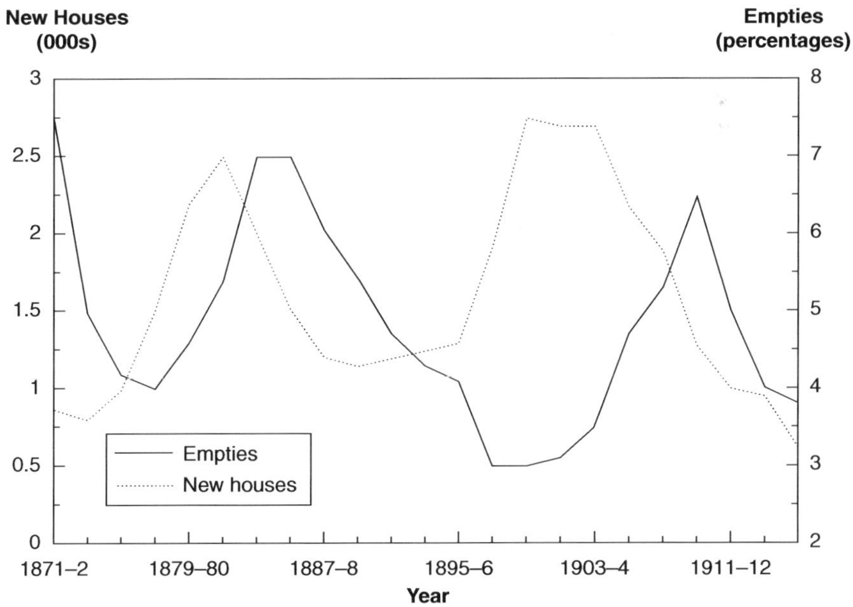

Figure 8.3 Variations in new houses and empty property, 1871–1916

Source: Spensley, 1918, 170.

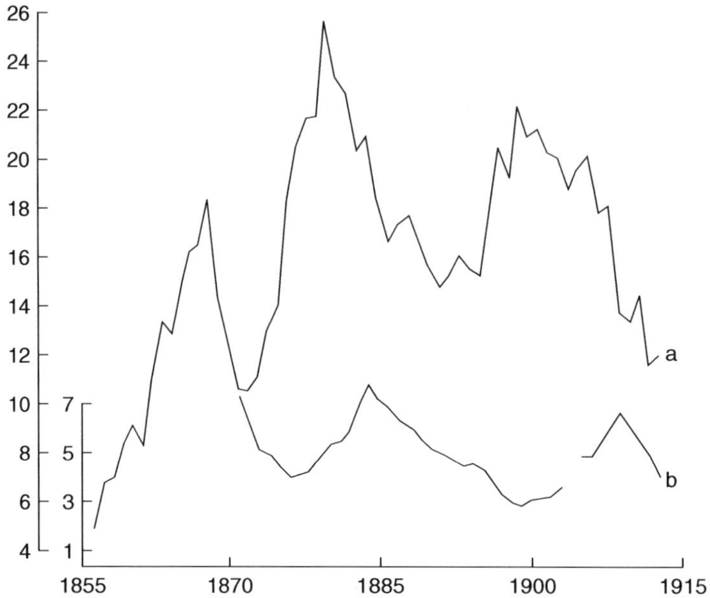

Figure 8.4 Surveyors' fees and empty property in London, 1855–1915

Source: Parry Lewis, 1965, 171.

Note: a = Surveyors' fees for new building in London £000. b = Empty property in London per cent.

For other parts of Britain, the nineteenth-century building cycle has been argued to have been caused by lagged responses to variations in the fortunes of the industries in those regions, with growth stimulating incomes and inward migration, and hence housing demand, and depressions bringing building to a halt.[42] The situation in London was somewhat different as the capital had a diverse economy where no industry predominated. Here, transportation innovations and the volume of unlet empty property seem to have had more influence, abetted by periodic financial crisis. The Overend and Gurney crash of 1866, in particular, sent London's new housing market tumbling as builders faced the sudden calling-in of loans.

Three transport-related metropolitan long building cycles have been suggested to have occurred from the 1860s, when public transport began to have a serious impact on residential location. The first peak was centred on the railway building boom of the 1860s; the second on the expansion derived from horse-drawn tram services around the 1880s; and the third and final one at the turn of the century was based on the new tube system and electric tramways.[43] The timing of the metropolitan building cycles appears to have been distinct from the national cycle from the 1860s to the 1890s, but it was more closely coincident after then. This may have been because prior to the 1890s provincial cities were sufficiently small that transport improvements had little impact on overall residential location. But the advent of the electric tram and then the motor bus changed all that and the rest of urban Britain came more into line with the influences on the metropolis.

The marked decline in the years after 1906–7 led the most eminent contemporary commentator, Spensley, to predict an upswing, but it was to be interrupted by the onset of war.[44] This prediction was undoubtedly accurate as so much was being invested in the transportation infrastructure at the time – with further tube lines, electrified tram routes and motor bus networks all coming into operation. The impact of the decline in housebuilding must have severely affected the fortunes of these new transport investments and, as Chapter 10 will show, their operators were in dire straits at the time. This suggests that the argument used about transport shifts earlier should not be regarded as a perfect explanation of building cycles; contemporary macroeconomic and political circumstances also had an influence. Property taxes, rearmament and the First World War then delayed the upswing, which in the 1920s and 1930s was to produce a record expansion of suburban London.[45]

Building cycles highlight the uncertainty involved in nineteenth-century housebuilding: variations in demand combined with changes in supply costs made development a risky business. The annual number of dwellings built fluctuated far more than today.[46] Bankruptcy amongst builders and losses to landowners when improving their estates were therefore commonplace. This, and the ease of entry into the building trade, kept housebuilding firm sizes generally small;[47] it was not until the 1930s that the large modern British estate developer emerged as a significant force in the industry.[48] Speculative housebuilders were also generally separate entities from building contractors. The latter built to contract for a client rather than for the general market as the speculative builder did. Contracting firms had grown up since the early nineteenth century,[49] and built the railways, other physical infrastructure, commercial buildings, grand houses and apartment blocks. Some of the building contractors were amongst the largest firms in the land, in contrast to speculative housebuilders. One reason why the two parts of the building industry were so distinct was that speculative builders had a terrible reputation for jerry-building and dishonesty;[50] whereas contractors wished to advertise their skills and probity. When Thomas Cubitt embarked on his audacious programme of estate development (see below), for example, his brother William split off his contracting firm from the family business and the two remained independent ever after.[51]

Edward Yates was one of the more successful nineteenth-century London housebuilders, and his success came from combining the functions of an estate developer, a builder and a landlord. Towards the end of his career he owned 2,345 houses, most of which he had built on his own developments. His wealth and capital backing enabled such a strategy – his largest development in Nunhead was built at a leisurely pace over forty years.[52] Another successful developer-cum-builder was Thomas Cubitt. He took even longer to build Pimlico, defaulting on his ground rent on the Grosvenor lease for over a decade after 1838, but the landowners had little option but to carry on with his leases because the poor state of the housing market at the time offered the prospect of no other takers. The scale of risk in nineteenth-century development can be seen in what is regarded as one of the most successful and prestigious London developments of the nineteenth century, Belgravia: of the three developers called in by the Grosvenor family to undertake this scheme on poorly drained land, only the astute or lucky Cubitt avoided bankruptcy.[53] Yates and Cubitt, none the less, were lucky exceptions because economic conditions in housing provision usually worked against the existence of such large, integrated enterprises.

Property taxes and the housing market

Property taxes were major sources of tax revenue in the nineteenth century. Between 1890 and 1900, they represented 39 per cent of central taxes and 89 per cent of local ones, excluding elementary education.[54] With regard to housing, they were levied on households directly in proportion to the rateable value of the dwelling, immaterial of its tenure; although, to ease collection, rates were often compounded into rents and paid by landlords. (Landlords received a discount for doing this, which itself became a subject of political controversy.)[55]

As a tax on housing, rates lower the effective demand for it. The final incidence of the tax, however, depends on the response of housing supply. For London as a whole, the supply of housing could be adjusted by altering the amount of new building and/or the quality of existing housing through improvement (rare) or disrepair (common). So a property tax imposed on the whole area would in the long run be borne partly by households and partly by landowners, but not by housing landlords, in line with standard tax incidence analysis. This is because the fall in effective demand lowers rents, and the supply of housing is cut back as a result. The housing supply reduction occurs through less new building and by landlords failing to maintain the quality of their existing properties. With less housebuilding, the demand for land is lower and its price falls. The fall in housing supply continues until rents rise to a level that ensures that housing landlord net risk-adjusted returns once again equal those in other possible investment outlets for them.

In nineteenth-century Britain, the target returns required from investing in housing can be assumed to be determined internationally in the long run because of the large export of capital. There is an opposing 'new view' of property tax incidence that suggests that the tax entirely falls on capital through the loss of investment opportunities in housing, but this assumes that capital cannot be imported or exported, which clearly is invalid for nineteenth-century Britain.[56]

Higher property taxes, in other words, raise household housing consumption costs and lower housing supply. Given the sticky nature of housing rents and lags in housing supply, the length of adjustment to new tax levels could be substantial. During the adjustment process, housing landlords may incur losses as well because they may not be able to adjust rents quickly; their tenants may default; or housing investments may have to be liquidated at capital losses. This explains periodic explosions of landlord anger at unexpected property tax increases, particularly when the housing market was depressed. In addition, property tax varied across the city, depending on the local authority in question, so the geography of property taxes affected housing supply.

Rates rose significantly during the nineteenth century as increasing demands were put on local government (see Chapter 16). The increases were greatest from the 1880s onwards as progressively greater obligations were put on local government bodies and as local politicians tried to improve the urban environment, transportation and housing through rate-funded expenditure. The impact of the rates on housing costs consequently was high and rising. In 1880, they represented 16 per cent of the total of working-class rent and rate payments combined; ten years later the share had risen to 20 per cent.[57] London, as a whole, was not particularly burdened, as similar percentages existed elsewhere – although Londoners did pay absolutely more in rates because housing costs were appreciably higher in the capital than the provinces. Such a large tax burden, none the less, had a significant depressing effect on the housing market: cutting new building and encouraging disrepair.

High rates in central areas, moreover, encouraged the better-off to leave them for cheaper suburban locations. A location across the city boundary was especially advantageous after the advent of the Metropolitan Board of Works in 1855, and even more so after the conception of the London County Council. It is interesting to note that inner city building around the West End for the rich was not particularly dynamic for most of the nineteenth century. Building in these districts failed to match the considerable growth in national wealth and the preference of the rich to live in or near London. Much of it, moreover, involved displacement from increasingly less fashionable areas, like Bloomsbury, into more fashionable ones, like Belgravia and Kensington. The considerable problems of developers in areas like Notting Hill and Pimlico, as they were developed, suggest that the spatial limits of this style of living were being reached. The property tax may well have played a part in its demise.

The end of a housing era

The years prior to 1914 saw a coming together of a number of depressing influences on a scale not previously seen, leading to a severe crisis in the

London housing market. Victorian Britain experienced an unprecedented property boom in the late 1890s and early 1900s. Vallis's land price series for England shows a sixfold real rise in auctioned land prices in the 1890s, only to be followed by an equally sharp fall.[58] This boom, when it collapsed, left the London market flooded with unlet suburban homes. The end of the boom was encouraged by inflation, which was eroding the real value of rental incomes and discouraging demand, and real wages were stagnating. Real interest rates and property taxes were also high. The combined effects plunged the housing market into a severe depression. It has been suggested that house prices fell by 40 to 50 per cent in the Edwardian era.[59] Unsurprisingly, there was a major slump in housebuilding.

These exceptional, but predominantly cyclical, effects were then overtaken by a dramatic structural break in the financial attractiveness of private landlordism. During the First World War, controls were introduced on nominal rents and mortgage interest rates, with the former maintained after 1918 despite high war-time inflation. These and other measures destroyed the pre-war structure of rental provision, which now faced new competition from subsidised council housebuilding and reformed and subsidised homeownership. With the virtual cessation of housebuilding since 1914, chronically low levels of new building lasted until the 1920s and disrepair mounted. Private landlordism, as the incumbent main housing provider, was an easy – if false – target for the post-war housing shortage and subsequent housing policies continued to discriminate against the tenure.

Landowners and leases

At the other end of the housing supply chain from the housing landlord was the ground landowner. When interested in profiting from housing development, landlords had a number of options. They could sell their land freehold or in fee for a perpetual rent charge; arrange for a builder to build houses and then sell them on freehold; or lease plots via a building agreement. Under a lease, the landlord let a site for a certain time at a stipulated ground rent and, at reversion, acquired all improvements to the land (that is, full rights to the site with any houses on it in a good state of repair). If changes in use occurred, or alterations were made to the building during the course of a lease, clauses in it would often stipulate that the landowner could charge a fee to permit the change. Leases, consequently, gave landowners continued rights over land use after the initial phase of building. There were, nevertheless, many badly drawn-up leases which kept leasing landowners from recovering much of the improved value of their land or left them with little control over its use until reversion. But landowners, by the nineteenth century, had generally learnt from the mistakes of their forebears, so that leases and the lawyers who drew them up exhibited considerable acumen and foresight over possible eventualities.

The most common form of building lease was for landlords to enter into direct contracts with builders for the erection of houses of a stipulated value, to be constructed within a certain time, at the charge of a site ground rent. Builders would then sell 'improved' leases of completed houses on the plots to house owners, profiting on the difference between their building and lease costs and the value of the improved leases they sold on. If builders failed to erect the stipulated dwellings, or to pay the ground rent when due, the lease would revert back to the landowner. Sometimes, especially when significant site infrastructure work was needed (for example, levelling, landscaping, roads and drainage), intermediary developers would enter. They lowered the capital needed by landowners to fund high-cost projects, and offered development expertise, at the price of sharing in the financial gains from building.

About a third of residential property in London in the last quarter of the nineteenth century was held freehold – although many property owners themselves let rather than actually lived in these freehold houses – with the rest of the housing stock held on short building leases of 99 years or less. Lease terms lengthened from around 31 years on average in the seventeenth century to about 80 years in suburban South London at the end of the Victorian era.[60]

A considerable literature has developed in recent decades over the impact of leasehold and freehold land on nineteenth-century residential development.[61] Practice varied considerably between towns and under the different legal arrangements of the constituent parts of the United Kingdom. This variation has been cited to highlight the importance of tradition and institutional arrangements, but the general conclusion of the literature follows the view of the (anti-landowner) Liberal Land Enquiry Committee of 1914 that landowners preferred to have leases and that the balance of demand and supply fixed whether they could. In areas of high land prices, leasehold was, therefore, more common and, as London had the highest land values, the prevalence of leasehold there was to be expected. Leasehold was consequently a product of land monopoly and shortage. This argument has a weakness, however, because the price of freehold land should have been commensurably higher in London. If the land market worked with reasonable efficiency, the discount on leasehold land should have been counterbalanced by the gains from retaining a leasehold interest in exactly the same way as elsewhere. Supply and demand, in other words, are likely to affect the general level of land prices, not the particular forms in which land, and associated property rights, are transformed from one use to another.

Rather than have recourse to poorly formulated arguments about the 'balance' of demand and supply, alternative hypotheses seem more credible. There might have been particular local economic reasons why London landowners preferred to use leases rather than to sell freehold. The potential benefits of leasehold over freehold, therefore, have to be examined in order to understand why London had such a high ratio of leasehold land.

Table 8.1 Present value of £40,000 at reversion

Target rate of return (per cent)	*Lease term in years* 31	50	80	99
2	21,560	14,860	8,200	5,630
4	11,860	563	174	820
6	6,570	217	380	120
8	3,680	850	80	20

Source: Own calculations.

Benefits of reversion to the landowning family

The usual reason suggested for landowners' preference for leasehold is that they, or their descendants, enjoyed the enhanced value of the property at the end of the lease. This is undoubtedly true but the value of such a benefit is far lower than is often suggested.[62] Assume when the land is first developed a landowner has a choice between selling freehold or on a 99-year lease. The expected returns from the lease are the annual rents over the period of the lease and the forecast reversionary value. These can be discounted at the prevailing real rate of interest and, in a competitive market, that calculated present value should be the same as the price that can be achieved by selling freehold, because freeholders will have made the same calculation about future returns when formulating the price they bid for the freehold. In the absence of widespread market inefficiencies, only when the landowner's view of those future returns is more optimistic than those of the market in general, or they accept a lower rate of return and hence a lower discount rate, will the present value of a lease to a landowner be greater than the selling price of the freehold land.

The present value of enhanced ground rents at the end of a lease may in any case be low. Table 8.1 gives the present value of an arbitrary £40,000 earned at reversion for a series of discount rates and lease lengths. It can be seen that the real benefit is a small fraction of what it notionally seems, especially as the target rate of return and lease length increase.

Landed family interests

Landowners, none the less, might in fact have had a lower rate of discount on assets in urban landed property than did average nineteenth-century investors. The social status of land and growing attempts, until the 1870s, by landed families to tie heirs to land through settlement devices suggest that landed interests had implicit lower discount rates for land. Leasehold was a beneficial form of property development for them, because it kept title within the family and lowered the risk of one descendant frittering the family wealth away. Settlement devices on land were probably easier to enforce on an errant heir than might have been the case with many other investments. Variations in risk-unadjusted target rates of return, moreover, can still be seen to have effects in property markets today. For instance, differences in implied discount rates between the users of offices and financial institutions holding portfolios of such properties help to explain why so many office blocks are leased rather than directly owned by the user.

The implicit social discount rate on land for the aristocracy in general, however, would probably have declined with the onset of agricultural depression and the gradual disposal of landed assets after the 1870s.[63] But the great landed estates in London had greater tenacity and held on to their highly profitable estates for far longer, so that the decline was probably not experienced with regard to London land in the same way as it was elsewhere.

Transactions costs

The transfer of land title in nineteenth-century England was an expensive and drawn-out business – a situation that was only resolved in a series of Property Acts between 1910 and 1925 when solicitors were persuaded to drop their opposition to reform.[64] Leasehold may have reduced transactions costs by avoiding the need to transfer full title to the seller. In London, this may have been particularly important as there were often unknown claims of rights to land use. Leasing kept potential problems associated with such claims in the hands of the original freehold owner, creating the possibility of a market where none was otherwise feasible.

Leasehold terms

The terms under which building leases were issued could, when expertly drawn up, impose significant conditions on the nature of housing developments, ensuring that housing of a particular type and style was built within stipulated time periods. It has been argued that this enabled landowners to indulge in early town planning, maintain building quality and avoid the threat of undesirable uses undermining neighbourhood property values.[65] Studies of land development in British cities during this period have tended not to support this view, generally concluding that leasehold or freehold made little difference to actual outcomes. Once the status of urban localities was established by the interaction of local demand and supply, particular types of housing would tend to be built in them whatever the land tenure. Moreover, if landowners were concerned about the effects of selling freehold on the value of adjacent land they owned, they could still stipulate conditions.[66]

As regards building control, in practice, it was difficult to keep builders to their lease agreements. Many nineteenth-century houses were shoddily built, even in the more salubrious districts. Poor-quality building was prevalent whatever the land tenure, reflecting unscrupulous builders' attempts to profit through misleading purchasers and ground landlords.

Land market monopoly

Another suggested reason for the prevalence of leasehold is that it enabled certain landowners to monopolise local land markets.[67] The great estates of London have been well documented and only a handful of landowners held much of the land developed in the West End and beyond. It is difficult, none the less, to claim that landowners had the ability to exercise extensive monopoly powers, particularly by the nineteenth century, because they faced the ever-present danger that, if they held out for excessive terms, development would leap-frog over their domains. Furthermore, as the urban fringe expanded, far greater numbers of landowners were drawn into the ambit of the London residential land market. Successive improvements in transportation systems greatly extended the spread of London, so the weakening of specific landowners' market positions accelerated during the course of the century. The situation of the Grosvenor family – one of the most extensive of inner London landowners – in relation to Cubitt in Pimlico, noted above, indicates that even the most powerful landed interests could find themselves in a poor negotiating position.

Increasing market liquidity

Leases were not only used by ground landlords but also by many lessees, so that a particular property could have a series of sub-leases and subdivisions of leases in between its final users and the ground landlord. This myriad of leases was much complained of when owners were chased for repairs, because the regulatory authorities frequently could not identify who was responsible. Yet such practices did have the practical advantage of breaking up the capital value of expensive leases. This allowed more people to invest in property and enabled them to spread their risks across a range of properties. By increasing competition amongst lessees, this benefited landowners as well – provided that they drew up the head lease satisfactorily.

Hedging against land market risk

The nineteenth-century land development process was a highly risky one. One risk was noted above: sharp fluctuations in overall market conditions as indicated by the wide variations in housebuilding rates. Furthermore, there was the threat that a particular development project might not gain favour, whatever the general state of the market. The outward expansion of the suburbs, in addition, was an uncertain business. Landowners often had little means of predicting when and in what form it would reach their land. Negotiations with potential builders would improve their knowledge of present market conditions but both parties would know that they were operating in conditions of great uncertainty. This riskiness of housing development was a reason why returns could be so handsome, but the downside carried the threat of bankruptcy.

Developers' expectations of development potential at a particular point in time as well as being inaccurate could be either too optimistic or too pessimistic. Yet the prevailing state of expectations would influence the freehold market price for land. If they were optimistic, the risk of a development failing was high, and such failure would then deter others from buying any adjacent land. If they were too pessimistic, the landowner would receive a lower than normal return. Leasing out land thus enabled landowners, in modern financial terminology, to take out options against such risks; whereas with freehold sales they were effectively taking the risk assessment the successful purchaser incorporated into their bid price. Under a lease, if the initial scheme proved too optimistic, the builder taking out the lease was likely to fail – so that the lease would revert back to the landowner and different tactics could be tried. Alternatively, if the land turned out at some time in the future to have a higher value use than initially envisaged, the landowner could charge a fine to permit the new use, thereby sharing in the unexpected development gain.

This option-like advantage of leases has not been pointed out in the historical literature but it would seem a potent one. London may well have had such a large proportion of its land developed on a leasehold basis because land prices were so high and suburban development particularly risky there. The sheer scale of the metropolis and uncertainties in the development of suburban transportation systems contributed to those risks.

The four main benefits of leases consequently would seem to be: differences in implicit discount rates when valuing the income streams from land by sellers and buyers of development land; transactions costs; greater market liquidity; and the ability to share in the scale and spread of subsequent development risk. None of these implies the need for any special market power on the part of landowners. With the advent of social housing and owner occupation after the First World War, the market conditions under which land leasing was made advantageous disappeared. Landowners by then were unlikely to have a low discount rate for land investments; land market transactions were significantly more efficient; and both social housing landlords and owner occupiers (encouraged by building societies) put a high premium on owning freehold.

Part 4

Infrastructure

9 To and from the capital

Introduction

Throughout the nineteenth century London was the focal point of the UK transport system, and, through its port, a centre of international trade. As transportation facilities improved, the capital's links were strengthened to even the most distant parts of the country. Both people and goods could move further, more quickly and at far less cost than in previous centuries. This helped to complete the formation of a national market for many goods and services – a characteristic that was vitally important for the development of metropolitan industries. Better communications also helped to make regional labour markets more competitive, because it was easier to migrate from one place to another. This was a factor encouraging greater regional convergence of wage rates in particular trades.

As London was the centre of the national transport system, a study of the development of its transport linkages could virtually be a history of British transport as a whole. This temptation is avoided here by concentrating on the implications of the transport revolution for the metropolis itself. Yet national implications can still be seen in the influence of the capital both on competitive structures in national transport and on the economic geography of Britain and its regions. Apart from the obvious fact that the capital was bound to become the hub of the national transport system, two other factors stand out in the national context. First, London was the most expensive place to build transport facilities – yet all major transport companies would feel the need to have a presence there. Second, it remained throughout the period a terminus point and also a barrier to the through-movement of passengers and goods between the North and Midlands and points beyond, including the Channel. Thus, London – because of its very existence and size – was either a destination or a transhipment point, which had significant implications for the economic geography of Britain as well as in the capital itself. London transportation activities gained considerably from this geographic fact and from the problem of crossing the capital for those who needed to continue journeys. Its place in the economic geography of England, furthermore, gave London's port an unprecedented importance that itself created considerable problems for the expansion of other activities in the capital by absorbing much land and labour in what were often hopelessly under-performing investments.

The means of travel for both passengers and goods are considered here: starting chronologically with the horse, then covering canals, sea coasters, steam packets and the railways. The final section examines the port.

Horse-drawn transport

Stagecoaches

Travelling by road was the age-old way of getting to and from London, but public coach services improved dramatically from the middle of the eighteenth century. The growth of stagecoach use was caused by higher speeds, better comfort and lower fares. The trip from London to Edinburgh, for example, could be completed in under two days in the 1830s, compared with almost ten days in the 1750s; while the time to Bristol fell from two days to nineteen hours. In 1821, there were 450 separate departures from London each week with a seating capacity of around 58,000.[1]

Much of the improvement in speed was due to the activities of private turnpike trusts. Charging users tolls, they paved roads, maintained them and built new ones. Roads to London were the most heavily used long-distance routes in Britain, so it is unsurprising that long-distance turnpikes were concentrated on them. Better methods of road construction, adopted by many of the trusts, were pioneered by civil engineers, such as Telford on his road from London to Holyhead. Speed was further aided by MacAdam's invention of tar-based surfacing materials. By the 1830s, trusts managed 22,000 miles of road – more than a sixth of the total national mileage.[2]

Higher speeds were assisted by developments in enterprise organisation and coach technology. Stagecoach companies became more sophisticated in their operations, for instance, by using several relays of horses per route; while the invention of the elliptical spring in 1804 meant that faster and more comfortable coaches could be introduced. As they grew in size, coaching companies could gain economies of scale, benefit from a network of routes, and invest in more and better coaches, so that a number of leading firms emerged. The London-based firm, Chaplin and Co., for example, in 1830 ran sixty-four coaches and had an annual turnover of half a million pounds.[3]

Costs were being lowered by several factors. Better roads, apart from making the ride smoother, also reduced wear and tear on vehicles and horses. The development of springed coaches enabled twice as many passengers to be carried. Their lower roofs also provided easier access to roof seats, and they were less prone to jolts, so more rooftop passengers could be accommodated. The coaching companies, however, still faced considerable variations in the running costs because of fluctuations in the prices of horses and fodder. Prices for both were particularly high in the 1800s, but the end of the Napoleonic Wars in 1815 then caused them to fall.

Reliability greatly improved, due to the faster speeds, competition and the example set by the mail coach. The quality of service depended on the grade of stagecoach used for travel. 'Flying machines' and mail coaches had the shortest journey times, for which they charged a premium rate, although their restricted luggage capacity and early morning departures discouraged some passengers. 'Old' or 'slow' coaches offered more leisurely journeys and lower fares. For those prepared to accompany parcels or goods, the 'caravan' provided very slow, but cheap, travel.

The heyday of the stagecoach was over as soon as the railways were built, but decline was far from instantaneous. The number of journeys grew impressively in the 1800s and remained high until the middle of the century. Both the number of services and passenger miles travelled increased fast during the French Wars, with passenger miles almost doubling in twenty years to over two million.[4] By 1840, however, routes were being cut, but overall passenger usage still expanded, compared to earlier decades, through a greater frequency of service on the remaining routes.

Road haulage

The rise in goods road traffic to and from London was equally notable. Ton mileage more than trebled between 1796 and 1840 and, unlike passenger traffic, the number of services grew rapidly, from 574 routes in 1816 to 1,081 in 1840.[5] The expansion was stimulated by industrial growth and the resultant expansion of internal UK trade, faster speeds, better reliability and falling costs.

Again, there were large operators as well as a multitude of smaller concerns. In London, two firms, Russel and Pickford, bought former inns from which to run their businesses. Another company, Marsh and Swan, acquired a site close to the City where they built stables, warehouses, granaries, a smithy and wheelwright shops. Like their passenger-carrying counterparts, the larger firms gained scale and network economies. They operated both fast and slow services.[6] Pickford's fast van service, introduced in 1814, reduced the journey time between London and Manchester from five days to thirty-six hours.[7]

Boats and ships

Rivers and canals

London had long depended on river transport. All movement out of the port moved east down the Thames Estuary, but the river was also used westwards – with Oxfordshire and Berkshire grain, for example, having been carried down the Thames since the middle of the sixteenth century.

The Lea had been navigable probably since Roman times, providing access to the rural hinterland of Hertfordshire, and the river was canalised in the early nineteenth century. A fillip to westbound river traffic was given by the canal boom.[8] The capital, however, was not to be the focus of the country's canal network, which tended to be concentrated in the new industrial districts of Britain.

London was first connected by canal to the North and Midlands in 1790 with the opening of the Oxford Canal, which ran from a junction with the Coventry Canal in the Midlands to Oxford, where it joined the Thames. The waterway was far from perfect, as it followed a narrow, winding course, and navigation on the Thames between London and Oxford could be difficult. These problems encouraged construction of a further canal a few years later, the Grand Junction (now known as the Grand Union), from a junction with the Oxford Canal in the Midlands to Brentford, west of London, and it was then extended to Paddington in 1801. The new route almost halved the Oxford Canal–Thames distance. To create a direct canal link to the port from the Grand Junction, another canal company was set up, the Regent's Canal Co., and a canal was built from Paddington to Limehouse. It followed a circuitous course to avoid built-up areas and the need for too many locks and tunnels, and after innumerable delays was finally completed in 1820.[9] It proved to be of limited success because the port could already be reached from the Grand Junction more easily via the Thames at Brentford. Later, a ten-acre dock was constructed at Limehouse Basin, where the canal reached the Thames opposite the Surrey docks.[10] Although planned as a transshipment point between the canal and the port, limited long-distance canal cargoes meant that it was mainly used instead for the unloading of coasters bringing coal by sea to London (see below, p. 208).

Until 1845, canal companies were unable to provide their own boat services without a specialist Act of Parliament, so most goods were transported by independent carriers.[11] There were three types: skipper-owners, general merchants, and large-scale, specialist transport companies. In 1800, on the key Manchester to London route, Pickfords and Bache and Co. of Coventry were the two largest hauliers. Others then competed on the route, though Pickfords still dominated.[12] As with road transport, there were two types of service. Slow boats, pulled by a single horse and tied up overnight, moved low-value goods. Fast or 'flying' vessels, generally owned by the large-scale operators, used relays of horses, double crews, round-the-clock sailing and lock priority licences to provide rapid, more expensive carriage of higher-value cargoes, such as groceries and manufactured goods.

Compared to canals in the rest of the country, those around London were under-used.[13] In 1845, the 14 per cent of Britain's canals located in the South-East transported only 6 per cent of the traffic by weight. The most used route was the Grand Junction route to the Midlands. In 1810, it carried 192,000 tons of cargo to London and 152,000 tons in the opposite direction. Coal was the major southbound commodity; paradoxically the same was also true for northbound traffic because London acted as an entrepôt for sea-borne coal. Other bulk commodities, particularly iron and building materials, made up much of the rest of the tonnage. Canal boats brought salt from Cheshire, glass from Stourbridge and non-perishable agricultural produce. The agricultural goods were sold at a thriving straw, vegetable and cattle market that developed close to the canal's Paddington Basin. Outward traffic, apart from coal, primarily consisted of London-specific products, groceries and manufactured goods, plus the city's leftovers of manure, ashes and breeze for agricultural use as fertiliser. The imbalance and variety in north- and southbound traffic raised costs, as many boats had to travel on return journeys with low-value goods, like manure, as ballast. The canal company from 1801 to 1810 also ran a regular passenger service from Paddington to Uxbridge, plus various holiday excursions.[14]

Canal transit for coal was restricted by the actions of the City Corporation, worried about a loss of tax revenue from its sea-borne coal levies. It managed to persuade Parliament to insert a clause in the Grand Junction's enabling act that forced all coal cargoes to be landed at Watford – then miles by road from the key London market. The constraint was weakened in 1805 at no expense to the City, when the Canal Act permitted up to 50,000 tons to pass through to Paddington on the payment of sea coal duties to the Corporation.[15] The tonnage limit was later increased and then abandoned, and the sea coal duties were finally abolished, but, by this time, railways had moved heavily into canal business.

The Regent's Canal was primarily used for local traffic, bringing from the port coal for general distribution and raw materials to the industries that sprang up along its route. Only a quarter of its more than 600,000 annual tonnage in 1835 originated from, or was sent to, non-London destinations. Two basins for cargo handling were built along the canal's route: the Cumberland next to Albany Street for the West End; and the City, next to Old Street. The former attracted a thriving hay and straw market, and around the latter clustered much canal-side industry.[16]

Railways were to blunt the use of canals but the unenterprising canal companies encouraged their own eclipse. They had first-mover advantage. Users and carriers had invested heavily in canal-side warehousing, loading equipment and barges, so they were reluctant to switch to the new transport mode. Long-distance rail transport initially was also more expensive than inland navigation, difficult to arrange because of the large number of small railway companies on routes, and rail companies did not have the contacts or expertise. As the railway companies amalgamated and improved their services, however, their competitive position improved. On the initial routes out of London, passenger traffic had dominated but soon freight became of growing importance. The canal companies failed to amalgamate or collude in face of the threat; the four companies on the London–Birmingham route, for example, only quoted through-prices late in the century. In dry spells, some were unable to maintain adequate depth for navigation, while frequent locks delayed transit.

Canal companies did make some attempts to resist the threat of rail. The Grand Junction, for example, made significant changes in the decade before the opening of the London and Birmingham Railway. It rationalised tolls, cut rates, tried steam power, extended reservoirs to ensure the canal stayed open, and doubled a flight of locks. With the arrival of the railway, a tariff war ensued. Tonnage on the canal actually rose by a fifth between 1838 and 1858, but cheaper tariffs and shorter distances cut revenue by 57 per cent so that the dividend was reduced from 10 per cent to 3.5 per cent. Under such pressures, the company unsurprisingly came to a rate agreement in 1857 with its two main rail competitors, the London and North Western (successor to the London and Birmingham) and the Great Western, and the agreed prices remained steady for thirty years after one increase in 1859.[17]

In general, by the 1840s and 1850s, the UK railway network was superseding the canals. Agreements not to compete with rail, or take-over by rail companies, then aided the canal system into industrial obscurity. Even though the London canal system was limited, its impact on the location of industry within the city and its environs was to be substantial throughout the nineteenth century, because the canals enabled local transshipment of bulky goods, provided plentiful supplies of water for steam power and other industrial processes, and kept land values low as a result of the environmental impact of canal-side industry.

Coastal shipping

The most important form of goods transport, in terms of tonnage, in the first part of the century was coastal shipping. In 1841, registered coastal tonnage of 3 million tons entered the Port of London – three times the coastal tonnage that sailed into Liverpool, the country's second port; 1.1 million tons also left London in coastal ships – the second largest amount in the country.[18] The leading port of origination was Newcastle, which mainly shipped coal (hence the phrase 'like sending coals to Newcastle'), with London the principal destination. Given the large number of ports around the British Isles, however, the capital by no means dominated coastwise trade.

Coal was the main London-bound cargo. Of the 2.2 million tons of merchandise imported in 1824, all bar 16 per cent was coal. After a dip in 1855, caused by coal wars with the rail companies, the trade expanded so that, by 1911, 9 million tons of coal were entering the capital on coasters,[19] a sixfold increase from 1818.

Each sailing brig carried approximately 220 tons of coal and made an average of ten round voyages per year. In the early part of the century, owners did not work their boats under freight contracts, with posted or negotiated freight rates, but rather bought cargoes, shipped them to the capital and sold them there. The coaster's control of the trade lasted until the mid-1840s, when it began to face increasing competition from rail. Rail companies by then could ensure rapid and certain delivery. The Great Northern Railway was the first to bring coal to London in quantity from 1850, and a price war with the sea carriers brought the cost of coal in London down from 30s to 17s a ton. Between 1845 – when they had a monopoly – and 1874, coasters lost 63 per cent of the coal trade to rail.[20]

Technical advances in shipping and handling, plus heavy investment, then enabled boat owners to claw back market share. For decades, the owners of coasters shunned the screw propeller because adoption of it would have necessitated scrapping their existing capital assets. When the steam, screw-driven, collier was finally first used in 1844, it could carry twice the cargo of a sailing brig and completed a round voyage between London and Newcastle far more quickly. Coaster freight costs tumbled as a result of such technical improvements: from around 10 shillings a ton from Newcastle to London in the early 1820s, to 6 shillings a ton in the early 1870s. (Up to the 1820s, the shortage of shipping and risks of the Napoleonic Wars had doubled the rate up to peak at almost £1 a ton, which significantly affected metropolitan heating and power costs in the first two decades of the century.)[21]

Ships increasingly concentrated on a growing bulk trade, leaving the retail business to the better equipped and located rail companies. To increase turnaround times, both in the North-East and in London, large amounts of capital were invested in steam-operated cranes and winders, culminating in 1863 in the launch on the Thames of a 250-foot floating derrick with six hydraulic cranes. Of no less importance, a new Coal Exchange was built in the City in the late 1840s to facilitate marketing and distribution.[22]

The revival of the coaster in coal shipment was only slowly achieved. At first, few ship owners bought steam colliers; so that even in 1863 three-quarters of coastal coal entered London under sail. The capital cost of steamers was high and the decline in Baltic business encouraged many sailing vessels to turn to the coastal trade, causing freight rates to plummet. The steamer, nevertheless, gradually grew in popularity, and by 1898 more coal was again imported into the capital by coaster than by rail.[23] As coasters now dealt in bulk, however, they were generally chartered by colliery owners, intermediate merchants or large industrial consumers, like the gas industry, and the coal was destined for use in the industries and gas works lining the banks of the Thames.

Coasters were important in integrating distant British agricultural regions with the London market in the period before railways. The second major commodity after coal carried by coaster, for example, was grain. In 1824, it accounted for 14 per cent of coaster traffic into London. Between 1819 and 1827, an average of 207,000 tons of grain a year entered the capital in this way: 37 per cent of which was wheat, 32 per cent oats, 18 per cent barley and the remainder malt. With the advent of railways, ship volumes inevitably fell and, by 1895, they were a tenth of those of 1825.[24] The fall, however, was partly offset by a rise in the carriage of hay, needed to feed the ever-expanding horse population. This commodity was transported in specially constructed flat-bottomed barges, loaded on their return voyages with horse manure. For a short period, from the 1830s to the 1850s, the Aberdeen Steam Navigation Co. also carried livestock; in the early 1830s, 7,000 cattle and 10,000 sheep a year were transported to London in this way. Business switched to rail when a line was opened to Aberdeen, though it recovered slightly in the 1860s and 1870s owing to the shipping company's success in obtaining return cargoes and an 1856 division of trade agreement with the railway.[25] Other goods imported by coaster included metals, jute and hemp from Dundee, salted meat, potatoes, sugar and building materials. The latter comprised bricks from Suffolk and Essex, Portland stone from Weymouth and Poole, and slates from Mid- and North Wales.

Coastal exports from London were dominated by the transhipment of foreign grain: almost 24,000 tons a year between 1819 and 1827, 43 per cent of which was wheat, 51 per cent oats and barley, and the remainder malt. Other outward cargoes were textiles, tea, wine and a wide selection of manufactured goods.[26]

Local sea passenger traffic only became important with the appearance of the steam packet in 1814. Although in 1802 there were passenger services from London to Leith and Berwick, the unpredictability of the journey times limited demand. By the mid-1830s, however, London had services to all the major British ports. Faster and cheaper than stagecoaches, steam packets in 1833 carried almost 400,000 people between London and Margate, 12,500 on the Dover route in 1836, 18,000 between London and Edinburgh in 1843, and over a million on the 'long ferry' to Gravesend, an important transshipment point for travellers to Kent including those journeying on the continental packets out of Dover and Folkestone.[27] Railways at first had little effect on this traffic, as the steamship was far more commodious and comfortable than the train, and the shipping companies responded to the new threat. In 1849, for example, almost twice as many passengers travelled from Leith, Edinburgh's port, to London by sea, as by rail from Scotland's capital, aided by the aggressive fare-cutting policy of the London and Edinburgh Steam Packet Company. But, subsequently, the superior speed and lower cost of railways were fatal to shipping, and steam packets were increasingly concentrating on the provision of holiday excursions.[28]

Boats also became integrated with rail for journeys to the continent and elsewhere. During the second half of the century, boat trains leaving central London stations would carry passengers to Dover, Folkestone, Newhaven and Harwich for Europe; to Holyhead and Fishguard for Ireland; and Southampton and Liverpool for non-European destinations. Charing Cross Station, in particular, became nineteenth-century London's equivalent of Heathrow.

Railways

Passenger traffic

London's first inter-city railway was the Birmingham line, completed in 1838. This was soon followed by routes to Southampton (1838), Bristol (1841) and Brighton (1841), and extensions of the Greenwich and Croydon lines out of London Bridge (1836) into Kent, Surrey and Sussex.[29] By the early 1850s, the rail network extended 6,600 miles and London was directly connected to most cities. Throughout the rest of the century, there was then substantial growth in the national network – rising to 15,376 miles in 1871 and 23,411 in 1912 – which was increasingly centred on London.[30] After the initial boom in rail lines, subsequent improvements that benefited the capital were better links to the north and a more extensive network in the metropolitan hinterlands. Improvements in comfort and speed also gradually occurred.

Rail increased the integration of the national economy and helped to heighten London's central role within it, and as the century progressed it enabled the better-off to commute longer distances into the capital and allowed some industries to decentralise away from the metropolis to smaller towns while still keeping in close touch with the huge metropolitan market.

As the discussion of previous modes of transport has shown, railways were not particularly strong competitors with other forms of transport out of London during their initial years. Gradually the situation changed, once teething troubles and capacity constraints were overcome, and new organisational practices invented. The railways have rightly become known as the first modern business corporations. The Railway Clearing House, which opened in 1842 and became fully operational in 1847, simplified payments for long-distance passenger and goods traffic.

Railway company amalgamations led to more uniform practices and policies and to a greater availability of capital for improvements. The 1846 merger of the London and Birmingham with the Grand Junction, to form the London and North Western, was of particular importance for the capital because of the formal link-up with the Liverpool–Manchester and Manchester–Birmingham lines. In general, however, mergers occurred to facilitate trunk routes into London or to develop regional monopolies, so that the areas around London were segmented into company territories. Ten major companies still served London following the amalgamations, so there was still potential for some competition, which was greatest to the south. The structure of the amalgamations of the early companies, none the less, reinforced the barrier effect of the capital, and no mergers occurred between companies with territories on opposite sides of the capital. This left little incentive for through-running across the metropolis or for the building of through mainline stations.

A plethora of stations

Parliament denied railways early central access to London for fear of the effect on the aristocratic residential quarters in the West End and the wrath of the Corporation of London. A Royal Commission on Metropolitan Termini in the mid-1840s drew a line along New Road (now Marylebone/Euston Roads), City Road, Finsbury Square and Bishopsgate Street, beyond which railways could not encroach.[31] Paddington, London Bridge and Nine Elms (and later Waterloo) arose next to similar invisible barriers. This encouraged rail companies to rely on independent termini rather than more efficient through stations or large combined termini. The Great Western, for example, in its act of incorporation was supposed to share Euston with the London and Birmingham, but broad gauge was chosen and the London and Birmingham proved difficult and so Paddington was built.[32] The large array of new stations, furthermore, were in the then rural fringes of the metropolis, a long way from where travellers wanted to be.

Early railway lines were costly to build, because the limited power of locomotives necessitated expensive civil engineering works. Companies partly compensated for this by building meagre facilities in the capital. Euston (1837), when built, was a sad affair behind the grand Doric arch and booking offices. For the first six years, trains were pulled up by cable to beyond the Regent's Canal in Camden, as the slope had been engineered too steeply for the weak steam locomotives; and then for many years afterwards trains had to be piloted up the slope by an extra engine. The London and Southampton similarly built a modest station at Nine Elms (1838), whence passengers had to catch a boat to take them to the West End and City – only building Waterloo ten years later in 1848. The Eastern Counties' terminus was at then distant Shoreditch, which was soon (1846) renamed Bishopsgate to give it a more central image – with Liverpool Street only opening in 1874.[33]

After the initial low investment in London termini, railway company strategies changed in subsequent decades, and by the 1860s, constrained by regulation on pricing, they competed for custom by providing magnificent, independent stations at central locations. Wherever possible, companies shunned attempts by competitors to share termini, so that each company ended up with one or more of its own. In some cases, they uncomfortably co-habited, as at Victoria (1860–2) and London Bridge, but generally they aimed at independence. They were encouraged in this by the prevailing financial climate and a weakening of City and Parliamentary resistance to new stations in central London. The enormous number of schemes proposed in the 1860s threatened to demolish much of central London, and companies felt forced to retaliate and offer their own schemes to blunt others' competitive moves.

During the 1860s, the previous southern barrier keeping railways out of central London was breached, following a Parliamentary Report that recognised the difficulties of existing arrangements south of the river. The decade saw an urban rail boom with the opening of Victoria on the site of the Grosvenor Canal. Having permitted the Victoria incursion across the Thames at the behest of one railway company (the London, Brighton and South Coast), Parliament was in no position to disallow the South Eastern's extension from London Bridge through to Cannon Street and Charing Cross. In the north, the extensions by the Midland to St Pancras and by the Great Eastern to Liverpool Street were also set under way.

Inter-company rivalry helped to spawn the proliferation of termini. But cost overruns were rife, partly caused by rising land values and the highly favourable compensation claims landowners could make, following legislation in 1845. For Britain as a whole, it has been estimated that railway companies commonly paid twice the current market value for land.[34] Misforecast investment costs were combined with over-optimistic projections of operating costs and additional traffic, so that few of these ventures paid. The South Eastern's scheme for Cannon Street and Charing Cross, for example, was three times over-budget and passenger numbers were far lower than expected. Despite the cost, facilities on the route were insufficient, so that congestion and delays to trains were rife for decades to come. Earlier the London and South Western had dismissed a similar extension from Waterloo as financially unviable. Both St Pancras and Liverpool Street also cost far more than anticipated, leading to cuts in dividends.[35]

In the following decade, Blackfairs Station was moved north of the river and renamed St Paul's, while Ludgate Hill opened – all as part of the Chatham's push through to Farringdon, the only central through-London route – and separately Holborn Viaduct Station was built and linked to it. These stations provided City connections for the London, Chatham and Dover's new line from Kent, though once again the cost of the route far outweighed its benefits to the sponsoring rail company.

Holborn Viaduct's location took advantage of the new road being built over the Fleet Valley, linking Holborn and the City, and its creation illustrates a common device used to promote new termini. An independent company would be set up to build a terminus station, to which the interested railway company would subscribe in association with independent backers. In the case of Holborn Viaduct, the Chatham's contemporary financial failure encouraged this approach; yet it was also the means used to promote both Victoria and Charing Cross (and used in other British cities). Kellett argues that this approach raised the cost of the new stations as the independent promoters could play off one railway company against another.[36]

The overall scale of the investment binge was huge. Between the mid-1850s and the 1870s, it has been estimated that the railway companies spent £40 million on routes and stations in London. This was a large slice of total national rail activity. This can be seen when compared to the £350 million spent on the whole of Britain's rail system up to 1860, by which time the national network was virtually complete.[37] The cost of the failure to limit metropolitan passenger and goods termini was thus high not simply in terms of its effect on London users but also in terms of the vast competitive rounds of unnecessary investment.

Terminus-building occurred in most major British cities during this period – one in Glasgow cost £2 million and another in Liverpool, £1 million. As the capital and end point of so many journeys, London received the greatest attention and its high land values imposed particularly high costs. Liverpool Street cost £2 million to build in order to push the Eastern Counties' terminus a short distance further into the City. The Cannon Street/Charing Cross extension from London Bridge required £4 million. These sums represent large shares of contemporary national investment – Liverpool Street and Charing Cross alone represented 0.75 per cent of mid-1860s national income.[38] The number of mainline termini in London would rise through the nineteenth century to an incredible fourteen. Other British cities were similarly richly endowed with stations – Manchester had six and Glasgow seven, for instance – and as they had smaller central land areas proportionately more of their central cities were absorbed in rail termini and associated land uses than in London. In absolute terms, rail land use in central London towered over other cities. In 1900, 776 acres of central land was owned by railways in London – so that they ruled over more metropolitan land than the Corporation of London.[39] This compares to 137 acres in Manchester and 85 in Glasgow.[40] Such expensive assets further limited the benefits of mergers between companies that already had a secure metropolitan base, so no company prior to nationalisation in 1948 had routes that ran the whole length of England.[41]

Competition was greatest to the south. The mistake of the South Eastern Railway in building a terminus at the distant Bricklayers Arms (1844) and the spread of long-distance commuting to and from the central districts encouraged encroachments across the river to serve the City and the West End. One reason for these surface expansions was that there were several owners of large tracts of relatively cheap land, which the rail companies could acquire for their schemes. The Marquis of Westminster owned most of the land for Victoria; the Archbishop of Canterbury and the Bishop of Winchester owned acres of slums in Southwark and Lambeth over which the Charing Cross extension was built. Charing Cross station itself was built on the site of Hungerford Market, and the sites of Cannon Street and Holborn Viaduct were owned by the Drapers' Company, St Thomas's Hospital and Emmanuel College.[42] The pattern of land holdings consequently helped to determine the location of termini. After the 1860s, there were few opportunities to acquire such large tracts, which virtually ruled out further change.

To the north of the centre, rail companies also tried to minimise costs by passing their routes through lower-value slum-housing land. This influenced the location of St Pancras (1868), for example, the grand end point of the Midland Railway, after it decided that sharing King's Cross with the Great Northern had become intolerable. By the early 1870s, the terminus building boom was finally over; only Marylebone was to come as a major terminus. Built for the Great Central Railway as the London station for a planned route from the North of England through to a Channel tunnel, Marylebone and associated goods yards were inconveniently located on land carved out of one of the last remaining, large inner city slum districts, Lisson Grove.

Few of the metropolitan surface rail projects after the 1850s would have been made without the spur of rivalry, over-optimistic traffic forecasts and gullible investors, with companies egged on by engineers and lawyers – who made fabulous incomes from the process of Parliamentary approval and in subsequent conveyancing and project management. Contractors were also willing to offer capital in exchange for contracts to build lines, but they were less willing to keep to cost estimates and tenders.

The costs to London

Much low-income living space was lost without replacement by the successive waves of terminus building. The losses were justified on the grounds that the demolitions were beneficial to health and that the inhabitants would filter up to better-quality accommodation. Instead, most of the remaining dwellings around the new termini and goods yards plunged in status and environmental quality, and the vast majority of the displaced moved into the remaining, already overcrowded, poor quarters. In the south, the engineer for the early London and Greenwich Railway in 1836 chose to build a viaduct over the slums and roads of Bermondsey, and the other southern railway companies followed suit on their inner city lines. This blighted yet further areas of working-class accommodation, as the evocative, if somewhat fictional, sketches of Gustave Doré show.

The other problems created by London's plethora of railway termini related to congestion and land supply. Through-passengers and goods traffic had to travel across central London to the various termini, slowing total journey times and adding greatly to London's already congested streets, especially prior to the development of the underground system. The loss of so much land to railways, and the blighting of even more, reduced inner city supply for other uses. This raised values in the core and restricted the outward movement of the central business areas. The high level of inner-London building rents, so criticised by industry and housing reformers, was given another upward push by the land demands of the railways. Large complex junctions were also needed in the inner suburbs to link railway companies' lines to each other and different termini. The two biggest were both in South London, where the Battersea and New Cross 'tangles' absorbed over 300 acres of land.[43]

Goods traffic

For the distribution of goods, most railway companies built large goods yards at central locations; for example, the Great Northern at King's Cross, the Midland at St Pancras, the London and North Western Railway at Broad Street and huge acreages in inner South London. Distribution centres were also set up by the large carriers. Pickfords, for instance, in 1841 built a large goods yard at Camden beside the London and Birmingham Railway, which five years later was handling approximately one-tenth of the line's goods traffic.[44] These facilities were also labour-intensive because goods needed to be loaded and unloaded, wagons needed to be made up into train loads and taken to their final destination, and all the transactions associated with them had to be recorded and filed and bills chased up. The Great Western, for example, employed only 193 at its main Birmingham station but 1,000 at its main goods yards in that city.[45]

The most important cargo transported by the railway was coal. Although the Great Northern Railway was the first shipper, it only transported and sold its own coal until 1860, when the practice was deemed illegal and independent carriers took over. By 1865, almost half of the coal was carried from Derbyshire and Nottinghamshire by the Midland, and a further quarter from Yorkshire by the Great Northern and London and North Western. The majority was for domestic use and distributed to 150 specialist coal depots, whence it was collected by retailers for delivery.[46]

An impact of rail goods traffic in London was to cheapen fuel and foodstuffs and to increase the range available. Railway freight costs, however, remained high. Productivity growth was low and the rail companies failed to reorganise their freight operations, even though the gains could be high. One reason in London was that, once having built their inner city yards, the railway companies were reluctant later in the century to invest in modern marshalling yards. The general use of slow-moving, small-capacity wagons has also been criticised. Coal wagons were generally despatched half full to minimise unloading times and, as they lacked automatic brakes and oiled axle boxes, they could only be pulled at low speeds. In contrast to this view, it has been argued that small, cheap wagons formed a good method of distribution given the density of the rail network and the high cost of horse transport from a single, central goods site.[47]

The policy of centrally located goods yards was driven by a need to fill the capacity of the new expensive urban rail lines and to compete with other rail companies for the London market. But the goods handled at these central facilities were rarely charged the true cost of providing such expensive transshipment points. Blackfairs Goods Station, for example, cost £600,000 in the 1860s and its annual running costs, including a capital charge, were just under £50,000. Meeting this cost would have added a charge of 4 shillings and 7 pence to each ton delivered there.[48] In the prevailing climate of price controls and regulation, such charges were never levied and represented a significant cross-subsidy from other rail business. (They would obviously have been prohibitive especially for heavier, low-value traffic like building materials.) This meant that users of such yards faced few spatial price variations between goods-handling facilities in the capital. If such charges had varied to reflect true differences in the costs of goods yards at different urban locations, they would have been much cheaper at the urban fringe because of the cheaper land there, and goods facilities undoubtedly would have been far more decentralised. Such greater decentralisation would have undoubtedly encouraged industry to be more decentralised, so that rail companies' policies of taking over large tracts of central land for the relatively low-value activity of goods handling probably helped to encourage metropolitan industry to stay in central locations more than would otherwise have been the case.

This locational influence was made greater by the lack of independent rail sidings, which forced firms to rely on railway companies' own goods yards, and the location of those yards became increasingly less favourable as parts of industry moved out from the inner core. Although much London industry was small in scale, it is remarkable how few businesses had their own railway sidings. Even in 1900, only approximately 100 had such facilities. Whether this indicates difficulties for firms wishing to connect to the rail system is unclear, but it is a major differentiation of nineteenth-century London from other British industrial cities, where such sidings were far more common. Heavy industry generally remained located along the Thames. It is interesting to hypothesise that rail companies in London encouraged the use of their own yards by limiting independent access to the rail system offered by sidings. The frequency of services on London lines would have, anyway, made shunting difficult. If such constraints on the availability of industrial sidings did exist, it would have discouraged the suburbanisation of the capital's industries during the railway age and forced more firms to relocate out of the capital altogether. There is no way of estimating the scale of this effect, but the rapid decentralisation of industry once road transport became generally in use suggests that it could have been high. Rail as a mode of transport paradoxically may have helped to keep London's industries locked into a narrow band of central industrial districts.

The Port of London

The growth of the port

London had for long been the centre of international commerce and the hub of sea trade, and the Port had for many centuries a disproportionate effect on the capital's economic life as a result. Its facilities were used for far more shipments than necessary to serve local industries and population because of a large and continuing entrepôt (re-export) role for north-west Europe as well as the rest of the UK.[49]

In the eighteenth century, Britain's sea trade had become increasingly concentrated on colonial trade. By 1794–6, the colonies were absorbing two-thirds of exports, and a quarter of imports came from the West Indies alone. London interests were the main instigators and beneficiaries of this trade. The East India Company, for example, had a monopoly of Indian trade until 1813 and Chinese until 1833.[50] The West Indies were another jewel and the monopoly of the West Indies Company. In 1798, between July and October when prevailing winds were propitious, a third of the ships entering the Thames came from the West Indies, and they tended to be the larger vessels, so that they accounted for two-thirds of the total tonnage of vessels.[51]

The industrialisation of Britain during the nineteenth century saw a rapid decline in these mercantilist practices – by 1844–6, for example, imports from the West Indies accounted for only 7 per cent of British imports. The pre-eminence of London was over. Sea trade initially expanded in the northern ports and later in the century in Scotland, Wales and along the south coast. This is unsurprising as manufactured exports from the rapidly expanding, new industrial regions, and the raw material and foodstuff imports required by them, were dealt with more conveniently from northern ports, such as Liverpool and Glasgow. Later, these were followed by coal exports from ports near to the mining regions. Yet, despite these changes, in the early 1820s London was handling 30 per cent of UK exports and by 1910 the share was still an impressive 15 per cent.[52] Liverpool experienced a corresponding, if somewhat smaller, relative decline, despite its proximity to the cotton-producing districts. London's share of imports displays a similar, if more variable, picture. In 1791, London stands supreme, edging Liverpool out because of its greater coastal trade, but, by 1900, London is merely one of many. Even though it experienced relative decline, the nineteenth century saw nothing but substantial growth for London's port, given the explosive growth of British international trade, with exports plus imports passing through the port rising from just under 1.5 million to over 24 million tons between 1820–4 and 1910–13.[53]

The causes of this absolute growth are fourfold. First, the city itself increased in size sucking in extra imports and producing more goods for export. Second, national transport improvements increased London's importance as a distribution centre. Third, from mid-century, the port developed important trade links with Australia and New Zealand; and, fourth, at the end of the nineteenth century it benefited from a surge in European trade and a growth in passenger liner traffic to the Empire and Orient. The port's re-export business remained strong throughout, with 54 per cent of the UK total value in 1913, largely owing to the presence in the City of many highly experienced merchants.[54]

Before the docks

Until the early nineteenth century, the port consisted of quays tightly located between London Bridge and a short distance down river from where Tower Bridge now stands. The 'Legal Quays', set up by Elizabeth I to ensure the payment of duties, ran from London Bridge to the Tower, and the 'Sufferance Quays', opened in the second half of the eighteenth century, covered the rest. These quays were privately owned and traders complained of monopolistic pricing in mooring and warehousing charges. The Corporation also licensed the lightermen, watermen and porters, all of whom used their monopoly position to improve their earnings and conditions of work. The port had been for long a major source of revenue for the City, as well as central government, because goods were taxed as they left or were loaded on to ships – coal being the most important source of revenue.

In 1800, the port was notoriously inefficient. The continual discharge of sewage into the Thames had reduced its depth. More importantly, the great expansion of trade had caused the number of vessels using the facilities to increase rapidly. In the Upper Pool by the legal quays some 1,775 vessels would moor in a space planned for only 545. A shortage of space for ships was matched by insufficient quays and wharves. There existed a mere 1,419 feet (432.3 metres) of legal quays – the same as in 1666 – and all were situated on the north side of the river. The Sufferance Quays trebled capacity but it was still woefully inadequate. Most vessels thus had to load and unload in the river and the port was further congested by an estimated 3,400 lighters, whose progress to and from quays was constrained by the mooring pattern of the port.[55] Whereas short-stay coasters were allowed to anchor close to London Bridge, larger foreign ships, which took longer to discharge their cargo, had to moor down river at Limehouse and Blackwall Reaches. The loading and unloading of such vessels were disrupted by coasters sailing up and down the river, while the lighters involved had to travel relatively long distances to reach quays and wharves.

There was also a shortage of warehousing within a reasonable distance of the port, particularly for the temporary storage of sugar. This seasonal import needed extensive storage facilities to ensure supply for the long months when no new cargoes arrived. Stealing was rife, despite the establishment of river police, with an estimated £506,000 of cargo stolen in 1797.[56]

The dock companies

By the end of the eighteenth century, London was trailing way behind Liverpool in investment and the introduction of new facilities; the northern port, for instance, had acquired enclosed docks in 1717. Although London merchants had long demanded improvements, action was only taken at the end of the eighteenth century, when the early stages of the Napoleonic Wars clearly demonstrated the inadequacies of the port. In 1796, a Parliamentary committee examined how facilities could be improved and recommended a series of enclosed docks to the east of the City. Neither the Corporation nor other vested interests were happy, but they finally failed to delay proceedings any further.[57]

In 1799, the government authorised the West India Dock Co. to build a new dock on the Isle of Dogs. To guarantee a reasonable capital return, it further decreed that for a period of twenty-one years all produce from and to the West Indies must be unloaded and loaded at the dock. Opened in 1802, the new facility extended over 24 acres, had its own legal quays and bonded warehousing, and was surrounded by a 20-foot high wall to prevent theft. The new design of London's port facilities cut theft dramatically, and led to less damage to cargoes and large gains in the speed of unloading and ship turnaround times. In order to satisfy the opposition from vested interests, the dock company had to compensate the owners of legal quays, porterage workers and others with £860,000. Customs dues in the new dock were based on bonding – payment when the goods were removed for consumption – rather than the old payment on arrival, so this gave merchants a strong financial incentive to store dutiable goods there. Goods were transported out of the dock on the new Commercial Road turnpike.[58]

The West India was followed by two more docks on the north bank of the river. The first, the London, was opened in 1805 at Wapping by the London Dock Co. It was given a twenty-one-year monopoly on the import of tobacco, rice, wine and brandy, except that imported from the East and West Indies. The second, at Blackwall, was opened in 1806 by the East India Company for its own ships and, as the company had its own secure City storehouse for its valuable cargoes, the dock contained no warehouses.

On the south bank, where the West European trade in timber, hemp and flax was traditionally dealt with, a number of docks were built. The bulky nature of these goods and the large dock space required made it infeasible for just one firm to provide sufficient accommodation. This precluded the granting of a monopoly of trade, as on the north side of the river. In 1801, the Grand Surrey Dock and Canal Co. created the Grand Surrey Dock. Six years later the East Country Dock Co. built the East Country Dock, specialising in timber, grain, salt and fruit; and in 1808 the Commercial Dock Co. converted an existing whaling stage into a further dock, concentrating on timber, hemp, flax and tar. As timber needed to be seasoned and so stored out of doors, none of these docks had a great deal of warehousing. They were also not enclosed by walls, because of the low value of the goods handled.[59]

These new docks failed to prosper after the initial years. Government policy towards the end of the French Wars switched away from mercantilism towards *laissez-faire*. This meant that the various dock company monopolies were not renewed when they fell due. The East India Company ceased trading after it lost its trade monopoly to India and China, selling its City warehouses to the dock companies. Ownership patterns then encouraged massive dock and warehouse duplication – a problem that was to persist throughout the century. In response to the imminent removal of the East and West India Companies' privileges, the St Katharine's Dock Company built a dock between the London Dock and the Tower for general traffic. This prompted the London Dock Co. to construct a seven-acre extension to its own facility. The resultant over-capacity cut profits and rival companies reduced their rates in an attempt to attract business. The competitive struggle and lost monopoly rights forced the East and West India Dock Companies to merge in 1838. The enclosed docks also began to face more serious competition from river wharves. They had the advantage of being closer to central markets and paradoxically benefited from the construction of the docks because of reduced Pool congestion. Coasters and near European shippers continued to unload there, storing their cargoes in riverside warehouses.

Another problem for the dock companies was that they could not impose total control over the handling of goods in their basins. The Acts authorising the construction of the docks all included a 'free water' clause to appease traditional port interests. This allowed lighters to enter and convey goods between ships moored in the docks and river wharves without the dock companies being able to charge them. For cargo unloaded in this way, the docks lost the quay dues that would otherwise have been paid to them. Even more important were the lost warehousing fees, as they made up the largest part of dock companies' income. At first, the problem was limited as most bonded warehouses belonged to the dock companies, so that foreign trade mainly went via the docks and coastwise trade was handled via the river wharves. As free trade dramatically reduced the number of goods that required customs clearance at the docks' legal quays, the amount of cargo lost by the enclosed docks to the wharves increased. The flow particularly accelerated from 1853, when the Customs Consolidation Act allowed legal quays and bonded warehouses to be built outside the docks. By 1856, fourteen riverside wharves had obtained these privileges and, by 1866, the number had risen to 116.[60]

The docks then faced a series of further problems throughout the century caused by changing technology. The Achilles' heel of enclosed docks is that once built each dock is essentially fixed in configuration and cannot economically be adapted to new requirements. The first major problem was the arrival of steamships and railways. No longer were large stocks of goods required to compensate for the uncertainty and seasonal variability of sail-boat journeys. The telegraph meant that orders for goods could now be dispatched around the world when required, once again lowering the need for storage. The demand for dockside warehouses was further cut by a fall in sugar imports caused by higher taxation.

The existing docks were too shallow, their quays too short and their entrances too narrow to accommodate the larger steamships. Moreover, they had insufficient space for railway lines to connect them to the expanding rail network, and lacked both the means and the will to develop new facilities. This gave an opportunity for two new entrants to capture a large share of the business of the docks. First, the railway contractors Thomas Brassey and Samuel Peto (with Peto's brother-in-law, Edward Betts) built the Victoria Dock; and, second, twelve years later the Millwall Dock was dug by the new Millwall Company. Directly linked to the main rail system, the hundred-acre Victoria Dock was sited on Plaistow Marshes, well down river of the existing docks. Vessels using it thus avoided the need to negotiate the congested and dangerous upper stretches of the Thames, while land and construction costs were low. Opened in 1855, the dock could handle the largest contemporary steamships. It used hydraulic cargo-handling machinery and contained eight jetties or piers. This configuration increased the number of ships that could be dealt with simultaneously and speeded unloading, since cargo could be rapidly transferred from a ship on one side of a pier to a barge on the other side. The L-shaped Millwall Dock was opened in 1868. It was slightly smaller than the Victoria at 36 acres and had a narrow entrance to its up-river location. But it could again deal with steamships, was adjacent to the Blackwall Railway, and had the first dry dock in London.[61]

Both docks offered relatively low port dues and rapidly siphoned off trade from existing facilities. By 1860, the Victoria Dock handled 854,000 tons of shipping, 70 per cent more than the East and West India Docks combined, double that of the London Docks, and four times that of St Katharine's. The result was that dock companies were forced into mergers. In 1864, anticipating the effect of the then uncompleted Millwall Dock, the older London and St Katharine's Docks joined forces with the new Victoria to form the London and St Katharine's Dock Co. In the same year, on the south bank of the river, the Commercial Dock Co., which in 1850 had taken over the East Country docks, amalgamated with the Grand Surrey Dock and Canal Co., the new concern being known as the Surrey Commercial Dock Co.[62]

Unfortunately for the profits of the dock companies, the mergers merely stimulated a further round of dock building as each company sought to keep up with the growing size of ships and to wrest business from its competitors. In 1876, the Surrey Commercial Dock Co. opened the 16-acre Canada Dock, which comprised 44 acres of timber sheds and warehousing sufficient to store 35,000 tons of grain. Four years later, the London and St Katharine's Dock Co. built the Royal Albert Dock. One and three-quarter miles long, it was then the largest in the world. Its construction, in turn, prompted the East and West India Co. to open Tilbury docks, built even further down river close to Gravesend. In retaliation, the Royal Albert Dock constructed an even larger lock entrance. This competition, along with Tilbury's unexpectedly high construction costs, the narrowness of its branch docks and the early boycott of the dock by lighter owners, forced the East and West India Co. into receivership in 1888. The company negotiated with the London and St Katharine's and the two firms merged in 1889 to form the London and India Docks Joint Committee. The north-side companies were finally united.[63]

By 1900, the Port of London had a substantial surfeit of dock space, a significant proportion of which was unsuitable for the steamships that were becoming larger by the year. The up-river docks had primarily become warehouse facilities served by lighters. In 1899, in a final attempt to destroy competition from riverside wharves, the London and St Katharine's and East and West India companies sought Parliamentary approval to levy a charge on lighters that entered their docks and a toll on the goods they carried. Although their initiative failed, it did much to draw attention to the problems of the port, and in 1900 the government set up a Royal Commission. The submission by the London Chamber of Commerce highlighted continual weaknesses: poor facilities and equipment, high charges, poor land communications and delays. The Commission's main recommendation, the creation of a new port authority, met with opposition, but was eventually implemented in 1908 with the creation of the Port of London Authority, the first major act of twentieth-century nationalisation. Public and press opinion voiced support for riverside quays and better dredging of the river, on continental lines, which would have left the unpopular dock companies unwanted and penniless, but Lloyd George supported the enclosed system and bought out the dock companies. The companies, anticipating their demise, had raised their charges and done little to improve their properties during the period 1902–8, so the new Authority spent the years up to the First World War improving the efficiency of the docks. However, it soon built itself an impressively grand headquarters suggesting that the principle of economy was not always uppermost in its strategies. It also commissioned a further dock, the George V, able to cope with the largest steamships, but its construction was delayed by the outbreak of war.[64]

Dock workers

For many years prior to the construction of the enclosed docks, four porterage brotherhoods had had a monopoly of dock labour. The dock companies broke this monopoly by hiring permanent men and the brotherhoods faded away. The West India Dock had some 200 permanent labourers when it opened in 1802. St Katharine's at its opening had 225 permanent men and 200 preferred labourers. By the 1860s, however, the work had become more casualised in line with fluctuations in workloads, which in the two India docks could vary from 4,000 to 1,300 men required each day.[65]

Dock labour in the 1860s was thus split into three groups. The 'permanent men', around 11 per cent of the workforce, had secure employment. 'Preference men', 22 per cent of the labour force, were given preference when casual labour was required, but had no guarantee of work, though most only experienced unemployment during exceptionally slack periods. The remaining two-thirds were 'casuals' employed on a daily and, after the arrival of the steamship, hourly basis. This residuum experienced by far the worst conditions and pay. They were generally former workers sacked from declining sectors, or they were workers in the gas, building, printing or cartage industries, who turned to the docks during seasonal downturns.[66] The perilous position of some of the dock companies and the under-utilisation of capacity helped to increase the variability of employment, because work was more widespread around the port's under-used facilities than would have been the case if fewer dock companies existed and older docks had been closed down or restructured to concentrate on specialist or lightering activities.

The 1889 dock strike coincided with the merger of the north-bank dock companies. The merger had enabled some rationalisation, so that greater stability of employment could be offered by using fewer men overall in a more rational allocation of ships between dock facilities. Those employed by the London and India docks were re-categorised into three groups by the new Joint Committee. There were permanent and 'A' class workers, who had regular work and weekly wages, with sick pay and pensions for the permanents; these did two-thirds of the work in 1894. In addition, another 29 per cent were 'B' men, who were registered and given numbered tickets of employment priority. They would be moved up and down the priority list according to their attendance rate and performance and would be employed after all the permanents and 'A's had work. A final 6 per cent of the work was done by 'C' casuals, hired for what work remained. This effectively policed the workforce and ensured that they were fit for the arduous work and could be punished if they slacked or stole.[67]

Permanent and preference staff and some specialist casuals were much better paid than ordinary casuals. Moreover, their wages were usually obtained over a three- to four-day week. Most casuals earned far less. The introduction of the steamship further depressed their pay. Unlike wooden sailing ships, steamers required little refitting and were unloaded rapidly. With more rapid turnarounds, the slack periods when no work was available grew. The highest casual incomes were received by dock workers based on the ship, because they had to be skilled in handling the various winches and ropes. Of the shore workers, those moving timber and corn – mostly in the Surrey Docks – obtained the highest salaries. This type of work required a certain amount of learnt technique, and the cargoes provided regular employment, because they took longer to unload and by the end of the century were arriving throughout the year.

Casual labour with daily hiring at the dock gate remained an important form of labour organisation throughout the period. Table 9.1 shows the maximum and minimum daily numbers employed in several of the dock facilities for 1891–2. An indication of the extent of underemployment caused by casualisation can be drawn by examining the percentage that the minimum employment is of the maximum (shown in the last

Table 9.1 Maximum and minimum daily employment in the Port of London, 1891–2

	Maximum	*Minimum*	*Minimum as percentage of maximum*
London and St Katharine's Dock	3,789	1,249	33
East and West India Dock	2,380	619	26
Surrey Commercial Dock	1,802	621	34
Victoria and Albert Dock	1,107	611	55
Wharves and private warehousing (north side)	3,865	2,675	69
Wharves and private warehousing (south side)	3,797	2,601	69

Source: Phillips and Whiteside, 1985, 22.

column). A lower rate of casualisation in a facility is presumably associated with a more stable employment pattern, and, hence, it can be seen that the older docks had the most variable employment, with the two Indias the worst; while the riverside wharves provided the least variable levels of employment, with in practice much permanent employment, even when it was not formally recognised as such. These data also provide an indication of the problems of the enclosed docks. They had by far the most variable workloads, because of their specialist facilities, and the greatest fixed costs – a dangerous financial recipe. Public opinion at the turn of the century, mentioned earlier, pushing for a switch back to quays, clearly had a point.

Many campaigned against dock casualisation in the nineteenth century and the practice was criticised and legislated against in the twentieth. Yet its existence was economically justifiable. Ships had uncertain arrival times and their cargoes needed to be rapidly unloaded. The latter was particularly true for perishable goods, but speed always helped to reduce dock charges. This meant that labour was only required at irregular intervals. Moreover, employing a completely permanent workforce would have led to considerable idle time for some skills, because of the skill range required by the large variety of cargoes handled at a single facility. Such skilled workers could be more fully employed by offering their services on a daily basis to separate employers, thereby both lowering costs and increasing their earnings. Permanency would also have enhanced the power of the trade unions. Such arguments are standard justifications for the large amount of casualised self-employment in the modern building industry and elsewhere.

In addition, it could be argued that both the employers and dockers preferred the system. Employers believed that casualisation improved labour productivity, because of the incentives offered by high piece rates and the desire of casuals to be re-employed. Many dockers also appear to have preferred the long spells of relatively well-paid, almost continuous work, followed by two or three days of idleness, to lower pay and regular hours. Additional advantages for nineteenth-century London dock workers arose from the structure of the capital's labour market, because casualisation allowed some of them to treat dock work as a secondary job to be undertaken when their primary occupation was seasonally unavailable. Finally, decasualisation would have forced the more specialised dockers to diversify their skills for fear of losing their jobs and, thereby, lose much of the status attached to their particular specialisations. Trade unionists, however, were – and still are – adamantly opposed to the practice, because they claimed it gave employers too much power to lower earnings, intensify the pace of work, ignore safety and provide poor working conditions. This argument, however, is more about the available supply of labour, which unions hoped they would be able to limit in order to raise pay and conditions. Their success in this venture, however, was limited during the period. A strike in 1912, under the new Port of London Authority (PLA), aimed at ensuring a union monopoly of labour, failed. The PLA, however, did take on about 3,000 men as permanent workers out of an average dock labour-force of around 4,500 – a similar ratio to that of the old Joint Committee. Strikes remained common up to the First World War.[68]

10 Moving around London

Introduction

One of the most significant technical developments affecting the size and functioning of London, like any other contemporary urban area, was the development of mass public transport. This chapter discusses the evolution of the means of motion in the capital from walking and private horse carriage through road-building, coaches, steamers, horse-drawn buses, surface railways, trams, tubes and motor buses.

The path of change was not simply dictated by technical innovations but also by the ways in which firms invested in the new forms of conveyance and competed with each other and alternative forms of travel. The nature of the investments, with high fixed costs and low short-run marginal ones, created a particular competitive context. Providers had the option of competing with each other or combining through cartel agreements or mergers. With competition, they faced low profits and potentially ruinous fare wars; whereas monopolistic practices would enable fares to be kept up and investment lowered, because new competing capacity was not added to the transport network. Circumstances periodically pushed firms into agreements and mergers. New inventions, and their application to metropolitan transport problems by risk-taking entrepreneurs, then threatened previously cosy relationships among the existing transport undertakings.

A clear cycle of innovation, competition and consolidation can thus be seen throughout the period. This culminated in the spectacular attempt by US entrants to monopolise all means of public transport in the capital in the 1900s. An integrated transport system, however, was not to be. This was despite the fact that, in the years prior to 1914, there was a virtually unanimous belief in its necessity, drawing on the new fashion for town planning. Each development is considered in turn in this chapter, with emphasis placed on how each transport mode came into being and the ways in which competition altered its provision.

The pedestrian city

Throughout the period most residents of the capital walked everywhere instead of using other means of transport. A traffic survey of the City in 1854 gives a good idea of the importance of this most ancient means of travel, with almost 70 per cent of people travelling into and out of the City daily doing so on foot (Table 10.1). Even as late as 1897, when extensive public transport systems had been developed, less than a quarter of South London trade unionists were regular users of them.[1]

Walking in a densely packed urban environment was generally the most sensible option. Despite its large population, until the 1860s, London was geographically small. In the first quarter of the century, the built-up area stretched for only four miles from north to south and six miles from east to west.[2] Traffic congestion was such, particularly from the 1850s, that walking was often the most rapid way of getting about. A survey of horse buses and four-wheeled carriages in 1863 found that they only moved at an average speed of 3 to 4.5 miles an hour.[3] Fares for the available public transport were also relatively high, and prohibitive for most working-class people until the introduction of subsidised services towards the end of the century. Most people, moreover, worked extremely long hours. This encouraged many to live close to their place of employment and so limited their transport requirements.

Walking was made easier as the century progressed by a series of improvements in road conditions and safety. Street lighting became commonplace from the 1830s onwards, making walking at night both easier and less dangerous. The extension of the police force further reduced the risk of mugging. Roads began to be better paved, drained and cleaned, improving journeys especially in bad weather. The extensive cutting of new roads through the centre, as discussed later in this chapter, also shortened journeys.

Table 10.1 Daily movement of people and vehicles into and out of the City, 1854

Mode	*Number*	*% of total persons*
Omnibus passenger	88,000	15
Steamer passengers	30,000	5
Walkers to and from Fenchurch Street and London Bridge stations	54,000	9
Walkers	400,000	69
Metropolitan Railway passengers	8,440	1
Total persons	580,440	100
Omnibus journeys	7,400	12
Other vehicle journeys	52,000	88
Total vehicles	59,400	100

Source: Kellett, 1969, 45–6, and own calculations.

Horses and carriages

Even the well-to-do generally walked, but they also could afford to travel on horseback or by private carriage. Growing congestion and the escalating cost of keeping and feeding horses in London, however, caused horseback riding and private carriages gradually to disappear. At mid-century, 5,000 horse-riders passed Temple Bar each day, but by the 1880s the sight of a man on horseback was uncommon.[4] Yet, even in 1891, the capital contained 23,000 private carriages.[5] Horse-riding retained its cachet as a wealthy leisure activity throughout the nineteenth century, with Rotten Row in Hyde Park the place to be seen.

The horse remained the main motive force in the movement of goods around the metropolis throughout the period. On the eve of the First World War, most of London's goods vehicles were still horse-drawn.

Horse transport had a profound effect on the nature of the urban form and street improvements in London. The difficulty and cost of horses and their stabling encouraged walking, which helped to keep the city small and dense. The limited travel span of the horse and cart further restricted urban expansion by constraining the outward movement of industry. An idea of the costs to households of private horse-based transport can be seen in the mews of the more expensive nineteenth-century West End neighbourhoods. Solely designed to house horses, carriages and livery servants, these back passageways behind the grand houses took up considerable expensive space; whilst working horses ate prodigious amounts of feed, and livery men were often some of the best paid domestic staff. Few could afford such luxury, so hardly any suburban developments contained such facilities. Compare, for example, Islington – which has few mews because it was designed for middle-class households leaving the City – with many West End streets and squares, which have mews, and were planned primarily for the landed aristocracy coming up to London for the Season. For the latter, conspicuous consumption was at a premium, of which a horse and carriage was an excellent demonstration; for the former, travel had more prosaic motives.

Road improvements had to take into account the requirements of horse-drawn carriages and carts. Steep gradients had to be avoided when making new roads for fear of slowing down horse-drawn traffic. Carriages and carts also take up considerable space and are not the most manoeuvrable of vehicles, so that congestion grew quickly as the numbers on London's roads rose. Horses also produce large amounts of excrement which fouls roads and pavements and blocks storm drains. On well-used routes, the nightly clearing of this by-product of travel was hardly sufficient. It has been rightly quipped that the invention of the motor car saved large cities in the nick of time from being engulfed in mountains of horse dung.

The horse was gradually replaced by other means of public transport throughout the period up to 1914. It remained the dominant means of road transport for a very long time, however, only losing out to the motor bus and electric tram in the decade before the First World War. It was then rapidly replaced in passenger transport, but declined much more slowly in goods traffic. A 1913 survey, for example, found that 88 per cent of goods vehicles were still horse-drawn.[6]

The growth of public transport and congestion

Congestion had traditionally been a bugbear of the capital but became worse in the centre over the course of the century, because road improvements failed to keep pace with the growth in traffic. Traffic was often reduced to walking pace or less, the rate of movement being determined by the slowest vehicles. Control of traffic flows at key junctions was minimal, adding further to delays. Huge traffic jams were commonplace, especially at bottlenecks such as Piccadilly, the Strand, Ludgate Circus and the Bank. In 1905, a survey showed that at the Princess Street junction next to the Bank, north–south traffic experienced an average of 337 delays a day, amounting to a total of six hours and five minutes lost time each day.[7]

The causes of increased congestion were related to changes in urban form and the means of movement. London's population grew and dispersed into suburbs, which meant that there were far more periphery–centre journeys than ever before. Industry, in contrast, predominantly remained in the inner ring around the city centre, so that many slow-moving carts clogged up central streets as they travelled to and from rail depots, the river, the docks and firms' metropolitan customers. National population and economic growth encouraged travel to the metropolis, adding more traffic to its roads. The metropolitan focus of the new national transport system exacerbated this trend, and the spread-out locations of the rail termini filled the central area with between-station traffic.

The second half of the century also saw a major increase in the number of public transport journeys made by Londoners. In the late 1860s, the average Londoner was taking more than twenty journeys a year on the various forms of public transport; by 1902, the number had risen to almost 140 a year.[8] The considerable improvements in public transport over the century, as described below, led to thousands of extra vehicles plying the streets, leading to the paradox from a modern perspective of congestion being exacerbated by improvements in public transport. As most were run by private operators, out to maximise returns, routes in the centre would cluster on to the roads where passenger flows were maximised, rather than being more evenly spread across the available road network. Traditional movement patterns consequently tended to persist, even when substantial road improvements were made. This effect can be seen, for example, with the Strand and Whitehall, which remained heavily congested after the opening of the nearby Victoria Embankment in the 1870s, while the latter remained under-used.[9]

Road improvements

The major central roads in 1800 generally ran from east to west to the north of the river, reflecting the geography of the West End and City. They were often narrow, poorly maintained and blocked by street markets and other local activity. The river was bridged only at a limited number of points, partly because powerful river-using interests had for centuries restricted plans for more crossings. By the early nineteenth century, however, their influence was on the wane, at least above the Pool of London – but the east and south-east continued to remain poorly connected across the river because of the port.

In the first few decades of the century, road conditions improved with increased expenditure on widening, paving and drainage, and on new routes. Local roads were the responsibility of the vestries and the City Corporation; the Commissioners of Woods and Forests was the main agency used by central government to finance central London bridge building and several road improvements (including Victoria Street and New Oxford Street); while many trunk roads out of the capital were under the control of private turnpike trusts. New construction in the central area in the period before the railways included Regent Street (1817–23) and Moorgate, cutting north–south thoroughfares through the traditional east–west pattern. Major trunk routes were constructed to the north of the built-up area – including New North Road (1812), Archway Road (1813), Caledonian Road (1826) and Finchley Road (1826–35); another new turnpike route ran from Marylebone to Tottenham, via Camden Town and Holloway. The number of river crossings similarly increased with the construction or rebuilding of five new bridges, principally financed by tolls – Vauxhall (1816), Waterloo (1817), Southwark (1819), and London (1824–31) – which, in turn, stimulated further road construction south of the river.[10]

In 1826, the fourteen North London turnpike trusts were amalgamated into one body, which introduced through-tolls, resurfaced many of its roads with macadam tar and stone, and built new thoroughfares. Four years later, the whole of the built-up area north of the river became a toll-free zone and the responsibility for the upkeep of roads was transferred to the vestries, though tolls continued to be charged in the outer areas. The growth of the rail network brought financial ruin to the national turnpike system and the remaining London companies were no exception. They responded by trying to exploit their local traffic, which was growing with the outward spread of the suburbs. The entrance to toll roads from side roads was blocked by further gates to force more vehicles to remain on the toll route, and charges were raised, which operators passed on to fare-paying passengers. This caused considerable agitation for the abolition of the turnpikes, with extravagant claims about their impact, of which Dyos (1961), for one, is sceptical.[11] In 1865, scores of gates were removed as responsibility for these roads was handed over to vestries.

The old turnpike routes, even so, still remained the principal thoroughfares of suburban London as vestries were reluctant to incur the expense of major road building; and the Metropolitan Board of Works (MBW), after it was formed in the 1850s, concentrated its extensive road-building programme on central districts. Only relatively minor schemes were undertaken in the suburbs, such as the widening of Camberwell Church Street and Peckham Road, and some of the suburban vestries complained bitterly about the Board's neglect. (As the MBW's rate was fixed equally across the whole County area, however, each vestry had an incentive to complain that its district was not getting enough of the Board's expenditure.) The consequences can still be seen in the street patterns of the nineteenth-century suburbs, which are noticeably mean in contrast to those of many other major European and North American cities. The occasional straight through-route, often constructed by a turnpike company, cuts through a mass of small streets and meandering routes, comprising old country lanes and the new residential streets thrown up by speculative developers.

Prior to the formation of the MBW in the 1850s, major road improvements and bridge-building were beyond the scope of existing local government. Instead, they were undertaken indirectly by central government, with the Commissioners for Forests and Woods the most common agency used for the purpose. It administered the Crown Estates and undertook, sometimes in combination with private developers, many of the great metropolitan improvements, such as the construction of Trafalgar Square, the Nash Regent's Park–Regent Street–Carlton House Terrace scheme and New Oxford Street. With the advent of the MBW, this implicit national subsidy to London's infrastructure ended, with new public works now funded by loans charged to the Board's rate account.

Over its life span, the MBW spent £7.5 million on roads, on average more per annum, even in nominal terms, than the London County Council (LCC) in its first forty-one years of existence.[12] Although its 1855 founding Act made the Board responsible for street improvements, each scheme required a separate application to Parliament for powers of compulsory purchase. The first application in 1857 resulted in the construction of Garrick Street and Southwark Street, and later Acts led to the building of Commercial Road, Clerkenwell Road, Charing Cross Road, Great Eastern Street, Hyde Park Corner and Shaftesbury Avenue. The construction of the Victoria Embankment led to the subsequent creation of Queen Victoria Street and Northumberland Avenue, and the Board also improved and widened other thoroughfares. With respect to bridges, the 1877 Metropolis Toll Bridges Act and subsequent legislation enabled the Board to take over eleven river crossings and free them from tolls. In addition, it rebuilt Battersea, Hammersmith and Putney Bridges, repaired and refurbished others, and in 1877 assumed control of Westminster Bridge from the Office of Works. The LCC's major road scheme was Kingsway in Holborn. Taken together, these schemes led to a transformation of the street structure of inner London, facilitating the shift to commercial uses as well as improving communications and giving the capital a far grander appearance.

Street improvements led to the demolition of many fine and historic buildings, and forced those who lived on the route of many new roads to move, exacerbating overcrowding. To prevent this, from the late 1870s compulsory purchase orders for street improvements that involved the destruction of fifteen or more working-class dwellings were only granted by Parliament if the MBW demonstrated that it had provided sufficient alternative accommodation. A further criticism was the poor planning and appearance of the completed streets. The MBW had no overall road plan and made little attempt to influence the design of street buildings; and its tendency to purchase the minimum amount of land for each scheme meant that adjacent building plots were small and unsuitable for ambitious projects. Under these conditions, a transformation of central London similar to that undertaken by Haussman in Paris was hard to achieve; yet, over a fifty-year period, a substantial physical re-ordering of the centre still resulted.

Coaches and hackney cabs

Short-distance stagecoaches, known as short-stagers, first appeared in the early eighteenth century. They carried four to six passengers inside and up to seven outside on the roof, and were used to provide regular services from the centre of London to the outskirts. This means of transport was introduced to serve the better-off when they moved out to the then desirable suburbs. By 1825, stagers had become commonplace, with probably around 600 such vehicles making around 1,800 journeys a day.[13]

The physical and social geographies of the city were important influences on the location of short-stager routes, and they closely followed what are now parts of underground or suburban railway routes. The downwards shift of these neighbourhoods is mainly attributable to later railway building that destroyed many inner-urban neighbourhood environments and made it possible for their more prosperous residents to move further out.

Regulation severely hampered the use of short-stagers. First, they were increasingly seen as a source of tax revenue, with duties rising from the late eighteenth century. Two further increases occurred in 1804 and 1815 – those having not more than six seats, for example, paying 3d per mile.[14] Road passenger transport continued to be a well-tapped source of tax revenue throughout the first half of the century. From the perspective of modern forms of congestion, taxing public transport seems perverse. But, in the early nineteenth century, such a tax was actually progressive, given the relative affluence of users, in an era when many other taxes were highly regressive, and it helped to reduce congestion by discouraging journeys. The second constraint was equally important: controls restricted the scope of stagers' business by obliging them to pick up or set down passengers within the central paved districts only at their termini. This exclusion from general street trade was aimed at protecting licensed hackney carriages from competition. Since the seventeenth century, only they could ply in the area covered by the Bills of Mortality (a system for registering deaths). They paid far less tax than the stagers but faced fare controls and other regulations from the Hackney Coach office.[15]

The most popular hackney was the four-wheeler, frequently second-hand gentlemen's coaches. With their monopoly, owners had little incentive to maintain or modernise their vehicles and many were dirty and in a poor state of repair, although a new, lighter chariot was introduced in the 1820s. In 1829, 1,100 coaches and chariots were licensed. The two-wheeled cabriolet (or cab) was introduced from Paris in the 1820s, but only 165 existed in 1829. They were faster and cheaper, but could only carry two people and could not be used in poor weather as they were open at the front.[16] The hackney's monopoly was finally lost in 1832, after which other types of vehicle could freely ply the streets for trade. The limit on the number of hackneys was also raised in 1833. The loss of monopoly led to a doubling of the number of hackneys and investment in new equipment and innovations, with the hansom cab eventually becoming the norm.

The hackney cab was remarkably resilient in the face of all the technical changes in public transport that took place over the rest of the period to 1914. Serving a different market from the underground and trams, the hackney was little affected by their introduction and gained from restrictions on the use of trams in the central area. It also benefited from main-line railway construction, which increased 'station to station' work and also the number of wealthy visitors to the capital. From 1870 to 1888, the number of hackney licences rose from 7,818 to 10,500, giving a seating capacity equivalent to that of the contemporary omnibus fleet.[17] Numbers then fell back – due to greater bus competition and the introduction of the telephone and the consequent reduction in business meetings. Hackney motor cabs were first introduced in 1903 and proved immensely popular, particularly after the 1907 introduction of the taximeter.

Steamboats

Steamboats began to sail the Thames from 1815, pre-dating by over two decades the application of steam in London's railways. The boats could carry hundreds of passengers and, unlike road transport, were not burdened by mileage duty. Nevertheless, they were subject to heavy wharfage fees, could not operate in bad weather or at night, were difficult to board and leave and, owing to congestion on the Thames, were involved in regular collisions. Despite these drawbacks, by the 1830s a regular service operated between London and Gravesend, Woolwich and Richmond. From 1837, smaller vessels, capable of carrying 120 passengers, sailed between

London Bridge and Westminster Bridge, Southwark Bridge, Chelsea and Nine Elms. In 1843, the Chelsea service alone carried over two million passengers a year. With high returns, competition grew and the extra capacity forced down fares.[18]

The advent of railways decimated steamboat demand, especially with the construction of the lines to Gravesend and Richmond and the building of the District Railway. Despite a merger of the existing operators in 1870, steamboats had all but vanished from the Thames by 1890.

Buses

Although bus services had probably already started in the eighteenth century, the first French-style omnibus was introduced to London in 1829 by George Shillibeer, based on his experience of them in Paris. It was drawn by three horses and eighteen passengers could sit on lengthways wooden forms. Others quickly followed. Drivers and conductors had to be licensed from 1838, and the deceitful behaviour of conductors soon caused their nickname, 'cad', to enter the general language. Shillibeer's buses ran from Marylebone to the Bank of England, mainly over the unpaved New Road (now Marylebone–Euston–Pentonville Roads), built as a by-pass to the north of the city in the mid-eighteenth century – and in this way avoided the monopoly restrictions granted to hackney cabs. Shillibeer did not prosper in the face of competition but others did.[19]

Omnibuses had several advantages. They could carry slightly more passengers than short-stagers and, having no outside seats, could be filled beyond their legal limit with less chance of detection. They were, therefore, more intensively used and fares per mile were nearly half those charged by the short-stagers. In addition, being simple they were lighter and, hence, faster than traditional coach-bodied vehicles. They were also more convenient. Passengers no longer had to book or clamber on to the roofs of carriages; there were no parcels to deliver; and the unpaved roads used were relatively traffic-free.

A drawback of horse buses was that, because of their size and heavy operating costs, their fares were beyond the reach of most working people. Furthermore, they generally ran from eight in the morning, when the majority of wage earners were already at work. The service was consequently, like stagers before them, largely used by the middle class.

During the 1830s and 1840s, the omnibus prospered with the abolition of the hackney carriage's monopoly. This legislative attempt to improve competition, however, was quickly met by the formation of cartels by the operators on each omnibus route. Their associations regulated the number of omnibuses that could run, competed against non-members, laid down strict timetables, and employed inspectors to monitor services and receipts. As the constraints were route-based, however, the network of routes could still expand. The associations could not stop others setting up and faced competition when returns were good.

Taxes on public transport were cut by up to a half in the wave of free-trade repeals in the second quarter of the century. In 1839, excise duty was reduced by a halfpenny to 2d per mile for coaches with thirteen seats; and, in 1842, it was further cut to 1½ d per mile, with the tax levied by vehicle rather than the number of seats. New safety regulations encouraged operators to increase seating capacity from fifteen to twenty-two per vehicle. Encouraged by lower taxation, nearly 1,300 buses were licensed by 1850 and seating capacity had doubled over the eleven previous years.[20] The extra competition stimulated by this growth in capacity led to substantial fare reductions in the late 1840s. The 1851 Great Exhibition gave a temporary fillip to demand – enabling fares to rise again – and, in that year, omnibuses carried around 20,000 passengers daily.

Rapid growth then came to an abrupt end. With the closure of the Great Exhibition, the number of visitors in London slumped. In response, intense competition broke out. Fares fell and operators went bankrupt. Buses were taken off the road to reduce capacity and firms campaigned for further reductions in mileage duty. They were eventually successful in 1855, securing a one-third cut in the tax. After a while, agreements were again formed between companies on the same routes, facilitated by the cuts in capacity. Trading conditions for most companies, however, remained poor and costs were rising because of a series of bad harvests and additional safety legislation.

The operators' problems were, in reality, structural, rather than cyclical, and similar to those of the modern bus industry. Running bus services means that most costs are fixed, because vehicles and their staff have to operate on the routes whatever the level of business. A two-horse bus, for example, actually needed 11–12 horses to keep it operating throughout the day, and horses had only relatively short – four-year – working lives.[21] Cartels on each route limited competition but were not the answer to the operators' problems. They meant that no operator could expand at the expense of others or switch buses to alternative routes in line with fluctuations in demand. They effectively froze the maximum capacity on any route and, hence, gave operators no incentive to invest. Fragmentation of ownership under the cartel arrangements also meant that economies of scale could not be achieved. Whenever profits rose, interlopers competed with the associations, and sharp falls in demand led to excess capacity, causing associations to collapse. There was also the threat of new forms of transport, such as the railway. What was needed to revive profits was an investor able to buy up individual operators in order to take excess capacity off the road; one having greater financial muscle to deter new entrants; which, through initiating mergers, could gain scale and network economies. A period of depressed demand is ideal for such a move, as the cost of buying out existing operators is then low because of their poor profitability.

In 1855, two Frenchmen, Leopold Foucard and Joseph Orsi, recognised the opportunity and formed the Compagnie Generale de Omnibus de

Londres, which four years later became the English-registered London General Omnibus Company (henceforth London General). With a capital of £600,000, raised largely in France, Foucard and Orsi began to buy up the capital's ailing operators. Influential support came from those, like Chadwick, who admired the better service provided by the single operator for Paris and hoped that consolidation would reduce road congestion. Soon the firm controlled 85 per cent of the London fleet with almost 600 buses and 6,000 horses.[22] It was now of a size that limited the threat of competition. Unsurprisingly, the total number of buses fell markedly to only 810 in 1856 – over a third less than four years earlier.[23]

London General was then able to improve services and could reap economies of scale in route networks, purchasing, foraging and garaging. Plants were opened for repairs and omnibus construction. New routes were organised, waiting rooms opened, new better-designed and ventilated vehicles purchased, and a short-lived 'correspondence system' was introduced based on Parisian experience, whereby passengers could transfer from one route to another without paying an additional fare. Feeder services began to run to and from railway stations. Many of these improvements, however, were only slowly introduced and limited in scale, partly because of London General's unexpectedly poor initial profitability and uncontrolled rises in costs.[24]

Trading conditions were difficult for a number of reasons. Opposition to the 'French monopoly' kept competition higher than had been expected. London General had 580 buses on the road in 1863 against 100 by its rivals, showing how difficult it actually proved to restrain entrants. Moreover, the London General had overpaid for many of the assets it had acquired, and it had given the owners of bought-out firms jobs as managers in the company, which limited rationalisation. Its founders were also discovered to have misappropriated 10 per cent of the initial capital.[25]

Despite these start-up problems, change eventually began to bear fruit. The bus, however, did lose out to the railways, which took away longer-distance passengers – as did the opening of the Metropolitan and District Railways. Fares had to be cut in face of this competition, sometimes by 50 per cent, and average journey lengths became shorter. By the mid-1870s, the number of rail journeys was probably two to three times that of buses.[26] As a result, London General's revenue fell from £601,324 to £516,905 between 1863 and 1875, despite passenger numbers rising by almost a quarter. Yet costs fell faster and, with the initial financial excesses no longer on the balance sheets, dividends of from 7.5 to 9 per cent were paid between 1870 and 1875 – a level far higher than that managed by the railways themselves, which earned meagre returns on London suburban investments.[27]

Substantial increases in overall demand for bus services occurred from the 1880s, after many years of stagnation, because of rising incomes and the movement of population out of the central city core. Between the early 1880s and the 1900s, the number of passengers travelling on the lines of the two main bus companies rose almost sixfold.[28]

General bus use was little affected by competition from the new forms of public transport that grew up in the last thirty years of the nineteenth century. The dominance of inner London journeys was largely retained, except on a limited number of underground routes, especially as trams were excluded from the central area. Buses, similarly, kept much of their suburban traffic because no competitor ran so close to so many commuters' homes, and falling costs enabled fares to be reduced. Suburban bus operators also set up connector services to surface and underground railway stations and to tram routes to increase business. Costs fell because of far lower road charges and cheaper feed for horses. Road tolls were abolished in the 1860s; while mileage duty was further reduced and, then, entirely removed in 1870. Horse feed prices fell because of the switch to imported grain.[29]

Indeed, such was the growth in London General's profits that, in 1881, a company promoter, London and Mercantile Association Ltd, set up a competitor, eventually named the London Road Car Co. It offered lower fares, more frequent services and new buses with stairs and a platform, suggesting that London General was failing to keep up with the new technology, market needs and investment.[30] The Road Car Co. tried to tap contemporary 'jingoistic' ideologies by branding London General as a foreign 'French' concern and adorning its own buses with a Union Jack logo. The existing associations, controlled by London General, retaliated by cutting fares and the new firm made poor profits. Even so, by 1890, the 'Union Jack' was carrying 37 million passengers a year[31] – about a third of the number using the London General's services – and its competition had forced the London General and its associates to invest and to become more up-to-date and efficient.

Most of the growth in bus use occurred prior to the major change in motive power from the horse to the petrol engine. But this switch, along with new competition from the tube and electrified tram routes, sparked off a new round of competition at the turn of the century. The history of the bus soon gets intermingled with other types of public transport, a story best left until the section on the underground below. But in the last decade of independence, a bus war was sparked off by the sudden surge in public transport capacity, driven by the two new motive powers of electricity for trams and railways and the petrol motor engine for buses.

Attempts to replace horses began almost as soon as buses became common in the 1830s, but the initiative was short-lived. The steam buses used were dirty, noisy and dangerous, with a resultant short life span. The steam bus reappeared in the late 1890s, again with limited success, but petrol-driven motor buses were to revolutionise public transport.

Motor buses first appeared in 1899 when the Motor Traction Co. for a short time ran two double-deckers between Kensington and Victoria.[32] With steel wheels and a standard horse-bus body the innovation failed to attract custom. Other companies then began to operate services with newly designed vehicles. In the early years, vehicles were unreliable and constantly breaking down. They had difficulty climbing even moderate gradients and, with solid chain-driven wheels, were noisy and uncomfortable. They skidded easily, had unbraked front wheels and, unsurprisingly, as a result were accident-prone. Accidents were increased by the employment as drivers of ex-horse-bus men, who, paid by journey, had a tendency to speed.

These initial problems were slowly ironed out, so that the advantages of motor buses came to the fore. They had greater carrying capacity than their horse-driven counterparts and travelled at somewhat higher speeds (though these were restricted by legislation), enabling routes to be longer. Running costs were lower and less variable. No stabling was required and the price of petrol, untaxed until 1909, was relatively low and unaffected by seasonal variations in supply, which could cause sharp fluctuations in the price of hay.

The success of earlier motor bus services encouraged an investment boom in 1905 with several new entrants and some established firms switching to the new technology. The London Motor Omnibus Co. was established in that year by investors enthusiastic about the new technology, which they thought could finally break the London General's monopoly. The new company, known as the 'Vanguard', was by far the largest operator of motor buses with fifty-eight vehicles.[33] The firm capitalised on its innovatory fleet by 'branding' its routes. It also offered low fares and new routes.

London General behaved as a classic monopolistic incumbent by reacting slowly to the introduction of the motor bus. It had large sunk costs in the old horse-drawn technology, which encouraged it to exercise caution with regard to motor developments. The risks associated with the new technology were also high, and several early motor bus operators soon went into liquidation. The company consequently delayed the switch over as long as it could, but it was less easy to stop new entrants taking advantage of their tardiness. London General was gradually forced to motorise its routes but the delay in switching had seriously damaged its competitive position. Soon, however, it would successfully retaliate and create its own technical advance in bus design.

By 1906–7, competition had become intense as the number of motor buses grew rapidly – nearly quadrupling, for example, from 242 in 1906 to 808 in 1907.[34] The old form of locomotion began to disappear rapidly from the streets as the number of licensed horse-buses fell, disappearing altogether in 1914. In places, motor bus rivalry reached substantial proportions, exacerbating congestion on key roads and increasing road accidents. In 1906, for instance, it was estimated that the Wellington Street junction with the Strand was served by 120 buses per hour. On many major central streets, an endless stream of buses slowly moved through the congestion all day long.[35]

A process of consolidation then occurred, similar to that of fifty years earlier. By 1907, many smaller companies were being forced out of business.

Forecasts, on which their investments had been made, proved to have been optimistic. Vehicle life expectancy was shorter and operating costs far higher than expected, partly because of new safety requirements. A serious crash in 1906 resulted in the introduction of tighter regulations governing the issue of Metropolitan Police licences and gave the police greater powers to stop and impound vehicles considered unfit to travel. Faced with ruinous competition, the remaining firms drew up fare agreements and began to amalgamate. The Associated Omnibus Co. sold its twenty-nine buses to the Great Western Railway, and London Motor took over three of its rivals, leaving it with a fleet of 310 motor buses. The 'bus war', however, only came to an end in 1908 when London General took over its two main rivals, London Motor and the London Road Car, to create a fleet of 899 vehicles, a quarter of which it promptly scrapped. London General had won out again – but this time only by sheer financial muscle. The outburst of competition had lasted only a few years.[36]

Regulation, for once beneficial to innovation, soon encouraged London General to experiment with new designs. New Metropolitan Police regulations on the weight of buses led to London General introducing a new B-type bus in 1910. Lighter than existing vehicles, the bus was also quicker and far more reliable, enabling the firm to cut costs and attract passengers. The buses were manufactured at the company's large Walthamstow works, where most components were made in-house, using the best modern techniques, and parts were designed to be interchangeable to ease repairs. The new bus type was highly advantageous in the London General's competitive fight for passengers against the remaining independent bus companies. (Its designer was not so lucky – he was summarily fired in 1911.) Soon small companies that had escaped earlier amalgamations came to terms with the London General – with only one, Thomas Tilling, remaining independent, after agreeing with the London General to limit the number of buses it ran.

The introduction of the B-type, however, alarmed independent bus manufacturers as they could see that they would now be excluded from the London market. One producer, Daimler, decided to set up its own London bus operator in competition with London General but lost out in a patent dispute. Another, Leyland, adopted a different tactic. It agreed to co-operate with London General in the centre but not in the outer districts where the latter was weak. Finally, the tram operator, MET, set up a bus company and ordered 350 new Daimlers in retaliation for bus threats along its tram routes. These developments threatened to bring even more over-capacity to London's public transport networks, and the fear of ruinous competition finally brought the various public transport undertakings under one ownership, as will be discussed later when the tube system is considered.

One outcome was that London General had to hive-off its bus manufacturing and promise to buy outside buses in order to stop vehicle manufacturers from threatening to set up competing operating companies again in the future. This was duly done in 1912, when the General's Walthamstow works became an independent bus producer called the Associated Equipment Company (AEC).[37]

By 1913, there were 3,522 licensed motor buses, many of them B-types. With reliable motor buses many new long-distance routes could be started, halting any further suburban tram development.[38] Bus use rocketed from 401 million passengers in 1911 to 757 million in 1914 as the public took wholeheartedly to the improved, cheap motor bus.[39]

Trains

Railways initially did not have much effect on travel within London. For example, the first station out of London on the new Birmingham line was Harrow, and, on the Great Western Railway, it was Ealing – distant places in the 1840s. This initial lack of interest was rational from the railways' point of view for several reasons.

In the first place, the early rail termini in London suffered from severe capacity constraints, making commuter traffic difficult to expand for a long time afterwards on a number of important routes. The problem of capacity is illustrated by the Great Northern Railway and its route into King's Cross. Opened in 1852, primitive braking and signalling meant that there were only nineteen departures a day in 1854, rising to thirty in 1862. This was hardly the frequency on which an extensive commuter system could be built. Later signalling and communication improvements, new platforms and the quadrupling of the line by digging expensive tunnels relieved the situation in the late 1870s and, by 1893, there were 539 movements daily into and out of the station and the associated link to the Metropolitan.[40]

Railways, secondly, were given little incentive to encourage suburban developments because they were denied the possibility of profiting from 'betterment' – rising land values on sites adjacent to their routes. Landowners dominated Parliament, which had to grant permission for lines to be built or extended. Perhaps unsurprisingly, therefore, Parliamentary legislation forbade the railway companies from speculating in land, so that adjacent landowners, rather than the railway companies, enjoyed any betterment arising from the new transport infrastructure. Only the Metropolitan, late in the century, managed to sustain a small development interest next to its line in North-West London.[41]

Criticism of the early railway companies for ignoring the commuter seems unfair in the circumstances. The cost of providing the necessary capacity would have been extremely high and uncertain. Companies would have had to wait years for a return from running services to sparsely populated areas, as some did. When, for example, the Great Western opened stations at Hayes and Acton they were only used by 40 to 50 passengers a day.

Some early railways, none the less, were initially built for essentially local journeys, such as the railway to Blackwall and the London and

Greenwich out of London Bridge. So rail commuting started to become commonplace from certain districts. In the 1850s, as many as 27,000 people commuted into the City by train, just over 10 per cent of those coming in by foot or bus (see Table 10.1, p. 244). At that time, the City contained only one terminus, Fenchurch Street (1841), though London Bridge (1836) and Shoreditch (1840) were within walking distance.

Travel by train became more popular from the 1860s. While rail companies fought over their central London estates during that decade, many new suburban stations were built on new and existing lines as the suburbs gradually moved outwards. As with the central stations, lines were not built on any rational plan but rather in reflection of inter-company rivalries and as a consequence of the tortuous process of Parliamentary approval. Competition was greatest in the south. This was partly because the upstart London, Chatham and Dover Railway encroached on South Eastern territory. Once in place, however, the new lines soon facilitated suburban expansion. The scale of provision to the south was such that pre-1914 middle-class development was given a strong southern bias with commuting stretching deep into the Kent and Surrey countryside.

By the 1870s, most railway companies were using their mainline routes into London to develop substantial mid-distance commuter traffic. Wider lines, better signalling and expanded termini all helped to create the capacity that had not been there earlier. Not all new investments were associated with the outer areas. The Midland, for example, when driving through from the north opened five stations in the last four miles into St Pancras.

With suburbanisation during the last thirty years of the nineteenth century, growth in intra-London rail travel was substantial. It outpaced the increase in bus travel in the 1870s, and between 1867 and 1902 matched overall the growth in bus use. Yet the rail companies made little or nothing from their urban investments. The scale of duplication was most ruinous in the south. Both the London, Chatham and Dover Railway and the London and South Eastern, for instance, fell into financial difficulty in the 1860s, largely because of their metropolitan schemes.

Commuter railways

Several railway companies specialised almost entirely in London commuter traffic, of which the East London and the North London are the most notable. Brunel's Wapping Tunnel, originally for pedestrians, was taken over by the East London Railway, which started running services in 1869. Soon an extensive network of suburban services, from as far away as Croydon, was passing through the tunnel to Liverpool Street. Financially, the company was unsuccessful and went into liquidation. Electrification finally reduced the route to a part of the Metropolitan network from 1913, with services from New Cross through to South Kensington and Hammersmith.

The North London Railway was already carrying 4.4 million passengers by 1853. Its prime route had been built to give the London and Birmingham Railway direct access to the docks, and it was two-thirds owned by the London and North Western, the successor to the London and Birmingham. The company had a policy of regular services and cheap fares, and the opening of its new City terminus at Broad Street sent passenger numbers soaring to 14 million in 1866. Further connections and suburban development along its lines both contributed to the company's peak years at the turn of the century, when 46 million passengers a year were carried. As with most other surface railways, once set up, investment and innovation on the North London were low. It failed to electrify or to improve the connections between its routes and the places where people wanted to go. Competition from trams and the tube then caused a massive loss of traffic, so that by 1921 traffic was down to only 11 million passengers a year and falling. By 1960, only 6,400 commuters arrived at Broad Street Station on a weekday morning, compared to over 40,000 in 1903, when it was one of the busiest stations in London, and in the 1980s Broad Street and the southern part of its City route finally closed.

The North London's story illustrates the catastrophic impact of the new forms of public transport on inner London rail passenger services. The biggest effects were felt in the decade prior to 1914. It is difficult with today's rail system to envisage the scale of the short trips around London by rail that existed from the 1860s onwards. Figure 10.1 gives some indication by comparing services out of Liverpool and Fenchurch Street Stations in 1904 and 1962. It can be seen that at the earlier date the inner routes were far more complex and extensive, with very frequent services, most of which had gone well before the 1960s. (The thickness of the lines is proportional to the number of weekday stopping trains.)

In some cases, rail companies did respond by electrifying routes. The London, Brighton and South Coast was badly hit by new tram routes, losing 1.25 million passengers to and from Croydon in a six-month period in 1905 alone. Its South London line also saw a decline in passengers from 8 million in 1903 to 3.5 million in 1908. Over a similar period, bookings from Peckham fell by a half. In response, the company embarked on a programme of electrification. It started first on the South London, completing the scheme in 1909 using an overhead system and multiple units. In 1913, the London and South Western adopted the now familiar third-rail system for schemes on its suburban lines. The London and North-Western, in contrast, in 1911 adopted the four-rail system of the underground in order that its electrification of the commuter route from Euston to Watford could link with the newly planned Bakerloo extension from Paddington to Queen's Park. Paradoxically, competition from the underground had initially stimulated this investment, but then co-operation with it made the venture financially viable.[42] The lack of a common type of electrification was to create problems in the future but, with the possibility of greater comfort, faster speeds and a more frequent service,

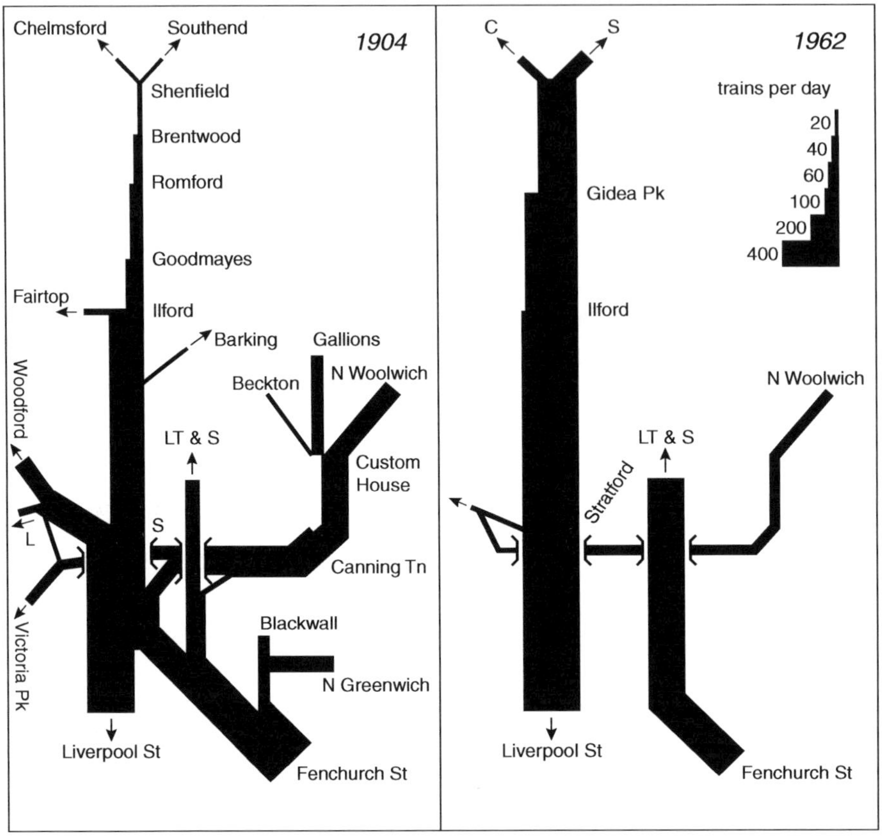

Figure 10.1 Services out of Liverpool Street and Fenchurch Street Stations, 1904 and 1962

Source: White, 1971, 197.

the railway companies began to win back business to their newly electrified lines.

Not all routes were lucky enough to receive such investment and most electrification of the southern lines was left until the inter-war years. Some companies could do nothing despite the obvious advantages. The by now merged South Eastern and Chatham Railway, in particular, was still in financial difficulties and so could not raise the capital to counteract the loss of traffic on its Metropolitan extension and North Kent lines to trams, despite seeking electrification powers in 1903.[43]

The Metropolitan and District Railways

The Metropolitan and District Railways were hybrids. They were precursors of the new underground lines in the city centre, but soon had extensive normal rail routes stretching way out into what was then countryside. The initial line, and the first passenger underground railway in the world, was constructed between Paddington and Farringdon via King's Cross from 1859 to 1863 for the Metropolitan Railway. The City Solicitor, Charles Pearson, had spent many years trying to raise support and funding for an underground railway in the Fleet Valley. The Metropolitan finally found backers in the Great Western Railway and the Corporation of London. The new company was soon to fall out with the Great Western, which precipitously withdrew all the equipment it had lent, leaving the Metropolitan without locomotives or rolling stock. But the company survived this setback.

Construction used the 'cut and cover' method, with streets being followed to minimise the demolition of property; while clearances for road improvements helped to contain costs from King's Cross to Farringdon, the most expensive part of the route. As elements of cost sharing, the station at Farringdon used land vacated by the Smithfield cattle market and the Great Western used the basement of the new Smithfield Market as a goods station.[44] The project as a whole was immediately successful, despite the soot-laden atmosphere. Almost 11 million passengers were carried in 1864 – rising to 28 million by 1868, only four years later.[45] Staff were said to find thick beards a useful filter for the smutty by-products of the steam trains used.[46]

Initially, dividends were good, at 7 per cent, but after several years it transpired in 1872 that a quarter of the amount was regularly being paid out of capital raised to fund line extensions. Moreover, costs were out of hand and suspiciously large sums went in property compensation. On discovery of these malpractices, Manchester interests were instrumental in ousting the previous board and in the appointment of Watkin, a Mancunian, as the new Chairman.[47] Further claims were made against the previous directors, and the civil engineer for the route, Fowler, was said to be the best-paid engineer in the world by Watkin because of his £152,000 fee. Fowler's fee may have been enhanced because he was more than an engineer and adept at winning Parliamentary approval for railway ventures. He was soon taking the initiative with the Metropolitan District (see below). He saved the scheme and was later rewarded by being paid a high engineering fee of £157,000 to oversee the building of it. Ever busy, he was also involved in the speculative promotion of Victoria Station.[48]

These tribulations at the Metropolitan overshadowed the extension of central London's new underground. Impressed by the success of the Metropolitan, Parliament proposed, soon after its opening, the construction of a further underground railway to serve the southern mainline termini and to be connected in the east and west to extensions of the original Metropolitan to form an 'inner circuit'. This scheme effectively blocked off any other schemes for underground railways including proposed ones that would have linked northern and southern main lines. The planned railway, the Metropolitan District (the first part of its name rarely being used), ran from South Kensington to Westminster Bridge by 1868, with the Metropolitan making a connection to it from Paddington. Part of the District's extension eastwards from Westminster was subsidised with free land from the Metropolitan Board of Works. This arose because the route followed the new Embankment built to hold Bazalgette's northern main sewer. Procrastination by the District, which had difficulty raising the money for the extension of its line beyond Westminster, was one reason why the Embankment was several years late in opening.

The point of setting up a new company rather than extending the powers of the Metropolitan was that it was felt that investors would regard the new company as less risky than an enlarged Metropolitan, and shareholders in the Metropolitan would not have their good – but, as has already been noted, fictitious – dividends threatened by the costs of the scheme. Once set up, a merger could then occur between the two companies. This prediction proved false. The District was badly affected by the collapse of Overend Gurney and Co. in 1866 which brought down its contractor backer, Peto and Betts, while the original South Kensington to Westminster part of its route was being built. After this it was unable to place all its share issue and remained chronically undercapitalised. These difficulties were compounded by the appointment of Forbes to run the District in 1870. He was also general manager of the London, Chatham and Dover Railway, the recent rival in the territory of the South Eastern Railway, whose chairman was also Watkin, who was appointed to run the Metropolitan Railway two years later. The two chairmen of the companies designated to complete the Inner Circle were consequently at loggerheads. So, unexpectedly, the District stayed independent of the Metropolitan, and the two companies' lines were only linked at the eastern end sixteen years later, in 1884, to form the Inner Circle.

The long delay in creating the Inner Circle, despite extensive public protest, arose in part because both firms were loath to co-operate and argued over how to apportion costs, revenues and train slots – a common affliction of most Victorian railways. Much has been made of the acrimonious relationship between the two railway barons in charge of the respective companies, but there were also good financial reasons why the merger never took place. First, with its reformed finances the Metropolitan was now honestly profitable and was experiencing growing traffic, whereas the District had much lower than predicted revenues from its less attractive southern route with which to finance a similarly-sized capital base. With such a divergence in returns, the Metropolitan had little cause to buy out the District and the District was in no position to do the opposite. The incentives to squabble thus stemmed from, rather than created, these differences in financial positions. The second problem was the sheer cost of building lines, whose route had been determined by Parliament rather than Mammon, through some of the most expensive parts of the capital with substantial property compensation claims. This meant that several sections of the Inner Circle could not possibly be justified on commercial grounds. The Aldgate to Tower Hill section was the last to be completed and only then because of the threat of another competing promotion being approved by Parliament and because of highly optimistic forecasts by the Metropolitan of through traffic from the East London line, little of which actually materialised. In such an array of circumstances, individual company gains could be made from attempting to pass capital costs on to the other party involved in the Inner Circle project and by arguing over operating arrangements and revenue sharing. In contrast, co-operation alone would not have made the venture much more profitable. The Inner Circle experience, rather than highlighting the frailty of human nature, makes it surprising that any subsequent underground railway was wholly funded by private enterprise – yet they were, in considerable numbers in the 1890s and 1900s.

Both the Metropolitan and the District were slow to modernise their rolling stock or to introduce new working methods or electrification. After 1882, each had powers to electrify. They experimented with a fourth-rail system for 0.75 miles in 1901 but full electrification was only completed in 1906.[49] This belated effort, however, enabled them to hold off competition from the new underground lines and trams and so they avoided the fate of the North London. Survival was further aided by the extensive suburban lines they had both built into different parts of Middlesex.

West London was one of the last areas to experience suburban expansion, partly because the heavy clay soils of Middlesex were thought to be unsuitable for housebuilding. Both the District and the Metropolitan, however, pushed lines into this part of London to drum up commuter traffic. The choice of this direction presumably was influenced by the limited competition from other companies, whereas most other directions were already heavily competed over. As the District was always chronically short of capital, its suburban extensions were piecemeal. The company became consummate at persuading others to help it. On occasion, local landowners proffered aid to the District on the prospect of enhanced land values. The company elsewhere made agreements to minimise capital costs with earlier railways in a locality, for joint use of stations or for running powers over their existing lines – particularly taking advantage of London and South Western routes north of its London to Southampton mainline. Through negotiating running powers, the District also developed an eastern service to Upminster in Essex.

The Metropolitan, in contrast, after the mid-1870s quickly pushed a virtually straight line out from Baker Street towards West Hampstead and Harrow. It eventually reached north of Aylesbury, over fifty miles from central London across mainly open countryside, to the bemusement of many. The reason became apparent when the Great Central began to move south towards London. Watkin, the company's chairman, was also chairman of the Metropolitan and of the South Eastern Railway, and the latter's routes from London to the Channel ports. The Metropolitan

Extension was probably part of his grand plan for a main line from Manchester to London, thence to continental Europe via a Channel tunnel. The continental connection was started but never completed, but the Great Central made use of part of the Metropolitan's suburban route for its entrance to London, although by then suburban traffic on the Metropolitan's tracks was too great to accommodate it. It had to rent newly built parallel lines south of Harrow from the Metropolitan and forge another route in alliance with the Great Western.[50]

The wisdom of Watkin's strategies was scant. The Great Central was the biggest failure, but the Metropolitan Extension was never used to its full capacity as a commuter line throughout its length. The land surrounding it beyond West Hampstead remained generally empty of homes until the inter-war years, and green belt controls have maintained pristine countryside beyond Rickmansworth to this day. To drum up traffic on the Extension, Watkin even started to build a pleasure ground and tower at Wembley. It was designed to be like the Eiffel Tower in Paris but slightly bigger. The failure of the pleasure grounds meant that the part-built tower was demolished, and the land was used later for housing and the Wembley stadiums.

Interestingly, as briefly mentioned above, the Metropolitan speculated in development land, as Barker and Robbins have shown, relying quite considerably on the profits from 'surplus lands'. Surplus lands arose from the statutory powers associated with the compulsory purchase of land. Railway companies were required to sell any land surplus to railway needs after a new route was completed. Usually, this process could proceed over ten years, but the companies could not grant building leases nor sell ground rents in the normal manner of building development. The Metropolitan Inner Circle Completion Act of 1874 was an exception to this – presumably in tacit recognition of the loss-making nature of this venture.[51] The Metropolitan's general exemption was significant: in 1885 it had 1,000 tenants and a rent role of £80,000 on its land holdings, plus more income from sales.[52] This ability to share in the gains of land betterment may have encouraged Watkin in his suburban line building. Despite the remaining empty acres, traffic for the Metropolitan and business in surplus lands were encouraged by the rapid growth of Willesden, Wembley and Harrow, and the Great Central meant little to the Metropolitan after Watkin's retirement in 1894.

Workmen's tickets

A final aspect of London rail commuting was the introduction of cheap workmen's trains. Pressure for them had begun in the 1840s and 1850s, because they were seen as a solution to central London overcrowding. This view was probably mistaken. Overcrowding was worst for the very poor, who were unlikely to move to the suburbs because they neither had the funds nor the time to live so distant from their irregular sources of work. The better-off working class had other travel options, a much wider choice of housing and, as was noted earlier, still often preferred to live near and walk to work at least until the end of the century. Even so, a clause compelling railway companies to run low-fare workmen's trains was inserted in all bills promoting London lines laid before Parliament after 1864. This had little effect as most lines had already been built, but nineteen years later the Cheap Trains Act required existing companies to operate them. The 1883 Act also proved limited in effect until the LCC started prodding the companies. The Board of Trade only took action after complaints were received, and a legal ruling absolved companies from the requirements of the Act if they could be shown to be against their financial interests.

Parliament was, in effect, forcing the railway companies to cross-subsidise workmen's trains from the profits made on other business. Unsurprisingly, many workmen's trains failed to pay and led to wasted capacity through the development of working-class suburbs with low off-peak traffic.[53] So, on particular routes, the cross-subsidy was substantial. Yet some operators to the south of the river and the Great Eastern Railway in the north-east wished to promote suburban development to utilise their vast over-investments in capacity, and they complied with the initiatives. By 1883, a hundred workmen's trains ran daily into central London, with about a third operated by companies with no legal obligation to run them. This suggests that many of the train services would have been run anyway, albeit probably with slightly higher fares.

Cheap fares were first made obligatory in the 1860s on new lines. The Chatham and Dover's Metropolitan Extension was the first route to introduce them, shortly followed by the North London Railway when it constructed its Broad Street route.[54] The Cheap Trains Act of 1883 heralded general compulsion of these subsidised services. By 1901, almost a third of the 410,000 arrivals at central stations from the inner and outer suburbs were travelling on cheap or workmen's fares.[55] The Great Eastern was the main provider of workmen's fares from the north-eastern and eastern suburbs with nearly half its daily arrivals travelling on cheap tickets, compared to a fifth or a third from elsewhere. Yet, to an extent, the high share of this business in the 1890s and 1900s partly reflected the fact that by then several railway companies' general suburban business was being decimated by new tram and tube lines.

The low profits from such activity may have been welcome to some hard-pressed railway companies, like the Great Eastern, but, all the same, it was not the sort of revenue on which new lines or other improvements, such as electrification, could be funded. It became increasingly difficult to ring-fence workmen's fare reductions on to a limited number of lines, so any new investments in their commuter business would almost certainly have had workmen's conditions imposed on them. This may help to explain a noticeable reluctance of the railway companies to invest to compete with the newer forms of public transport.

The divergent response of railway companies to working-class commuting had a causal influence on the spatial expansion of the metropolis. The north-eastern spread of working-class suburbs to Tottenham and beyond is a well-cited example. Although other factors obviously had an influence, the importance of rail lines to suburbanisation and the strategic nature of railway companies' behaviour do suggest that the effect was there.

Trams

Trams initially benefited from the low surface resistance of metal wheels on smooth rails, so that horses could pull far greater loads than with omnibuses. More passengers could be carried in greater comfort and safety on vehicles that were easy to get on and off. Track laying and purchase of cars entailed high initial investment, but overall unit costs were far lower than for buses, so fares could be commensurately reduced. This enabled public transport finally to be affordable down into the middle echelons of the working classes, so horse trams were the first truly mass transit system.

Attempts to introduce trams to London were thwarted by local political opposition from 1857 to 1868. The first proposal was by the London General for a route from Notting Hill Gate to Bank via the New Road, but its bill failed in Parliament.[56] If this route had been laid, the structure of London public transport would undoubtedly have been radically different, because it traversed most of the route of the soon-to-be-built Metropolitan Railway and would have made the latter unviable.

The first actual tram service was introduced in 1861 by the American, George Train. He laid tracks down Bayswater Road and Victoria Street and opened a route from Westminster Bridge to Kensington Gate, but they were torn up again after a few months. Another attempt at persuading Parliament failed in 1867–8. Finally, with routes open across the world and in other British cities, Parliament acquiesced. Three companies were licensed to operate – using capital raised overseas. The London General had been vehemently opposed to tramways after its rebuff in the 1850s, but then switched to support once it came to an arrangement with one of the new companies to supply horses for its trams.[57] Soon trams were attracting millions of passengers and earning high returns. The North Metropolitan's dividend in 1870 was an impressive 12 per cent, and some tram companies were pressing for new routes, particularly in the city centre.

Rapid expansion in light of such initial success soon ran into political opposition. In a complex series of legislative moves, the supporters of further tram extension failed to get an all-London authority to sanction future lines, and saw a strengthening of local interest as owners of property fronting a proposed route could now object as well as local authorities themselves. Tram owners had to maintain the part of the road that lay between their tracks and one and a half feet on either side of them –

costing, it was estimated, up to £500 a mile each year. Furthermore, local authorities were presented with the right to veto construction, charge wayleaves, and require ancillary road improvements, and they were able to purchase lines compulsorily at scrap values after twenty-one years of operation.[58] Finally, in 1872, central areas were declared a prohibited zone.

Without central connections to each other's routes, the three sanctioned firms operated in distinct parts of the suburbs. In 1875, the North Metropolitan carried 28 million passengers on its northern and eastern network; the London transported 16 million on 20 route miles in South London; and the smaller London Street plied over 5.5 miles from Euston to Archway, King's Cross and Holloway, serving 5 million passengers. Yet, in a short six years, despite the severe constraints on their operation, trams were carrying virtually the same number of passengers as the whole omnibus system and generally continued to earn good returns of 7 to 9 per cent throughout the rest of the century.[59]

Further companies entered the business, starting up tram routes on the remaining available suburban main roads. They were not very profitable, because the initial three had already taken the best routes and they lacked economies of scale. By the 1890s, moreover, the prospect for the Big Three was uncertain as they soon faced municipal take-over by the new London County Council as their leases came due. Under the Progressives, LCC policy was for immediate take-over: optimistically seeing both good profits to keep down rates and cheap subsidised services to the suburbs so that the working classes could benefit from greater suburbanisation. The existing trams had already been a major impetus to the outward movement of working-class residences, especially as workmen's concessionary fares were written into their charters and the trams operated for much longer periods of the day than did buses. As political chance would have it, however, the Progressives were only tenuously holding on to power in 1896 when negotiations over the first major reversions occurred, and on the casting vote of the Highways Committee Moderate chairman the northern systems were leased out again at a fee to the North Metropolitan to operate until 1910. But two years later, with the Progressives fully back in power, the LCC in 1898 took over the operation of the whole South London system.[60]

Electrification

Horse-drawn trams survived into the twentieth century. Although electric trams were a practical proposition from the late 1880s, their widespread introduction in the capital did not occur until the 1900s (Bristol was the first British city to have electric trams in 1895).[61] Electric-powered trams were faster than their horse-drawn equivalent and could be used on longer routes. Despite higher capital costs, they had relatively low operating expenses, were mechanically reliable and could carry more passengers than horse-drawn cars.

Electrification saw a new surge in route-building, particularly in the ever-expanding suburbs. The new technology encouraged further enterprises into the tram business, particularly through buying up the smaller, unprofitable horse-tram companies and using them as a base for route expansion, as London United Tramways (LUT) did, or by leasing lines from local authorities, as British Electric Traction did – creating its London subsidiaries, the Metropolitan Electric Tramways and the small South Metropolitan. Operating outside the County area, these companies had less to fear from municipalisation but, even so, the LCC still managed to block an early attempt by the LUT to electrify a Hammersmith to Shepherd's Bush line in 1895. So electric trams first appeared in London in 1901, when the LUT finally succeeded in electrifying its West London services and started building new lines deep into the suburbs. None the less, the familiar tram story of local authority demands forced the company to restrict the number of routes it developed.[62] Local authority tram operators in the east and south quickly electrified or planned new lines and other private operators began electrification in 1904. By this time, tram routes were acting as feeder services for the new, rapid transit, underground rail system.

As with horse-drawn trams, each area was dominated by a single operator. The need for local authority approval effectively stopped competitors setting up. Given the dispersed nature of routes and their inability to be connected via the centre, few economies of scale could anyhow have been gained by combining tram operation under one ownership; nor with local spatial monopolies could finances and services be improved through cartel agreements as had occurred on the buses. At this time, trams were far cheaper than horse-drawn buses, whose only advantage was that they travelled to the centre from which trams were banned.

In 1895, a syndicate offered to buy up all the tram lines in the metropolitan area, electrify them, turn routes in the County area over to the LCC and then lease them back on an operating basis. But the LCC turned them down, preferring to negotiate itself with the existing companies.[63] The resultant delay in electrification was significant and the LCC trailed the private operators – only opening its first electric line from Westminster to Tooting in 1903 and extending electrification through to all its lines by 1913. Part of the reason for the delay was that the LCC insisted on using a conduit system, rejected by the private companies as too expensive, whereby trams ran along an electric rail embedded in the road surface. The system avoided aesthetically unsightly overhead cables, but was expensive because it necessitated the diversion of underground pipes and the lowering of roadways and took twice as long to construct.

Arguments over technology were not the only constraint on electrification. The introduction of trams on the Council's northern routes was delayed by its operating lease with the North Metropolitan. The latter refused to electrify the lines itself because of the impending loss of its routes to the LCC but would have reaped an unfair financial advantage under the terms of the lease if the LCC had undertaken the task. After much discussion, the stalemate was eventually broken in 1906 when the lease was ended four years early and the company compensated. The last LCC horse-tram travelled in 1915, but by 1913 few of these by now heavily loss-making vehicles remained.

Overall the LCC spent £13.5 million on its tramway system in the course of less than a decade. This huge sum was not far off the cost of building the three main new Yerkes tubes (see below).[64] The early optimism about profits turned out to be false as the Council's policy of low fares and high wages for staff ate into profits, as did tube and motor bus competition. Growth was dramatic in the first half of the 1900s, with LCC journeys rising from 117 million in 1903 to 505 million in 1910, with another 250 million or so for the other operators. This compared with around 400 million journeys by bus, so the tram was outstripping the bus.[65] The year 1910 was to be the peak because the advent of the motor bus soon reversed these trends and trams started to lose business.

Not all tram companies suffered prior to 1914. The MET in the outer suburbs and many council systems in the outer east and south (namely, Bexley, Dartford, Erith, Ilford, Leyton, Walthamstow and West Ham) managed to sustain their traffic or even increase it and thereby stay profitable.[66] These systems, however, were in the expanding suburbs and connected to rail transit to the centre; whereas the LCC system suffered from the loss of population from the County area and the absence of the routes through the centre that motor buses enjoyed. The London United in the less densely populated west was also in difficulties from 1909. LCC tram passenger journeys fell slightly from 1911–12, and traffic became more concentrated in the morning and evening peaks, leaving the LCC's large, inflexible cars to travel around heavily under-used during the rest of the day. It foolishly spurned London General overtures to co-operate. Operating costs as a result rose dramatically, fares and revenues could not be raised and so the system plunged into its first overall loss in 1913–14. Losses continued throughout the inter-war years and by the 1940s the tram system was to be closed down altogether.

Nor was the LCC's experience with its tram system an entirely happy one in terms of social policy. First, the LCC had failed to stop local authority self-interest from curtailing tram growth or to break the ban on central routes. Second, co-operation between the operators was also a long time in coming and the situation was not helped by the LCC's aggressive social policy stance with regard to subsidised fares, which would have imposed losses on the private operators. Third, technical improvements were delayed. An expert witness told the 1905 Traffic Commission that electrification was over ten years late because of the 1870 Tramways Act and resultant local authority interference, and that many suburban lines had been lost.[67] Divisions between the interests of the LCC and the vestries/boroughs contributed to the confusion of objectives. Furthermore, the LCC's procrastination and adoption of an expensive conduit system led to more delays and to technical difficulties in joining up with suburban systems.

These policies, by restricting tram development, negated the social role assigned to this form of transport. The working men's fares policy also soon became an albatross as more and more people took advantage of them at a considerable subsidy. The issue of such tickets rose from 10 million in 1904 to 42 million in 1910–11 and to 77 million in 1913–14, at a loss of £65,000 in 1910–11 (which pro rata would have been almost £120,000 in 1913–14). These costs had to be borne by the rates and as they did not actually benefit the poor were likely to be regressive in incidence.

The final area where the LCC's tram policy brought difficulties was in relation to other modes of public transport. In 1902, the LCC stood a good chance of becoming the transport authority for London but lost the opportunity in 1902–3 when opponents pointed out its partisan support for trams.[68] As owner of one mode, it was hardly likely to be impartial. Moreover, the Council as it turned out backed the wrong mode of transport. The newly improved motor bus was to sweep the board for reliable, cheap, fast road transport from 1910. This might not have been envisaged in the 1890s but the Council did not use the informational advantages caused by the delays to its tram investments, noted above, to reconsider its policy.

Its tram policy, nevertheless, remained the lynchpin of the LCC's transportation, supplemented by vigorous encouragement of workmen's fares. With the County Council's cajoling, the 1905 Royal Commission on Transport in London called for the amalgamation of the different tram operators, through routes along major central thoroughfares, and for two new major cross-city roads with surface trams and electric rail tracks beneath them; none of which happened. The Progressives also championed a network of sub-surface tram lines running through central areas, but failed to convince experts of their viability. The only north–south connection through the centre was made by the LCC in 1906 as part of the building of Kingsway and Aldwych, and the tram system never achieved central focal points – a fact that must have brought much relief to the new tube promoters.

The relative weakness of the London system can be seen from the 1905 Commission's finding that the capital, overall, in 1905 had one route-mile of tramway for roughly every 34,000 of its population, as opposed to one mile for every 9,000 in Manchester and one mile for every 13,000 in Liverpool.

The LCC's championing of the tram was always couched in terms of efficiency, cost-effectiveness and social policy. Yet one stark piece of institutional chance must not be overlooked. Of all the various transport modes, the tram was the only one with the municipal reversion clause inserted in its charter – the only one, in other words, that the LCC could expect to obtain full control of and operate on municipally determined criteria. Once the own-running tram policy was embarked upon it was politically difficult to reverse – a large workforce and asset base was created and much intellectual and political capital had been invested in this 'solution' to London's transport and housing problems. Public–private partnerships had been shown to work in suburban tram systems, but after the MET fiasco, noted above, they were anathema to the LCC.

After 1900, it did not require an enormous amount of forecasting ability to recognise that the future was not simply the tram. Why did the LCC not set up motor buses to compete with the London General's monopoly or encourage others to do so? (It finally tried to obtain powers in 1920 but failed to get them.) Why not build a tube or, at least, threaten to build one with or without a private sector partnership? Why not try and find an accommodation with the mainline rail companies? Alternatively, the LCC could have retreated, selling off its tram system as the price of becoming the London Traffic Authority.

The tram turned into a juggernaut that left the LCC effectively, and expensively, powerless over the future of London's transport. Even public ownership, when in came in the 1930s, led to the setting up of a body outside of the control of the LCC, the London Passenger Transport Board – a turn of events of which even the unions, erstwhile champions of the Progressive strategy, approved, because by then LCC tram workers were badly paid.

The underground

Underground railways had been proposed for London since the 1830s and, as was noted earlier, the Metropolitan became the world's first underground railway in the 1860s. The expense of the cut-and-cover method, however, deterred others from investing in further lines built in this way after the Metropolitan and District. An alternative was the construction of deep-level tunnels – the tube as it quickly became known – which became technically feasible towards the end of the nineteenth century with the introduction of robust electrical motors. The soft, but watertight, London clay is often ideal for tunnelling – so the new technology brought into existence the central London tube network much as it exists today. After a hesitant start, due to technical problems and investor reluctance, a comprehensive network under virtually unified ownership emerged within the space of two decades – with most lines opened in just seven years between 1900 and 1906. The structure of the modern central underground system was founded, with the exceptions of the much later Victoria and Jubilee lines and major alterations to what is now the City branch of the Northern line.[69]

The tunnelling shield had been used to build the 1843 Wapping Tunnel and the short-lived – because of a lack of adequate means of traction – 1870 Tower Subway. With further improvements, it allowed tubes to be constructed rapidly and relatively cheaply. Divided into cells to permit several workers to excavate the clay simultaneously, the shields were jacked through the cut clay and gave support while the earth was excavated. The tunnel was lined with iron segments as the shield was moved forward. Electric traction, proved to be feasible in 1879, solved the problem of ventilating tunnels carrying steam trains. Most of the new electric trains were bought from US companies and shipped over to London. Electric lifts also made access to the lines easier for passengers, although they were slow by modern standards. Controversy raged over whether cut-and-cover or deep tunnels were preferable. The 1905 Royal Commission on London's Traffic reckoned the costs were fairly even.[70] In this case, the tubes may have been an inadvertent mistake as they were not built to mainline standards and, hence, could not accommodate through-running from the surface system. The initial tube promoters would not have been much concerned about this as they had few direct connections with the mainline rail companies, but the subsequent social cost was high.

Construction costs were reduced by an 1892 Parliamentary ruling that underground companies were no longer obliged to purchase the property above their works, greatly reducing the capital costs of a scheme. Private landowner permission, for which recompense could be demanded, however, was still necessary, though this requirement was circumvented by lines following public roads, wherever possible. This necessitated some sharp curves and, on occasion, one line running above the other where a street narrowed, to minimise compensation claims. This piggyback arrangement, for example, can be seen in the layout of the Central line platforms at Notting Hill Gate and Chancery Lane. Vibration was particularly bad in the first tubes, as was the smell before ionisation was introduced in the 1920s, so compensation was a recurrent issue. Tube companies could not claim betterment from landowners for enhancing their land values, even though values increased on a grand scale, nor did they indulge themselves in property development.

The first line was a small-bore one between the City and South London, which ran between Stockwell, then a leafy suburb, and the City. It was completed in 1890, with subsequent extensions to Clapham Common (1900), Angel (1901) and Euston (1907) – rebored, it is now part of the Northern line.[71] It was followed in 1898 by the Waterloo and City line. This short route was built by the London and South Western Railway as a belated substitute for its original desire to site its terminus in the City. The Central London Railway (Central Line) opened in 1900 – running from Shepherd's Bush to the Bank of England. It charged a standard twopenny fare initially and was highly successful for the first few years, but traffic dropped off after 1905 as bus companies retaliated. This encouraged the company to abandon the uniform fare in order to increase revenue. Initially, however, it was highly successful, paying the international investors that funded it a dividend of 4 per cent between 1901 and 1906.

Although the first tube was in the south, it proved also to be the last before 1914 – apart from the short spur of the Bakerloo between Waterloo and the Elephant and Castle. This may be accounted for by the experience of the City and South London, which not only suffered higher costs by being the pioneer but also intense competition from surface transport, which kept returns low. Districts south of the Thames were well provided with overground lines following the earlier competition between the southern rail companies. Much of the soil in the inner south, moreover, was water-bearing and expensive to tunnel. Tram routes were extensive in South London and the LCC in the 1890s had ambitious plans for them. Yet the situation north of the river was still highly competitive, although the banning of trams from the central district kept at bay the gravest threat in the 1890s. Unsurprisingly, lines developed after the City and South London concentrated on the central core.

Apart from the costs of compensation, two major problems faced tube promoters in their quests to start their schemes. The first was obtaining the necessary Parliamentary approval for the proposed scheme. This was both uncertain and time-consuming. The criteria depended on the whim of the Parliamentary Committee assigned to deal with it, and were affected by the contemporary political composition of Parliament and the lobbying influences of opponents. These were often transport operators threatened with a loss of business or allies of a competing scheme. Success was risky and the costs of achieving it high; yet, once obtained, the rights proved to have considerable market value because they avoided the cost, uncertainty and delay that promoters of new schemes would face in overcoming the Parliamentary hurdle. So the several schemes approved in 1891 and 1892 developed a longevity that in several cases outlasted their initial supporters, and were built under circumstances not initially intended.

Funding of tubes at the turn of the century proved to be the major problem, with lines delayed or abandoned. Investors were generally wary of these investments, which could easily turn sour – like the modern Channel Tunnel. As noted earlier, the original formation of the District, for example, in the 1860s, was encouraged by the belief that it would be easier to raise capital in this way than if the Metropolitan had tried to do it alone. Tube construction was expensive: estimated to be over a quarter of a million pounds per mile in 1900.[72] Tubes also took many years to build, while no revenue could be earned, at a time when other forms of public transport were also being transformed by new technology and changed ownership patterns. The short Waterloo and City line, for example, was sanctioned in 1893, so the decision to invest must have been made shortly after the opening of the City and South London. There was no difficulty in raising the necessary capital, because the London and South Western Railway (LSWR) guaranteed the share issue of £540,000 and gave full support to this 1.5 mile feeder into the City. The line was built mainly under the river, thereby avoiding extensive compensation claims, and with no possibility of mainline through-running. This may have been accounted for by the LSWR's slowness in electrifying its routes out of Waterloo, so at the time there was nothing to connect to. Even so, the line was not opened for business until 8 August 1898 – almost four years after the initial start of construction of the tunnels.[73] In light of such gestation costs and the number of schemes looking for backers, the problems of raising finance were perhaps understandable.

Even once financial backers were found, difficulties could still arise. The original Bakerloo line company, for example, which also had the support but not the financial backing of the LSWR, was not started until 1898, five years after it had received approval. The problem was finance. Finally, financial backers – the London and Globe Finance Corporation – were found, but then the tube company collapsed in 1901 following their failure and work stopped until Yerkes bought the Bakerloo a year later (see below).[74] The London and Globe's commitment to the Bakerloo was an important contributory factor in its own collapse as the investment indicated that this firm and its colourful chairman, Whitaker Wright, had over-extended themselves. After its demise, Wright was charged with financial malpractice and sentenced to seven years' penal servitude, but chose to commit suicide instead.[75] This much-publicised case must have further discouraged domestic investors from contemplating investments in tubes.

The need to persuade investors of the viability of schemes gave mainline rail companies considerable potential leverage over the new tubes, and the spread of mainline stations helps to explain the lines that were built and those that were not. Even so, most mainline companies stayed aloof, but the LSWR, as noted above, and the Great Northern Railway took a particular interest in tubes as a means of improving their suburban services. The Great Northern and City tube, opened in 1904, was founded by the Great Northern Railway to encourage commuter traffic north of Finsbury Park and divert the existing overcrowding on Great Northern suburban services. This tube, unlike the others, was consequently built to mainline dimensions. Like the District before, the sibling soon fell out with the parent (this time it seems to have been the parent's fault), had problems raising the finance, and through-running never occurred until the 1980s. The Great Northern also encouraged the flotation of the Great Northern and Strand, which was taken over to form the northern section of the Piccadilly line (see below).

The new tubes faced considerable competition from other contemporary forms of public transport, so routes with assured high-density use were preferred rather than recourse to any rational overall plan for a mass transit network for the world's largest city.

American intervention

The situation for the tube system at the turn of the century was highly uncertain, but then a United States entrepreneur, C. T. Yerkes, backed by a New York/London finance house, Speyer Bros., transformed the situation. Speyer were not novices in London, having had a City office since 1861 in order to market American securities on the continent and undertake large-scale exchange deals.[76] By 1899, the colourful Yerkes had spent almost two decades assembling, then selling, a unified tramway system in Chicago, but he left all this for some reason to come to London for the remaining five years of his life. His predictions in 1900 that by 1920 people would travel twenty miles or more by electric train and that the horse-bus was doomed were classified as those of a dreamer by the contemporary editor of the *Daily Express*, in an apparent echo of the views of most British investors.[77]

Yerkes's first venture into the tubes was to purchase in 1900 the rights of the Charing Cross, Euston and Hampstead – a company that had lain moribund for the previous seven years because of lack of investor interest – for the substantial sum of £100,000. He then applied for extensions from Hampstead and Kentish Town to Golders Green and Highgate respectively, with the Golders Green station located on what was currently farmland. The American system was coming to London not simply in terms of the new-fangled electric technology and syndicated finance but also in the type of suburban development. Yerkes then used his shareholding in the District to set up the Metropolitan District Electric Traction Company (MDET) in 1901, again with American backers, to finance electrification of the District Railway, which at the time was in a poor financial state, and to build the Brompton and Piccadilly line that had been approved in 1893 and come into the District's possession. The tube route was then extended, for the MDET quickly began negotiations to acquire the Great Northern and Strand. Finance for the latter was still not in sight, two years after approval, until an arrangement in 1901 between the above-mentioned Great Northern Railway and the MDET led to transfer of the proposed route to the latter. At transfer, the planned route was cut north of Finsbury Park, where it was supposed to relieve mainline congestion, in order to protect the Great Northern's own commuter business – so the original justification for the line, the current overcrowding north of Finsbury Park, seems to have been quietly forgotten in these manoeuvrings. The Great Northern and Strand cost Yerkes £131,016, a price set by the costs and Parliamentary deposits of the route to date plus a 5 per cent return.[78] The Hampstead tube's shares were then also transferred by Yerkes to the MDET and it bought out the works of the failed Bakerloo.

Within eighteen months, these events transformed one weak, one failed and several hardly-built or paper schemes into a powerful force. The MDET itself was then acquired by a new company in 1902, in a piece of financial engineering underwritten by Speyer interests. The new enterprise, Underground Electric Railways Company of London (UERL), which would then be able to issue stocks and shares to fund the by now £16 million that had been committed to building underground lines. Shares were then issued in a complex way that meant that they would receive no return until profits exceeded 5 per cent, but there were no difficulties in finding buyers.[79] How much Yerkes and others made out of these financial dealings is unclear but, by the end of them, the main financial risks were being taken by those who bought UERL stock – and they were to lose most of their money in the next few years.

A major competitive threat to UERL emerged with the attempt by another US financial group, the Morgan banking interests, to float another London tube network. Like Speyer, Morgan had close links to the City and good experience of London – so the firm did not embark on this venture without good knowledge of the city.[80] Its initial interest was sparked by the activities in 1900 of British Siemens in wanting to build a tube as an outlet for its electrical products. Negotiations then switched to the then highly profitable London United Tramways (LUT), which wanted further links to its West London tram network after the success of its connection to the Central London at Shepherd's Bush. Knowledge of Morgan interest from 1900 to 1902 must have spurred on Yerkes and his associates in their own activities. The Morgan proposal was to build 38 miles of new tube line stretching from Hammersmith in the west to Southgate and Waltham Abbey in the far north-east suburbs. Their mistake was to form a joint partnership with LUT, which would provide three-eighths of the capital, but they did not acquire control of LUT as the Yerkes interests had done with the companies they invested in.

The relationship with LUT proved fatal. During 1902, the Morgan scheme seemed set to pass through Parliament, until the chairman of LUT unexpectedly sold his shares at a good price to Yerkes, who promptly withdrew LUT from co-operation with Morgan. As Parliament had stipulated that the Morgan lines had to be built in their entirety, the whole Morgan scheme collapsed and Parliament, at a time when feeling about American financial manipulation was running high, did nothing to enable Morgan to rescue the situation.[81] Whether the Morgan system would actually have been built is highly uncertain. Competition between the competing underground lines would have been substantial and surface transport was already showing that it could fight back. Once having got permission for its lines, the Morgan interests, rather than actually build them, might also have been happy to sell out to the Yerkes Group, which would have had a strong interest in squeezing out a potential competitor.

Why such financial interest in the London underground? London tube building in the early 1900s, for investors, especially overseas ones, seems to have had the characteristics of a modern internet stock. The surface railways, the Metropolitan and District companies, and the first tube, the City and South London, all gave no indication that new underground rail schemes would be highly profitable, but the success of the Central London, though in fact relatively modest and as it turned out short-lived, encouraged a flood of enthusiasm. The new electric technology finally seemed improved enough to offer a comprehensive service, and expected passenger numbers were talked up to highly optimistic levels, without regard for parallel technical developments in motorised road transport. The Central London had shown that investment banks could earn handsome profits by gathering a syndicate together and floating an underground company. Furthermore, those in the know within such syndicates could secretly buy development land around new stations before routes became public knowledge.

Public policy towards transport had switched considerably since the 1860s, when Parliament had seemed interested in sustaining competition – as indicated in the widespread permissions it gave to railway companies to build new stations and metropolitan routes. By 1900, industrial policy was switching towards the large industrial combine. The impact of congestion on London streets caused by bus competition, the uncertainties of new transport schemes and the call for unification under municipal ownership all pushed public and political opinion towards the need for consolidation in metropolitan public transport. The history of tube building in the 1890s and 1900s does suggest that Parliament, if it had wished, could have set up competing groups in the London underground by specifying ownership structures as well as routes, but it had no interest in doing so. The huge fixed costs of constructing an underground line, moreover, and the need to fill trains with large numbers of passengers paying fares high enough to cover amortisation as well as running costs, pushed towards consolidation. With consolidation would come monopoly, whereas competing groups in a regulated environment might have been a more socially beneficial outcome.

Yerkes died in 1905, though Speyer remained the financial *éminence grise* to the UERL. By 1906, the situation for companies both above and below ground had become financially dire. Motor bus competition, described above, ate into tram, bus and tube profits. Passenger numbers on the underground lines were well below earlier forecasts. The new equipment did not always work – the District, now virtually bankrupt, had electric trains that kept on breaking down. The UERL contacted the LCC with a view to selling out to the Council but the Progressives spurned them. To avoid further ruinous competition, the bus and underground companies came together in the London Passenger Traffic Conference in 1907 to fix fares and share traffic, but the bus and underground companies could not agree.[82] This pushed the remaining underground companies closer together – with joint marketing exercises and co-operative technical improvements, especially in signalling, which led to increased speeds and frequency.

The UERL narrowly avoided financial collapse in 1908 when investors who had sustained high losses on their investments in the company accepted a financial and organisational restructuring. The London General in the same year, as noted above, had managed to bring most bus companies under its wing. Both the underground and the bus company had a strong incentive to co-operate and, by 1911, the UERL managed to acquire the London General by offering it extremely attractive terms.[83] Other remaining bus companies quickly came to agreements or were absorbed by the new Combine, as did the independent tube companies, the City and South London (1912) and the London Central (1913), which were both acutely aware of the damage that the Combine's buses could do to them. The other independent tube company, the Great Northern and City, went in 1913 to the Metropolitan, which managed to stay independent and saw the potential for combining routes in the City with its new acquisition, but then failed to achieve Parliamentary approval for these schemes and so was left with this odd outpost to its north-western empire.[84]

London's public transport network had been partially unified by private enterprise, using predominantly foreign capital – an act officially sanctioned by Parliament. That the UERL would win out in the end was by no means certain prior to its success. Instead, through good management, luck and the ability to raise funds when needed, it outmanoeuvred others. The tube was to be the focus of metropolitan public transport from now on. Competition, however, was not completely removed. In some areas, the new London Traffic Combine's services would compete, or come to accommodations, with surface railways, including the Metropolitan. The LCC tram system continued to be a significant rival, against which the Combine used loss-making, cross-subsidised buses. Private bus companies could also still set up and, in the early 1920s, there were about sixty of them.[85] For most of its costly tube routes, however, the group had a clear run and could raise fares to profitable levels with little threat of retaliation. Another problem was that future investment and innovation would be constrained as the new monopoly had an incentive to limit them in order to maximise the returns from its existing assets. The Underground Group set up office in St James, which was to become the home of London Transport after its formation in 1933.

The timing of the impetus to merger was also significant in bringing it about. The building of the underground network, the electrification of tramways and to an extent suburban railways, and the advent of the motor bus suddenly and dramatically increased public transport capacity. Although annual journeys per head of resident population increased from 165 in 1896 to 300 in 1913, the increase in capacity was probably still far above that which could be viable without monopoly pricing.

The competitive scramble for London's commuters in the two decades prior to the First World War was perhaps a unique period in British urban history. Huge sums were spent on transport systems, running on new technologies, that in reality could never be profitable as independent entities. They changed the city's urban structure, greatly encouraged decentralisation and facilitated the turn-of-the-century housing boom. The implicit contemporary subsidy to London travellers and property owners was huge. The big losers were shareholders in many of these new ventures, the overground railways and the LCC, especially following its investment in trams. Forty years before, mainline railways had been castigated for failing to provide enough cheap, suburban services. Now, they experienced large losses of passenger traffic and major investments in London services were abandoned. They concentrated where possible, instead, on longer-distance commuting. The fate of the North London Railway and of inner-city rail services in general has already been highlighted. Even more so than the Metropolitan and District, the rail companies failed to electrify their services, despite the fact that others abroad were showing the benefits of doing this. Significant electrification did not come until after the First World War, by which time any potential battle with the underground had been irretrievably lost, and old rail suburban branch lines were slowly incorporated into the underground network in the inter-war years.

It is interesting in this context to think of a 'what if' scenario. What if the mainline companies had built tunnels in the 1890s through central London linking their inner city networks and providing fast through electric suburban services? The tunnelling distances in general would have been far less than those of the new underground routes. The latter in such circumstances would probably never have been built on the scale they were by private enterprise, because then they would have faced irrepressible competition.

The failure of the rail companies to pick up the ideas and technologies used by others in London could be put down to entrepreneurial failure. More likely reasons, however, are institutional. The rail companies had been locked in bitter competition since their inception and would probably have found it impossible to co-operate voluntarily in such high-cost ventures. The geography of ownership meant that no company had routes on opposite sides of the city that could be beneficially connected and they had, on a number of occasions, been denied cross-centre link ups by Parliament in earlier decades. They faced price controls and were forced to operate extensive cheap workmen's services that did not make investment pay. They would also have been less able to avoid property compensation as larger tunnels with gentler curves than existed in the underground would have had to have been built. Moreover, the tube system, once it had entered the time-consuming process of Parliamentary approval, property compensation and construction, had first-mover advantage. With the added competition of trams, this made sure that extensive mainline rail investment in inner London would never pay. Nevertheless, the District did propose to build an express route below its existing lines from Earl's Court to the City – an idea that was dropped, unfortunately for future generations, when it was absorbed by the Yerkes Group. The Great Northern and City, the half-hearted link of the Great Northern Railway to the Square Mile, from Finsbury Park to Moorgate, also gives a hint of what might have been. An absence of express rail tunnels through London has remained a major contributory factor in slowing public transport journeys in the metropolis.

11 Utilities, communications and markets

Introduction

Transportation facilities are not the only important aspects of the physical infrastructure in a city. Clean drinking water and sewage systems to carry away unhealthy waste are necessary to maintain health. Power is needed for industry and homes, so the means to produce and distribute sources of it must be available. Information and documents need to be circulated within the city and elsewhere via communications systems. Finally, distribution networks have to be in place to enable the exchange of produce to feed the urban population.

Substantial change occurred in all these aspects of metropolitan infrastructure during the nineteenth century. In 1800, many of them did not exist – in the case of gas, electricity, the telegraph and telephones, they had yet to be invented. Others were in a rudimentary or a worsening state – namely, the post, water and sewerage. Each component, moreover, exhibited natural monopoly characteristics because each, in one way or another, involved expensive network connections and high fixed costs in production facilities. Optimal scales of provision, furthermore, became much larger over time. Water and sewerage required pipes to be laid through the urban area and for health reasons they needed to serve the whole population. Gas, electricity, the telegraph and telephones did not necessitate such wide coverage but cables still had to be laid throughout the city and expensive production and distribution facilities had to be created. The market distribution of foodstuffs required an array of wholesale markets, linked into the evolving transport system, to serve the newly emerging mass retailing system. The postal system had to have similar links to national transport and also an urban network of sorting and delivery facilities.

Duplication would cause ruinous competition but monopoly contained its own dangers as well. As a result, the state had to intervene and regulate all of these industries. Powers were also needed to purchase land compulsorily to create plant and to enable the laying of pipes and cables. The very existence of the organisations involved in these areas of infrastructure, therefore, required Acts of Parliament or a regulatory licence, and through these mechanisms the state helped to formulate the rules through which provision would operate. There were various state controls in these areas on quality, price, availability, investments and profit levels. Fluctuations in predominant political philosophies meant that various ownership models were adopted. Communications was the first to adopt the public ownership model – with the post, telegraph and telephone all becoming public monopolies over the course of the period, for reasons that seem the opposite of Victorian *laissez-faire*. Private monopolies existed in water supply and gas for most of the period, despite extensive campaigns for municipal control; eventually an independent public body was set up to supply water. Electricity remained small-scale, mainly private and partly competitive. Wholesale markets mainly became the subsidised prerogatives of railway companies and the Corporation of London. Sewerage was unquestioningly seen as a municipal matter. The sheer cost of a sewer system and the need to encompass the whole population led to a restructuring of London's local government – for this reason, consideration of sewerage is left until the chapter on local government (Chapter 16).

Several infrastructure activities became ensnared in a long political debate about the claimed superiority of municipal provision. At the beginning of the period, for local government to claim better organisational skill than private initiative would have been laughable. But, by mid-century, the persuasive talents of some key figures had drawn sewerage into the municipal net and from then on there was a clamour to bring in water, gas, electricity and the telephone system. This 'Gas and Water socialism' was a national phenomenon during the last quarter of the century but had particular characteristics in the capital, because of the latter's sheer size and unique political structure.[1] Yet, by the 1900s, enthusiasm for municipalisation was on the wane and London continued to have a unique and varied institutional framework for infrastructural services.

Institutional structures determined the development of infrastructure provision over the course of the century. On occasion, technical change or new regulations aimed at overcoming the failures of earlier legislation altered the institutional framework. The gas industry, for example, was transformed by technology; whilst water had a whole series of legislative measures aimed at overcoming abysmal failings. Analysis thus has to put emphasis on changing institutional frameworks. Each aspect of infrastructure is considered in turn: water, gas, electricity, post, telegraph, telephone and wholesale markets. Clear parallels emerge.

Water

Water supply was a source of irritation, poor health and death in London throughout the nineteenth century. Part of the problem was the sheer cost of providing the enormous amounts of water required by the largest city in the world. The nine private companies in existence in 1876 supplied an estimated 116 million gallons (526 million litres).[2] Although this is only a quarter of the 2,000 million litres or so currently consumed in the London area, the capital cost of extraction, reservoirs, cleaning and piped supply to dwellings was daunting.

From the late seventeenth century onwards, capital was forthcoming for water supply through the floating of private companies. They increasingly undertook the task of supply for a fee, or water rate, paid by those who connected to their systems. These commercial companies superseded the medieval system of well-supply and a limited number of free gravity-fed conduits financed by the Corporation of London. At an early stage, therefore, London's local government showed more interest in keeping property taxes low than in providing good-quality, universal water supplies. Added to this was the role of Parliament in legislating, or failing to legislate, in attempts to improve the condition and extent of metropolitan water supply. Arguments also raged over whether a private monopoly of supply was desirable, or whether a publicly owned, unitary, city-wide water authority was preferable. And, when that public body seemed in sight at the end of the century, dispute centred on whether it should be independent or part of the newly created London County Council. The case of water, consequently, provides a good example of the governance of London during this era, as well as of the history of a resource so inadequately provided for most of the nineteenth century that many hundreds of thousands of Londoners must have been taken ill or died unnecessarily from cholera and other water-borne diseases.

In 1800, the largest of the private companies providing the capital's water were, to the north of the Thames, the New River (1619) supplying the City and Islington, and the Chelsea (1723) covering Westminster and surrounding districts; and, on the south side, the Lambeth (1785) and the Southwark (1760). The earliest, the New River, illustrates the scale of investment and the associated risk. It was founded after the City had obtained Acts of Parliament in 1606 and 1607 to build a channel bringing fresh water from Hertfordshire into reservoirs just north of the City and then to pipe it to paying customers. The first promoter foundered after the Corporation refused to subsidise the venture. Underestimating the cost, the next promoter, Hugh Myddleton, a wealthy goldsmith and member of the Parliamentary Committees considering water supply, was forced to ask for half the funding from James I (who wanted an equal share as a sleeping partner). Reminiscent of concerns in modern Britain, a quarter of the water was then lost from leakages in the Company's pipes that ran through the City from 1613. Once established, however, the Company was highly profitable.[3]

Later operators made extensive use of water pumped from the Thames, but still had the expense of reservoirs, pumping and pipe-laying. The Chelsea Company's operations for extracting and storing water from the Thames, for example, had spread across 89 acres (36 hectares) of present-day Pimlico and Victoria by the late eighteenth century. Its extensive use of land arose partly from a tidal pumping system that raised water out of the Thames.[4] This had minimal running costs but showed the lack of interest in investment.

The rapid growth of London, and James Watt's improvements in the design of pumping machinery, then led to the creation by statute of five further firms – the West Middlesex (1806), the East London (1807) and the Grand Junction (1811) to the north of the Thames, and the Kent (1809) and Vauxhall (1805) on the opposite bank. The statutes were necessary to limit competition and, thus, encourage private investment. The Acts, however, defined imprecise boundaries. This caused for a few years expensive, multiple laying of pipes in streets and fierce competition between the companies, which depressed water rates below profitable levels. In response, the water companies began to collude. Following the lead of the New River and the East London Company in 1815, all the companies had agreed by 1817 to operate within specific areas and significantly raise their charges.[5]

In economic terms, the situation is a classic instance of competition under conditions of natural monopoly. As natural monopolies, the marginal cost to each of the water companies of supplying a new customer was below the average cost of supply. Firms would consequently always benefit from cutting their price of supply to capture households' business from other water companies – forcing the general price of supply below average costs, leading to permanent losses. If the average costs of London's water companies were markedly different, the one with the lowest marginal cost curve would eventually have captured the whole market. It would have reaped economies of scale as it moved down its cost curve, putting further pressure on competitors that did not have such economies of scale, and once in a monopoly position would have been able to raise prices and further enhance profitability through price discrimination. Fear of this happening would presumably encourage the weaker firms to come to agreements with the stronger ones. The stronger were likely to be the older ones that had already invested heavily in equipment and distribution networks.

But why should the stronger firms have colluded, when in a few years they could have seen the new entrants off ? The answer probably lies in limits to the extent of economies of scale. These may partially have been technical. High leakage rates in particular would have forced restrictions on the geographical extent of piping from one major facility, putting a cap on technical scale economies. The other constraints to scale were political. Water supply was a contentious issue, subject to extensive interest from politicians. A monopoly water supplier, given its likely characteristics, would have been subject to even more opprobrium than was actually heaped on London's companies during the nineteenth century. The risk of political pressure to supply unprofitable services would also have been far greater. For these reasons, it seems likely to have been in the self-interest of the water companies to collude rather than for one to swallow up the others. The statutory existence of each one anyway limited the possibilities of mergers, but the statutory rules are likely to have been in accordance with the industrial structure wished for by the companies. Statute anyway did not stop several mergers between them.

Public complaints of the effects of the new cartel led to a Parliamentary Committee in 1821. Its recommendations supported monopoly supply by the private companies, but with statutory control of water rates and referees to arbitrate between consumers and the companies. These recommendations have a similarity to the system in operation in the UK since water privatisation in the 1980s, but the 1821 proposals failed to reach the statute book.

The firms invested in considerable new facilities and pipe-laying. The New River Company, for example, supplied water for the first time to first-floor premises from 1805 and started to replace its wooden pipes with cast-iron ones from 1811; while the Chelsea cut the Grosvenor Canal (site of today's Victoria Station) and expanded its reservoir in Green Park in the 1820s. Yet the companies had little incentive to invest sufficiently in improvements in the quantity and quality of the water supplied to match increases in demand, or to supply water to low-income households, which would face difficulties in paying water charges.

Many poor areas thus remained unconnected to the mains, including parts of the City. In Southwark, in 1843, 30,000 residents were forced to depend on wells and rainwater butts. As late as 1862, courtyards of poor housing in Whitechapel were served by stand-taps switched on for a quarter to half an hour a day, except Sundays when there was none.[6] Those living in the working-class districts supplied by communal standpipes and without water tanks had to store water in any receptacle available. Frequent recourse was made to stagnant water butts fed intermittently from the running water supply. In the poorer districts where the facilities were shared, these were recognised as an appalling health hazard. If away from home when the supply was turned on, some families went entirely without water or had to borrow from neighbours. Even when water was piped into homes, supply was intermittent. Companies ran water through their pipes for only a few hours or less a day and for three to six days per week, ostensibly to minimise leakages from inadequate pipes. Even in 1876, only 53 per cent of London houses had a constant water supply.[7]

The overall situation was extremely deleterious to health, allowing infection to spread rapidly throughout the population. Amongst other water-borne illnesses, cholera struck in London in 1831. The connection to contaminated drinking water was decisively proved by the late 1840s, but the disease still infected Londoners for decades to come – a situation that could have been avoided if fresh water supplies had been provided.

The quality of the supplies was equally poor. In the first half of the century, apart from the East London and New River Companies, water was drawn from the stretch of the Thames where the city's sewage and industrial wastes were discharged. Even the New and Lee Rivers were heavily polluted. There was also little filtration. The first successful sand filter bed was brought into use in 1829 by the Chelsea and, even though in 1834 Parliament required firms to incorporate filter beds into all new works, quality remained poor.

Criticism of the companies' performance led to successive, but generally unsuccessful, Parliamentary interventions. Criticism of Parliament's response was rife throughout the century. Many MPs were identified as having shareholdings in the companies; most had limited London interests; and voters, until electoral reform in the last quarter of the century, were property owners who would have had to pay for any improvements and so would not have taken kindly to their MP being too strident in the push for reform.

No real action was taken until 1852, when the first Metropolitan Water Act prohibited the extraction of Thames water from below Teddington Lock, and obliged all companies to filter river-derived water, and to cover all service reservoirs within a radius of five miles of St Pauls. A London Water Examiner was also appointed as a regulatory agent. The Lambeth quickly moved its intake upstream in 1853. The death rate in its area fell to 37 deaths per 10,000, less than a quarter of the Southwark and Vauxhall's 130 deaths. Maximum constraints on the water rate charges were also set. Unfortunately, the legislation controlled only the rate poundage, so that water charges rose substantially as the assessed values of London properties grew. As property revaluations occurred every five years from the 1870s, the water companies were guaranteed substantial revenue increases for supplying exactly the same service to each property. This was reflected in growing profits and dividends. The lucky New River, serving the City where property values rose the fastest, could boost its dividend as a result from 7.3 to 11.5 per cent between 1871 and 1881.[8]

A few years after the 1852 Act, the companies were further required to provide a constant water supply, though only if this was requested by four-fifths of households, and a 10 per cent cap was put on their profits (though the extent to which these financial powers were used seems limited in view of the subsequent high profits of the companies). A second Metropolitan Water Act in 1871 forced the companies to submit their annual accounts for inspection by the government auditor, and provided for the appointment of an impartial water inspector to submit monthly and annual reports on water qualities to the Local Government Board and to make periodic inspections of company works. In 1877, the companies were finally forbidden to cut off supplies for non-payment of water rates.

The result of these government initiatives was a gradual improvement in both the supply and quality of London's water. There remained, however, much disquiet over company profits, the service provided, and the supposed higher costs that resulted from the existence of several suppliers. Despite the amalgamation of the Southwark and Vauxhall firms in 1845 and the 1856 absorption of the Hampstead River by the New River, water provision was still split between eight undertakings. In 1850, the General Board of Health, with Chadwick chairing, produced a report on London water supply. In typical Chadwick centralising fashion, it recommended a single metropolitan enterprise covering water and sewerage, a technically suspect system of delivery and an entirely new long-distance source of fresh water.[9] Whether a single body was required is unclear. Sewerage and water only needed combining because of Chadwick's misguided technological enthusiasms. For water alone, it is unlikely that the scale economies were sufficiently large, as yet, to justify the existence of such a large body. In gas supply – an industry with somewhat similar characteristics – city-wide organisations arose only several decades later with the advent of new distribution technologies and, even then, the north and south were supplied by separate companies, as is shown later.

Attempts to bring water under the control of one organisation began in earnest in 1851, when the government unsuccessfully endeavoured to amalgamate the suppliers, and pressure for reform continued throughout the rest of the century. In 1878, the Metropolitan Board of Works (MBW) introduced a bill for the acquisition of water supply. After lobbying by the water companies and growing Parliamentary mistrust of this metropolitan first-tier body, the MBW failed to obtain sufficient support. Two years later, in 1880, a government bill aimed at their purchase by a trust was rejected by the Select Committee appointed to consider it. Bills introduced by the vestries and the City Corporation in 1891, again designed to establish a trust, were referred to the Ridley Committee, which reported adversely.

Earlier failures to regulate the private companies swung sentiment round to the need for a publicly owned, unitary water body; while technical improvements made the logic of a London-wide institution far more compelling than it had been at the beginning or middle of the century. The London County Council repeatedly and unsuccessfully sought to obtain powers to purchase the companies in the 1895, 1897, 1899 and 1900 Parliamentary sessions. Finally, prompted by the failure of its own bill for the creation of a water trust, the government in 1896 set up the Llandaff Commission to investigate the whole question of control. The inquiry's 1899 report recommended the creation of a public authority outside of the control of the new structure of metropolitan local government, despite much lobbying from the London County Council. In 1902, the London Water Bill created the Metropolitan Water Board, which took over the water companies' 8,000 miles of 2-inch to 60-inch pipes and set up home on the site of the New River Company's headquarters in a symbolic demonstration of continuity amidst change. Acquiescence was rewarded with around £40 million compensation.[10] This figure had been inflated by rising property values in London and, given their lack of investment to achieve desired objectives, might seem over-generous to the old water companies.

The new public body had less incentive to circumvent legislation and the needs of the population than had the previous private companies because it had simply to break even, while achieving an array of physical measures of performance (comprehensive coverage, quality, regularity, etc.). To achieve these ends, it had the right to impose a compulsory rate charge, essentially at a level of its own choosing. Water was thus municipalised but left outside of the normal checks and balances of a municipality. By keeping the Board out of the maelstrom of disputes over local taxation and expenditure, the legislators accepted that water supply mattered more than cost and political fashion. Resource allocation to London's water was now primarily a question of negotiation between the Board and central government. Yet, in doing so, Westminster had clipped the centralising wings of London's new municipal authority. The performance of the new Board seems to have been far better as agitation ceased. However, the weaknesses of financial incentives and cost accountability inherent in such organisational models, and the constraints on investment caused by periodic public expenditure crises, were subsequently to be prime justifications for the privatisation of water supply again around seventy-five years later in the 1980s.[11]

Gas

Gas was another new industry of the nineteenth century. It was first used for lighting in London in 1807, when the German Frederick Winsor illuminated the south side of Pall Mall. Five years later, in 1812 he formed, by special Parliamentary Act, the Gas Light and Coke Co. to provide light for Westminster, the City and Southwark. The firm constructed gas-making plants in Great Peter Street, Westminster and, later, in Curtain Road, Shoreditch. Successfully winning public street and bridge lighting contracts, by 1815 it had built 26 miles of main and erected 4,000 gas lamps.[12]

Other firms entered this new industry on seeing the profitability of this innovatory enterprise. Five more statutory companies were formed – the City (1816), the Imperial (1820), the Ratcliff (1823), the Phoenix (1824) and the Independent (1829) – plus a number of smaller undertakings working under private deeds of trust. These invested in their own infrastructure, so that, by 1823, London had 250–300 miles of main, which by mid-century had risen to 2,000 miles.[13] As coal was the main input and water was needed in production, gas works tended to locate next to the river or canals. Four, for example, set up along the route of the Regent's Canal – providing much needed business.[14] Not all the start-ups survived – a small company in Camberwell, for example, had only a brief life in the 1820s – indicating the riskiness of the early years of the industry.[15]

London companies also became promoters of gas companies elsewhere in Britain and builders of the necessary works. London iron merchants John and George Barlow, for example, had done this in over ten towns and cities by 1822, and in 1815 Preston hired an engineer with the Chartered Company in London to build its facilities.[16] This characteristic illustrates two general themes about London-based enterprises: first, they may have been in a position to benefit from the propensity of innovations to be developed in large cities; and, second, that the relationships between London enterprises and the rest of Britain were often much closer in the first decades of the nineteenth century than is credited in segmented views of the nineteenth-century national economy.

The success of the surviving first gas suppliers, in turn, encouraged further entry into the sector, greatly increasing the level of competition and lowering the initial high price of gas. By the 1840s, charges had fallen from the earlier 15s to only 4s per thousand cubic feet, as companies reaped scale advantages with expanding networks and cost savings from technical improvements, and faced severe competition for the first time. Connections also began to domestic homes, which increased territorial competition. The effects of competition were the most obvious, with rival companies laying mains in the same streets, leading to much congestion, inconvenience and waste. During the 1840s Oxford Street and Tottenham Court Road were supplied by four different companies from five gas stations, and Walworth Road had four companies' mains on each side of the road.[17] The natural monopoly characteristics of gas supply were exerting themselves in the same way as they had done twenty years earlier in water supply.

The response of the gas companies to the outbreak of competition was similar to that of the water companies: collusion. Again, it was unlikely at this time that economies of scale were such that one single London producer could gain a natural monopoly. The four companies that operated to the south of the Thames divided the area into four separate districts in 1853. A year afterwards, the principal firms agreed to raise prices from 4s to 4s 6d per thousand cubic feet, and in 1857–8 the North London companies followed their example and agreed to restrict their activities to specified districts.

The political reaction to these cartels was distinct from that in the case of water. On the one hand, vestries combined to pressurise Parliament into legislating against the gas companies' new monopoly powers. On the other hand, the companies wanted the new situation formalised, and the arrangements that they had made with each other were subsequently given statutory authority by the 1860 Metropolis Gas Act. In return for recognition of the monopolies, the Act imposed maximum charges on gas supply, limited dividends to 10 per cent, and obliged the companies to supply all consumers whose premises were within fifty yards of a main. These conditions were more stringent than those imposed upon the water companies, particularly the obligation to connect, and may have reflected the earlier experience with water. Gas, of course, was not so essential as water, and was not used in many homes, which still relied on candles and coal. The gas companies did not have to deal with the poorest households and the highest-risk payers, and so may have been more amenable to the regulations devised for them. Another factor in their acquiescence was developments in the bill's committee stage, when these apparent stringent controls were weakened by the gas interest.

London users thus remained unhappy with the new cartel arrangements, which received widespread condemnation. The Corporation of London, in marked contrast to its position on water, often threatened to take over gas companies operating in its area. As the main market for gas was street lighting, followed by the lighting of large public and private buildings, a few large public sector consumers should have acted as countervailing powers to the gas monopolies. But there is no evidence of such consumers trying to increase their purchasing muscle through joint purchasing agreements. The Corporation of London, for example, did not combine with some of the vestries to force better terms on the gas companies. There was no success for moves towards municipalisation, a trend that was growing in other parts of urban Britain.

Individual initiative was to be the next source of pressure for change. Charles Pearson was one of those energetic Victorians who concerned themselves with urban public affairs not by entering politics but through attempts to get statutory acceptance of socially-useful private schemes. He was the promoter of the world's first underground – the Metropolitan – as a means to relieve traffic congestion in the capital. He also tried his hand at the reform of gas supply. His first suggestion was that the distribution system of pipes and mains should be owned and maintained by co-operatives of consumers. Suppliers would then feed into this network gas they produced at competitively determined prices. The obvious problem was to acquire the mains system and ensure that co-operatives could fund its maintenance and any necessary investment in its extension and improvement. This difficulty made the approach a non-starter but the broad sense in the proposal can be seen by comparing it to modern practice. If the co-operatives are replaced by a tightly regulated, privately owned distribution system, and some controls over collusion between suppliers are added, it approximates closely to the reforms introduced into the British gas market in the 1990s.

Making no headway with the proposal for a gas market, Pearson teamed up with Alexander Croll, and several investors, to form the Great Central Gas Consumers' Co. in order to challenge the existing producers. The co-operative ideal was carried over as the new firm was partly owned by its customers. The company started to sell gas at lower prices but, in a classic response by a cartel to an interloper, the other gas companies matched those prices and adopted other tactics to drive the new firm out of business. Workmen from Commercial Gas Co., in a well-publicised event, deliberately stopped the Great Central laying a pipe over Bow Bridge, part of the proposed route of the Consumers' Company's main trunk line. In the face of such pressure, Pearson was forced to admit defeat. The company began to toe the cartel's line and was eventually taken over by Gas Light & Coke.

Technology was stagnant in the gas industry for many years after the 1830s. The brute force of skilled men and labourers, as stokers, firers and haulers, shifted and burned coal and drew off the coke in small retorts, with little in the way of mechanisation. Two twelve-hour shifts were the norm, with periods of intense effort during the day interspersed with ones of complete inactivity after a demand peak. Working conditions were hard, but gas workers were relatively well paid. Seasonal fluctuations were substantial, with winter demand three or more times the summer load. Casual hiring in such circumstances was high and shifts were long and variable, although men could claim a vested right to a job when re-hiring took place – a tradition with which firms were reluctant to interfere.[18]

Technical developments then occurred in distribution in the form of larger mains pipes. Pre-payment meters also greatly increased the extent of the gas market in the last decades of the century. A new mantle made gas far better for domestic light, so that more and more London homes were connected to gas mains. Demand was smoothed out more over the course of a day and over the year, as gas was increasingly used for other things apart from lighting, both in the home and by industry. Casualisation decreased as the difference in the summer and winter employment levels halved. Most importantly, marked economies of scale in gas production emerged, with significant unit cost savings when production was based in giant works, on cheap land away from points of consumption but next to quayside facilities for the delivery of coal.

Many of these developments, by increasing the scale of the natural monopoly, stimulated consolidation of the industry into two major concerns – one north of the river and one in the south. In the third quarter of the century, northern gas supply became dominated by the Gas Light & Coke Co. It built a giant gas works at Beckton in East London at the end of the 1860s, and distributed gas through new large 48-inch mains. The Imperial, which previously had been a far larger company, responded by building a similar plant at Bromley-by-Bow but failed to achieve the same cost economies. Gas Light & Coke then absorbed its main northern competitors: in 1871, it took over the Equitable, in 1872 the Western, and in 1876 the Imperial and Independent.

In the south, the South Metropolitan undertook a similar strategy to that of the Gas Light & Coke. A 150-acre site was acquired in East Greenwich (now the site of the Millennium Dome). From this base, it gradually amalgamated with the other South London producers. Prices fell and demand rose fast: in the fourteen years between 1874 and 1888, for example, the gas produced by London works increased by 87 per cent.[19]

The capital's gas sector in the last quarter of the nineteenth century consequently was an example of a London industry displaying what are often called Schumpeterian innovation characteristics.[20] Schumpeter, rather than suggesting that competition was the best means of achieving technical progress, argued the opposite. The creation of giant firms encouraged innovation in order to keep out competitors; the innovatory lead would then be copied, so the monopolist had an incentive to continue innovating. The behaviour of the two successful firms, north and south of the river, in building giant works and absorbing competitors displays such Schumpeterian characteristics. Previously, firms had been reluctant to scrap outmoded equipment; now take-over by a new giant forced through a rationalisation.

Hobsbawm, in contrast, argues that labour militancy encouraged firms along the route of improving their technology.[21] In the late 1880s, as part of the surge of new mass unionism, Marx's daughter, Eleanor Marx, and Will Thorne set up the London 'Gas-Workers and General Labourers Union', with many provincial workers joining it along with their metropolitan brethren. Demands for an eight-hour day and other benefits would cost the Gas Light & Coke a substantial £50,000 a year, the company claimed; yet most firms quickly acquiesced to the unions' demands for fear of the disruption to services. This mass union then survived in the industry, when most other 'new unions' elsewhere soon fell away. Hobsbawm notes the rapid increase in investment in the years after this successful strike, with British firms adopting new machinery faster than in other countries – identifying unions' efforts to raise the price of labour as the cause and investment the effect. His argument, however, is probably overstated and the Schumpeterian-style reasoning seems more plausible. The technological changes were coincidentally happening. Furthermore, many developments had occurred prior to 1889. In fact, gas employers needed to protect their new, expensive investments and to conform to regulatory requirements over the quality and permanence of supply. These concerns, their monopoly powers and a wish to generate greater commitment from their workforces, in combination, may have helped to sustain the union rather than the other way round.

Subsequent, greatly enhanced, natural monopoly advantages may then have weakened further incentives to innovate. The new threat from electricity was weak in London, as the following section will show. The gas companies themselves could have entered this new business, using a similar strategy to that which dampened competition in public transport, but they showed no interest in electricity generation, despite the common use of coal and similar distribution networks and consumer bases. They may have been discouraged from such diversification by the political threat to the large monopoly over London's power that they would have achieved.

National evidence exists of further efficiency gains through to the First World War. Labour productivity continuously increased: for instance, a commentator could point to a four- to sixfold reduction in the number of retort-house men by 1913. The amount of gas extracted from a ton of coal also rose. This meant that London firms could increase their output after the 1890s, despite a slight fall in the amount of coal they used. This offset somewhat for the gas industry the growing problems in British coal production and the concomitant rise in the price of coal.[22]

The existence of two new enlarged gas monopolies encouraged further attempts to bring them under local government control. The City

Corporation and the MBW co-operated in 1875 to introduce three bills aimed at metropolitan gas supply. One suggested the acquisition of the companies' plant; another gave powers for alternative sources of supply; and a third wanted to regulate the companies' prices and profits. The cost of the first measure and a disinclination to give the MBW any more powers gave neither of the first two measures much hope, but the threats encouraged the companies to enter a voluntary arrangement by which dividend increases would be matched by price reductions to consumers. How much of a real burden this agreement was on the companies is unclear, but it could have only been limited because, as noted above, their production and distribution costs were falling substantially and continued to do so up to 1913. Subsequent LCC manoeuvring, under the Progressives, to acquire gas, met with little success in Parliament.

The relative price of gas in London in comparison with other parts of the country is unknown. Provincial municipalities owning gas producers were pricing in order to transfer substantial profits to general municipal accounts, so that municipal ownership for the gas consumer was a mixed blessing. London firms, furthermore, were more able to reap economies of scale than elsewhere, because of the much larger size of the capital and its continued rapid growth.

The impact on employment of the gas industry was high. In the peak winter months, for example, about 10,000 men would be employed at Beckton. The scale of its operation had a strong effect on the expansion of East London, and the districts surrounding the plant, such as East Ham, had a disproportionately high male population for decades afterwards.[23] Although casual employment had fallen, 14 per cent of workers in the national industry were still seasonal labourers in 1906.[24]

With its new-found low-cost production and distribution systems, the gas industry began to look for new business beyond the staple of street lighting. It intensified the domestic market for gas by encouraging more households to adopt gas lighting and use gas appliances. In 1881, the Gas Light & Coke set up a depot for the exhibition of domestic gas appliances and began to hire out cookers and water heaters. Its lead was followed by the other companies, and by the end of the period significant quantities of gas were being used in the home. The company also established its own tar and ammonia products works at Beckton in 1881. The distillation of tar for creosote and other chemical by-products expanded alongside the gas industry, and one firm in the 1870s distilled 12 million gallons of tar a year. Knock-on industrial effects occurred – timber imported to the port from the Baltic was cut up and creosoted for railway sleepers. One plant could produce 1.5 million sleepers a year, much of which was exported.[25]

As municipalisation never came to London's gas supply, the two gas giants remained independent until nationalisation after the Second World War.

Electricity supply

Electricity supply grew relatively slowly in London and the rest of the country, but the development of electricity was especially fraught in the metropolis. Electricity is useful both as a means of lighting and power. After a poor start, lighting provision expanded, such that London had 473,000 incandescent lamps by 1891 compared to Berlin's 75,000 and Paris's 67,600 – even so, the city was still predominantly gas-lit until well after 1918.[26] Power was another matter. By 1911, only 39 per cent of London's supply was used for stationary and traction motors, in contrast to 66 per cent in Berlin and 81 per cent in Chicago. Worst of all, overall per capita electricity consumption was only 65 per cent that of Berlin and 35 per cent of Chicago's.[27] This was despite the sheer size of the metropolis in contrast to those other two cities, the scale of the capital's manufacturing base and the widespread use of electric power by transport utilities from the 1900s.

Suppliers in London, moreover, failed to keep up with technical developments, hampering application in industry and failing to make the transition from small-scale localised supply to much cheaper large-scale generation and city-wide distribution, in contrast to cities like Chicago and Berlin. The degree of fragmentation was phenomenal. Within the Greater London area in 1913, there were 65 suppliers, 70 generating stations, 49 types of supply system, 10 frequencies, 32 voltage levels for transmission and 24 for distribution, and around 70 ways of pricing and charging.[28] The deficiencies of metropolitan provision were widely known and fiercely debated but political stalemate inhibited change.

The supply of electricity was in its earliest days an unproved and highly speculative investment. Expansion was hampered by the fact that electric lighting was often more expensive than gas and, after the introduction in the 1890s of the Welsbach mantle, the quality of gas illumination greatly improved. Promoters were also initially discouraged by the 1882 Lighting Act, which allowed statutory firms to break up streets and lay cables, but gave local authorities the right after twenty-one years to buy the companies at written down values. Designed to allow any emerging competitive problems to be solved by future municipalisation, or at least the threat of it, this regularity framework was misguided. It neither forecast increasing economies of scale in generation and distribution, despite clear evidence of its likelihood in the previous history of the gas industry; nor, by failing to standardise voltages, did it recognise the possibility of future amalgamations amongst producers, despite previous experience in both water and gas. (Although, to be fair, many innovations were yet to come and a battle of the voltages raged for several decades in the technical literature.) The pay-back period of twenty-one years was far too short for such an expensive and risky investment, and the fear of municipalisation would further limit amalgamations as the operating leases shortened. National monopoly characteristics were consequently only recognised in the threat of monopoly rather than in the potential benefits of scale – an intellectual myopia that continued to dog policy debate.

London's first electricity generating station was established at Holborn Viaduct in 1882. Financed by the Edison Co., it lit the City Corporation-owned viaduct and the premises of thirty private customers, including the City Temple church. Uncommercial, it lost money and was closed after only two years. The next station, built in 1886, lit a new development of almost 100 houses in Kensington Court. Its success was copied by another firm that set up in this wealthy area of London. The Cadogan Electric Lighting Co., was formed in 1888, and the following year, using a DC system, began to supply other parts of Kensington and Knightsbridge, plus Chelsea and Brompton. Relatively successful, the company was taken over in 1889 by the Chelsea Electricity Supply Co.[29]

Six years after the first legislation, the 1888 Lighting Act extended the life of statutory private companies to forty-two years – although it was still difficult to expand across municipal boundaries thereby limiting scale economies. This, plus falling costs, encouraged other firms to enter the sector. By 1891, London contained 17 central generating stations out of the 54 in Britain as a whole; in 1905 generating capacity had risen to an annual output of 160 million kWh.[30] The metropolis thus initially led the rest of the country in the provision of the new source of power. This illustrates the point, made in Chapter 2, that very large cities tend to lower the risk of such investments. London contained sufficient wealthy inhabitants able and willing to try electricity regardless of its cost, and sufficient population to create a large demand for the new power once it had become established. Yet the early failure to standardise, multiple ownership, and uncertainties over ownership rights then held back investment, so that the capital had a less satisfactory electricity supply framework than many other urban areas.

Early ventures distributed electricity via direct current. This limited the range of transmission, so that plants could only be small, supplying a local neighbourhood or an individual plant. Much early supply up to the early 1890s, therefore, was expensive and a luxury item for the enthusiast and the rich. During the 1890s a variety of municipal and private firms sprang up, providing supply to local areas from small stations. Some ingenuity can be seen. The Westminster Electricity Supply Corp., for example, collected rainwater from the roof of Victoria Station to cool its equipment, and powered ice-cream-making machines in its plants in summer when demand was low. St Pancras and Ealing Boroughs had refuse-burning plants.[31]

The innovation of transmission via higher-voltage alternating current (AC) opened up the development of the modern electricity industry. Its first use arose from co-operation between Sebastian Z. de Ferranti and Sir Coutts Lindsay, an art gallery owner in Bond Street. The latter had in 1883 installed a small generator in the basement of his gallery and had begun to supply direct current to his neighbours. Ferranti was instrumental in the switch to AC transmission and the setting up of the London Electricity Supply Corporation (LESC) in 1887. In 1890, the company had 312 customers, spread over a wide area of the West End. Keen to avoid the problems of working from Bond Street, Ferranti proposed a solution similar to the evolution of the metropolitan gas industry – a giant plant down river, relying on cheap, bulk coal and river water for cooling. His Deptford plant would generate enough to light two million bulbs and power would be transferred along 10,000-volt cables, where previously they were all below 2,500. The company avoided the difficulties of negotiating with twenty-four London authorities over cable-laying by putting them alongside railway lines, but Ferranti still complained of municipal interference in creating local competition that negated the potential scale economies of the operation.[32] The impending arrival of the 1888 Act meant that the LESC easily raised its start-up capital of £1 million. Ferranti, however, made an unsustainable technological leap in generating capacity, and his choice of generators and AC system was soon overtaken by new technical developments. The power station failed to achieve its potential due to technical problems and poor-quality water and coal. By 1898, the company had lost over £400,000 of its initial capital[33] and only paid a dividend on its ordinary shares from 1904. This experience must have chastened investors when contemplating subsequent calls for capital by other firms.

The early start in electricity generation may have involved penalties of fragmentation and incompatible systems but the conflicts of London politics added further stultifying dimensions. Unlike in the country as a whole, where electricity was under the control of a single local authority or a small number of companies, in London it was sold by a multiplicity of undertakings. In 1905, there were twelve municipal and fourteen corporate suppliers in London, which generated AC and DC on a variety of distribution systems, voltages and frequencies.[34] Even in the 1920s, the situation had not improved, with sixteen metropolitan boroughs and fifteen private companies active in the LCC area, plus separate plants supplying transport organisations.[35]

Private sector supply dominated in the wealthy central and west areas, where electricity was first generated. Municipal ownership was most prevalent in the East End, the south and some of the outer suburbs, where the Progressive Party was in power. The municipal undertakings were concentrated in the less profitable areas – supplying industry, working-class neighbourhoods (though working-class domestic electricity consumption was uncommon until after 1945) and spread-out suburban districts.

Because of the small size of most power stations, the average cost of production was relatively high. This particularly discouraged business use. In 1905, only 10 per cent of the electricity generated was used by London's industry;[36] just 7 per cent of whose motive power was electric.[37] This lack of use occurred even though many early power stations were located near to industry alongside waterways in order to cheapen the cost of coal and have a ready supply of water, like their gas-works predecessors. On the banks of the Regent's Canal, for example, there were five stations – at

St John's Wood (1904), Marylebone (1906), St Pancras, City Road Basin and Shoreditch.[38]

Early regulations recognised the distinctiveness of electricity supply in the capital. Many enterprises were competing against each other, in contrast to the rest of the country. Yet the regulatory environment was muddied by a Board of Trade report in 1889. It aimed at the impossible by simultaneously arguing for more competition, through allowing firms to cover wide areas, and for less competition, by specifying areas to be allotted to the existing private companies in order to avoid excessive duplication. The spectre of the fight between private and municipal provision can be detected behind this odd compromise and many contemporary and modern commentators blamed uncertainty over the role of the public sector for the slow evolution of electricity provision. Paradoxically, the Conservatives under the influence of Chamberlain were more pro-local government than the Liberals were by the 1900s, so when a Liberal government came into power in 1905 the pendulum again swung in favour of private enterprise.[39]

Political infighting continued to produce stalemate. Successive attempts, by either municipal authorities or private interests, failed to unify the system or to achieve the generating economies available by building large riverside plants. With neither private nor municipal lobbyists sufficiently strong to gain the upper hand, fragmentation remained as the compromise option. A Schumpeterian-style strategy, which had been so successful earlier in the gas industry, would have found it hard to succeed within this framework, as Charles Merz (see below) was to find out.

The London County Council in 1902–3 proposed to buy out the private undertakings in combination with the London boroughs. Its attempt to obtain statutory powers was defeated by anti-LCC and anti-municipal lobbies. A private initiative arose two years later when Merz – already responsible for a highly successful pioneering electricity scheme around Newcastle upon Tyne – presented a bill that proposed the erection of three giant power stations on the south bank of the Thames to supply electricity to the existing distributors and large users. His plants would reduce costs from contemporary levels that could be as high as 1.46d per kWh to only 0.15d per kWh, indicating the scale of the extra costs imposed by sub-optimal generating sizes.[40] This time the initiative was opposed by the London County Council and the boroughs, so this bill failed as well. A compromise 1906 plan of Lloyd George's, then President of the Board of Trade, for the creation of a public–private partnership was abandoned in 1907, when the Progressive Party lost control of the London County Council.[41] Although some co-operation between corporate and municipal undertakings subsequently occurred, the electricity supply system remained incoherent and expensive until well after the First World War. Electricity reform was consequently blocked by the politics of London.

It can be argued that in the early years of electricity the industry was in no position to compete with gas for lighting but, by the 1900s, that argument was beginning to wear thin. London's myriad of small industrial enterprises could not economically generate their own electricity and so would have benefited from a large-scale supply network. When Merz proposed his scheme in 1905, he raised the already evident fact that manufacturing firms would leave London in search of cheaper power, but to no avail.[42] Overall, the knock-on effects of the early legislative mistakes, and the subsequent failures to remedy them, must have had large, if incalculable, effects on metropolitan consumers, transport undertakings and industry. All were faced with higher energy costs and were discouraged from switching to this new source of light and power. The drift to the suburbs of industry, already apparent in the forty years before 1914, was undoubtedly slowed.

Alongside nascent electricity supply developed an electrical engineering industry. Yet, up to 1914, Britain's electrical engineering industry was overshadowed by the world activities of industrial giants from the USA and Germany, and was hampered by the contemporary problems in electricity generation and distribution, as the experience of Ferranti illustrates. Most of the major firms set up in the UK were subsidiaries of overseas companies and, like early multinationals in other industries, they often chose a London location for their plant. In the 1880s and 1890s, the capital was home to much of the industry as a result, but the concentration was far less by 1911 as plants had been set up elsewhere in the country and, apart from cable and light-bulb production, no large-scale plants developed in the capital. Ferranti & Co. initially had premises in Hatton Garden from 1885, and then in 1887 moved to Charterhouse Square, where the company produced electricity meters, generators, transformers and alternators and placed an unusually high emphasis on research and development. Then, requiring room for expansion, it relocated to Oldham in Lancashire where there was cheap space and a plentiful supply of skilled labour. Despite the absence of the newly emerging electrical giants, nevertheless, metropolitan employment in the industry rose from a mere 1,300 in 1881 to over 22,000 in 1911.[43]

The most important London manufacturer was the German firm, Siemens Bros., set up in 1863 to take advantage of the spread of the electric telegraph. Based in Woolwich, it employed between 400 and 1,000 in its cable division. In the ten years between 1873 and 1883, it made and laid 12,600 nautical miles of cable. This, and its position in the dynamic German electrical engineering industry, placed it in a good position with the expansion of electricity supply.[44] The greater use of electricity also led to the development of firms manufacturing batteries, light cables, electrical instruments, generators, switch-gear, accumulators and domestic items such as lights and stoves. Location tended initially to be in Clerkenwell and then in an area stretching from Camden to Dalston, both of which could offer supplies of the necessary highly skilled workforce.[45] Scale economies in manufacturing, however, were hampered by the multiplicity of suppliers and varied voltages and systems used by them and endured by domestic and commercial customers.

Post and telecommunications

Post

Public postal services became available in 1635 and local deliveries in 1680. By the nineteenth century, the capital's postal system was run by the Post Office as a public monopoly. During the early 1830s, it comprised three offices: the Inland Office, which was in charge of the entire country's postal network; the Foreign Office, which dealt with overseas correspondence; and the Twopenny Office, which handled mail within the capital and its environs. All of these were separate organisations and Londoners could therefore receive mail from each. Unlike in many smaller towns, letters in London were usually delivered to the door. In 1794, the Postmaster General's Office had organised delivery walks in the capital and seven 'rides' from London serving Brentford, Edmonton, Finchley, Mitcham, Mortlake, Woodford and Woolwich. Postage was paid on receipt of the letter. In 1800, a penny was charged for inner London deliveries and twopence in the outer area, with higher charges for other towns and cities. The letters were transported by mail coach and, from the late 1830s, railways were increasingly used – giving greater speed and enabling letters to be sorted in transit.[46] The cost of the postal service was high.

Reform occurred in the 1840s and 1850s. Costs were considerably reduced as the Post Office improved the organisation of the post and reaped the benefits of scale. In 1840 a uniform penny post was introduced. This cut transaction costs dramatically. Before, a postman could deliver only seventy letters on each one-and-a-half-hour walk, and recipients often refused to pay the required charge. By 1841, less than a tenth of letters delivered in London were posted unpaid and around half of the pre-paid correspondence was stamped.[47] Further reform took place in the 1850s when the Inland and Twopenny Offices were amalgamated, ten separate postal districts were created and an hourly delivery service was established. The result of these changes was a further rise in efficiency. By 1857, 65 per cent of letters were delivered by 9 a.m. the next day, as compared to only 5 per cent in 1856.

London was the main source of postal business in Britain. In 1854, for example, letters delivered there accounted for almost a quarter of the country's total correspondence.[48] Large investments in postal services continued, including a purpose-built underground railway between Paddington and Whitechapel via Mount Pleasant, started in 1913.[49] The Post Office was one of the largest employers in the metropolis.

Parcels were largely handled by the rail companies and road carriers, such as Pickfords and the 1837 London Postal Delivery Co. There were also a large number of messenger companies, circumventing the 1837 Post Office (Management) Act monopoly.[50]

Telegraph

London's first experimental telegraph line was set up around the Inner Circle of Regent's Park in 1837, at the same time as Samuel Morse gave his first public demonstration in the USA. A real line soon followed between Euston Station and Camden Town as part of the signalling system out of Euston in 1837. It failed, and was replaced by traditional signalling, but the clear potential of the new invention was such that its developers, William Fothergill Cooke and Professor Wheatstone, entered into partnership and began to construct commercial networks. Brunel recognised the benefits of the system and had telegraph signalling lines laid under the new Great Western Railway from Paddington to West Drayton. By the 1860s, the Post Office had organised an extensive network in London. Private firms also developed, so that by 1868 there were 91,000 miles of wire in Britain and 3,381 telegraph stations. The unsightly overhead wires soon proved a menace in the crowded centre of the capital.[51]

Two firms came to dominate in London: the London District and the Universal Private Telegraph Companies. The list of activities offered by the companies reads like that of a modern internet service provider – messages, commercial and financial news, alarms, betting services and weather forecasts were among them. Cables were also laid around the world, facilitating for the first time rapid international communication between London and the rest of the world.

Private provision, however, lasted for thirty years only. State take-over was advocated by those associated with the telegraph, mixing patriotism and profit. They argued that its national defence and other public good characteristics were too strong to be left in the hands of private ventures. In 1868, the various telegraph companies were nationalised and, in 1870, they were placed under the control of the Post Office. The Post Office paid £8 million, making the fortunes of the previous owners.[52] The Post Office had an extensive telegraph network by 1890, centred on the City with links to the West End. The Post Office's own branches constituted the main connections from which thousands of runners would deliver messages. To improve connections to the telegraph offices, the Post Office tore up London's streets to install a network of two-and-a-half-inch pneumatic tubes that linked seventy of its post offices into the telegraph system.[53]

Fate was soon to make nationalisation a hopeless investment as the telephone was invented soon afterwards. The sunk costs of the telegraph, locked as they were into the accounts of a public enterprise, were not to be written-off. So, the prime effect of nationalisation of the telegraph, rather than actually being a public benefit, was to delay severely diffusion of telephone services, because the Post Office tried to protect its investment by delaying replacement of the telegraph by the telephone for the next forty years.

Telephones

One of the earliest experiments with the Edison carbon telephone in Britain was undertaken in 1878 by Colman, the mustard firm, between its Norwich factory and its London offices in Cannon Street. This again illustrates the importance of London, at the top of the British urban hierarchy in the adoption and diffusion of new innovations but, once again, highlights the problems innovators in urban infrastructure faced – because London and the rest of Britain, despite their wealth and commerce, were not to be leaders in the adoption of the telephone but rather laggards. It was calculated in 1910 that Britain would have had 2.5 million telephones by then if progress had been similar to that in the USA; whereas, in reality, only 600,000 existed. The rapid development of a national rail network earlier in the century is in marked contrast with the slow pace in telephones. Patent disputes and incompatible systems played a part, but the nature of competition and state/private relations seem to be the main culprits, and London one of the greatest losers. Telephone technology required high throughputs to gain economies of scale and generate network externalities. The more customers were connected to one system, the greater the number of reciprocal connections, and hence benefit, each one had. Unfortunately, regulation was inhibiting, so a unified system was slow in coming.[54]

The role of the Post Office

The Post Office soon became involved in the development of telephone services. It failed to persuade Parliament to define telephones as telegrams but, shortly after, in 1880, obtained a court ruling that the new telephone companies were infringing its telegraph monopoly.[55] Firms had to obtain fixed-term licences from the Post Office to operate services and to open new exchanges; they also had to pay it a 10 per cent royalty on their revenues. The Post Office began its own services by converting some telegraph lines, but these were not particularly successful. The telephone was primarily seen as a competitor to the telegraph network it had expensively invested in since nationalisation in 1870. With the power to slow down developments, the Post Office was prone to refuse telephone companies' licences and to distrust consolidation. It permitted new entrants in order to stop private operators gaining monopolies in specific localities and developing network benefits that would threaten use of the telegraph, as with the Globe example in London cited below.

The threat of public ownership also existed from the earliest days, but the investment-reducing uncertainty generated was not resolved until 1901 in London (1905 elsewhere) – when it was made known that the licensee would be taken over by the Post Office at the expiry of its term, with compensation only at the replacement cost of the equipment. This would have discouraged extensive marketing as the licensee would get nothing for goodwill – the implicit value of a larger network. In a big, dense city like London, the network effects of a substantial customer base could be achieved for far less investment in actual hardware than in more spread-out localities, so the disincentive was greatest there. Only when taken over by the Post Office in 1912, thirty-four years after the first use of the telephone in Britain, could the true network benefits be reaped. The improvement was due to the creation of a monopoly rather than because the new owner was the Post Office, which, as has been shown above, was previously the inhibitor of such effects in its desire to protect the telegraph. By 1912, this impediment presumably was less as the cost of the investments in the telegraph would by then have been written-down in its accounts. In the new, truly national, network that was then finally formed, London was the inevitable kingpin.

Municipal authorities added their constraints to the spread of telephones by adopting parochial attitudes, by a widespread refusal of wayleave rights to telephone companies to lay their lines, and by harbouring desires to run their own services. Strenuous attempts to persuade the LCC to allow the use of underground cables in central London were to no avail, so an extensive overhead system of cables existed. This had to conform to the 1891 London Overhead Wire Act and local by-laws, and was prone to both collapse and fire. Pressure from the LCC, amongst others, led to government legislation in 1899 enabling any local authority to apply for a licence to operate a municipal telephone service. Only six were opened in the country, with all but one, Hull, rapidly disappearing after losses.

Telephone operators in London

The first telephone exchanges were introduced almost simultaneously in London, Manchester and Glasgow, primarily for business use. By 1881, London had fifteen exchanges, although the areas they covered were small and served few subscribers – the situation for several years.[56] With regard to trunk lines, London was initially poorly served. Trunk networks were quickly developed in Lancashire and Cheshire, in the Yorkshire area and in the North-East, with good connections between all of them. In contrast, London was only connected to the north in 1890 and had few trunk lines radiating from it even two years later.

The early development of the London telephone system was dominated by competition between two firms: the Telephone Co., which used the technology developed by Bell; and the Edison Telephone Company of London, using rival technology. The capital's first telephone exchange was opened by the Telephone Co. in 1879. Although the firm at first only had seven or eight subscribers, demand for its services grew rapidly and before the end of the year it had established two further exchanges. The Edison Co. opened its first exchange at around the same time, and subsequently established three branch ones. Aggressively marketing its services, the company undercut its rival's rate, charging an annual subscription of

£12 a year, as compared to the Telephone Co.'s £20.[57] For some months the two firms competed. Financial losses, however, forced them in 1880 to combine to form the United Telephone Co. Ltd. The new firm greatly expanded its services and opened new exchanges but soon, in 1881, faced fresh competition from the London & Globe Telephone & Maintenance Co. This interloper charged a subscription fee of £10 a year, half United's, and began to sabotage its rival's operations – for example, deliberately cutting, tying and shorting its cables. In an attempt to halt these activities, United took legal action against the Globe Co. but failed to resolve the problem satisfactorily by this means. It finally silenced the threat by purchasing the firm for £25,000 in 1884. This history once again has similarities with other infrastructural sectors. Initial competition was followed by consolidation and, in this case, further Post-Office inspired competition.[58]

Consolidation occurred nationally in 1889 when United Telephone merged with the National Telephone Co. and the Lancashire & Cheshire Telephone Co. The new country-wide operation, known as the National Telephone Co., traded until 1911 when its licence expired and it was compulsorily purchased by the Postmaster General. Initially the new company decentralised its London service into separate districts, but the lack of co-ordination between them led it to establish a single central metropolitan administration in 1905. From 1890 the firm also introduced new technology, such as the horizontal multiple exchange, the self-restoring indicator board, and motor generators to ensure a uniform line voltage. The latter allowed subscribers' instruments, each of which had had its own battery, to be replaced by non-battery telephones, which were cheaper to maintain.

To operate the exchanges, the National and, later, the Postmaster General recruited young women. Training, wages and employment conditions were good. As with domestic service, wedlock was frowned upon because employment was terminated on marriage – though highly skilled operators were placed on a reserve list and called upon in emergencies and at times of peak demand.[59]

Wholesale markets

London had had large produce markets since time immemorial. But during the nineteenth century, the scale of activity increased as the population grew and transportation and retail patterns changed. A result was that large sums were spent on new facilities and a greater distinction was made between retail and wholesale. Wholesale markets sold fruit, vegetables, meat and fish to shops, restaurants and street traders. Centred around them were many ancillary activities, warehouses and the offices of the firms using them. Additional jobs were provided for a multitude in associated transportation, porterage, cleansing, and scavenging and in providing drink, food and sometimes accommodation for those active in the markets. Markets, consequently, had a substantial influence on surrounding employment activities. As London grew during the nineteenth century, the throughput of business in these markets expanded rapidly – as figures for Smithfield, discussed later, indicate – enabling them to reap substantial economies of scale.

Ownership varied between the Corporation of London, other local government bodies, railway companies and private individuals. This meant that competition existed between the wholesale markets, but the extra costs of travel to more distant ones implied that customers had a strong incentive to use the most convenient ones. Markets also specialised to reap scale economies. Competition, consequently, only tended to occur between those active in similar products and in close proximity to each other, or between central markets and suburban ones. Not all prospered and some central markets were eventually closed. Over time, it would seem that the suburban outlets gained business at the expense of their inner city counterparts, unless those at the centre had one or a mixture of scale and scope economies, regulatory laxity, or a generous patron that continued to give them a competitive edge.

The markets at railheads also prospered because they were located at the transshipment points between two modes of transport. There was limited competition between them because their rail connections came from separate parts of the country, so each tended to specialise in the produce of the regions through which their lines passed.

Fruit and vegetables

The most important fruit and vegetable market was Covent Garden, which in the late eighteenth century was predominantly used by market gardeners selling their own crops. As market gardens moved further away from the centre, independent wholesalers developed as intermediaries. By 1850, only some of the market's flowers were sold directly by growers.

The market had initially been set up in the environs of Bedford House and spread to the Russell family's adjacent prestigious residential development of Covent Garden, which had been built earlier in the seventeenth century but whose residents were abandoning it for newer developments to the west. The Russells acquired a Royal Charter for a fruit, vegetable and flower market in 1670. It then slowly gained business from the closure of other central markets; while non-vegetable traders moved in as well. Complaints about the nuisance and orders for improvements and better regulation were commonplace. In 1828, its owner, the Duke of Bedford, built the famous half-acre market building in the middle of the original residential square. Trade continued to expand and, by 1859, ninety wholesalers conducted business there with many more in the surrounding streets. Some developed a national presence by diversifying upstream to produce-growing areas and by developing wholesaling operations in other major conurbations. George Munro (1862), for example, had expanded by 1907 to cover the North-West from Manchester, and to Guernsey – the source of early-season vegetables.[60]

Investment in the market continued – the Floral Market being opened in 1861 and the Jubilee Market building in 1904. Yet, perpetual criticism was made of the congestion and impact of the market on the local area and of the inadequacy of the facilities. Sensitive to criticism and the cost of improving the market, the 9th Duke tried to sell it to the Metropolitan Board of Works and the City Corporation, neither of which was interested in the responsibility or the expense of making improvements. The family finally divested itself of the market in 1918.[61]

Other important fruit and vegetable markets were situated at Borough, Spitalfields, Brentford and Greenwich, each serving the areas adjacent to them. Others were set up at Farringdon Street and various other railheads. The original Borough market was under City control and had been located just south of London Bridge since the Middle Ages. The City closed it in the second half of the eighteenth century and the local parish set up a new one nearby. The proximity of London Bridge Station and the expansion of South London greatly increased its turnover. As part of the extension of the London and South Eastern Railway from London Bridge into the heart of London, the market was extensively rebuilt. Spitalfields flourished with the nearby industrial development and was privately owned. It was rebuilt in 1872 at a cost of £80,000 and served inner East London. Brentford was redeveloped in 1893 beside the railway junction at Kew Bridge, supplying south-western districts.

On a smaller scale were the central Farringdon Street, Portman and Cumberland markets. Farringdon Street market was built in 1856 on the site of the old Fleet market, which had closed in 1829, but it failed to take off. Portman market, opened in 1831 off Edgware Road, concentrating on hay and straw and later fruit and vegetables, also disappeared; a similar fate befell the Oxford Street Pantheon (1834), which specialised in pot plants and cut flowers. Cumberland market was a hay and straw market originally in the Haymarket but moved after 1830 to York Square, next to Regent's Park and the canal. Small central markets lacked the economies of scale of their larger competitors and unless highly specialised or subsided in some way they could not compete with the new rail-based markets. Their land, furthermore, was highly valuable in other uses and so many gradually closed.

The major railhead markets including the Great Northern's at King's Cross, the Midland's at Somer's Town and the Great Eastern's at Bishopsgate and Stratford. King's Cross opened in 1865 and took over from Tooley Street as the main potato market, though it also handled large amounts of celery, green peas and rhubarb. The potatoes were brought by rail from Lincolnshire and Yorkshire and, by 1879, the market was selling 85,000 tons a year, rising to 124,000 tons by the 1920s.[62] Close by, Somer's Town, built in 1892 by the Midland Railway, dealt in vegetables brought into St Pancras from Bedfordshire and, later, bananas landed in Southampton, Liverpool and Avonmouth. Stratford, established in 1879 by the Great Eastern Railway, supplied a wide range of flowers, fruit and vegetables to the new residential areas in the outer east; Bishopsgate was developed in the inner east on the site of the old Shoreditch station in a vast network of arches below the original structure.[63]

These markets generally formed part of wider purpose goods stations, which have already been examined in Chapter 10. There, it was noted that central goods facilities failed to charge full costs to users. This subsidy undoubtedly encouraged the level of activity of the wholesale markets on railway premises and discouraged decentralisation.

Meat

Meat was sold both as livestock and after slaughtering. The capital's main meat market was Smithfield but there were two other central ones. Newgate concentrated on slaughtered meat, and closed in 1849, while Leadenhall's wholesale activities specialised in slaughtered meat and hide. This market was also shut in 1871 to be replaced ten years later by a new £99,000 poultry and sundry products market. The closure of Newgate and Leadenhall markets was influenced by public health concerns and tightening regulations plus a loss of competitive edge against Smithfield's growing economies of scale, investment in new technologies and good rail links. From 1833 to 1845, there was another large, fifteen-acre, slaughtered meat market at Islington.[64]

By far the largest meat market was Smithfield. Extending over four to five acres in a densely-packed part of the centre, it initially dealt mainly with live animals. As an indication of its size, in 1810, 140,000 cattle and one million sheep were sold. From the 1800s, there were serious campaigns to have the market moved but change was blocked by the Corporation of London. Yet, by the 1840s, the market had reached saturation point. There was a crescendo of complaints about cattle stampedes, causing disruption to other businesses and acting as a source of cover for pickpockets, and about the fouling of roads. In 1849, a Royal Commission recommended that live animals should be sold elsewhere and, after strong opposition from the City – which by then earned £10,000 a year from the market – the Smithfield Removal Act was passed in 1854. In its last year, Smithfield sales had reached 277,000 live cattle and 1.6 million sheep.[65] The wholesaling of live meat was relocated northwards to the Metropolitan Cattle Market erected on the site of Copenhagen Fields, off Caledonian Road. It was expensively designed and built with grandly designed pubs, vast cast iron halls and an ornate clocktower (which can still be seen). It was six times larger than Smithfield, served by the London and North Western, Great Northern and Eastern Counties Railways, and able to accommodate over 50,000 animals. The market proved less successful than its predecessor, mainly because, with the coming of refrigeration, meat was increasingly transported by rail already slaughtered, and, to prevent the spread of livestock diseases, restrictions were placed on the movement of live animals. Even so, this new market soon brought the quality of the surrounding neighbourhood tumbling down because of the movement of livestock.

At Smithfield, dead meat continued to be sold and, in 1868, a grand new market hall was constructed with direct rail access below. The reconstituted market went from strength to strength – adopting new technologies and becoming the headquarters of the world's largest meat traders (see Chapter 6).

The Corporation's strategy in spending so much on its three new central and suburban wholesale meat markets (and on Billingsgate fish market) was presumably encouraged by the fact that their locations would then become unassailable, so that the City would retain a key link in the capital's food businesses rather than see them drift out of its range to the cheaper, less congested suburbs. The guild basis of political influence on the Corporation of London may have encouraged this desire to retain wholesale markets, when otherwise they might have decentralised more. If this was the case, the approach worked well for the City – keeping these functions under City control far into the twentieth century. Smithfield still survives today – though the Caledonian market ceased effectively to operate as a meat market after the First World War, and Leadenhall has lost its wholesale functions.

Fish

The main fish market was Billingsgate, which, until the Thames became too polluted, sold the catches of the 400 fishing boats that worked between Deptford and London Bridge; and later, fish caught by the 2,000 vessels operating from eleven ports on the south, south-east and East Anglian coasts. By the early 1870s, the market handled 98 million sole, 18 million whiting, 24 million mackerel, 1,050 million herring and 10 million eels per year, plus oysters and salmon. To deal with the great expansion of business, in 1877 a new one-acre market was constructed, followed in 1888 by a further dry fish market. Nevertheless, the rebuilt market still attracted criticism and, in 1883, was described as deficient and 'a scandal to London'.

Part 5

Industrial and commercial change

12 Manufacturing

Introduction

Earlier chapters have examined some of London's manufacturing but this chapter focuses more directly on it. A prime reason for doing this is to consider the types of industry active in London in light of the theories in Chapter 2. Particular attributes were said to make a large city like London advantageous for production. Moreover, as markets and technologies changed over time, a gradual change in the types of metropolitan industry should be observed. Businesses in general do not conveniently display information about why they located where they did. Yet informed conjectures can still be made by considering the input and output market contexts in which firms operated, which is done for the industries covered in this chapter.

When doing this, it needs to be remembered that the general range of consumption goods was far smaller and the products unsophisticated compared to those of today, so that the expectation is of a narrower range of industries with simpler production processes. Furthermore, prevalent technologies still often relied overwhelmingly on workers using hand-tools or relatively simple labour-assisted machinery. Most of the making up of cotton, iron and other products of the industrial revolution into useful goods was done by handicraft workers in the clothing, iron-working and other industries. This labour intensity of production increased the attractiveness of cities with their pools of labour and, therefore, it is to be expected that labour-intensive production processes would be over-represented in city activities.

A large expense within production, moreover, was skilled labour and it was in general short supply, especially given the low educational attainment of most of the contemporary workforce. Producers would have incentives, therefore, to organise production in ways that economised on the direct employment of skilled labour, either through out-working or through changing production processes in ways that circumvented the particular skill shortages in question. New nineteenth-century technologies mixed machinery and skilled and less skilled labour, and it is to be expected that the more labour, rather than machinery, oriented ones would benefit most from a large city location.

Transport was another key locational factor in a situation where the relative cost of moving either people or goods between two places was high. Two examples of the costs of moving heavy building materials dramatically illustrate the point. A five-mile road journey early in the century would add 40 per cent to the cost of Bedfordshire bricks; and even later, after considerable improvements in rail and sea transport, the cost of shipping Yorkshire stone added a third to its London price.[1] Improvements in transport over the course of the century exposed metropolitan producers to far greater domestic and foreign competition, and changes in the capital's industrial structure over the course of the period should be seen as a result.

A final locational aspect is state regulation. In earlier centuries, regulation had required local production of many goods consumed in the capital, and competing imports were banned or discouraged by high tariffs. Most guild constraints had disappeared long before 1800, but some publicly ordained monopolies had survived and industries collapsed when they were removed – most notably, silk. Other industries declined rapidly with the move to free trade: fine shoes, watch- and piano-making and optical instruments are examples.

Agglomeration economies, changes in markets and production processes, transportation developments and state regulation, therefore, are factors that are emphasised in the industrial histories below. The first section explains in some detail how production of several key consumer goods – especially clothes and furniture – was reorganised from around the middle of the century. The histories of the clothing, furniture and footwear industries are then examined in light of these factors, and the loss of the silk industry is described. The narrative then switches to the engineering industries – where the mechanical, shipbuilding, vehicles and precision instruments industries are examined. A final section describes the shifting pattern of building materials industries. Overall, these histories illustrate that the earlier theories of urban economic dynamics provide plausible explanations for the changing urban industrial landscape.

A new sub-contracting system

During the nineteenth century large numbers of British households for the first time began to consume standardised, mass-produced goods, particularly clothing, shoes and furniture. One of the main ways in which they were produced was a new organisation of work that developed from around the middle of the century and, in Britain, it was centred on London. It involved a complex division of labour, whereby the manufacturing process was broken down into component parts and passed around to various types of worker. In several industries many also worked at home. Outworking was by no means new. The differences that made the system new instead stemmed from the changed relationship to the market place and the introduction of new technologies. The processes using expensive machinery, such as the cutting of materials, tended to be located in main workshops or small factories; those parts that used cheap or no machinery were also carried out in main workshops but, in addition, they were often sub-contracted out to smaller workshops or home-workers. In clothing, in particular, the sewing machine revolutionised production because it was cheap, relatively easy to use, and could be used at home as well as in workshops and larger factories. These changes led to a new urban geography of production and consumption.

Detractors of this new organisation of production quickly labelled it 'sweating', because of the long hours some workers had to spend in miserable conditions at home or in a cramped workshop to earn even the smallest pittance. In the sense of making people sew for very long hours for little reward, sweating in clothing trades had undoubtedly been going on since time immemorial. The same would have been true for particular tasks in many other trades. Yet the existence of sweating became notorious in the nineteenth century because of well-publicised resistance by some trades to de-skilling,[2] and via the growing pressure exercised by reformers from the mid-century onwards. The worst cases of exploitation were brought to the attention of the public through political agitation that led to the setting up of Parliamentary Commissions of Enquiry, and through popular pamphlets and books aimed at highlighting the evils of sweating. Rather than poverty being a cause of people accepting badly-paid jobs, the badly-paid jobs were argued to be the cause of poverty. The worst cases in the popular mind soon became the common experience of all those working in the 'sweated industries'.

Academics until the mid-1980s tended to reproduce unquestioningly the arguments put forward by those Victorian social reformers campaigning to abolish sweating.[3] The crux of the 'evils of sweating' argument was that London's traditional craft-based industries had declined into this form in order to fend off competition from the provinces and this led to mass impoverishment of a large section of the working population. In contrast, a number of recent commentators have noted that the organisation of 'sweated' production is remarkably similar to the organisational forms that became common in many industries in the late twentieth century: 'flexible production.'[4] The characteristics of nineteenth-century flexible production, of course, were somewhat distinct from latter-day forms because of the differences in prevailing technologies and goods and labour markets across time. To avoid confusion, and prior negative judgement, the organisation of these nineteenth-century industries is here called the 'new sub-contracting system', and it probably operated on a greater scale in London at the time than anywhere else in the world.

The analysis first examines the general context of the new sub-contracting system, contrasting it with earlier industrial forms and with the nature of contemporary factory production methods. After this contextualisation, the clothing, shoe and furniture industries and some of their sub-branches are examined.

Some economics of nineteenth-century consumer goods production

One of the central hypotheses of modern supply theory is that firms aim to minimise the costs of production because by doing so they maximise profits. Cost minimisation in the nineteenth-century clothing, shoe and furniture industries has traditionally been interpreted as pushing wages down as far as possible by substituting plentiful unskilled labour for scarce skilled labour. There was, however, more to a cost minimisation strategy in these industries than that, as an analysis of the overall contemporary conditions of demand and supply for these producers indicates.

Traditional practices

The demand for durable consumer products at the beginning of the nineteenth century was limited. Most were bought by the wealthy, who demanded high quality and unique designs and were prepared to pay high prices for them. Their preferences were strongly influenced by ever-changing fashion and so many spent heavily on luxury items and conspicuous consumption. This encouraged producers to use skilled handicraft methods for most of the tasks, although many unskilled male and female workers would work alongside the more highly trained men doing the simpler tasks in workshops or as out-workers. Small masters and journeymen might use apprentices and family members for these less skilled tasks. The spatial organisation of production and selling was varied. Workshops could act as retail outlets, with clients coming to look at products and designs, to be measured, or to have completed clothes adjusted for fit. Independent shops existed for some luxury products, and ready-to-wear goods already existed for items such as shoes. Haberdashers were also common as they sold the sewing materials used to make up clothing at home – a task done by servants where they existed.[5] Another route to clients was for masters to visit the homes of the wealthy to win orders and note down measurements, taking the instructions back to small workshops.

Within the labour-force, the prime distinctions were between large masters, who were often significant members of the relevant guilds; small independent masters, who had often risen up through the trade; other skilled workers who stayed as journeymen; apprentices; and the unskilled. Apprentices could be indentured for many years without monetary payment and their families would generally have to pay masters or journeymen to take them on. Businesses were usually small, although some masters developed extensive concerns. Some trades, such as tailoring, could be entered without an apprenticeship, and orphan boys were often bound to tailors by parishes and charities.[6] Masters had to extend considerable trade credit to clients and, as numerous novels attest, this was a risky activity.

By the early nineteenth century, the system had changed only slowly over a long time period, according to George.[7] Based as it generally was on time-served skills, this organisation of production maintained quality, but it had the considerable advantage for producers of restricting supply by limiting entry into trades. This kept prices high, although probably with little effect on the level of demand, as the wealthy were relatively insensitive to price. Life, however, was not always pleasant for journeymen and apprentices, let alone the unskilled. Many worked long hours in workshops or at home and piecework was prevalent. Supervision, none the less, was limited and they could organise their work themselves, taking time off for such events as traditional saints' days and fairs. Journeymen were unsurprisingly keen to maintain restrictions on the number of apprentices and they, rather than the guilds, were active in trying to enforce them – though often with limited success.[8] Apprentices were forced by indentures to live in meagre accommodation under the watchful eye of often unsympathetic employers for little or no pay. When not at work, they unsurprisingly spent much of their time on the street and were a ready source of high jinks.[9]

Several changes took place in this craft system from the late eighteenth century. By the 1860s, the changes were so substantial that they could be regarded as a new organisation of production, though one which clearly had evolved from earlier practices.

The first significant shift was that clients began increasingly to visit salons and shops in order to see a range of wares. This encouraged several enterprises to grow in size and farm out more of their tasks to out-workers. From the 1820s, furthermore, the trend of skilled real wages started to rise and continued to do so for the rest of the century as the demand for skilled labour outstripped the available supply.[10] Producers, therefore, had a strong incentive to economise on skilled labour. General rises in earnings, furthermore, greatly expanded the market for cheaper-quality products. To accommodate these supply and demand changes, trades tended to split into a bespoke sector, producing more expensive one-off products for the luxury market, and a cheaper ready-made sector, where lower quality and a much finer division of labour became prevalent. Less concerned with quality, the latter utilised as much as possible more abundant supplies of unskilled labour. Again, this bifurcation between luxury and general markets was not entirely new but spread across a wider range of consumer products and deeper down the social strata.

In the fabrication of long-lasting consumer goods, factory production was generally a poor or non-existent contemporary substitute for traditional craft methods. Although mechanisation had come to textile spinning by the late eighteenth century, it only slowly moved down the production chain to the making of clothes. Even weaving was a skilled handicraft process until the 1830s–1840s. Clothing production was increasingly mechanised as the century progressed, but quality at first was low, although it slowly improved. Production lines once set up, moreover, could produce only a limited number and variety of items. Economies of scale were necessary to derive the benefits of mechanisation, which required continuous production runs; yet demand was frequently of a form that made such continuity difficult to achieve. Machines generally needed skilled operatives to work them, making production even less flexible in face of varying demand. Skilled workers, in short supply, were also more able to combine for higher wages or to restrict changes in production methods. These characteristics have discouraged extensive mechanisation of some sectors of the clothing industry through to the present time.

In the context of nineteenth-century London demand, the varying attributes of the different production systems available led to the simultaneous existence of three methods of production. The first was factory production of simple items. Such plants were frequently located in the provinces to take advantage of lower wages and rents; yet a number were built in the capital. The other two methods both involved small workshops and out-working, and they were the central focus of activity in the capital. This small-scale production was subdivided into luxury and mass production: the former focused on skilled employees and the latter used far more unskilled workers in a complex division of labour, labelled here as the new sub-contracting system.

A large amount of shoe production left the capital, even before the nineteenth century, as it was more profitable to mechanise and locate elsewhere. Clothing and furniture, however, generally remained there. As the century progressed, the mix of workshop and metropolitan/provincial factory production changed with new innovations, changes in taste and increases in demand, all permitting higher continuous output runs, but the new sub-contracting system remained dominant in several sectors.

Demand

During the nineteenth century, there was a huge increase in the demand for clothes, shoes and furniture. In 1800, the majority of the population either made their own clothes or wore second-hand garments and shoes. Apart from in the homes of the well-to-do, furniture was rudimentary. Rising real incomes then enabled first the expanding middle class and by the end of the century the skilled and semi-skilled to buy new products. This demand was highly price-sensitive, unlike that of the wealthy, so supply-side changes that cheapened output were important in stimulating the new demand. Falling input prices helped. The cost of textiles was tumbling as were the prices of many other manufactured inputs, as the benefits of industrialisation were being felt. Cut timber was also cheaper when North American and Russian imports were added to the traditional Scandinavian ones.

Changes in distribution were important in stimulating demand and cheapening supply. Transport improvements that extended the market have already been considered in earlier chapters. The retailing revolution played an important role. Ready-to-wear clothes, shoe and furniture shops made purchases less time-consuming and easy comparison of goods feasible.

Comparison of shop goods was important, because quality was now more variable, and there was a clearer, but imperfect, association between quality and price. Towards the end of the century further demand stimulus was given by the emergence of the multiple store.

Demand was further stimulated by employment and social changes, such as the expansion of white-collar employment and the growing significance of clothing and furniture as symbols of social status. Affluent workers took to wearing stiff collars to workshops, for example, to indicate their respectability.[11] Population was also increasing fast, particularly in the major cities like London. New private organisations, like the railway companies, retailing establishments and hotels, required furniture and also shoes and uniforms for their staff. Public sector demand fell with the rundown of the armed forces after the Napoleonic Wars, but rose again with the Crimea campaign and the expansion of Empire. Moreover, as Britain was turned into a single market, much London produce could be sold elsewhere in the country through multiples and networks of travelling salesmen. Exports rose as well, particularly to South Africa and Australia. From 1881 to 1914, for example, the value of clothing and apparel exports rose from £3.7 million to £8.6 million, a large proportion of which comprised cheap men's outerwear.[12]

A problem for producers was that this substantial increase in demand was associated with considerable variations in its level. Some of this variability was caused by fluctuations in the trade cycle; seasonal factors contributed; and fashion added another dimension. Within each broad product range, moreover, there could be considerable uncertainty when predicting the demand for particular lines. Stock holding to smooth these fluctuations would have been expensive and would have led to much unsaleable produce when demand turned against the particular line in question. A more efficient and cheaper response was to organise production in a way that minimised stocks through an ability to switch production from one item to another and to organise it in a way that enabled firms to vary rapidly the amount of capital and labour used.

The sub-contracting of production did precisely this. As production was labour-intensive and most capital was tied up in work-in-progress, sub-contracting meant that it was easy to vary both of these inputs in line with the level of output. Resources in each sector could also be utilised to the maximum extent that prevailing demand allowed, because when one firm's products were not selling well, labour and capital could switch to producing for those firms that had been more lucky in spotting market trends.

Using a predominantly unskilled workforce that was in plentiful supply also minimised the cost effects of sharp fluctuations in demand. As skilled labour was in limited supply, surges in clothing demand would lead to a bidding up of skilled earnings. In contrast, more unskilled workers could be used with little effect on their wage rates because their supply was highly elastic. This cost stabilisation effect in the face of fluctuating demand does not depend on unskilled wages being at a particular absolute level; instead, it is the differences in supply elasticities between skilled and unskilled labour that are important. Hence, poverty wages were not necessary for sub-contracting to expand. This helps to explains why it continued to thrive for decades into the twentieth century, long after the worst conditions and pay were eradicated through legislation and a general rise in unskilled pay. Contrary to what the Victorian reformers believed, the argument presented here suggests that the new sub-contracting system did not generate poverty, but rather took advantage of changes in technologies and the benefits of agglomeration economies to expand use of the available pool of unskilled labour.

It is worth noting that a large pool of low-wage, unskilled labour in London (or anywhere else in Britain) was hardly a new nineteenth-century phenomenon. Because of the intense competition for unskilled work, low wages and extensive hours had long been common. Out-working had existed in millinery, button-making and many other activities for centuries. What was different about the industries considered here was their new organisation of production, which created a new mass of unskilled jobs for women and immigrants. Thus, the enormous growth in employment in 'sweating' helped to keep people out of even worse jobs or the workhouse.

The division of labour and technical change

Adam Smith in his *Wealth of Nations* (1776) recognised that the division of labour, and with it labour productivity, was limited by the extent of the market. The greatly increased demand of the nineteenth century enabled a more complex division of labour to be introduced into London's consumer goods industries. The first important new division was that between shops and wholesalers. Under the traditional craft system of production, there was less distinction between retail and wholesale, but the emergence of mass retail outlets for consumer goods led to equally large wholesalers emerging. In some cases, larger shops would set up their own workshops when they had enough steady business, rather than rely entirely on independent wholesalers. Small independent masters also remained, so there was still considerable organisational variety in the ways in which consumer goods were produced and sold.

Wholesalers became the linchpins of the way in which the new system of production operated. They chased orders and broke down the work involved in producing clothes, shoes and furniture into a large number of standardised tasks, each performed by a worker who did nothing but the assigned operation. This increased output and productivity permitted the wider introduction of cheap unskilled labour – a process facilitated by the continued use of piece rates. Piece rates encouraged an intensity of effort unlikely to occur under hourly or daily rates of pay. They removed, moreover, the need for direct supervision of effort, enabling some aspects of production to be completed in workers' own homes. Constant monitoring of quality was unimportant, as the garments produced were sufficiently simple for workmanship to be judged quickly by eye, and fines could easily be introduced for imperfections. Home-work reduced wholesalers' lighting, heating, rental and capital costs, and enabled them to escape costly factory and workshop legislation. It also facilitated greater productive flexibility and, by isolating workers, prevented their effective organisation.

This new broader division of labour was facilitated by the introduction of improved technology. In clothing, for example, the power-driven bandsaw was adopted from the late 1850s. It cut several layers of cloth simultaneously and thus sped up the process. Relatively expensive and difficult to operate, these machines were largely wholesaler-owned and operated by skilled workers employed on the wholesalers' premises. Once the cloth was cut, the pieces were then passed to others less skilled in the workshop, to sub-contractors or to home-workers.

Out-workers themselves generally had to acquire their own simple tools and machines – in clothing and footwear manufacture a hand- or treadle-operated sewing machine. The invention of the sewing machine was one of the most important industrial discoveries of its era. It removed much of the skill in sewing, aided the subdivision of work and greatly increased output.[13] In the manufacture of shirts, for example, a machinist was thirty times faster than a hand sewer. The machines were cheap, small enough to be used at home and relatively easy to operate, enabling easy entry into home-working. From 1861, when the first patents expired, sewing machine use expanded and was commonplace by the 1870s. Machines could be purchased in instalments from Singer or rented from organisations like the Jewish Board of Guardians. Training could be obtained from wholesalers or sewing machine manufacturers.[14]

Clustering and agglomeration economies

The wholesalers when putting out tasks to other workshops or home-workers were passing on work-in-progress in which they would have a great deal of working capital invested. They would consequently want to monitor out-workers to ensure timely return of the goods. They would also not want time wasted in the transport of semi-completed items between processes. In order to achieve this, sub-contractors and home-workers had to be located near to wholesalers' premises. Home-workers, similarly, would be keen to live near to wholesalers in order to find out what work was available. Particularly in the years before the telephone, wholesalers would, furthermore, want to be in close proximity to competitors to compare what lines were selling well and to be available to bid for any excess work that a competitor might have from a large order. All of these are typical agglomeration economies.

This created a new geography of production. Each ready-made consumer goods trade tended to cluster in particular areas of the city near to places where their low-paid, home-based workforces could afford to live. It is not surprising, therefore, that most were located somewhere in the inner East End. The most concentrated activity was the one with a relatively expensive and difficult to transport raw material – furniture. It was clustered in Hoxton, just north of the City. The bespoke sectors of these trades, conversely, would tend to be located near to their retail customers and so were centred on the West End, the affluent suburbs and, to a lesser extent, the City.

Labour supply in a segmented labour market

The workers employed to operate the new machinery and perform the other processes in the new mass-market sectors were largely indigenous East End women and recent male immigrants. Women were almost the entire workforce in dressmaking; over 80 per cent in shirtmaking; 40 per cent in tailoring; and slightly under 10 per cent in boot- and shoe-making.[15] The figures include both bespoke and ready-to-wear, and the proportion of women would have been greater in the latter. Poorly educated, these East End women and their daughters had little choice but to became unskilled factory, workshop or home-workers. As home-workers, they were joined by widows with children, spinsters too old for domestic service, the ill and the destitute.[16]

The immigrants were largely Jewish men – Jewish women tended not to work after marrying at a young age. Anti-Semitism restricted the activities that these workers could enter. As adults, moreover, their age made it impossible to acquire the apprenticeship training necessary for most skilled trades. Language and low education were further barriers to clerical work. They also often had previous experience in the garment industry of their home country. Between 1895 and 1908, for instance, former clothing workers made up almost 30 per cent of new arrivals entering the Poor Jews Temporary Centre, a sleeping place for recently arrived immigrants. Entrepreneurial and hardworking, many became masters themselves, to the extent that some activities became almost exclusively run by Jewish enterprises. An understanding of traditional religious requirements attracted fellow Jews to these trades.[17]

One unfashionable way of looking at the development of the new subcontracting system of production was that it was partly a distributional struggle for jobs and income amongst the general workforce. Male supremacy and racism played parts in that power struggle, leaving the best-paid skilled work for English men throughout the period and, even for them, many points of entry were carefully guarded. Craft unions, unsurprisingly, used their power only for the benefit of their skilled members and the opponent was often the unskilled. Reformers played down these complex issues of working-class divisions and market forces. This is perhaps unsurprising as most were influenced by the Webbs, who themselves took a great interest in these industries – believing that strong unions were essential and that casual employment stopped their existence. They also held the misguided belief that the working class, whatever their sex or ethnic origin, had a natural, common interest in the reform of 'sweating' – which they did not because only worse jobs beckoned for many. This is not to say that arguing for reforms and minimum conditions in these industries was morally wrong, but those morals had a price for some of the poorest in society – an even worse job or none at all. One modern quip used in Third World studies is that the only thing worse than being exploited by a multinational is not being exploited by one; the joke could also have been applied to the nineteenth-century 'sweater'.

Spatial differences in production methods

The adoption of out-working was not unique to the capital. Clothing manufacturers in Leeds, Manchester and Glasgow all sub-contracted work out and used home-based unskilled workers. In 1850, over two-thirds of tailors in Glasgow were estimated to work for sub-contractors.[18] London's adoption of powered machinery and factory production was also far slower than in the provinces. By 1904, for example, only just over a quarter of its clothing workers were employed in factories, as compared to two-thirds in Leeds and almost a half in the UK as a whole.[19] Factory production was less appropriate for the old inner city. The East End lacked sufficient low-cost space, and existing buildings were too insubstantial to withstand the vibrations of large-scale machinery. After the formation of the Office of Metropolitan Buildings and London County Council, there was also stringent and strictly enforced building and factory legislation. London producers could have chosen to build factories in the non-LCC suburbs, away from the eye of the factory inspector, as other industries did, but it was probably less profitable to do so because key agglomeration economies would have been lost.

A regional spatial division in the organisation of these industries is suggested by these findings, with London concentrating on higher value-added activities that for technological or demand reasons could not be done more cheaply in provincial factories with a lower-cost labour supply. Evidence for this comes from two clothing industry surveys. In a 1907 survey, clothing workshops, a large proportion of which were in the capital, were 12 per cent more efficient in terms of the value of their net output per worker than clothing factories. In a later 1930 survey, when regional figures were more available and factory technology greatly improved, the fragmented London industry was still found to be more productive than elsewhere.[20] Further evidence is provided by the fact that some London clothing firms themselves utilised this spatial division within their own businesses, with factories in the provinces for some lines and a London production network for others.

Wages

Historical accounts of these industries tend to put emphasis on the low pay of the workforce, in keeping with the belief that these industries had degraded into sweating. More realistically, as with every other industry, wages and out-work payments varied considerably, which can be seen if Booth's survey data from the 1880s are consulted. In determining differences in labour payments, the demand and supply of particular types of worker were the prime determinants. The profitability of each type of labour to firms (more precisely, their marginal revenue products) determined whether firms were willing to hire them. Some of the worst-paid workers, sadly for all their efforts, added little value to the product and so would only be employed at pittance wages.

Institutional factors played a part. Firms would generally respect traditional differentials and would sometimes pay over the odds to keep key staff or to have sufficient labour at peak times. On the supply side, the availability of alternative employment opportunities and the degree and scarcity of skills were significant factors. Hierarchies caused by skill, tradition and prejudice gave workers good information about the likely earnings they could receive and sustained differentials. Overall differentials, none the less, were primarily influenced by workers' skill levels, sex, ethnic origin, whether they were recent immigrants or not, the work they performed and the economic position of the sector in which they were employed. Other determining factors included the degree to which trades were seasonal and workers' ability to find alternative employment in 'slack periods' and, if labour was hired on piece rates, the hours of employment that could be achieved or were required.

The clothing industries

There were three important parts of the clothing industry: tailoring, dressmaking and shirtmaking. Their shares of employment indicate their relative importance in London. These, along with boot and shoe manufacture, are shown in Figure 12.1, where these sectors' employment shares are presented for the census years from 1861 to 1911. Dressmaking was the most important, followed by tailoring which grew strongly in the last two decades of the nineteenth century. Boot and shoe manufacture was next, although it declined almost continuously over the period; and last in importance is shirtmaking, which also shrank somewhat. This was the sector that had always used out-workers the most and estimates associated with the first census of production in 1907 suggest that they constituted half of the workforce.[21]

Tailoring

The sector comprised two branches – the bespoke and the ready-made trades. Each will now be considered in turn.

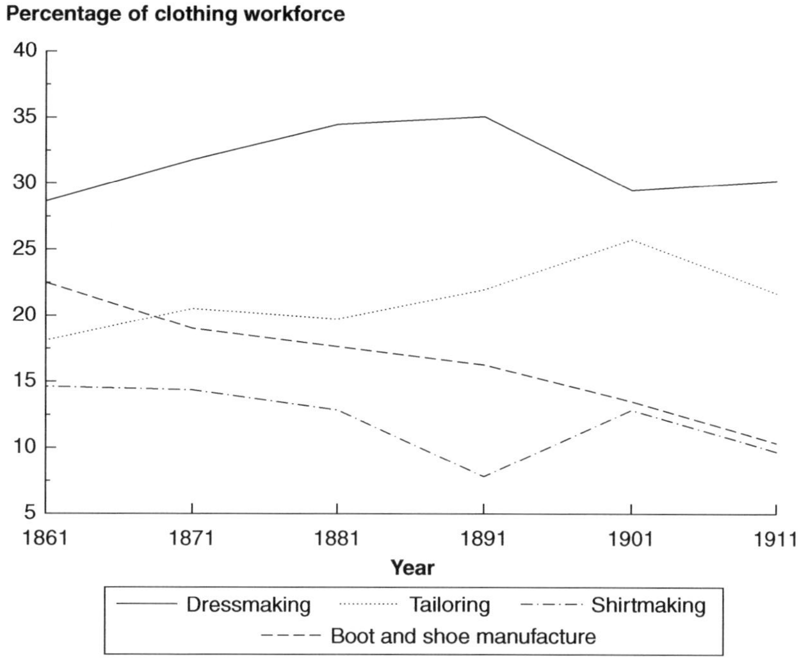

Figure 12.1 Percentage of London clothing workers engaged in the main clothing sectors, 1861–1911

Source: Schmiechen, 1984, 39.

Bespoke

In the eighteenth century, bespoke tailoring was based in the City and produced ladies' outerwear – that is, costumes, coats and skirts – and men's and boys' suits, trousers and uniforms. Its employees comprised highly skilled, well-paid foremen, who cut cloth and finished work, and less skilled and worse-paid tailors, who sewed seams and buttonholes and prepared work for finishing. Both groups laboured in their employers' own premises, were highly unionised, and were almost wholly male. With the migration of its wealthy clientele westwards, this sector gradually relocated, and by 1800 was concentrated around Savile Row. Tailors producing for the civilian market congregated around Regent Street, while army tailors stayed closer to the clubs of Pall Mall.[22]

Employment of less skilled male workers in workshops and female home-workers gradually increased. This de-skilling was encouraged by the 1814 repeal of the Elizabethan apprenticeship statutes, though enforcement had been lax for a long time; heightened competition from the ready-made sector; and the rise of the 'show shop', in which garments were displayed and then the orders made up elsewhere. Trade unions attempted to oppose these changes, but were generally unsuccessful. In 1827, a strike to prevent the spread of the use of female out-workers collapsed; further industrial action in 1834 failed to restrict out-working and maintain artisan wages.[23]

Women performed relatively simple tasks and girls were used as sewing machinists. Approximately half of the male workers were journeymen, concentrating on the more skilled processes, and others operated machines. Both the men and the women were generally English. As late as 1881, just sixty-eight Eastern European tailors were employed in the West End, and in 1901 the figure was still relatively small at 421.[24]

Medium-sized production units appeared in the 1850s, set up by retail bespoke tailors. For example, Henry Poole and Son at the height of the Season employed 500 workers, but had only 85 permanent staff – a third of them in the cutting room plus others in sales, clerical and portering tasks. Senior cutters and sales staff were on generous commissions – presumably to stop them leaving and to act as a work incentive.[25]

Ready-made

In 1800, the ready-made trade catered largely for government and institutional orders but, for reasons described above, the market for ready-to-wear garments expanded dramatically. Wholesalers sometimes had factories in the provinces and often owned several retail shops.[26] Employing mostly unskilled women, the trade was concentrated in the East End and the City. By 1861, the East End contained 34,000 tailors and tailoresses; in 1911, there were 65,000, with employment increasing most rapidly between 1881 and 1901.[27] Of the women working in the ready-to-wear trade, 46 per cent were machinists and the rest were sewers, finishers and pressers. Of the men, 35 per cent were cutters, 10 per cent machinists, and the remainder were pressers, warehousemen and packers.[28]

The gender and workshop/home divisions of work varied according to the type of clothing produced. As men's suits and trousers were easy to make and less subject to fashion, manufacturing could be broken down into many simple processes undertaken by women and girl home-workers. The production of women's wear was more difficult and machinists were generally male; women only being employed as finishing handworkers. The manufacture of simple lightweight garments, such as waistcoats and boys' trousers, required little skill and machinery and so was undertaken by women working at home. The employment of immigrant workers similarly varied between trades. Jews tended to be especially prominent in the production of women's clothing and in the coat and jacket sections of the men's tailoring trade.

There was little call for women's ready-to-wear coats, skirts and suits in the first half of the century. But greater female social freedom, new modes of retailing and innovations in transport, particularly the bicycle, gradually generated higher demand for such apparel. In the late 1850s, Charles Selincourt of Pimlico began to produce women's wear for large retail outlets, such as Harvey Nichols and Marshall and Snelgrove. Another successful entrepreneur, Morris Cohen, began making women's clothes in 1877. He opened a factory in the inner East End in 1895 and employed 180 workers eight years later. His success encouraged others into the trade.[29]

Dress- and shirt-making

Dressmaking grew strongly from the middle of the century. From 1861 to 1911, the number of dressmakers in the capital rose from 55,000 to 80,000 and London accounted for around a third of the UK workforce. Those employed were almost all women, working either in West End dressmaking establishments or at home in the East End.[30]

In the mid-1860s, around 17,500 women were employed in the West End's dressmaking houses.[31] There were four grades of establishment based on the social class of their clientele. First- and second-class ones had customers from the nobility and upper middle classes respectively and specialised in silk court dresses, trains and ball gowns. Both only made bodices, sending the dresses to be made up by out-workers. Below them, the third- and fourth-class houses dressed the wives of the middle class and the labour aristocracy. They produced silk and cotton garments and made both the bodices and the dresses on the premises.[32]

All classes of dressmaker employed young women aged between 14 and 25, and at least until mid-century generally required their skilled staff to live-in. A small number of women entered the trade as apprentices, who after paying a premium of £30 to £50 obtained two to three years' training. Most, however, were 'learners', the daughters of tradesmen and artisans, who after an apprenticeship in the provinces received nine months to two years further instruction in return for a premium of £10 to £15.[33]

Young women were attracted to dressmaking for a number of reasons. It was regarded as a genteel occupation and most of these women had few skills other than the sewing learnt in childhood. For those from the provinces, living-in additionally provided protection from the dangers of urban life and offered the prospect that the cachet of a London training would allow them to start up their own business when they returned home. The sector also offered greater independence than domestic service and was better paid. The hours were long – twelve a day was quite common. The more skilled women would often live-in at the more up-market establishments but the lower-paid had to find accommodation elsewhere.

The majority of dressmakers were home-workers, producing dresses either for the dressmaking houses or the slop trade. Slop was the general term for clothing manufacture for independent wholesalers. Those working for dressmakers lived close to those establishments in the poorer residential districts around St Martin's-in-the-Fields, the Strand and St Giles, and were employed by the day. The slop workers were concentrated in Stepney and, to a lesser extent, Shoreditch and Bethnal Green. They obtained sewing from middlemen, who often charged a fee for providing the work.

When times were hard, many dressmakers were forced to turn to shirtmaking, the third clothing sector, which also included the manufacture of blouses, overalls, collars, ties and underwear. This was organised by wholesalers. Women did the bulk of the sewing, with girls as machinists and elderly women as finishers (buttonholes and buttons). At first, the activity was concentrated in Stepney, but it gradually moved to Bow and West Ham as the docks relocated down river and the dockers – with their wives and daughters – migrated with them.

Shirtmaking was undertaken at home, in workshops and increasingly in London-based factories. In 1911, the scale of some shirtmaking plants was large, employing from 500 to 800 staff, because technology had made inroads into the handicraft processes in this trade. Wages were generally low, and producers faced competition from prisons and workhouses.[34]

The urban location of clothing manufacture

In the early part of the century, tailors were predominantly located in the City, West End and the western suburbs near their clientele. Slop-sellers and clothing warehouses were based in the City and the east. There was virtually no activity in South London, which at this time was hardly built up. By the 1850s, the number of tailors had grown substantially and had spread throughout the metropolis, although they were still concentrated near their clients, many of whom had moved to new suburbs in the north-west and west. Slop-sellers and warehouses also proliferated, but tended to remain to a greater extent in their traditional City and East End locations. Some activity can also be seen by this time in South London.[35]

Silk weaving

The silk industry dated from the sixteenth century, but had all but gone by the 1840s. The fall of Antwerp to the Spanish in 1585 prompted many silk merchants and manufacturers to flee to London, where, after the 1685 revocation of the Edict of Nantes, they were joined by Huguenot weavers, who emigrated to England to escape persecution. In the late 1700s, it was estimated that the capital contained 12,000–15,000 looms operated by around 40,000 weavers, most of whom worked in their own homes in Spitalfields and Bethnal Green.[36] Decline was the result of domestic and foreign competition. Silk had always been thrown, twisted and dyed outside London, and by the late eighteenth century the provinces, in particular Coventry, Macclesfield, Manchester, Stockport and various Essex towns, were beginning to take up weaving as well. Their great advantage was that their labour costs were around a third of those found in the capital.

The London industry was controlled by the 1773 Spitalfields Acts, under which wages were fixed at a relatively high level, each weaver was allowed just two apprentices, which restricted entry to the trade, and weavers were banned from contracting work outside of London. The response of London manufacturers to provincial competition was to concentrate on satisfying the high local demand for finer and more fashionable silk materials that required more skill in their manufacture than the coarser provincial products. Others began to send a proportion of their orders to other centres, contrary to the stipulations of the Spitalfields Acts, and a few moved out of the capital altogether.[37]

Collapse occurred during the 1820s with the repeal of their protective legislation. After pressure from provincial silk masters, the Spitalfields Acts were abolished in 1824. As a result, more work was placed outside London and a large number of extra workers entered the sector. More importantly, in 1826 the ban on the import of foreign manufactured silks was replaced by a customs duty of 25 to 40 per cent.[38] The inflow of low-cost, high-quality fashionable French silks decimated the London industry and by the end of the year 8,600 looms were idle and 30,000 weavers were unemployed. Working long hours for subsistence wages, a number of weavers stayed in business, so that, in 1838, the East End still contained 10,000 silk looms. Yet these strategies did not enable the industry to survive indefinitely. The introduction of steam-powered machines in the provinces and the repeal of all import duties in 1860 reduced the numbers still active to negligible levels. By 1914, probably only 114 weavers remained, mostly working in Bethnal Green.[39]

Footwear manufacture

The numbers employed in the London boot and shoe industry declined from 43,000 to 28,000 between 1861 and 1911, with the largest falls occurring in the decades 1861–71 and 1901–11. The result was that the capital's share of the England and Wales footwear workforce fell between 1841 and 1911 from 17 per cent to 11 per cent.[40] Like the clothing industry, footwear manufacture comprised two geographically separated sectors. There was a similar pattern of location in the footwear trades to that in clothing, with the up-market bespoke side predominantly in the west and the ready-made side in the east. Warehouses, however, were more concentrated in the City than was the case for clothing.

The smaller of the two sectors was the bespoke trade, which produced all types of boot and shoe. Throughout the period, it was located in the West End. The ready-to-wear trade in 1800 was concentrated in the City and East London and then spread outwards, reaching as far as Hackney and Clapton.[41]

The London shoe trade was far less successful at adapting to change than the clothing trade. Some types of shoe-making had already moved out of the capital before 1800 – men's boots, for example, were now produced in the provinces. This is unsurprising as such shoes were easy to transport and were less prone to the dictates of fashion. The London-based bespoke sector was soon to suffer from foreign competition, which took a large market share after successive tariff reductions from the 1820s to the 1860s.

For several lines, London producers successfully set up out-working arrangements. Leather cutting had to remain in-house – initially because it was highly skilled and later because of the expense of the machines that replaced the craft labour. Machinery again encouraged factory production as mechanisation gradually spread through the elements of shoe-making previously sent to out-workers – including finishing, the sewing of uppers, and the joining of sole and insole to the upper.[42] Technical change and international trade, therefore, left a metropolitan location with little advantage. Producers there, consequently, faced only its higher costs and metropolitan production inexorably declined.

The introduction of machinery was far more gradual than in the provincial centres, where firms had mechanised as early as the early 1860s. In the late 1880s, competition from the highly mechanised US industry spurred them to adopt even more machinery and, along with a trade union campaign to outlaw home-working, this encouraged a further move into factories. By 1895, 70 per cent of footwear workers in England and Wales were employed in factories and, by 1905, the proportion had risen to over 80 per cent. The resultant fall in the prices of provincial manufacturers reduced the demand for London-made shoes and the sector contracted. The remaining London firms concentrated on those products where they possessed an advantage – namely, the manufacture of babies' footwear, slippers and shoes with elaborate uppers, which all required extensive handwork. By 1911, the East London industry employed 12,000 shoe-makers, a substantial number but only half that of Leicester, where the industry was most concentrated.[43]

Furniture manufacture

In 1841, the furniture and timber industry employed 20,000 workers, and employment more than trebled in the next seventy years to almost 67,000 in 1911.[44] The industry comprised five trades – timber merchanting and cutting, the production of bespoke furniture, high- and low-class hand-made products and, finally, factory production. Not only did a London location offer similar benefits to those in the clothing industry, but also furniture could be bulky, which reinforced the incentives to locate in the major market; moreover, wood was imported via the docks, so that sawn wood could be obtained cheaply in whatever quantities or forms required.

Timber merchants were located on the south bank of the Thames and later the Surrey Docks, where wood was brought in from abroad and elsewhere in the UK. With the construction of the Regent's Canal, yards were also established along its banks and in Shoreditch to supply the Curtain Road furniture firms. The larger dealers supplied cut wood directly to furniture manufacturers and also to smaller merchants. Sawyers were either employed directly or on contract by the timber merchants and some worked independently. Mechanisation in the form of the circular saw had been introduced in the eighteenth century and by the 1820s the saws were being steam driven. By mid-century hand sawing had all but disappeared.[45] Many more sawyers were employed in the furniture trade itself.

The West End bespoke sector was relatively unimportant except for upholstering, a highly specialised trade that gradually declined, virtually disappearing by 1900. The wealthy preferred to purchase high-class ready-made furniture, which was produced by a large number of specialist manufacturers in workshops attached to shops in West End. In the early nineteenth century, they employed 40–50 people, on average, with the number rising to 100–350 by mid-century in the larger establishments.[46] This indicates that scale economies were becoming more important. The shops were initially located in the St Martin's Lane district but, after 1800, rising rents encouraged them to move north to the streets around Tottenham Court Road and Euston Road.[47] In the 1840s, large stores, such as Maples and Heal's, appeared in the area and opened up their own workshops – Maples employed 1,295 men in its workshop in 1888.[48] From the 1870s, they also began to sub-contract work to small master manufacturers, who by specialising in one object could undercut the stores' workshop prices. Customer demand for rapid delivery encouraged the use of nearby firms, so that Tottenham Court Road became an important furniture manufacturing district – of which the workshops at the side of Heal's and some converted buildings on Stephen and Gresse Streets are modern reminders.

As the high-class, ready-made trade expanded in the West End, a similar sector producing poorer-quality goods emerged in the East End.[49] Although a small sector existed in the eighteenth century, it took off after 1820 as the market for furniture expanded and skill wages rose.[50] Its manufacturers by the 1860s were largely found around Curtain Road and the Old Street area of Shoreditch, after they had been displaced by the building of Broad and Liverpool Street stations. Firms then gradually moved east towards Bethnal Green and north into Hoxton. By the end of the century, they had began to spread north of the Regent's Canal towards Hackney. Like the ready-to-wear clothing industry, the sector was organised by wholesalers. On receiving orders, they sub-contracted tasks to small manufacturers, who either worked alone or had small workshops.[51] Little machinery was used, as demand was highly volatile, depending as it did on the building cycle, season and fashion, and the equipment available was too costly for most workshops to bear.[52]

Having received an order from a wholesaler, manufacturers purchased the necessary wood from timber yards on credit or with the earnings of recent work. They then had the wood cut into the required shapes and planed by sawyers – passing the pieces on to turners, fret cutters, carvers and others before putting the item of furniture together. The small manufacturers organised and paid for the transportation of pieces of furniture between the different processes as well as undertook their assembly. This encouraged the clustering of these processes. The completed piece was then returned to the wholesaler, who arranged for it to be polished and, when necessary, upholstered – either in-house or by further out-workers. The furniture was sold to retailers in the UK and abroad.[53] In 1888, £750,000 of furniture was exported, a third to Australia and the remainder to South Africa, Argentina and the USA.[54]

The furniture factory grew in significance in the 1880s. By the 1890s the East End contained half a dozen works employing more than fifty men, each of which produced whole pieces of furniture in-house. By-passing the wholesaler, they sold direct to retailers in the West End and elsewhere. Lacking sufficient space to expand production and for sales, and wishing to escape new stringent fire regulations, these larger firms began to move away from the East End to the suburbs in the early 1900s. Harris Lebus, for example, relocated to Tottenham in 1899, and another producer, Greaves and Thomas, shifted production to Clapton in 1908.[55]

Engineering

General mechanical

At the start of the nineteenth century, London was an important place in the UK mechanical engineering industry. In 1825, the capital contained approximately 400 engineering firms, giving employment to more than 10,000 men.[56] Most establishments were small and the industry was based on the skills of the traditional independent millwright. Industrialisation in the north and the diffusion of machine tools meant that London lost out to Lancashire and elsewhere but a significant industry remained.

There was some spatial differentiation with inner city firms concentrating on heavy constructional engineering, such as cranes, hydraulic apparatus, boilers and tanks; while Deptford, Greenwich, Lewisham and Woolwich had larger plants concentrating on marine boilers and engines, railway equipment, armaments and other space demanding activities. The huge government-owned Royal Arsenal in Woolwich, for example, grew to employ 3,211 men in 1911.[57] By the end of the century, engineering had spread up the Lea Valley, stretching to the outer reaches of the capital, in particular to Edmonton.[58] Even further up the Lea Navigation, the publicly owned Enfield Small Arms factory was established in 1815, employing from 2,400 to 3,200 for the rest of the century.[59] Several engineering industrial districts, consequently, existed in the metropolis.

In keeping with British production practices, engineering was predominantly a craft activity. The 'American System' of standardised, interchangeable parts and flow-line production only had an impact in a limited number of sectors, such as small arms production. Engineering companies employed many well-paid craftsmen, often trained in the provinces, working in small workshops. Once again, therefore, as with many consumer goods industries, London's nineteenth-century engineering enterprises were characterised by flexible production technologies – local networks of small-scale producers, using craft labour as needed and locally produced inputs (in this case iron from foundries) in order to respond to the varying requirements of the market place.

Alongside the mass of small engineering workshops were several larger firms that had adopted new engineering technologies developed during the first half of the nineteenth century. These innovations included the self-acting drill and power-driven lathes and planers. Some firms went under with the collapse of shipbuilding in the 1860s but, overall, mechanical engineering experienced substantial growth with employment in the capital rising from around 10,000 in 1841 to 33,000 in 1911.[60]

Shipbuilding

Shipbuilding contained some of London's largest enterprises employing up to 2,000 men. London and the Thames Estuary dominated British shipbuilding in the early nineteenth century but all was at an end by 1912. Even so, there was a long see-saw process of expansion and decline. Around 2,500 men were employed in the industry in 1831 and the number rose to 6,000 by 1851. Then for the next fifteen years there was a massive boom with 16,000 working in 1856 and a peak of 27,000 in 1865 – more than ten times the number in 1831 – but after that date decline was just as meteoric, dropping by a third in six years, but still remaining at over twice the level of 1831 in 1901 at 5,500.[61] Shipbuilding finally ended shortly before the First World War as a Dreadnought battleship sailed down the Thames in 1912.[62]

Until the middle of the century, London producers benefited from a high local demand for merchant vessels and warships, as the metropolis was the biggest port in the country and the home of the Admiralty. Wood was imported through the port. Large numbers of skilled shipwrights and 'amphibian' workers also existed – the latter were joiners, painters and other building workers who could be called upon in times of high demand.

The introduction of iron and steam ships at first had little negative impact. London firms rapidly developed a technological lead over the rest of the country in the new construction methods. Initially, the distance from iron and coal supplies was relatively unimportant, because only a small amount of iron was actually used in ship construction and transport costs formed an even smaller proportion of its cost. What is more, local scrap iron could easily be substituted for forged iron. Problems, none the less, were soon to emerge. In the 1850s, the price of forged iron fell, more was used in the construction process and Lloyds, the ship insurers, began to set limits on the amount of scrap iron permissible in high-grade metal ships. The cost scales consequently were tipping against London towards other British shipbuilding centres, where firms had caught up in the technological race. London firms' labour costs were also far higher than those of their provincial rivals, caused by traditional wage-setting practices and trade union activity.

The extraordinary boom in the decade from the mid-1850s to mid-1860s resulted from a temporary surge in demand. One stimulus was war – in the Crimea and the civil war in the United States. Mid-century developments also greatly increased the need for new ships – especially the rapid growth in imported foodstuffs, emigration, and the replacement by the Navy of its wood and sail vessels with iron and steam ships. London yards expanded and new firms were established, often on a financially unsound basis.[63] From the mid-1860s the demand for ships fell, and in 1866, after the bankruptcy of the discounting house Overend Gurney, which had advanced large sums to shipbuilders, the sector collapsed. By November of that year, almost all the estimated 27,000 shipbuilding workers were unemployed,[64] and in 1867–74 the tonnage of merchant ships launched on the Thames amounted to only 2 per cent of total UK output, as compared to 27 per cent in 1852–3.[65]

What remained of the London industry survived by concentrating on the construction of high-cost vessels, the price of which was unimportant, government contracts, marine engineering and bridge-building. Some new firms even entered the industry but, from the 1890s, these new activities also began to disappear.[66] Yards lacked sufficient space for the latest technologies. Firms faced high rents and rates and the new 'fair wages clause' forced government contractors to pay the current salaries of the districts in which they were located, pricing London-based firms out of the market. In 1904 and 1906 respectively, Thorneycroft and Yarrow moved away from London to Southampton and Glasgow, to be followed by J. and G. Rennie in 1908 and, in 1912, by the Thames Ironworks. The few remaining firms undertook repair work, often entering into long-term contracts with shipping lines.[67]

Vehicles

Road vehicle production has a long history in London and, by 1861, employed 9,500 people, almost 20 per cent of the total England and Wales workforce.[68] In the era of the horse, carriages, carts and omnibuses were the main products of vehicle builders. Most of the activities involved some form of woodworking, so the technology was simple and production units tended to be small. Wood supplies were good in the capital but the nature of production gave no exceptional locational advantage – apart from a proximity to local demand.

There were two centres: the West End and South-East London. West End producers built for a general market consisting of wealthy individuals and trades people. A central location tapped the luxury market and maximised the catchment area for the trade business. Space-demanding workshops and showrooms encouraged firms to seek out central neighbourhoods with lower rents. South-East London firms concentrated on the production of heavy goods vans for the nearby docks.[69]

Commercial motor vehicle manufacture only started in Britain in 1896. The early British motor car business was craft-based and made luxury vehicles. The majority of firms were assemblers, buying both the engine and chassis, though some larger companies manufactured chassis in-house. The car industry retained the characteristic of having many small assembly firms and components suppliers until the development of large plants in the inter-war years. Ford's assembly plant for the Model T set up in Manchester in 1911 was an exception, and by the end of the First World War Ford dominated British car sales. It only moved its plant down to Dagenham in the 1930s and Dagenham initially was not a success.[70]

Prior to the success of Ford, London producers were significant in the nascent industry, with the capital in 1911 containing a quarter of the country's motor manufacturers. The most famous name today is Vauxhall. Originally marine engineers, the firm from 1901 to 1903 made cars at a plant on Wandsworth Road in Vauxhall before moving to Luton. Further centres developed in West London. In Chiswick, the shipbuilders Thorneycroft made steam wagons until 1899, when their plant was relocated to Basingstoke. From the turn of the century, Willesden and Acton became a focus for the manufacture of cars. North-East London also contained several producers of components. J. P. Prestwick opened a large plant in Tottenham in 1911 producing engines and motor cycles.[71]

Many of the components used by assemblers were produced in the capital, although most engines came from France or French subsidiaries set up in London. Car bodies were purchased from former West End carriage makers. The earlier bicycle boom had benefited Coventry producers, which switched to car production but, at this stage of development of the car industry, the metropolis offered several locational benefits – good demand, supplies of skilled engineering labour, a tradition of flexible networks of suppliers and a pool of enthusiastic innovators. When production line methods became commonplace in the inter-war years, however, expensive London locations were less attractive. Many London engine, chassis and component producers also supplied the nascent aircraft industry.

Precision instruments

In the eighteenth century, precision instrument making and the related watch and jewellery trades were based in Fleet Street. Precision firms then began to congregate in Clerkenwell. In the 1820s, a further centre had developed in inner South London. The jewellery and diamond trades clustered in Hatton Garden. By the end of the century, the pull of agglomeration economies was weakening as greater mechanisation was introduced, and many firms moved to the Lea Valley. The Ensign Camera works, for example, relocated from High Holborn to Walthamstow. Others, however, stayed in the inner city. Gas meters, for example, where manufactured in Finsbury until the 1960s. New nineteenth-century industries spawned the need for specialist measuring equipment, which became an important component of the London engineering sector. Firms were largely comprised of small masters operating from workshops, but there were several bigger concerns.[72]

Industrial and building materials

Most materials industries existed in London because they provided inputs into other industries active in the capital. Building materials are heavy and, therefore, suffer from high transport costs. Shipping raw materials into the capital, especially via the port, and processing them for distribution to the near market was often a transport cost minimising solution. Building materials were also a rare case of the environs of the capital containing the necessary raw materials, so bricks and cement could be made locally. As production methods became more mechanised, and raw materials were exhausted, many of these industries gradually left London to set up in the outer suburbs or nearby towns where the new, more efficient, production methods could still outweigh the cost effects of greater distances.

Many of the materials industries were highly polluting and operated from central locations. For much of the period, for example, both a large pottery and an artificial stone-making facility operated on the banks of the Thames virtually opposite the site of the Houses of Parliament. Legislation towards the end of the nineteenth century encouraged some to leave, but the principal impetus to the relocation of polluters was the market mechanism itself. Transportation improvements slowly made it possible to serve metropolitan markets from more distant locations. So, as wages and land values rose, these industries were encouraged to move elsewhere, or else they failed when their metropolitan input costs rose and they could not compete with non-London producers.

The industrial geography of the capital, moreover, was affected by such relocations because the empty banks of the Thames downstream of the city were viable areas for such producers – with low land values and weaker regulation outside of the County – and the more noxious industries gradually congregated there, benefiting from external economies of clustering as they did so. These market processes were extremely slow and applied only to the more land-intensive activities – the small forges, iron foundries and other heavy polluting activities stayed in their beneficial central locations. It is, therefore, unsurprising that the inner southern industrial district was simultaneously one of the most polluting areas for much of the period and the location of some of the worst poverty. Low-income groups could take advantage of the lower land costs caused by the negative externalities of both industry and the railways in that part of the city – but at the cost of a poor-quality life.

In contrast to the centrifugal forces discussed so far, some polluting industries had been set up initially in out-of-town locations but were then gradually absorbed into the fabric of the city. Leather and tanning are good examples. The treating of skins was based in Bermondsey and Southwark, where in the first half of the century around a third of all the leather output of England and Wales was treated. These areas were then drawn into the urban nexus by the rapid city growth, so that by the mid-nineteenth century they were inner suburbs rather than the outer suburbs they had been in previous centuries. Market and input considerations continued to encourage their location in the capital, as tanneries obtained hides locally from metropolitan slaughter-houses, with additional skins imported from overseas. Even here, the heavy leather tanneries – the worst polluters – gradually moved north to Yorkshire and Lancashire to avoid high rents and rates, but light leather and the working up of leather goods generally remained in London.

Pottery was not a speciality of the capital – many luxury items had been imported for years. During the industrial revolution production grew elsewhere, particularly in the Stoke region of North Staffordshire. Even so, there were producers – especially in the district on the south bank of the Thames between Lambeth Bridge and Vauxhall – and production largely consisted of stoneware: that is, lower-priced, heavier pottery items with high transport costs. Some output was for the building trade – drainage pipes, chimney pots and Coadestone, an artificial stone. Others were for industry, particularly crucibles – pots made of clay and graphite used for the melting of metals and chemicals. The largest stoneware producer was Doulton, which in 1878 employed 600 at its Lambeth works.[73] Coade, the producer of Coadestone, was set up in 1769 and continued in its Lambeth factory until the 1840s. It provided decorative features for many of London's major buildings and new houses during that time. The stone was prized for its cheapness and durability.

Crucibles were manufactured by the five Morgan brothers. In 1856, they bought the UK rights to a process of crucible production developed by an American firm and opened a small factory in Battersea. Their firm, the Patent Plumbago Crucible Co. (from 1880, the Morgan Crucible Co.) rapidly expanded, so that by the 1880s it was the largest producer of crucibles in the world. In 1900, it employed 421 workers in the capital and, from 1903, it began to diversify into the manufacture of electric motor parts.[74]

Iron foundries

The capital contained a large number of iron foundries supplying castings to its various engineering works and iron goods to the building industry.

Lambeth Marsh in 1872, for example, contained approximately twelve foundries.[75] Domestic and architectural markets were the most important. St Pancras Ironworks made street lights, while another firm's coal-hole covers were sold throughout the country.

Bricks

Cement production ceased to be a local activity after the invention of Portland Cement in the 1820s.[76] Local stone hardly existed, but good brick-making clay was abundant, so most housing and many other built structures were made of brick. Production was itinerant, with clay often dug up, hand-moulded and fired before land was built upon. The trade was carried out by itinerant gangs of brick-makers, who would move from site to site. As an average modest house early in the period required around 30,000 bricks in its construction and some 3 million bricks could be extracted from an acre of ground,[77] each acre yielded enough bricks for 100 houses. Given the huge demand for bricks during the expansion of London, it follows that many thousands of acres must have experienced brick production before being developed.

Brick-making was a handcraft process and remained so in the capital far longer than elsewhere. The bricks were fired in 'clamps' – heaps of coal and ash covered by previously overbaked bricks. Ash was often put into the clay to aid firing, giving London bricks a varied, mottled appearance. Elsewhere in the country kilns were used during the period and these became increasingly mechanised, but the London gangs continued with their traditional ways. This could have been conservatism or, alternatively, the older approach may have been more flexible, leaving little trace of production, and it may have been less polluting and, therefore, may have been required by landowners interested in subsequent development.

Red bricks went out of fashion in the metropolis towards the end of the eighteenth century, so that for most of the nineteenth century the natural red of the clay was treated when bricks were made. The lead of the capital was not followed in much of the rest of the country where red remained predominant, so that London houses became distinguished by their colour. 'Grey' bricks (brown, yellow and only rarely grey) were made by adding chalky clay and a special sand from the Thames at Woolwich to the brick paste. When these sources ran out, chalk alone was added.

The problem faced by non-London producers was the cost of transporting their product to the capital, even after the advent of railways. Some production moved out to Essex and Kent whence bricks were transported to London via river and canal, and the cost equation was improved by shipping metropolitan ashes and refuse in the returning boats to fuel the firing. New, mechanised, large brick works in Bedfordshire and Cambridgeshire utilising excellent local clays were built towards the end of the century to serve virtually a national market. They gained substantial scale economies in both production and distribution. No longer able to compete on cost, this led to the demise of the 'London' brick after 1900.[78]

By mid-century, brick production could require quite significant investments of capital in equipment and stocks of semi-made and completed bricks on large brick-making sites. Firms set up to exploit the more extensive clay deposits to the west, acquiring the rights to extract clay from landowners for longer periods of time. The Stamford Brook Brickfield, for example, was in operation from 1876 to 1889 and supplied most of the bricks to the Bedford Park estate. The financial requirements of such enterprises were much greater than those of the early producers and they also tended to use more mechanised processes.[79]

13 Domestic, clerical and professional services

Introduction

This chapter considers three important service industries. Domestic service was a substantial employer of women especially, as was the associated laundry industry. Its peak share of metropolitan employment was reached by mid-century and the sector was declining in absolute terms by the end of the period. In contrast, administrative services were growing from mid-century and growth accelerated from then on, so that by 1911 employment in administration had reached around a tenth of total employment. This reflected contemporary growth in public services, education, finance and industry. New organisational practices emerged, ones which put more emphasis on efficient administration and the recording and monitoring of transactions. New technologies, such as the typewriter and paper copying, encouraged these trends by making them both cheaper to implement and more effective in their outcomes. The professions also grew through the period, although with varying histories. It would be tedious to cover the whole range of professional activities, so two only are considered here: lawyers and accountants.

Domestic service

No middle-class household in the nineteenth century was complete without a servant. As London was the centre of the aristocratic Season and had a disproportionate share of Britain's middle class, it is unsurprising that domestic service also formed a disproportionately large part of metropolitan employment. By mid-century there were around 200,000 domestic servants, representing around a quarter of the workforce, as compared to only 13 per cent in the country as a whole. Numbers then rose to 262,000 in 1871, but overall employment growth was even faster, so the share fell to 19 per cent of those employed and continued to decline for the rest of the period. In absolute terms, the number of servants remained stable in the 1880s and 1890s, after which it started to decline, falling by almost a fifth to 214,000 in 1911.[1] The end of the nineteenth century consequently marked the peak of service employment, and mid-century was when its significance in London employment was greatest – with an incredible 1 in 4 workers in domestic service. Change in the twentieth century was very rapid. During the First World War and its aftermath there was a major decline, and servants were virtually non-existent forty years later.

The majority of servants were to be found in West London and the suburbs, areas with a large proportion of middle-class residents. In the 1850s, Kensington and St James contained four times as many servants as Shoreditch, Bethnal Green and Bermondsey.[2] Most worked alone or in pairs. In 1897, for example, 27 per cent of servant-employing households had just one servant and another 35 per cent only two servants.[3]

Employers had particular perceptions about what made a good servant, while employees also had clear views of what was men's and women's work and who should go into service. Geography, gender and age all influenced the supply of labour for domestic service. Domestic service, therefore, was a fragmented labour market where the opinions and practices of employers and employees determined who was employed on what tasks. Such views and habits then helped to influence the nature of jobs and their conditions. To an extent, however, these prejudices merely corresponded to contemporary conditions of servant demand and supply, so it is difficult in practice to identify the real impact of such views on the functioning of this labour market. One clear example of prejudice, however, occurred in the negative attitudes of employers to older and married women, which forced many of them to seek alternative, less remunerative employment elsewhere.

Only around 20,000 out of 185,000 indoor servants in 1851 were men,[4] indicating that service was a predominantly female occupation. The most prestigious and well-paid service jobs were held by men, but male servants gradually declined in number.[5] The higher cost of employing men encouraged the decline. Fashion also no longer insisted on the presence of a man in fine livery to greet callers. As other new job opportunities were created in hotels and elsewhere, men grew more reluctant to enter service or would leave after a short period to move in to such activities.

Generally, London servants were slightly older than those in the rest of England and Wales, though female servants tended to be younger than their male counterparts. It was still a young person's job, with only a small proportion staying in the occupation past the age of 40.[6] The job was also a highly mobile one. Before they left service, most servants had worked for a large number of households. In 1899, more than a third of domestic servants in the capital had been employed by their employer for less than a year, and over half for less than two years – a pattern similar to that in the rest of the country.[7] Movement presumably minimised the monotony of the work and, as in so many modern occupations, enabled the aspiring servant to move up the career ladder.

London-born women were employed less as servants, so that only a quarter of female metropolitan servants were born there. 'Town girls' were reluctant to enter service, and employers were disinclined to appoint them, because they were believed to be more dishonest and insubordinate. Many country girls possessed the necessary skills for ordinary posts, often gaining experience locally before moving to the metropolis. By the 1870s, further specialised training could be obtained from London's twenty-two charity-funded domestic training schools. Work was found through personal recommendation, newspaper advertisements or employment agencies, such as the Metropolitan Association for Befriending Young Servants (1875), which in the 1880s placed 5,000 girls per year.[8]

Service was even seen as a beneficial experience for a new young migrant. Living-in provided protection from the dangers of urban life, and service was thought to improve the prospects of a good marriage. Girls learnt domestic skills, habits of punctuality and obedience, were often taught basic arithmetic and reading skills, and avoided the crude habits that were supposedly picked up in factories. Through their everyday activities, they came into close contact with shopkeepers and artisans, from whose ranks marriage partners could be found.

By the standards of nineteenth-century pay for women, servants did quite well. Demand for staff was high and supply tight, so servants were paid higher wages in comparison to both their provincial counterparts and similar occupations. In a 1906 survey, for example, female servants earned respectively 31 per cent and 39 per cent more than clothing machinists and laundresses.[9] They were also less likely to suffer unemployment or work-related illness than in other potential activities and, with little need or opportunity to spend their salaries, they could save, which again improved their marriage prospects.

Drawbacks to service were that the food and accommodation were often sub-standard, most servants were expected to work long hours, and those employed in single-servant households often experienced great loneliness. Perhaps worst was the loss of personal freedom resulting from being in service. Even the limited leisure time available had to be negotiated continually and taken under the watchful eye of the employer. The fact that dismissal meant the instant loss of a home and the reference essential for a new post made the position of many servants difficult – although the mobility figures considered above suggest that this effect should not be exaggerated. Yet the fact that women, when able, left the occupation in droves despite its apparently high financial compensation suggests that these personal constraints and psychic costs were strongly resented.

Women servants in their thirties could hope for a decent marriage or to return home to their family village; otherwise, once their savings were exhausted, they were forced into the poor jobs in the clothing industries or shop work. Marriage and childbirth patterns must have been affected by the sheer scale of the number of eligible women in London required to stay single and childless in order to keep their posts. It was all very well to argue that the respectable domestic could save and hope for marriage to a nice male shopkeeper or skilled worker, but most would have had to accept less. Poverty could soon beckon for those who married young for love.

The decline in the number of servants from the 1890s appears to have a number of explanations. On the supply side, urban migration reduced the pool of rural women from which London drew most of its servants. The various Education Acts took girls under 15 out of the labour market and gave them basic skills that expanded their occupational options. The growth of administration and of the leisure and retail industries created new female jobs, as well-paid but less physically demanding and more socially respectable than service. On the demand side, despite a rise in middle-class incomes, there was less need for domestic help. Families were becoming smaller and parents increasingly wished to take more personal care of their children. New suburban houses were similarly getting smaller and lacked servant accommodation. Labour-saving technologies, such as gas for heating, lighting and cooking, electric lighting, piped hot water, improvements in cleaning materials and polishes, and changes in the technology of shopping greatly reduced the amount of housework to be undertaken. Improvements in the postal service and then the advent of telephones also obviated the need for servants to run messages.

The fall in servant supply forced those who wished to obtain domestic help at relatively low cost to turn to charwomen. These lived out and were generally married or widowed. A small number of middle-class households additionally began to search further afield for new sources of labour. Lady helps, gentlewomen who had fallen on hard times, were recruited, as were servants from Scotland and abroad, particularly France, Germany and Switzerland.

The growth of laundry services

A further large employer of women was the laundry industry, which grew rapidly, particularly in the second half of the century. Until the end of the period, most laundry was done by hand – a labour-intensive process that absorbed many women in London's labour market. Expansion of this activity was not only spurred by population growth and rising real incomes, but fashion also played its part. Upper working- and middle-class aspirations to gentility required greater attention to appearance, for which freshly washed and perfectly pressed clothes were paramount. In addition, the growth of large public and private institutions, such as hospitals, hotels and restaurants, required the laundering of thousands of sheets, towels and napkins, plus various types of garment.

Because of the large number of wealthy inhabitants, institutions and lodging houses, and its highly polluted atmosphere, London contained proportionately more laundresses than anywhere else in the country. In 1851, there were 51,018 according to the census, and 67,506 according to the Women's Trade Union League. The census figure then fell to 39,100 in 1911.[10] Important factors were the substitution of silk and artificial silk for starched calico in women's underclothing, the arrival of the domestic washing machine and laundry mechanisation.

In 1901, almost three-quarters of all laundry establishments were hand laundries. These small workshops employed on average six workers in 1904, used little machinery, and were concentrated in West London.[11] There, they were close to the households of the rich and enjoyed the drying benefits of the prevailing, pollution-free, westerly winds. Many laundries grouped together on single streets. The setting up of one establishment generally caused the value of surrounding property to plummet, because of the pollution, heat and smell, so fellow laundries were quick to take advantage of the fall in property prices.

Apart from a small number that specialised in silks, most hand laundries washed only cotton, linen and some flannel items. By tradition, they collected, soaked and washed and mangled and starched in the first part of the week and then ironed, aired, folded and packed and delivered in the second half.

The hand laundry began to disappear in the 1890s, to be replaced by establishments using power-driven machinery, such as steam presses and washing and drying machines. By 1912, these new firms were rapidly displacing hand laundries, and accounted for almost half of the capital's laundry businesses. They generally avoided the domestic market and concentrated on washing from institutions. The combination of quality and cost was such that they received work from as far afield as Scotland and Paris. Even when mechanised, laundries were generally quite small in scale. In 1904, each had an average of only thirty-three employees. The western emphasis in their location continued after mechanisation, and they were concentrated in districts like Fulham, Hammersmith and Acton. Kensal New Town became popularly known as 'Soap Suds Island' and Notting Dale as 'Laundry Land'.

The women employed by power and hand laundries had distinctive characteristics, which suggests once more that institutional factors were creating a segmented labour market. Most were over the age of 30[12] – that is, getting too old for service – and in 1901 over half were married or widowed. Laundry work required little skill, and the seasonal peaks in demand coincided with troughs in the male employment cycle. Laundries could therefore take advantage of the need to sustain household incomes by employing the wives of temporally unemployed men. The early summer upturn in female recruitment, for example, matched the period of male lay-offs in the gas industry; while the winter peak paralleled the beginning of seasonal unemployment in the building trades.

The majority of workers were employed on a temporary basis, reflecting the seasonal nature of the demand for laundry services. Women might work for four or five days a week in the Season, yet only for a few hours during the slack months of August and September. Until the 1895 Factory Act, average hours were long and conditions poor. Wages inevitably were low.

Throughout the whole period, there were large numbers of washerwomen who took in other people's washing to do in their own homes. Their number is unknown but, with such ease of entry to this activity, the remuneration was poor, the hours long and the conditions hard.

Clerks

As the capital of the United Kingdom, the seat of government and the site of the Royal Court, London contained more administrative and professional workers than the rest of the country put together.

Clerks were the main workers in administration, although a growing band of overseers and managers existed alongside the expansion of clerical work. For much of the century, administration as an activity was relatively unimportant as an employer of labour. Government was limited and the typical business enterprise was small, employing only a few clerks plus some premium-paying clerical apprentices. As they needed to be literate, clerks generally came from artisan or lower middle-class backgrounds. They were relatively well paid, and, given the size of firms, had close relationships with their masters – often hoping to become employers themselves. Book-keepers-cum-cashiers dealt with financial records; whilst the ordinary clerk was responsible for correspondence, filing, elementary book-keeping and routine office matters.

Considerable changes occurred in the nature and content of clerical work from the 1880s. The size of organisations and range of functions they undertook enlarged substantially, and with these developments the amount of clerical work grew exponentially. Some large business enterprises appeared, especially in financial services – often with a headquarters in the capital and operations throughout the country, all of which had to be co-ordinated, facilitated, recorded and accessed via the actions of armies of clerks. Government also considerably expanded its functions at central and local levels, especially in the field of education. Administrative needs were further increased by the arrival of scientific management and a greater accounting of production costs and market revenues. Improved communications led to more dispersed activities and to less reliance on word-of-mouth and casual record-keeping. The telegraph, telephone and refined postal service also promoted the recording of new types of information. Mechanisation in the form of the typewriter, the calculating machine and other devices provided the means by which that could occur and, by substantially increasing the productivity of clerks and secretaries, encouraged their use over a wider range of administrative activities. Thus, the greater size of firms, scientific management and mechanisation all led to greater specialisation and division of work within organisations and within the small, specialist entities that were set up to feed into larger firms' needs. Central city locations were ideal for the spread of such networks and the source of large pools of clerks commuting in from the suburbs.

Data are only available for the later part of the period. The rapid growth in administration meant that, by 1891, London and the Home Counties contained almost 180,000 clerks – with the number doubling over the next twenty years (see Table 13.1). Only 15 per cent worked in the public sector in 1891, though the percentage rose to 19 per cent by 1911. Administrative workers were overwhelmingly men, but employment of women developed fast, so that they represented 25 and 20 per cent of clerical workers in the public and private sectors respectively by 1911.[13] A large number were young: 46 per cent of commercial clerks in 1911 in England and Wales were under the age of 25.[14] Those in the metropolis tended to commute, living in the northern and southern fringes of the County area and in the newer suburbs beyond. In 1901, in Stoke Newington and Lewisham, for example, clerks represented 13 per cent of occupied males, as compared to less than 3 per cent in Shoreditch and Bethnal Green.[15]

Wages and conditions of employment varied both within firms and between industries. Office boys earned little more than a pittance and were often employed on a short-term basis. In contrast, corresponding clerks were paid well and given numerous perks. The best employers were banks and insurance companies.[16] Their clerks additionally benefited from job security, job mobility, a high social status associated with such employment, regular promotions, and in some cases pensions and half days on Saturdays. The older private banks offered other valuable perks. At Hoares, for example, junior clerks lived in part of the family mansion and received free meals.

Jobs were rarely advertised and largely filled by personal recommendation, though occasionally by exam.[17] From the 1870s, candidates for all Civil Service and some local government appointments had to sit an examination. Public sector wages were lower than in banking and insurance, though all posts were pensionable and secure. The worst-paid sectors were

Table 13.1 Employment in administration in London and the Home Counties, 1891–1911

	Year	*Total*	*Women (%)*
Public sector	1891	26,900	17
	1901	41,900	24
	1911	68,400	25
Private sector	1891	152,000	7
	1901	218,100	13
	1911	292,000	20
Total	1891	178,900	8
	1901	260,000	15
	1911	360,400	21

Source: LSE, 1935, 72.

in manufacturing industry and transport, where in 1910 male clerks earned little more than an artisan.[18] Their pay fell by 10 per cent in the next four years, reflecting the growing competition for such work. Employment for these clerical workers was often insecure, job mobility limited because of the specialised nature of some of the tasks performed, and working conditions poor.

Declining pay

From the 1890s, clerical wages appear to have fallen, largely owing to an oversupply of potential clerks. Much administrative work could be performed by anyone with basic literacy, and educational reforms were raising general literacy standards. For the more skilled posts, the number of candidates grew as a result of the expansion of technical education. From the 1880s, private colleges began to provide training in shorthand, typing and book-keeping and, in the 1890s, many school boards took advantage of government grants and other funds to begin offering commercial courses in evening classes, technical schools and even secondary schools.

Other reasons for the worsening conditions include the continued employment, by many firms, of gentlemen, whose objective was to learn the ropes before entering a business themselves, and who were thus content to work for low wages. Clerks, furthermore, were proud of their status and so were reluctant to form trade unions or to demand higher wages, because such actions went against their conception of gentlemanly behaviour. English clerks also had to compete with well-educated foreign workers, particularly Germans, coming to Britain to gain commercial experience and again willing to accept low salaries. In 1887, a London Chamber of Commerce survey found that 35 per cent of leading City firms employed such overseas clerks.[19]

A further development depressing male wages was the inflow of women from the 1890s. By 1911, women accounted for over a fifth of the clerks in London and the Home Counties.[20] In the private sector, most were found in commercial companies; banks, insurance companies, legal practices and transport firms remained largely male bastions until the inter-war period. The vast majority of women performed tasks that were routinised or not deemed 'masculine', such as typing and the operation of telephone and telegraph exchanges. They worked in separate rooms from their male colleagues, and were generally required to leave employment on marriage, usually receiving a lump sum based on their length of service. Their wages were half to three-quarters of those of their male counterparts.[21]

Professions

The growth of middle-class professions in the nineteenth century has been well documented.[22] They were strongly over-represented in London because of its wealth and the range of activities taking place there. Professional bodies, moreover, had not really made it in public recognition and respectability until they had a London headquarters. The Royal Institute of British Architects, for example, after several moves eventually settled in Conduit Street (until the 1930s); while the Chartered Surveyors Institution and Institution of Civil Engineers opened grand buildings in Great George Street.

The functions of professional societies were several. The most publicly beneficial aspects concerned the introduction of rules of conduct and knowledge, so that clients could be better assured of the efficiency and probity of the professional they were hiring. Sanctions existed but they were weak and rarely used, with personal conduct and the opprobrium of colleagues regarded as more effective and gentlemanly. The Victorian equivalent of continuing education was provided through lectures and papers for members. Self-interest was also a driving force. Apart from the benefits of networking, a professional body, particularly if it could gain a royal charter, considerably raised the status of the work – architects were regarded as a dastardly lot, for example, before their Royal Institute was formed. Self-regulation contained the fear of state regulation and the professional institute could return the threat by lobbying politicians in their members' interests – a business at which some were extremely successful. Finally, professional rules limited the entry of new recruits. Such constraints on supply did wonders for earnings, though some occupations were far more successful at this restriction of trade than others.

Scientific and artistic associations blossomed as well as the more commercially oriented bodies. The Royal Society occupied rooms in Somerset

Table 13.2 Selected male professions in England and Wales, 1880–1911 (thousands)

	1880	*1891*	*1901*	*1911*	*% change 1880–1911*
Clergy	33.5	36.8	39.6	40.1	20
Barristers & solicitors	17.4	20.0	21.0	21.4	23
Physicians & surgeons	15.0	18.9	22.4	24.6	63
Dentists	3.5	4.6	5.1	7.4	108
Authors & journalists	5.6	7.4	9.8	12.0	113
Scientific	1.1	1.9	3.1	6.2	427
Architects	6.8	7.8	10.8	11.1	61
School masters & lecturers	44.0	49.1	57.8	68.7	55
Civil service officers and clerks	21.3	31.3	42.4	57.4	169
Local government (excl. police)	18.0	19.7	26.3	54.3	201
Total for 10 professions	166.7	197.6	238.6	303.1	81

Source: Perkin, 1989, 80.

House before moving to Burlington House; the Royal Academy of Arts followed a similar route with an intervening sojourn in the new National Gallery; the Royal Institute of Painters of Water Colours opened spacious galleries in Piccadilly; and the Royal College of Music set up in Marylebone Road. These and many others started or expanded during the period. They not only greatly enhanced the cultural life of the city and heightened the professional status of academics, artists and musicians, but also offered a wide range of employment opportunities for less esteemed Londoners as attendants, janitors, clerks and administrators.

Exact numbers of professionals active in London are hard to come by. National numbers were rising at a rapid rate, as the data for ten professions given in Table 13.2 show – and several of them would have had a strong London bias. Here, lawyers are examined in some depth, as one of the oldest of the London professions and one that was the largest consumer of inner city land in the Inns of Court and offices around Chancery Lane and elsewhere in Holborn. Accountancy – a new nineteenth-century activity – is also considered.

Lawyers

Solicitors and attorneys

The legal profession comprised solicitors, attorneys and barristers. Solicitors were originally Chancery officials and attorneys practised at common law but, by the start of the century, both performed similar functions. Later, in 1870, attorneys assumed the title of solicitor. Growth in the profession was substantial in the early part of the nineteenth century. One source suggests that, in 1775, the capital contained 1,087 attorneys and solicitors; and, by 1832, their numbers had virtually trebled, employing a further 3,000 clerks.[23] Another source comes to similar conclusions, reckoning that, in 1780, there were 1,236 attorneys in the metropolis and 2,430 elsewhere in the country.[24] These sources indicate that London contained a third or more of all those working in law in England and Wales. There was further growth throughout the century, roughly in line with population expansion. The 1851 census, for example, found 32,500 persons in law, though this included a large number of clerks and others.[25]

From the fifteenth to the eighteenth century, solicitors were based in the various Inns of Chancery, such as Clifford's Inn (1345), Staple's Inn (1415) and Barnard's Inn (1445). They were distinct from the Inns of Court which housed barristers and other court advocates. Such 'Inns' originated from the hostels used in the Middle Ages for lawyers and students, located within easy reach of the Court in Westminster. They were subsequently centres of legal education. By the end of the eighteenth century, however, they were of limited significance and had largely become dining clubs. Although most survived into the nineteenth century, one by one they disappeared to be taken over by other urban uses – for example,

Clement's Inn was sold in 1884 and demolished, and part of the London School of Economics now stands on the site; and New Inn was acquired in 1899 as part of the LCC's Kingsway scheme – Australia House now occupies its site.

The role of the Inns of Chancery was taken over by the Society of Gentlemen Practisers. This was formed in the early 1730s and had a membership of less than 200, despite London having an estimated 7,000 attorneys and solicitors during this period. In essence, it was little more than an informal club meeting in local taverns in the Fleet Street area.[26] In 1819, the Metropolitan Law Society was also founded to raise professional standards. The Law Institution was established in 1827, and it quickly became the leading body, receiving a Royal Charter in 1831, and became known as the Incorporated Law Society. It opened its own premises in Chancery Lane, with an extensive library, and began to establish itself throughout Britain, regulating and registering legal practices. Its social and educational functions hastened the demise of the Inns of Chancery. Yet many solicitors and attorneys remained outside the aegis of any professional body.

Entrants were largely middle-class and only had a secondary education. Even in the 1870s, no more than 5 per cent of solicitors possessed a university degree. After 1729, when the Act for the Better Regulation of Attorneys and Solicitors came into force, all had to serve a five-year apprenticeship with a qualified practitioner. Before the Law Society's introduction of a series of weekly lectures, they received no formal legal training. Examination was by a judge, but was generally perfunctory until 1836, when those who did not attend the Society's lectures had to undergo a more stringent test. From 1860, greater formality was introduced and all had to pass a preliminary, general knowledge exam. Later, in 1877, judges handed their examining role over to the Law Society.

Lawyers associated with the Ecclesiastical Courts were based around St Paul's, but disappeared by the mid-nineteenth century with the abolition of the remaining public functions of such courts.[27]

Some of the most important solicitors' practices had already been formed in the eighteenth century. London practices acted as agents for their provincial counterparts and, as the century progressed, they began to specialise in particular aspects of the law. Remuneration took the form of item fees and, from 1883, *ad valorem* charges. Earnings for the leaders of the profession were high, though for others incomes could be precarious. For example, those who specialised in real property and were not of particular reknown were subject to the vagaries of the building cycle and to attempts at reforming the tortuous process of conveyancing.[28] Finance and business could provide lucrative work. There were 2,026 firms of solicitors in the City in 1891, and company promotions and share issues, in particular, could be highly profitable for them.[29] At the top, Freshfields in 1820 earned £57,000 in fees from the Bank of England alone;[30] and Gregory Rowcliffe in the early nineteenth century made annual profits of

£6,000, rising in the 1830s to £11,000.[31] In the 1830s, times were good, so that even medium-sized firms had profits of £3,000 to £4,000 a year.[32]

Barristers

The division between solicitors and barristers was established in the 1790s by the Inns of Court. Like the Inns of Chancery, these had declined by the end of the eighteenth century – with the Bar containing between 290 and 300 practitioners in 1780. By 1911, there were over 4,000, most of whom worked in London. They reasserted themselves as part of the push for improvements in legal education and, in doing so, formalised the criteria for those who could represent clients in the higher courts (barristers only) and those who could not. Solicitors were also forbidden to become judges and enter high office. In reciprocation, by 1800, barristers were shut out from areas reserved for solicitors: conveyancing and direct dealings with clients. With these reforms, legal skills improved but the entry to the world of client representation in court became severely restricted and barristers' work more lucrative as a result. Unsurprisingly, the number of barristers grew throughout the nineteenth century.[33]

Recruits were largely upper-class, having achieved a basic secondary education – increasingly from one of the growing number of public schools. As with solicitors, they underwent a period of apprenticeship, or pupilage, with a qualified barrister to whom they paid a premium of £100 plus £10 a year. There was, at first, no formal training and no qualifying test, apart from the requirement that a certain number of meals should be eaten in the Inns of Court. Further reforms were introduced from the late 1840s, with lectureships set up in the Lower and Middle Temple and at Gray's Inn. In 1851, the Legal Education Council was established, which represented all four Inns and, in the following year, it initiated a system of voluntary qualifying exams, which were made compulsory in 1872. The supply of barristers was further limited by the tendency of many who qualified to quit the profession, preferring to go into business or obtain a public appointment. Those who did become barristers earned high incomes: in 1850, eight made £8,000 a year, twenty-four £5,000 and five £11,000. Queen's Councils earned, on average, between £1,500 and £3,000 a year, and junior barristers £500 to £1,200.[34]

With their need to have ready access to the courts, the Inns remained tied to Holborn and expanded in scope, so that the unique legal quarter of London grew substantially in size. Symbiotically, when the decision was made about the location of the new 1870s Law Courts, dealing with non-criminal cases, a site near to the Inns at the eastern end of the Strand, rather than traditional Westminster, was chosen. The Old Bailey, rebuilt in 1910, remained just to the east, expanding on to the site of the demolished Newgate Prison. The Law had come to the lawyers.

Accountancy

The City's various activities spawned numerous ancillary services. The most important was accountancy. At the start of the century, accountancy was usually practised as a sideline to some more lucrative occupation, such as auctioning, rent collecting or stockbroking. The profession only emerged in its own right in the 1830s, after the 1831 Bankruptcy Act, which required qualified officials to liquidate assets on the behalf of creditors. Further legal developments strengthened accountants' roles. The 1862 Companies Act established the role of official receiver; the 1861 Bankruptcy Act introduced the concept of voluntary bankruptcy; and another related Act eight years later enabled accountants to be appointed as trustees of debtors' estates. Through these measures, insolvency work greatly increased, and to undertake it relatively large accountancy firms developed.

Once established, many of these partnerships began to provide investment advice to individuals, became involved in the financial restructuring of businesses and undertook company audits. At first, audit business came only from railway companies and private banks but, after audits were made compulsory, all limited liability firms needed accounting services. Insolvency, none the less, remained the main source of income for much of the second half of the century, although it was cyclical in nature as more firms failed during slumps. Whinney, Smith & Whinney, for example, gained 94 per cent of its fees from this source in 1870 and 46 per cent in 1890. Audits then grew in importance in the 1900s: 53 per cent of Whinney's income in 1900 and 35 per cent in 1910.[35] Margins were high because office and staff costs were low. In Price, Holyland and Waterhouse, for example, profits were 81 per cent of fees in 1870 and 69 per cent in 1885, so that senior partners earned substantial incomes.[36]

Professionalisation did not occur for many years. In order to reduce the threat of misconduct and poor standards, which could damage the whole profession, the main London firms in 1870 finally formed the Institute of Accountants. In 1871 it had only thirty-eight members but, by 1880, it had merged with various provincial societies to form the Institute of Chartered Accountants. This association, in turn, encouraged the setting up, in 1885, of the Society of Accountants and Auditors, for those who lacked the desire, resources or ability to become a member of the Institute. A few years later, in 1891, the Corporation of Accountants came on the scene; and, in 1905, the London Association of Accountants, which accepted members without examination. All the various institutions and societies set up headquarters in the capital.[37]

By 1880, London contained 500 accountancy practices and 50 auditors, many of which had been attracted from the provinces.[38] Growth continued in the following decades – the City had 701 practices in 1891. Insolvency business was especially profitable, with Whinney, Smith & Whinney earning over £43,000 during the course of winding up Overend, Gurney & Co. in the twenty-six years after its failure in 1866.[39]

In the 1900s, London practices were expanding into the provinces and overseas. Waterhouse, for example, established branch offices in Liverpool in 1904 and Newcastle in 1912; undertook work in Australia from the 1880s; opened a New York office in 1890; and entered into further partnership or agency agreements with firms in Australia in 1896, Egypt in 1907, and Buenos Aires in 1912. The company's overseas work contributed 18 per cent of its total fees in 1914.[40] This internationalisation, however, related specifically to the needs of British clients throughout the world and was influenced by the enormous export of capital from the UK, rather than being a case of London firms setting up from scratch in new markets. Touche set up offices in Argentina, Canada and the USA in the 1900s, for example, because these were the areas where the investment trusts he managed were investing.[41] At the same time, for similar reasons, overseas firms set up branches in the City, the contemporary centre of world finance: an example was the New York company Marwick Mitchell and Co., which arrived there in 1911.

Financial agents

Accountants and lawyers were part of the institutional network of financial services, and they often took on a more active role than the reactive one of dealing with company accounts, liquidations and legal matters. Attorneys as stewards of estates and trustees for wills could easily put lenders and borrowers together and charge a fee for doing so. They were particularly important in funding industry in the eighteenth century, and were, for example, predominant over banks in finance in Yorkshire until the second quarter of the nineteenth century.[42] Their roles in mortgage markets were even more significant, given the information advantages they had from undertaking conveyancing work. Accountants took part in company promotions, offered investment advice to clients, managed investment trusts and formed key components of personal networks in finance. By doing this, both professions helped to forge national and international capital markets centred on London.

Cottrell has examined in detail the activities of David Chadwick, and his accounting firm, Chadwicks, Adamson and Collier.[43] This Manchester-based practice undertook most of the important iron, coal and steel promotions of the 1860s and 1870s – channelling savings from the North-West into the shares of companies converting from personal to equity ownership. Chadwick became the Manchester agent for the London-based Globe Insurance Company in the 1850s, which brought him into contact with clients in the North-West with savings seeking investment outlets. In 1860 he started to practise as an accountant, which reinforced his connections in Manchester and the cotton towns, and in the following year a London office was opened to complement the Manchester one. This brought him into contact with City circles and he had a series of partners with City links at his London office into the 1890s, and was involved in the establishment of at least forty-seven limited companies between 1862 and 1874. The wheels of British finance, consequently, had complex and varied institutional structures, most of which involved the City but, as in the case of Chadwick, not all of them emanated from there. And it is to the City that the next chapter goes.

14 Financial services and the City

Introduction

The growth of London as the centre of British and international finance is one of the better-known aspects of the nineteenth-century London economy. Expansion from relatively modest beginnings took place across a wide variety of financial activities – government finance, the stock exchange, national banking, merchant (or investment) banking, insurance, international finance and commercial trade. All of these sectors underwent rapid growth, particularly after 1860, caused by expanding opportunities offered by the world market and the possibility of moving into new areas of business. Each financial sector increasingly became more specialised and international, incorporating many foreign-based rivals.

The role of the financial sector is that of intermediation in money and capital markets. There are many such roles: creating safe and secure means through which transactions can be conducted; operating markets where the prices of financial instruments are uniform and known; covering temporary shortfalls in government, business and personal cash-flows by short-term lending; bringing together those that have capital to lend and those that need to borrow it; and providing a variety of other services, such as insurance and foreign currency exchange. The direct success of a financial sector depends on the returns made from these intermediation roles, rather than simply on the scale of funds that pass through them. The wider economic and social implications of financial services, furthermore, relate to the efficiency of these activities and whether they channel funds to the most economically and socially desirable ends.

Financial intermediation problems in early nineteenth-century Britain were substantial, because of the localised and frequently rudimentary nature of contemporary financial institutions. The seasons and periodic trade cycles would leave either agricultural or industrial districts with surfeits or deficits of funds, which later helped to stimulate national banking activity, centred on the City. Owners of capital, particularly when small-scale, were forced to rely on trusted advisors, such as a local solicitor, who might have only limited expertise in finding the best or safest returns. Borrowers similarly had to rely on local and personal contacts. Financial panics and bank runs were commonplace. Mechanisms were slowly put in place during the nineteenth century that limited the appearance of panics and reduced the scale of their impact, although without entirely eradicating them. An increasing concentration of financial services in London created a sophisticated national market that overcame some of these intermediation problems and helped to increase the stability of Britain's financial system.

The City directly depended for its existence on the expansion of the national economy, the important role of nineteenth-century Britain and its currency in the world economy, and the vast export of capital to other industrialising nations during the fifty years or so before 1914. Its impact on London's economic life itself is less clear. For, although the City of London became closely associated with these financial activities and 'the City' became a phrase synonymous with British finance, many other activities apart from finance took place in the City.[1]

The scale of employment in financial activities was also modest in terms of total employment in the capital – the typical City firm before 1914 employed fewer than ten staff,[2] but the wealth channelled through, and generated in, the City was substantial. The impact of this wealth on the London economy, none the less, should also not be exaggerated. The gains were for the few rather than the many and the few often lived in country mansions rather than town houses. Most financial employment was in clerical work, which provided for a modest lifestyle only.

Geography is an important element in understanding the role of metropolitan financial services. The types of financial activities taking place by 1914 in the City clearly conform to the predictions of central place theory, which would suggest that they exist in the city at the top of the urban hierarchy because of the need for a large national market to sustain them. Agglomeration economies were similarly important. The means by which information could be transmitted were limited, though they improved throughout the century, and financial activity thrives on being first with 'news'. Growing economies of scale and an expanding market led to specialisation and greater activity at the national and international scales. All of these factors and more led to close clustering of activities in the City and, also, of particular financial services within it as they grouped around the physical market places that they served, such as the Stock Exchange or the Baltic Exchange. London, furthermore, had well-established personal and institutional networks of a scale unrivalled elsewhere in the world and, with them, a stock of 'expertise'; it also had excellent pools of ancillary services, from printers to lawyers; and the largest mass of clerical workers and other financial specialists.

The City, thus, conformed to the notion of an industrial district as set out in Chapter 2 (or, in fact, a set of overlapping industrial districts for different types of financial activity). There is no need consequently for peculiar British cultural or social class factors to explain its existence or to understand why it drew most national financial activity into its net.

The City's locational attractiveness increased over the century as developments in transportation and communications lowered the friction of distance, reducing national regional barriers and opening up the world as a whole to its remit. Furthermore, over the course of the century the British and world economies grew and changed significantly, bringing with them new financial needs which the financial services industries responded to in a variety of ways. Some effects were cumulative. Greater scale, for example, created progressively more liquid markets as the number of buyers and sellers expanded. The agglomeration benefits of an available pool of skilled labour were similarly multiplied. Once the City achieved its national ascendance over British financial services, these cumulative effects multiplied and no other location in Britain could compete.

This did not mean, however, that London was the sole source of financial service activity in Britain: the national concentration in the capital was less than for a number of other industries. In the early years of the century, the barriers of distance meant that many financial markets were local or regional in nature (although interest rates etc. were still influenced to varying degrees by national factors). As the British economy developed, these markets became more nationally oriented and focused on London; yet, at the same time, there was a deepening of financial needs, with many services having to be located near to their clients. A good example is the development of banks into national networks: each with a headquarters and several functions in London but a wide national network of branches and, hence, employment. Metropolitan financial services were similarly split between serving the needs of the local population and higher-order activities. The geographic development of financial services in Britain during the nineteenth century, therefore, should not be seen solely in terms of a growing concentration of activity in the City; although when concentrating on it, as this chapter does, the overwhelming impression is of its importance in British finance.

Many of the agglomeration economies existing in the City took particular social and institutional forms. 'Institutional' here describes the network of formal and informal rules and practices linking a set of organisations and agents together. They prescribe particular rules of behaviour, strategies and ways of doing business.[3] One outcome in the context of the City, for example, was that transactions costs were reduced considerably through the operation of degrees of trust and some procedures for redress when they failed. Analysis of the growth of finance within the context of the subject matter of this book, therefore, has to look at the development and operation of the institutions and organisations active in the various markets that made up financial services in the City. This is done below by, first, examining the growth of banking and discounting, the capital markets and insurance. The extensive commercial trade of the City forms the subject of the penultimate section concerned with other activities taking place in the Square Mile. A final section describes how its physical structure was transformed and redeveloped.

Banking, discounting and the money market

The growth of a national system

Prior to the industrial revolution, English banks were overwhelmingly based in London. Many had emerged from goldsmith origins from the seventeenth century onwards, but other new private banks had been set up in the eighteenth century. By 1800, there were seventy in London – divided into a 'West End' group, which concentrated on dealing with the gentry, the aristocracy and lawyers, and a 'City' group, which concentrated on commercial paper and providing services for stockbrokers and country banks.[4] Outside London, country banks had grown up to finance the needs of the industrialising regions from the 1750s onwards, and had been set up by attorneys, merchants and others to serve local areas. By 1800, there were 370 of them, reaching a peak of 1,100 in 1838.[5] Private note issue was unregulated, so many different bank's notes circulated freely, which helped to overcome chronic shortages of means of payment. By 1833, there were 430 private banks issuing their own notes.[6] The exception was London, where the Bank of England (the 'Bank') had a monopoly of note issue within a 65-mile radius of the City, and the Bank's notes did not circulate much beyond the metropolis before the 1830s.[7]

English banking, thus, was essentially local and London by no means played the leading role. Local banks had key informational advantages, at a time when it might take days to contact the capital from the more remote areas. Yet, if local bank pricing was too much out of line with national trends, arbitrage opportunities would have opened up for financial intermediaries from outside the locality. So a local basis to banking did not negate the existence of a national market. As the barriers of distance were reduced over time, moreover, such localised benefits were diminished so that wider spatial presences by banks became more feasible.

Centralising tendencies can be seen clearly in nineteenth-century English banking, especially after the widespread adoption of the telegraph. By the First World War, most of the country's major banks had headquarters in the City and the Bank was the prime currency issuer. Improvements in communications, however, cannot be the sole explanation of the changing geography because, as will be shown below, state regulation and institutional structures played an important part in the evolution of the banking system.

Regulatory barriers to lending remained from previous centuries. Lending to the private sector, unlike government borrowing, was still subject to the usury laws, which limited the interest rate to a 5 per cent maximum. There were ways around the restrictions but their existence discouraged commercial lending. Changes were introduced in 1833 and 1837 as a result of financial developments, but controls on debt over three months' maturity were not finally abolished until 1854. The usury constraints had effects on the contemporary structure of financial markets.

The relaxations in the 1830s, for example, arose because of the impediments that were imposed on institutional changes in the discount market. Other constraints on institutional practices had arisen with the 1720 Bubble Act, which had been introduced after the fiasco of the South Sea Bubble with the implicit aim of limiting the circulation of company shares, as a draconian measure to avoid further bubbles. One result was that joint stock company status was hard to achieve and so most British firms were organised on an individual owner or few partners basis, with unlimited liability. Partnerships remained the main form of firm organisation until the last quarter of the nineteenth century – long after the Bubble Act had been repealed in 1825. This type of firm structure had important implications for the stock market because it meant that only small parts of British industry had shares that were issued or transacted – a situation that persisted through the nineteenth century.[8]

The small, localised nature of banking in the 1800s was encouraged by further legislative constraint. Until 1826, all note-issuing banks were forbidden to have more than six partners and note issue was a profitable opportunity that few bankers would voluntarily forgo. The only exceptions to this rule were the Bank of England and two Scottish banks, both of which were permitted joint stock status. The Bank of England, in addition to its own select list of clients, acted as the government's banker and had the only gold reserve in the country. These last two roles gave it influence over government monetary policy.

In order to meet exceptional demands for funds during financial crises, private banks maintained a reserve of 'call' money, part of which was kept in cash and the remainder was invested on a short-term basis. They sent the funds to the City where their agents used them to buy bills of exchange (known as 'bills' for short). Bills were financial instruments that had developed to finance international trade in the seventeenth and eighteenth centuries and were commonplace in Britain during the eighteenth century. They were drawn on a bank by the purchaser of goods and given to the seller prior to delivery, who then took the bill to the bank, or its corresponding one, for acceptance that the bill would be paid at a specified date. The bill could then be used as a means of exchange until it expired, because bills under English law were negotiable, with payment made to the bearer, which meant that they could easily be exchanged between parties. A discount on the face value of the bill provided the means of profit for the financial intermediaries involved.

The advantages of bills were that they overcame currency exchange problems in national and international trade; provided trade credit so that a firm's receipts and expenses could be smoothed out; and offered an investment outlet for those, like banks, that wished to lend short-term funds. As successive governments failed to increase the money supply in line with economic expansion, for much of the second half of the eighteenth century and into the nineteenth, bills formed the bulk of the English money supply and were the dominant medium of exchange. Small bills, in particular, circulated as money in face of a lack of small denomination notes and coin. With the growth of bills of exchange, the influence of London was felt throughout the national market because of its central-place role in discounting them. The credit needs of the Lancashire cotton industry, for example, were primarily met via bills discounted in London.[9]

But why were these inter-relationships linked via London, rather than some other place in Britain? The historical scale of finance in the capital was one factor. Other influences were the port and associated historic links with other European and American finance centres, such as Amsterdam and Baltimore, over trade in foreign bills of exchange and international loans. Napoleon's conquests in continental Europe and the British blockade led to the demise of centres like Amsterdam, and more business moved to London, increasing further its scale advantages. Last but not least, the Bank of England was located in the capital and had the country's only stock of gold. Private banks needed to go to the Bank for help from time to time to make up imbalances in their receipts and out-goings. With only rudimentary regulation and monitoring, personal contact and a bank's reputation were important in persuading the Bank to lend in such circumstances. So, for these reasons and more, the banking system was inevitably centred on London.

The regionally fragmented nature of the banking system gave further encouragement to the use of City facilities. The small country banks could not balance a surplus of demands for funds in one locality with deficits in others through internal transfers between branches, as can banks with nation-wide branch networks. This gave London banks a key intermediation role in the country's banking system. Glyns, a 'City' private bank, for example, had sixty country bank relationships in 1849 and, earlier in 1802, the twelve leading London banks in the field all together corresponded with 205 provincial banks.[10] Banks with surplus funds would send the money to London for purchase of bills of exchange; while banks with a greater demand for loans than available funds would send bills to London for rediscount. In these ways, London acted as a conduit for the reallocation of funds between deficit and surplus areas. There thus developed a 'correspondence' relationship between country banks and the metropolitan financial system: business between them included the transfer of bills and bank notes, the purchase of government securities or dividend payments for customers, and the financing of local trade via inter-bank transfers. In addition, London agents acted as important conduits of information on investment opportunities and market titbits for the country banks. In this way, an early integration of the national banking system was achieved. As the country banks were generally weak and undercapitalised, however, a crisis occurring in one region would rapidly affect the London bill market and could cause a national financial crisis.[11]

As well as the correspondence system, businesses in London themselves needed bills discounted, as the capital was the major commercial centre in the country. Spatial specialisation of London-related banking business occurred within the City and its environs and it was influenced by the location of commercial markets. Smithfield bankers, for instance, were unsurprisingly heavily involved in the droving trade, and banks in Southwark concentrated on hops, which were bought and sold in the area. Such proximity was presumably necessary in order to have the most up-to-date market information and to be able to meet clients in the general course of their business.[12]

The emergence of discount houses

During the Napoleonic Wars, two new financial specialists emerged in London: first, merchant banks that discounted and issued foreign bills of exchange and underwrote government debt;[13] and, second, specialist bill brokers that began to intermediate between the buyers and sellers of bills.[14] Further developments followed a severe financial crisis in 1825; one of which was the gradual emergence of discount houses.[15] Discount houses played a key role in binding the English money market together and in determining the role of the City within it, so it is worth considering the implications of their evolution.

When pressed for cash, the London private banks had previously relied on the Bank of England to buy – that is, rediscount – the bills in their possession. The Bank was thus their lender of last resort, helping them to avoid failure at times when they could not sell enough bills to meet the demands for cash put on them. During the 1825 crash, the Bank had to stop doing this because it ran out of funds. Recognising the finite resources of the Bank, prudence encouraged the banks from then on to increase their own reserves. Most of these new reserves were then lent on call to City bill brokers. The interest rate paid by brokers for this call money was half a per cent or so below bank rate in normal times, and the lowest-risk bills were used as security – so that in normal times the business was both profitable and low-risk.

Bill brokers previously had only been intermediaries between sellers and buyers, but they had then turned into dealers by using these call loans from banks to buy bills on their own account: profiting from the difference between the cost of their borrowings and the returns on bills. By doing so, they created a deeper and more liquid market for bills and thereby improved the earlier role of London in smoothing out surpluses and deficits in the English banking system. The strength of the new system was reinforced when the Bank of England agreed from 1830 to discount bills for a select number of bill dealers – thus, acting as their lender of last resort. The last resort role would be required most in financial panics when bill dealers would have difficulty selling bills and be pressed for call money to be repaid. Such bill dealers had created embryonic discount houses. As these discount houses were principally obtaining their funds by borrowing the reserves of private banks, this meant that the Bank was effectively reaffirming its previously uncertain role as lender of last resort for the whole British financial system, and the modern (pre-1980s 'Big Bang') London money market was beginning to form. Four leading firms, including Sanderson & Co. and Overend Gurney & Co., were given the privilege of a Bank discounting facility in the 1830s.[16]

Discount houses were now increasingly important in the financial system, but periodic financial crises brought some of them perilously close to grief and several folded. One difficulty was the ambiguous relationship between the Bank and the money market because the Bank was caught in a dilemma. On the one hand, its privileges rested on its special role in the British financial system and, on the other hand, it was a private bank and as such in competition with the discount houses for bill business. It competed particularly vigorously for bills between 1844 and 1847, but a financial crisis occurred in 1847. The resultant calls on its funds made it clear that the policy of competing in the bill market had made that market more risky. This led to a new policy of holding the Bank's discount rate generally above the market rate and varying it in line with prevailing interest rates and market conditions.[17] Faced with the penalty of a higher interest rate, the discount houses would only come to the Bank for assistance at times of real need. In this way, variable Bank Rate was born and greater control exerted over the money market.

Yet there was still a notable weakness in the discount market, because individual discount houses could disadvantage competitors by taking extra risks in the knowledge that if things went wrong, with a lender of last resort facility at the Bank, they would be bailed out. And there was little in the system as it existed to contain the moral hazard of discount houses taking unreasonable risks. The potential fragility of the discount houses came to a head within the space of a decade.

During the financial panic of 1857, caused primarily by bank failures in America, the discount houses were again in trouble. Sanderson failed and Overend Gurney had to be lent £700,000.[18] After this threatening experience, the Bank changed its lending policy and refused to offer further facilities to discount houses and brokers. This move again brought uncertainty to the Bank's implicit role as lender of last resort to the financial system and subsequent events were to force the Bank to reverse its decision, because the unilateral loss of Bank support, rather than limiting the risk-taking of the discount houses, turned out instead to increase it.

The reaction of the discount houses to the Bank's new policy was influenced by changes in their ownership and financial structures. Restrictions on the formation of joint stock companies were relaxed between 1855 and 1862, and several discount houses took advantage of these developments to adopt limited liability status. The National Discount Co. and London Discount Company were founded in 1856 and their success in weathering the 1857 crisis, combined with the Bank's reaction to that crisis, encouraged others to take up joint stock status. Financially, discount houses after the withdrawal of the Bank's credit line faced the need to raise and hold higher reserves, which, in turn, reduced the profitability of the bill business.

At a personal level, partners had operated with unlimited liability and they now had no lender of last resort and so they faced far greater personal financial risks at times of general market panic. Going public would ameliorate these difficulties, though not all took that route quickly – Alexanders, for example, delaying it until 1891.[19] But, in the absence of clear financial accounts and explicit or implicit regulatory constraints, the costs of the moral hazard of excessive discount house risk-taking were merely extended from the Bank as lender of last resort (even if at the time it did not want to be) to shareholders as potentially gullible investors in the new joint stock discount houses.

The weakest link by the 1860s was the firm of Overend Gurney & Co. It successfully floated as a joint stock enterprise in 1865, having previously failed to merge with the National Discount Co., but it did not tell investors about the huge losses it was making in non-discount activities. The firm had in recent years diversified away from the now less profitable discount business into reckless lending of substantial funds on a partnership basis in shipbuilding, ship-owning, grain, iron, railways and other unlikely ventures. Although rumours were circulating long before its final collapse, intervention was impossible because of the absence of a regulatory structure. When financial uncertainty struck in 1866, the Bank refused to lend it money and the firm went under, causing an enormous financial panic that then forced the Bank to lend £4 million to other discount houses, banks and merchants. The ambiguity in the Bank's behaviour, therefore, was brought starkly into the open in this crisis and subsequent debate. The collapse of Overend Gurney had forced the Bank of England to play its hand as lender of last resort and it was subsequently always expected to do so when required, though the discount houses were also expected not to take such risks again.[20]

This episode in the history of the London money market illustrates that changes in the institutional structure of City finance had important consequences for the stability of the financial system of the country as a whole. Far greater stability was subsequently achieved because of significant organisational changes in the geography of British banking, which diminished the previously pivotal role of the discount houses. This occurred through the growth of national branch banks centred on London, and was primarily induced by technological advances. But, before turning to this, the subsequent history of the money market to 1914 can be briefly summarised.

The stock of bills of exchange declined from the mid-1870s to the mid-1890s,[21] reflecting changes in financial intermediation and trade. New large national banks could deal with surpluses and deficits within their own branch networks by offering overdrafts rather than by recourse to bills. In addition, the volume of credit needed in trade was falling as transportation and other developments reduced the need for stocks and working capital to finance it. All banks, however, continued to lend some of their funds on call or short notice – 14 per cent in 1914, most of it lent on the London money market.[22]

As domestic bills business declined in relative importance, the demand for bill facilities from abroad grew dramatically, through the functioning of the gold standard and as overseas countries industrialised or joined the world economy as primary producers. Much late nineteenth-century international trade was funded on bills drawn on London, so that by 1913–14 two-thirds of outstanding commercial bills were foreign.

Bill brokers and discount houses remained at the centre of the money market after the 1880s, but had to share the greatly expanded foreign business with merchant banks, whose ranks had been increased by the expansion of this line of activity. Merchants banks had good overseas contacts, which gave them an edge. Foreign enterprises, like Morgan from the USA, set up or expanded London-based merchant banks, bringing their networks of overseas contacts with them.[23] By 1913, merchant banks were undertaking 40 per cent of London's trade finance business.[24]

Joint stock banks

The 1825 crisis was blamed on undercapitalised country banks – eighty English ones had failed[25] – so legislation was passed ending the Bank of England's monopoly of joint stock banking south of the border. Joint stock banks were permitted outside of the Bank of England's 65-mile sphere of influence and, later, in 1832 the Parliamentary Committee charged with examining renewal of the Bank's own charter imposed the condition that non-note-issuing joint stock banks could set up in London itself – made law in the 1833 Bank Charter Act.[26] The result of these legislative measures was a rapid growth of joint stock banks and a decline in the importance of private ones. By 1844, joint stock banks numbered 107 nationally, compared to 286 private banks.[27] Six operated in London in 1841, including the London and Westminster (1834) and the London and County (1839).[28] The London ones were set up to cater to the metropolitan middle class and were successful, but most early joint stock banks in the provinces were little different from their private banking predecessors – small, local and undercapitalised – and they utilised the traditional correspondence system with London. Only the National Provincial Bank of England quickly achieved a wide coverage through England and Wales, while the rest were regional or local and remained so until the 1870s. Expansion of joint stock banks' deposits was substantial, none the less, nationally averaging almost 6 per cent a year between the late 1840s and the 1870s.[29] The London-based ones increased their deposits from around £9 million to £43 million in the decade after 1847, despite being excluded from the Clearing House by the private banks until 1854.[30] But the overall banking system, particularly in industrial areas, remained weak.

The Bank Charter and the Joint Stock Banks Acts of 1844 aimed to strengthen the banking system, but their impacts slowed down the decline of private banks and the expansion of joint stock ones. No new banks were allowed to issue notes and it was expected that this would eventually leave the Bank as the only note issuer, as older banks amalgamated or switched to joint stock status. But the loss of the profits on note issuance discouraged banks from changing their status. At the same time, stringent new rules were imposed on the setting up of new banks. The combined result was that only one new joint stock bank opened between 1846 and 1860 and few private banks merged with joint stock ones.[31] The Bank was empowered to issue £14 million of notes plus any amount backed by bullion, whose volume at the Bank depended on foreign exchanges. The Bank could no longer issue money as and when it wished, and thus lost its flexibility over extending credit at times of trouble. In the panics of 1847, 1857 and 1866, the Act had to be waived to allow the Bank to act as lender of last resort. After 1866, however, the Act was never suspended again before 1914 – indicating the degree to which the banking system had finally stabilised in the last third of the nineteenth century.

The growth of joint stock banks eventually transformed British banking. Deposit banking led to the introduction of the overdraft and the provision of cheque accounts. Cheque writing was facilitated by an 1853 reduction in the stamp duty charged on cheque writing and by the admittance of the London joint stock banks to the London Clearing House. The lull in joint stock bank formation ended in the 1860s, especially after the Companies Act of 1862 which repealed the remaining constraints on joint stock banking from the 1844 Act and, amongst other things, granted limited liability to insurance companies.[32] This legislative change encouraged private banks to switch status through conversion or merger. The pull of London also increased, with the National Provincial Bank, for example, deciding in 1866 to forgo its £0.5 million provincial note issue in order to get a London office.[33] The significance of the London money markets and better means of communication gradually encouraged other banks to set up London offices or headquarters, while serving other regions or the country as a whole through an extensive branch network.

From the late 1880s, joint stock banks began to acquire each other at an accelerated rate. London firms moved into the provinces and provincial firms took over London banks to obtain a City foothold. Then the newly merged banks would open branches in regions where they were underrepresented. (The Midland is a well-studied case.) In many ways, the banks were acting in a similar fashion to the new multiples in retailing. In banking, a national presence offered economies of scale and scope, a clear brand image, and a 'balanced' regional network of branches. Locationally, a London headquarters placed these banks at the centre of the nation's money and capital markets, at the gateway to international activity, and gave them the image of competence, respectability and security.

Many private and smaller joint stock banks disappeared in these takeovers. For instance, there were thirteen City private banks in the London Clearing House in 1870, yet only five in 1891.[34] As a result of the merger movement, by 1911, London-based banking groups controlled 56 per cent of UK branches and 65 per cent of deposits, as compared to only 18 per cent and 36 per cent respectively in 1871.[35] The era of regional banking was over and London-based organisations now predominated – in 1895, the value of provincial clearings was only 5 per cent of that of London. Subsequent bank growth was spectacular with London clearings rising from £6.3 billion in 1894 to £16.4 billion in 1913.[36] This geographic structure of banking then lasted for much of the twentieth century, with London gradually increasing its centralising position.

Banking also extended its international role. The position of merchant banks in the foreign bill market has already been mentioned, and the UK clearing banks competed by developing their own overseas links. The City became home to a number of British-owned overseas banks – forty in 1900, with an international network of over a thousand branches – and the offshoots of foreign banks – approximately twenty-eight in 1913.[37]

The impact of distance on nineteenth-century financial markets

In 1820, a stagecoach journey from London to Liverpool would have taken around thirty hours. Using the fastest means of transport, therefore, a correspondence to Liverpool initiated by some London banker or broker to enquire about some matter of finance of concern to them would have generally taken a week or more for the round journey, and there was always the risk of delays. There was also no guarantee that the questions would have been satisfactorily answered or that the response would not stimulate the need for further information. The ease with which a telephone conversation, or other means of communication, can deal with such matters today can make it hard to understand how difficult and unreliable was the transfer of information across distances in the early nineteenth century.

London financiers, therefore, were at an informational disadvantage with regard to much of their own national market, even though they would have been generally better informed about national and international events than many of their provincial counterparts. Trusted agents could be used in distant towns but there were limits to such relationships, which were much better at dealing with routinised events than at dealing with rapidly changing situations or in grabbing unexpected opportunities that could make or break fortunes. Accounting systems and rules of disclosure were also rudimentary, so that publicly available information was poor. These information constraints reinforced the need to have someone with their ear to the ground, searching out vital information, and this reinforced the barrier of distance. The correspondence system enabled extensive, but usually routine, financial exchanges to occur and this enabled much integration of the national market, but distance barriers still made it impossible for individual organisations to gain a competitive advantage through having a national presence.

By the early years of the nineteenth century, consequently, there existed regionally distinct financial markets linked via the contemporary transport and communications systems. Price differences between these markets would exist that could not be instantaneously overcome because of communication barriers and, even where information was available, transaction costs could make arbitrage unprofitable. Such barriers, however, have limits and are more easily surmountable in the long run. By the end of the eighteenth century, there is evidence that regional markets were reacting to London interest rates.[38] An integrated national capital market seems to have emerged by then, albeit with important local differences in terms of the organisational structure of financial services. The huge financial demands by the state during the Napoleonic Wars and the increasing use of domestic bills of exchange further helped to integrate the financial system.

The problems of distance were compounded with overseas transactions. London had long been bound up with the financial aspects of international trade and in advancing large foreign loans, particularly to governments. The Atlantic crossing is a good illustration of the slow communications prevalent in the early part of the century. A ship from Liverpool to New York in the years 1791 to 1815 on average took 21–28 days eastbound and, against the prevailing winds, the westbound trip lasted 35–84 days. These times gradually fell, and the advent of steamships, which overcame the westbound disadvantage of sail, cut the trip down to eight days eastbound and nine west.[39] Along with greater speed came lower cost, greater reliability and security, and an improved availability of insurance so that insurance rates tumbled. The freight rate on a shipment of specie, for example, fell from 0.5 per cent of value on a voyage from New York to London in 1827–8, to 0.16 per cent in 1896–1900; while the associated insurance rate dropped from 0.63 to 0.13 per cent.[40]

The impact of the communications revolution from the 1860s was, unsurprisingly, dramatic as it allowed information to be passed nearly instantaneously between distant markets, altering the organisation and geography of financial services. London was connected to all the major British cities by telegraph in the late 1860s, though technical difficulties at first limited its usefulness. Communications were then further improved by the arrival of the ticker tape machine in 1867, the telephone in the 1880s, direct telegraph links with provincial exchanges in the 1890s, and private telephone lines in the 1900s. In 1851, the first submarine telegraph cable was laid between Dover and Calais. This enabled London dealers to be almost instantly aware of prices on the Paris Bourse. Cables were subsequently laid to other European countries and then further afield: to New York in 1866, Melbourne in 1872 and Buenos Aires in 1874. The international telegraph was followed by the telephone, with the first London to Paris link appearing in 1891.[41] These new forms of communication were immediately used by the financial community for information, to place orders in foreign markets and to transfer funds.[42] Such innovations lowered both risk and transaction costs and created new market relations. Enhanced use of cable communication across the Atlantic after 1882, for example, created integrated price movements on the New York and London stock and bond markets – it had a greater impact on drawing prices together in these two markets than in US regional markets themselves.[43] Both real and nominal interest rate differentials between the two countries also narrowed, as suggested by evidence for sixty-day sterling bills.[44]

As communications improved and markets became more sophisticated, therefore, price differences between markets were greatly narrowed, limiting arbitrage opportunities. Better communications also encouraged further spatial concentration of many aspects of financial services. Greater clustering arose because of the need to be aware of recent information or that which was available only informally. With prices between markets narrowing and a much faster speed of reaction to changing market events, proximity to the main dealing places became of even greater importance. Cumulative effects would then enhance the clustering in a typical process of increasing agglomeration economies – with knock-on developments in labour markets, specialist services, etc.

The communications revolution, therefore, is of considerable importance when examining both national and international capital market developments and it will be a theme of what follows.

Stocks and shares

The domestic market

The first and continuing locational advantage of the City as a place for financial services was that its near neighbour was the biggest debtor in the country – the government. Specialist dealers in government stock developed in the 1690s with the advent of a permanent national debt. A London location for the market in already existing stock was strengthened by the fact that the capital was the only place in England where the ownership of government stock could formally be transferred. Originally, dealers worked from the coffee houses of Change Alley and then they moved to premises in Threadneedle Street, where members of the public were charged 6d to enter in order to do business.[45] In 1801, the modern Stock Exchange was born, regulated by a deed of settlement, and membership was restricted to candidates chosen by the ballot of an elected overseeing committee; a purpose-built exchange was opened a year later.

In the early 1800s, holders of public debt were principally located in London and the Home Counties, reinforcing the concentration of stock dealing in the capital. Provincial savers, in contrast, tended to invest in local mortgage markets[46] (although common price effects were observable, as noted earlier). In 1840, government stock accounted for 89 per cent of the securities quoted on the Stock Exchange,[47] with the rest consisting of the shares of the narrow range of bodies that had won joint stock status in the Parliamentary charters that had set them up – the chartered merchant companies, the Bank, canal owners, turnpikes, water and gas enterprises, insurance companies, and, just appearing, rail companies and joint stock banks. Scale advantages were apparent in the operation of the Stock Market, with numerous specialised brokers, extensive daily trades so that extreme fluctuations in price were limited, and a growing network of ancillary services – law, accounting, printing and so on.

Over time, the relative importance of central government debt declined as public policy switched to a regime of lower borrowing. This led to a reduction in the supply of government stock as the outstanding national debt fell significantly – declining from £794 million to £680 million between 1850 and 1913.[48] This contraction, however, was countered by the substantial growth of other public sector borrowing, with the great capital works of local authorities and statutory agencies, including the Metropolitan Board of Works.

The funding of the newly formed provincial joint stock banks and the first rail boom led to the setting up of stock exchanges in many large provincial cities and towns. Formal markets started in Liverpool and Manchester in 1836 and fourteen were added elsewhere during the 1840s. In 1840, for example, only 37 per cent by value of Scottish securities were quoted in London.[49] The emergence of so many regional exchanges reflected the localisation of capital markets at the time, but many of them were short-lived and disappeared in the aftermath of the collapse of rail share prices in 1845.[50]

Stock Exchange members were not allowed to partake in new share issues but only to deal in second-hand stock. Merchant banks did much issuing and joint stock banks and short-lived finance companies were involved in the early 1860s share-issue boom, but the 1866 financial crisis then squeezed them out. With the growth of company flotations from the 1870s, a variety of promotion companies emerged in the new issues market – advertising their wares and drumming up commentary in the press. Unable to organise the underwriting of issues, many promoters manipulated share prices at flotation in order to make money, so that a share would initially trade at an artificially high price before falling. In the late 1870s, 75 per cent of all public company formation was found to be affected by such premiums by an 1878 Royal Commission investigating the Stock Exchange.[51] This practice affected provincial exchanges as well, and would have discouraged investors from subscribing to such shares at least in the initial period of their existence.

The Stock Exchange was not the only dealer in existing company shares in the City, because not all companies could get their shares listed on the Stock Exchange, so secondary markets emerged. A Stock Exchange listing was important for the liquidity it conferred, meaning that investors would be attracted to a firm's shares as they could buy and sell them in a broad market. Exchange members, however, found it unprofitable to deal in companies with a small share circulation, so smaller issues tended not to be listed. This encouraged two developments. First, in London, brokers who were not members of the Exchange developed a secondary market in smaller issues and these and other shares were bought and sold at auctions outside of the Exchange's remit, which threatened but did not supplant the Exchange's activities. Second, a new lease of life was given to provincial exchanges by dealing in these smaller issues and tapping local sources of finance for larger issues. Several new local exchanges were opened in the 1870s, and several of the thirteen provincial exchanges in the early 1880s specialised in particular industries – Manchester and Sheffield, for example, dealt in iron companies.[52]

Although many company shares were only quoted on a local exchange, as London was by far the largest exchange, it was convenient to have parallel quotations for some larger share issues on both the relevant local and the London exchanges – and the practice increased over time. By 1900, 99 per cent of the securities found on the Glasgow market were also quoted in London.[53] One result of the development of multiple quoting on different exchanges was the adoption by brokers of 'shunting' – the monitoring of security prices in a number of markets to make arbitrage profits. When a price difference emerged between exchanges, the security in question would be purchased in the lower price market and almost simultaneously sold in the higher price market. Common in the 1850s, this practice became widespread in the 1860s – and was aided by the introduction of the telegraph.

By permitting City brokers to discover prices on provincial markets almost immediately, communications improvements during the decade enabled them to make alliances with provincial brokers in order to trade in commercial stocks on behalf of clients with no risk of sudden, unknown price fluctuations. The introduction of private telephone lines, however, then restricted this activity to the ten or so brokers able to afford such lines. Instantaneous communication gave these brokers an advantage that the others could not match.[54] This contributed to the decline of the provincial exchanges. The amount of shunting fell further after new London Stock Exchange rules, introduced in 1909, put severe restrictions on the practice. These prevented jobbers from dealing with non-members of the Exchange, including provincial exchange personnel, and forbade brokers to sell or buy on their own account.[55] None the less, such practices had helped to integrate members of provincial exchanges with the London market, and the number of brokers grew in London, completely dwarfing the scale of activity in the provincial exchanges.

In terms of the overall involvement of the British stock exchanges in funding the capital requirements of private companies, their roles were relatively small. The limited scale, however, was demand- rather than supply-driven. In addition, once the national rail system was more or less in place by the 1860s, there was relatively little effective private British demand for infrastructure capital. The infrastructure needs may have been there, but the organisational forms in which they came to market frequently did not impress investors, as can be seen with the underground system which relied on US funds for the development of the tube (see Chapter 10).

The providers of social infrastructure – transport, communications, power, water and sewerage, etc. – and housing were by far the greatest consumers of capital in the country and so needed the intermediation facilities offered by the City far more than did manufacturing enterprises. As an approximation of the types of demand for capital, Table 14.1 breaks down the 1856 and 1913 national capital stocks into their sectoral components. Services constituted by far the largest share – almost a half in 1913 – and housing added another 24 per cent, but the City had little to do with that. Even so, almost three-quarters of the capital stock was in these two sectors rather than in manufacturing, mining or agriculture. Social overhead capital dominates over the manufacturing capital stock. As this was the case it is unsurprising that railway shares dominated the stock market, that private utilities were significant, and that much funding of social overhead capital was done through the public sector bond market.

In respect of manufacturing investment, there was little demand for City finance and what was on offer was often highly risky. Most new British firms were small and required limited start-up capital. Such sums could more cheaply be obtained from savings, friends, relatives or local investors. Similarly, firm expansion generally occurred through investing retained profits or by the introduction of a 'silent' partner. Trade debt was covered by issuing bills of exchange or by borrowing from local provincial banks, and later through overdraft facilities at one of the new national banks. Many manufacturing firms, as a result, remained private companies rather than converting to joint stock company status with a listing on the London or a local exchange. Conversion to joint stock status occurred in specific industries rather than randomly throughout industry.

Nevertheless, by 1907, the Stock Exchange share listings contained 570 domestic industrial and commercial concerns, worth around £500 million.[56]

Table 14.1 The capital stock of the United Kingdom, 1856 and 1913

	Percentage shares	
	1856	*1913*
Agriculture	19	6
Manufacturing	13	19
Services	39	49
Construction	1	1
Mining, etc.	2	2
Existing dwellings	27	24
Total	100	100

Source: Millward, 1990, 424.

Note: Rounding errors may affect summations.

Yet few of them had adopted joint stock status simply to raise capital. Rather, for banking, insurance and other financial enterprises, the incentive for issuing share capital was to spread risk. The breweries were reacting to the high cost of pub properties. Among industrial, commercial and mining concerns, the purpose was generally to facilitate a growing division between ownership and management. The need for this arose when problems emerged in founding families or because of the increasing complexity of organisational structures in some industries. Even so, the vast majority of British firms remained relatively small-scale, family businesses, using only limited amounts of fixed capital, until after the First World War, unlike contemporary developments in the USA.[57]

The trend towards restricting competition evident in a number of late nineteenth-century industries also stimulated flotation on the London exchange. Attempts by firms in an industry to limit competition by setting up cartels often led to disagreements; whereas joint stock status of a merged enterprise solved many such conflicts of interest. Once a new firm was established, shares could be issued to previous owners, giving them a common interest in the firm's success, and competent staff could be employed to manage the merged businesses.

One factor associated with limited involvement of capital markets in the funding of investment and innovation in British industry was the poor accounting and regulatory environment, which meant that markets could not function effectively. Firms could hold back vital investor information because of laxities in disclosure and accounting procedures; insider information could be used extensively to the detriment of the ordinary investor; the over-pricing of share issues has already been mentioned; and it was virtually impossible for shareholders to sack managements or for hostile take-overs to be successful.[58] The shareholding principals, therefore, often could not trust their management agents. The result was both credit rationing and higher costs of capital for all firms, as investors had little means of distinguishing between the duds and the diamonds in the mantle of industrial enterprise. This failure can hardly be blamed on investors or the Stock Exchange, but rather on public policies that, despite successive piecemeal reforms, did not create an adequate institutional framework for better functioning of domestic capital markets – though the scale of the consequences is hard to discern from other factors influencing the ownership structure of firms.

International share dealing

International dealings began in the eighteenth century, when British securities were bought and sold on behalf of foreign clients, particularly the Dutch. The long period of European warfare from 1789 to 1815 led to a fall in the foreign possession of British securities, but there was a compensatory increase in British holdings of foreign securities. By mid-century, however, London's involvement in foreign business remained small. In

1853, only 8 per cent of the £12.5 million of paid-up securities quoted on the Stock Exchange were foreign.[59] Trading in overseas securities was largely confined to government stock from continental Europe, the USA and South America. These were issued in London and bought and sold by British investors.

Like domestic trading, international dealing was transformed by the communications revolution. The result of these innovations was that the London financial community increasingly began to act for both British and foreign clients, buying and selling stocks in London and on foreign exchanges.[60] Initially, this international business was dominated by merchant banks, because they generally possessed good contacts abroad and had geographically dispersed funds. From the 1860s and 1870s, however, merchant banks gradually became less involved in international stock dealing, because it distracted them from their more lucrative issue work and was believed to involve excessive risk. Their place in the international arena was taken over by stock exchange brokers, who generally formed alliances with foreign brokers and international banks.

The 1860s and 1870s saw a substantial increase in the value of internationally traded securities in parallel with economic development and industrialisation elsewhere in the world. The first internationally traded stocks were those issued by the governments of countries of recent development, such as Canada, Brazil, Argentina and Australia; later they were joined by issues from governments in underdeveloped regions, for example, China, Mexico and Japan. Most of these loans were raised for the construction of infrastructure and other public works. International government issues were complemented by corporate bonds and stocks issued by US railroad companies and subsequently by Canadian and Argentinian railways. Added to these, in turn, were mining securities issued by companies, such as Rio Tinto, and by industrial and commercial stock floated by international firms, such as the Nobel Dynamite Company and United States Steel. Eventually, such corporate stock formed the largest part of the international securities business.

The creation of an international market provided opportunities for London brokers to profit from price differences in international stock markets. Such arbitrage operations were at first centred on the differences between London and the Paris Bourse, but then they expanded to encompass other European exchanges. The activity was initially confined to European government debt, and then London firms gradually began to deal in all markets and securities. Because of their complex nature, such operations were undertaken by only a limited number of broking firms – 262 in 1909.[61] Most concentrated on a particular country and specialised in a certain class of business, like railroad stocks. The success of these brokers attracted foreign dealers to London, who tended to retain strong links with their countries of origin, giving them an informational advantage. Foreign banks, such as Credit Lyonnais and Deutsche Bank, set up branches in London and they captured a significant part of the arbitrage business in some types of foreign share, such as US corporate bonds, South African gold mining issues and Malaysian plantation stock.

These developments, however, did not lead to perfect price equality across international stock exchanges. The Amsterdam and London capital markets had been closely integrated since the eighteenth century, and Amsterdam led London in the local trading of foreign securities. (Of the 87 securities listed on the Amsterdam Beurs in 1855 only 16 were domestic or colonial.) Paris joined in from the 1850s. Even so, the evidence suggests that substantial price differences still remained into the 1900s, so that (risky) arbitrage possibilities were still available.[62]

The export of capital

The City's involvement in overseas investment was immense, with the greatest outflow of funds occurring in the second half of the century. Between 1870 and 1914, a net average of 4.3 per cent of British national income was invested abroad, so that by 1913 overseas assets represented 32 per cent of the stock of net national wealth and British investors earned £200 million in foreign income alone. The flow of net overseas investment varied and was significantly reduced by domestic investment booms, but was particularly high in 1871, 1888–90 and 1909–11.[63] Britain was not the only European country to export capital – considerable sums went abroad from France and Germany. They were not quite at the scale of British investments, however, but still very large by modern standards (see Table 14.2), and they mainly went to different countries from British exports, notably central Europe and Russia.

The majority of the capital exported from Britain during this period was channelled to the temperate regions of recent settlement and around 70 per cent of it was used to finance infrastructure. Less than a fifth went directly to agricultural, mining and manufacturing activities, although the proportion did increase in the last quarter of the century.[64] The focus of overseas investment consequently was to open up temperate areas of the world to meet the large demand for primary products generated by Western industrialisation. Of the £4.1 billion invested in foreign securities issued in London from 1865 to 1914, a third went to South America and Australasia and a further third to North America.[65]

Foreign investment occurred in two ways. A small proportion of funds was used to purchase the share issues of British firms that owned and managed foreign operations. The vast majority, however, was invested in loan debentures/stock issued in London and to a lesser extent abroad, largely by foreign governments, other institutions whose loans received government guarantees and railway companies. The share of lending to non-government bodies grew substantially to reach 60 per cent of the total in the 1905–14 period.[66]

Institutional specialisation existed in overseas new issues. Loans to non-colonial governments were floated through well-established merchant banks

Table 14.2 Net foreign investment as a percentage of domestic savings, 1850–1913

	UK	*Germany*	*France*
1850–4	12.3	–	20.1
1855–9	30.2	–	21.6
1860–4	21.5	1.4	24.8
1865–9	32.2	3.4	25.9
1870–4	38.0	7.3	29.0
1875–9	16.2	13.1	18.7
1880–4	33.2	18.3	–1.1
1885–9	46.5	19.3	11.3
1890–4	35.3	12.6	10.0
1895–9	20.7	11.5	23.0
1900–4	11.2	9.0	16.1
1905–9	42.7	7.6	22.0
1910–13	53.3	7.3	12.5

Source: O'Rourke and Williamson, 1999, 209.

such as Rothschilds and Barings. Within the Empire, self-governing colonies' loans were handled by the Bank of England and the London and Westminster Bank; while the issues of the dependent Crown colonies and protectorates were initiated by the Crown Agents, a quasi-government body under the supervision of the Colonial Office. Private sector loans were generally dealt with by, amongst others, the newer merchant banks, which tended to specialise in issues for particular areas or purposes. J. P. Morgan, for example, concentrated on US railroads and, later, industrial flotations. Despite such specialisation, competition still existed – the joint stock banks, for example, increased their share from virtually nothing in the 1870s to 17 per cent of all overseas issues between 1910 and 1914.[67]

The principal influence on the export of capital was the return achieved relative to investments in Britain – when overseas investments were more profitable, capital flowed abroad. Edelstein has estimated that, between 1870 and 1913, the average risk-adjusted returns on overseas investments were almost a quarter greater than on domestic ones (5.72 per cent overseas to 4.6 per cent domestic). Arguments that either the City or British investors had an irrational bias towards the international over the domestic economy seem misplaced in face of such evidence. The surplus of savings over investment in the UK, instead, was directed to the opportunities offered by the opening up of the resource-rich areas of new European settlement, in what was an approximately integrated world capital market.[68] British investments, therefore, had roughly to match returns overseas, and the scale of the export of capital indicated that diminishing returns were being experienced by investments in Britain.

Insurance

Insurance had evolved well before the nineteenth century but expansion was considerable after 1800.[69] The history of insurance in the City requires its subdivision into several types: marine, fire and life.

Marine insurance and Lloyds

Marine insurance had developed out of London's role as a port. Both vessels and cargoes were initially insured by shipping agents and shipping brokers, who then began to specialise in providing insurance alone. After meeting at the Royal Exchange and later in a room in Cornhill, underwriters finally settled in Edward Lloyd's coffee house in Tower Street. Lloyds gradually provided services that its clientele would otherwise have been unable to afford individually, such as the provision of shipping news and experienced clerical staff, in a classic instance of agglomeration economies.

For much of the eighteenth and early nineteenth century Lloyds underwriters prospered. The 1720 Bubble Act gave Lloyds and two chartered companies, the Royal Exchange Assurance and London Assurance, a monopoly of the insurance of ships and goods at sea. Lloyds prospered at the expense of the other two because the latter charged rates 20–30 per cent higher, limited their cover to £10,000 on any one ship and were reluctant to insure cross-risks – such as voyages taken between two ports outside the UK. By 1810, the two assurance companies possessed only 4 per cent of marine business.[70]

Prosperity faltered at the end of the Napoleonic Wars. The marine insurance market contracted and rates fell by 75 per cent due to the disappearance of war risks. Then, in 1824, Lloyds lost its monopoly and this led to new joint stock companies being formed, such as the Alliance and Indemnity. These new firms soon captured part of the London business and, more importantly, the growing insurance needs of northern ports, such as Liverpool and Glasgow. The result was a rapid reduction in underwriters from a peak of 2,000 in 1800 to only 189 in 1849.[71]

Lloyds responded to the increased competition in four ways. First, it turned to the international shipping market, which because of the growth of world trade was undergoing rapid expansion. Clients were offered highly competitive rates, foreigners were admitted as members, and a network of overseas brokers – generally merchants and shippers – was established. Such was the success of this strategy that others followed their lead and, by 1900, two-thirds of world marine insurance was handled in Britain, half by Lloyds and most of the remainder by other City institutions.

Lloyds, secondly, moved into fire reinsurance. Reinsurance involves underwriters taking the risk of policies for a share of the premium. This could not be done prior to 1865 because of imposition of fire insurance duty and the Inland Revenue would not recognise Lloyds as an agent for its collection.[72] With the duty abolished, non-proportional reinsurance was developed, whereby risks were pooled across policies. In doing this, underwriters agreed to pay claims in excess of an agreed figure in return for a percentage of all the premiums received by the original insurer, without concerning themselves with the detail of every policy. As the large fire insurance companies were reluctant to allow rival firms to participate in their policies and non-proportional reinsurance reduced their costs, Lloyds' share of the business grew rapidly.

The third initiative was to develop new lines of insurance. A number of underwriters began to cover against burglary, loss of goods in transit and motor and aviation accidents. In the 1900s, these lines became the main businesses of several underwriters, who reinsured their risks with marine counterparts.

The fourth change was organisational. With the Lloyds Act 1871, it became an incorporated society – a legal entity with its own rules and self-governing constitution.[73] New members were required to provide securities, while insolvency, bankruptcy or a conviction for fraud were automatically followed by expulsion. To fund and spread the risks of new ventures, individual underwriters were superseded by syndicates. These comprised an active member and a number of others, called 'names', who pledged their wealth as security for the insurance granted, for a share of the premium. The result of these developments was that by 1913 around 20 per cent of premium income came from non-marine insurance and membership had risen again to 621.[74]

Life insurance

Stimulated by the 1799 exemption of premiums from tax, life insurance underwent rapid expansion in the early nineteenth century. By 1806, London contained eight life offices and between 1806 and 1839 a further 100 were opened, though 32 of them failed. They either concentrated solely on life policies or additionally transacted fire and marine business. The number of policies held by each firm was relatively small. Sun Life (1810) in the 1830s, for example, sold 200–250 new policies a year; even as late as 1841 it only issued 478.

At first, the policies came in two forms: an assurance payable on the death of the life insured or an endowment payable at the end of the agreed period provided the person was still alive. Later, in the 1840s, endowment insurance policies appeared, which combined these two elements. Companies also began to offer bonuses on policies.[75]

During the second half of the century, life insurance extended its market to include the middle and the upper working classes, who used life policies to fund retirement at a time when private pension schemes were rare.[76] Underwriting became a more orderly and predictable business due to advances in actuarial practice and legislation requiring companies to furnish accounts and actuarial returns.

London's lead in the industry, however, was gradually challenged by provincial firms, particularly those based in Edinburgh and Norwich. In earlier years, the size of the market for life insurance in the capital had made the London firms unassailable, but improvements in communications meant that the whole UK market could be served from one location. The pull of the City was thereby reduced because insurance companies' long-term investments in land mortgages and government stock did not require them to be close to a financial market.

With the advent of the international telegraph, international business was made feasible. Sun Life, for example, appointed agents in Spain, Hamburg, Belgium and Baden in the late 1880s and early 1890s, transacted business in the Near East through branches of the Imperial Ottoman bank, and established a separate company in India in 1891.

Firms developed new products as market opportunities opened. Railway accidents were covered from the 1840s and, in the 1890s, bicycling injuries and occupational hazards. Business in the latter grew particularly after the 1901 Workman's Compensation Act with its obligations on employers over injuries at work. In 1900, Sun Life introduced a monthly premium scheme aimed at artisans and a non-medical policy whereby it provided life insurance without a medical examination.[77]

Fire insurance

Fire insurance dated from the Great Fire in the seventeenth century, which led to the formation of a number of firms. By 1800, the capital contained seven fire offices, the largest of which were the Sun, the Phoenix and the Royal Exchange, with market shares of respectively 34, 22 and 16 per cent. The City's early lead in the industry, however, was slowly challenged by provincial firms as industrialisation had generated as fire risks many factories and warehouses in the North. By the 1860s, two of the largest fire insurers were based in Liverpool, with London covering only 56 per cent of the fire risks insured in Britain, as compared to 66 per cent in the 1830s and 90 per cent in 1800.[78]

Fire companies developed overseas business much earlier than their life counterparts. In the 1820s and 1830s, several companies appointed agents in Germany and France and, from the 1850s, there was a movement into other countries, particularly in North America. Provincial companies also developed overseas business, so that by 1888 a fifth of all the fire insurance in the US was in British hands.

Consolidation again increased the role of London. By 1850, the Phoenix had taken over thirteen companies, the largest being Protector Fire, which had 7 per cent of the fire market; Sun Insurance had merged with twelve firms; and the Alliance had bought out three other smaller ones.[79]

Investment portfolio diversification

From the 1870s, British insurance companies began to extend the areas in which they invested their funds. At mid-century, most firms wished to obtain a combination of liquidity and high yields and so bought a mixture of land mortgages and government stock. Land mortgages gave a high return but were illiquid, and government stock provided low yields but could easily be sold. As returns in agriculture collapsed with the onset of competition from world markets, this strategy had to be reassessed. Investments were made, instead, in overseas mortgages and in non-government and foreign government securities. By 1913, 56 per cent of life insurance assets were in securities, as compared to 34 per cent in 1870, and only 1 per cent was in UK government stock. The new investment strategy required far more skill and expertise than its predecessor. This encouraged more provincial companies to move to the City in order to be close to the money market.[80]

Commercial trade

The nineteenth-century City contained thriving businesses in commercial trade and also some manufacturing enterprises – the two would often merge together under one proprietor. Overall, according to the 1891 census, such enterprises constituted up to two-thirds of the firms operating in the City. They included manufacturing chemists and 435 commercial brokers dealing in such commodities as tea, cotton and ivory. Textile and clothing businesses – merchants, warehouses and manufacturers – added another 652 firms. There were 207 'makers' of a wide variety of goods including chronometers and revolving-shutters; and 602 manufacturers – making things as un-City-like as sausage machines, springs and sheep dips. A further 2,461 merchants could be added dealing in a wide variety of goods.[81] The list is as long as it is varied and illustrates the dangers of simply seeing the City as a place for high finance.

Commercial activities can be split into four sectors – physical trade, office trade, futures trade and ship management. Physical trade involved goods moved through the port. Given the continued importance of the nearby wharves and the warehouses behind them, and the difficulty of working in the enclosed docks, a City location continued to be the obvious and most proximate place for such firms to locate.

Major changes occurred in physical trade from the 1850s. The port and its merchants lost business, particularly in bulky commodities, to its northern rivals; while its re-export trade was affected by the growth of European ports, such as Amsterdam. The telegraph and steamship further undermined the merchants' traditional role because they permitted direct trade between consumers and producers. The response of the merchant community was to concentrate on the import and re-export of high-value goods, such as platinum, diamonds, furs, etc., where transport costs were of less importance than marketing and specialised knowledge. They also became involved in new products – rubber, petroleum and manufactures – and new markets such as Latin America. To improve their competitive advantage, they began to employ foreigners for their knowledge and contacts, and to specialise in particular goods, markets or countries of supply. Their success attracted foreign merchants to the City – for example, Germans, who specialised in the sugar and tea trades, and Greeks, who concentrated on shipping and grain.

Office trade was associated with the movement of goods that never physically passed through London. The business grew rapidly in the second half of the century because the telegraph made available good supply-and-demand information. This enabled produce to be sold world-wide on the basis of newly formed world prices. Linked by telegraph with most major countries and with unparalleled expertise in products and markets, London merchants soon began to dominate. A City location was important in this activity in order to take advantage of the communications facilities, expertise and information available there. The success of existing traders attracted others to the City from both within the UK and overseas. As business expanded, there was also increasing specialisation in particular markets or products. To gain further agglomeration economies, those concentrating on particular sectors began to congregate – Mincing Lane, for instance, became the haunt of firms dealing in coffee, tea, sugar and spices. Specialised markets then developed, such as the Metal Exchange, dealing in tin, copper and lead; the Baltic Exchange, concentrating on shiploads of grain for international sale; the Corn Exchange, handling smaller grain consignments for domestic sale; and the London Commercial Sale Rooms, covering a variety of produce.

Similar growth was experienced in futures trade, in which commodity contracts are traded in advance of their completion. The telegraph reduced the uncertainties of this type of trading, so firms wishing to ensure regular supplies at known prices began to buy goods in the forward market. Risks, however, were still high. Purchasers of commodities could be left with supplies that they did not want at prices above the prevailing rate; whilst sellers could face sudden surges in demand for goods that they had already sold at relatively low prices. There consequently developed markets in the contracts themselves in which there was no expectation of final delivery of the physical product by the parties involved; rather they facilitated the spreading of the risks away from those actually involved in the physical trades. Other refinements occurred. Purchasers of contracts for future delivery, for example, often took out reverse contracts to sell the same amount of goods bought in the buy contract in order to hedge their risks. Losses on the latter, if the price of the commodity fell, were therefore offset by a corresponding rise in the value of the sell contract and vice versa. As with office trade, various official futures markets were established – in corn in 1878 and coffee and sugar in 1888.

Finally, ship management also underwent considerable change during the second half of the century. The telegraph removed much of the autonomy of ships' captains, with decisions on journey time, return cargoes and other ships' matters increasingly made in the UK. Simultaneously, the expansion of world trade encouraged many firms to specialise in particular types of ship, cargo or route. There was a drift of shipping management firms from other parts of Britain to the City, because it provided access to a world-wide communication system and proximity to those operating in the physical and office trades. They were followed by ship owners and managers from other countries – in particular, from Germany and Scandinavia.

The redevelopment of the City

The decline in the City's resident population accelerated from mid-century onwards. From 130,000 in 1851, it fell to 112,000 in 1861, and the out-migration accelerated so that only 27,000 were left by the turn of the century.[82] Some residents were lured by the attractions of the suburbs; while many others had to make way for the new offices and warehouses that arose throughout the Square Mile. The ancient characteristics of the City were lost in the throng of new commerce and transportation. It has been estimated that four-fifths of the City's buildings standing in 1905 were not there fifty years before. Only 7 per cent remained in use as residences by 1911.[83] The exceptions to the transformation, though few, had a surprising impact in keeping the district more domestic and 'London' in style than would otherwise have been the case. This is particularly true of the many small churches, splendidly sustained by ancient City charities; a handful of public buildings and monuments; and the old street pattern behind the new broad thoroughfares cut through by the Corporation and the Metropolitan Board of Works.

The two decades between 1857 and 1877 were a time of active new building with headquarters erected in an opulent manner for banks, insurance companies and firms whose business spread across the UK. Equally grand new stations opened up to ferry workforces from suburban home to office and back again. Office rents rose rapidly towards the end of the century – by 60 per cent between 1887 and 1910, according to Turvey's calculations.[84] Such rent rises stimulated a boom to an extent that severe overbuilding occurred. One result was that the Edwardian nature of the City survived for decades afterwards.

Property companies started to appear from the 1860s to supply firms' office and warehousing needs, though most buildings continued to be owned directly by occupiers themselves. Lifts began to be introduced, but the City, like the rest of Europe, shunned the new, steel-framed, high-rise office building which were developed in Chicago in the 1890s and quickly diffused throughout North America. The few steel-framed buildings that were built failed to pierce the skyline and were disguised in heavy masonry casings. Building regulations helped to maintain a uniform height, though it is unlikely that the rules would have remained the same if large numbers of enterprises had wanted high-rise structures.

The first lifts were water-powered, thanks to the London Hydraulic Company. (At the time of writing, such a lift still existed in St Pancras Chambers.) Water under pressure also powered theatre machinery and cranes and had other industrial uses, such as hat presses. What was eventually a 187-mile network of high-pressure pipes ran throughout the central areas and the East End, fed by five pumping stations spread along the Thames and the Regent's Canal. In 1895, the London Hydraulic Company provided 221 passenger lifts and over 500 goods lifts and cranes in the City.[85] The high number for goods indicates the importance of warehousing as a City land use. The London Hydraulic Company itself provided a Victorian technology that was soon to be overtaken by electricity, though it survived until 1971. Founded a hundred years before, it was given a statutory monopoly over its role at its inception – like the earlier water and gas monopolies but unlike the electricity and telephone companies that were to follow.

Activities in the City as they expanded from their earlier roots, or developed as new parts of the City economy, were highly clustered. The tiny area of the City thus itself became divided into specialised districts of financial and commercial activity. This highlights the importance, even at the centre, of tight clustering and illustrates the dual agglomeration benefits for many urban activities of being part of an industrial district and, at the same time, located to share in the benefits of a large urban area as a whole. The pull of centrality led to high land values in the Square Mile, so that only activities that gained the most profit from being there survived. The high rents and external economies, as well as the nature of the service activities involved, meant that most of the businesses were small in size, with over 11,000 recorded in the City in 1901.

The 673 acres of the City became a goldmine for the Corporation of London, as well as for many of the owners of the firms active there. The average rateable value of an acre of City property was estimated to be around fifteen times more than that in the rest of the capital. This rate base was tenaciously kept for the Corporation's own expenditures against threats of redistribution from the rest of the capital and Parliament; although a judicious use of philanthropy brought several London parks, Epping Forest and some other non-City-based activities into its fold. City charities were also encouraged by the Corporation to be generous outside of the Square Mile.

The scale of the rise in City land values can be glimpsed in the growth in rateable values, which increased 161 per cent between 1861 and 1881 and by another 40 per cent between 1881 and 1901. The rise in property values benefited the seventy-six traditional Livery Companies, whose membership in 1880 had dropped to 9,000 but whose property was worth a total of £15 million. Their annual trust and corporate income made them some of the richest and most influential institutions in the capital. By 1900, the Companies' annual income was £600,000, with a third devoted to charitable or trust purposes.[86]

Part 6

Welfare and government

15 Welfare and social policy

Introduction

Welfare and social policy in the late twentieth century have come to mean state involvement in the provision of minimum incomes and unemployment programmes, and interventions into the family life, health, education and housing of the nation. These things did not exist in early nineteenth-century Britain in the forms in which they are known today. The New Poor Law of 1834 set out the rather unpleasant consequences of relying on state benevolence to ensure personal survival, and most other aspects of welfare had to be found somehow by individual family endeavour or not at all. In the years up to 1914 considerable change took place. A mass of voluntary organisations, friendly societies and non-profit institutions grew substantially in savings, insurance, health, education, housing and the alleviation of poverty. London shared disproportionately in their expansion and attention. The state, at local and central levels, moreover, was forced to confront problems that governments previously were expected to leave to private interests. The origins of the modern welfare state system and social policies can be seen in these various movements because, once in existence, by creating a degree of path dependency they passed on a legacy.

It would be wrong, however, to see the process of change as a rational one, with a variety of experiments devised and tested until the best ones were found after a long period of search. Nineteenth-century sensibilities affected the forms of welfare that emerged and nineteenth-century taxation policies imposed limits on what could be done. Welfare reform, moreover, was implanted within a market-based economic system and its consequences had repercussions within specific markets, such as housing and labour, that were often ignored or only poorly understood. In the London context, welfare debates were wide-ranging but focused on the four principal issues that form the basis of the modern welfare state: poverty, education, health and housing. The actual extent to which policy aims were achieved and the costs of doing so are matters of evaluation based on the available information, in which London's unique place in British society and its own economic, political and social geography play important roles. Yet, what perhaps stands out most clearly are the severe constraints on a city-level approach to welfare – a theme that is taken up further in the following chapter on local government.

Not all aspects of the welfare activities of government and private bodies are covered in this chapter. For one thing, many books could be, and have been, written on this broad subject.[1] Here, several aspects of welfare are considered – health care, including prevention of disease in the form of public sanitation; education; income support via the private provision of income for periods of unemployment or ill-health or for old age; charity and the public relief of poverty through the Poor Law; wages and unemployment relief; the employment and unemployment policies of local government; and, finally, social housing which was provided by a mix of private and public agencies. In their various ways, they illustrate the contexts, successes and dilemmas of the city-level approach to welfare provision and the complexity of the public/private nexus.

Health care

Doctors

Owing to the presence of the large teaching hospitals and many of the well-to-do, there was a national concentration of the medical profession in London. It was divided into three specialisms: apothecaries, physicians and surgeons.

Apothecaries sold and prescribed medicines, often from their own shops, and were under the supervision of the Society of Apothecaries. They were in competition with druggists and chemists for sales but had the advantage over them of being able to prescribe. Surgeons also prescribed drugs as well as undertaking general surgery, and were required to be members of the Royal College of Surgeons. Largely middle-class, their education involved a system of apprenticeship, courses in anatomy and surgery, and a period of 'walking the wards' of the major London hospitals. Physicians, finally, prescribed medicines and offered advice. They either possessed degrees in physics or were fellows/licentiates of the Royal College of Physicians, which was able to grant its members the right to practice within seven miles of the capital. Physicians were few in number: from 1771 to 1833, the College admitted 168 fellows and a similar number of licentiates. Their members were largely drawn from the upper middle class, with admission to the College being restricted to Oxbridge graduates.[2]

The existence of these three types of doctor led to much confusion, so, in 1858, the Medical Act created registered medical practitioners. To achieve that status, doctors had to satisfy one of the existing licensing bodies of their capabilities in either medicine or surgery, and, after the 1886 Medical Act, in both subjects.[3] As well as a register, and rules for being put on it, the Act also established a disciplinary body, the General

Medical Council. The Act gave a legally enforceable requirement to doctors that many other professions were adopting voluntarily in the codes of their professional institutions. This may have been because of the importance of competence in health matters. Yet, given the poor state of medical knowledge at the time, the shift may more accurately be ascribed to the rivalry between the three branches of the profession, which were suddenly catapulted into one unitary entity with knowledge requirements that not all of them would have possessed in their earlier guises.

Doctors in London earned considerably more than elsewhere. New practitioners earned from £800 to £3,000 a year as compared to £500 to £1,500 in the provinces. The chance of improvement was also greater in the metropolis and the more distinguished metropolitan medic could receive up to £6,000 a year.[4] Centrality was of key importance to aspiring doctors, enabling them to be close to hospitals, a pool of wealthy West End residents, and to others who might wish to travel to London. Harley Street in Marylebone became a choice location for doctors from around the middle of the century. The disparity in medical supervision between rich and poor districts was substantial. In 1900, for example, Bethnal Green possessed one doctor for every 3,000 residents; whereas Kensington had a doctor for every 480 people.[5]

Hospitals

Many of London's major hospitals had been founded as charities prior to the nineteenth century and there was considerable extension of provision during the period. Hospitals were funded either by the Poor Law or charitable contributions, or privately for the wealthy.

Poor Law hospitals tended to treat fever cases, the old, the mentally ill and patients with venereal disease and other chronic disorders.[6] Voluntary hospitals were centrally located and played a national role in teaching medical practice. They concentrated on acute cases, which were more suited to treatment in a hospital environment and of greater interest to medical teachers and researchers. Such conditions were also more likely to lead to sudden death or a rapid return to health – ensuring rapid patient turnover. Such hospitals had a clear market incentive in that good recovery rates led to higher charitable subscriptions, although contemporary medical knowledge lamentably let them down.

By the 1860s, all the major general hospitals had been founded and the basic structure of the metropolitan system until this day was set up.[7] Then, from mid-century, all kinds of hospital expanded. The Metropolitan Poor Act of 1867 permitted the establishment of infirmaries independent of workhouses, and medical men wishing to advance their careers increasingly set up their own voluntary ones. Most of the latter were small and were concentrated in central London. A plethora of doubtful establishments grew up as a result. A Lord's Committee in 1890 found that sixty-seven special hospitals existed in 1890 and subjected them to strong criticism, especially the small ones. They were said to draw funds away from the general hospitals to the benefit of doctors rather than patients and to provide inferior treatment.[8]

Hospital provision failed to decentralise with expansion of the metropolis, and remained centrally concentrated with hospitals staying in their original locations, or moving only short distances when rebuilding – as in the case of St Thomas's shift from near London Bridge to adjacent to Westminster Bridge in the 1860s. Virtually all hospitals were sited within a two-square-mile area of the centre, so that the sick had to travel long distances and, if they were poor, could not afford the journey. Within a one-mile radius of the Middlesex Hospital, by the 1890s, there were eight general hospitals and twenty-six specialist institutions. They did not co-operate with each other, nor did they concentrate on specific catchment areas. The lack of provision was worst in the south. In 1902, the *Daily Mail* campaigned for Barts to be moved to Clapham, the Charing Cross to Woolwich and the Westminster to Tottenham, pointing out that the hospitals would profit handsomely from the difference in land values between centre and suburbs, but all to no avail. King's College Hospital, however, did move south to Denmark Hill at the turn of the century.[9]

The difficulty of moving hospitals was great. Ancient endowments and the charitable giving on which they relied were often linked to provision in specific localities, and existing local communities, hospital staff and consultants were all generally opposed to moving. Because there was little co-operation between hospitals and no central authority to direct them, hospitals on the basis of their individual interests gained from central locations. This self-interest encouraged those that ran each hospital to oppose co-operation or decentralisation, even though the latter would have been in the interests of patients as a whole.

The agglomeration benefits of a central location for hospitals are similar to those of other enterprises. The labour market benefits of centrality, for example, apply to hospitals as much as to other activities. This was particularly the case because many medical practitioners working in hospitals also had centrally located private practices. Specialist medical and research facilities and ancillary medical services were in the centre as well. It was easy to acquire informal information about new techniques within the medical milieux of the City and West End. Centrality also maximised the catchment area for obtaining charitable donations. A suburban move by one hospital would limit its catchment area and so reduce the number of potential donors, especially if it moved to a working-class suburb. Many wealthy districts were in the West End from whose residents substantial subscriptions could be gained and hospital management committees could be packed with worthy and influential local residents. Centrality also maximised the catchment area for patients for the specialised hospitals and for the special departments of the general hospitals. The pull of the centre for hospital providers, therefore, was strong and not simply a product of vested interests.

Early on in the century, hospitals would rarely feature in Londoners' lives, but towards the end of the period medical advances and growing recognition of the benefits of hospital treatment had greatly increased per capita demand. Problems arose because medical advances and rising standards of care were simultaneously increasing costs. Charitable giving could not cope. In 1893, the city's voluntary sector treated 1.7 million patients at a cost of £790,000, but raised only £766,000. The overall deficit may not seem much but some of the major hospitals were in severe financial difficulties.[10] Some relief, however, came from the establishment in 1897 of the King's Fund, which raised money for London hospitals and tried to rationalise provision.[11] But a poor geographic spread and perennial money problems remained.

Income support

Friendly societies

Self-help is often classified as a Victorian virtue, and many Londoners in the nineteenth century adopted the rational strategy of providing for periods when regular earnings dried up through illness, unemployment or old age.[12] The better-off had their investments in shares, bonds, mortgages and real estate. Such savings mediums, as has been noted in earlier chapters, were also used by some members of the artisan classes, but the main vehicle for them increasingly became savings accounts at one of the many friendly societies represented in London. Some were related to the housing market, such as the building societies. Others provided sick pay, death benefits or paid for medical attention.

The number of such societies was always substantial throughout the period but greater use was made of them as the century progressed. In 1800, Middlesex and the City contained 909 registered societies, perhaps a third of the country's total.[13] At first, most were locally organised and trade-based, though they could still be relatively large. The City Shoemakers' Society, for example, had 600 members, its West End equivalent 600–700, and the carpenters' five London societies supposedly had a total membership of 2,500.[14] The significance of their role can be seen in information for 1803, when a third of the adult male population belonged to a friendly society.[15]

The societies were mutual insurance organisations, so to encourage membership they had to relate benefits closely to contributions and ensure financial stability. This encouraged them to serve a relatively homogeneous group of subscribers and to introduce rules that excluded the riskiest participants. Membership was generally restricted to the semi-skilled and skilled, via the setting of a minimum wage for admission. In the case of the Woolwich branch of the Ancient Order of Foresters, 53 per cent of new members from 1845 to 1876 were skilled and only 30 per cent unskilled, and many worked in the secure employment environment of the Arsenal.[16]

In addition, many societies excluded workers over the age of 55 and trades that involved a great risk of unemployment, or employed men believed not to be sober or industrious.

A trend towards national coverage developed, as it enabled societies to grow larger. Risks were further diminished by such a strategy, as it left societies less exposed to the risks of specialised regional economies. Through this process, branches of national affiliated orders began to appear in place of local concerns.

The causes and relief of poverty

Poverty was mitigated in London, as elsewhere in the country, by charity and the Poor Law. The particular structures and problems of London, none the less, gave the issue of poverty in the capital specific dimensions.

Two interpretations of the causes of poverty dominated debate, as they still do today, and were expressed most clearly in the majority and minority reports of the Royal Commission on the Poor Laws, published in 1909.[17] The first highlights individual failure, and is often called the individualistic or moral view. The poor are so because of individual moral failings, such as laziness, drunkenness, and a lack of personal and civic pride. Generous state help to such people only makes matters worse by encouraging more applicants; it weakens self-help and determination further through the creation of a cycle of dependency; and undermines the virtues of work and self-reliance in the rest of society taxed to fund the poor relief. The policy prescription consists of draconian measures to discourage the feckless poor from acts of immorality and applying for relief, and simultaneous attempts to identify the good in the chaff and to offer them ways of helping themselves to improve their economic and moral lot.

The alternative, systemic, view suggests that poverty is not the fault of individuals but of the highly varied circumstances they are in: caused by factors such as unemployment, health, age and poor education or combinations of these. The causality between morality and poverty may be switched around entirely in this view by arguing that anti-social behaviour is a product of the hopelessness of the poor's situation. The systemic interpretation's policies focus less on punishment and more on relief of immediate causes – such as providing income support and work schemes in trade depressions – and on tackling longer-term structural problems, such as bad housing and poor education. Intervention is also beneficial to all because it removes health hazards and, by drawing more into work, increases total national wealth.

The two perspectives, however, are not as starkly opposed as they seem because the systemic argument recognises an inherent problem that applicants for benefits may not be genuinely in need. This difficulty can only be overcome by offering expensive universal benefits to all or by operating selection, or 'means testing', schemes – which, in another way, again divide the deserving from the undeserving. The practical distinctiveness of the two approaches is consequently more one of emphasis and the direction of remedial action than of total difference.

In the context of nineteenth-century London, as in the rest of Britain, the moral outlook held firm sway from the 1830s into the twentieth century. Yet the systemic interpretation increasingly gained ascendancy, especially after Booth's and Rowntree's surveys at the end of the century, which highlighted large-scale poverty and argued that the vast majority of the poor were such through no fault of their own. The route through which the systemic view initially entered policy was via action on longer-term structural causes: education, housing, social insurance and, most vigorously, health – via compulsory vaccination, inspection and health-related public works. These developments helped to weaken gradually the dominance of the moral view from the 1860s onwards. Many of these proto-welfare state measures became the responsibility of local government, and the systemic view formed the basis of many of the major urban local authorities' social policies. The voluntary sector, in contrast, tended to hold to the moral view.

Attempts at significant redistributions of income towards the poor, via local publicly provided benefits in income or kind, faced immense difficulties, because they had to be almost entirely funded out of property taxes. The connection can be seen in the optimistically naive slogan for the Progressives in the early LCC, which Sidney Webb borrowed from Chamberlain's early Birmingham campaigns: 'High rates and healthy cities.'[18] Chamberlain, in fact, managed to keep rates at the same level, but metropolitan local government was associated with ever-escalating taxation. Rates were hugely unpopular and increasingly seen as a burden on enterprise, with consequences that are explored in the following chapter.

Voluntary associations

Voluntary philanthropic activity in the capital in the early 1860s amounted to between £5.5 million and £7 million annually. Although not solely concerned with alleviating poverty, this sum was still more than the total Poor Law expenditure for England and Wales as a whole.[19] Donations continued at a high level: in the late 1880s, *The Times* boasted that the annual income of the various London charities was around £5 million, 'twice that of the Swiss Confederation'. The voluntary approach consequently dwarfed official relief of poverty in the capital.

The money was raised through a variety of means, such as individual donations, church collections, charity balls and public appeals. In one exceptional case, the 1886 Mansion House appeal raised £78,000 because of the scale of the prevailing distress and a fear of severe rioting. Yet regular giving was large-scale, as can be seen for the 1860s and the 1870s, when an annual collection on a June Sunday in London churches for local hospitals would bring in £30,000 on average.[20]

The money was distributed in a variety of ways. Large amounts were used to finance free dispensaries, the free treatment of outpatients, schools, soup kitchens, homeless poor asylums and, during slumps, the distribution of clothing, footwear and small sums of money to the unemployed. Charity, consequently, was not a direct substitute for public relief, as the money was generally spent in distinct ways and focused upon particular groups in poverty. Direct income subventions were made by the voluntary bodies, though they were generally not continuous, reliable or adequate sources of relief. The 1886 Mansion House appeal relieved almost 41,000 families, representing 160,000 individuals, in the form of small doles averaging 13s 1d per head.[21]

A drawback of this huge voluntary activity was that there was neither co-operation nor co-ordination either between the charities themselves or with the Poor Law authorities, so that much of the money was used ineffectually. The ways in which the funds could be spent, moreover, were influenced by the widespread distinction on donators' parts between the 'deserving' and 'undeserving' poor. The idea of a huge, unruly, feckless residuum, or underclass, that could even be a danger to urban stability, dominated early views on poverty and persisted even after the evidence suggested otherwise. One result was that many believed that philanthropic organisations were often hoodwinked, leading to the demoralisation of the respectable poor.[22]

In light of such criticisms, in 1869 the Charity Organisation Society (known fully as the Society for Organising Charitable Relief and Repressing Mendicity) was formed to rationalise charity disbursements across England and to impose a strongly moralistic view of poverty on social debate and policy. The poverty of the undeserving, it argued, was caused by bad moral character and they should be left to a punitive Poor Law. Instead, the Society aimed to help the deserving poor from slipping into moral degeneration, by using sympathetic casework and financial help to aid them in regaining independence. In the event, many charities refused to co-operate with the Society. Yet its London branches were industrious: distributing to vetted paupers grants in cash or kind; offering loans – 1,039 in 1872 alone; helping with emigration; providing pensions and widows' funds; and re-using cast-off clothing and books.[23] Its views tempered over time, but had considerable influence in the formation of social attitudes and policies towards the poor.

Poor relief

Prior to the introduction of the New Poor Law measures, poor relief largely took the form of monetary assistance to people who continued to live in their own homes. This practice changed to 'indoor relief' in a workhouse following the 1834 Poor Law Amendment Act, which created a centralised bureaucracy in the form of the Poor Law Commission. The Poor Law Board, set up in 1847, applied further pressure on parish Poor Law unions to provide relief only within the workhouse. Outdoor relief, it was argued, increased Poor Law expenditure by discouraging paupers from searching for work or investing in benefit clubs, or by reducing family charity. Moreover, such relief depressed wages and hindered the free flow of labour by tying the poor to their current place of settlement. When paupers applied for relief they could be forceably sent back to their place of origin – a measure aimed, in particular, at avoiding influxes of poor to one particular locality and, in general, at sparing the large cities from a flood of the rural poor.[24]

In London, the Commission's efforts to encourage the introduction of indoor relief were relatively successful, with around a third of those applying being sent into the workhouse. As can be seen from Table 15.1, this form of relief was proportionately far more important in the capital than in Lancashire and the West Riding, in both 1850 and 1860. There were, nevertheless, substantial disparities in the kind of relief offered by metropolitan unions. Indoor relief was particularly pronounced in the West End and older western/north-western suburbs and in the inner industrial areas. This was because of the characteristics of their poor as much as any ingrained difference in philosophy. On the one hand, the wealthy, western areas had relatively few long-term paupers but many domestic servants. When servants became unemployed, they also lost their home and so the workhouse offered the only refuge. On the other hand, in the inner industrial crescent, there were large numbers of poor and a limited rate base, so the workhouse was used as a disincentive to restrict applications for relief. Not all low-income areas, however, adopted such a strategy: Lewisham, Poplar and Rotherhithe, in particular, maintained a policy of outdoor relief. Poplar was the most enthusiastic, typically spending 50 to 75 per cent more on outdoor than indoor relief in the 1850s and 1860s.[25] These atypical policies reflected local politics and a greater degree of social homogeneity in these localities.

From the 1850s, however, the number of dissident parishes gradually fell as central control tightened. In 1852, the Poor Law Board forbade London unions from providing outdoor relief to able-bodied men already in employment. If a man was unemployed, outdoor relief could only be given in return for work. It was further laid down that a third of the relief given to the outdoor poor should consist of help in kind, with an even greater proportion for the able-bodied. When these measures proved insufficient, measures to discourage outdoor relief were tightened in the 1867 Metropolitan Poor Act. This gave the Poor Law Board powers to nominate pro-workhouse guardians to unions and permitted the creation of separate sick asylum districts for the establishment of infirmaries and dispensaries. Local districts and the Metropolitan Asylum Board built large numbers of hospitals and asylums, institutionalising many of those previously receiving monetary payments. Indoor relief was additionally promoted by the 1871 Pauper Inmates Discharge and Regulation Act.[26] This set up further deterrents by requiring separate wards for vagrants. Anyone

Table 15.1 Percentage of poor relief spent on indoor and outdoor relief in London, Lancashire and the West Riding, 1850 and 1860

	1850			*1860*		
	Indoor	*Outdoor*	*Other*	*Indoor*	*Outdoor*	*Other*
London	34	35	31	33	25	42
Lancashire	17	54	29	19	41	40
West Riding	10	73	17	13	62	26

Source: Green, 1995, 215.

discharged from the workhouse was almost by definition a vagrant, unless they had the support of an extended family or charity, as they must have been destitute before succumbing to the harshness and humiliation of indoor relief. Now they could no longer qualify for outdoor relief as they were vagrants.

Despite the relatively high use of indoor relief, London at first built few extra workhouses. By 1847, for example, only eight unions had sought permission from the Poor Law Commission to construct new premises, and most of these were located in rapidly growing suburbs.[27] A deterrent was the high cost of construction in the capital, which caused many unions to balk at such large investments. Instead, parishes preferred to alter or add to their existing premises. By the 1860s, the demand for indoor relief forced a switch in policy, and an expanded programme of building started that carried on for most of the period. Much of the increase was related to special needs, however, such as infirmaries and vagrant wards – keeping the standard of the normal workhouse overcrowded and grim.

The initial impact of the New Poor Law in London was to reduce real total expenditure sharply. The fall was short-lived, however, because from the late 1830s expenditure grew rapidly, outstripping that of England and Wales as a whole, so that by the late 1850s it had surpassed the pre-1834 levels.[28] This, however, still represented a considerable per capita saving because of London's population growth.

The causes of poverty

The reasons for the growth in poor relief have some bearing on the debate over causes of London's poverty. The data for London (Middlesex) in Figure 15.1 are compared with those of two northern industrial districts, Lancashire and the West Riding of Yorkshire, and with England as a whole. London, like the northern industrial districts, experienced much faster trend growth in poor relief than the rest of England. The West Riding's increase was far less than the capital's. Yet the trend in the growth of poor relief in Lancashire is similar, even though it had a smaller population, and it is worth considering why.

Lancashire's industry was dominated by the new factory systems of the

Figure 15.1 Poor Law expenditure by county, 1813–68

Source: Green, 1995, 219.

Note: Middlesex encompassed London north of the river and so acts as a proxy for London as a whole when data are available only on a county basis prior to the setting up of the County of London in 1889.

cotton industry and its towns were experiencing even faster rates of urban growth and immigration than London in the early years of the century. A difference can be seen in Figure 15.1 in Lancashire's greater cyclical variation in the amount of poor relief compared to the other two regions. Both London and Lancashire were hit by the unemployment effects of general downturns in the business cycle, but after 1837 London's fluctuations were noticeably smaller in amplitude – with Lancashire's distress greatest during the American Civil War. This suggests that the cyclical benefits for the metropolitan poor of having a larger and more dispersed industrial structure actually did exist. Lancashire's one-industry economy generated more cyclical poverty than London's multi-industry one.

Local variations in Poor Law taxation

Within London, parishes were responsible for raising the funds for their expenditure by levying a Poor Law rate on all taxable local property. Expenditure in the capital consequently varied geographically according to the mix of wealth and poverty and local policies towards the scale and form of relief. In the 1830s and 1840s, Poor Law unions in the inner industrial belt set far higher Poor Law rates than their counterparts in the West End, City and outer suburbs, with parishes in inner Southwark charging the most. In 1840, for example, rates in poor Bethnal Green were 2s 1d in the pound, as compared to 5½d in the pound in wealthy St George, Hanover Square.[29] Part of the reason for the difference is attributable to the far higher property values in the West End, so that the regressive disparity in the taxes paid by wealthier inner city households was not what the raw rate poundage figures would suggest. Suburban localities with their combination of low property values and rate poundages, however, contributed a far lower share of the total urban-wide burden than their income distributions would imply. The City had the particular benefit of the high rateable value of business premises located there, relieving the charge on residential property.

The burden on the parishes that could least afford it intensified between 1840 and 1860, even if account is taken of changing differences in property values. By 1858, residents in St George-in-the-East were paying a rate of 3s 9d in the pound; whereas those in St George, Hanover Square, at 6d, were charged only a halfpenny more than in 1840. The City, by then, had fallen into one of the cheapest rate poundage categories because of continued out-migration and rising property values.

The worsening situation in the poorer districts arose for two main reasons: legislative change and the impact of suburbanisation.

Before 1846, unions could remove paupers who had not lived long in their parish back to their place of settlement. Although the process was costly and cumbersome, many unions used this provision, particularly with the poor who had recently arrived from Ireland or Scotland. The 1846 Poor Law Removal Act created a new category of 'non-settled but irremovable' poor. This status was conferred on widows whose husbands had died less than a year before and on those resident in a parish for five or more consecutive years. The poorer East End unions had large numbers of immigrants, so their expenditure rose rapidly. By the 1850s, Whitechapel, Poplar and some inner southern districts were having to commit a third of their Poor Law expenditure to the irremovable poor.[30]

At the same time, better-off households were migrating out of these poorer inner areas to the suburbs, lowering the income base on which rates were collected. Rate income fell and, as larger houses were subdivided into flats and rooms to let, there was an even greater inflow of the poor to these inner districts. Land-use change in the City and West End was also pushing the poor from there into the surrounding low-income neighbourhoods. Poor Law expenditure, as a consequence, was redistributed from the centre to the inner poor districts to the benefit of the wealthy residents in the centre and the distress of ratepayers elsewhere. There was some local adjustment to compensate for these population moves, as with the decision of the City of London Poor Law Union in the 1850s to continue to support 1,500–1,600 paupers now resident in adjacent parishes.[31]

Crisis point was reached in 1866, when a cold winter, high bread prices and the financial panic after the failure of Overend Gurney led to the collapse of many industries, including shipbuilding, and to a large increase in pauperism. In East London, the number applying for relief at year end almost doubled between 1865 and 1867 to 36,407.[32] In order to meet this expenditure, unions increased their rates – Bethnal Green's rose by 75 per cent in four years. Few were confident that ratepayers would not revolt and that the necessary revenue could be collected. In Shoreditch, 15,000 summons were issued in 1868 for non-payment of rates.[33] In response to this fiscal crisis, the 1867 Metropolitan Poor Act created the Metropolitan Common Poor Fund to redistribute rate income from the wealthier to the poorer districts – the first instance of spatial municipal income and expenditure smoothing in the capital.

Redistribution of the Poor Law burden was financed by contributions from individual unions according to their rateable value. Initially, it applied only to the cost of maintaining lunatics, pauper children and the casual poor, various forms of medical expenditure and the salaries of Poor Law officials. But, from 1870, it provided additionally a subsidy equivalent to 5d a day for each adult indoor pauper, which had the subsequent effect of further discouraging outdoor relief and funding the construction of more workhouses. The Act led to a substantial transfer of funds to the poorer unions and falls in their rate demands. From 1867 to 1877, for example, 25 per cent and 33 per cent of poor relief spending in St George-in-the-East and Bethnal Green respectively came from the fund.[34]

Another unintended consequence of the Act was that it gave a boost to the attractions of living in the suburbs for the better-off, where property taxes were lower. This was especially the case for far-flung neighbourhoods outside of the County area, because residents there completely avoided paying the imposed equalised Poor Law charges.

Employment and wages policies

Local government in London in various ways tried to raise employment conditions through factory legislation; by improving remuneration by using their own staff rather than contractors and paying them well; and by adopting schemes for the unemployed. These developments occurred from the 1880s onwards and reflect the stimulus to metropolitan local government politics provided by attempts to emulate the 'municipal socialism' of several successful provincial authorities. Most was done by vestries when they were under Progressive control and by the LCC during the Progressive era. The Progressives were the London embodiment of the New Liberalism of the era, drawing on its roots in older Radicalism, with a small contingent of the growing labour/socialist movements.[35] Their policies focused on labour market and social reforms, a believed superiority of municipal enterprise and attacks on what they saw as privilege and monopoly.

An area over which Progressives had immediate control was the employment conditions of municipal employees and the use of contractors. Since the 1860s, vestries had increasingly been employing workers direct rather than using contractors. With the growing politicisation of the vestries, this policy was intensified, so that by 1890 it was claimed that 60 per cent of the labour used by vestries was employed directly by them. In strongly Progressive Battersea, all work was undertaken by direct labour by 1895.[36] The LCC adopted a similar programme, setting up its own building workforce, for example, in the 1890s. Council manual workers were also paid well, at above comparable private sector rates. 'Fair wages' clauses, encouraged by national legislation, were introduced and made compulsory in contracts with the private sector.

Vestries of whatever political persuasion had for many years been concerned to offer local, small-scale unemployment relief by hiring the unemployed for street sweeping and the like. Some more ambitious programmes were floated towards the end of the century but they foundered because of their cost and the difficulty of funding them through the rates. One development only appeared towards the end of the period – it was the use of local government capital expenditure in a counter-cyclical way to create employment at times of downturn in the business cycle. This arose from a provision of the 1909 Budget setting up a Development Commission and a Road Board, empowered to encourage public authorities to concentrate capital works in times of depression. These had little effect up to 1914, but were to have a major impact on London's suburban transport infrastructure after 1918.

Housing the poor

Prior to the 1850s, little was heard of the 'housing question' in London. The poor mainly lived in low-quality, inner city accommodation but they did not agitate for improvements and no one else took much notice. Although never at the forefront of politics, from the 1850s on, concern and intervention grew up to the First World War. London during this period played a leading part in the evolution of national housing policies. Newspapers, books, pamphlets and reports tended to focus on its problems and, in the absence of a London-wide government, the issue was taken up in Parliament, which passed a series of housing-related Acts from the 1850s onwards. This section documents and evaluates this surge in concern and action.

The origin of the 'slum'

During the nineteenth century, slums came to be defined as such by commentators on the housing conditions of London's poor. Slum was a slang word for a room where low goings-on occurred in buildings found in the quiet backwaters behind main streets – giving the etyomological link to slumber. It came to replace older phrases such as 'rookery' as its usage widened to cover a whole neighbourhood of bad housing. Cardinal Wiseman in 1850 popularised the term in his condemnation of the housing around Westminster Abbey. The word consequently has roots replete with a moral view of bad housing. Wiseman, for instance, called slums 'nests of ignorance, vice, depravity and crime', and this moral view of housing explains the popularity of the housing question with middle-class reformers. Their consciences were awoken by the sensational reports from 'hidden' London and a number of social surveys in the 1850s and 1860s, vividly portraying the extremes of poverty that could be found in the capital, by Mayhew, Hollingshead, Mearns, and others.[37] Housing policy aimed to root out these problems and was as much about changing what were seen as undesirable aspects of the lives of the working classes as about improving their living conditions. Increasingly throughout the century the emphasis focused on overcrowding, rather than on other physical features such as house condition, because it was seen as a broad indicator of morally unsatisfactory lifestyles as well as of poor housing.[38]

Many London nineteenth-century slums were street blocks entered by a few narrow passageways from main thoroughfares. Inside they contained an array of short passages, blind-alleys, and the occasional break in a row of housing – sometimes less than three feet wide – to allow access to further poor-quality accommodation behind. Sanitation and running water were limited or non-existent, unlike the rubbish, stench and noise. Mortality rates were found to be much higher than in better districts. These densely packed neighbourhoods were often small in geographic area. This enabled an early conception of the slum problem as a physical phenomenon of isolated trouble spots that needed clearing, with only a belated recognition that householders had to be re-housed in new dwellings or they would simply go and exacerbate overcrowding elsewhere.

There were other types of bad housing that were more integrated into the broader social fabric. The mews behind grand houses, for example, contained small workshops and terribly overcrowded rooms for the poorest of households – often cheek-by-jowl with the horses they were intended for. All the smart neighbourhoods had such pockets of poverty, particularly when they had declined somewhat, as happened in Paddington. Other slums arose when wealthier inhabitants moved on leaving their old homes to rent-farmers who crudely subdivided the houses – offering little in the way of sanitation or fresh water. With no maintenance, the buildings quickly fell into disrepair. Finally, as the century progressed, areas of cheap dwellings thrown up earlier slowly declined in quality and into total disrepair.

Quite how many slums existed in nineteenth-century London is unknown. Even the most balanced of surveys tended to exaggerate merely by describing the worst rather than average housing circumstances. Modern writers have similarly been prone to overstate the problem. Wohl's (1977) survey, for instance, is an essential part of the literature but, on occasion, he gives the impression that bad housing affected most of London's working classes, which is hardly likely to have been the case – particularly from the mid-nineteenth century onwards:

> Thus far from being untypical and the condition of just an unsuccessful minority of workmen in the metropolis, overcrowding was in fact the state of the majority of workmen who, for one reason or another, could not benefit from the development of working-class suburbs.[39]

Yet his only data are for 1911, when 10 per cent of the capital's (County) population lived in what was classified as overcrowded accommodation. This may represent a severe problem but it is still that of a minority. Moreover, bad housing, like poverty, is a relative term so it is hard to set a fixed, immutable standard for it.

In terms of the number of rooms in each dwelling for the population as a whole, London does not look particularly bad at the turn of the century compared to many English cities, as shown in Table 15.2 (and certainly not when compared to Scottish ones). Moreover, the 40 odd per cent of the metropolitan population living beyond the County boundary, mainly living in the new suburbs, were far better housed on average than those in the County area on which the data in Table 15.2 are based. It is probable, therefore, that the average Londoner actually had better space standards than virtually any other large British town dweller, despite the far higher housing costs of the capital.

Although average housing standards had risen during the nineteenth century, social consciences may well have been pricked by the failure of some to keep up with them. Relativity can be seen in the minimum socially acceptable standard for housing prior to the First World War, which was far lower than it is today. And social reformers, by the 1880s, had made it clear that they felt that housing had a special place above many other aspects of life. Those actually suffering the bad housing may have had other priorities, but they were not given much say in determining social policy goals.

Table 15.2 Comparative dwelling sizes for selected cities, 1901

	Number of rooms (% of total stock)		
	1 to 3	*4*	*5 or more*
Birmingham	32	13	55
Bradford	42	21	37
Manchester	9	40	51
Leeds	26	25	49
Newcastle	53	19	28
London	39	15	46
England and Wales	18	22	60

Source: Burnett, 1978, 153.

Filtering and the options for housing policy

If Victorians had a theory of low-income housing supply, it was based on filtering. As more suburban houses were built for the better-off, those lower down the scale could move up into the higher-quality dwellings they vacated. Unfortunately, this can only happen if the rents of those better-quality dwellings fall to levels that the poor can afford. If prices do not fall, the quality of the vacated houses has to drop: either by reducing space standards, say by renting off single rooms to families, or through disrepair. In reality, continued population increases meant that filtered-down houses quickly became as bad as the previous slums, and overcrowding spread outwards into adjacent inner city districts, such as previously middle-class Islington. Filtering theory, in other words, is wrong, as it assumes that the supply side does not adjust to new circumstances. The theory was not only used by railway companies and the advocates of *laissez-faire*. Keir Hardie, the first Labour MP, also adopted it in 1903 to justify municipal housing for the better class of artisans: 'housing vacancies would be created right down to the lowest slums'.[40]

If filtering theory ignores housing market dynamics, so did other explanations for slum conditions. One culprit was identified in the unscrupulous behaviour of private landlords (as exemplified in Shaw's *Widowers' Houses*). Many reformers suggested that this market failure could be resolved by philanthropic bodies or municipalities taking over the responsibilities of being a landlord. Yet both of the latter found it financially impossible to re-house the lowest-income families, despite subsidies, until the large, centrally funded, slum clearance subsidy schemes of the 1930s. The philanthropic bodies were also more liable to police the behaviour of their tenants, keeping non-payment of rents to minuscule levels; whereas private landlords faced greater default. This does not imply that landlords were angels, rather that extreme poverty in a private housing market offers little other option but bad housing. The alternative route of land invasion and squatting, commonly used by the modern Third World urban poor, was virtually impossible in nineteenth-century England.

Other problems were raised by those opposed to philanthropic and municipal endeavour. Providing good-quality, subsidised housing in the inner city in effect sanctioned and subsidised low-wage employment there. The incidence of the housing subsidy, consequently, might not remain with the poor it was supposed to help but, in part, depress their wages – increasing the profits of the 'sweaters' and other exploiters of casual labour. If the housing of the poor were subsidised in inner London, moreover, this would attract the poor from other regions and foreign immigrants to fill up the slums vacated by their companions. If those slums had been cleared as part of the re-housing, more poor would still have been drawn to London by the better prospects – creating new slums to replace the old, and putting further downward pressure on casual wages. The link to the labour market and migration was an Achilles' heel that housing reformers never effectively managed to rebut. In part, the callousness or ingenuousness of the many proponents of these links, however, helped them to lose the argument. The economist, Alfred Marshall, for example, suggested strict sanitary enforcement to reduce the supply of sub-standard accommodation and compulsory expulsion of the poor to the countryside.[41] (Others would have preferred rural labour camps.)

Octavia Hill argued differently. She relied on intensive personal education of the poor in self-improvement; opposed philanthropic model dwellings and municipal building on grounds similar to those cited above; and argued for piecemeal improvement of existing dwellings to reverse the negative consequences of filtering-down.[42] By her death in 1912, she was managing possibly 1,800 dwellings.[43] Despite her fame, she was widely labelled by contemporaries as an eccentric, latter-day Samuel Smiles – though her principle of housing renovation rather than redevelopment has a surprisingly modern resonance.

Another reason why the links between housing and labour markets never came to the fore was the view that the urgency of the housing shortage made such rational argument seem heartless. Yet housing reform, rather than increasing the quantity of low-income housing, actually made its supply in the inner city fall. This was because only the better-off artisan could afford most of the new housing erected, or put up with the regimentation. The Kingsway and Clare Market LCC schemes of the turn of the century, for example, removed 6,000 and provided re-housing for only 500.[44] The displacement of the poor, not surprisingly, became a running sore for housing reformers.

The loss of inner city housing land to other urban uses, nevertheless, was a potent argument in housing reformers' favour, even if retaining it was not necessarily the best strategy. Much of central London and its pre-nineteenth-century housing stock was turned over to railways, street improvements, new public and commercial buildings and model dwellings. Re-housing obligations were slow to come and were weak once imposed. Estimates of the displaced vary, and must inevitably be circumspect as they assume no change in the absence of the building works, but they are still dramatic – up to 120,000 people removed by the railways,[45] many more by street improvements, and countless others by the switch from residential to commercial and public land uses. Where were those tied to the inner city supposed to live?

Most modern accounts suggest that the number of low-income employees stuck in central residential areas by the nature of their work was high, citing evidence such as an LCC survey from just prior to the First World War, reporting that many of the working men living in Bethnal Green, Holborn, Southwark and Westminster said that they preferred central living, despite the higher rents, because of the convenience of getting to work. Earlier, in the 1880s, a model dwelling company with central tenements had reported that almost half of those living in its dwellings lived under a mile from their place of work.[46]

In reality, there is little hard evidence and there is also a problem of identifying cause and effect because city-centre jobs requiring local residence may have existed in large numbers when local low-income housing was there, but would have moved further out if such housing was absent from the urban core. Yelling, although he comes down himself on the side of necessity, provides some counter-evidence that shows rather limited numbers tied to the city centre through employment.[47] Moreover, contemporary critics of 'trapped by necessity' view included that most famous surveyor of poverty, Charles Booth, who favoured a suburban solution of encouraging, through improved transport, more of the working classes to commute in from the suburbs. This would have the added benefit of reducing city-centre housing demand. The LCC, by the turn of the century, itself was convinced that many more both could afford to move to the suburbs and had hours of work compatible with commuting. Another informed contemporary commentator suggested that many of those living centrally did so through habit, proximity of friends or the allurement of endowed or voluntary charity, and wondered why society at large should subsidise such preferences.[48] With the list somewhat extended, his statement could be reinterpreted as saying that the poor wanted to live centrally because the London-related agglomeration economies of particular benefit to them were greatest there. If that was the case, suburban solutions would have had to encompass more than housing and transport to compensate for the loss of central agglomeration benefits.

When local authorities built houses, they imposed extra burdens on the rates to fund the new developments. This raised others' housing costs and discouraged new private development. With no central exchequer subsidy, the impact on local public finances was significant. The Metropolitan Board of Works towards the end of its life, as illustration of this point, claimed that it had lost over £1 million on the slum clearance and rebuilding schemes it was encouraged to undertake – a charge put on London ratepayers.[49] After initial enthusiasm, the Board tired of the delays, cost and opprobrium associated with the task and wanted to be able to clear slums, sell the land commercially and use the proceeds for new housing elsewhere in the city – going along with rather than against the grain of contemporary urban change. Under the contemporary 'replacement on site' arrangements, it argued, existing populations were untraceably scattered at the time of demolition; then the long gap between demolition and completion of the new housing cut into currently available supply; and, when completed, non-locals were likely to be re-housed. The MBW's difficulties highlighted the scale of the funds required and the long delays before anything was seen for their expenditure; yet the rate costs were immediate, substantial and soon subject to criticism. By the time of its critique of prevailing wisdom, it was too late for the Board to have much influence on future housing policy, and with its demise, the new LCC, at least initially, continued to encourage inner city rebuilding.

Even the much-vaunted policy of encouraging additional suburbanisation had drawbacks. This policy was put into practice from the 1890s in three ways: by building new municipally owned tram routes, by developing social housing, and by encouraging the railway companies to issue more workmen's tickets. In each case, at least some private investment may have been choked off – by private tram companies, suburban developers of working-class housing, and the rail companies. So the net social benefit was far less than it seemed, especially if the additional rate burden was high.

Model dwelling companies

The earliest approach to housing policy was an extension of the principles of the various Building Acts, which since the seventeenth century had set minimum standards for new buildings. Under this policy regime, existing housing should have had minimum standards based on the state of repair, overcrowding and hygiene. A series of Housing and Health Acts adopted this approach, which, though often criticised for their weakness, did much to clean up and improve the sanitary condition of the older housing stock. The first measures were introduced by Lord Shaftesbury in 1851. He steered through two Housing Acts, having failed earlier to introduce a measure restricting overcrowding, because its inspection rights were argued to limit personal freedom. The first Act required minimum standards for common lodging houses – these were the insanitary dormitory quarters of transients, long disliked by the police as harbingers of crime. Some 82,000 people were thought to live in 10,800 common lodging houses in London in 1854, more than the population of most English towns. The Act's requirements of compulsory registration and inspection were carried out by an enthusiastic police force, with the worst sanitary abuses cleaned up. Shaftesbury's second Act (Labouring Classes Lodging Houses Act) permitted vestries to borrow money, buy land and build houses for the labouring classes. What came to be council housing was thus permitted during the heyday of *laissez-faire*. A remarkable range of opinion supported such non-market intervention, including *The Times* and the *Medical Times*, with the latter calling for large numbers of model dwellings to be purchased by the state. The drafting of the Act, though, meant that it was virtually impossible to use.[50]

Non-profit model dwellings then came to the forefront as a solution to the housing question. The 'model dwelling' was a phrase that came to mean the tenement blocks, generally four to six storeys high, built to minimum standards across austere courtyards, which appeared throughout central London over the next sixty years.[51] As a built form, they were pervasive in the city centre. Around 40,000 tenements with a total of 105,000 rooms were erected up to 1914[52] – many of them still exist today, although they now house much smaller household sizes with far better amenities. Population densities were often extremely high – higher than the densities of the overcrowded slums they replaced. One building in

Farringdon Road in the 1880s reached an awesome density by London standards of 1,625 people per acre[53] – indicating the extent to which concern over overcrowding was about privacy rather than space. These schemes were designed and operated as 'a controlled environment of enforced respectability' – highlighting the moral concerns of the philanthropic bodies that built them. They were expensive to build, which helps to account for their minimal standards – Peabody, one of the cheapest builders of model dwellings, only managed £90 a room on subsidised central city land; suburban speculative builders could produce for less than half that amount at vastly lower population densities.[54] The price of central city housing for the labouring classes was high, and once it became the new land-use, the projects were themselves open to the retort that they were stealing expensive land from better uses.

Philanthropic housing bodies had existed in England since the Middle Ages, providing almshouses for the elderly and destitute, for example. The rise of Victorian philanthropy and permissive legislation gave them a substantial boost from the 1860s onwards – and most of their actions were directed towards the metropolis, although housing conditions were undoubtedly worse elsewhere in Britain. Over thirty model dwelling companies and trusts were set up in London in the second half of the nineteenth century, and many reconstituted ones still exist today as part of the housing association movement.[55] The principle of these new housing charities was that they had to show a small profit on their operations – hence they have often been characterised somewhat sarcastically as 'five per cent philanthropy'. The need for the offering to Mammon was justified on the grounds that private enterprise rather than the state was better in housing provision and that such a rule avoided demoralising the recipients of the new dwellings. These organisations filled a need that local government could not then provide for and soon proved to be vigorous opponents of the municipal housing model.

In reality, the model dwelling companies operated in a subsidised and uncompetitive environment. Housing Acts in 1866–7 enabled them to borrow cheaply from the state, which they did; charity donations protected their finances; they had privileged access to land sites, so they could bid low prices for them; and excess demand existed for their products. There was some rivalry between the trusts, with others complaining, for instance, about Peabody's low costs and rents. Yet there were no inducements for the others to follow Peabody's example, to be efficient or to provide the housing their consumers actually wanted. Some model dwelling companies received land donations from concerned land magnates, which explains the odd appearance of such structures in the wealthiest neighbourhoods. These philanthropic bodies also left a substantial legacy for later social housing: via design criteria, their voluntary status and the foundation of an influential housing profession.

Slum clearance by public bodies started in Liverpool, Glasgow and Edinburgh but soon legislation was introduced to legitimate and facilitate its adoption in other cities, especially London. The Torren's Act of 1868 proved ineffectual and was replaced by the Cross Act of 1875. Slums were to be removed by compulsion, with adequate compensation for loss of property, and the cleared land sold to private developers for new working-class housing. The Metropolitan Board of Works was encouraged to take the lead, selling the cleared land to model dwelling companies. It eventually undertook fourteen schemes. Optimistically, at the time of the passing of the Cross Act, it was argued that spending £2 million would solve the problem of London's slums. The MBW, in fact, managed to spend over £1.5 million but, in doing so, hardly scratched the surface.[56] The sheer cost of removing slums, intractable difficulties over compensation and betterment, and a failure to do anything for the worst-housed had sobering effects on other pre-1914 experiments.

The LCC

The LCC initially carried on the previous slum clearance policies and encouraged vestries in their endeavours, although conflicts soon arose between the enthusiasm to direct of the former and the reluctance to spend of the latter. The new County Council's flagship scheme at Boundary Street, Shoreditch, was opened in 1900 and marked a departure in improving the design standards of inner city working-class flats while keeping to a tight budget. But it faced the same old problems of high costs and homelessness. The scheme, for example, housed 5,500 but displaced 5,700, few of whom could wait or afford to move into the new accommodation.[57]

The Council then switched to a policy of building suburban estates in line with its pre-existing policy of making commuting more accessible and cheaper. Thus, in 1900, it obtained Parliamentary permission to buy land outside its boundaries and proceeded to build four new estates at Norbury, Old Oak, Tooting and Tottenham: two of them outside of the LCC area. It broadly adopted the design criteria of the emerging Garden City movement in these schemes and, by doing so, unwittingly helped to ensure that the mass of later suburban owner occupiers would reject them.

By 1914, the Council had spent almost £3 million on constructing 9,800 tenements. The Corporation of London had built 490 and other boroughs in the Greater London area just over 5,000.[58] All together local authorities had yet to match the model-dwelling companies by 1914, but the stage had been set for a massive expansion of public housing provision in the inter-war years.

16 The government of London

Introduction

Local government in nineteenth-century London had an entirely different history from the rest of the country. From mid-century, a two-tier system evolved. The first tier covered city-wide activities – most famously in the formation of the London County Council in 1889 but earlier with the Metropolitan Board of Works and a variety of single-function statutory bodies. The second tier consisted of local vestries – based on parish districts – and other minor local entities. The Corporation of London had a special position in the second tier. This situation was unique in contemporary urban Britain because, since 1835, most large towns and cities had had their own, single-tier, councils.

Justification for the difference in London related to its size. It was just too big to allow any reasonable sense of democratic representation with only one tier. It was also commonly felt amongst politicians that a city-wide body would create an alternative, quasi-national government. Why this should be so is unclear, as local government at the time had very limited and parochial functions and, as the USA showed, in practice there was little to fear. The potential platform for London Radicals and others, none the less, was too much for national politicians to stomach. Economically, a single-tier body would anyway have been well above the optimal size for many prevailing local government functions.

Controversy over London's government in the nineteenth century was primarily articulated in debates among a narrow band of interest groups: those sitting on the various functional bodies; politicians in Parliament, the Cabinet and party machines; intellectuals and others interested in the 'local government' question and issues, such as sanitation, housing and education; and bodies claiming to represent hard-pressed ratepayers. What is noticeably missing from this list of combatants are ordinary Londoners. General political concern over local government was minuscule – local elections rarely excited much interest and the only serious attempt to raise a mass demonstration about London's governance by Radicals in the 1880s was an embarrassing damp squib, even though such events were by then fashionable.

Over the course of the century, the scale of metropolitan local government activity grew substantially. At the same time, controversy raged over the forms it should take, what services should be provided and how they should be financed. The issues under debate are similar to those of today. Local government needed to be democratic and representative of local populations, undertake its roles efficiently, keep tax levels down and respond to nationally determined minimum standards of provision.

Wider democracy (at least, for men) came to the first tier in 1889 with the formation of the London County Council (LCC). It had spread into the vestries somewhat earlier, and at both levels political divisions appeared on party lines from the 1880s onwards. The vestries were reformed on several occasions, becoming municipal boroughs in the 1900s. Yet several functions that were part of democratic local government elsewhere in Britain remained in the private sector or were run by non-elected statutory bodies, with water being the most important example.

Local government and statutory body activity, moreover, was almost entirely funded by property taxes in the metropolis; whereas, today, much local government expenditure is financed through central government grants, and other expenditures, such as social security, are the sole responsibility of central government. Rate bills consequently were a major political issue in a way that, the 1980s poll tax apart, they have never been since. Erroneously, rates were generally thought to be borne only by the owners of properties rather than those who rented them. This gave a narrow band of property-owner interests considerable influence over local government, with ratepayers' groups closely aligned with petty bourgeois property interests. Especially contentious areas of local government were social programmes that required large-scale redistributive taxation. Overall, it should be remembered that property taxes were the most prevalent form of direct taxation during the period. Central government swallowed all the sales, import and income taxes levied and some of the revenues from real property, yet provided few services in return. Those services, instead, were the prerogative of local activity, if any public bodies were to supply them at all – and rates had to finance most of them.

This chapter focuses on the economic issues surrounding the government of London. It does this first by considering some general economic principles about local government – using London examples to illustrate them. Then the evolution of metropolitan government in the nineteenth century is examined and contrasted with those principles. This is not naively to assume that economics did determine, or should have determined, the changes that actually occurred. Rather it is done to provide some criteria against which to evaluate the reforms that took place. In reality, the shifting political structure was a path-dependent one. As well as influencing contemporary politics, the organisations and institutional practices already in place influenced the ones that followed in far more ways than impatient reformers would have liked.

Some economics of local government

What goods should local government provide?

Economic theory examines government as a process of public, or collective, choice. Governments are the means by which certain actions can be undertaken. Voters can be regarded as consumers of those actions, who are taxed to pay for them. Consumer utility maximisation in the face of resource constraints, the standard tools of economics, can therefore be applied to government activity.[1]

In a market economy, government provision of some goods is necessary because markets have insufficient incentive to provide them. They are termed public goods and come in three types – pure, impure and local. Pure public goods are ones that are consumed by many people at the same time but where it is impossible to exclude those who do not pay. Disease prevention programmes, clean air and national defence are three commonly cited examples. Impure public goods are similar to pure ones but are subject to congestion – most inter-urban roads are classic instances. Finally, local public goods are those where the benefit is geographically limited. The benefit of a street light exists in a highly localised manner; parks cover a wider area and fire and police services have even broader spatial effects. Local public goods may also be subject to congestion, such as occurs with good schools.

Some market-provided local goods may also generate benefits beyond those for which their users pay. In the modern world, public transport systems may reduce road congestion, benefiting those who still use a car as well as those using a new facility. Such external benefits provide justification for local subsidies to their producers and, when for some reason such subsidies are infeasible, may provide justification for municipal provision. The opposite may also occur in that external costs are created locally – pollution and threats to public health are two such cases. Municipal government can intervene to limit or proscribe them, possibly implementing nationally laid-down standards. There are some goods that are classified as merit goods – those which people have a moral (or politically determined) right to consume to a certain standard. Libraries and some cultural facilities had this characteristic in the nineteenth century. Housing came to be considered a merit good in Britain after the First World War and the advent of centrally funded council homes.

A final means used to justify local government provision – one particularly popular in the nineteenth century – is that of natural monopoly. If a locally produced and consumed good is associated with technologies that lead to declining average costs as output rises, private provision, if it exists, will quickly evolve into a cartel or single firm that can abuse its market position (as happened in transport, see Chapter 10). Public ownership of key services, by definition, removes the threat of private monopolistic abuse. It cannot be assumed, however, that public provision always works in the consumer's interest. A monopoly public provider may still generate many of the feared consequences of a private monopolist. They may under-invest for political or managerial reasons; they may have limited incentives to be efficient; or they may evolve organisational structures that limit adaptability and innovation or favour particular sectors of the population over others. Given these potential problems, regulations that alter the incentive structures of monopoly providers (be they public or private) towards more efficient outcomes are the current vogue in economic theory. The various privatisations in modern Britain have been influenced by such regulation theory. Nineteenth-century central governments used similar regulatory devices but much more crudely. Their impact on public transport and the utilities in the capital was profound, as earlier chapters have discussed. Such regulation was a prime example of the importance of Parliament for the local government of London. In relation to complaints of monopolistic practices in provision of metropolitan services, however, Parliament tended to be sanguine and left many private concerns alone.

How big should a local government district be?

The particular characteristics of a local public good determine the best spatial size of the jurisdiction of a government agency providing it. The agency should cover an area large enough to include all those benefiting from a local public good; each user therefore pays their share of providing it. As every type of public good is likely to have differential optimal spatial spread, this would suggest that the ideal arrangement for local government would be a large number of local agencies providing distinct public services, each covering a distinct spatial area of the city. To an extent, this is what occurred in nineteenth-century London, especially in the early years when there was a multitude of distinct bodies dealing with burials, paving and other matters in often highly localised ways. There were over 300 separate local government-type bodies operating within London in the 1840s, with the number shrinking rapidly thereafter as centralising tendencies came to the fore.[2]

One problem in real life is that the benefits of local public goods may spread beyond the jurisdictions of the agencies producing them. The classic instance is the resident of a free-standing suburban community using public facilities in an adjacent city centre. Some users are thus able to free-ride and not pay for the existence of these facilities. This is one justification for regional or central government subsidies for local public goods, through grants to city governments, to ensure optimal provision. In nineteenth-century London, this was infeasible, so free-riding was prevalent and uncompensated for, especially as the suburbs expanded.

A multitude of separate bodies for each type of public good, nevertheless, may not be perfect. For one reason, economies of scale exist in the provision of some public goods. If such scale economies exist, it may be better to produce the services in question over a larger area than that determined by demand, so that those scale economies may be recouped – in, say, refuse collection. This production factor expands the ideal area of a jurisdiction above that determined by consumer use alone. By the mid-century, such scale considerations became important in a number of key areas, most notably with respect to sewage disposal. This encouraged the formation of a formal London-wide body to undertake the provision of services where economies could be reaped at the city level: the Metropolitan Board of Works.

Further justification for centralisation can be given in terms of the administration of local public goods. As nineteenth-century experience showed, a multitude of small, single-function bodies may easily become unaccountable, self-serving and inefficient. They thereby raise the transaction costs of providing public goods, so it may be cheaper to provide a variety of services via larger, more efficient and transparent, multi-function bodies. (This is an argument that economies of scope exist in the provision of local public goods.)

The two-tier system of local government in London can be seen as a rough and ready compromise to these divergent pressures. Yet, in the upper tier, the logic of combining all functions under the aegis of one democratically elected body was at the centre of heated political dispute in the nineteenth century. Democracy (or consumer sovereignty) is better served by small, local government units than by large, amorphous city political machines. Should city-level functions, moreover, be provided by a series of independent bodies or by one combined body? The transaction cost argument is far weaker for combining bodies that are already large and bureaucratically organised on a city-wide scale. Where the desired standard of service is fairly clear-cut, moreover, the need for direct democratic input to determine service levels may also be unnecessary. Quite a number of single-functional metropolitan first-tier agencies appeared in the nineteenth and early twentieth century: some unelected as with water and the police; but another, the London School Board, was subject to elections.

So far, no account has been taken of differences in consumer preferences and levels of income and wealth amongst the urban population. The implications of these two factors are considerable for the organisation of local government.

Voter mobility

One influential economic theory of local government is that it can operate like a club (known as the Tiebout hypothesis). If there are a multitude of local governments spread across a particular urban area, like-minded people with similar incomes and preferences can group together spatially and vote in a local council that provides them with the level of public services they desire, given the charges they will incur. (The analogy is with non-profit private clubs, such as those for tennis and golf.) Jurisdictions that cover large areas of a city are likely to include a heterogeneous array of urban residents and thus cannot create those effects. The club approach suggests that local authority districts should be relatively small, enabling like-minded consumers to group together and vote for the local public services they want.

The vestry system of nineteenth-century London (the second tier) has some correspondence with this theory. Social segregation was marked between vestry districts and so was the scale of the services provided. Davis's (1988) analysis of vestry accounts in 1880–1, for example, shows a strong positive relationship between expenditure per head on streets, lighting and local drainage and rateable value per head.[3] The better-off areas, in other words, spent and taxed more. By all accounts, vestries were not particularly democractic, at least not until the later years of the period, but even unrepresentative vestrymen must have been subject to considerable local pressure. There might consequently be some truth in the applicability of this club-style view to nineteenth-century London. It should be remembered, however, that people choose to live in a particular locality for many reasons other than the provision and cost of local public services, which weakens the Tiebout model's predictive effect substantially.

One area where voter mobility is strongly influential is where local government takes on, or is required to implement, substantial programmes that redistribute local income. A case in point, discussed in the previous chapter, was the operation of the Poor Law. Areas where Poor Law Guardians needed to charge a high rate tended to be the districts where the poor lived, while the wealthier districts paid less. This could be interpreted as the wealthy taking advantage of distinct local jurisdictions and high land values to isolate themselves from the costs of poverty. Alternatively, it could be seen as the expression of consumer preferences, with the vestries acting as rough and ready club-style jurisdictions. The same could be said of council housing and some other services, where at the end of the century the vestries in working-class districts were far more active than the middle-class ones. The local vestry structure made such divisions possible – separations that were severely weakened when the vestries were amalgamated into boroughs in 1902, and through rate equalisation (see below).

The ability of the better-off to avoid paying for services consumed by the poor may be regarded as socially unjust. This is a matter of moral judgement. But the discussion illustrates a general principle that local areas are bad places to implement redistributive policies. If such policies are extensive, leading to high levels of taxation, they encourage those that pay the most and receive none of the benefits to move elsewhere, be they businesses or better-off residents. As Chapter 15 noted, poor rate equalisation was introduced to force the better-off districts to pay more for the poor, but this was only within the County of London area. This gave the better-off an additional incentive to move to suburbs beyond the County boundary. Even there, rate levels varied considerably, with prosperous Bromley charging a rate of 6s 8d in the pound and working-class Walthamstow, 10s 8d, in 1910–11.[4]

Redistributive policies fail at the local level because of this mobility effect and, in consequence, are better funded at national level. Urban land, though, is immobile and therefore a local land values tax is not subject to the above criticism. (The LCC's Progressives did push central government for land values taxation but got nowhere.)[5]

The types of taxes collected to pay for producing local public goods add extra distortions to the urban economy. Property taxes fall hard on built structures and discourage both their use and supply. (They do not correspond to land values taxes because the value of the building may often bear a poor relation to the value of the land on which it stands.) Many economists would argue that the best local taxes are user charges at long-run marginal cost for the identifiably specific services provided (like refuse collection), and a land values tax to cover any other requirements associated with public goods (in the sense defined above of non-excludability) and the external benefits of other publicly or privately provided goods – like transport services.[6] This local tax structure never existed in nineteenth-century London (nor, to put this in context, does it operate anywhere now), and disputes over the level of rates were a major driving force in organisational reform.

The history of government in London can hardly be said to have been determined by the economic principles discussed above, but the principles do highlight some of the dilemmas and pitfalls that existed. That history will now be gone through with the points they identify in mind. Throughout the century, the public administration of the capital was dispersed among a wide range of bodies. They are shown in Figure 16.1. The dates indicate the formation and life of particular agencies during the period. The arrows indicate which agencies were merged into what larger bodies. The bodies shown were mainly first-tier ones. The second-tier ones in the figure are marked by lines and arrows to the vestries/metropolitan boroughs as they were slowly merged together. The Corporation of London stands as a distinct, second-tier, entity. To facilitate discussion, the period is divided into three, designated by major changes in the first-tier bodies. The initial period covers the years before 1855 and the formation of the Metropolitan Board of Works (MBW); the second covers the era of its functioning, 1855–89; and, finally, come the twenty-five years of the LCC up to 1914.

Reform passed by: before 1855

Public services up to 1855 were provided by the City Corporation, vestries – local government based on parish districts – and various statutory bodies. By 1838, the capital contained around 100 statutory trusts that paved, lighted, cleansed and, up to 1829, even policed specific districts. All set rates, but none were locally accountable and there was little co-operation

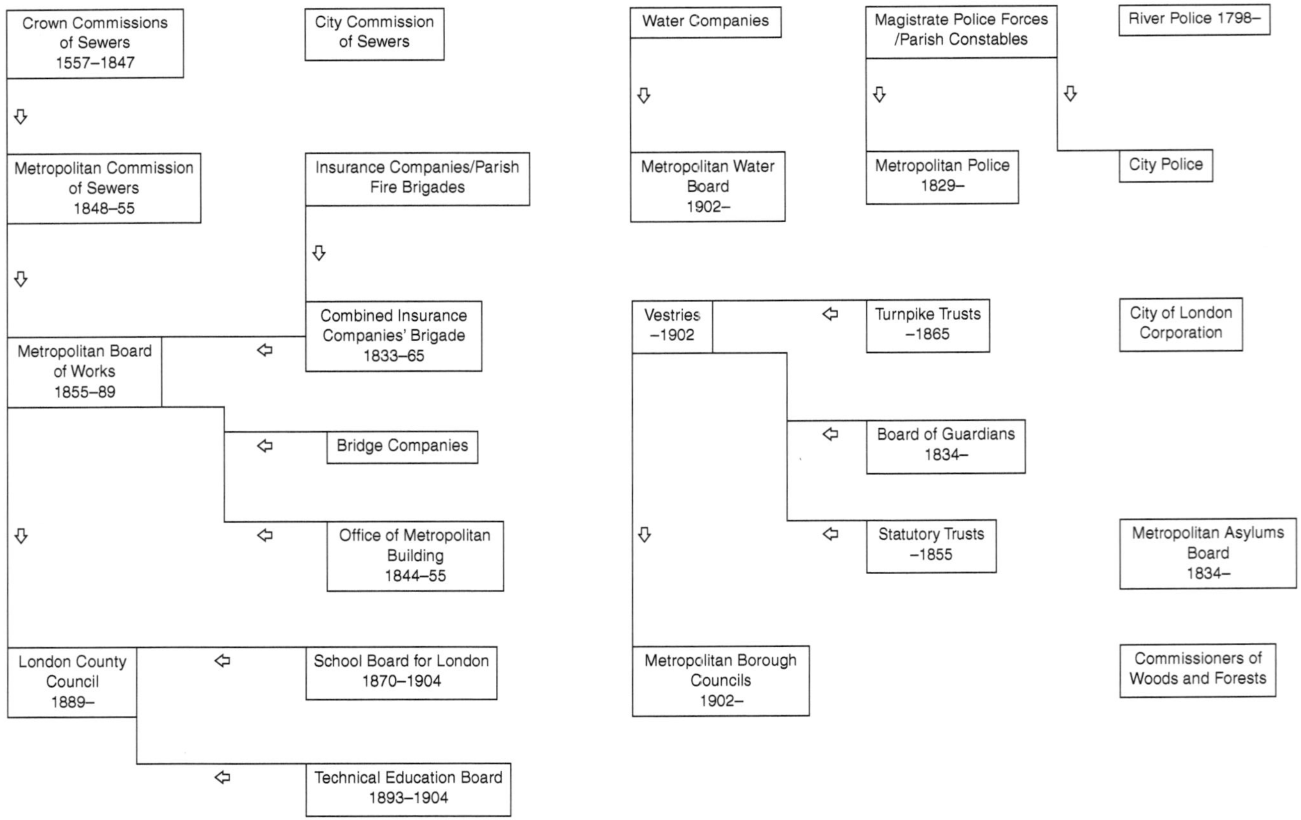

Figure 16.1 The major London public sector bodies, 1800–1914

either between the trusts or between them and the vestries. Each is now considered in turn.

In the City, lighting was undertaken by the City Corporation and paving by the City's sewer commission. The Corporation, in addition, carried out normal vestry duties; governed the Thames for eighty miles from Staines to the Medway; had a monopoly of markets within a radius of seven miles; and collected coal duties over an area of twelve miles. Immensely rich, it was also comparatively representative. Day-to-day matters were dealt with by the Court of Common Council. This comprised 26 aldermen, who were elected for life and had their own court, and 200 councillors, who were elected by freemen of the City's wards and, after 1867, by all £10 ratepayers in the Square Mile. Lesser powers rested with the Court of Common Hall, composed of the Lord Mayor, the aldermen and some 12,000 liverymen of the City Corporation. A further Court of Wardmote was held separately in each of the City's twenty-six wards and every local ratepayer could attend. It dealt with parochial matters and elected ward officials and aldermen.[7]

The Corporation's counterpart in the rest of the capital was the vestry. In 1838, the capital contained 172 of these authorities, the size of which varied from the tiny liberty of the Artillery Ground near Bishopsgate with a population of 1,500 to St Georges, Hanover Square with over 60,000 residents. Two types of vestry existed. The most democratic were the 'open' parishes. In these, all decisions were made either by a show of hands at meetings open to all male ratepayers or, if a majority of a meeting required it, by a poll of ratepayers. The democracy of such parishes, in practice, was more apparent than real. Held on weekday mornings at irregular intervals, meetings were poorly attended and, because of their cost and tendency to lead to delay, polls were rare and attracted few voters.

These vestries, even so, were far more representative than their 'closed' counterparts. Decisions were made by a council of 30 to 100 residents and vacancies were filled by nomination.[8] Owing their existence to immemorial custom or to Acts of Parliament, there were around fifty such parishes in 1800 and they were found in the more populous areas and in fashionable West London. Many were corrupt and inefficient. From the 1820s, they were the subject to criticism over their exclusivity and claimed extravagance. Agitation eventually resulted in the passage of the 1831 Hobhouse Act. This permitted ratepayers in such parishes to elect vestrymen, though only when a majority voted for the adoption of the Act in a special poll. In practice, such was the apathy towards local politics that few ratepayers participated in these polls and elected councils were only introduced in five parishes. It is interesting to note that in these five parishes, open elections encouraged programmes of what Sheppard has called 'the most vigorous and repulsive economy'.[9] The narrowness of the property-owning electorate caused this. From this, it may be surmised that 'closed' vestries actually raised the probability of higher expenditure over 'democratic' ones in an era when local beneficiaries of public goods were far greater in number than those who both paid and voted for them.

The main function of vestries in the early part of the century was the provision of poor relief. After the 1834 Poor Law Amendment Act, this duty was transferred to local Poor Law unions (see Chapter 15), leaving them with purely local public good responsibilities. Vestries were also the conduits for collecting and distributing local rates in order to reduce collection costs. The public goods they produced were limited, involving the repair and maintenance of local highways not owned by turnpike trusts; paving, lighting and cleaning pavements under their administration; and providing and maintaining cemeteries.

Such vestry activities were theoretically managed by Church Wardens and Poor Law Overseers. In fact, as both positions were unpaid and subject to annual election, the incumbents generally devoted little time to their duties and there was little continuity of knowledge and experience. Appointments were made to committees to deal with specific matters, such as highways and burial grounds. Such committee members were again unpaid and annually elected. The Poor Law committees established in this way gained a reputation for jobbery and corruption. Only a few salaried staff were appointed by vestries. The most senior was the clerk, who attended and kept minutes of all meetings and committees, dealt with all correspondence and kept a check on vestry finances, but was generally underpaid and overworked; below him were rate collectors, inefficient and claimed to be often corrupt; and surveyors, following the 1835 Highways Act. Vestry administration, therefore, was cheap but not particularly efficient or honest.

There were several further independent bodies that provided public goods and services to Londoners, as shown in Figure 16.1. There were eight Sewers Commissions (see below). The Commissioners of Woods and Forests and the Turnpike Trusts have already been discussed in Chapter 10. There were the fire and police services (see pp. 406–9). There were also the water companies, which were private during this period but are mentioned as they were eventually municipalised in the 1900s (see Chapter 11). No other city in Britain had such an array of bodies.

Pressures for reform

Local government change passed London by in the reforming 1830s through a mixture of neglect and apathy. The first report on the national situation of urban governance, by the Royal Commission on Municipal Corporations, dealt only incidentally with London. The 1835 Municipal Corporations Act, unsurprisingly therefore, excluded the capital from its far-reaching urban measures. By the time of the Commission's second report two years later, which did deal with London, the impetus for reform had dissipated. That report also failed to recommend a strong alternative to the existing system; in part, because the current structure of local government in the metropolis, as was noted above, already embodied a semblance of democracy, one of the main tenets of the 1835 Act. The subsequent prime impetus to reform came from what seems to the modern mind an unlikely source – the woeful inadequacy of the capital's sewers.

The sewer question

Sanitation in London was in a poor state in the early years of the nineteenth century. Of the eight Commissions of Sewers that existed, seven were appointed by the Crown and the eighth, covering the City, by the City Corporation. The system had numerous drawbacks. The Commissions had originally been established by a statute of Henry VIII for the disposal of surface water and this remained their primary concern, rather than sewage, into the nineteenth century. In Westminster until 1815, it was an offence to discharge domestic sewage in to the local Commission's system, and similar bans lasted elsewhere in the metropolis for even longer.[10] Six of the Commissions obtained additional statutory powers to dig up streets and lay sewers, but two of them, Westminster and Tower Hamlets, were still legally unable to build sewers, though both circumvented the law.[11] There was no conformity in the size and form of the sewers each Commission built and, owing to jobbery and technical incompetence, many works were excessively expensive and prone to collapse. When Commissions with no independent outlet to the Thames improved the sewers in their districts, this increased the flow of sewage in other neighbourhoods towards the river, flooding their sewers.

Even in the 1840s, by which time technology had improved, a large proportion of metropolitan householders were still forced to rely on cesspools – two-thirds of them in Holborn and Finsbury. At this date, such a traditional system of disposal was wholly inadequate. Greater volumes of effluent caused by population growth and increasing use of water closets, combined with the high costs of emptying the pits, meant that cesspools increasingly overflowed, with a resultant contamination of fresh water supplies. This situation remained much the same until after the building of the new city-wide sewer system in the late 1850s. As late as 1856, no more than a tenth of houses were connected to a main sewer. By 1876, the situation was reversed with less than a tenth unconnected,[12] but it would take some time more before all benefited from this obvious health measure.

The campaign for the reform of the Sewers Commissions was led by the Poor Law Commissioner, Edwin Chadwick. In 1842, he published *The Sanitary Condition of the Labouring Population of Great Britain*, highlighting the connection between poor sanitary conditions, disease and poverty. Such was the force of his advocacy that two Royal Commissions were appointed to examine the issues he raised. Once again, London was dealt with separately, with investigations in 1843 and 1847 respectively into the health of towns and sanitation in the metropolis. Both reports fiercely attacked the Sewers Commissions and, in 1848, the City Sewers Act established a new body, the Metropolitan Commission of Sewers, which took over the duties of the seven Crown Commissions. Aware that reform was imminent, the City Commission of Sewers a few months earlier had obtained an Act of Parliament, which had greatly increased its sanitary powers, and was thereby excluded from the Act.[13] But, the Square Mile apart, a major new city-wide body was set up to provide a key local public service to replace a claimed local inefficiency. It was not hard to conclude that the other powers of the vestries might soon follow – with the figment of local democracy sacrificed to the apparent reality of utilitarian efficiency.

As it turned out, the new centralised Commission proved largely ineffective. The planning of a new sewer system was delayed by the need to draw up a detailed survey of the existing system. Disagreement then broke out, largely due to personal animosities and technical disagreements over the form of sewer construction. At the same time, the Commission's reputation was severely damaged by an ill-informed decision to flush all the sewers, which caused cholera-infected excrement to be poured into the Thames and contributed to the 1849 cholera epidemic. With the consequent expulsion of Chadwick and the recruitment of more engineers, the Commission's performance improved. Progress, however, remained slow and, by 1855, the Commission had built only a few miles of main sewer, and its major work, the Victoria Street sewer, had collapsed through bad workmanship. Although some of the ideas guiding the Metropolitan Commission were fanciful, such as the belief that London's effluent could be profitably sold once efficiently collected, charitably it could be argued that this first tier-body had arrived before the economies of scale were there to justify its existence. This might help to explain why it failed, whereas its smaller City counterpart flourished, bringing fame to its chief. The personalities of the two leaders, however, are usually given prominence – dour, scheming Chadwick against clever, urbane Sir John Simon.

Another reason why the City body was more successful was because it had greater powers than the Metropolitan Commission. Its private Act laid down that all new houses should be connected to a street sewer and had to contain a water cistern. Powers of compulsion were given to bring existing housing up to the same standards. Programmes were introduced for the cleansing of privies, the removal of dung and excrement, and the suppression of cesspools. Furthermore, the New River Water Company was persuaded to supply water twice a day rather than the previous once. As a result of these innovations, when London was afflicted by cholera in 1849, only 211 of its 11,000 victims lived in the City.

The two-tier system from 1855 to 1889

The formation of the Metropolitan Board of Works

The failure of Chadwick's Sewers Commission was used as the basis for an attack by the City and the resurgent vestries on the arguments for a greater centralisation of metropolitan local government. Vestries were, thus, able to remain the centre of political power after the reform of metropolitan governance in the 1850s. The 1855 Metropolis Local Management Act created the world's first two-tier urban administrative system. It reorganised the vestries and created a new city-wide body, the Metropolitan Board of Works, to undertake what were by then obvious needs that could only be provided at the city level. Sewers were its primary initial duty but, in addition, it was empowered to undertake major street improvements, administer building regulations and perform duties such as naming streets and numbering properties along them.

The Act abolished the statutory trusts and Metropolitan Commission of Sewers, but kept the City Corporation. It defined the functions of vestries, gave them a uniform franchise and transferred to them previously independent local trusts and bodies set up under a variety of Acts for baths and libraries. Vestries also indirectly elected the members of the MBW, a third of whom were subject to re-election in a year but, in practice, they all served for long periods.

A strong tension was set up between the two tiers, which grew over the Board's lifetime until abolition and replacement by the London County Council. On the one hand, pressures on the Board to contain costs were not the same as they would have been on a directly elected body. Its members faced little fear of voters dismissing them because of their policies, especially after it became clear that vestries would continue to nominate the same people to the Board for many years at a time. Moreover, its rate charges were spread across a large number of electoral districts rather than limited to the jurisdiction of any single representative on it, so the costs of any of its actions were dissipated. In addition, the Board faced strong pressures to spend. These were driven by central government, local interests and its own assessments of need. On the other hand, the political complexion of vestries caused them to emphasise economy and keep rates down, especially before the extension of the franchise. They had only partial control of rate-funded expenditure, however, because of the first-tier charges over which they had, at best, indirect influence only.

First-tier expenditures, unsurprisingly in view of these arrangements, kept on rising as a proportion of total rates from the 1850s onwards. In 1863–4, 24 per cent of vestry-raised rates went to the first tier and, by the MBW's last year in 1888–9, it and the added first-tier London School Board together accounted for 54 per cent. The growing demand for public goods, moreover, was increasingly about city-level functions, as will be described below. Further pressures would come in measures to redistribute the burden of the poor rate and other public expenditures more evenly across the capital, so that by 1893–4 in a wealthy vestry like St James only 19 per cent of rate income was used locally.[14]

This tension between the two tiers of local government drove further metropolitan reform up to 1914. Furthermore, the national government was physically in the same city and took a persistent and interfering interest in metropolitan amenities and services and its structure of local government – sometimes viewing them in a national context and at other times being far more parochial. These tier relationships have underpinned London local politics ever since.

The vestry revival

Of the 78 existing vestries, 23 were deemed to be suitable for self-government. The remaining parishes were grouped into fifteen district boards, whose members were elected by the component parishes, which were retained merely to provide a franchise. In terms of the earlier theory, it could charitably be argued that the 1855 reforms were catching up with the greater economies of scale and scope existing in the provision of local public goods by mid-century; while retaining a wide number of second-tier bodies, in the form of vestries, to maximise local accountability. The optimal size of such bodies, however, was a matter of dispute. A year earlier in 1854, the Royal Commission on the Corporation of London had argued for eight larger ones, corresponding to the number of metropolitan areas electing Members of Parliament, but thirty-eight distinct units were deemed to be viable in the 1855 legislation.[15]

Each vestry and district board was made responsible for sewage, cleansing, the removal of rubbish and local improvements, and they had to appoint at least one medical officer of health and one inspector of nuisances. Their duties were financed by rates levied yearly for distinct purposes and through loans borrowed on the security of those rates. The vestries and boards have been argued to have been obsessed by economy, largely due to the absence of party politics and the domination of the vestries by tradesmen, who often retained their seats for decades. In the 1885 elections, only 90 of the 200 electoral areas were contested and merely 40 polled, with in 32 cases candidates topping the poll with fewer than 50 votes.[16]

The vestries varied considerably in wealth – the variations arising because of the patterns of property values and population densities across the urban area. The differences were exacerbated over time as the poor migrated from the centre and as the property values there rose immensely. By the 1900s, the Cities of London and Westminster together contained 40 per cent of the capital's rateable value. Population sizes also were still highly uneven: in 1861, the six largest parishes each contained more people than Bradford, while the four smallest contained under a thousand residents apiece.

Despite their supposed emphasis on economy, the vestries could not avoid large outlays on infrastructure works. The laying of sewers by them largely occurred after 1860, by which time the MBW had laid down much of the main system. The most extensive programmes were found in the suburbs as population decentralised, but some older parishes also incurred substantial expenditure. The vestries similarly greatly enhanced their road systems – constructing, improving and taking over from toll companies many hundreds of miles of highway. In contrast to their image of parsimony, the vestries spent more per head on highways than any other public authority in Britain between 1856 and 1900. They generally obtained up to a third of the costs from the MBW, which until its demise gave vestries and district boards over £1 million for this purpose. They also invested heavily in parks, open spaces, public baths and housing. The image of Scrooge-style second-tier metropolitan government, therefore, may be misplaced.

With regard to current spending, one of the main activities, the removal of refuse, was frequently put out to contractors, which in some areas undertook the work for no charge as they profited from the sale of the rubbish collected. Such contractors were criticised as being often poorly monitored and inefficient – which may indicate the difficulty of running vestry activities on a shoestring. Some parishes, such as Battersea, later in the century when vestries were becoming both more professional and political in their operations, none the less, did cancel contracts.[17] At mid-century, however, parsimony and partisan interest took a different turn – particularly in trying to minimise the new regulatory roles being imposed by Parliament on local government, especialy with regard to health matters. Most notably, few medical officers and inspectors of nuisance were employed and, when in post, they were often used ineffectually for fear of threatening landlord interests. In 1858, the capital contained only forty-eight medical officers, many part-time and poorly paid, though their numbers generally increased during epidemics. As the 1855 Act failed to lay down the amount and type of work to be undertaken and the parishes merely possessed powers to abate nuisances, the few inspectors employed at first merely reported, investigated and acted upon complaints rather than initiated investigations themselves. Gradually, though, the number of officers employed rose and their duties were extended to include deterrent activities, such as the inspection of bakeries and lodging houses, and work that resulted in long-term improvements – as, for example, by requiring the paving and drainage of yards and through the provision of dustbins. Even in 1885, nevertheless, many parishes employed few inspectors. In Bermondsey, for example, there was only one sanitary inspector per 86,000 residents and in Mile End one per 105,000, as compared to one per 11,000 in St Olaves and one per 9,000 in St Giles.[18]

Disease prevention was obviously a city-wide public good, which could not be effectively undertaken at the second-tier level, as the foregoing has shown. Consequently, the retention of its main means of implementation in the second tier can only be put down to political factors at the time of the 1855 reforms. The resulting inefficiencies rebounded back on the vestries, paradoxically, as failings with regard to health constituted a major weapon for their critics.

The functioning of the MBW

The MBW comprised forty-five members appointed by vestries. Its activities were primarily financed through charges levied on ratepayers and collected via sometimes reluctant vestries. The organisation's administrative costs were small, aided by the use of vestries as rate collectors, which meant that the Board needed only eight clerks to oversee rate collection and enforcement. Initially, it had an establishment of only fifty. Its total employment in 1861 was 136, rising to 300 in 1867–8 with the addition of those working on the Board's new drainage and sewerage systems.[19] These numbers are tiny by modern standards – the era of large-scale employment in London local government would only begin in the 1890s.

Money was raised in the capital markets, particularly from insurance companies, and repaid out of the MBW's rate precept. Financial organisations understandably were reluctant to fund a body with potentially open-ended commitments. A significant number of large-scale projects, especially if several ran over budget, could conceivably strain the patience of metropolitan taxpayers, so that at worst a rate revolt would force the Board to default. This difficulty had to be met. One device was to find special sources of funds for large projects, although they required Parliamentary legislation. A £2 million loan for most of the works surrounding the creation of the Embankment was raised in this way. Conveniently for the Embankment scheme, the ancient duties on wine and coal had just been renewed for ten years in 1861, with 4d of the coal duty allocated to improvements in and around the City. Minus that 4d, the rest of these duties were then diverted to fund the Embankment and Queen Victoria Street schemes under the Embankment Act of 1862. Even so, most of the costs on the south side of the river still had to be paid from the rates.[20]

A more permanent solution was to put a cap on the MBW's expenditure. For example, the Drainage Act of 1858, which funded the major sewer programme, put a ceiling on its loans for this purpose at £3 million, giving a government loan guarantee up to this sum to lower borrowing costs. Yet pressures for expenditure generally exceeded the imposed limits, so that periodic revisions were made – with the drainage-related cap, for instance, raised to £4.2 million in 1863.

Such programme-based financial constraints, however, were gradually weakened as they became less efficient at dealing with the MBW's widening range of activities. For one thing, as the Board's activities expanded, it could pool risks. Thus, it was less threatened by the fortunes of one individual scheme, lowering the need for Parliamentary loan guarantees and the time and expense it took to get them. The value of its rate base also grew dramatically as metropolitan land values rose. Between 1856 and 1886, rateable value across the capital rose almost threefold from £11 million to £30 million. These developments helped to make possible the 1869 Loans Act. This allowed the Board to pool its loan costs by issuing metropolitan consolidated stock, repayable in sixty years, and to raise a single general rate instead of the previous three distinct ones for general expenses, fire and drainage. The MBW's new stock was easily tradable and was popular with investors – allowing its loan charges to fall by almost a quarter from 4.5 per cent to 3.5 per cent. Soon, it was acting as the conduit for loans raised by other metropolitan-wide bodies, such as the London School Board, and for local vestries and Boards of Guardians. Under a new Loans Act of 1875, constraints were again put on its borrowing powers and now potentially open-ended expenditure by requiring the MBW to go annually to Parliament for approval of its finance bills.[21]

The Board added its own share of delays to the construction of an adequate sewer system. At first, the cause was disagreements between its engineers and interested parties over the system's design and, then, arguments between the Board and the government regarding the scheme's scale and cost. Board members, for example, wanted to keep costs down by keeping the final outlet into the Thames as close to the city as possible but the government wanted it further downstream. The bureaucratic wrangling only came to an end in 1858, when an unusually dry and hot summer caused 'the Great Stink' – a terrible stench from the Thames, so overpowering that Parliament was forced to make the Board indépendent of direct central control and give it guaranteed borrowing powers with loan costs chargeable as a uniform metropolitan-wide sewer rate.

The project, finally completed in 1868, involved the construction of five east-to-west, large-diameter, intercepting sewers, 82 miles in all, three of them to the north and two to the south of the Thames with several pumping stations along the way where gravity could not be used. This network diverted the north–south flow of the existing sewers into an easterly movement so that sewage would now enter the river well below the built-up area. The finished system, the largest in the world, was able to deal with 400 million gallons of rainwater and sewage a day. Its final cost at £4.6 million, however, was considerably more than the envisaged £2.8 million.[22]

The Board also reconstructed and repaired 165 miles of existing sewers at a cost of £75,000, built additional storm drains at an extra cost of £700,000 and, after problems with the scale of effluent discharged into the Thames, built a precipitation works in the late 1880s which separated the liquid and solid materials, with the latter being taken out to sea and dumped.[23]

Suggestions had been made since the mid-1840s to improve the urban environment by reclaiming land from the river through construction of embankments on either side of the Thames. Opposition by wharf owners and other interests blocked any feasible move until the plan for the construction of the sewers came to fruition. The MBW then embarked upon its first and most successful exercise in urban planning by constructing embankments on either side of the Thames to the west of the City. The new riverside structures carried highways and footpaths on top of them and, apart from the main sewers, contained piping for gas, water and telegraph wires. On the north side, the eastern end was linked to a new road, Queen Victoria Street, running into the heart of the City, and the underground in the form of the District Railway was to run from Westminster into the City along the new route. The Victoria Embankment on the north side was completed in 1870 and the Albert on the south in 1869, with over 30 acres reclaimed from the Thames. The Chelsea was to follow to the west in 1874.

The Embankment project illustrates the fact that battles over major urban improvements were as much a feature of Victorian times as they are in modern society. The MBW, for instance, wished to embank all of the south side of the river from London Bridge to Vauxhall, but had to be content with the section to the west of Westminster following successful protests by vested interests, which not even prescient fears of flooding could dislodge from their opposition. On the north side of the river, intra-local government conflict flared with the City Corporation outraged at the incursion of another agency into its territory with the MBW's Queen Victoria Street scheme. However, its attempt to be the agency empowered to undertake the works failed despite a vociferous campaign. Contractors added to their woes by failing to undertake specified works, overcharging or going bankrupt and threatening the completion of schemes. Partners, such as the District Railway, caused additional delays.

The final area of dispute, and perhaps the most damning to the long-term prospect of metropolitan improvement, was the issue of compensation. With regard to the Embankment, property compensation claims came from wharf owners and other businesses that would lose access to the river, and from nobles concerned at having a new road running past their riverside houses. Each claim was high relative to actual land values and they took a long time to settle. The Board, for example, spent £2 million on compensation claims for Queen Victoria Street alone.[24] The MBW could recoup some costs by reselling cleared vacant land adjacent to its schemes at its new improved value (the enhanced value is known as 'betterment'), but such plots were generally small and were worth only a fraction of the original purchase price, including compensation, of the land used in projects. No betterment tax, furthermore, could be charged to the owners of land whose value was substantially increased by such schemes, to offset the costs of compensation and the necessary public works. On occasion, large plots could be sold off – such as the 8.5 acres of land sold to St Thomas' Hospital for £90,000 to facilitate its displacement by railway building from near London Bridge to its present site.[25] But valuable open public spaces could not often be provided, even when the cost was relatively trivial – as at the Mansion House end of Queen Victoria Street where a triangle of land that became the centre of a major planning dispute in the 1980s and 1990s had to be sold off at less than the asking price rather than become a much desired open space in the heart of the City. Even by the Palace of Westminster an enormous campaign had to be waged to avoid land that is now Victoria Tower Gardens being sold off for commercial development. Such compensation issues stymied further grand town planning schemes and helped to give London that sense of piecemeal haphazard development when other major nineteenth-century cities were undertaking major 'city beautiful' projects, most notably in Paris. In an attempt to raise funds for further grand schemes, the MBW tried in 1866 to persuade Parliament to allow it to institute an improvement rate charged to landlords and occupiers throughout the capital, but failed to do so.[26] Private developers were similarly hampered by compensation costs, as the rail companies experienced with their new central stations. The significance of the delay and cost caused by compensation procedures must have had a notable effect on slowing and altering the trajectory of the redevelopment of central London.

On occasion, private interest could be transcended without compensation. This occurred when 1879 legislation gave the Board the authority to require the construction and maintenance of adequate river flood defences on private premises at the owner's cost. This case also illustrates the gradual growth of a broader 'public interest' – with public officials deciding, within guidelines, where the public interest lay and enforcing it at private cost.

The substantial expenditures incurred by the Board on roads, bridges and working-class housing have already been documented in Chapters 10 and 15. Further works included the creation and acquisition of new parks and open spaces, and over 2,600 acres were being managed by the Board in the late 1880s. The first parks laid out by the Board were Finsbury and Southwark Parks. Finsbury Park was originally supposed to be in the district of Finsbury but circumstances led to it being laid out several miles to the north. Moreover, less than half the land authorised for purchase in the 1857 Act was actually bought, as an economy measure. Southwark Park followed in 1869. In both cases, the Board wished to recoup part of the cost by selling off some land for building and was only stopped from doing so by the ensuing public outcry. The Board then obtained control of many parks and open spaces, particularly with the aid of the 1866 Metropolitan Commons Act, which gave the MBW powers to acquire commons and open spaces. Gifts from City and other charities, landowners (for example, Blackheath) and wealthy individuals (one of whom funded improvement of Leicester Square), plus joint schemes with vestries (such as the purchase of Parliament Hill), were among the devices used to create and maintain open spaces. Battersea, Kennington and Victoria Parks were transferred by central government from the Office of Works in 1887. Preserved from being built over, among others, were Hampstead Heath, Clapham, Streatham and Wandsworth Commons, Blackheath and Highbury Fields. Yet again, far more could easily have been done if expenditures had been greater, particularly in the suburbs as they grew, while land there was still cheap. The geography of open spaces in London consequently represents a haphazard array rather than systematic provision in line with metropolitan growth.

Parks and open spaces illustrate another aspect of the expanding role of first-tier metropolitan governance. The Board became a focus for interest group lobbying over the provision of free public goods in situations where property owners could only be expensively bought out. Pressures to purchase Hampstead Heath from its owner, for example, were applied to the Board by the Commons Preservation Society, public figures and some vestries, from the MBW's inception. Other vestries opposed the purchase and the landowner was reluctant to sell. Only by 1870 was the Heath in public ownership, and only after the owner was paid a handsome sum – the Board thought they could get it for £45,000–50,000 but had to pay £295,000, though half of the sum was paid by charities and public subscription.[27] Similar situations arose over the freeing of river bridges from tolls – long periods of campaigning and lobbying and eventual purchase by the Board of the bridges with substantial compensation, way above feasible market prices, for their owners.

Other functional duties involved the regulation of private activities for the public good. Statutory responsibilities conferred on the Board included the enforcement of the 1872 Infant Life Protection Act, which concerned child-minders; the 1869 Building Act, which involved the supervision of dangerous structures; the 1866 Cattle Diseases Prevention Act; and a variety of legislation controlling inflammable and explosive substances.[28] In 1870 and 1871, the Board became the designated local authority for London, apart from the City, under the Tramway Act and the Metropolis Water Act.[29] The first-tier role was gradually expanding and often given to the MBW for lack of any other body rather than because of its original terms of reference. Its supervisory roles, however, were constrained. In the case of building regulation, for example, much discretion was left with local building surveyors outside of the Board's control and its powers were insufficient to impose effective city-wide controls.

The fire service

The MBW became the controller of another obvious first-tier activity, the fire service. At the start of the nineteenth century, public fire-fighting duties were undertaken patchily by vestries, by a charity – the Royal Society for the Protection of Life – and by private insurance companies. The latter had an obvious incentive to limit the effects of fires but their role had expanded to a wider responsibility for ten square miles of central London, which they were reluctant to adopt. The insurance companies' brigades amalgamated in 1832 to form the London Fire Engine Establishment. This cost £8,000 a year to operate, indicating the value to the insurance companies of its existence, and it ran 19 fire stations with 80 men and 2 river fire floats. The new brigade grew rapidly and was highly successful. Between 1833 and 1865, it dealt with 32,376 fires, a third of which were serious. By 1861, 117 firemen were employed to operate 27 horse-drawn manual engines, one steam engine, 28 hand pumps and 2 steam-powered floats.[30] The continued use of manual pumps for decades after steam ones had shown their worth was said to be a product of the conservatism of the force, but it also helped to lower the companies' contributions.

The fire service was made into a metropolitan-wide organisation in 1865. After they suffered a loss of £2 million in a Tooley Street fire, the insurance companies lobbied Parliament for the formation of a metropolitan fire service, pointing out that such a service existed in every other British city. After considering the question, the government instructed the Metropolitan Board of Works to provide fire cover in 1865. The new brigade was financed through a special rate; by the insurance companies, who contributed £35 annually for every £1 million of London fire insurance they held; and by the Treasury, which provided a yearly grant of up to £10,000. Growing rapidly, the brigade's staffing increased from 130 at inception to 674 in 1888. New stations were built and equipment bought, so that the number of serious fires fell dramatically from 1865.[31] However, London still had a higher death rate caused by fire relative to population size than other British cities.[32]

The fire service under the Board was continually hampered by a lack of funds. The shortage of staff and inadequacy of the fire service was commented upon by coroners.[33] A proposal was made to resolve the problem by increasing the fire rate and raising the contribution made by the insurance companies. The latter would have none of it and the income shortfall dragged on for years until abolition of the Board. More success was had with the water companies, which in the 1860s did not supply water on a constant basis, so that when a fire occurred the brigade had to wait for an official to come and turn the water on. Gradually through the 1880s, a constant supply was achieved and the Board set up nearly 9,000 hydrants.[34]

The financing and actual organisation of an effective metropolitan fire service, it can be seen, lagged far behind advances in technology and organisational practices. Tradition and conservatism in technology were continued under the Board from the earlier insurance company period. Only ex-sailors were hired – some went to sea merely to meet the requirement – and obsolete manual pumps continued to be used.

On the disappearance of the MBW, control of the brigade passed to the LCC, which in 1904 changed the fire service's name to the London Fire Brigade. But it retained many practices of the previous administration and was the subject of periodic criticism.

The London School Board

Another first-tier body, but this time elected, was set up to improve education. The London School Board, created by the 1870 Education Act and financed by a special rate, provided and maintained elementary schools and also developed schools for older children. Attendance was compulsory for 5- to 9-year-olds but truancy was common, running at 20 per cent in 1900. The Board was city-wide covering the MBW area, thanks to an amendment to the Education Act tabled by a London MP.[35] Until 1891, parents had to pay a weekly fee of 2d to 3d, after which time education was free. The School Board's role augmented and replaced those of the existing schools run by the National Society, the British and Foreign Society, the churches and the Ragged Union, which together in 1870 provided places for only half the capital's child population. By 1903, the Board had made available a school place for every child, built many schools and hired many teachers and created a system to try to enforce compulsory school attendance. National legislation abolished the Boards in 1902 and responsibility passed to the LCC.[36]

The police

One early, independent city-wide service to develop was policing, which has remained under the auspices of the Home Office until the present day. In 1800, the policing of the city was undertaken by parish constables and various magistrate groups. The most famous of the latter was the Bow Street Runners, formed in 1748. They operated foot patrols extending over an area stretching four miles from the centre. In 1805, they were supplemented by the Bow Street Horse Patrol, formed to deter highway robbery, covering an area from 4 miles to 20 miles outside the capital. The river was patrolled by the Thames Police Force, established in 1798, which was financed by West India merchants, and from 1801 by the government.

Concerned about the quality of the policing of London, Robert Peel in 1829 pushed through Parliament the Metropolitan Police Bill. This established a Metropolitan Police Force, with a strength of 3,000 men, whose beat included the whole of the metropolis – except the City, which retained its watchman system, and the Thames, which remained under the jurisdiction of the River Police. Ten years later, further reform occurred when the City established its own police force and the Bow Street Runners and River Police were absorbed into the metropolitan force. The Bow Street Runners, in turn, in 1842 were transformed into a detective department, though, due to public suspicion and internal professional jealousy, this unit grew only slowly. By 1868, it contained only 15 men out of a force of 8,000. Expanded by a new Commissioner, in 1877 it was found to be highly corrupt and after an inquiry it was separated from the uniform branch, given its own leader and renamed the Criminal Investigation Department.

By 1900, the Metropolitan Police Force contained nearly 16,000 men, had 21 divisions and covered an area of nearly 700 square miles. New developments included the establishment in 1885 of a Special Irish Branch, renamed the Special Branch, a fingerprint bureau in 1901, a detective training school in 1902, and a police training school. The City of London Police in 1910 employed 1,181 men, and was divided into six divisions.

The end of the MBW

The popularity of the MBW was never high, despite the evident fruits of its labours. Its high expenditure caused rates to rise and led to agitation from ratepayers, who also resented its undemocratic basis. The City Corporation had also long been an opponent because of the fixed, city-wide rate charged by the Board, which bore heavily on property in the City, and because of recurrent encroachments on its perceived jurisdiction. Pressures were growing for a unified, democratic city-wide government, although its form was still problematic as it could easily step on the democratic operation of the second tier. The theoretical conflicts over the appropriate size of local government, raised earlier in the chapter, were having very real impacts in late nineteenth-century London. Nevertheless, scandal not logic provided the catalyst, because change eventually occurred in 1888 when it emerged that a number of the Board's officers had personally gained from dealings in surplus lands. Unable to prevaricate any longer, the government used impending legislation on urban government in British cities to establish a new body, the London County Council (LCC), as a replacement for the Board.

Creation of the Council meant that its 118 councillors were directly elected every three years. (They, in turn, chose nineteen aldermen, who served for six years.) The composition of first-tier politicians was altered substantially as a result of direct elections. Most were now affiliated to a political party and were relatively young, male professionals, managers and businessmen. (The three women who tried to stand at and won in the 1889 LCC elections were subsequently disenfranchised by the courts.)[37] Apart from these electoral factors, the LCC covered the same geographical area, even though the suburbs had already outgrown it, and possessed the same limited set of functions as the MBW.

The shift satisfied the aspirations of both the economisers and those that saw metropolitan government as a way of radically improving urban social policy and creating a new London political identity. Directly elected councillors, for the economisers, would be more open to the concerns of ratepaying voters; whereas control of the LCC was optimistically seen by radicals as a launching pad for social change. As it turned out, at least until 1914, the pendulum swung between expenditure and austerity, but the economisers were probably more correct in that the LCC's circumscribed powers and fear of the wrath of the electorate severely limited the changes that occurred.

The London County Council years, 1889–1914

The LCC

One factor that hamstrung the activities of the LCC was the large number of other governmental bodies, often with conflicting duties, that existed in the capital. To effect any change, negotiation was required with many of them, and perhaps with central government as well. So many of these other bodies could, in effect, veto LCC policies. Two cases in point were the refusal to allow the through-running of trams by some vestries and a frequent vestry reluctance to undertake slum clearance, with both stymying key LCC initiatives.

The empowering Act for the LCC had, perhaps deliberately, failed to clarify the tangle. It created six new second-tier councils to administer the remainder of the ever-expanding capital, but it did not change the structure nor the roles of the vestries, boards and other public bodies. London governance in the early 1900s was a bewildering tapestry. To quote Waller:

> Seven central bodies operated within the LCC area, spending £16 million per year: the LCC itself, the Metropolitan Water Board, Metropolitan Asylums Board, Central Unemployed Body, Thames Conservancy, Metropolitan Police (Home Office), and City Corporation (controlling markets, etc.). There were also 94 local bodies, spending £9 million per year: 28 Borough Councils, 31 Boards of Guardians, 4 School District Boards, 2 Sick Asylum Boards, and 29 Distress Committees. If we take Greater London, we find some 262 authorities spending about £34 million per annum: 6 County Councils, 38 Borough Councils, 61 Urban District Councils, 14 Rural District Councils, 50 Boards of Guardians, 54 Parish Councils, and 39 Distress Committees.[38]

Furthermore, the setting up of the Port of London Authority created yet another important agency. The LCC had representation on it and on the Water Board but in both cases the effects were limited.

From 1889 to 1907 the Council was under the control of the Progressives, a collection of radical Liberals and socialists. Despite their promise of a 'new start' for London and an era of municipalisation, they mainly continued with the policies of the MBW. The rhetoric the Progressives used, moreover, helped to discourage central government from increasing the Council's powers. A series of attempts by the LCC to acquire the utilities and the port, commonly run by other equivalent city councils in the land, foundered, as did proposals for the reform of local finance. By the mid-1900s, the popularity of the Progressives was on the wane.

Rates were the perennial issue. According to Millward and Sheard's (1995) study, nominal expenditure by all London local authorities increased by a third between 1897–8 and 1907–8 – somewhat more than for county boroughs on average in the rest of the country. Rate demands in this ten-year period also rose faster in the metropolis, with a rise of 72 per cent as against 63 per cent in the county boroughs (though in this inflationary period the rises were less in real terms). London's per capita annual expenditure was also much higher (63 per cent more in 1907–8 than in other cities in England and Wales). What is unclear is the extent to which this reflected the higher costs of providing services in the capital because of higher wages, rents and land values; metropolitan inefficiencies; or genuinely higher levels of service provision. There was a steady rise in London local authority expenditure from the mid-1880s up to the 1900s from just over £2 million to £3.5 million in nominal terms, then a sharp upwards shift as the metropolitan boroughs were founded in 1902, peaking at over £5 million in 1904–5; this was followed by stagnation up to 1914, which in real terms represented a notable decline as councils became reluctant to raise rate bills any further.[39] At the first-tier level, both capital and current expenditure grew rapidly in tandem from the mid-1880s to the early 1900s, rising from under £1 million each in 1886 to over £7 million in 1904–5. Then capital expenditure fell away to around £3 million in 1910–11, while current expenditure continued to soar to £12 million.[40] This experience was common in other British cities.

The LCC's prominence and Progressive ideologies ensured that its rate demands drew attention, rather than those of the second tier. The Council, additionally, had to endure much newspaper criticism over several controversial policies, such as its unsuccessful pursuit of the capital's water supplies; and its 1902–3, again failed, attempts to acquire London's electricity undertakings. Electors were also unimpressed by the Progressives' puritanical paternalism. This was reflected in the banning of park games on Sundays, and in the suppression of music halls and public houses, especially in poor areas.[41] Few, therefore, were surprised when the Progressives were defeated in the 1907 elections by their long-standing opponents, the Moderates, under a new name, the Municipal Reform Party. Elected on a manifesto that pledged rate reductions, the Municipal Reform Party stabilised the rate at 1s 5d in the pound but failed significantly to reduce expenditure. The Muncipal Reformers then ruled for twenty-seven years until 1934. They were closely allied to the Conservative Party on its by then protectionist policy of Imperial Preference. To this end, the LCC gave preference to British goods in their purchasing policy and paid good wages in, for example, clothing contracts as part of an attempt to attract the working class to the benefits of protectionism. Preference was also given to employers of London men, except in the incongruous case of furniture which was bought more expensively from the provinces as the London trade was dominated by 'aliens' and so tantamount to a purchase from abroad.[42]

The Council's activities up to 1914 encompassed five main areas – housing, education, transport, parks and public health.[43] Some of these have already been dealt with in earlier chapters.

In the field of education, the Council was permitted by the 1889 Technical Instruction Act to levy a penny rate for technical education. Parliament also earmarked a duty on beer and spirits for this purpose in the 1890 Local Taxation (Custom and Excise) Act. With these new resources, the LCC in 1893 set up a Technical Education Board (TEB), comprised of twenty Council members and fifteen experts. By 1904, when the Board's duties reverted back to the LCC along with the London School Board, the TEB had helped to create a variety of institutions involved in technical education, particularly the polytechnics; it subsidised the University of London; provided scholarships for bright Board schoolchildren to go to grammar schools; and had set up evening classes in a wide variety of subjects. It was less successful with secondary education, failing to embark on a large school building programme because of the cost, so only a few grant-aided grammar schools existed instead.[44]

Road expenditure continued in the manner of MBW, but with less emphasis on city-centre schemes. Many of the streets on which the trams and other vehicles travelled were improved and, under pressure from the Post Office, many were renamed – thereby removing the formerly confusing duplication of street names. The woeful connections between east and south-east across the Thames were tackled with costly tunnels – the Blackwall in 1897, the Rotherhithe in 1908 and the Greenwich pedestrian tunnel in 1902 – and in 1905 a Thames steamboat service was introduced. This, however, proved unsuccessful and was discontinued in 1907.

The Council continued its predecessor's parks and open spaces policy. In 1901, Lincoln's Inn Fields were purchased, followed by Hackney Marsh, Waterlow Park and, in 1903, Hainault Park. Conservation tentatively began. Following protests over the destruction of Edwardes Square in 1904, the Council managed to pass through Parliament the 1906 London Squares and Enclosures Preservation Act. To prevent flooding, from 1901, it duplicated most of the city's intercepting sewers and enlarged the size of outflow sewers. Its 1894 London Building Act finally created a single building code for the capital; in 1909, this was extended to cover metal-framed buildings and reinforced concrete construction. Finally, public health was tackled through a myriad of statutory controls and initiatives. Among other things, the Council began to license and inspect nursing homes, provide maternity services, organise treatment for venereal disease, investigate complaints of river and air pollution, etc.

From vestries to municipal boroughs

Changes came to the vestries in several ways. In the first place, a widening franchise and growing national interest in local politics transformed these previously sleepy political backwaters. Some were taken over by Progressives and the new members tried to transform local urban expenditure in the ways open to them, as their colleagues were doing on the LCC.

Progressive and Moderate fights over control of vestries, moreover, heightened popular awareness of them and their powers. The LCC had considerably more supervisory and co-ordinating powers over the second tier than the old MBW and was minded to use its muscle vigorously. Relations between the two tiers remained bad as conflicts arose over housing, transport, rateable value assessments and health legislation. There were also conflicts within the second tier, with those areas gaining from increases in social local expenditure at loggerheads with those whose residents were only going to pay for them – through first-tier levies and equalisation accounts.

Equalisation of the rate burden across the vestries and districts was taken further in 1894 with the passing of the London Equalisation of Rates Act. The first act of rate distribution had occurred with the Poor Rate in 1867, but the new Act proposed a levy of 6d in the pound across the whole County area to be paid out to parishes in proportion to their populations. The wealthy districts were consequently being taxed to fund the expenditure of the poorer ones, at a level that would increase with the growth in the value of the property located in them. To the equalisation scheme, Kensington would provide £18,000, St George, Hanover Square, £31,000, and the City, £96,000. This added to the erosion of any Tiebout-style principle in local government within the County area. Overall, taking into account both first-tier and equalisation charges, it has been calculated that, in the thirty years after 1863, the share of metropolitan taxation taken by uniform city-wide charges rose from 27 to 62 per cent and the equalisation measures of 1894 pushed it up to almost 70 per cent. The option of moving out of the County, consequently, became increasingly attractive to those that felt aggrieved by these developments.[45]

Throughout the 1890s, there was considerable agitation and dispute over the structure of the second tier. There was a general desire for local representativeness, but there was a high risk without further equalisation that a multitude of small bodies would be financially unviable, or offer restricted services. The compromise outcome in 1899 was the amalgamation of many of the central vestries, an avoidance of extra equalisation, and the conversion of the second-tier authorities into twenty-eight municipal boroughs, which came into force in 1902. The idea was also to devolve certain powers from the first tier, but borough reluctance led to nothing happening in practice.

It is sometimes argued that the metropolitan boroughs were set up simply as a cynical act by central government to clip the wings of the LCC. This interpretation, as Davis (1988) shows, is far-fetched because the greatest debate was over the preservation of local autonomy without denying a role for the first tier. The resultant boroughs were compromises – ones that were frequently too large to provide a clear local identity but sufficiently homogeneous to ensure that one party, and its machine, would be in power for decades to come. The inherent conflicts between the first and second tier, if anything, had been exacerbated by consolidation amongst the second tier, because this led to more powerful boroughs that still balked at the power of Big Brother. The outer suburbs, furthermore, remained outside the ambit of city governance as single-tier entities, free of metropolitan responsibilities and expense.

It could be argued that the result of the 1889 and 1899 reforms was a bias towards public service provision at the expense of economy. Although most councils were constrained by fear of ratepayer revolts, this threat only set an upper limit to expenditure. In practice, furthermore, the growth of the party system and the remote large size of local government ensured that particular political parties were in power for long periods of time. Both first- and second-tier councils, therefore, competed for metropolitan favour with limited threat from economising ratepayers; while a minority of the second tier picked up a disproportionate share of the bill via equalised and uniform rates, and the suburbs were set free. Thus, it could be argued that neither democratic accountability nor the efficient delivery of public services were really achieved under the final structure of local government existing in London prior to 1914. Yet it was to be one that had a very long subsequent life.

Part 7

An assessment

17 Conclusions

Introduction

It is useful to start with a quote to illustrate the paradox contained in so many studies of nineteenth-century London – the development of the capital is often criticised; yet the end result is generally admired. The quote is from the late David Eversley commenting in 1975 on *The Victorian City*, edited by Dyos and Wolff (1973). He found its two volumes of readings full of the failures of London and asks incredulously:

> How did it come about that something that was so frightful, apparently, as a habitation and a workplace for the mass of the people, something that smelt so offensively, and was so manifestly unjust, which was the joint product of the speculators' greed, and the second-hand delusions of grandeur of hack architects, came to be also the symbol of solid virtue, the zenith of our national achievement, the masterpiece of civic success, against which all our modern efforts to improve the [built] environment are now judged, and found wanting?
>
> (Eversley, 1975, 104)

Eversley's incredulity was expressed over a quarter of a century ago but it still has relevance today.

To declare for metropolitan success in opposition to such views, however, would be to miss a central point that the London economy was an interconnected entity operating in a wider British context. Explaining those inter-relationships is the key to comprehending its development and outcomes. The problem of understanding nineteenth-century London, therefore, is one of theory as much as assembling the available historical information. In many interpretations, as previous chapters have argued, there are misleading theories of urban change that lead to heaven and hell-fire style conclusions. In contrast, this study has tried to apply modern economic theories about cities and industrial change to its analysis and has used such theories to evaluate critically the available contemporary data.

Despite the claim of a better theoretical basis, reluctance still has to be exercised in coming to conclusions about successes and failures. In part, this is because the data are insufficiently robust. Yet more important is that even the thousands of words written above have not been able to place all the components of change in their appropriate setting. In particular, emphasis has been put on technical change and market competition – highlighting institutional and other political constraints on their interaction. This has been done because of a belief in the importance of these factors; yet they are unlikely to tell the whole story. Other theoretical perspectives might disagree with this approach. To a postmodernist this approach might seem too deterministic, but that is economic theory. To the populist and believer in the overriding importance of the cultural context, the sins of omission probably refer instead to the actions of people. Yet, people are here, albeit mainly in the simplified behavioural contexts of economic analysis. The argument here would suggest that this treatment most accurately synthesises the daily existence of contemporary Londoners, because it identifies key aspects of how they lived. Most are historically silent as individuals, with little or no political involvement. Instead, they anonymously worked, consumed housing, travelled, shopped and took their leisure in the multitude of markets and institutional frameworks that made up the London economy. To describe people's existence otherwise, and downplay such factors, is surely to distort reality. Even so, of course, more than the economic has to be considered when asking questions about how they lived, felt about their situations and their attitudes to the city in which they resided.

An evaluation of economic success and failure, furthermore, does not solely depend on getting causal relationships and their consequences right. Some criteria by which to characterise them are also needed. They are inevitably going to be flavoured by personal value judgements, which, in this context, means that the measures are affected by the comforts and problems of the early twenty-first century. The temptation to indulge in criticism of such sort, however, is hard to resist, because there were abundant problems that our forebears failed to resolve. Partly, such puzzles existed because their nature was misunderstood, but another contributory factor was that many issues involved resource allocation and, hence, potentially irresolvable conflicts of interest. Many of the issues, moreover, still constitute serious challenges today. How, for example, should urban infrastructure and public transport systems be optimally provided, financed and run? How can the inherent productivity advantages of cities be enhanced without damaging the quality of urban life? The list is endless. But one of the lessons of history is that the answers are not easy – they may not even exist – and that many alternative approaches have been tried before and found wanting. Historical contexts may change but urban dilemmas often do not.

Furthermore, the conclusions of this study are as much about processes as end results. How did the London economy function? What were its constituent parts? Were there any major surprises within it, given the endowments of the metropolis and the predictions of modern urban economic analysis? Was the metropolis so distinctive in the British urban structure? Did it hold back the rest of the British economy? Would more public sector intervention have made transport, utility and housing provision better? Was its wealth built on the shoulders of a mass of working poor?

Many of these themes have already been covered but the main threads of growth, industry, living standards, infrastructure provision and governance still need some drawing together. This is done below, and a final section looks towards the rest of the twentieth century by considering whether London had become too big by the First World War.

A centre of industry

One of the principal themes of the book has been the development of industry. In many recent histories, it has been argued that London industry was exceptional in the context of Britain at the time. According to these accounts, a relatively narrow range of consumer goods industries was at its industrial core, locked into production processes predicated on cheap labour and sweating. In contrast, this book has argued that there were a wide range of industries and that London became industrially less specialised over time. Those industries had a variety of histories – yet the majority prospered, so that overall employment grew at a rate that was somewhat faster than population growth, decade after decade.

General techniques of production, as well as the range of goods produced, inevitably improved over the 115-year period, and many metropolitan industries adopted contemporary advanced techniques. The firms that prospered did so because of the importance of the local market and the ability to utilise significant agglomeration economies. The result was often dense networks of small producers, rather than large-scale plants, but these networks were highly productive in a context where communications and transport were much slower and more expensive than they are today. Large plants, however, existed in the sectors where technology made them the preferred method of production but locational advantages still favoured London and its environs, such as in brewing and piano-making. Plants grew larger over the period, moreover, in gas, water, chemicals, clothing, food processing, printing and transportation utilities, to name but a few.

London industry did not require extremely low wages for its survival and success. It was the technologies associated with urban production that primarily determined the types of production methods used rather than the low earnings of the unskilled. Arguments that 'sweating' was the dominant industrial form because of the low-paid, trapped pool of unskilled labour fail to ask a key question. If low wages were so important, why did these industries not migrate to other towns and cities in Britain, or even overseas, where unskilled wages were lower? In fact, as was shown earlier in Chapter 12, attempts to introduce such organisations of production in similar industries in Leeds and Glasgow were comparative failures. Arguments based on agglomeration economies, as used here, in contrast, do provide an explanation for the metropolitan success of this method of production, even if it represented a declining share of the city's total employment.

An integrated industrial structure

Metropolitan industrial change was inter-connected in several important ways:

Demand pull

The relatively higher general standard of living in the capital encouraged firms to set up there to supply its rapidly expanding market – one that required an ever-wider range of products and services as time progressed. From this base, other markets could be served as well, at home and overseas. Many manufacturing industries as well as service ones evolved in this way. The financial services of the City at the beginning of the period, for example, were primarily focused on its home base – the British government (debt), the population of London (banking and insurance) and commerce (bills of exchange and insurance). By 1914, the City was at the apex of a much expanded, world financial system.

Agglomeration economies

Because agglomeration economies were important for so many metropolitan firms, their existence and improvement were central to economic growth. The continual birth and death of firms, with new entrants far exceeding demises, helped to encourage the expansion and transformation of those agglomeration benefits. Concomitant city population growth contributed its beneficial agglomeration effects.

Competition over city resources

Competition between firms over scarce land and labour helped to determine which metropolitan industries would continue to prosper and which would fail or relocate elsewhere. It also influenced the economic geography of the metropolis through the resulting patterning of its industrial districts.

Suburbanisation

The dynamic interaction between employment and housing further helped employment to expand. Without suburbanisation, housing shortages would have brought urban growth to a halt. The general ease with which the suburbs could be opened up and the relatively low cost of their creation kept both the rise in metropolitan labour and other input costs down. Labour and land rents remained more expensive than elsewhere in Britain, which was only sustainable if the productivity of metropolitan industries was sufficiently high to absorb them.

This last conclusion provides a general answer about the role of the metropolis in the British economy. It was the location of a significant proportion of total economic activity and those activities, taken as a whole, were more productive than they would have been elsewhere. In the sense of the capital's contribution to national income, therefore, London must have played a positive role in British economic development. This was because it embodied, as an urban agglomeration, mechanisms that raised total factor productivity.

This result may not be valid in a dynamic context, if it is argued that London-based activity somehow blocked particular paths of national economic development. The studies of particular industries in this book do not suggest that was likely to have been the case. The issue, however, strays into debates about the trajectories of the pre-1914 British economy and their causes, which cannot be adequately addressed here.

Utilities and public goods provision

The London economy relied on transportation systems, a functioning urban area and an effective public health framework conducive to urban living. With some important provisos, outlined below, these services expanded sufficiently well to accommodate continued expansion. Besides this, the costs of providing public goods and the distribution of their benefits contributed to the detailed economic geography of the city. Taxation through rates charged on buildings according to their value, however, put constraints on supply in the housing market, and led producers to economise on plant sizes or to relocate elsewhere.

Path dependency

The industries that evolved throughout the nineteenth century depended to an extent on what existed before. This, perhaps, is most clear with the development of the enclosed docks and the associated expansion of the East End. There, the prior role of London as a port, the ways in which the port functioned and the position of the mercantile trade monopolies all had significant effects on dock growth. But, the same can also be seen in the histories of many manufacturing industries and services.

Institutional factors

Along with path dependency, institutional arrangements were of equal significance. The nature of the metropolitan brewing industry, for example, was much affected by a structure of ownership carried over from the eighteenth century and the behaviour induced by it. Labour markets were also affected. Yet, perhaps, the most significant areas where institutional factors were important were in the provision of transportation services, the utilities and urban public goods. Parliament, in particular, laid down rules within which organisations had to function, and the outcomes of their subsequent behaviour produced a series of problems which are considered in further depth later.

London's service economy

The broad structure of London's economy became progressively more like that of the rest of Britain over the course of the period. This is one conclusion of the location quotient analysis presented in Chapter 4, which, using employment data from the census, measured the relative concentration of particular British industries in the capital. It found that the most highly represented in 1911 were seven manufacturing industries. The level of aggregation implied by the Standard Industrial Classification categorisation used may have helped to create this result, but it still highlights the importance of urban agglomeration economies for many manufacturing activities during the era. The consequence was that the relative attractiveness of the capital was sometimes higher for manufacturing sectors than it was for many services, including the much vaunted banking and finance sectors.

Taking into account population differences, most service activities, on average, employed a third more people in the capital than was the case across Britain as a whole. Even so, the difference between the share of employment in services in the metropolis and elsewhere was narrowing over time. This occurred because service activities were expanding and widening in scope in other towns and cities. Migration from rural to urban areas ensured that the labour was available to take up the new jobs on offer. Continued urbanisation outside of London thereby increased the scale of national service activity – with many services closely related to urban population sizes. The rest of Britain, in other words, was catching up with the service economy that the capital already partly possessed. Consumer-oriented manufacturing, moreover, was expanding elsewhere. London remained unlike other towns and cities, however, but part of the distinctiveness of its industrial structure was associated with its sheer size and the diversity it generated.

Within particular services, London had specific roles. It had a mix of functions attending to the needs of the local population in a similar way to much of the rest of Britain but, in addition, it had more 'higher-order' functions than other regional centres, such as Manchester and Birmingham, and greater employment of domestic servants. Alongside local shopping districts, for instance, there were disproportionately more city-centre shops; the same could be said of mainline stations and local transport systems;

and, in similar fashion, the City co-existed with residentially oriented High Street banks and friendly societies. These special higher-order service roles, however, were simply not big enough to explain the trajectory of the capital's economic growth. Rather, a more plausible scenario is that many developments in the metropolitan economy were a consequence of simultaneous changes in population service and manufacturing activity. This is seen most clearly in the joint transformation of retailing and many consumer goods industries.

The standard of living and poverty

The employment structure obviously had strong implications for the general standard of living. Many manufacturing enterprises relied on skilled and semi-skilled labour and the service sector provided other good job opportunities. Both manufacturing and services enabled many to earn incomes that provided relatively comfortable existences by the standards of the day and, on occasion, extremely good ones. Most people, therefore, prospered; which is one of the reasons there were so many migrants to the city throughout the period, at a rate undiminished until the first decade of the twentieth century.

It is much less clear what the exact standard of living of particular social groups actually was. Estimates provided in Chapter 5 suggested substantial real increases in living standards over the period. Once housing costs are taken into account, there is some evidence that skilled earnings were converging between the capital and other large English cities. Health and life expectancy also improved significantly adding to the quality of life.

What is hopelessly unknown is the distribution of income and wealth amongst the metropolitan population. Extensive information exists on particular wealthy individuals and poor people, but those descriptions can say nothing about the relative scale of either. Booth's much misunderstood survey of poverty at the turn of the century was so full of methodological and measurement difficulties that it hardly warrants the accuracy sometimes attributed to it. The famous 'more than 30 per cent of people in London lived in poverty' soundbite-style summary of his findings is more 'two nations' imagery than proven fact. In reality, far fewer people were likely to have been in dire want by the standards of the day. Furthermore, in contrast to the theoretical prediction that many poor people would be drawn to the capital, Chapter 15 suggested that the reality of social control mechanisms tended to keep them away. Poverty was generally avoided when people worked, particularly if several members of low-income households simultaneously had jobs. Some unskilled wage levels, nevertheless, were abysmally low; yet prejudice and segmented labour markets tended to keep such outcomes of excess unskilled labour from affecting unskilled labour markets overall. This was the case, for example, with the worst women's home-working jobs and also when waves of overseas immigration threatened to flood the metropolitan labour market.

Public transport and the utilities

The transformation of public transport and the port, the improvement of water and sanitation, the introduction of gas and electricity, and developments in the means of telegraphic and telephone communication all required substantial, high-risk investment and state regulation. Together these activities can be classified as the urban built infrastructure. Each of them exhibited natural monopoly characteristics, network gains and considerable external benefits and costs. Sanitation apart, all of them were developed by the private sector, subject to Parliamentary sanction. As a result, the public sector played a smaller role in the London economy than it did in many other contemporary large British cities. Some sectors were bought out, with the state taking over water supply, the docks and telephones late in the period, and coming partly into electricity generation and tramways.

The role of government and the public sector

Parliamentary regulation was a mixed blessing. On the positive side, its existence imposed some constraints on monopolistic abuse, set some minimum standards of operation, and channelled investment into approved schemes, which limited, though did not negate, duplication. On the negative side, national government's domain and interests stretched far beyond the capital; its procedures on comparatively minor urban governance issues were time-consuming and cumbersome; its members were prone to respond to self-interested lobbying; and, not least, the politics of the capital were treated by Parliament and successive governments as an object exercise in divide and rule. London-specific pressures and wishes, therefore, could often be brushed aside or ignored.

With hindsight, Parliament made some poor decisions over metropolitan development. The worst were undoubtedly over water, where investment was hampered, costs raised and health ruined by the failure to regulate adequately the private water companies. To be fair, though, the solutions were not easy to find. If the public sector had become involved earlier, it does not seem likely that all problems would have been resolved, and some may have become worse. The only public bodies around before 1855 were the vestries and, if water had been given to them, significant scale economies would have been lost, unless they had co-operated and spent heavily – both of which were unlikely. Facing up to the need for a city-wide body for sanitation at mid-century forced city government on a reluctant vestry system and Parliament alike. It is improbable that water would have done the same in any earlier period.

It is interesting, even so, to think of the 'what if' scenario of the existence of such a city-wide public metropolitan water body in 1800. Given the contemporary ignorance of health matters, poor technologies, high costs of improvement and the designated monopoly power, such an entity would probably have been the subject of opprobrium in the way that the private companies were. Privatisation, or the licensing of private competitors, might then have been outcomes, as they had been in an earlier century when the Corporation of London was reluctant to embark on the expense and risks of expanding the public water supply and so encouraged the setting up of the New River and other private companies. Water was too vital to leave to the market; yet too expensive for politicians to contemplate properly. The contradiction took a long time to resolve.

The issue of whether public bodies, municipal or otherwise, would have generally done a better job with urban infrastructure than private near, or complete, monopolies has light thrown on it by the cases of telephones and tramways. The monopoly powers conferred on the publicly owned Post Office undoubtedly restricted the expansion of the telephone in the metropolis in order to protect its telegraph investments. Similarly, conferring powers on a wide variety of local government bodies with regard to tramway construction led to a failure to create an integrated and extensive tram system and discouraged private investment. LCC-owned tramways, furthermore, trailed rather than led to switchover from horse to electric motive power. Vesting powers in public bodies, in other words, does not make the problems of monopolistic abuse go away. Public bodies, in addition, were subject to strong constraints on expenditure in order to avoid imposing charges on the rates, as the LCC Progressives discovered to their cost.

In contrast to many other British cities,[1] the movement towards municipal ownership was achieved in only a limited way. Some did occur. Many main roads and bridges across the Thames were provided (or constructed) by private interests charging tolls during the early decades of the nineteenth century, and were gradually brought under local government control up to the 1860s. Sewage disposal also switched from being a private household matter (primarily using cesspits) to a major public expense financed by municipal agencies. The Post Office, apart from short periods of private telegraph and telephone services, also managed to keep its grip on communications. Yet, in the main, infrastructure provision was a private matter.

Frequently, a political explanation is given for this extensive use of the private sector. Two arguments are mustered to support this. The first is that vested interests were able to influence Parliamentary debate and government action. This implies that private ownership interests won out because of special, possibly corrupt, group pleading against a common interest that was better satisfied by public provision. The second relates to national politics, where it is argued that central government was too scared of the potential scale and, hence, power of a London-wide municipal government that provided most urban services. As a result, local government was kept fragmented, and relatively weak city-wide bodies were introduced to fulfil a minimum centralising role from 1855 onwards, so that local government did not have the scale to provide adequate city-wide infrastructure.[2] Not only do these two arguments implicitly suggest without demonstration that public provision is necessarily better but they also over-politicise the political with the power it assigns to special interests.

It can be argued, in contrast, that three economic factors helped to contribute to the greater use of the private sector in London. The first point is the scale of the costs associated with the provision of many services. It would have been extremely difficult for local government to have raised such sums or to have funded them out of the rates. The upheaval in local government and its finance just over the need for a public sewer system in the 1850s illustrates this point.[3] To have included many of the other infrastructural investments taking place at the same time within the public sphere would have strained public finances beyond breaking point. The second factor is that many projects were highly risky. Many nineteenth-century infrastructure programmes in the capital were well over-budget (including the Metropolitan Board of Works' major 1850s sewer scheme); whilst managing contractors to keep costs under control was equally hard.[4] Technical change was also substantial and innovations were risky to fund and they led to large losses for older technologies. Public monopoly is not conducive to such dynamics because it is hard to deal with entrenched interests in the public utilities – as can be seen with the Post Office and telephones and local authorities and electricity generation.[5]

The final economic factor suggesting that private infrastructure provision might have frequently been a better option was that many infrastructural services were overwhelmingly used by the middle class – especially public transport until the 1890s/1900s, plus electricity and telephones. To have funded such services out of local taxation would, therefore, have been highly regressive.

The broad balance between public and private provision by the 1900s, thus, does not seem so exceptional. Services with more public good characteristics were generally in the public domain and others were not. Housing and trams were added to the public sector in the 1890s and 1900s as, by this time, the political pendulum had swung in favour of municipal ownership, but the results were by no means an unquestionable success.[6]

What was noticeable about infrastructure was that it stimulated a variety of 'big solution' proposals and differences arising purely on grounds of political ideology. The big ideas often did not work or produced unexpected outcomes. Chadwick with sewers and health and the LCC with trams and housing are two clear examples. Electricity is another illustration. Big ideas and conflicting political ideologies lead to stalemate, as can often be seen in the history of London's infrastructure. Lost in the complex world of metropolitan politics were such vital skills as the art of compromise or of setting up contexts where self-interest could lead to greater social good.

New projects

An obvious mistake was to allow the mainline railway companies to build so many terminals at such great distances from each other. The expansion of London would have been very different if there had been a handful of stations rather than the multitude that there were. It could be argued that the surfeit was the price that had to be paid for preserving the old urban core; yet much of that was to be refashioned anyway, and most other large European and American cities over the following decades did a better job of integrating their rail systems.

Similarly, when new docks were approved, no attempt was made to force any rationalisation on the port as part of the price of approval – leading to further, extensive, land-consuming duplication. Yet the need for rationalisation was clear and the cost to the state at such times would have been minuscule, especially in comparison to subsequent nationalisation. Nationalisation created a parochial body interested primarily in preserving the dock system as it was. So, the port's dock facilities were strung out down the Thames to the long-term detriment of the East End and expansion of the City. Two consequences were that land values were forced higher and suburban expansion to the east had to be that much further out for working-class households that could least afford it. The marshes of East and South-East London were dug out for an excessive number of docks, whereas those elsewhere were often drained for housing or for more productive industries.

Parliamentary control, in addition, was reactive. Investors made application for monopoly rights or compulsory land purchase abilities. No attempt was made, beyond a little sensible standardisation, to impose rational urban plans. With the tube, for example, one modern approach in other countries is for the public sector to propose routes and ask for bidders to build, operate and transfer the facility to the public domain at the end of a long lease. Such an approach to planning was used, for example, for some colonial transportation projects, but it was never used in London. Investors instead made uncoordinated guesses as to which routes would pay and would obtain Parliamentary approval – at least until the advent of the Underground Group. Profit-maximising routes may not bring the highest social returns when considerable externalities are present as they tend to be with urban infrastructure. The disjuncture between the interests of investors and the needs of a city can thus be high.

One means, land values gains, by which metropolitan investors could have been encouraged to take account of such externalities, furthermore, was neglected, because urban infrastructure providers had few possibilities of profiting from the enhancement in land values their investments often created. Regulation, similarly, was poorly enforced – as the history of the water companies attests. Modern-style independent regulatory agencies did not evolve. *Laissez-faire* apart, perhaps it was felt that they would be too open to influence – a factor that is not lost on modern regulation theory with its notion of regulatory capture (whereby a regulator comes to associate too closely with the regulated monopoly's point of view).

Enterprise behaviour

Firms operating in the provision of nineteenth-century metropolitan urban infrastructure had strong incentives to collude, as the histories in earlier chapters showed. Cartelisation, moreover, was becoming an increasingly fashionable industrial strategy. New technologies would then give interlopers a chance, threatening the previous relationships. In this way, competition kept on asserting itself. What weakened this process was the growing expense of investments.

In urban public transport, the shrinking opportunities for competition continually to reassert itself encouraged an entrepreneur, Yerkes, to try to control the whole network of competing systems. Once this happened, existing competitors or new entrants could only prosper if they had low fixed costs – which, in practice, meant small motor bus firms. Yerkes could be regarded as a Schumpeterian-style hero, creating a monopoly in order to invest and shake up an industry. But the subsequent behaviour of the monopoly he created suggests otherwise. Overall, it is likely that public transport fares were higher, and areas of new investment lower, to pay for the tube system that had been devised in a few years at the turn of the century. Whether that represented a good contemporary trade-off is questionable.

Uneven regulation played an important part in stifling competition. With transport, the surface railways, for example, were subject to requirements to provide many cheap services, and tramways were taxed and constrained in a variety of ways. However, it would have required considerable ingenuity and foresight to have devised and repeatedly changed a regulatory system – a process which was probably beyond the scope of the contemporary body politic. A principal modern argument for urban public transport is that it reduces congestion by taking private motor cars off of city streets, thereby generating considerable external benefits. This justification did not exist prior to 1914. Instead, more difficult to quantify impacts on the housing of the working classes were the most common justifications for transport subsidies. In practice, this meant low fares cross-subsidised out of operators' other businesses.

Would land-use planning have done much better?

Extra surface public transport often generated more congestion and associated public investment in inner urban roads to take higher traffic loads was generally insufficient. These issues nowadays fall within the remit of land-use planning under the Town and Country Planning Acts. It was also suggested earlier that one option was to auction the rights to run new transport links, which would require prior planning and evaluation of routes. New systems of transport, as has been seen, eventually changed the urban form, raising further issues about the planning of suburban areas.

The difficulties of the planned, centrally directed alternative to the piecemeal, uncoordinated way in which nineteenth-century London developed have been raised by a number of commentators. This was the essence of Rasmussen's (1937) influential view of London's uniqueness, which somewhat sentimentally identified a village feel to its constituent parts as a result of the unplanned spread. Yet, far from singular, this taking over of surrounding communities could be said of most other cities and so was neither unique to London nor even to England. The neighbourhoods swallowed up, however, in the London context were usually the quite substantial suburbs of the mainly well-to-do that had evolved previously; the scale of which was unique to London. The compliment embodied in the village metaphor, therefore, should more accurately have been given to earlier suburbanisation.

The general theme of the lack of publicly orchestrated town planning was developed by Olsen (1979), who earlier had come out with a strong private planning role for the landed estates but had modified that conclusion (Olsen, 1964). It has been revived recently by a British planner in a book subtitled 'There but for fortune' (Hebbert, 1998), who contrasts the state-directed transformation of Paris and other European capital cities during the era with the experience of London. The difference, however, should not simply be put down to an absence of planning but to the presence in England of that bugbear of planning – heavy compensation to land and property owners whose rights of use were infringed by urban improvements. This affected the evolution of transport routes, for instance. Most importantly, it generally turned the efforts of the Metropolitan Board of Works and other public bodies to restructure central London into mealy-mouthed affairs, although there were some exceptions. The Board, for example, could not afford the high costs of buying up properties to a considerable depth on either side of its routes, so the new developments along its new thoroughfares were frequently dismal because there was insufficient space or financial incentive to do much else. Its involvement in providing land for model dwellings also did not help the aesthetics.

Paradoxically, one area where an absence of planning was, perhaps, particularly beneficial was in the suburbs. Suburban expansion was despised and regretted by many influential Victorians and Edwardians, in the same way as it is today, so that any planning authority endowed with strong powers would probably have constrained urban growth considerably. The building by-law characteristics of much late nineteenth-century suburban housing, moreover, were used as a critique by those arguing for planning;

so the suburban expansion that remained would have been very different in form, with unknown effects on housing supply.

The point to note here is that an omnipotent urban planner would have been hard-pushed to devise a successful plan for London in such circumstances, and would have been forced to impose tight controls on private activities. Lacking the necessary foresight, furthermore, any such plan would have tended to be backward-looking and based on the experience of already existing technologies. During the period in question, and especially after the 1870s, such a situation would have been particularly unfortunate given the extent of the technical changes taking place.

These critical comments are not arguments against planning but rather suggest that the interconnectedness of urbanisation and the uncertainties associated with it are generally too simplistically treated in British land-use planning theory and practice. Although relieved of the problems of compensation by the 1947 Act, the complex economic and social situations into which planning intervention is made and the difficulties of forecasting urban change are usually still ignored in much modern planning practice, which hankers for the technical fix in place of real world uncertainty.

Local government and real estate

Government was the facilitator of economic change in London rather than the prime determinant of it. This was not simply because the years from 1800 to 1914 included the high tide of *laissez-faire* ideologies, especially from the 1850s onwards. The state in various guises was always keen to impose its influence on metropolitan development but governments had neither the resources nor the powers to revise the capital city to their own preferences. London was just too big, the expense of even minor schemes too great, and property owners too powerful. As the provider of public goods and a grantor of property rights, government inevitably played a key role in urban development. Its role in general infrastructure development was considered above. Most of what it did by-passed, rather than required reform of, local government. Public health measures, especially sanitation, and the provision of cleansed, paved, well-lit roads, however, forced governance on to the urban agenda; and the public sector was the vehicle generally used for urban and social reform.

Up to the 1890s, the tendency had been to set up new public bodies to deal with specific problems. These extended from the New Poor Law in the 1830s to the London School Board in the 1870s. From the late 1850s, centralising tendencies began to win out, with first the Metropolitan Board of Works and then the London County Council being set up. Once in existence, they then drew extra functions into themselves. For forty years subsidised housing was kept out of the public sector by pressure from the philanthropic movement but, from the 1890s onwards, that argument began to be lost as well. From a trickle prior to 1914, moreover, council housing became a flood in the inter-war years – built by both tiers of metropolitan government. Only the Metropolitan Water Board, the police and the port slipped through the municipally centralised net of first-tier activities allocated to the LCC – each retaining its independence due to national politics.

The much-maligned vestries and other lower-tier public bodies were similarly caught up in the pressures for greater scale in local government. Amalgamation came in two great waves in the 1850s and 1900s. These second-tier bodies have received a remarkably poor press as being controlled by undemocratic skinflints, insensitive to the needs of the metropolitan populace. It is difficult not to be influenced by this view of the vestries but a decent history of them does not exist, so it is hard to make robust conclusions about their actual behaviour; and the other, politically insignificant, but functionally important, minor second-tier bodies rest in total obscurity. In contrast to the common parsimony critique, it is clear that vestries actually spent much on metropolitan improvements. On some areas, such as roads, they were actually high spenders by contemporary British standards – partly because of the scale of new suburban growth. They also experimented with urban innovations – such as mass libraries, baths and electricity generation – which suggests that more than a little civic pride resided in them; which was spurred on by a spate of town hall building from the 1870s onwards. The descriptions of jobbery and corruption attributed to vestry behaviour, moreover, are generally drawn from contemporary political polemics rather than hard evidence and, even if they existed, may be more attributable to the prevailing narrow franchise than to this particular organisational form of local government.

Democracy, efficiency and countervailing power against the first tier are the usual explanations of why the vestries were amalgamated and subsequently transformed into enlarged municipal boroughs in the 1900s. Efficiency arguments did induce the introduction of the first-tier bodies, but alone they do not adequately explain the assignment and duplication of functions, nor the actual geographical spread of the first- and second-tier entities. As Chapter 16 argued, reform left the new municipal boroughs in the 1900s as large machines for one political party or another to rule for years on end, which party winning out depending on the overall class composition of the municipal area in question. Once the boroughs came to be key providers of working-class housing, furthermore, the voting propensities of particular parts of the city could be affected by whether and where council housing was erected or slums removed. In the inter-war years, for the Labour Party, building houses won votes; for the Conservatives, not to build dwellings was the best strategy. In this way, the mosaic of the city was gradually transformed on the basis of political propensities.

The newly created municipal boroughs, because of the large areas they covered, were remote from local populations that were inevitably diverse in a large city, but not disparate or politically active enough actually to affect the composition of local government. The greater democracy supposed to go along with municipal reform was thus mainly a sham. The efficiency criteria themselves were, at best, only partly met. Again, no detailed studies exist, but local public services in London have persistently cost far more than elsewhere. The extent to which this is more a function of the structure of metropolitan local government than of any claimed distinctive production characteristics of local public goods there has never been effectively investigated. Suspicion, however, has to alight on the political process, because within it there were great incentives to placate supporters and other political machine minders and far fewer pressures to be efficient.

Why did London local government end up like this? One possible explanation is the growth of party politics after national electoral reform. By the 1880s, national political parties were increasingly more active and effective in attracting votes. The politicisation of the vestries during this decade was noted in Chapter 16, and the advent of the LCC created a major political forum with national, as well as metropolitan, influence. Could it be that, rather than seeing the first tier and second tier of local government as evolving as political counterweights to each other, they both were transformed to suit the operations of the new political parties? The standard 'two tiers as counterweights' argument faces the problem that a party on gaining national government could have reformed London politics once more to reflect its particular interests. Yet this never happened – at least not until the 1960s.

An argument that suggests simultaneous benefits for all national political parties of the structure of local government devised in the 1880s and 1890s, therefore, may be more plausible. A multiplicity of democratic bodies providing public services in the metropolis would surely have been anathema to the new national political parties that were evolving after national franchise reform. Far more resources would have had to have been devoted to a greater number of local elections, raising their costs considerably. Moreover, control of party members in a much more fragmented local polity would have been even harder than it already turned out to be – threatening the presentation of a unified national programme. The radicals/left ended up with the urban core and the conservatives/right with most of the suburbs in a stable, and machine-efficient, political equilibrium. On this argument, politicians picked the structure of London's government for their own interests; while dressing up the reforms with arguments about democracy and efficiency. The causes of the structure of metropolitan local government were probably multi-faceted, rather than simply a political carve-up. Yet it would be naive to assume that politicians do not take their own interests into account when restructuring local government.

One area where metropolitan politics had little success was in trying to implement major social reforms. By ignoring the feedback effects of local taxation, the radicals intent on change may well have exacerbated the problems that they were trying to solve. This is especially the case as solutions were seen to lie predominantly with housing, and with the means of transportation necessary to get to and from it. Yet housing and business premises were singled out as the main source of local government income. In this sense, to see local government initiatives as precursors of the future welfare state is only to look at the outputs and not the organisational structures and their costs. Municipalisation of this type rather was a blind alley. Most important for the functioning of the capital and other British cities, the battle to shift at least part of the cost of social policies to the national level failed, and other necessary public goods had to be curtailed and urban expansion cut back as a result. The spreading metropolis, in addition, was divided between a County area that increasingly paid for the capital's public services and a suburban area that did not. The costs of social welfare and of funding local public services are highly topical subjects a century on, but it is clear that the Victorians and Edwardians did not get it right.

Was London too big?

Rapid and virtually continuous city growth was a new phenomenon of the nineteenth century and, up to 1914, it did not lead to much lower densities in inner urban cores. London exhibited these characteristics without parallel. Apart from the occasional campaigns to save public open spaces, there was little government constraint on city growth. Even so, informed opinion despised expansion and wished to contain it. The call for containment was to continue after the First World War and it started to have a strong effect on urban policy in the 1930s and, by the late 1940s, became a catchword with the advent of a revamped town and country planning system and strongly interventionist new towns and regional policies. With ups and downs, that containment policy is still at the forefront of British land-use politics today – though nowadays in the guise of protecting the environment as well as the countryside. The decades of unrestrained metropolitan expansion prior to 1914, within the containment remit, should be castigated as failures.

It is obviously not within the scope of this study to deal fully with the consequences of urban policies that came into existence only after 1914. Yet some useful commentaries on them can still be made, because in many respects they were introduced as critiques of the late nineteenth-century approach. In the introductory chapter, an analogy was made with modern geological theories that treat solid mountains as being in a permanent state of flux. Nineteenth-century London certainly illustrates such a process of perpetual change in what, at any point in time, seemed to observers to be a fixed state of affairs. Urban expansion, in particular, was one of the keys that led to the economic growth of the capital, as Chapter 8 explained. This has been argued here to have been to the general benefit of its economy and population and British economic growth as a whole during the period.

The thrust of the criticisms made here of the provision of urban infrastructure, transportation, the property tax, social policies, local government structures and the limited suburbanisation of industry, taken together, suggests that suburbanisation would have been even greater if the city somehow had managed to function more efficiently. This result can certainly be seen in the 1920s and 1930s when renewed bursts of suburbanisation occurred after some of these constraints had been removed. London was thus not too big prior to 1914 but rather the opposite.

This view was also shared by most social reformers by the turn of the century. Although detailed criticisms of their views have been made here, they were certainly right that low-income groups were less able to enjoy the benefits of urban change in their inner city locations. Their optimism suggested that transport reform could facilitate their suburbanisation as well. Local government and some of the model dwelling companies began to build at the urban fringe in consequence. A more equitable London would probably have been an even bigger one.

Along with post-1920s containment went social policies that further constrained the fluidity of the city. By the 1930s, the suburbanisation of public housing was being replaced by the earlier nineteenth-century policy of dealing with housing problems *in situ*, and where this was not possible of 'decanting' populations out of the capital. Rent control introduced in 1915 then froze tenancies across the pre-1914 housing stock and discouraged landlords from maintaining their properties. By the 1970s large areas of inner London were covered with public housing, built to replace the slums often caused by such long-term disrepair. Firms were discouraged for many years from setting up or expanding in London by regional and local planning policies – again as part of the containment of the capital. Corollaries of restricting suburban growth were thus attempts to freeze land-use patterns in the pre-existing city. This was despite the fact that jobs in general have been decentralising from the urban core since the 1920s onwards. Unsurprisingly with such long-term policies, an inner city crisis was discovered by politicians in the 1970s; one exacerbated by a concomitant collapse of inner city manufacturing.

Subsequent policies, nevertheless, have still retained their spatial fix. Modern urban regeneration projects, although ostensibly about solely dealing with deprived people's social and economic problems, are predicated on resolution of them *in situ*. Urban policy, from being a relatively minor player in urban change in the nineteenth century, has thus come to have a major impact on metropolitan change. Yet is modern policy so wise? Or has the apparent fixity of the built environment mesmerised policy makers into thinking that city structures should, and can, be made to stay the same? Perhaps late nineteenth-century acceptance of greater urban fluidity may have been a wiser course.

Notes

1 This city

1 Keynes, 1973, 383.
2 Cannadine, 1997, Chapter 15, 'London History'.
3 Cannadine, 1997, 159.
4 Many of the numbers presented in subsequent chapters have been rounded to improve comprehension. This may lead to some minor errors when they are added together.

2 Economics and London's history

1 Economic does not simply mean work undertaken by economists because urban geographers and others have played important parts in developing and testing these theories. Some recent work has been dubbed the 'new economic geography' by its proponents (Krugman, 1991 and Fujita *et al.*, 1999).
2 Turvey, 1966.
3 Cannadine, 1997, 147–58.
4 For introductions to the issues, see Ball *et al.*, 1998; Glaeser, 1998; Krugman, 1991; and Quigley, 1998.
5 With economies of scale, unit costs of production fall as output rises; with diseconomies of scale, unit costs rise. Many goods and services will have cost curves that exhibit falling average costs over certain ranges of output and rising ones over others – giving rise to a U-shaped average cost curve.
6 Gatrell, 1977; Lloyd-Jones and Le Roux, 1980.
7 As argued, for example, by Hall, 1962a, and Sheppard, 1998.
8 For example, Chandler, 1990.
9 See Pollard, 1994.
10 Marshall, 1919.
11 Hall, 1962a.
12 Stedman Jones, 1971.
13 See Chapter 3.
14 See Chapter 10.
15 The definition of a pure public good is that consumption of it is non-rival. Consumption by one person, in other words, does not affect consumption by others. Roads are impure public goods because of potential congestion.
16 Hennock, 1963.
17 North, 1990.
18 With regard to the motor bus, substantial destruction to the roads and bridges over which they travelled occurred. The roads were designed for much lighter horse transport and early buses had solid wheels and were heavy. Their groundwork costs were thus borne by local authorities in their road repair and improvement budgets (Jackson, 1991, 8–9).
19 The 1863 Select Committee on Metropolitan Railway Schemes, for example, had 13 bills before it which together would have added 174 route miles through the metropolis and demolished a quarter of the City (cited in Kellett, 1969, 51).
20 Kellett, 1969, Chapter 11.
21 See the special issue of *Urban Studies*, 1998, on city competition.
22 Krugman, 1996.

23 See, for example, Hudson, 1992 and Langton, 1983.
24 The literature is surveyed in Chapter 4.
25 Hunt, 1986.
26 Hudson, 1992, 104.
27 Langton, 1983.
28 Lee, 1986; Cain and Hopkins, 1993.
29 For an explanation and application to the nineteenth century 'Atlantic economy', see O'Rourke and Williamson, 1999.

3 Population and migration

1 Wrigley, 1967 and 1987.
2 Ball *et al.*, 1989, 50.
3 Waller, 1983, 1, 8.
4 Lampard, 1973; Weber, 1899.
5 Woods, 1985, 650.
6 Woods, 1985.
7 Woods and Hinde, 1987, 37.
8 Wrigley and Schofield, 1981, 166.
9 Schwarz, 1992, 133.
10 Matossian, 1985, 190–4.
11 Galloway, 1985; Landers, 1987.
12 Matossian, 1985.
13 Hardy, 1988, 391.
14 Luckin, 1997.
15 Winter, 1982.
16 McKeown, 1976, 153–4.
17 McKeown and Record, 1962, 120.
18 Oddy, 1982, 125.
19 Burnett, 1983, 254.
20 McKeown and Record, 1962, 120.
21 Luckin, 1984, 120.
22 Luckin, 1984, 117.
23 Woodward, 1984, 69–70.
24 Woods and Hinde, 1987, 50.
25 McKeown and Record, 1962, 119.
26 Mooney, 1994.
27 Woodward, 1984, 76.
28 Woodward, 1984, 76.
29 Crafts, 1978, 22.
30 Anderson, 1985, 69–87.
31 Lawton, 1990.
32 Samuel, 1973.
33 Calculated from Baines, 1994, 52.
34 Boyer and Hatton, 1997, 703.
35 Shannon, 1935, 84–5.
36 Pooley and Turnbull, 1998.
37 Cited in Stedman Jones, 1971, 137.
38 Stedman Jones, 1971, 136–42.
39 O'Rourke and Williamson, 1999, 138.
40 Swift and Gilley, 1989.
41 Rude, 1971, 7.
42 Davis, 1991.
43 Jackson, 1964, 295.
44 Hohenburg and Lees, 1995, 256.
45 Lees, 1979, 62.
46 Engels, 1845.
47 Wohl, 1977, 9–10.
48 Merriman, 1993, 142.
49 Pollins, 1982, 134.
50 Hall, 1962a, 62.

51 Hall, 1962a, 62.
52 This section is based on Merriman, 1993, and contributors to that edited book.
53 Baines, 1985, 144.
54 Wareing, 1981.
55 Baines, 1994, 49; Baines, 1991.

4 Work and industry

1 Hall, 1962a, is an influential proponent of this view.
2 For example, Sheppard, 1971, 1985 and 1998.
3 Berg, 1985; Crafts, 1987 and 1995; Daunton, 1995.
4 Aldcroft and Richardson, 1969.
5 Lee, 1979, 3–4; Lawton, 1978; Drake, 1972.
6 Lee, 1979, 5.
7 Employment data from Lee, 1979.
8 Cain and Hopkins, 1993, 62.
9 For example, Rubinstein, 1981, 1986 and 1987.
10 Feinstein *et al.*, 1982.
11 Millward, 1990, 424.
12 All data in this section are calculated from Lee, 1979.
13 Bradley, 1989.
14 Chandler, 1977.
15 Green, 1995, 110–11.
16 Green, 1995, 111.
17 Green, 1996, 22.
18 Price, 1980; Clarke, 1992.
19 Prothero, 1978.
20 Hobsbawm, 1964, 7–15.
21 Green, 1995, 26.
22 Waller, 1983, 24.
23 Hannah, 1983.
24 Green, 1995, 18.
25 Bostock and Jones, 1993a and b.
26 See George, 1966; Green, 1995; Schwarz, 1992.
27 O'Rourke and Williamson, 1999, 11.
28 Platt *et al.*, 1993.

5 Wealth, living standards and poverty

1 Rubinstein, 1987.
2 See, for example, Daunton, 1989 and Daunton and Rubinstein, 1991.
3 Rubinstein, 1987, 25–7.
4 Calculated from Table 5.1.
5 Berghoff, 1991.
6 Perkin, 1989, 257–8.
7 Nicholas, 1999.
8 Cannadine, 1992, 8–11.
9 See Chapter 14.
10 Pollard, 1994, 79.
11 Rubinstein, 1986, 46–51.
12 Cannadine, 1980, 23–4.
13 Rubinstein, 1993, 26.
14 Rubinstein, 1993, 31.
15 Perkin, 1989, 98.
16 Schwarz, 1992, 57.
17 Routh, 1980.
18 Atkinson, 1975, 22; Rubinstein, 1986, 70–2.
19 Lindert, 1994, 378–81.
20 Mitchell, 1988, 769–70.
21 Alexander, 1970, 39.
22 Parl. Paper, 1908, CVII, xv.

23 For example, Stedman Jones, 1971.
24 See, for example, Stedman Jones, 1971.
25 Royal Commission of Housing for the Working Classes, 1884–5, 17, cited in 1905 Board of Trade study.
26 See Chapter 8.
27 See the map of London housing rents in R. J. Morris, 1986, 171.
28 Schwarz, 1992, 179.
29 Stedman Jones, 1971, 216–17.
30 Parl. Paper, 1905, lxxxiv, 47.
31 Stedman Jones, 1971, 216.
32 Parl. Paper, 1905, lxxxiv, 30.
33 Crafts and Mills, 1994, 190.
34 Schwarz, 1985.
35 Phelps-Brown and Hopkins, 1954; Lindert and Williamson, 1983.
36 Available in Mitchell, 1988.
37 Feinstein, 1990.
38 Schwarz, 1985, 33; Schwarz, 1990.
39 Booth, 1902, vol. ix, 381.
40 Stedman Jones, 1971, 44.
41 Tebbutt, 1983, 122.
42 Stedman Jones, 1971, 56.
43 Booth's Categories A, B and 50,000 odd in C, Stedman Jones, 1971, 55–6.
44 Brodie, 1999.
45 Green, 1995, 251; 1996.
46 See Chapter 14.
47 Schwarz, 1992, chs 4 and 7.
48 Schwarz, 1992, 322.
49 Schwarz, 1992, 84–9.
50 Green, 1995, 88.
51 Estimated by dividing the 200,000 skilled in 1848 by total male employment in the 1851 census: 705,000.
52 Routh, 1980.
53 Barro and Sala-i-Martin, 1991 and 1992.
54 Hunt, 1973, 1986a and b; Boyer and Hatton, 1994.
55 Hunt, 1986a, 937.
56 Hunt, 1973.
57 Hunt, 1986a, 938–45.
58 Boyer and Hatton, 1994, 93; 1997.
59 Pooley and Turnbull, 1998.
60 Mayhew, 1861.
61 Greenwood, 1869.
62 Mearns, 1883.
63 Booth, 1902.
64 Rowntree, 1901; Perkin, 1989, 32–3.
65 Gillie, 1996.
66 See O'Day and Englander, 1993 and Englander and O'Day, 1995.
67 See Englander and O'Day, 1995; Hennock, 1976 and 1987.
68 Englander and O'Day, 1995, 61.
69 Hennock, 1987, 210.
70 See Harris, 1994, ch. 8 and Hennock, 1987.
71 Green, 1995, 195.
72 Green, 1995, 195.
73 Green, 1995, 230.
74 MacKinnon, 1994, 284–7.
75 Lindert, 1994, 383.
76 Boyer, 1990.
77 Schwarz, 1992, 50.

6 Retailing and the new mass market

1 Schwarz, 1992, 56.
2 Adburgham, 1964 and 1979.
3 Davis, 1966.
4 Alexander, 1970, 63.
5 R. W. Rawson, cited in Alexander, 1970, 62.
6 Forshaw and Bergstrom, 1983, 27.
7 Mayhew, 1861, quoted in Burnett, 1978, 137.
8 Robertson, 1958 and 1959.
9 Weinreb and Hibbert, 1983, 92.
10 Forshaw and Bergstrom, 1983, 32.
11 Weinreb and Hibbert, 1983, 399.
12 Simmons, 1986, 50.
13 Sheppard, 1971, 192.
14 Simmons, 1986, 50.
15 Atkins, 1980, 530.
16 Whetham, 1976.
17 Schwarz, 1992, 61–2.
18 Winstanley, 1983.
19 MacKeith, 1985.
20 LSE, 1935, 38.
21 Burnett, 1978, 15.
22 Munby, 1951, 66.
23 Burnett, 1978, 244.
24 Hugill, 1978, 27–30.
25 Stoddard, 1974.
26 Hugill, 1978.
27 Alford, 1973.
28 Alford, 1977, 137, 263.
29 Warren, 1980, 11.
30 Musson, 1965.
31 Hardie and Pratt, 1966.
32 Tweedale, 1990.
33 Slinn, 1984, 23, 79.
34 Glenny Crory, 1876, 66–7.
35 Chandler, 1990, 374–5.
36 Chandler, 1990, 278.
37 Chandler, 1990, 376.
38 Chandler, 1990, 377–8.
39 Fraser, 1981, 112.
40 Fraser, 1981, 115.
41 Nevett, 1977.
42 Jeffreys, 1954, 29–30.
43 Burnett, 1978, 123; Chandler, 1990, 382–3.
44 Hough, 1949.
45 Fraser, 1981, 124.
46 Fraser, 1981, 128.
47 Fraser, 1981, 129.
48 Weinreb and Hibbert, 1983, *passim.*
49 Shaw and Wild, 1979, 282.
50 Lambert, 1938, 67–75, 242.
51 Dale, 1995, 46–7, 82, 87.
52 Honeycombe, 1984, 42.
53 Peel, 1960, 36.
54 Corina, 1978.
55 Barty-King, 1992, 4, 83, 97.
56 Lambert, 1938, 139.
57 Lambert, 1938, 147–8.
58 Jeffreys, 1954, 29–30, 74.

7 Leisure and pleasure

1 Watney, 1976.
2 George, 1966, 41–54.
3 Bernard, 1987, 457.
4 Burnett, 1978,
5 Burnett, 1978, 50.
6 Harrison, 1973, 162.
7 Based on information in Schwarz, 1992, 55.
8 Burnett, 1979, 175.
9 Gourvish and Wilson, 1994, 285.
10 Corran, 1975.
11 Green, 1995, 30.
12 Gourvish and Wilson, 1994, 136–9.
13 Gourvish and Wilson, 1994, 76.
14 Burnett, 1978, 16.
15 Gourvish and Wilson, 1994, 76.
16 Cottrell, 1980, 168.
17 Gourvish and Wilson, 1994, 76.
18 Munby, 1951, 67–8.
19 Chandler, 1990, 267.
20 Burnett, 1978, 225.
21 Gourvish and Wilson, 1994, 78–81.
22 Cottrell, 1980, 168.
23 Cottrell, 1980, 169–70.
24 Cottrell, 1980, 170.
25 Cottrell, 1980, 169.
26 Gourvish and Wilson, 1994, 271.
27 Gourvish and Wilson, 1994, 300–1.
28 Gourvish and Wilson, 1994, 610–12.
29 Graves, 1963, 21, 28, 32.
30 Purvis, 1986, 197.
31 Briggs, 1985, 43.
32 Wainwright, 1990, 22, 47.
33 Waugh, 1957, 8, 33, 43; Whitehead, 1999, 60–6.
34 Briggs, 1985, 44, 51.
35 Borer, 1972, 187.
36 Simmons, 1984, 5.
37 Simmons, 1984, 6–7, 14.
38 Borer, 1972, 190.
39 Leapman, 1987, 82–3.
40 Sheppardson, 1991, 26, 53.
41 Sheppardson, 1991, 17.
42 Hope, 1990.
43 Richardson, 1976.
44 Delgado, 1971, 67.
45 Judd, 1983, 14–15.
46 Wroth, 1896.
47 Sheppard, 1971, 357.
48 Weinreb and Hibbert, 1983.
49 Bailey, 1987.
50 LSE, 1935, vol. 1, 291.
51 Booth, 1991, 34–40.
52 Booth, 1991, 38–40.
53 Bailey, 1987, 154–6.
54 Bailey, 1987, 160.
55 Harrison, 1971, 324–5.
56 Mander and Mitchenson, 1965.
57 Gray, 1996, 22.
58 Smith, 1933, 290.
59 Gray, 1996, 23.

60 Sorensen, 1996.
61 Sorensen, 1996, 84.
62 Weinreb and Hibbert, 1983.
63 Lawton, 1978, 275, 279.
64 McLeod, 1986, 217.
65 Weinreb and Hibbert, 1983.
66 Hibbert, 1988, 17–18.
67 Whitehead, 1999, 56.
68 Whitehead, 1999, 58.
69 Wainwright, 1982, 135, 165, 184.
70 Elvin, 1984, 76.
71 Baines, 1985, 330, 338.
72 Harris, 1994, 199–200.
73 Lee, 1979.
74 Boyce *et al.*, 1978, 24–5.
75 LSE, 1935, 311.
76 Handover, 1960.
77 Green, 1995, 28.
78 Gibberd, 1992, 61.
79 F. Hunt, 1986.
80 LSE, 1935, vol. 1, 301.
81 Green, 1995, 80.
82 Hall, 1962a, 104.
83 Vamplew, 1988.

8 Suburbanisation and housing

1 Winter, 1993.
2 Daunton, 1983; Knowles and Pitt, 1977.
3 For example, Bowley, 1944; Gauldie, 1974.
4 For example, Daunton, 1983.
5 Dyos, 1982.
6 Wohl, 1977, appendix IVa, where all local authority schemes prior to 1914 are listed.
7 Finlay and Shearer, 1986; Porter, 1994, ch. 5.
8 Dyos, 1961, 37, 84.
9 Weber, A. 1899; Park *et al.*, 1925.
10 Marriott, 1988.
11 Pollins, 1964, 43–4.
12 Ashworth, 1964, 73.
13 Dyos, 1961, 58.
14 Pooley, 1984.
15 Best, 1981, 68–9.
16 Dyos, 1961, 63.
17 R. J. Morris, 1986, 178.
18 Ihlanfeldt, 1982.
19 Wohl, 1977, 319.
20 Yelling, 1986, 139–42.
21 Kellett, 1969, 379 (no data for women available).
22 Perkin, 1970, 245–57.
23 Wohl, 1977, 295.
24 Muthesius, 1982, 11.
25 A modern model of this process can be found in Black and Henderson, 1999.
26 Hall *et al.*, 1973.
27 Feinstein, 1988, 387.
28 Summerson, 1978, 65–6.
29 Dyos (1961, 127–37) illustrates this longevity with the history of Edward Yates, a South London builder/developer.
30 Summerson, 1978; Jenkins, 1975.
31 For example, Jenkins, 1975; Roebuck, 1979; whilst Saint, 1999, is a good recent survey.
32 Jackson, 1991, 12.
33 Daunton, 1983, 103.

34 Land Enquiry Committee, 1914.
35 Daunton, 1983, 98.
36 Buchinsky and Polak, 1993, 14–18.
37 Jackson, 1991.
38 See DiPasquale and Wheaton, 1996, for a modern treatment of such vacancy models.
39 Sheppard *et al.*, 1979, 179.
40 Abramowitz, 1968; Isard, 1942; Ball *et al.*, 1996.
41 Sheppard *et al.*, 1979; Feinstein, 1988.
42 Parry Lewis, 1965.
43 Sheppard *et al.*, 1979, 179.
44 Spensley, 1918.
45 Jackson, 1991; Edwards and Pigram, 1986.
46 Ball and Morrison, 2000.
47 Dyos, 1968.
48 Ball, 1983.
49 Cooney, 1955.
50 Summerson, 1973, 17; Dyos, 1968.
51 Hobhouse, 1971.
52 Dyos, 1961, 132.
53 Hobhouse, 1971.
54 Daunton, 1983, 218.
55 Daunton, 1983; Davis, 1988.
56 See Netzer and Drennan, 1997.
57 See the discussion in Chapter 5.
58 Vallis, 1972 – cited in Ball, 1983.
59 Offer, 1977.
60 Dyos, 1961, 87–91.
61 Daunton, 1983, provides a literature survey.
62 Both Dyos (1961, 87–9) and Daunton (1983, 74–5) discuss reversionary values without discounting them.
63 Cannadine, 1992, ch. 3.
64 Offer, 1977 and 1981.
65 Olsen, 1979, 129–31 and Olsen, 1982.
66 Cannadine, 1980, 391–429.
67 Daunton, 1983, 73–4.

9 To and from the capital

1 Freeman, 1986, 80.
2 Albert, 1972.
3 Thrift, 1990, 458.
4 Chartres and Turnbull, 1983, 69.
5 Chartres and Turnbull, 1983, 85.
6 Chartres and Turnbull, 1983, 83, 97.
7 Turnbull, 1979, 67.
8 Cove-Smith, 1977.
9 Hadfield, 1970, 127–31.
10 Herbert, 1961.
11 Bagwell, 1988, 13.
12 Turnbull, 1979, 81.
13 Hadfield, 1969.
14 Hadfield, 1970, 119–20.
15 Hadfield, 1970, 118.
16 Hadfield, 1970, 131–2.
17 Pollins, 1971, 61.
18 Bagwell and Armstrong, 1988, 176–7.
19 Bagwell, 1988, 61.
20 Bagwell and Armstrong, 1988, 185.
21 Harley, 1988, 854.
22 Bagwell and Armstrong, 1988, 187.
23 Bagwell and Armstrong, 1988, 187.

24 Bagwell, 1988, 60.
25 Bagwell, 1988, 62.
26 Armstrong and Bagwell, 1983, 164.
27 Armstrong and Bagwell, 1983, 164.
28 Bagwell and Armstrong, 1988, 197–8.
29 Dyos and Aldcroft, 1974, 119.
30 Pollins, 1971, 116.
31 Barker and Robbins, 1963, 50.
32 White, 1971, 110.
33 White, 1971, 118–19, 112–13, 171–2.
34 Kellett, 1969, 391.
35 Kellett, 1969, 275–6.
36 Kellett, 1969, 267.
37 Barker and Robbins, 1963, 163.
38 Kellett, 1969, 79.
39 1 square mile = 640 acres; although, in fact, the City covers 673 acres.
40 Kellett, 1969, 290.
41 Kellett, 1969, 278–9.
42 Kellett, 1969, 15.
43 Kellett, 1969, 294.
44 Turnbull, 1979, 119.
45 Kellett, 1969, 82.
46 Freeman, 1986, 93.
47 Irving, 1978, 62–3.
48 Kellett, 1969, 82.
49 Port of London Authority, 1974.
50 Jackson, 1986, 96.
51 Pudney, 1975, 22.
52 Bagwell and Armstrong, 1988, 176–7.
53 Bagwell and Armstrong, 1988, 220, 240.
54 Jackson, 1988, 244.
55 Jackson, 1983, 54–5.
56 Pudney, 1975, 20.
57 Pudney, 1975, 22–4.
58 Broodbank, 1921, vol. 1.
59 Pudney, 1975, 56–8.
60 Pudney, 1975, 91.
61 Pudney, 1975, 93.
62 Pudney, 1975, 93–4.
63 Pudney, 1975, 104.
64 Pudney, 1975, 144–7.
65 Pudney, 1975, 76–79.
66 Lummis, 1994, 56.
67 Stedman Jones, 1971, 318–19.
68 Pudney, 1975, 150, 152.

10 Moving around London

1 Dyos, 1961, 62.
2 Barker, 1988, 135.
3 Kellett, 1969, 50.
4 Richardson, 1995, 165.
5 Barker, 1988, 142.
6 Barker and Robbins, 1974, 190.
7 Parl. Paper, 1905, xxx, 8.
8 Parl. Paper, 1906, xli, 127.
9 Inwood, 1998, 554.
10 Barker and Robbins, 1963, 12.
11 Dyos, 1961, 65.
12 Owen, 1982, 115.
13 Barker and Robbins, 1963, 15.

14 Barker and Robbins, 1963, 6.
15 Barker and Robbins, 1963, 7.
16 Barker and Robbins, 1963, 7.
17 Barker and Robbins, 1963, 245.
18 Barker and Robbins, 1963, 40–3.
19 Barker and Robbins, 1963, 14–22.
20 Barker and Robbins, 1963, 59.
21 Barker and Robbins, 1963, 39.
22 Morris, 1953, 8.
23 Barker and Robbins, 1963, 64.
24 Barker and Robbins, 1963, 89, 98.
25 Barker and Robbins, 1963, 94.
26 Barker and Robbins, 1963, 167.
27 Barker and Robbins, 1963, 166, 175.
28 Parl. Papers, 1906, xli, 127.
29 Day, 1973.
30 Barker and Robbins, 1963, 246–50.
31 Barker and Robbins, 1963, 253.
32 Barker and Robbins, 1974, 122.
33 Morris, 1953, 42.
34 Barker and Robbins, 1974, 133.
35 Morris, 1953, 45.
36 Klapper, 1978, 67.
37 Barker and Robbins, 1974, 173–81.
38 Jackson, 1991, 6.
39 Barker and Robbins, 1974, 185.
40 White, 1971, 155.
41 Kellett, 1969, 391–8.
42 White, 1971, 122.
43 White, 1971, 61–3.
44 White, 1971, 82.
45 Barker and Robbins, 1963, 111–15, 125, 134.
46 White, 1971, 84.
47 Barker and Robbins, 1963, 159.
48 Barker and Robbins, 1963, 161; Kellett, 1969, 273.
49 White, 1971, 92.
50 White, 1971, 163.
51 Kellett, 1969, 393.
52 Kellett, 1969, 397.
53 Kellett, 1969, 374.
54 Barker and Robbins, 1963, 173–4.
55 Calculated from Kellett, 1969, 378.
56 Barker and Robbins, 1963, 90–1.
57 Barker and Robbins, 1963, 186.
58 Barker and Robbins, 1963, 190–5.
59 Barker and Robbins, 1963, 196–7.
60 Barker and Robbins, 1963, 268–70.
61 Barker and Robbins, 1974, 21.
62 Jackson, 1991, 3.
63 Barker and Robbins, 1974, 25–6.
64 Barker and Robbins, 1974, 102.
65 Barker and Robbins, 1974, 99.
66 Barker and Robbins, 1974, 190.
67 Jackson, 1991, 3.
68 Barker and Robbins, 1974, 86–8.
69 Croome and Jackson, 1993.
70 Parl. Paper, 1905.
71 Barker and Robbins, 1974, 55–6.
72 White, 1971, 96.
73 Barker and Robbins, 1974, 50–1.
74 White, 1971, 101.

75 Kynaston, 1994, 216–19.
76 Kynaston, 1994, 226.
77 White, 1971, 99.
78 Barker and Robbins, 1974, 69.
79 Barker and Robbins, 1974, 71–3.
80 Chernow, 1990.
81 Barker and Robbins, 1974, 77–84.
82 Barker and Robbins, 1974, 143–4.
83 Barker and Robbins, 1974, 173–7.
84 Barker and Robbins, 1974, 182–3.
85 Gillespie, 1989, 116.

11 Utilities, communications and markets

1 Briggs, 1963.
2 Weinreb and Hibbert, 1983, 932.
3 Weinreb and Hibbert, 1983, 541–2.
4 Weinreb and Hibbert, 1983, 148.
5 Weinreb and Hibbert, 1983, 929.
6 Davis, 1988.
7 Weinreb and Hibbert, 1983, 932.
8 Davis, 1988.
9 Hall, 1999, 690.
10 Davis, 1988.
11 Metropolitan Water Board, 1953, 1961.
12 Everard, 1949.
13 Falkus, 1967, 504.
14 Faulkner, 1990, 49.
15 Dyos, 1961, 147.
16 Falkus, 1967, 505.
17 Weinreb and Hibbert, 1983, 304; Dyos, 1961, 147.
18 Hobsbawm, 1968, 161–2.
19 Hobsbawm, 1968, 163.
20 Maddison, 1992.
21 Hobsbawm, 1968.
22 Hobsbawm, 1968, 167.
23 Ashworth, 1964, 64–5.
24 Hobsbawm, 1968, 170.
25 Glenny Crory, 1876, 28–9.
26 Hughes, 1993, 247.
27 Hughes, 1993, 228–9.
28 Hughes, 1993, 227.
29 Bowers, 1982, 139–40.
30 Bowers, 1982, 158, 161.
31 Hughes, 1993, 235, 237.
32 Hannah, 1979, 11.
33 Hughes, 1993, 246.
34 Bowers, 1982, 161.
35 Gillespie, 1989, 112.
36 Hannah, 1979, 45.
37 Bowers, 1982, 161.
38 Faulkner, 1990, 53.
39 Bowers, 1982, 374.
40 Hannah, 1979, 45.
41 Davis, 1988, 214.
42 Hannah, 1979, 45.
43 Lee, 1979.
44 Scott, 1958, 42.
45 Hall, 1962a.
46 Daunton, 1985, 5–7.
47 Daunton, 1985, 40.

48 Daunton, 1985, 46–7.
49 Trench and Hillman, 1993, 181–2.
50 Daunton, 1985, 51.
51 Trench and Hillman, 1993, 175–6.
52 Trench and Hillman, 1993, 178.
53 Trench and Hillman, 1993, 177.
54 Robson, 1973, 224.
55 Trench and Hillman, 1993, 178.
56 Robson, 1973, 169–70.
57 Occomore, 1995, 6.
58 Occomore, 1995, 17.
59 Occomore, 1995, 69, 71.
60 Webber, 1969, 115.
61 Webber, 1969, 117.
62 Passingham, 1934, 114–15; Thorne, 1990, 104.
63 Forshaw and Bergstrom, 1983, 169.
64 Passingham, 1934, 21, 78.
65 Forshaw and Bergstrom, 1980, 54.

12 Manufacturing

1 Muthesius, 1982, 29.
2 Green, 1995; Schwarz, 1992.
3 For example, Hall, 1962a; Stedman Jones, 1971 and Schwarz, 1992.
4 Piore and Sabel, 1984.
5 Schwarz, 1992, 186–7.
6 George, 1966, ch. 4.
7 George, 1966, 202.
8 Schwarz, 1992, 217–19.
9 George, 1966, 168–78.
10 See Chapter 5.
11 Schmiechen, 1984, 39.
12 Feldman, 1994, 191.
13 Mokyr, 1990, 141–2.
14 Schmiecheon, 1984, 25.
15 Schmiechen, 1984, 41.
16 Pennington and Westover, 1989.
17 Newman, 1982.
18 Morris, 1986a, 38, 50.
19 Morris, 1986a, 55.
20 Godley, 1996, 40.
21 Schmiechen, 1984, 196.
22 Waugh, 1964.
23 Green, 1995, 124, 162, 166.
24 Kershen, 1995, 116.
25 Walker, 1988, 70.
26 Green, 1996, 18.
27 Schmiechen, 1984, 38–9.
28 Morris, 1986b, 48.
29 Kershen, 1995, 102.
30 Schmiechen, 1984, 38, 41.
31 Walkley, 1981.
32 Alexander, 1983, 35.
33 Alexander, 1983, 35.
34 Martin, 1966, 49.
35 Green, 1995.
36 Gibson, 1958, 4.
37 Green, 1995, 158–9; Gibson, 1958, 5.
38 Sheppard, 1971, 167.
39 Gibson, 1958, 6.
40 Schmiechen, 1984, 39–40.

41 Hall, 1962b.
42 Hudson, 1968.
43 Bythell, 1978, 113.
44 Lee, 1979.
45 Schwarz, 1992, 199.
46 Schwarz, 1992, 200.
47 Heal, 1953.
48 Barty-King, 1992, 37–8.
49 Oliver, 1961 and 1966.
50 Schwarz, 1992, 200.
51 Hall, 1962a, 87–8.
52 Hall, 1962a, 89.
53 Kirkham *et al.*, 1987.
54 Hall, 1962a, 87.
55 Hall, 1962a, 90.
56 Crossick, 1978, 51.
57 Hogg, 1963, appendix 10.
58 Hall, 1962a.
59 Putnam and Weinbren, 1996, 46, 49.
60 Lee, 1979.
61 Pollard, 1950, 89.
62 Pollard, 1950, 88.
63 Pollard, 1950, 81.
64 Sheppard, 1971, 180.
65 Pollard, 1950, 89.
66 Pollard and Robertson, 1979.
67 Crossick, 1978, 50.
68 Hall, 1962a, 154.
69 Nockolds, 1977, 111.
70 Chandler, 1990, 346.
71 Hall, 1962a; Georgano *et al.*, 1995; Lewis, 1999, 61–4.
72 Williams, 1994.
73 Sheppard, 1971, 162; Atterbury and Irvine, 1979.
74 Morgan Crucible, 1956.
75 Gibberd, 1992.
76 Bowley, 1960.
77 Clarke, 1992, 101, 132.
78 Muthesius, 1982, 28–9, 208.
79 Harper Smith, 1991, 407.

13 Domestic, clerical and professional services

1 McBride, 1976, 36.
2 Green, 1995, 151.
3 McBride, 1976, 20.
4 Schwarz, 1992, 258.
5 Sheppard, 1971, 368.
6 McBride, 1976, 45.
7 McBride, 1976, 76.
8 Horn, 1975, 44, 48.
9 McBride, 1976, 63.
10 Malcolmson, 1986, 8.
11 Malcolmson, 1986, 8.
12 Schwarz, 1992, 47.
13 LSE, 1935, vol. VIII, III, 276.
14 Lockwood, 1989, 43.
15 McLeod, 1974, 143.
16 Holcombe, 1973, 151.
17 Anderson, 1977.
18 Holcombe, 1973, 151.
19 Holcombe, 1973, 150.

20 LSE, 1935, vol. VIII, III, 276.
21 Holcombe, 1973, 151.
22 For example, Carr-Saunders and Wilson, 1933; Gourvish, 1988; Lockwood, 1989; Perkin, 1989.
23 Kirk, 1976, 108, 114.
24 Corfield, 1995, 82.
25 Schwarz, 1992, 27.
26 Kirk, 1976, 31.
27 Slinn, 1984, 97.
28 Offer, 1977.
29 Kynaston, 1996, 21.
30 Slinn, 1984, 36.
31 Davis, 1984, 13, 15.
32 Kirk, 1976, 89.
33 Corfield, 1995, 90; Reader, 1966, 211.
34 Reader, 1966, 201.
35 Michie, 1992, 177.
36 Jones, 1995, 465.
37 Institute of Chartered Accountants, 1966.
38 Michie, 1992, 177, 180.
39 Kynaston, 1996, 21.
40 Jones, 1995, 396–7.
41 Michie, 1992, 177.
42 Hudson, 1986.
43 Cottrell, 1980, 112–41.

14 Financial services and the City

1 Borer, 1977; Gibson-Jarvie, 1979.
2 Kynaston, 1996, 31.
3 North, 1990.
4 Black, 1996, 115.
5 Neal, 1994, 168.
6 Cottrell, 1986, 146.
7 Black, 1996, 119.
8 Cottrell, 1980, 7–10.
9 Neal, 1994, 157–62.
10 Cottrell, 1986 152; Black, 1996, 116.
11 Black, 1989 and 1996.
12 Black, 1996, 115.
13 Chapman, 1984.
14 Sheppard, 1971, 57.
15 Scammell, 1968; Fletcher, 1976.
16 Kynaston, 1994, 88–9.
17 Sheppard, 1971, 67–8.
18 Sheppard, 1971, 74.
19 Kynaston, 1996, 39.
20 Kynaston, 1994, 235–43.
21 Cottrell, 1986, 145.
22 Michie, 1992, 72.
23 Morgan's failed intervention into the tube system is examined in Chapter 10.
24 Michie, 1992, 72–3.
25 Cottrell, 1986, 148.
26 Kynaston, 1994, 84–5.
27 Cottrell, 1986, 148.
28 Kynaston, 1994, 86–7; Sheppard, 1971, 59.
29 Cottrell, 1986, 151.
30 Kynaston, 1994, 181.
31 Sheppard, 1971, 64.
32 Cottrell, 1980, 53.
33 Sheppard, 1971, 72.

34 Kynaston, 1996, 39.
35 Michie, 1992, 71.
36 Mitchell, 1988, 456.
37 Michie, 1992, 73.
38 Buchinsky and Polak, 1993.
39 Officer, 1985, 572.
40 Officer, 1985, 569.
41 Michie, 1987, 42.
42 Garbade and Silber, 1978, 829.
43 Officer, 1985.
44 Obstfeld and Taylor, 1998, 362, 366.
45 Kynaston, 1994, 16.
46 Cottrell, 1980, 6.
47 Michie, 1987, 4.
48 Michie, 1992, 104.
49 Michie, 1987, 4–5.
50 Cottrell, 1986, 154.
51 Quoted in Cottrell, 1980, 147.
52 Cottrell, 1980, 153.
53 Michie, 1987, 25.
54 Michie, 1987, 14–16.
55 Michie, 1987, 85.
56 Michie, 1992, 115.
57 Hannah, 1983.
58 Kennedy, 1982, 113–14; 1987.
59 Michie, 1987, 37.
60 Michie, 1987, 42–5.
61 Michie, 1987, 76.
62 Neal, 1985, 226.
63 Edelstein, 1994, 173; Michie, 1992, 112.
64 Simon, 1968, 42–3.
65 Michie, 1992, 109.
66 Simon, 1968, 43.
67 Cottrell, 1975, 31.
68 Edelstein, 1982; 1994.
69 Clayton, 1971.
70 Cockerell, 1984, 11–15.
71 Sheppard, 1971, 200.
72 Cockerell, 1984, 21.
73 Cockerell, 1984, 19.
74 Michie, 1992, 152–3.
75 Dickson, 1960, 6, 16–18.
76 Ogborn, 1962.
77 Dickson, 1960, 188–233.
78 Trebilcock, 1985, 461.
79 Trebilcock, 1985, 495.
80 Michie, 1992, 159.
81 Kynaston, 1996, 13.
82 Waller, 1983, 28.
83 Summerson, 1977.
84 Turvey, 1998.
85 Turvey, 1998.
86 Waller, 1983, 54–6.

15 Welfare and social policy

1 Mandler, 1990, focuses on London.
2 Reader, 1966, 16.
3 Reader, 1966, 67.
4 Reader, 1966, 200.
5 Prochaska, 1992, 7.

6 Ayers, 1971.
7 Powell, 1996, 165.
8 Prochaska, 1992, 5.
9 Powell, 1996, 165–7.
10 Prochaska, 1992, 9.a
11 Powell, 1996, 169.
12 Johnson, 1984 and 1985.
13 Green, 1995, 97.
14 Green, 1995, 98.
15 Schwarz, 1992, 56.
16 Crossick, 1978, 183.
17 See the discussion in Harris, 1994, 240–1.
18 Harris, 1994, 200.
19 Fraser, 1976, 97.
20 Stedman Jones, 1971, 298; Fraser, 1976, 97.
21 Stedman Jones, 1971, 299.
22 Stedman Jones, 1971, 299–300.
23 Humphreys, 1995, 119.
24 Crowther, 1981.
25 Green, 1995, 219–20.
26 Driver, 1993, 89.
27 Green, 1995, 214.
28 Green, 1995, 215.
29 Green, 1995, 226.
30 Green, 1995, 226.
31 Green, 1995, 226.
32 Green, 1995, 235.
33 Green, 1995, 240.
34 Green, 1995, 241.
35 Davis, 1988, 119.
36 Davis, 1988, 159.
37 Mayhew, 1861; Mearns, 1883; Hollingshead, 1986.
38 Wohl, 1977, 5; Dyos, 1982.
39 Wohl, 1977, xiv–xv.
40 Quoted in Yelling, 1986, 58.
41 Marshall, 1884, quoted in Yelling, 1986, 55.
42 Wohl, 1977, 179–99.
43 Malpass, 1999, 48.
44 Yelling, 1986, 146.
45 Dyos, 1955, 13; Kellett, 1969, 327.
46 Wohl, 1977, 30.
47 Yelling, 1986, 146.
48 J. Parsons writing in 1903, cited in Yelling, 1986, 146.
49 Wohl, 1977, 136.
50 Wohl, 1977, 74–8.
51 Tarn, 1973.
52 Wohl, 1977, appendix III.
53 Wohl, 1977, 168.
54 Wohl, 1977, 168.
55 Wohl, 1977, 146.
56 Wohl, 1977, 133.
57 Yelling, 1986, 38.
58 Wohl, 1977, appendix III.

16 The government of London

1 See, for example, Netzer and Drennan, 1997; Cullis and Jones, 1992.
2 Boyne and Cole, 1998.
3 Davis, 1988, 38.
4 Waller, 1983, 64.
5 Davis, 1988, 155.

6 Netzer and Drennan, 1997, 193.
7 Owen, 1982, 228–9.
8 Sheppard, 1982, 24.
9 Sheppard, 1982, 25.
10 Sheppard, 1982, 25.
11 Darlington, 1970.
12 Owen, 1982, 223.
13 Owen, 1982, 28.
14 Davis, 1988, 200.
15 Davis, 1988, 12.
16 Davis, 1988, 28–9.
17 Davis, 1988, 159.
18 Owen, 1982, 223.
19 Owen, 1982, 161.
20 Owen, 1982, 80.
21 Owen, 1982, 165–8.
22 Owen, 1982, 59, 65.
23 Owen, 1982, 63–73.
24 Owen, 1982, 93.
25 Owen, 1982, 91.
26 Owen, 1982, 106.
27 Owen, 1982, 150.
28 Owen, 1982, 127.
29 Davis, 1988, 40.
30 Holloway, 1992.
31 Owen, 1982, 127–30.
32 Segars, 1989, 171.
33 Segars, 1989, 168–9.
34 Owen, 1982, 137.
35 Inwood, 1998, 690.
36 Bryant, 1986.
37 Clifton, 1992, 8.
38 Waller, 1983, 62.
39 LCC Abstract of Statistics, 1897 to 1914, *passim.*
40 Parliamentary Papers, 1884–1914, *passim.*
41 Waters, 1989,
42 Laurence, 1989, 94–5.
43 Gibbon and Bell, 1939; Jackson, 1965; Ruck and Rhodes, 1970.
44 Saint, 1989, 77–87.
45 Davis, 1988, 168, 174.

17 Conclusions

1 See Briggs, 1963.
2 See Davis, 1988; Young and Garside, 1982; and Chapter 18.
3 See Chapter 18.
4 Owen, 1982.
5 The history of telephones is a good example- see Chapter 11.
6 See Chapter 17.

Bibliography

Parliamentary Papers

Local Taxation Returns, 1884, lxvii; 1887, lxix; 1893–4, lxxvi; 1898, lxxvi; 1903, lviii; 1909, lxxiv; 1914, lxviii.

Her Majesty's Commissioners for Inquiring into the Housing of the Working Classes, First to Third Reports, 1885.

Report of the Metropolitan Board of Works for the Year 1888, 1889, lxvi.

Metropolitan Board of Works Enquiry Committee, 1889.

Report on Wholesale and Retail Prices in the UK 1902 with Comparative Statistical Tables for a Series of Years, 1903.

Memoranda. Statistical Tables and Charts Prepared by the Board of Trade with Reference to Various Matters Bearing on Britain and Foreign Trade and Industrial Conditions, 1905, lxxxiv.

Royal Commission Appointed to Inquire into and Report upon the Means of Locomotion and Transport in London, 1905. Minutes of Evidence, 1906.

Report of the Enquiry by the Board of Trade into Working Class Rents, Housing and Rental Practices, 1908, cvii.

Books and articles

Abramowitz, M. (1968) 'The passing of the Kuznets cycle', *Economica*, 45–58.

Adburgham, A. (1964) *Shops and Shopping 1800–1914: Where and in What Manner the Well Dressed English Women Bought her Clothes*, London: Allen & Unwin.

Adburgham, A. (1979) *Shopping in Style: London from the Restoration to Edwardian Elegance*, London: Thames & Hudson.

Albert, W. (1972) *The Turnpike System in England 1663–1840*, Cambridge: Cambridge University Press.

Aldcroft, D. and Freeman, M. (eds) (1983) *Transport in the Industrial Revolution*, Manchester: Manchester University Press.

Aldcroft, D. H. and Richardson, H. W. (1969) *The British Economy 1870–1939*, London: Macmillan.

Alexander, D. G. (1970) *Retailing in England during the Industrial Revolution*, London: Athlone Press.

Alexander, S. (1983) *Women's Work in Nineteenth Century London: A Study of the Years 1820–50*, London: Journeyman Press.

Alford, B. W. E. (1973) *W.D. & H.O. Wills and the Development of the UK Tobacco Industry 1786–1965*, London: Methuen.

Alford, B. W. E. (1977) 'Penny cigarettes, oligopoly and entrepreneurship in the UK tobacco industry in the later nineteenth century' in Supple, B. (ed.) *Essays in British Business History*, Oxford: Clarendon Press.

Anderson, G. L. (1977) 'The social economy of late Victorian clerks' in Crossick, G. (ed.) *The Lower Middle Class in Britain 1870–1914*, London: Croom Helm.

Anderson, M. (1985) 'The emergence of the modern life cycle in Britain', *Social History*, 10, 69–87.

Armstrong, J. and Bagwell, P. S. (1983) 'Coastal shipping' in Aldcroft and Freeman, 1983.

Ashworth, W. (1964) 'Types of social and suburban development in suburban Essex' in Centre for Urban Studies (ed.) *London: Aspects of Change*, London: MacGibbon & Kee.

Atkins, P. J. (1980) 'The retail milk trade in London 1790–1914', *Economic History Review*, 33 (4), 522–37.

Atkinson, A. B. (1975) *The Economics of Inequality*, Oxford: Clarendon Press.
Atterbury, P. and Irvine, L. (1979) *The Doulton Story*, Stoke-on-Trent: Royal Doulton Tableware.
Ayers, G. M. (1971) *England's First State Hospitals and the Metropolitan Asylums Board 1867–1930*, London: Wellcome Institute of the History of Medicine.
Bagwell, P. S. (1988) *The Transport Revolution*, London: Routledge.
Bagwell, P. S. and Armstrong, P. (1988) 'Coastal shipping' in Freeman and Aldcroft, 1988.
Bailey, P. (1987) *Leisure and Class in Victorian England: Rational Recreation and the Quest for Control 1830–1885*, London: Methuen.
Baines, D. E. (1985) *Migration in a Mature Economy: Emigration and Internal Migration in England and Wales 1861–1900*, Cambridge: Cambridge University Press.
Baines, D. E. (1991) *Emigration from Europe 1815–1930*, Basingstoke: Macmillan.
Baines, D. E. (1994) 'Population, migration and regional development 1870–1939' in Floud and McCloskey, 1994.
Ball, M. (1983) *Housing Policy and Economic Power*, London: Methuen.
Ball, M. and Morrison, T. (2000) 'Housing investment volatility: a long-run international comparison', *Housing, Theory and Society*, 2, 5–12.
Ball, M., Gray, F. and McDowell, L. (1989) *The Transformation of Britain: Contemporary Social and Economic Change*, London: Fontana.
Ball, M., Lizieri, C. and MacGregor, B. D. (1998) *The Economics of Commercial Property*, London: Routledge.
Ball, M., Morrison, T. and Wood, A. (1996) 'Structures investment and economic growth: a long-term international comparison', *Urban Studies*, 33, 1687–706.
Barker, F. and Jenkins, P. (1990) *The History of London in Maps*, London: Barrie and Jenkins.
Barker, T. C. (1988) 'Urban Transport' in Freeman and Aldcroft, 1988.
Barker, T. C. (1989) 'Business as usual: London and the Industrial Revolution', *History Today*, xxxix, 49–51.
Barker, T. C. and Robbins, M. (1963) *A History of London Transport: Passenger Travel and the Development of the Metropolis. Volume I: The Nineteenth Century*, London: Allen & Unwin.
Barker, T. C. and Robbins, M. (1974) *A History of London Transport: Volume II The Twentieth Century*, London: George Allen & Unwin.
Barro, R. J. and Sala-i-Martin, X. (1991) 'Convergence across states and regions', *Brookings Papers in Economic Activity*, No. 1, 107–82.
Barro, R. J. and Sala-i-Martin, X. (1992) 'Convergence', *Journal of Political Economy*, 100, 223–51.
Barty-King, H. (1992) *Maples, Fine Furnishers: A Household Name for 150 Years*, London: Quiller Press.
Berg, M. (1985) *The Age of Manufactures. Industry, Innovation and Work in Britain 1700–1820*, London: Fontana.
Berghoff, H. (1991) 'British businessmen as wealth holders, 1870–1914: a closer look', *Business History*, 33, 24–41.
Bernard, A. (1987) *The Whisky Distilleries of th United Kingdom: The Centenary Edition*, Edinburgh: Mainstream.
Best, R. H. (1981) *Land Use and Living Space*, London: Methuen.
Black, D. and Henderson, V. (1999) 'A model of urban growth', *Journal of Political Economy*, 107, 252–84.
Black, I. (1989) 'Geography, political economy and the circulation of finance capital in early industrial England', *Journal of Historical Geography*, 15, 366–84.
Black, I. S. (1996) 'The London agency system in English banking 1780–1825', *London Studies*, 21, 112–30.
Booth, C. (1902) *Life and Labour of the People of London*, London: Macmillan.
Booth, M. R. (1991) *Theatre in the Victorian Age*, Cambridge: Cambridge University Press.
Borer, M. I. C. (1972) *The British Hotel Through the Ages*, Guildford: Lutterworth Press.
Borer, M. I. C. (1977) *The City of London: A History*, London: Constable.
Bostock, F. and Jones, G. (1993a) 'The growth of foreign multinationals in British manufacturing 1850–1962', *University of Reading, Discussion Papers in International Investment and Business Studies*, No. 181.
Bostock, F. and Jones, G. (1993b) 'The characteristics of foreign multinationals in British manufacturing 1850–1962', *University of Reading, Discussion Papers in International Investment and Business Studies*, No. 182.
Bowers, B. (1982) *A History of Electric Light and Power*, London: Peregrinus in association with the Science Museum.
Bowley, M. (1944) *Housing and the State*, London: Macmillan.

Bowley, M. (1960) *Innovations in Building Materials*, London: Macmillan.

Boyce, G., Curran, J. and Wingate, P. (eds) (1978) *Newspaper History from the Seventeenth Century to the Present Day*, London: Constable.

Boyer, G. R. (1990) *The Economic History of the English Poor Law 1750–1850*, Cambridge: Cambridge University Press.

Boyer, G. R. and Hatton, T. J. (1994) 'Regional labour market integration in Britain, 1850–1913' in Grantham, G. and MacKinnon, M. (eds) *Labour Market Evolution: The Economic History of Market Integration, Wage Flexibility and the Employment Relation*, London: Routledge.

Boyer, G. R. and Hatton, T. J. (1997) 'Migration and labour market integration in late nineteenth century England and Wales', *Economic History Review*, 50 (4), 697–734.

Boyne, G. A. and Cole, M. (1998) 'Revolution, evolution and local government structure: an empirical analysis of London', *Urban Studies*, 35, 751–68.

Bradley, H. (1989) *Men's Work, Women's Work: A Sociological History of the Sexual Division of Labour in Employment*, Cambridge: Polity in association with Basil Blackwell.

Briggs, A. (1963) *Victorian Cities*, London: Odhams Press.

Briggs, A. (1985) *Wine For Sale: Victoria Wine and the Liquor Trade 1860–1984*, London: Batsford.

Brodie, M. (1999) 'Artisans and dossers: the West End riots and the East End casual poor', *London Journal*, 24, 34–50.

Broodbank, J. G., Sir (1921) *History of the Port of London. Volumes 1 and 2*, London: Daniel O'Connor.

Bryant, M. E. (1986) *The London Experience of Secondary Education*, London: Athlone Press.

Buchinsky, M. and Polak, B. (1993) 'The emergence of a national capital market in England, 1710–1880', *Journal of Economic History*, 53, 1–24.

Burnett, J. (1978) *A Social History of Housing 1815–1970*, Newton Abbot: David and Charles.

Burnett, J. (1983) *Plenty and Want: A Social History of Diet in England from 1815 to the Present Day*, London: Routledge.

Bythell, D. (1978) *The Sweated Trades: Outwork in Nineteenth Century Britain*, London: Batsford.

Cain, P. J. and Hopkins, A. G. (1993) *British Imperialism: Innovation and Expansion*, London: Longman.

Cairncross, A. K. (1953) *Home and Foreign Investment 1870–1913: Studies in Capital Accumulation*, Cambridge: Cambridge University Press.

Cannadine, D. (1980) *Lords and Landlords: the Aristocracy and Towns, 1774–1967*, Leicester: Leicester University Press.

Cannadine, D. (1992) *The Decline and Fall of the British Aristocracy*, London: Picador.

Cannadine, D. (1997) *The Pleasures of the Past*, Harmondsworth: Penguin.

Carr-Saunders, A. M. and Wilson, P. A. (1933) *The Professions*, London: Frank Cass & Co.

Carter, H. and Lewis, C. R. (1990) *An Urban Geography of England and Wales in the Nineteenth Century*, London: Edward Arnold.

Chandler, A. D. (1977) *The Visible Hand. The Managerial Revolution in American Business*, Cambridge, Mass.: Belknap Press.

Chandler, A. D. (1990) *Scale and Scope. The Dynamics of Industrial Capitalism*, Cambridge, Mass.: Belknap Press.

Chapman, S. D. (1984) *The Rise of Merchant Banking*, London: Allen & Unwin.

Chartres, J. A. and Turnbull, G. L. (1983) 'Road transport' in Aldcroft and Freeman, 1983.

Chernow, R. (1990) *The House of Morgan. An American Banking Dynasty and the Rise of Modern Finance*, New York: Simon & Schuster.

Clark, C. (1951) 'Urban population densities', *Journal of the Royal Statistical Society*, Series A, 114, 35–56.

Clarke, L. (1992) *Building Capitalism. Historical Change and the Labour Process in the Production of the Built Environment*, London: Routledge.

Clayton, G. (1971) *British Insurance*, London: Elek Books.

Clifton, G. C. (1992) *Professionalism, Patronage and Public Service in Victorian London: The Staff of the Metropolitan Board of Works 1856–89*, London: Athlone Press.

Cockerell, H. (1984) *Lloyds of London: A Portrait*, Cambridge: Woodhead-Faulkner.

Cooney, E. (1955) 'The origins of the Victorian master builders', *Economic History Review*, 8, 167–76.

Corfield, P. J. (1995) *Power and the Professions in Britain, 1700–1850*, London: Routledge.

Corina, M. (1978) *Fine Silks and Oak Counters: Debenhams 1778–1978*, London: Hutchinson.

Corran, H. S. (1975) *A History of Brewing*, Newton Abbot: David & Charles.

Cottrell, P. L. (1975) *British Overseas Investment in the Nineteenth Century*, London: Macmillan.

Cottrell, P. L. (1980) *Industrial Finance, 1830–1914. The Finance and Organisation of English Manufacturing Industry*, London: Methuen.

Cottrell, P. L. (1986) 'Banking and Finance' in Langton and Morris, 1986.

Cove-Smith, C. (1977) *London's Waterway Guide: A Complete Guide to the Rivers and Canals of Greater London*, St Ives: Imray, Laurie, Norie and Wilson.

Crafts, N. F. R. (1978) 'Average age at first marriage of women in mid-nineteenth century England and Wales: a cross-section study', *Population Studies*, 32, 21–5.

Crafts, N. F. R. (1987) 'British economic growth 1750–1850: some difficulties of interpretation', *Explorations in Economic History*, 24, 245–68.

Crafts, N. F. R. (1995) 'Exogenous or endogeneus growth? The Industrial Revolution Reconsidered', *The Journal of Economic History*, 55, 745–72.

Crafts, N. F. R. and Mills, T. C. (1994) 'Trends in real wages in Britain 1750–1913', *Explorations in Economic History*, 31, 176–94.

Croome, D. F. and Jackson, A. A. (1993) *Rails Through the Clay: A History of London's Tube Railways*, Harrow Weald: Capital Transport.

Crossick, G. (1978) *An Artisan Elite in Victorian Society: Kentish London 1840–80*, London: Croom Helm.

Crowther, M. A. (1981) *The Workhouse System 1834–1929: The History of an English Social Institution*, London: Batsford.

Cullis, J. and Jones, P. (1992) *Public Finance and Public Choice*, Maidenhead: McGraw-Hill.

Dale, T. (1995) *Harrods: A Palace in Knightsbridge*, London: Harrods Publishing.

Daley, A. and Benjamin, B. (1963) 'London: a case study', *Population Studies*, 17, 26–37.

Darlington, I. (1970) *The London Commissioners of Sewers and their Records*, Chichester: Phillimore.

Daunton, M. J. (1983) *House and Home in the Victorian City*, London: Edward Arnold.

Daunton, M. J. (1985) *Royal Mail: The Post Office Since 1840*, London: Athlone.

Daunton, M. J. (1989) 'Gentlemanly capitalism and British industry, 1820–1914', *Past and Present*, 122, 24–33.

Daunton, M. J. (1995) *Progress and Poverty: An Economic and Social History of Britain 1700–1850*, Oxford: Oxford University Press.

Daunton, M. J. and Rubinstein, W. D. (1991) 'Gentlemanly capitalism and British industry, 1820–1914: a debate', *Past and Present*, 132, 44–61.

Davies, R. and Grant, M. D. (1983) *London and its Railways*, London: David & Charles.

Davis, D. (1966) *A History of Shopping*, London: Routledge & Kegan Paul.

Davis, G. (1991) *The Irish in Britain 1815–1914*, Dublin: Gill & Macmillan.

Davis, J. (1988) *Reforming London: The London Government Problem 1855–1900*, Oxford: Clarendon Press.

Davis, P. (1984) *Number One: A History of the Firm of Gregory Rowcliffe and Co. 1784–1984*, London: Gregory Rowcliffe & Co.

Day, J. R. (1966) *The Story of London's Underground*, London: London Transport Board.

Day, J. R. (1973) *The Story of the London Bus. London and its Buses from the Horse Bus to the Present Day*, London: London Transport Executive/Greater London Council.

Delgado, A. (1971) *Victorian Entertainment*, Newton Abbot: David & Charles.

Dennis, R. (1978) 'The social geography of towns and cities 1730–1914' in Dodgshon, R. A. and Butlin, R. A. (eds) *An Historical Geography of England and Wales*, London: Academic Press.

Dickson, P. G. M. (1960) *The Sun Insurance Office 1710–1960: The History of Two and a Half Centuries of British Insurance*, London: Oxford University Press.

DiPasquale, D. and Wheaton, W. (1996) *Urban Economics and Real Estate Markets*, Englewood Cliffs, NJ: Prentice Hall.

Dodgshon, R. A. and Butlin, R. A. (eds) (1978) *An Historical Geography of England and Wales*, London: Academic Press.

Drake, M. (1972) 'The Census 1801–1891' in *Nineteenth Century Society: Essays in the Use of Quantitative Methods for the Study of Social Data*, Cambridge: Cambridge University Press.

Driver, F. (1993) *Power and Pauperism: The Workhouse System 1834–1884*, Cambridge: Cambridge University Press.

Dyos, H. J. (1955) 'Railways and housing in Victorian London', *Journal of Transport History*, ii, 11–21, 90–100.

Dyos, H. J. (1961) *Victorian Suburb. A Study of the Growth of Camberwell*, Leicester: Leicester University Press.

Dyos, H. J. (1968) 'The speculative builders and developers of Victorian London', *Victorian Studies*, XI, 640–90.

Dyos, H. J. (1982) 'The slums of Victorian London', in Cannadine, D. and Reeder, D. (eds) *Exploring the Urban Past: Essays in Urban History by H. J. Dyos*, Cambridge: Cambridge University Press.

Dyos, H. J. and Aldcroft, D. H. (1974) *British Transport: An Economic Survey from the Seventeenth Century to the Twentieth*, Harmondsworth: Penguin.

Dyos, H. J. and Wolff, M. (eds) (1973) *The Victorian City: Images and Realities, Volume 1*, London: Routledge & Kegan Paul.

Edelstein, M. (1982) *Overseas Investment in the Age of High Imperialism. The United Kingdom, 1850–1914*, London: Methuen.

Edelstein, M. (1994) 'Foreign investment and accumulation, 1860–1914' in Floud and McCloskey, 1994.

Edwards, D. and Pigram, R. (1986) *London's Underground Suburbs*, London: Baton Transport.

Elvin, L. (1984) *Bishop and Son, Organ Builders: The Story of J. C. Bishop and his Successors*, Lincoln: L. Elvin.

Engels, F. (1845) *The Condition of the Working Class in England in 1844*, Harmondsworth: Penguin (1987 edition).

Englander, D. and O'Day, R. (eds) (1995) *Retrieved Riches. Social Investigation in Britain 1840–1914*, London: Scolar Press.

Evans, A. W. (1985) *Urban Economics. An Introduction*, Oxford: Blackwell.

Everard, S. (1949) *The History of the Gas Light and Coke Company 1812–1949*, London: Ernest Benn.

Eversley, D. (1975) 'Searching for London's lost soul', *London Journal*, 103–17.

Falkus, M. E. (1967) 'The British gas industry', *Economic History Review*, 20, 494–508.

Faulkner, A. (1990) 'The Regent's Canal' in Hunter, M. and Thorne, R. (eds) *Change at King's Cross. From 1800 to the Present*, London: Historical Publications.

Feinstein, C. H. (1988) 'Residential dwellings' in Feinstein, C. H. and Pollard, S. (eds) *Studies in Capital Formation in the UK, 1750–1920*, Oxford: Oxford University Press.

Feinstein, C. H. (1990) 'New estimates of average earnings in the UK 1880–1913', *Economic History Review*, 43, 595–632

Feinstein, C. H., Matthews, R. C. O. and Odling Smee, J. (1982) *British Economic Growth 1856–1973*, Oxford: Clarendon Press.

Feldman, D. (1994) *Englishmen and Jews: Social Relations and Political Culture 1840–1914*, London: Yale University Press.

Finlay, R. A. P. and Shearer, B. (1986) 'Population growth and suburban expansion' in Beier, A. L. and Finlay, R. A. P. (eds) *London 1500–1700: The Making of a Metropolis*, London: Longman.

Fletcher, G. A. (1976) *The Discount Houses in London: Principles, Operation and Change*, London: Macmillan.

Floud, R. and McCloskey, D. (eds) (1994) *The Economic History of Britain Since 1700. Volume 2: 1860–1939*, Cambridge, Cambridge University Press.

Forshaw, A. and Bergstrom, T. (1980) *Smithfield: Past and Present*, London: Heinemann.

Forshaw, A. and Bergstrom, T. (1983) *The Markets of London: A Complete Guide with Maps and Photographs*, Harmondsworth: Penguin.

Fox, C. (ed.) (1992) *London World City 1800–1840*, London: Yale University Press.

Fraser, D. (ed.) (1976) *The New Poor Law in the Nineteenth Century*, London: Macmillan.

Fraser, W. H. (1981) *The Coming of the Mass Market 1850–1914*, London: Macmillan.

Freeman, M. J. (1986) 'Transport' in Langton and Morris, 1986.

Freeman, M. J. and Aldcroft, D. H. (eds) (1988) *Transport in Victorian Britain*, Manchester: Manchester University Press.

Freeman, P. and Essam, B. (1994) *Bricks and Rollers: A Story of the Faircloughs Pioneers in the Early Development of Clacton*, Saffron Walden: East Anglia Traction Engine Club.

Fujita, M., Krugman, P. and Venables, A. (1999) *The Spatial Economy. Cities, Regions and International Trade*, Cambridge, Mass.: MIT Press.

Galloway, P. R. (1985) 'Annual variations in deaths by age and deaths by cause, prices and weather in London 1670–1830', *Population Studies*, 39, 487–505.

Garbade, K. D. and Silber, W. L. (1978) 'Technology, communication and the performance of financial markets: 1840–1975', *Journal of Finance*, 33, 819–32.

Garside, W. R. (1980) *The Measurement of Unemployment: Methods and Sources in Great Britain 1850–1979*, Oxford: Blackwell.

Gatrell, V. A. C. (1977) 'Labour, power, and the size of firms in Lancashire cotton in the second quarter of the nineteenth century', *Economic History Review*, xxx, 95–139.

Gauldie, E. (1974) *Cruel Habitations: A History of Working Class Housing 1780–1918*, London: Allen & Unwin.

Georgano, N., Baldwin, N., Clausager, A. and Wood, J. (1995) *Britain's Motor Industry: The First Hundred Years: The Fluctuating Fortunes of Britain's Car Manufacturers from Queen Victoria's Time to the Present Day*, London: G. T. Foulis & Co.

George, M. D. (1966) *London Life in the Eighteenth Century*, Harmondsworth: Penguin.
Gibberd, G. (1992) *On Lambeth Marsh: The South Bank and Waterloo*, London: J. Gibberd.
Gibbon, G. and Bell, R. W. (1939) *History of the London County Council 1889–1939*, London: Macmillan.
Gibson, A.V. (1958) 'Huguenot weavers' houses in Spitalfields', *East London Papers*, 1 (1), 3–14.
Gibson-Jarvie, R. (1979) *The City of London: A Financial and Commercial History*, Cambridge: Woodhead-Faulkner.
Gillespie, J. (1989) 'Municipalism, monopoly and management: "the demise of socialism in one county 1918–1933"' in Saint, A. (ed.) *Politics and People of London: The London County Council 1899–1965*, London: Hambledon Press.
Gillie, A. (1996) 'The origin of the poverty line', *Economic History Review*, 49 (4), 715–30.
Glaeser, E. L. (1998) 'Are cities dying?', *Journal of Economic Perspectives*, 12, 139–60.
Glass, D. V. (1963) 'Some indications of the difference between urban and rural mortality in England, Wales and Scotland', *Population Studies*, 17, 44–63.
Glenny Crory, W. (1876) *East London Industries*, London: Longman.
Godley, A. (1996) 'Immigrant entrepreneurs and the emergence of London's East End as an industrial district', *London Journal*, 21 (1), 38–45.
Gourvish, T. R. (1988) 'The rise of the professions' in Gourvish, T. R. and O'Day, A. (eds) *Later Victorian Britain, 1867–1900*, Basingstoke: Macmillan.
Gourvish, T. R. and Wilson, R. G. (1994) *The British Brewing Industry 1830–1980*, Cambridge: Cambridge University Press.
Graves, C. P. R. (1963) *Leather Armchairs: The Chivas Regal Book of London Clubs*, London: Cassell.
Gray, R. (1996) *Cinemas in Britain: One Hundred Years of Cinema Architecture*, London: Lund Humphries.
Green, D. (1991) 'The metropolitan economy: continuity and change 1800–1939' in Hoggart, K. and Green, D. (eds) *London: A New Metropolitan Geography*, London: Edward Arnold.
Green, D. (1995), *From Artisans to Paupers: Economic Change and Poverty in London 1790–1870*, Aldershot: Scolar Press.
Green, D. (1996) 'The nineteenth century metropolitan economy: a revisionist interpretation', *London Studies*, 21, 9–26.
Green, O. (1987) *The London Underground: An Illustrated History*, London: Ian Allan.
Greenwood, J. (1869) *The Seven Curses of London*, London: Blackwell (1981 edition).
Hadfield, C. (1969) *The Canals of South and South East England* , Newton Abbot: David & Charles.
Hadfield, C. (1970) *The Canals of the East Midlands (including part of London)*, Newton Abbot: David & Charles.
Hall, P. (1999) *Cities in Civilization. Culture, Innovation, and Urban Order*, London: Orion Books.
Hall, P. G. (1962a) *The Industries of London Since 1861*, London: Hutchinson University Library.
Hall, P. G. (1962b) 'The East London footwear industry: an industrial quarter in decline', *East London Papers*, 5 (1), 3–21.
Hall, P. G. *et al.* (eds) (1973) *The Containment of Urban England: Volume 1*, London: George Allen & Unwin.
Handover, P. M. (1960) *Printing in London from 1476 to Modern Times*, London: Allen & Unwin.
Hannah, L. (1979) *Electricity Before Nationalisation: A Study of the Development of the Electricity Supply Industry in Britain to 1948*, London: Macmillan.
Hannah, L. (1983) *The Rise of the Corporate Economy*, London: Methuen.
Hardie, D. W. F. and Davidson Pratt, J. (1966) *A History of the Modern British Chemical Industry*, Oxford: Pergamon Press.
Hardy, A. (1988) 'Diagnosis, death and diet: the case of London 1750–1909', *Journal of Interdisciplinary History*, xviii, 387–401.
Harley, C. K. (1988) 'Ocean freight rates and productivity, 1740–1913: the primacy of mechanical invention reaffirmed', *Journal of Economic History*, 48, 851–76.
Harper Smith, A. and T. (1991) *The Brickfields of Acton*, London: A & T Harper Smith.
Harris, J. (1994) *Private Lives, Public Spirit: A Social History of Britain, 1870–1914*, Harmondsworth: Penguin.
Harrison, A. E. (1969) 'The competitiveness of the British cycle industry, 1890–1914', *Economic History Review*, 22, 287–303.
Harrison, B. (1971) *Drink and the Victorians: The Temperance Question in England 1815–72*, London: Faber & Faber.
Harrison, B. (1973) 'Pubs' in Dyos and Wolff, 1973.
Heal, A., Sir (1953) *The London Furniture Makers: From the Restoration to the Victorian Era 1660–1840*, London: Batsford.
Hebbert, M. (1998) *London: There but for Fortune*, London: Wiley.

Hennock, E. P. (1963) 'Finance and politics in urban local government in England, 1835–1900', *Historical Journal*, VI, 212–25.
Hennock, E. P. (1976) 'Poverty and social theory in England, the experience of the 1880s', *Social History*, 1, 75–6.
Hennock, E. P. (1987) 'The measurement of urban poverty: from the metropolis to the nation 1880–1920', *Economic History Review*, 40, 2, 208–27.
Herbert, M. (1961) *London's Canal: The History of the Regent's Canal*, London: Putnam.
Hibbert, C. (1988) *London's Churches*, London: Queen Anne Press.
Hobhouse, H. (1971) *Thomas Cubitt: Master Builder*, London: Macmillan.
Hobhouse, H. (1976) *Lost London. A Century of Demolition and Decay*, London: Macmillan.
Hobsbawm, E. J. (1964) 'The nineteenth century labour market in London' in Centre for Urban Studies (ed.) *London: Aspects of Change*, London: MacGibbon & Kee.
Hobsbawm, E. J. (1968) 'British gas workers 1873–1914' in Hobsbawm, E. J., *Labouring Men: Studies in the History of Labour*, London: Weidenfeld & Nicolson.
Hogg, O. F. G. (1963) *The Royal Arsenal: Its Background, Origin and Subsequent History, Volumes 1 and 2*, Oxford: Oxford University Press.
Hohenberg, P. M. and Lees, L. H. (1995) *The Making of Urban Europe 1000–1994*, Cambridge, Mass.: Harvard University Press.
Holcombe, L. (1973) *Victorian Ladies at Work: Middle Class Women in England and Wales 1850–1914*, Newton Abbot: David & Charles.
Hollingshead, J. (1986) *Ragged London in 1861*, London: Dent.
Holloway, S. (1992) *Courage High: A History of Firefighting in London*, London: HMSO.
Honeycombe, G. (1984) *Selfridges, Seventy Five Years: The Story of a Store 1909–84*, London: Park Lane Press.
Hope, A. (1990) *Londoners' Larder: English Cuisine from Chaucer to the Present*, Edinburgh: Mainstream.
Horn, P. (1975) *The Rise and Fall of the Victorian Servant*, London: Gill & Macmillan.
Hough, J. A. (1949) *Co-operative Retailing, 1914–45*, London: International Co-operative Movement.
Hudson, K. (1968) *Towards Precision Shoemaking: C. and J. Clark Ltd and the Development of the British Shoe Industry*, Newton Abbot: David & Charles.
Hudson, K. (1982) *Pawnbroking: An Aspect of British Social History*, London: Bodley Head.
Hudson, P. (1986) *The Genesis of Industrial Capital: A Study of the West Riding Wool Textile Industry c. 1750–1850*, Cambridge: Cambridge University Press.
Hudson, P. (1992) *The Industrial Revolution*, London: Edward Arnold.
Hughes, T. P. (1993) *Networks of Power. Electrification in Western Society, 1880–1930*, Baltimore: Johns Hopkins University Press.
Hugill, A. (1978) *Sugar and All That: A History of Tate and Lyle*, London: Gentry Books.
Humphreys, R. (1995) *Sin, Organised Charity and the Poor Law in Victorian England*, Basingstoke: Macmillan.
Hunt, E. H. (1973) *Regional Wage Variations in Britain 1850–1914*, Oxford: Clarendon Press.
Hunt, E. H. (1986a) 'Wages' in Langton and Morris, 1986.
Hunt, E. H. (1986b) 'Industrialisation and regional wage inequality: wages in Britain 1760–1914', *Journal of Economic History*, 46, 935–61.
Hunt, F. (1986) 'Opportunities lost and gained: mechanisation and women's work in the London bookbinding and printing trades' in John, A. V. (ed.) *Unequal Opportunities: Women's Employment in England 1800–1918*, Oxford: Blackwell.
Ihlanfeldt, K. R. (1982) 'Income elasticities of demand for rental housing: additional evidence', *Urban Studies*, 19 (1), 36–48.
Institute of Chartered Accountants (1966) *The History of the Institute of Chartered Accountants in England and Wales 1880–1965 and of its Founder Accountancy Bodies*, London: Heinemann.
Inwood, S. (1998) *A History of London*, London: Macmillan.
Irving, R. J. (1978) 'The profitability and performance of British railways 1870–1914', *Economic History Review*, 31, 46–66.
Isard, W. (1942) 'A neglected cycle: the transport-building cycle', *Review of Economics and Statistics*, 24, 149–58.
Jackson, A. J. (1991) *Semi-detached London: Suburban Development, Life and Transport 1900–39*, Didcot: Wild Swan.
Jackson, G. (1983) *The History and Archaeology of Ports*, Tadworth: World's Work.
Jackson, G. (1986) 'Sea trade' in Langton and Morris, 1986.
Jackson, G. (1988) 'The ports' in Freeman and Aldcroft, 1988.
Jackson, J. A. (1964) 'The Irish' in Centre for Urban Studies (ed.) *London: Aspects of Change*, London: MacGibbon & Kee.

Jackson, W. E. (1965) *Achievement: A Short History of the London County Council*, London: Longman.

Jeffreys, J. B. (1954) *Retail Trading in Britain 1850–1950*, Cambridge: Cambridge University Press.

Jenkins, S. (1975) *Landlords to London. The Story of a Capital and its Growth*, London: Constable.

Johnson, P. (1984) 'Self-help versus state help: old age pensions and personal savings in Great Britain 1906–1937', *Explorations in Economic History*, 21, 329–50.

Johnson, P. (1985) *Saving and Spending: The Working Class Economy in Britain 1870–1939*, Oxford: Clarendon Press.

Johnson, P. (1996) 'Economic development and industrial dynamism in Victorian London', *London Journal*, 21 (1), 27–37.

Jones, E. (1995) *True and Fair: A History of Price Waterhouse*, London: Hamish Hamilton.

Jones, E. and Woodward, C. (1992) *A Guide to the Architecture of London*, London: Weidenfeld & Nicolson.

Judd, M. (1983) '"The oddest combination of town and country": popular culture and London fairs 1800–60' in Walton, J. K. and Walvin, J. (eds) *Leisure in Britain 1780–1939*, Manchester: Manchester University Press.

Kellett, J. R. (1969) *The Impact of Railways on Victorian Cities*, London: Routledge & Kegan Paul.

Kennedy, W. P. (1982) 'Economic growth and structural change in the United Kingdom, 1870–1914', *Journal of Economic History*, 42, 105–14.

Kennedy, W. P. (1987) *Industrial Structure, Capital Markets and the Origins of British Economic Decline*, Cambridge: Cambridge University Press.

Kershen, A. J. (1995) *Uniting the Tailors: Trade Unionism Amongst the Tailoring Workers of London and Leeds 1870–1939*, Ilford: Cass.

Keynes, J. M. (1973) *Collected Works*, vol. VII, Basingstoke: Macmillan.

Kirk, H. (1976) *Portrait of a Profession: A History of the Solicitor's Profession 1100 to the Present Day*, London: Oyez Publishing.

Kirkham, P., Mace, R. and Porter, J. (1987) *Furnishing the World: The East London Furniture Trade 1830–1980*, London: Journeyman Press.

Klapper, C. F. (1961) *The Golden Age of Tramways*, London: Routledge & Kegan Paul.

Klapper, C. F. (1978) *The Golden Age of Buses*, London: Routledge & Kegan Paul.

Knowles, C. C. and Pitt, P. H. (1977) *The History of Building Regulation in London 1189–1972 with an Account of the District Surveyors' Association*, London: Architectural Press.

Krugman, P. (1991) *Geography and Trade*, Cambridge, Mass.: MIT Press.

Krugman, P. (1996) *Pop Internationalism*, London: MIT Press.

Kynaston, D. (1994) *The City of London. Vol. 1: A World of its Own 1815–90*, London: Pimlico.

Kynaston, D. (1996) *The City of London. Vol. 2: The Golden Years 1890–1914*, London: Pimlico.

Lambert, R. S. (1938) *The Universal Provider. A Study of William Whiteley and the Rise of the London Department Store*, London: Harrap.

Lampard, E. (1973) 'The urbanizing world' in Dyos and Wolff, 1973.

Land Enquiry Committee (1914) *The Land: Report of the Land Enquiry Committee, Vol. II: Urban*, London: Hodder & Stoughton.

Landers, J. (1987) 'Mortality and the metropolis: the case of London 1675–1825', *Population Studies*, 41, 59–76.

Langton, J. (1983) 'The industrial revolution and the regional geography of England', *Transactions of the Institute of British Geographers*, 9: 145–67.

Langton, J. and Morris, R. J. (eds) (1986) *Atlas of Industrialising Britain 1780–1914*, London: Methuen.

Laurence, S. (1989) 'Moderates, municipal reformers, and the issue of tariff reform' in Saint, A. (ed.) *Politics and People of London: The London County Council 1899–1965*, London: Hambledon Press.

Lawton, R. (ed.) (1978) *The Census and Social Structure: An Interpretative Guide to Nineteenth Century Censuses for England and Wales*, London: Cass.

Lawton, R. (1990) 'Population and society 1730–1914' in Dodgshon, R. and Butlin, R. (eds) *An Historical Geography of England and Wales*, London: Academic Press.

Leapman, M. (ed.) (1987) *The Book of London*, London: Guild Publishing.

Lee, C. H. (1979) *British Regional Employment Statistics 1841–1971*, Cambridge: Cambridge University Press.

Lee, C. H. (1981) 'Regional growth and structural change in Victorian Britain', *Economic History Review*, 34, 438–52.

Lee, C. H. (1984) 'The service sector, regional specialisation and economic growth in the Victorian economy', *The Journal of Historical Geography*, 10, 139–55.

Lee, C. H. (1986) *The British Economy Since 1700: A Macroeconomic Perspective*, Cambridge: Cambridge University Press.
Lee, C. H. (1994) 'The service industries' in Floud and McCloskey, 1994.
Lees, L. H. (1979) *Exiles of Erin: Irish Migrants in Victorian London*, Manchester: Manchester University Press.
Lewis, J. (1999) *London's Lea Valley. Britain's Best Kept Secret*, Chichester: Phillimore.
Lindert, P. H. (1994) 'Unequal living standards' in Floud and McCloskey, 1994.
Lindert, P. H. and Williamson, J. G. (1983) 'English workers' living standards during the industrial revolution: a new look', *Economic History Review*, 36, 1–25.
Lloyd-Jones, R. and Le Roux, A. A. (1980) 'The size of firms in the cotton industry: Manchester 1815–41', *Economic History Review*, 32, 72–82.
Lockwood, D. (1989) *The Blackcoated Worker: A Study in Class Consciousness*, Oxford: Clarendon Press.
LSE (1935) *New Survey of London Life and Labour* (under direction of Hall, H. L., Sir), London: London School of Economics.
Luckin, B. (1984) 'Evaluating the sanitary revolution: typhus and typhoid in London 1851–1900' in Woods, R. and Woodward, R. (eds) *Urban Disease and Mortality in Nineteenth Century England*, London: Batsford.
Luckin, B. (1997) 'Perspectives on the mortality decline in London 1860–1920', *London Journal*, 22 (2), 123–41.
Lummis, T. (1994) *The Labour Aristocracy 1851–1914*, Aldershot: Scolar Press.
MacKeith, M. (1985) *Shopping Arcades: A Gazetteer of Extant British Arcades 1817–1939*, London: Mansell.
McBride, T. M. (1976) *The Domestic Revolution: The Modernisation of Household Service in England and France*, London: Croom Helm.
McKeown, T. (1976) *The Modern Rise of Population*, London: Edward Arnold.
McKeown, T. and Record, R. G. (1962) 'Reasons for the decline of mortality in England and Wales during the nineteenth century', *Population Studies*, 16, 94–122.
MacKinnon, E. M. (1994) 'Living standards, 1870–1914' in Floud and McCloskey, 1994.
McLeod, H. (1974) *Class and Religion in the Late Victorian City*, London: Croom Helm.
McLeod, H. (1986) 'Religion' in Langton and Morris, 1986.
Maddison, A. (1992) *Dynamic Forces in Capitalist Development: A Long-run Comparative View*, Oxford: Oxford University Press.
Malcolmson, P. E. (1986) *English Laundresses: A Social History 1850–1930*, Urbana and Chicago: University of Illinois Press.
Malpass, P. (1999) 'Continuity and change in philanthropic housing organisations: the Octavia Hill Housing Trust and the Guinness Trust', *London Journal*, 24 (1), 38–58.
Mander, R. and Mitchenson, J. (1965) *British Music Hall: A Story in Pictures*, London: Studio Vista.
Mandler, P. (ed.) (1990) *The Uses of Charity: The Poor Relief in the Nineteenth Century Metropolis*, Philadelphia: University of Philadelphia Press.
Mariott, J. (1988), 'West Ham: London's industrial centre and gateway to the world: industrialisation 1840–1910', *London Journal*, 13 (2), 121–42.
Marshall, A. (1884) 'The housing of the London poor', *Contemporary Review*, XLV.
Marshall, A. (1919) *The Economics of Industry*, London: Macmillan.
Martin, J. E. (1966) *Greater London: An Industrial Geography*, London: G. Bell & Son.
Matossian, M. K. (1985) 'Death in London', *Journal of Interdisciplinary History*, 16, 183–97.
Mayhew, H. (1861) *London, Labour and the London Poor: Selections made by Victor Neuburg*, Harmondsworth: Penguin (1985 edition).
Mearns, A. (1883) *The Bitter Cry of Outcast London*, London: James Clarke & Co.
Merriman, N. (ed.) (1993) *The Peopling of London: Fifteen Hundred Years of Settlement from Overseas*, London: Museum of London.
Metropolitan Water Board (1953) *London's Water Supply 1903–53*, London: Metropolitan Water Board.
Metropolitan Water Board (1961) *The Water Supply of London*, London: Metropolitan Water Board/P. S. King & Staples.
Michie, R. C. (1987) *The London and New York Stock Exchanges 1850–1914*, London: Allen & Unwin.
Michie, R. C. (1992) *The City of London: Continuity and Change 1850–1990*, London: Macmillan.
Michie, R. C. (1997) 'London and the process of economic growth since 1750', *London Journal*, 22 (1), 63–90.
Millward, R. (1990) 'Productivity in the UK services sector: historical trends 1856–1985 and comparisons with the USA 1950–85', *Oxford Bulletin of Economics and Statistics*, 52, 423–36.

Millward, R. and Sheard, S. (1995) 'The urban fiscal problem, 1870–1914: government expenditure and finance in England and Wales', *Economic History Review*, 48, 501–35.

Mitchell, B. R. (1988) *British Historical Statistics*, Cambridge: Cambridge University Press.

Mitchell, B. R. (1992) *International Historical Statistics: Europe 1750–1988*, Basingstoke: Macmillan.

Mokyr, J. (1990) *The Lever of Riches: Technological Creativity and Economic Progress*, Oxford: Oxford University Press.

Mooney, G. (1994) 'Did London pass the sanitary test: seasonal infant mortality in London 1870–1914', *Journal of Historical Geography*, 20 (2), 158–74.

Morgan Crucible Co. Ltd (1956) *Battersea Works 1856–1956*, London: Morgan Crucible.

Morris, J. (1986a) 'The characteristics of sweating: the late nineteenth century London and Leeds tailoring trades', in John, A. V. (ed.) *Unequal Opportunities: Women's Employment in England 1800–1918*, Oxford: Blackwell.

Morris, J. (1986b) *Women Workers and the Sweated Trades: The Origins of Minimum Wage Legislation*, Aldershot: Gower.

Morris, O. J. (1953) *Fares Please: The Story of London's Road Transport*, London: Ian Allan.

Morris, R. J. (1986) 'Urbanization' in Langton and Morris, 1986.

Munby, D. L. (1951) *Industry and Planning in Stepney*, London: Oxford University Press.

Musson, A. E. (1965) *Enterprise in Soap and Chemicals: Joseph Crossfield and Sons Ltd 1815–1965*, Manchester: Manchester University Press.

Muthesius, S. (1982) *The English Terraced House*, London: Yale University Press.

Neal, L. (1985) 'Integration of international capital markets: quantitative evidence from the eighteenth to the twentieth centuries', *Journal of Economic History*, 45, 219–26.

Neal, L. (1994) 'The finance of business during the industrial revolution', in Floud and McCloskey, 1994.

Netzer, D. and Drennan, M. P. (1997) *Readings in State and Local Public Finance*, Oxford: Blackwell.

Nevett, T. (1977) 'London's early advertising agents', *Journal of Advertising History*, 1, 15–17.

Newman, A. (1982) *The Jewish East End 1840–1939*, London: Jewish Historical Society of England.

Nicholas, T. (1999) 'Wealth making in nineteenth- and early twentieth-century Britain: industry v. commerce and finance', *Business History*, 41, 16–36.

Nockolds, H. (ed.) (1977) *The Coachmakers: A History of the Worshipful Company of Coachmakers and Coach Harness Makers 1677–1977*, London: J. A. Allen.

North, D. C. (1990) *Institutions, Institutional Change and Economic Performance*, Cambridge: Cambridge University Press.

Oakley, E. R. (1989) *The London County Council Tramways: Volume 1, South London*, London: London Tramways History Group.

Oakley, E. R. (1991) *The London County Council Tramways: Volume 2, North London*, London: London Tramways History Group.

Obstfeld, M. and Taylor, A. M. (1998) 'The Great Depression as a watershed: international capital mobility in the long-run', in Bordo, M. D. *et al.* (eds) *The Defining Moment: The Great Depression and the American Economy in the Twentieth Century*, Chicago: Chicago University Press.

Occomore, D. (1995) *'Number Please! A History of the Early London Telephone Exchanges from 1880 to 1912*, Romford: Ian Henry.

O'Day, R. and Englander, D. (1993) *Mr Charles Booth's Inquiry. Life and Labour of the People of London Reconsidered*, London: Hambledon Press.

Oddy, D. J. (1982) 'The health of the people' in Barker, T. and Drake, M. (eds) *Population and Society in Britain 1850–1980*, London: Batsford.

Offer, A. (1977) 'The origins of the Law of Property Acts, 1910–1925', *Modern Law Review*, 40, 505–22.

Offer, A. (1981) *Property and Politics, 1870–1914: Landownership, Law Ideology and Urban Development in England*, Cambridge: Cambridge University Press.

Officer, L. H. (1985) 'Integration in the American foreign exchange market, 1791–1900', *Journal of Economic History*, 45, 557–85.

Ogborn, M. E. (1962) *Equitable Assurance: The Story of Life Assurance in the Experience of the Equitable Life Assurance Society*, London: Allen & Unwin.

Oliver, J. L. (1961) 'The East London furniture industry', *East London Papers*, 4 (2), 88–101.

Oliver, J. L. (1966) *The Development and Structure of the Furniture Industry*, Oxford: Pergamon Press.

Olsen, D. J. (1964) *Town Planning in London: The Eighteenth and Nineteenth Centuries*, London: Yale University Press.

Olsen, D. J. (1979) *The Growth of Victorian London*, Harmondsworth: Penguin.

O'Rourke, K. H. and Williamson, J. G. (1999) *Globalisation and History. The Evolution of the Nineteenth Century Atlantic Economy*, Cambridge, Mass.: MIT Press.

Owen, D. (1982) *The Government of Victorian London 1855–1889: The Metropolitan Board of Works, the Vestries and the City Corporation*, London: Belknap Press.

Palmer, M. and Neaverson, P. (1994) *Industry in the Landscape 1700–1900*, London: Routledge.

Panayi, P. (1994) *Immigration, Ethnicity and Racism in Britain, 1815–1945*, Manchester: Manchester University Press.

Park, R. E., Burgess, E. W. and MacKenzie, R. D. (1925) *The City*, Chicago: Chicago University Press.

Parry Lewis, J. (1965) *Building Cycles and Britain's Growth*, London: Macmillan.

Passingham, W. J. (1934) *London's Markets: Their Origin and History*, London: Sampson Low & Co.

Peel, D. W. (1960) *A Garden in the Sky: The Story of Barkers of Kensington 1870–1957*, London: W. H. Allen.

Pennington, S. and Westover, B. (1989) *A Hidden Workforce: Homeworkers in England 1850–1985*, Basingstoke: Macmillan.

Perkin, H. (1970) *The Age of the Railway*, Newton Abbot: David & Charles.

Perkin, H. (1989) *The Rise of Professional Society: England Since 1880*, London: Routledge.

Phelps-Brown, E. H. and Hopkins, S. V. (1954) 'Seven centuries of the price of consumables compared with builders' wage rates' in Carus-Wilson, E. M. (ed.) *Essays in Economic History. Volume II*, London: Edward Arnold.

Phillips, G. and Whiteside, N. (1985) *Casual Labour: The Unemployment Question in the Port Transport Industry 1880–1970*, Oxford: Clarendon Press.

Piore, M. and Sabel, C. (1984) *The Second Industrial Divide: Possibilities for Prosperity*, New York: Basic Books.

Platt, D. C. M., Latham, A. J. H. and Michie, R. (1993) *Decline and Recovery in Britain's Overseas Trade 1873–1914*, Basingstoke: Macmillan.

Pollard, S. (1950) 'The decline of shipbuilding on the Thames', *Economic History Review*, 3, 72–9.

Pollard, S. (1994) 'Entrepreneurship 1870–1914' in Floud and McCloskey, 1994.

Pollard, S. and Robertson, P. (1979) *The British Shipbuilding Industry 1870–1914*, London: Harvard University Press.

Pollins, H. (1964) 'Transport lines and social divisions' in Centre for Urban Studies (ed.) *London: Aspects of Change*, London: MacGibbon & Kee.

Pollins, H. (1971) *Britain's Railways: An Industrial History*, Newton Abbot: David & Charles.

Pollins, H. (1982) *Economic History of the Jews in England*, London: Associated University Press.

Pooley, C. (1984) 'Residential differentiation in Victorian cities: a reassessment', *Transactions of the Institute of British Geographers*, 9, 131–44.

Pooley, C. and Turnbull, J. (1998) *Migration and Mobility in Britain Since the 18th Century*, London: UCL Press.

Port of London Authority (1974) *The History of the Port of London up to the Advent of the Port of London Authority*, London: Port of London Authority.

Porter, R. (1994) *London: A Social History*, London: Hamish Hamilton.

Powell, M. (1996) 'A century of hospital planning in London: from the House of Lords Enquiry to the Tomlinson Report', *London Journal*, 21 (2), 164–80.

Price, R. (1980) *Masters, Unions and Men. Work Control in Building and the Rise of Labour 1830–1914*, Cambridge: Cambridge University Press.

Prochaska, F. K. (1992) *Philanthropy and the Hospitals of London: The Kings Fund 1897–1990*, Oxford: Clarendon Press.

Prothero, I. (1978) *Artisans and Politics in Early Nineteenth Century London: John Gast and His Times*, Folkestone: Dawson.

Pudney, J. S. (1975) *London's Docks*, London: Thames & Hudson.

Purvis, M. (1986) 'Popular institutions' in Langton and Morris, 1986.

Putnam, T. and Weinbren, D. (1996) 'The Royal Small Arms Factory and industrial Enfield 1855–1914', *London Journal*, 22, 46–63.

Quigley, J. M. (1998) 'Urban diversity and economic growth', *Journal of Economic Perspectives*, 12, 127–138.

Rasmussen, S. E. (1937) *London: The Unique City*, London: Jonathan Cape.

Razzell, P. (1993) 'The growth of population in 18th century England: a critical reappraisal', *Journal of Economic History*, 53 (4), 743–71.

Reader, W. J. (1966) *Professional Men: The Rise of the Professional Classes in Nineteenth Century England*, London: Weidenfeld & Nicolson.

Richardson, D. J. (1976) 'J. Lyons and Co. Ltd: Caterers & Food Manufacturers, 1894 to 1939' in Oddy, D. J. and Miller, D. S. (eds) *The Making of the Modern British Diet*, London: Croom Helm.

Richardson, J. (1995) *London and its People: A Social History from Medieval Times to the Present Day*, London: Barrie & Jenkins.

Robertson, A.B. (1958) 'The open market in the City of London in the 18th Century', *East London Papers*, 1 (2), 15–22.

Robertson, A. B. (1959) 'The suburban food markets of 18th century London', *East London Papers*, 2 (1), 21–6.

Robson, B. T. (1973) *Urban Growth: An Approach*, London: Methuen.

Roebuck, J. (1979) *Urban Development in Nineteenth Century London: Lambeth, Battersea and Wandsworth 1838–1888*, London: Phillimore.

Routh, G. (1980) *Occupation and Pay in Great Britain, 1906–79*, London: Macmillan.

Rowntree, B. S. (1901) *Poverty: A Study of Town Life*, London: Macmillan.

Rubinstein, W. D. (1981) *Men of Property: The Very Wealthy in Britain Since the Industrial Revolution*, London: Croom Helm.

Rubinstein, W. D. (1986) *Wealth and Inequality in Britain*, London: Faber & Faber.

Rubinstein, W. D. (1987) *Elites and the Wealthy in Modern Britain: Essays in Social and Economic History*, Brighton: Harvester.

Rubinstein, W. D. (1993) *Capitalism, Culture and Decline in Britain 1750–1990*, London: Routledge.

Ruck, S. K. and Rhodes, G. (1970) *The Government of Greater London*, London: Allen & Unwin.

Rude, G. (1971) *Hanoverian London, 1714–1808*, London: Secker & Warburg.

Saint, A. (1989) 'Technical education and the early LCC' in Saint, A. (ed.) *Politics and People of London: The London County Council 1899–1965*, London: Hambledon Press.

Saint, A. (ed.) (1999) *London Suburbs*, London: Merrell Holberton.

Samuel, R. (1973) 'Comers and goers' in Dyos and Wolff, 1973.

Scammell, W. M. (1968) *The London Discount Market*, London: Elek.

Schmiechen, J. A. (1984) *Sweated Industries and Sweated Labour: The London Clothing Trades 1860–1914*, London: Croom Helm.

Schwarz, L. D. (1985) 'The standard of living in the long run: London 1700–1860', *Economic History Review*, 38, 26–41.

Schwarz, L. D. (1990) 'Trends in real wage rates, 1750–1790, a reply to Hunt and Botham', *Economic History Review*, 43, 90–8.

Schwarz, L. D. (1992) *London in the Age of Industrialisation: Entrepreneurs, Labour Force and Living Conditions 1700–1850*, Cambridge: Cambridge University Press.

Scott, J. D. (1958) *Siemens Brothers 1858–1958: An Essay in the History of an Industry*, London: Weidenfeld & Nicolson.

Seaman, L. C. B. (1973) *Life in Victorian London*, London: Batsford.

Segars, T. (1989) 'Working for London's Fire Brigade' in Saint, A. (ed.) *Politics and People of London: The London County Council 1899–1965*, London: Hambledon Press.

Shannon, H. A. (1935) 'Migration and the growth of London 1841–91', *Economic History Review*, 5, 79–86.

Shaw, G. and Wild, M. J. (1979) 'Retail patterns in the Victorian city', *The Institute of British Geographers, Transactions*, 4 (2).

Sheppard, F. (1971) *London 1808–70: The Infernal Wen*, London: Secker & Warburg.

Sheppard, F. (1982) 'Vestries' in Owen, 1982.

Sheppard, F. (1985) 'London and the nation in the nineteenth century', *Transactions of the Royal Historical Society*, xxxv, 51–74.

Sheppard, F. (1998) *London: A History*, Oxford: Oxford University Press.

Sheppard, F., Belcher, V. and Cotterell, P. (1979) 'The Middlesex and Yorkshire Deeds Registeries and the study of building fluctuations', *London Journal*, 176–217.

Sheppardson, C. (1991) *The Luxury Hotels of London*, Lewes: Book Guild.

Simmons, J. (1984) *The Victorian Hotel*, Leicester: University of Leicester.

Simmons, J. (1986) *The Railway in Town and Country 1830–1914*, Newton Abbot: David & Charles.

Simon, M. (1968) 'Pattern of new British portfolio foreign investment 1865–1914' in Hall, A. R. (ed.) *The Export of Capital from Britain 1870–1914*, London: Methuen.

Slinn, J. (1984) *A History of Freshfields*, London: Sweet & Maxwell.

Smith, D. H. (1933) *The Industries of Greater London*, London: P. S. King & Son.

Sorensen, C. (1996) *London on Film: One Hundred Years of Film Making in London*, London: Museum of London.

Spensley, J. C. (1918) 'Urban housing problems', *Journal of the Royal Statistical Society* lxxxi, 161–210.

Stedman Jones, G. (1971) *Outcast London: A Study in the Relationship between Classes in Victorian Society*, Oxford: Clarendon Press.

Stevens, J. B. (1993) *The Economics of Collective Choice*, Boulder, Colo.: Westview Press.

Stoddard, J. (1974) *Manbre: A Hundred Years of Sugar in Hammersmith 1874–1974*, London: Fulham & Hammersmith Historical Society.

Summerson, J. (1973) *The London Building World of the 1860s*, London: Thames & Hudson.

Summerson, J. (1977) 'The Victorian rebuilding of the City of London', *London Journal*, 3 (2), 163–85.

Summerson, J. (1978) *Georgian London*, (rev. edn), Harmondsworth: Penguin.

Swift, R. and Gilley, S. (eds) (1989) *The Irish in Britain 1815–39*, London: Pinter.

Tarn, N. (1973) *Five Per Cent Philanthropy: An Account of Housing in Urban Areas Between 1840 and 1914*, Cambridge: University of Cambridge.

Tebbutt, M. (1983) *Making Ends Meet: Pawnbroking and Working Class Credit*, Leicester: Leicester University Press.

Thorne, R. (1990) 'The Great Northern Railway and the London coal trade' in Hunter, M. and Thorne, R., *Change at King's Cross. From 1800 to the Present*, London: Historical Publications.

Thrift, N. (1990) 'Transport and communication 1730–1914' in Dodgshon, R. A. and Butlin, R. A. (eds) *An Historical Geography of England and Wales*, London: Academic Press.

Trebilcock, C. (1985) *Phoenix Assurance and the Development of British Insurance: Volume 1, 1782–1870*, Cambridge: Cambridge University Press.

Trench, R. and Hillman, E. (1993) *London Under London: A Subterranean Guide*, London: John Murray.

Turnbull, G. L. (1979) *Traffic and Transport: An Economic History of Pickfords*, London: Allen & Unwin.

Turvey, R. (1966) *The Economics of Real Property*, London: Macmillan.

Turvey, R. (1998) 'Office rents in the City of London 1867–1910', *London Journal*, 23, 53–67.

Tweedale, G. (1990) *At the Sign of the Plough: 275 Years of Allen and Hanburys and the British Pharmaceutical Industry 1715–1990*, London: John Murray.

Vallis, E. (1972) 'Urban land and building prices', parts I–IV, *Estates Gazette*, 222, 1015–9, 1209–13, 1406–7, 1604–5.

Vamplew, W. (1988) *Pay Up and Play the Game: Professional Sport in Britain 1875–1914*, Cambridge: Cambridge University Press.

Village London Atlas (1987) *The Village London Atlas: The Changing Face of Greater London, 1822–1903*, London: Guild Publishing,

Wainwright, D. (1982) *Broadwoods By Appointment: A History*, London: Quiller.

Wainwright, D. (1990) *Stone's Ginger Wine: Fortunes of a Family Firm 1740–1990*, London: Quiller.

Walker, R. (1988) *The Savile Row Story: An Illustrated History*, London: Prion.

Walkley, C. (1981) *'The Ghost in the Looking Glass': The Victorian Seamstress*, London: P. Owen.

Walkowitz, J. R. (1992) *City of Dreadful Delight: Narratives of Sexual Danger in Late-Victorian London*, London: Virago.

Waller, P. J. (1983) *Town, City and Nation: England 1850–1914*, Oxford: Oxford University Press.

Wareing, J. (1981) 'Migration to London and transatlantic emigration of indentured servants 1683–1775', *Journal of Historical Geography*, 7 (4), 356–78.

Warren, K. (1980) *Chemical Foundations: The Alkali Industry in Britain to 1926*, Oxford: Clarendon Press.

Warren, K. (1986) *The Motorbus in Central London*, London: Ian Allan.

Waters, C. (1989) 'Progressives, puritans and the cultural politics of the LCC 1889–1914' in Saint, A. (ed.) *Politics and the People of London: The London County Council 1889–1965*, London: Hambledon Press.

Watney, J. (1976) *Mother's Ruin. A History of Gin*, London: Owen.

Waugh, A. (1957) *Merchants of Wine: Being a Centenary Account of the Fortunes of the House of Gilbey*, London: Cassell.

Waugh, N. (1964) *The Cut of Men's Clothes 1600–1900*, London: Faber & Faber.

Webber, R. (1969) *Covent Garden: Mud-Salad Market*, London: Dent.

Weber, A. F. (1899) *The Growth of Cities in the Nineteenth Century*, New York: Greenwood (1969 edition).

Weinreb, B. and Hibbert, C. (eds) (1983) *The London Encyclopaedia*, London: Macmillan.

Whetham, E. (1976) 'The London milk trade 1900–1930' in Oddy, D. J. and Miller, D. S. (eds) *The Making of the Modern British Diet*, London: Croom Helm.

White, H. P. (1971) *London Railway History*, Newton Abbot: David & Charles.

Whitehead, J. (1999) *The Growth of Camden Town AD 1800–2000*, London: Jack Whitehead.

Williams, M. E. W. (1994) *The Precision Makers: A History of the Instrument Industry in Britain and France, 1870–1939*, London: Routledge.

Winstanley, M. J. (1983) *The Shopkeeper's World 1830–1914*, Manchester: Manchester University Press.

Winter, J. (1993) *London's Teeming Streets 1830–1914*, London: Routledge.

Winter, J. M. (1982) 'The decline of mortality in Britain 1870–1950', in Barker, T. and Drake, M. (eds) *Population and Society in Britain, 1850–1980*, London: Batsford.

Wohl, A. (1977) *The Eternal Slum: Housing and Social Policy in Victorian London*, London: Edward Arnold.

Woods, R. (1985) 'The effects of population redistribution on the level of mortality in 17th century England and Wales', *Journal of Economic History*, 45 (3), 645–51.

Woods, R. and Hinde, A. (1987) 'Mortality in Victorian England: models and patterns', *Journal of Interdisciplinary History*, xviii, 27–54.

Woodward, J. (1984) 'Medicine in the city' in Woods, R. and Woodward, J. (eds) *Urban Disease and Mortality in 19th Century England*, London: Batsford.

Wrigley, E. A. (1967) 'A simple model of London's importance in changing English society and economy, 1600–1750', *Past and Present*, 37, 44–70.

Wrigley, E. A. (1987) *People, Cities and Wealth: The Transformation of Traditional Society*, Oxford: Blackwell.

Wrigley, E. A. and Schofield, R. S. (1981) *The Population History of England 1541–1871: A Reconstruction*, London: Edward Arnold.

Wroth, W. (1896) *The London Pleasure Gardens of the Eighteenth Century*, London: Macmillan.

Yelling, J. A. (1986) *Slums and Slum Clearance in Victoria*, London: Allen & Unwin.

Young, K. and Garside, P. L. (1982) *Metropolitan London: Politics and Urban Change 1837–1981*, London: Edward Arnold.

Index